Janaé

[illegible] Lukes

6 am - 8 pm

M-F ifant tod

6:30
6:P FT Sub

wed
2nd 2:30

124 Little Lukes
Bannock preschoo

white house
parking Lot

through playground

THE SURVIVOR'S GUIDE TO THEOLOGY

M. James Sawyer (Ph.D., Dallas Theological Seminary) has taught theology for over twenty years. He is professor of theological studies at Western Seminary's Northern California Campus in San Jose. He is the author of *Taxonomic Charts of Theology and Biblical Studies* and *Charles Augustus Briggs and Tensions in Late Nineteenth Century American Theology*, coauthor of *Reinventing Jesus?*, and coeditor of *Who's Afraid of the Holy Spirit?*

THE SURVIVOR'S GUIDE TO THEOLOGY

M. JAMES SAWYER

GRAND RAPIDS, MICHIGAN 49530 USA

ZONDERVAN.COM/
AUTHORTRACKER

ZONDERVAN™

The Survivor's Guide to Theology
Copyright © 2006 by M. James Sawyer
Requests for information should be addressed to:

Zondervan, *Grand Rapids, Michigan 49530*

Library of Congress Cataloging-in-Publication Data

Sawyer, M. James.
The survivor's guide to theology / M. James Sawyer.
p. cm.
Includes bibliographical references and index.
ISBN-10: 0-310-21150-6
ISBN-13: 978-0-310-21150-1
1. Theology, Doctrinal—Popular works. I. Title.
BT77.S32 2006
230—dc21
2002000787

This edition printed on acid-free paper.

All Scripture quotations, unless otherwise noted, are taken from the *Holy Bible: New International Version®*. NIV®. Copyright © 1973, 1978, 1984 by International Bible Society. Used by permission of Zondervan. All rights reserved.

Scripture quotations identified as NET Bible are from the *New English Translation Bible*, copyright © 1995–2001 Biblical Studies Foundation. All rights reserved.

Scripture quotations identified as NRSV are from the *New Revised Standard Version of the Bible*, copyright 1989 by the Division of Christian Education of the National Council of the Churches of Christ in the USA. Used by permission.

Scripture quotations identified as REB are from the *Revised English Bible* (Oxford, England: Oxford University Press; New York: Cambridge University Press, 1989).

Scripture quotations identified as RSV are from the *Revised Standard Version of the Bible*, copyright 1946, 1952, 1971 by the Division of Christian Education of the National Council of the Churches of Christ in the USA. Used by permission.

The website addresses recommended throughout this book are offered as a resource to you. These websites are not intended in any way to be or imply an endorsement on the part of Zondervan, nor do we vouch for their content for the life of this book.

All rights reserved. No part of this publication may be reproduced, stored in a retrieval system, or transmitted in any form or by any means—electronic, mechanical, photocopy, recording, or any other—except for brief quotations in printed reviews, without the prior permission of the publisher.

Interior design by Todd Sprague

Printed in the United States of America

06 07 08 09 10 11 • 18 17 16 15 14 13 12 11 10 9 8 7 6 5 4 3 2 1

For Kay, my soulmate, confidante, and co-laborer in the Kingdom

CONTENTS

PART III: SIGNIFICANT PEOPLE AND TERMS

PREFACE

WHY ANOTHER INTRODUCTION TO THE STUDY OF THEOLOGY?

In twenty years of teaching theology to graduate students, I have used a number of texts I thought were appropriate to the subject and the background level of the students. My constant frustration has been that as soon as I find a text I like, it goes out of print. Thus I decided to write my own.

A second reason for my writing this book was to direct beginning students to the resources available for the study of systematic theology. For although many resources are available, they are widely scattered and difficult for beginning students to locate.

A third issue that led to this new textbook on systematic theology is that many systematic theologies recommended to students begin with content without giving any hint that there are preliminary issues that must be sorted out. By way of comparison, a good exegetical commentary always begins with a detailed introduction to the background issues, including the state of the text (textual criticism), the history of the interpretation of the book, critical problems, and the literary and historical/cultural background of the book. It is vital to deal with all of these issues if the book is to be accurately understood and interpreted. In the case of shorter books of the New Testament, these introductions may at times be as lengthy as the commentary itself.

As a young student, I found this material tedious and often wanted to hurry up and get to the "really important stuff." I now realize that getting to the "really important stuff" without dealing with the preliminary issues is naive at best, dangerous at worst. The same principle holds true for the theologian, perhaps more emphatically so. Medieval theologians called systematic theology "the queen of the sciences" because in some sense it encompassed all other areas of knowledge, not just biblical knowledge. That fact led to the understanding that the theological enterprise was comprehensive and involved a synthetic mind-set different than that in any other discipline.

We live in an age of specialization. The idea of a twenty-first-century individual writing a medieval *summa* that would encompass all human knowledge is laughable. Specializations, whether secular or sacred, all have their own peculiar lenses for looking at the study of their discipline and their own jargon for discussing it. This often locks nonspecialists out of any meaningful discussion (and often even out of all but the most rudimentary understanding), since they have no mental map, do not understand the jargon, and do not know the literature.

In one sense, the study of theology is still comprehensive. It still must incorporate truth from any and every source into its consideration. So theologians must have at least a passing knowledge of many disciplines, although they normally will not be expert in any of them other than their own. In another sense, the discipline is technical, like any other. Theologians have developed jargon that they use to talk to one another. To the novice, understanding the jargon that we use on a daily basis can be a daunting task. Terms like *hypostatic union* (Is it part of the AFL-CIO?), *economic trinity* (What does economics have to do with the study of God?), *vicarious substitution* (Is this when you use margarine in place of butter in a recipe?), and *justification* (Doesn't that have something to do with word processing?) can sound as foreign and incomprehensible as Latin catchphrases (of which there are plenty in theology). Yet each term is densely packed with theological meaning. We employ these terms, not to be obtuse, but because they provide a shorthand in communicating.

Likewise, we have our own set of authorities that we quote, and the uninitiated can be lost as they hear the names of Calvin, Luther, Barth, Augustine, Origen, Anselm, Schleiermacher, and the like tossed offhandedly into a conversation or lecture. If students do not have some kind of scorecard, they will be hopelessly lost trying to keep track of who taught what and whether it was considered orthodox or heretical.

Other factors also led me to undertake the writing of this volume, including:

1. *Introductions currently available are geared toward the advanced student.* Strangely, in biblical and theological studies, one must have a grasp of the discipline to understand introductory issues! I have tried to present introductory issues at an introductory level. My aim is to simplify without becoming overly simplistic. Perhaps an analogy will prove helpful here. When my wife

was pregnant with our second son, our first son (twenty months old when his younger brother was born) wanted to know where babies came from. We tried showing him pictures of fetal development in utero but finally had to settle for the explanation that "the baby is in Mommy's tummy." We shared with him as much as he could grasp given his stage of intellectual development. We did not share untruth with him ("the baby is brought by the stork"), nor did we give a detailed explanation of conception, gestation, and the birth process. We did give accurate information on which he could build as he matured. Likewise, my goal in this volume is to give developmentally appropriate information about the greatest study of all, that of our God and Father as he has revealed himself in his Word and his works.

2. *Introductory issues are vital to beginners to alert them to the minefields of theological study.* As noted above, in biblical studies much time is spent on introduction. Theology has often been assumed to be a contextless discipline that presents eternal truths that never change and therefore does not need the kind of introduction that is found in the exegetical disciplines. While we often proceed with the unstated assumption that "what we don't know can't hurt us," this is manifestly not true. I have observed numerous instances of individuals, well trained at seminary in *the truth* as understood by their particular theological tradition, who proceed with further study and have their faith shaken and in some cases overthrown because their training had not prepared them for what they would face once they moved outside their narrow tradition. A little knowledge is a dangerous thing, and too little knowledge can be very dangerous indeed. If we go into a field thinking that a single book is going to present us with the truth, we easily can be blindsided by unknown material, and our confidence can be radically shaken. While hackneyed, the aphorism "forewarned is forearmed" is still true.

3. *Theology involves far more than doctrine or a straightforward summary of biblical teaching.* Theology involves secondary reflection on doctrine to see its implications and applications. Its issues are complex. Too often the beginner is tempted to adopt the attitude, "God said it; I believe it; that settles it." While this attitude is commendable insofar as it truly reflects obedience toward God and his self-revelation, it is woefully inadequate when it comes to understanding God's revelation and explaining it to our culture. This approach too often looks at the form but fails to cut to the heart of the meaning and significance of what was said.

4. *We live in an age in which philosophy is ignored, even by seminarians.* Few major evangelical seminaries in the United States maintain a philosophy prerequisite, a requirement that was standard as recently as fifteen years ago.

Quite simply, theology and philosophy go hand in hand. One cannot understand, explain, or do theology without an acquaintance with philosophy.

5. *Understanding the nature of truth is vital.* Evangelicals affirm as a first principle that truth exists and that God has given it to us in the Scriptures. Yet we have historically failed to come to grips with the fact that the church has always seen two books of revelation, the book of Scripture and the book of nature, and that since God is the author of both, there must be a mutual relationship, an interdependence between them. We need to understand the nature of the interrelationship between these two books written by God and their implications.

6. *We often speak of "human thinking" or "human wisdom" in a disdainful manner.* Yet we fail to take into account that we, as we interact with the revealed text of Scripture, are humans, and what flows from that interaction is fallible human interpretation of infallible, inerrant divine truth, not infallible divine truth itself. In short, we fail to see a distinction between the truth itself and our understanding of that truth. Even in our redeemed state, we remain both finite and fallible at our best. To equate our understanding of God's truth with God's truth in its fullness is unmitigated arrogance. Yet we all fall into this trap.

7. *We need to understand the true nature of orthodoxy.* Orthodoxy involves right belief, but that belief is not static, since God has revealed untold amounts of truth to us. We must start with the faith once delivered to the saints and then incorporate progressively discovered truth into that underlying faith. Orthodoxy should be growing and progressing, open to correction and growth, not static, defensive, and dead.

8. *Each generation is called to reappropriate the eternal truth of God afresh.* This means that we must critically examine the shape of the faith we have inherited and check it against the revelation of God itself. Our attitude must be that of the Bereans, who neither simply accepted Paul's teaching because he was a persuasive preacher nor rejected it out of hand because it was new. Rather, they searched the Scriptures to see if the things Paul was saying were so. This reappropriation process might be compared to the intellectual growing pains of an adolescent entering adulthood. At some point, the adolescent must examine the teaching of his or her parents and consciously evaluate the legitimacy or illegitimacy of the things taught. Human fallibility operates on many levels. Most often much that has been taught will be accepted, while other things, some very dear to the parents, will be rejected.

9. *We tend to take ourselves too seriously.* We are engaged in serious business, for the eternal destiny of individuals depends on our being right. Yet in

our seriousness we set ourselves up as the guardians of God's truth (that is, of our understanding of God's truth). We must realize in our theologizing that we do not hold the substance of reality together by our teachings. We simply describe that which exists apart from ourselves. As a theologian aptly observed more than a century ago, "No one is totally orthodox save God himself." If we see ourselves as having to be right on every detail, we succumb to the temptation of Adam and Eve in the garden in wanting to be as God.

10. *We have historically tended to see all truths as equally important.* Doctrines such as a recent creation or the pretribulation rapture of the church are often seen as being equally as important as the deity of Christ or his atoning death. Because we have not learned to prioritize doctrines, we tend to consign to outer darkness those who mispronounce our pet shibboleths. We will examine the wisdom of establishing a taxonomy of doctrine founded on the fundamental Christian faith as expressed in the ancient creeds and summed up in the statement that teaching that is truly Christian must have been "held by the whole church in all places and at all times."

11. *We have not in recent generations had the ability to be self-critical.* Early-twentieth-century theological battles have bred a defensive mentality: "We have to preserve the ancient faith against the onslaughts of modernism." We owe our forefathers a debt of gratitude in that they were willing to contend for the faith against a religion that, under the name of Christianity, denied every cardinal doctrine of the historic faith. As one contemporary evangelical has put it, we have been content to settle in the valley of paradox and erect our fortresses rather than press on toward new discovery. As those settled in the fortress, we tend to measure ourselves by ourselves, a practice the apostle Paul calls unwise (2 Cor. 10:12).

12. *We have a rich history.* Bernard de Chartel said in the twelfth century, "We are like dwarves on the shoulders of giants. And as dwarves, we shall be able to see only so long as we do not climb down from the giants' shoulders." Young or beginning theologians must be aware that their own tradition is not the only one in which God has worked. All who call themselves Christians stand on a common heritage, whether we realize it or not. We dare not ignore those who have been taught by the Spirit down through the ages, even if they look different from us.

- - -

These are some of the issues that have prompted this volume. My hope is that this book will prove valuable as an introduction to the greatest study of all, theology. Remember, it is not necessary to agree with a position to learn from it. Often the greatest learning and growing come through interacting with those with whom we disagree, if for no other reason than that they cause us to think rather than take shelter in pat answers and inherited—but untried—truth. We have no need to fear those who would assail our faith if it is established on the living foundation of Jesus Christ.

ACKNOWLEDGMENTS

No project of this type is ever accomplished alone. Many individuals have helped in various ways to see this work to completion. Among those who deserve special thanks are Ed van der Maas, former senior acquisitions editor at Zondervan, for his help in shaping and honing the scope of this project as well as his encouragement and many hours of interaction as we discussed various questions of philosophy, epistemology, and theological systems.

I also thank Dan Wallace for his careful reading of many chapters and insightful questions and criticisms that have helped sharpen the focus in numerous places and for his contribution on establishing a doctrinal taxonomy from an exegetical perspective.

My colleagues Roy Low and Gary Tuck have been unceasing in their support and encouragement.

Jeffrey and Merilyn Hargis and J. Daniel Sawyer provided helpful suggestions that made some of the more arcane material more accessible.

Eric Sorensen, Joe Childs, and Van Brollini provided invaluable assistance in preparing the chapters on Reformed theology, Wesleyan-Arminianism, and Orthodoxy respectively.

Jon Olson and Jerry McCarn provided key help in the production of the reference section.

Greg Herrick and Troy Dameron read key parts of the manuscript for clarity and coherence.

John Luke provided his expertise and criticism particularly in the area of accurately presenting the scientific examples and analogies.

Kathleen Rocheleau, Lynx Crowe, Jonathan and Stephanie Sawyer, and Kay Sawyer assisted in compiling the indexes.

The questions from and dialogue with students from my Theology I classes over the last fifteen years gave rise to and helped shape the work.

My wife, Kay, provided constant encouragement and support for what at times seemed to be an interminable project. It is to her that I dedicate this work.

CHAPTER 1

WHO NEEDS THEOLOGY ANYWAY?

The great nineteenth-century evangelist D. L. Moody was at one time challenged by a woman who reportedly said, "I want you to know that I don't believe in your theology." Moody's response: "I didn't know I had any!"[1] This just goes to show that even great men of God can be wrong.

The word *theology* is a compound of two Greek terms: θεός (*theos*, "God") and λόγος (*logos*, "word, statement, discourse, a line of argument"). Therefore, in simple terms, a theologian is someone who knows about or speaks about God, and theology is what is thought or said about God.

When I was about five years old, my beloved pet dog died. Shortly thereafter I was talking with my friend Chuck about death and what happens afterward. As we dug in the dirt and filled our toy dump trucks, we came to the conclusion that when you died you went to heaven and lived there. Then when you died in heaven, you went to the next heaven and lived there, and so on. Even as young children, confronted with questions of life, death, and God, we were in the most basic sense practicing theologians developing a theology (a rather unusual one, but a theology nonetheless) as we dug in the dirt and played with our trucks.

Whenever we think about God, we are involved with theology. The question therefore is not *whether* we will be theologians—we have no choice in the matter. Rather, the question is *what kind* of theologians we will be—good or bad, responsible or irresponsible.

But, you say, if we all are theologians anyway, can't we be good and responsible theologians by just being good and sincere Christians? Most Christians over the last two millennia (including D. L. Moody!) have hardly been aware of the discipline of theology, and if they were, they saw it as something abstract, theoretical, more than a bit daunting, and unrelated to everyday life. Theirs was a *practical* faith. So why should we even study theology? Why isn't it enough to just love Jesus and obey him?[2]

Scripture calls us to disciplined learning. Paul admonishes in 1 Corinthians 14:20, "Brothers, stop thinking like children. In regard to evil be infants, but in your thinking be adults." Yet many of us never take the responsibility for theological maturity seriously. While we may put great effort into our profession, perhaps even earning a Ph.D., many of us are like the astronomer who said to the theologian, "I don't understand why you theologians fuss so much about predestination and supralapsarianism, about the communicable and incommunicable attributes of God, imputed or infused grace, and the like. To me Christianity is simple—it's the Golden Rule: "Do unto others as you would have others do unto you." (To which, incidentally, the theologian replied, "I think I see what you mean. I get lost in all your talk about exploding novas, expanding universes, theories of entropy and astronomical perturbations. For me astronomy is simple: It's 'Twinkle, twinkle little star …' ")

We can illustrate the importance of theology by means of the skeleton and the jellyfish. When we look at a skeleton, we can be reasonably sure it is dead. The life that once held these bones together is gone, and these bones are now held together with pins and wires. This is how many people view theology: lifeless and a collection of ideas that are held together by the artificial means of complex rationalizations and arguments. Then there is the jellyfish. A jellyfish can live for a time on the beach but cannot do anything. It lies on the sand in a pulsating blob, unable to do anything except possibly sting a passerby. The jellyfish, like the skeleton, has a problem. While the skeleton has structure without life, the jellyfish has life without structure. The lack of structure, or a skeletal system, causes it to be ineffective at doing anything on land.

While it is true that theology alone may be lifeless, spiritual life without structure is at best ineffective and is for all practical purposes useless. The answer to the dilemma is to bring together the life with a structure that will support it.

A structure such as a skeleton will allow us to accomplish the task of living life, but this does not mean that just any structure will do, that one structure is as good as another. Years ago I worked with a person who as a child had fallen from a tree and broken his arm. The physician who attended to him was drunk and set the arm improperly so that in the healing process a deformity developed. My colleague could still use his arm, but it was not fully functional because the structure that supported his arm inhibited his movement.

Improper theological structures may give the illusion of being intellectually and spiritually harmonious and in line with Scripture, but the reality shows otherwise. In the pilot episode of the original Star Trek series, broadcast as "The Menagerie," Captain Christopher Pike (Captain Kirk's predecessor) is imprisoned on the planet Talos 4. The inhabitants of the planet exhibit him and a beautiful young woman in their zoo. The plan is for them to mate and ultimately populate the planet. Pike learns that the Talosians are experts at illusion and that this is why his escape attempts keep failing. When he is finally successful and is about to leave the planet, he tries to take the young woman as well, but she refuses to leave. He discovers that she, like everything else he has experienced, is not as she appears. She is human, but she is not young and beautiful. She is the sole survivor of a scientific expedition stranded on the planet years before. Badly injured in the crash of her spaceship, she had been nursed back to health by the Talosians. But they had never seen a human before and consequently did not properly set her broken bones, and she ended up hunched over with twisted limbs. In this ugly condition, she could not face other humans. She could live a functional life, but the underlying structure of her body could not support normal existence. Her twisted structure cut her off from contact with normal humans.

To extend our analogy a step further, our theology should have not only a functional structure but also a beauty and attractiveness that reflects the beauty of God, who is himself the source of beauty. Astrophysicists who are searching for a "unified field theory" that will explain and unify our knowledge of how the universe came into being and how the fundamental forces of nature are related speak of the "beauty principle." They have discovered in their advancing knowledge significant new insights that have an "elegant simplicity" about them. It is this very elegance that is a compelling feature in the acceptance of the new theory. Likewise, our theology should have a compelling beauty about it. If it does not, we probably need to do more reflection to grasp more fully who God is and what he has done.

During our first trip to England, my wife and I visited the medieval walled city of York and the York Castle museum. Particularly fascinating was the exhibit showing the history of warfare, with displays arranged in chronological order, beginning in the Stone Age. We saw the progress in weaponry during the Bronze Age and into the Iron Age, including spears, bows and arrows, and chariots. In the medieval displays, we saw broadswords, body armor, and chain mail. Then, in a display that was dated only fifty years later than the preceding one, we saw a profound shift. The armor was nearly gone, and now cannons and muskets were used. The defensive weaponry of previous decades was ineffective against the new gunpowder-powered weapons. In order to survive under these new conditions, both the defensive and the offensive weapons had to change.

While theology is rightly seen as an intellectual activity that seeks to bring all things under the lordship of Christ and is rightly seen as an act of worship, it also involves interaction with our contemporary culture. In this sense, we might think of our theology as an armory that provides us with weapons to do battle with a world that is hostile to the lordship of Christ. If we do not retool our weapons to meet the current battlefield conditions, we face defeat. This has been a real problem for the evangelical community in that we have not recognized changing conditions and have carried muskets into battle when the opposition totes M16s and AK–47s.

Our theological understanding comes from the Bible but not from the Bible alone. Many of the questions, categories, and thought forms that are incorporated in our understanding are drawn from the dominant philosophy of the culture we inhabit. Professional theologians have recognized this fact for centuries and have acknowledged that it is unavoidable. When the culture changes, as it does continuously and is doing now at an unprecedented rate, persisting in using the thought forms and categories and explanations and defenses of the faith that have been effective in a previous generation is akin to charging into battle astride horses with sabers drawn, only to be met by machine guns, tanks, fighter jets, bombers, heat-seeking missiles, and the like. While it may be courageous, it is hardly wise.

Our theology has consequences. What we believe matters. History reveals that our belief system determines whether we live wisely or naively. One of the most tragic events of the medieval crusades was the Children's Crusade. Since the previous crusades had ended in dismal failure, some reasoned that it was because the crusaders were sinners and God would not bless a venture undertaken by sinners. If an army of pure individuals were raised, surely God would bless and give victory. Who is purer and more innocent than children? So an army of children was put together with the objective that they would rescue the Holy Land from the infidel Turks. But when the army of children reached the Holy Land, instead of defeating the Turks, they were captured and sold as slaves.

Love of Jesus, while vital, is not enough. Theology is not just for the professional, the professor, the pastor, or even the Sunday school teacher. Each of us is responsible to become a competent theologian. Rather than viewing our theology as propositions to be learned, we ought to view it as an *act of worship*. God has entrusted to us his divine revelation in all its multifaceted richness and fullness, but he has not given us a theology. He has revealed himself through his works and his words in human history, in his encounters with individuals at various times and places. He has revealed himself most fully in the person and work of Jesus Christ, but that revelation is in narrative, or story, form. Our job is to organize the material and bring it into a coherent whole so that we can more fully grasp who God is and what he has done. We offer back to him the fruit of our labor in understanding him and his work. The task of theology is to bring all things under the lordship of Christ. While we may rely on the work of others who have gone before us, we have a personal responsibility before God for our understanding.

Our call is not to remain babes, but to grow continuously. While there is far more to spiritual maturity than theological knowledge, this knowledge is a definite part of maturity. Jesus commanded us, "Love the Lord your God with all your heart and with all your soul and with all your *mind*" (Matt. 22:37, italics added). The goal is to always be ready to give an answer to those who ask us about our faith (1 Peter 3:15). This demand puts us squarely in the midst of the discipline of theology, a discipline that is and will always be dynamic, a work in progress, because our finite human understanding cannot by definition grasp completely and once and for all infinite truth.

NOTES

[1]Cf. Stanley N. Gundry, *Love Them In: The Life and Theology of D. L. Moody* (Chicago: Moody Press, 1976; reprint 1999), 67.

[2]By our basic definition of a theologian, one need not even be saved to be a theologian. Scripture itself testifies that every human being has some knowledge of God, a knowledge gleaned from the created order as well as from conscience (see especially Ps. 19 and Rom. 1:18–20). The theology being spoken of here is not formal or technical, but it is nonetheless real theology. Thus, while it is possible to be a theologian without being saved, it is not possible to be saved without being a theologian, since salvation involves not just a mystical spiritual experience and encounter with "spiritual reality," but is found in the person and work of Jesus Christ.

PART 1

ON BEING A THEOLOGIAN

OUTLINE OF CHAPTER 2

A. **The Theologian as Guardian of Truth**
   1. What Is Faith?
      a. Thomas Aquinas
      b. Martin Luther
      c. John Calvin
      d. Faith Seeking Understanding
   2. What Is Heresy?
   3. The Theologian as Preserver of Tradition

B. **The Theologian as "Scientist/Explorer"**
   1. The Theologian as "Scientist"
      a. The Analytical and Critical Task
         (1) The Text of Scripture
            (a) The historical nature of divine revelation
            (b) The limits of translation
            (c) The cultural context
         (2) General Revelation
         (3) Earlier Theologians
      b. Paradigms
         (1) Kuhn's Structure of Scientific Revolutions
         (2) Three Types of Paradigms
         (3) Changing Paradigms in Theology
         (4) Worldview and Incarnation
         (5) The Role of Models and Paradigms in Theology
   2. The Theologian as "Explorer"

C. **The Theologian as Contextualizer**
   1. The Origins of Contextualization
   2. The Roots of Contextualization
      a. Biblical Roots
      b. Historical Roots
      c. Form versus Content
   3. Objections to Contextualization
   4. Implications of Contextualization
      a. A Call for Creativity and Innovation
      b. Integrating the Academic and Practical Theological Disciplines
      c. Understanding the Sources of Theology
      d. Rethinking the Nature of the Authority of the Scriptures
      e. Rethinking Denominational and Ecumenical Relations
   5. Evangelical Contextualization in the Contemporary World

D. **Conclusion**

CHAPTER 2

THE THEOLOGIAN'S CONTRADICTORY JOB DESCRIPTION

During his tour of the United States near the end of his life, the great twentieth-century Swiss theologian Karl Barth was asked at a press conference what the most profound theological idea was that had ever entered his head. Barth replied, "Jesus loves me this I know, for the Bible tells me so." Yet Barth wrote more than six million words in his *Church Dogmatics* to explain his theological understanding. Christianity is simple at its heart, but it is anything but simplistic. Theologians are finite and sinful human beings, yet they are called to study the Infinite and ultimately to attain a knowledge of God in all his various aspects.

When we are confronted by our first course in theology, we generally try to learn the basic doctrines and to "get our theology down." In so doing, most of us trust our teacher and adopt uncritically what we are taught. Initially this is not a problem. The basic message of Christianity is simple, and a first course in theology also tends to be fairly straightforward. The difficulties begin when we realize that the basic message of Christianity has over the centuries been understood and interpreted in a variety of ways. What sometimes makes it even more intimidating is that over the centuries many Latin and German terms have found their way into the standard vocabulary of theological studies, as the following chart shows.

Theology is most commonly understood as *sapientia*, *scientia*, or *orthopraxis* (see chart on next page).

John Jefferson Davis has noted of these three models of theology:

> A healthy evangelical theology, to properly equip the people of God for the work of ministry (Eph. 4:11–16) needs all three elements: *sapientia*, *scientia*, *orthopraxis.*

FIGURE 2.1.

Models of Theology	
Theology as *sapientia* (wisdom)	The aim of theology as *sapientia*, or wisdom, is pointing the believer to God in a relational fashion. In this model, theology is seen as being more than just propositions about God, more than an acceptance of abstract beliefs. Rather, theology points toward a relationship with God based on personal trust. This was the model employed by Augustine and later by the Puritans. William Ames, the theological father of the New England Puritans, defined theology as the "teaching of living to God."[1]
Theology as *scientia* (science)	During the Middle Ages, with the rise of scholasticism, theology was conceived of as *scientia*, as science—in fact, as the "queen of the sciences." Medieval scholastics composed the great *summas*, theological works that were the summing up of all theological knowledge or, in some cases, the sum of all human knowledge. Theology was the reigning academic discipline and exercised hegemony over all other areas of study.
Theology as *orthopraxis* (right action)	More recently, with the rise of liberation theology, a new model of theology has emerged that sees *orthopraxis*, right action in the world rather than right doctrine, as the goal of the theological task. But it is not just the liberation theologians who are embracing this theme. Even within the evangelical community some have adopted this perspective, albeit with a significantly different emphasis. R. J. Rushdoony has insisted that the task of systematic theology "cannot simply be an exercise in thinking, and a systematization of Biblical thought. It must be thinking for action in terms of knowing, obeying and honoring God by fulfilling His mandate to us.... It is related to what happens in church, state, school, family, the arts and sciences, the vocations, and all things else."[2] In other words, systematic theology is not an end in itself; it is a means to an end, namely, the furtherance of the kingdom of God, the bringing of all things under the lordship of Jesus Christ.

> A theology that loses touch with the dimensions of personal spirituality and Christian growth becomes sterile and academic.
>
> A theology that rejects the heritage of the great medieval and seventeenth-century scholastic systems will find itself in danger of losing the precision of thought and intellectual rigor that are essential to the theological task.
>
> A theology that loses sight of the dominion mandate (Gen. 1:28) and the Great Commission (Matt. 28:19–20) forgets that Christian knowledge is not an end in itself but an instrument for bringing about the "obedience of faith" (Rom 1:5) among the nations. Evangelical theology's proper context is the ministry and mission of the church, and its goal is to extend the reign of Jesus Christ to the uttermost parts of the earth.[3]

These models of theology are helpful, even necessary, and they serve as the foundation for the following discussion. But they fail to capture the unavoidable dynamics and the tensions inherent in the theological enterprise. So instead of focusing immediately on a theological system or a theological construct that is the product of the theologian's labor, we must first look at some of the dynamic and even contradictory responsibilities that pull at the student of theology. There are at least three central aspects of the theologian's task that to a greater or lesser extent pull in different directions and at times seem mutually contradictory. These three factors are at work in the individual theologian as well as in the theological community. If we make the mistake of emphasizing one of these over the other two, the result can be great misunderstanding and (often unnecessary) debate among theologians. The three aspects of the theologian's job are *guardian of truth*, *scientist*, and *contextualizer*.

A. THE THEOLOGIAN AS GUARDIAN OF TRUTH

> The things you have heard me say in the presence of many witnesses entrust to reliable men who will also be qualified to teach others.
>
> (2 Tim. 2:2)

> Contend for the faith that was once for all entrusted to the saints.
>
> (Jude 3)

Christianity is founded on the conviction that truth exists and that God is its source and author. God's truth concerning humankind's spiritual condition and the remedy for that condition has been revealed in God's Word, the Scriptures. The Scriptures are normative for faith and life. But the Bible is not a systematic theology, and it does not present us with organized doctrinal

WANTED

Theologian to communicate the truth of God to the church of the next generation. Must be thoroughly versed in the Scriptures and unwaveringly committed to preserving "the faith once delivered to the saints." Must have insatiable curiosity and the mind of a dedicated scientist. Must also have courage to follow the evidence toward truth wherever it leads no matter what the consequences. The successful candidate will recognize the culturally bound nature of human communication and be so fully immersed in cultural thought as to be able to boldly reshape his or her communication into the thought forms and language of the day.

expositions. It is a book that deals with concrete issues and with God's activity in history, culminating in the life, death, and resurrection of Jesus Christ. Scripture points to Jesus as the only way to enter into relationship with God (John 14:6), and it is the message of the redemption in Jesus that has been given to the church to proclaim. This is the faith "once for all entrusted to the saints." Yet the early church discovered that even the simple proclamation, "Christ died for our sins," was undergirded by a host of formal theological assumptions. These assumptions were teased out of the biblical text and made explicit, a process that gave birth to the more formal discipline of theology that we recognize today.

The early church took its responsibility to preserve the truth of the apostolic tradition seriously. Moving away from the teaching of the apostles was considered the gravest of offenses. From its earliest days, the church has regarded itself as the guardian of the truth of the gospel. The earliest formal theological statement preserved for us is *The Demonstration of the Apostolic Preaching*, written by Irenaeus, bishop of Lyons, around A.D. 200.

1. What Is Faith?

> Now faith is being sure of what we hope for and certain of what we do not see.
>
> (Heb. 11:1)

J. I. Packer says this about the link between knowing *about* God and knowing God:

> I question the adequacy of conceptualizing the subject-matter of Systematic Theology as simple revealed truths about God, and I challenge the assumption that has usually accompanied this form of statement, that the material, like any other scientific data is best studied in cool and clinical detachment.... "Detachment from what," you ask? Why from the relational activity of trusting, loving, worshipping, obeying, serving, and glorifying God: the activity that results from realizing that one is actually in God's presence, actually being addressed by him, every time one opens the Bible or reflects on any divine truth whatsoever.... This ... proceeds as if doctrinal study would only be muddled by introducing devotional concerns; it drives a wedge between ... knowing true notions about God and knowing the true God himself.[4]

Any discussion of theology and theological study—if it is to be done properly—*must* begin with a precommitment of faith. But what is faith? The answer seems obvious: faith is a belief in something. However, if we take as our starting point the Greek, rather than the English, terms used for *faith* and *believe* in the New Testament (πίστις [*pistis*] or πιστεύω [*pisteuo*]), the question becomes a bit more complicated. The Greek terminology encompasses both the cognitive (*what* we believe) and the personal (*in whom* we believe). Both these aspects appear in the history of the church in the emphases of the works of diverse theologians.

The dual aspect of the New Testament understanding of faith can be seen simply by looking at several passages.[5] The notion that *pistis* involves *belief in a statement* can be seen in the Gospels as well as in Hebrews and James; for example, "If you *believed* Moses, you would *believe* me, for he wrote about me. But since you do not *believe* what he wrote, how are you going to *believe* what I say?" (John 5:46–47, italics added). Even in Paul, who perhaps more than any other New Testament author stresses the trust aspect of faith, we find this cognitive stress: "For this reason God sends them a powerful delusion so that they will *believe* the lie" (2 Thess. 2:11, italics added). In this case, the belief is false! The more common usage is that the object of belief is the affirmations of the gospel, for example, "Now if we died with Christ, we *believe* that we will also live with him" (Rom. 6:8, italics added). These few examples demonstrate that the New Testament concept of belief as expressed in the terminology of *pistis* had specific intellectual content.

On the other hand, the verbal form *pisteuo* regularly carries the idea of personal trust, a trust that involves a disposition of the will. In the New Testament we see this expressed by the verb *pisteuo* in combination with a preposition that introduces the object of that trust εἰς (*eis*, "in" or "into") or επί (*epi*, "on" or "upon"). This construction stresses the personal commitment to the object of faith, commonly Jesus or God. "Whoever *believes in* the Son has eternal life, but whoever rejects the Son will not see life, for God's wrath remains on him" (John 3:36, italics added). "They replied, '*Believe in* the Lord Jesus, and you will be saved—you and your household'" (Acts 16:31, italics added). "For it stands in scripture: 'See, I am laying in Zion a stone, a cornerstone chosen and precious; and whoever *believes in* him will not be put to shame'" (1 Peter 2:6 NRSV, italics added). Occasionally some translations will render πιστεύω επί (*pisteuo epi*) as simply "trust," as, for example, in, "To one who ... trusts him who justifies the ungodly, his faith is reckoned as righteousness" (Rom. 4:5 RSV; cf. NRSV).

Clearly the New Testament envisions faith as including both belief *and* trust. When the term is used, it usually includes elements of both rather than referring to either belief *or* trust. When it comes to "saving faith," both elements must be present, but when we look at various theologians, we see that one or the other element often takes precedence.

a. Thomas Aquinas

Thomas Aquinas (c. 1225–74) stands as representative of the Roman Catholic tradition. His teaching on faith is complex and highly nuanced. His most important themes see faith as *assent* and faith as *formed by love.* On the one hand, faith is an intellectual *assent* to a proposed belief—to propositions—but this faith is not mere knowledge, because knowledge as such does not compel the mind to *believe* a proposition as such. In Thomas's estimation, the truths of faith are not self-evident. The mind must be moved to assent by a deliberate choice of the will.[6] Thomas then proposed that the essential content of belief, the Nicene Creed and the Apostles' Creed, must be believed *explicitly*, while other teachings of the church must be believed *implicitly*. Such faith achieves its certainty from the infallible authority of the Roman Catholic Church. "To have faith thus means, in practice, to give your assent to the articles of belief defined by the church's creeds and, at the same time, to be ready to accept anything else that may be proposed for your belief by those who exercise the church's teaching office."[7]

For Thomas, faith becomes a habit of mind as opposed to a series of disconnected acts. It is at this point that the second aspect of faith is seen: *faith formed by love.* A good habit is one infused by God rather than self-generated. As such it is a theological virtue. It is a habit of mind that gives lively intellectual assent to things unseen. The source of this habit is love, or friendship with God.

b. Martin Luther

It was specifically to this "faith formed by love" that the Reformers objected. The Reformers, Martin Luther in particular, objected to the intellectually oriented teaching on faith and in response emphasized the trust side of the equation. Luther's teaching on faith has been called *fiducia*, "confidence." Critics of Luther's teaching claim—wrongly, I believe—that his position finds security, not in sacraments or doctrines, but in subjective feeling, in a seeking after a sense of *feeling* forgiven. Luther did emphasize the *trust* aspect of faith, in response to the overintellectualization of Thomistic faith. He did not deny that faith is assent, but he insisted that it is something more. What concerned Luther is what he called *historical faith*, mere intellectual assent to the gospel account. (Even Satan believes in this sense, and such a faith does not save.) Luther insisted that one must have a *trust* that risks everything on the promise of the gospel. At one point Luther said:

> We should note that there are two ways of believing. One way is to believe *about* God, as I do when I believe that what is said of God is true; just as I do when I believe what is said about the Turk, the devil or hell. This faith is knowledge or observation rather than faith. The other way is to believe *in* God, as I do when I not only believe that what is said about Him is true, but put my trust in Him, surrender myself to Him and make bold to deal with Him, believing without doubt that He will be to me and do to me just what is said of Him.[8]

Luther clearly affirmed the dual nature of faith seen in the New Testament—both the cognitive aspect as well as the personal appropriation of the truth. Unbelief is not heresy, as it is in Thomas's understanding, but rather a lack of trust. Luther recognized the propositional nature of faith, that it involves "right thinking about God."[9] That right thinking arises out of a grasp of the content of the gospel, the revelation of God.

c. John Calvin

In John Calvin we find yet another emphasis, that of "recognition." Calvin saw the term *faith* as ambiguous,[10] and in keeping with his exegetical method, he did not try to tie all his conclusions into a tidy framework. While Calvin's discussion lacks the precision of Thomas's, it breathes an existential realism that is absent in Thomas. In this Calvin sounds strangely modern. He stated at one point, "Surely while we teach that faith ought to be certain and assured, we cannot imagine any certainty that is not tinged with doubt, or any assurance that is not assailed by some anxiety."[11]

Calvin saw four components of faith:

1. Knowledge
2. God's goodwill as the object of the knowledge
3. The grounds of that knowledge
4. Inward means by which the knowledge is imparted

Note that the object of faith here is not a list of propositions, but God's benevolence, his goodwill, toward us. This faith has an existential component resembling the knowledge of a personal acquaintance rather than scientific empirical observation. *Knowledge* is actually *recognition*. Faith is so conceived because its knowledge is a response to God's disclosing of his will and is unlike other types of knowledge that arise from things available to us by sense perception.

In Thomas's system, the concept of implicit faith made faith in some sense rests on ignorance, but Calvin was emphatic that this is not an adequate conception.

> Faith rests not on ignorance, but on knowledge. And this is, indeed, knowledge not only of God but of the divine will. We do not obtain salvation either because we are prepared to embrace as true whatever the church has prescribed, or because we turn over to it the task of inquiring and knowing. But we do so when *we know that God is our merciful Father*, because of reconciliation effected through Christ [II Corinthians 5:18–19], and that Christ has been given to us as righteousness, sanctification, and life. By this knowledge, I say, not by submission of our feeling, do we obtain entry into the Kingdom of Heaven.[12]

Faith, in Calvin's understanding, involves not only the head but also the heart. Genuine faith will endure, having seen him who is unseen through trial and persecution. Unbelief for Calvin is the belief that God is against us. It is seeing God as our enemy. In Jesus Christ the believer sees God as he really is and understands that even in discipline he is not the enemy but a good parent who is working for his child's best interests.

d. Faith Seeking Understanding

While explanations of "what faith looks like" differ, they also bear a "family resemblance." Faith involves an intellectual element and an element of personal trust. When it comes to the discipline of theology, theologians must stand within the realm of faith. The proper attitude would seem to be that of Augustine and Anselm, *fides quaerens intellectum*, "faith seeking understanding," as opposed to the rationalistic perspective that states, "I understand in order that I may believe." Theologians begin and continue within the context of faith. Even when they are using critical tools to verify truth, it is within the context of a relationship with the living God revealed in Jesus Christ. They understand their own finiteness and fallenness, and they realize that the finite cannot grasp the infinite, which is shrouded in mystery. And even in the area of the finite, the task of incorporating all knowledge into one's theological understanding is ultimately unattainable. Furthermore, theologians understand that the effects of sin have warped the perspective of even the most devout believer, affecting one's perceptions and articulations. All theological work done is in some measure provisional and in need of criticism.

Although theology is by definition an intellectual discipline, the practice of the discipline begins and continues in faith. As the intellectual content is more fully grasped, knowledge of God is more fully apprehended, and faith, far from being left behind, is enriched and nurtured. The growth of theological knowledge within the context of faith leads not to the danger of heresy, but to true maturity that more adequately grasps the proper object of faith and dethrones idolatrous misconceptions. Such a perspective seeks to test all things, hold on to what is good, and reject that which is wrong.

2. What Is Heresy?

The roots of individualism in American society go deep into its cultural soil. It is out of this individualism and the insistence on personal liberty and freedom of conscience that America's greatness arose. However, individual liberty has a dark side. One need only glance at the book of Judges to see that if individual liberty exists without a guiding center of accountability to God and to fellow humans, chaos reigns.

Western culture today appears to have lost its spiritual center. With the birth of the postmodern world, the very concept of truth itself is denied. The church is marginalized and has become increasingly irrelevant even in the lives of those who call themselves Christians. Belief systems are exchanged for "worship experiences," and theological understanding, even among evangelicals, stands at an all-time low. In the late 1990s, sociologist George Barna conducted a poll of evangelicals and concluded that a majority of the people who adopt the label *evangelical* and attend evangelical churches are "more likely to think that 'evangelical' refers to being passionate about faith or religion, perhaps even fanatical, but that the term has little to do with theological perspectives."[13] A New Testament professor at a major evangelical seminary has commented on several occasions that while evangelical scholarship has never been at a higher level, it is as if in the churches we have entered a new "dark ages" with reference to the knowledge of Scripture. I would add that the darkness extends to the knowledge of theology.

Most Christians view theology as abstract discussions of such topics as "How many angels can dance on the head of a pin?" and dismiss it as irrelevant to life. This is not a new phenomenon, but theological anti-intellectualism has become a virtual avalanche that has buried the church. The concept of orthodoxy, the basic doctrines of the church that identify it as Christian, and the creeds that arose out of the great ecumenical councils of the fourth and fifth centuries are largely deemed irrelevant.

The ideas of orthodoxy and its opposite, heresy, are virtually unknown.[14] In fact, pride is often taken in adopting theological positions opposed to the doctrines the church has always affirmed. What is not recognized is that heresy—teaching rejected by the church—was rejected for a reason: it ultimately undercuts a key element of the gospel. The question must be asked, "What happens to a person who embraces and lives by heretical teachings?" C. FitzSimons Allison contends that while heresy is prevalent in the world today, it is ultimately cruel to the person who adopts it. "Victims of these teachings have been encouraged either to escape the world and their basic humanity into some form of flight and death or to use religion to undergird and isolate further their own self-centered self from the need to be loved and to love."[15]

The problem with heretical teaching is that it panders to the natural desire of the fallen human heart. Heresy reflects the way we would like things to be rather than the way God has established them. Allison notes, "Heresies pander to the most unworthy tendencies of the human heart. It is astonishing how little attention has been given to these two aspects of heresy: its cruelty and its pandering to sin."[16]

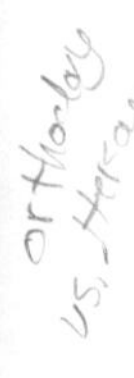

The rap against orthodoxy is that it is dull, unimaginative, and defensive, while heresy is bold, creative, and innovative. While there may be some truth to this charge, in that defenders of orthodoxy have at times been dull, intolerant, and even cruel, and that heretics have sometimes been sincere and selfless in promoting their beliefs (often beliefs that contained a partial truth while ignoring the wider context and the implications of the belief), the other side is also true. Heretics have at times also been repressive, cruel, and intolerant while the orthodox have been selfless and magnanimous. Athanasius, fourth-century bishop of Alexandria, suffered years of persecution for his defense of orthodoxy while his heretical opponents rode the wave of popular and imperial support.[17]

Contemporary examples of the elevation of heresy to a virtue abound. The late Episcopal bishop James Pike's defense of his beliefs was entitled *If This Be Heresy.* Walter Kaufman wrote *The Faith of a Heretic*, and Robert Van de Weyer issued *The Call to Heresy*, contending that orthodoxy and heresy are dictated by the fact that the "victors write history." In this scenario, orthodoxy becomes simply the victor's version of the truth.

The term *orthodoxy* generally has been used to refer to the decisions of the first four ecumenical councils of the church. The creedal statements coming out of these councils did not define doctrine so much as set the boundaries around the subsequent discussions of the Trinity and the person of Christ as both God and man. While these statements are not perfect and reflect the thought forms of the early church, they have stood the test of time. The truth of orthodox doctrine prevented Christianity from "being absorbed into paganism" and from degenerating into merely another legalistic sect.[18]

Having said this, I must admit that there is a tendency for orthodoxy to drift into another kind of "heresy." While a creed is a statement of belief, it is not an end in itself. It is a road map, a pointer to a greater reality, but too often the map becomes identified as the reality itself. Enforced subscription to a creed or doctrinal statement is sometimes substituted for vital faith in the God to whom the creed points. Thus "correct" orthodoxy gives birth to "a new kind of heresy, a heresy of the spirit rather than of doctrine." This phenomenon is yet another criticism against orthodoxy.

The whole reason for distinguishing between heresy and orthodoxy arises from the fact that ideas have consequences, as do teachings. The ultimate question involved here is one of truth, an unpopular concept in our postmodern world. Lesslie Newbigin says of this flight from truth, "The relativism which is not willing to speak about truth but only about 'what is true for me' is an evasion of the serious business of living. It is the mark of a tragic loss of nerve in our contemporary culture. It is a preliminary symptom of death."[19]

Underlying this entire discussion is the truth to which the prophet Jeremiah witnessed: "The human mind is more deceitful than anything else. It is incurably bad" (Jer. 17:9 NET Bible). John Calvin put it another way: the heart is a "perpetual factory of idols." Every heresy in some way encourages an aspect of the fallen human nature. The term heresy is derived from the Greek αἵρεισθαι (*haireisthai*), to choose.[20] It does not imply a neutral choice;

there is an underlying spiritual-moral factor. Neither heresy nor orthodoxy is simply an intellectual exercise; there is an inescapable heart factor. Anglican bishop Jeremy Taylor observed, "Heresy is not an error of the understanding but an error of the will."[21] To this Samuel Taylor Coleridge added its converse, "Faith is not an accuracy of logic, but a rectitude of the heart."[22]

3. The Theologian as Preserver of Tradition

Despite the current darkness, the evangelical tradition has in the past self-consciously built its theological understanding on the Scriptures, but in so doing, it has not had a sense of historical continuity with the broader Christian tradition. This is particularly true in America. Church historian Kenneth Scott Latourette observed that nineteenth-century American Protestants tended "to ignore developments which had taken place in Christianity in the Old World after the first century."[23] A common assumption was (and is) that theology is simply built on the Bible, or that our system of theological understanding is simply "the Bible's own view of itself." In some camps, the cry "No creed but the Bible" has in effect cut groups off from their heritage as Christians and evangelicals. Yet this implies that the Holy Spirit has taught the church nothing over the past twenty centuries.

This mentality that the Bible alone is the authority for and source of theology has sometimes had a divisive result that has seen groups split over differences in their understanding of Scripture—often without any benchmark or guiding principle other than a commitment to biblical authority.[24] The "Bible alone" mentality has often been accompanied by a naive biblicism that assumes that the text has a "plain meaning" and that denies, usually implicitly, that all reading of the biblical text involves interpretation.

During the last decade and a half of the twentieth century, a renewed emphasis on the enduring nature of the central core of the Christian faith arose within the evangelical community. Thomas Oden, Methodist theologian at Drew University, became the catalyst. Trained in the liberalism of the Bultmann tradition, he ultimately rejected the liberal project as bankrupt.[25] In the destruction of his liberal optimism, he discovered the ancient sources of Christian theology in the writings of the early church fathers (patristics). These writings laid the foundation of and set the parameters for the development of later Christian understanding. He grasped the true nature of the Christian heritage and came face-to-face with the fact that much modern exegetical and theological scholarship had manipulated Scripture to say whatever the exegete/theologian wanted it to say. Ultimately his conviction of the importance of the church's common theological heritage became so compelling that he produced a three-volume systematic theology in which his stated goal was *to say nothing new.* His rationale bears repeating:

> I prefer consent-expressing ancient exegetes to those whose thoughts are characterized more by individual creativity, controversial brilliance, stunning rhetoric, or speculative genius. The weighting of references may be compared to a pyramid of sources with canonical Scripture as the firm foundation. The stable center of the pyramid is the consensual Christian writers of the first five centuries. Atop these are the best of the medieval writers followed by the consensual teachers of the Reformation and Counter-Reformation at the narrowing heights, and more recent interpreters at the tapering apex, but only those few who best grasp and express the one mind of the believing historical church of all cultures and times.
>
> I am pledged not to try to flip that pyramid upside-down, as have guild theologians, who tend to value only what is most recent. Earlier rather than later sources are cited where pertinent, not because of an antiquarian nostalgia for that which is older, but because antiquity is a criterion of authentic memory in any historical testimony....
>
> My purpose is to delineate points of substantial agreement between traditions of East and West—Catholic, Protestant, and Orthodox—on the power of grace in spiritual formation. I will be listening intently for the historical ecumenical consensus received by believers of widely varied languages, social locations, and cultures, whether the consensus is of African, pre-European, or European Christian traditions, whether it is expressed by women or men of the second or first Christian millennium, whether it is post or pre-Constantinian....
>
> Who are the principal consensual exegetes to whom this argument constantly appeals? Above all they are the ecumenical councils and early synods that have come to be so often quoted as representing the mind of the believing church; the four preeminent ecumenical teachers of the eastern Christian tradition (Athanasius, Basil, Gregory of Nazianzus, John Chrysostom), as well as the western (Ambrose, Jerome, Augustine, and Gregory the Great); and others whom the church has perennially valued for accurately stating broad points of ecumenical consensus.[26]

The Christian's appeal to the authority of Scripture is vital and foundational—but it cannot adequately stand in isolation from other factors. Even heretics and cults claim to hold to the authority of Scripture, yet they proclaim doctrines that are at variance with the received faith of the church. On what basis can we make a decision as to who is right and who is wrong? The claim that an accurate exegesis of the Bible is the final arbiter is attractive yet ultimately fails, since it does not recognize that the exegetical decisions made by any interpreter are made from within an interpretive tradition rather than from an objective, value-neutral stance.

While the exegete may legitimately tell us what the text meant to a particular author and to his audience, the text cannot legitimately be said to assume or teach, for example, a foundational doctrine of the faith such as the Trinity or the hypostatic union, since these are *postbiblical structures imposed on the data of the biblical text.* An illustration may help clarify this point. During my first year as a professor, I was teaching on the doctrine of the Trinity. The point of my lecture was that our understanding of God as three *hypostases* (ὑποστασις, "person") who share a common *ousia* (οὐσια, "essence") had emerged out of more than two centuries of theological controversy and wrestling with the implications of the biblical material. At this point, one student's hand shot up. "What do you mean they didn't believe in the Trinity?" he demanded. "I open my Bible and see the Trinity everywhere!" And that is precisely my point. We who live on this side of the councils of Nicea and Constantinople open the Bible and see the doctrine of the Trinity everywhere. But those who lived before those councils *did not have the categories that allowed them to see what we take for granted.* While the data from which the doctrine of the Trinity is constructed are found within Scripture, the formal doctrine itself is not an explicit teaching of the Bible, since it is not a category of the Bible. It is a human construct that has stood the test of time as a model that faithfully reflects, organizes, and interprets the scriptural data in a coherent, self-consistent manner.

The concept of an authoritative tradition arose early in the history of the church as new teaching challenged the received doctrine. In fact, this was key in the rise of the concept of apostolic succession. As originally understood, apostolic succession referred not to the spiritual authority of the apostles being passed down, but to the apostolic doctrine being passed from generation to generation. Very early on the bishops assumed the teaching office and saw themselves as entrusted with the preservation, protection, and proclamation of the truth of the gospel. The seed of this concept is found in Scripture, where Paul admonishes Timothy, "And what you heard me say in the presence of many others as witnesses entrust to faithful people who will be competent to teach others as well" (2 Tim. 2:2 NET Bible). Thus there is a core of apostolic doctrine that is to be passed on from generation to generation.

As the church grew and matured, it faced opposition from those who claimed to have "secret traditions" handed down from Jesus but not entrusted to the apostles. Against these claims the church stressed its historic connection to the apostles and the fact that Jesus would not have entrusted his truth to unknown persons rather than to those who accompanied him in his ministry. The truth that Jesus taught was then committed to writing and preserved in the New Testament. "Rules of faith" such as the "Old Roman Symbol,"[27] were drawn up to summarize the apostolic doctrine. Origen, the great if often idiosyncratic early-third-century theologian from Alexandria, said that the teaching of the church was founded on "either the evidence to be found in the sacred Scriptures, or that to be discovered by the investigation of the logical consequences of the Scriptures and adherence to accuracy."[28] Likewise, Irenaeus, in his *Demonstration of the Apostolic Preaching*, demonstrates from the Scriptures the truth of the rule of faith. As challenges to the faith arose from within the church, councils were called to debate the opinions. The councils did not invent new doctrine; they clarified, explained, and drew out, much in the manner Origen had described a century earlier, the implications of the teaching that the church had held since the apostles first delivered their doctrine. The process of doctrinal development was largely a clarifying of the message the church had always proclaimed. The difference was that before this time individual fathers of the church had done the "unpacking." Now the whole church officially put its imprimatur upon this unpacking and published the results of the councils in the form of creeds that regulated the teaching of the church.

The doctrinal development of the first four centuries formed a historic benchmark for the church. All who call themselves Christian today, whether Roman Catholic, Orthodox, or Protestant, adhere to the doctrinal truth contained in the ecumenical creeds of the first four centuries.[29] Many evangelical Protestants bypass the creedal statements and ground their doctrines directly in Scripture, but even here the truth of the content of the creeds is affirmed even though the authority of the creeds is denied.

We have looked at how the apostolic doctrine was handed down and codified, but we have not yet touched on the assumption that the living Holy Spirit is the teacher of the church. Unless we affirm that theology is merely an intellectual exercise, we must recognize that the Holy Spirit is a dynamic presence, teaching the church. Indeed, Abraham Kuyper insisted that the "mysticism of the Spirit" is a necessary component of the theological enterprise.[30] If this is the case, then ignoring the work that went on in the ancient church and deeming the conclusions it reached unimportant may reveal, not so much a high view of the Scriptures as a culpable, spiritual arrogance and may bring the theologian under the apostle Paul's rebuke against the Corinthians: "Did the word of God originate with you? Or are you the only people it has reached?" (1 Cor. 14:36).

A key component of the theologian's job is the preservation and defense of this apostolic tradition. He or she stands in the stream of the church's fathers and like Timothy of old has a responsibility to pass on the teachings received. If this were the extent of the job, the theologian would simply have to repeat what was received in the form in which it was received. However, the picture is more complicated. What the theologian receives is not limited to the apostolic tradition only; it is more comprehensive and often has a different focus than the "fundamental Christian faith."[31] Over the centuries, the apostolic tradition has been interpreted and "refined" from various perspectives, such as the Reformed, Arminian, Lutheran, and Dispensational. Thus it becomes necessary to check the form of the tradition we have received against the original. We cannot assume that what has been handed down has not been changed. Change may be nearly imperceptible, but it is change nonetheless.

As a youth, I worked for a time with my father, a contractor. One of my first jobs was to cut a pile of boards to the same length. I carefully measured the first cut from the proper side of the blade and made the cut. I checked the length of the board, and it matched the specifications my father had given me. I then measured the next board using the freshly cut one as a template. Since I knew the template was the right length, I didn't measure again. I then measured the next board by the one I had just completed, and so forth. In about a half hour I had finished the task. But when my father examined the job, he was frustrated and upset. Each succeeding board was shorter than the previous one. Instead of measuring each cut against the original template, I had measured each cut against the previous cut. I had not realized that this procedure didn't take into account the width of the blade; and over the course of the job, the final boards grew almost imperceptibly but steadily shorter. The final board was a full one and one-half inches shorter than the first. By using succeeding copies as opposed to the original as my standard of reference, I had made the boards unusable for their intended purpose.

The theologian must know the parameters of the received faith and be able to detect that which falls outside those parameters, even by a small amount. It is at this point that the theologian's job shifts focus from preserver to critical inquirer.

B. THE THEOLOGIAN AS "SCIENTIST/EXPLORER"

The theologian is, as we have seen, a *guardian* of the truth. He must also be a *communicator* of the truth (see "The Theologian as Contextualizer," below). Between these two tasks lies the theologian's mandate to pursue two interrelated tasks: to be *a researcher* of *truth* as well as *a searcher* for *truth*.

1. *"Scientist."* Being a researcher of truth involves the analytical and critical investigation of the theologian's sources of truth (*critical* in the sense of examining and evaluating carefully). The most helpful metaphor to describe this aspect of the task is that of *scientist*. Theology is not a fuzzy discipline that can get by with sloppy thinking and a casual handling of the available data. Yet on the other hand, doing theology is not simply doing science, which is why "scientist" is a metaphor here and is put in quote marks.

2. *"Explorer."* As searcher for truth, the theologian can be compared to an *explorer*. We cannot simply presume that the content and boundaries of our theology are "*the* truth, the whole truth, and nothing but the truth." The boundaries of theology continue to expand and change, as they have for the last two thousand years—while its foundation and core remain steady as a rock.

1. The Theologian as "Scientist"

a. The Analytical and Critical Task

In 1989 two researchers in Utah, Dr. Martin Fleischmann and Dr. Stanley Pons, announced to a stunned world that they had produced "cold fusion," which promised energy without the high cost and danger associated with nuclear reactors. Skeptical but fascinated, the media and the scientific community heralded it as a breakthrough discovery, which it would have been if research scientists around the world had been able to successfully reproduce the experiments of Fleischmann and Pons. The consensus was that there was a flaw either in Pons and Fleischmann's procedure or in their observations.[32]

One of the key facets of the scientific method as it is applied in the physical (or hard) sciences is that of the *reproducibility of experiments*. Individuals in different locations, using the same materials and the same method, must get the same results. While theologians do not deal with research results that can be experimentally verified, the principle of public verifiability is very much applicable to theologians. They are not free to spin theological theories out of bits of data from randomly selected sources. Theologians must always give a clear account of their sources and (to the extent possible) of their assumptions and presuppositions. In other words, theologians must be intellectually honest and transparent so that their readers can go back to the sources underlying the conclusions and understand the basis for them.[33]

Theologian-scientists look in three directions: at the text of Scripture, at general revelation, and at the work of earlier theologians.

(1) The Text of Scripture

The first order of work for the scientist/theologian is an encounter with the text of Scripture itself. Even when discoveries in the text confirm the general parameters of the belief they have inherited, this phase gives those understandings a new richness and depth. In the mid-1960s, color television began to enter American homes. What we saw on the screen were the same images we had been watching for over a decade in black and white, but now they came alive in a new, vivid way. For the first time, we saw the subtle details, and we never wanted to go back to the old black and white again. I would liken this process to what I discovered when I first learned to exegete the text of Scripture and saw firsthand the nuances of the Greek language and some of the features that are lost in translation. And when I learned the historical part of the exegetical process, it took my understanding and appreciation of the text to a new level. Whereas before I had been listening to a melody, I now heard the symphony.

(a) The historical nature of divine revelation. The question arises, "Why, if God's Word is meant for his people, must we undertake such study? Shouldn't his message be readily apparent?" The answer to this question is severalfold. First, because the message of the biblical text was given largely in ancient Hebrew and koine Greek, languages no longer in use, the assumption that "I should be able to open the Bible and understand it because it is the Word of God" fails at the outset. This assumption does not take into account the historical nature of divine revelation. If a student were given a Greek or Hebrew text, it would be meaningless to him or her. Those who identify their English translations with the written, inspired, inerrant Word of God regularly overlook this fact. When we pick up and use an English translation, we are in a real sense dependent on scholars and their views in the various areas of critical study, such as linguistics and hermeneutics. Since scholars may be more or less accurate in their translation from the original language, peers must critically evaluate the quality of the translation.

(b) The limits of translation. On the other end of the translation process is another variable: the "receptor language." While the original text is fixed in that the biblical Hebrew and Greek do not change over time,[34] the same cannot be said for the receptor language. Any spoken language is living and dynamic. Words, modes of expression, and even grammar are in a constant state of flux. Recent dictionaries incorporate many new terms as well as new usages of existing terms. Other terms become obsolete and fall out of usage. If a translation is to communicate in the most complete way possible, it must take contemporary idiom into account and render into English the meaning of the original in a way that best represents contemporary usage without sacrificing the original intent.

(c) The cultural context. Another reason why we must study the text of Scripture is to attempt to discover the meaning that was clear and even obvious to the original hearers, who shared a common language, a common cultural heritage, and a common context of conversations with, for example, the apostle Paul. Twenty-first-century humanity does not share either the language or the cultural perspectives and values of first-century humanity.

To assume that we understand what a text says simply because it is accurately translated is a grave error. Terms and concepts that are used in both the ancient and contemporary world do not necessarily involve the same meaning or nuance. For example, the term *adoption* is often used in the New Testament as an explanation of the nature of the believer's relationship to God. *Adoption* is also a contemporary concept. But without further study, we would not know that in the ancient world adoption did not have reference to childless couples seeking to have a family of their own. Nor did it refer to infants. Adult males rather than infants were adopted in the first-century Roman world. Members of the older generation would adopt a person who would care for them in their elder years and would inherit their property. The adoptee was brought into the family with full status and legal rights as an adult son. Adoption involved a severing of all legal ties with the adoptee's past life, even to the point of erasing all criminal charges and legal debts. Before the law that person was quite literally a "new man" without a past. His identity was totally linked to the new family. To read the Pauline texts concerning *adoption* from our perspective and our cultural practice of adoption is to miss the point that Paul is making about the nature of the believer's standing before God.

Perhaps the clearest example of this is found in the New Testament Epistles. In these inspired documents of the apostolic authors, we have only half the conversation. We do not know with certainty the circumstances prompting the letters; these must be inferred from the letters themselves. Furthermore, the letters contain for the most part only issues under discussion. Shared assumptions remain implicit because there was no need to discuss them: a first-century reader would readily understand much of that implicit information, since both the writer and the reader inhabited the same world. But the twenty-first-century reader inhabits a different world with different assumptions, which is why there are so many, often radically divergent, interpretations of the Epistles.

(2) General Revelation

The concept of general revelation as it is discussed usually has reference to that which can be gleaned about the nature of God directly from the created order, apart from special revelation (the Bible). The concept of general revelation is in reality far broader than this. It involves an understanding of God as the author of all truth found in the created order since he is its source and author. This concept forbids pitting the truth of creation against the truth of the Bible as is commonly done, for example, in the debate about creation. (This concept is developed at length in chapter 4, "Sources and Authority in Theology.")

(3) Earlier Theologians

Theology involves, not reproducing the results of an experiment, but checking the results of other theologians' work against the data of Scripture. This checking entails applying recognized exegetical and logical methods to the Scriptures and checking the results of that application with the theological results of a previous generation as well as to contemporary proposals. A caveat is in order here. In studying the works of earlier theologians, students must be diligent to understand the historic and sociological context of the theologian being studied and deal with that person according to the standards of his or her time rather than anachronistically imposing current standards on the analysis or reading one's own preconceptions and prejudices into the person's work.

b. Paradigms

Likening the task of the theologian to that of the scientist is not a new thought. This was precisely the analogy made by Charles Hodge in his *Systematic Theology* when he first published it in the 1870s. What has changed, and changed radically, is the conception of the task of the scientist. During Hodge's time the task of the scientist was conceived within the larger assumptions of Baconian inductivism.[35] The world was objective and "out there," and the task of the scientist was simply to discover the world as it actually was. The scientist was to discover the facts, draw inductive conclusions, and in so doing expand human knowledge of the created order piece by piece.

(1) Kuhn's Structure of Scientific Revolutions

But this view of the orderly progress of knowledge was derailed in the latter half of the twentieth century. The catalyst was Thomas Kuhn's pivotal book *The Structure of Scientific Revolutions.*[36] This work marked the beginning of a new era in the way science viewed itself and in our understanding of our progress in knowledge. Its implications have had profound significance for the theologian/exegete as well.

Kuhn observed that when a science is *immature,* there are competing models, explanations, or paradigms. No one disciplinary matrix is able to win the day. Eventually one theory or perspective will gain dominance, but that dominance comes from the superiority of the theory rather than the imposition of that theory by the scientific community. The dominant theory (paradigm) is able to account for all the data and offer direction for future research in a more cogent, comprehensive, and fruitful way than competing theories. Once it has gained ascendancy, a consolidation process takes place, during which other theories are marginalized as unscientific.

The paradigm becomes the sole recognized disciplinary matrix and is viewed as "the way science is done" in the discipline in question. At this point, the situation is one of *mature* science, and the mature paradigm exercises hegemony over the entire discipline. A revolution creates a divide between those who accept the new paradigm and those who do not. These two groups have different conceptions of the problems, standards, and goals of research and even of what constitutes relevant data. When one group is sure that the revolution has triumphed, those still unconvinced are effectively marginalized, and the victors turn their attention from debating foundations to new areas of research.

This hegemony continues, but as time goes on, anomalous data that do not fit the paradigm accumulate and eventually bring the discipline into crisis. At this point, a new model will be proposed that will account for all the known data as well as the anomalous data. This new paradigm will exist alongside the old paradigm for quite some time. The establishment generally regards the newly proposed paradigm as heretical because it challenges key assumptions that have guided researchers for years. Thus an intellectual battle ensues between the old, accepted paradigm and the new proposal. Eventually—usually a generation later—the new paradigm is adopted and the revolution is complete. Those who still cling to the old paradigm are marginalized, repeating the process that brought the previous paradigm into dominance.

A concrete example of this process can be seen in the acceptance of plate tectonics as the dominant paradigm in geology. Early in the twentieth century, as Alfred Wegener (1880–1930) studied the shape of the continents, he observed that the shape of the east coast of South America looked as if it would fit nicely into the west coast of Africa. Further musing over the shape of the continents led him to the conclusion that the entire world had at one time been a single continent, which he called Pangaea. Wegener proposed the theory of continental drift and with it "plate tectonics, one of the most important and far-ranging geological theories of all time; when first proposed, it was ridiculed, but steadily accumulating evidence finally prompted its acceptance, with immense consequences for geology, geophysics, oceanography, and paleontology."[37] Wegener's theory is a classic example of the kind of revolution Kuhn discusses. After initial skepticism and hostility, the geological community was confronted by a mass of accumulating evidence that could not be accounted for by the previous theory. When the data reached a critical point, the previous theory was overthrown and plate tectonics became the new reigning paradigm.

(2) Three Types of Paradigms

Kuhn's use of the term *paradigm* can be boiled down into three main categories.

The first use of the term *paradigm* is that of "artifact" or "construct." These are specific scientific achievements embodying crucial advances in science that have become models having a key role in the puzzle-solving process that is the normal work of the research scientist.[38]

The second sense in which he uses the term is with reference to sociological paradigms. He also identifies this level of paradigm as a disciplinary matrix involving the background and assumptions of a particular discipline. This level is analogous to a theological system.

The third meaning is metaphysical and is the most important one for our purposes. Metaphysical paradigms have to do with assumptions about the nature of the world. These are analogous to the normal usage of the term *worldview*. There is much talk about "worldviews" in the wake of postmodernism and the emergence of pluralism, so it is important to define what the term implies. A worldview is the network of assumptions, values, customs, and ways of coping with the world that are common to one's culture or subculture, held largely subconsciously.[39] We absorb a worldview during the socialization process, and our primary worldview is never consciously chosen but is absorbed from childhood. A worldview is implicit in every culture. Like the air we breathe, it surrounds us, but we usually are unaware of its presence. A change in worldview is a self-conscious shift in perspective of the first order, involving changes of viewpoint that were once held inviolable. Because of the intellectual and emotional trauma involved, very few people ever truly change their worldview.[40]

As human beings we are creatures of habit. More than this, our experience has conditioned us in terms of what we can see and how we do things. The way we have always done it is "*the* right way." We infer conditions in situations due to our past experiences. Often these inferred conditions will be legitimate, at other times they may actually prove to be a hindrance to grasping a new reality or to solving a problem. In the figure below, try to connect all nine dots by placing a pencil on one dot and then drawing four straight lines without once lifting the pencil from the paper.

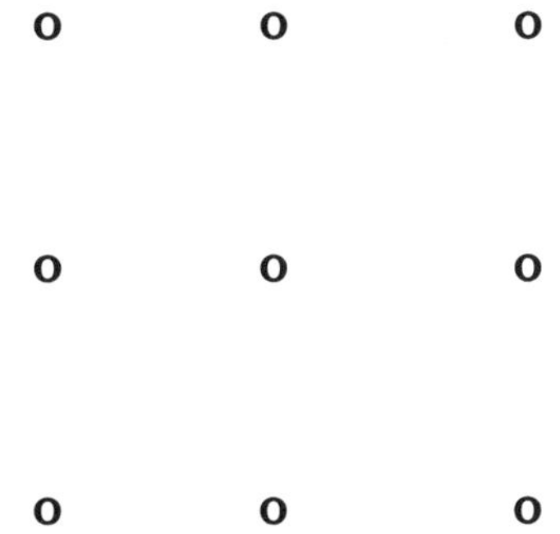

This puzzle is solved only when the natural but unjustified assumption that the lines drawn cannot extend beyond the dots is questioned. Our thinking falls into ruts, and only by extricating our thinking from the ruts can we see new perspectives. A key part of the scientist's work is in observing, in learning to take off the blinders of preconceptions and look afresh at the evidence. This process is key in the pursuit of truth as well as in confirming or disconfirming what is already held as truth. "If progress is to be made in theology ... it will not be made by staying in old lines of thought or by digging new ones deeper, but in lateral and synthetic developments. The preservation and development of what is good in the old lines may involve the questioning of some deeply rooted assumptions."[41]

(3) Changing Paradigms in Theology

The history of theology and biblical study reveals a series of changes in paradigms.[42] The patristic consensus culminating with Augustine gave Western theology a unified perspective that dominated until the High Middle Ages. At that time, however, the Augustinian synthesis fell into crisis and the

Thomistic perspective emerged. Thomas's synthesis competed for dominance until the Council of Trent, at which point it became official Roman Catholic doctrine.[43] The Reformation brought about a radical change in the way theology was done and asserted the priority of the text of Scripture. The next true paradigm shift, the rise of the historical-critical method, was not primarily theological but methodological, in that it purposed to study the Bible scientifically like any other document. This amounted to a first-order Kuhnian revolution in the realm of biblical studies. No longer could the Bible be viewed as simply divine and as having a facile surface harmony. Rather, the text was viewed as essentially human and as embodying the variant perspectives of its human authors as well as the sources used by those authors. The theological world still operates largely under the influence of the historical-critical method to this day.

While less radical than first-order paradigm changes, changes in theological systems (sociological paradigm shifts) have profound influences over the way theologians perceive their reality. Changes in the framework affect not only doctrines themselves but are felt even down to the level of exegesis and the interpretation of discrete passages of Scripture.

(4) Worldview and Incarnation

Sometimes we hear devout believers ask, "Can't we just adopt the worldview of Jesus? He was after all God himself. Surely that is a safe way to order one's life and view of reality." If by "worldview of Jesus" we mean that the contemporary Christian can share with the biblical writers their view of nature and physical reality, the answer is no. While spoken out of a desire for obedience to God and imitation of the Savior, such a longing can never be realized, because we do not live in the first-century world. The biblical writers lived in a prescientific world, and their knowledge of that world was "primitive" by our standards. Thus we cannot with intellectual honesty participate in their view of the world. The discoveries about the nature of physical reality that have been made in the past several centuries cannot be dispensed with any more than we can uninvent the atomic bomb.

The incarnation involved a self-limitation of God in a particular human being at a particular place and time in history. Jesus entered history at a particular place and time to reveal God and to provide salvation, not to unlock the mysteries of the created universe. This was a task God delegated to humankind at the creation when he commanded humans to have dominion over the earth. However, if by this question we are asking whether there are underlying assumptions about reality that form a continuity throughout the

Bible and history, the answer is an emphatic yes. The Bible assumes and presents a view of God, the created order, the nature of humanity, redemption, and so on that are at the core of any view of reality a Christian may hold.

So what does all this have to do with theology? Insofar as theology has to do with the redemption of humanity from its sinful condition, this aspect of the theological truth remains unchanged from age to age. Insofar as the task of theology is bringing all of creation under the lordship of Christ, it has everything to do with the theologian's task. As we learn more about the created order, we discover further information that must be incorporated into theological understanding.

(5) The Role of Models and Paradigms in Theology

An ancient pagan emperor who visited the Jewish rabbi Joshua ben Hannaniah demanded that the rabbi show him his God. The rabbi replied that the request was impossible. Not to be put off, the emperor continued to insist. Ben Hannaniah took the emperor outside and told him to stare at the sun. "That's impossible!" protested the emperor. Ben Hannaniah replied that if the emperor could not even look at the sun in its brightness, how could the emperor expect to behold God in his glory?

The work of Kuhn described above has profound implications for theology. The subject matter of theology, God, is ultimately beyond our grasp. The problem is twofold: human finitude and fallenness. The finite cannot by definition grasp the infinite. In addition, sin has darkened human understanding and made it impossible to comprehend accurately who God is.[44] This desire to comprehend God with the human mind has been a constant temptation to theologians and philosophers throughout the ages. Martin Luther called this attempt the "theology of glory" and added that the proper way to find God is in the "theology of the cross." In other words, we are to find and understand God as he has revealed himself in Christ and his work on the cross rather than try to grasp him as he is in himself, in his unveiled glory and apart from the humiliation of the cross.

We do not learn things univocally; we learn by analogy. We incorporate new understanding into our store of knowledge by comparing it to things we already know. Thus models and analogies are vital. In science abstract concepts often are stated in mathematical formulae. Models are constructed as an aid to understanding.

Models are not literal "things"; they are human constructs that help us organize and make sense of the world around us. Scientists do not believe in the literal truth of the models; they believe in the truth expressed in the mathematical formulae. In theological study, doctrines are often erroneously understood, by theologians and laypeople alike, as literal realities. In fact, figurative language is used even in the Scriptures to describe God and his relationship with humankind. A concept such as adoption is drawn from human life and applied to God in an analogical manner. God does not go to the courthouse and legally adopt individuals when they trust Christ as Savior. But the metaphor of adoption communicates a profound reality concerning the believer's relationship to God.

The concept of *natural law* as it was originally employed was metaphor. Those who first used the terminology did not conceive that God has actually written laws concerning the natural universe, much less think that he would necessarily be obliged to abide by them. Yet over the next century, the concept of natural law came to be understood literally. This scientific understanding had immediate theological overtones. Miracles became impossible since God would not break his own laws. During the past century, the concept of natural law has shifted back from being prescriptive to being a descriptive metaphor.

This principle also holds true in more complex areas of theology. For example, the doctrine of the Trinity is not formulated as such in Scripture. The Bible does not *explicitly* teach that God is three persons sharing a single nature; the Bible *does* explicitly teach monotheism (Deut. 6:4 et al.). But it also presents much data concerning the plurality of God. Jesus, for example, receives worship, and he is said to be the Creator, but he is also seen as distinct from God the Father. The church constructed its doctrine of the Trinity over a period of two and a half centuries, trying to present a model that was faithful to the biblical data without being self-contradictory. What emerged from this process was the Nicene-Constantinopolitan doctrine of the Trinity. The doctrine as it is formally stated is a human construct, a model that attempts to show the unity and plurality of the personal God who has revealed himself in Scripture. This model has passed the test of time, enduring since the early days of the church. This is not to say that the model is perfect, but there has never been a proposal put forth to replace it that hasn't fallen into one of the ancient heresies.

Analogies, models, and paradigms are as much a part of the theologian's work as they are of the scientist's. There are, however, several dangers.

The first, as stated above, is the danger of understanding models and paradigms as literal realities.

The second danger involves pressing analogies and models beyond their legitimate function. Analogies by definition are both similar and dissimilar to that which they are related as explanations. Misunderstandings arise when either incidental or dissimilar parts of the analogy are pressed as integral parts of the reality. Thus the theologian and student must carefully ascertain what aspects of analogies and models are or are not relevant to the reality that is being described.

Conversely, as discussed above, all human knowledge exists within a framework of understanding. The "facts" we understand are not simply value-free pieces of information. Every fact we grasp has already been interpreted by our worldview to give it meaning. This is our paradigm of reality. If we receive data that do not fit that paradigm, our minds will initially ignore them, but if enough data accumulate that do not fit into our paradigm of reality, our minds will force us to create a new paradigm that will account for both the old *and* the new data. In the 1998 film *The Truman Show*, Truman Burbank is the unknowing star of a hit television show; his whole life has been aired for the world to see—but he himself has no hint that his life is not real. During the film, the carefully constructed fantasy comes unraveled as Truman progressively discovers one anomalous piece of data after another that makes him question the nature of the world he inhabits. As *The Truman Show* ends, Truman discovers the nature of his reality. "Was nothing real?" he asks. "You were real," comes the reply. All the experiences of his life were still his experiences, but now they underwent a radical reinterpretation as to their nature and meaning.

As was the case with Truman, as we discover new knowledge, it may alter the framework within which the received core of theology is interpreted and applied. This does not imply that new knowledge is final and not open to further clarification and discovery. Rather, the nature of human knowledge is that it is heuristic and open to correction and clarification.

- - -

How does this fit with the theologian's job description? Theologians, as people who must think critically, must maintain an intellectual honesty about their work. They cannot with integrity proceed on the assumption that what they have been taught, even by the greatest masters, is the final word. Every generation is called to check the theological structure it inherits against the foundations. "If theologians proceed in the belief that they need neither examine nor even acknowledge their inherited metaphysical commitments, they will simply remain prisoners of whatever philosophical school was in the ascendant thirty years earlier, when they were first-year students."[45] There is more to be learned, both from the text of Scripture and from the created order. Theologians proceed with commitments and assumptions, but having these commitments and assumptions, they recognize that their understanding is not infallible. It is both finite and fallen. Thus they must have the intellectual and spiritual courage to follow the evidence, even if it challenges their perspectives.[46]

2. The Theologian as "Explorer"

In addition to being a "scientist," the theologian's job also involves being an "explorer." He or she must be a modern-day Columbus, Magellan, or Marco Polo. The theologian must set out to discover more of the nature of the world, either by "going boldly where no one has gone before" or by studying in greater detail that of which only the general parameters are known.

Theology is dynamic rather than static. Dyed-in-the-wool preservationists will shrink from talk of change in theology: "Is this not a letting go of the truth for a new fad?" But to deny the possibility of dynamic change is to implicitly claim that one has achieved the pinnacle of all theological knowledge. The Eastern Orthodox claim, "If it's new, it's heretical" is hardly an adequate perspective.[47] The metaphor of the scientist/explorer recognizes that while what has been handed down may be good, true, and right, it is not the *totality* of truth. The theologian's theology must not become a fortress in which he or she can dwell safe from potential attack, protected by doctrinal towers and turrets. Rather, it must function as a compass for further exploration. Much of God's revelation remains to be explored and incorporated into our understanding.

Theologians/explorers discover new territory and relate it to the known world. They begin with the backpack of received truth and strike out beyond the pale with a burning desire to extend their horizons in search of new knowledge. They will discover fantastic new things that have to be incorporated into their structure of reality. They may even change the world. While they remain close to home, their discoveries will generally be of the curiosity variety, the "Oh, isn't that interesting?" type of discovery that adds color and depth to their intellectual and spiritual world. But as they venture into areas uncharted by their community, as they "boldly go where no one has gone before," their vision of reality itself will go through radical readjustment. The old vision of what reality was cannot contain what has been discovered. This is the phenomenon of paradigm shift articulated by Thomas Kuhn.[48] Explorers are going beyond the theological and ecclesiastical fortress out into the world of broader general revelation, a world their discipline and training in exegesis has often left them unprepared to meet and incorporate into their understanding of reality.

A telling example of this phenomenon was a series of articles in *Christianity Today* during the mid-1980s on how quantum physics was revolutionizing the concept of the nature of reality.[49] To those with no previous exposure, the subject of the discussion was in some cases quite unnerving. The telling point here is not primarily in the articles themselves, but in the reactions that appeared in the letters to the editor in the following issues. One pastor wrote: "Mass that exists, then becomes non-existent in transit, then exists again according to our will? I don't have to listen to this! Beam me up, Lord!"[50] A layman complained: "How do the three articles discussing the New Physics apply to evangelical conviction? I wonder how many subscribers put their magazine down with disappointment and dismay because they lacked the knowledge and interest to cope with the far-out ideas."[51]

But perhaps most disturbing was the example the author of the original article cited in his opening paragraph: "A few weeks ago an acquaintance of ours, a theologian, remarked in the course of a stimulating dinner conversation that he considered quantum mechanics the greatest contemporary threat to Christianity. In fact, he said if some of the results of this theory were really true, his own personal faith in God would be shattered."[52] Those responding to the new ideas reacted strongly to having their view of creation challenged with the new paradigm because, I suspect, their own faith and understanding of God himself were tied in an almost absolute way to their view of the nature of the created order, the physical world. To assent to the truth of quantum physics would be to destroy God himself. These reactions did not just come from laypeople. They came from pastors and theologians as well, and therein lies the problem.

In the Middle Ages, theology was the queen of sciences; it exercised hegemony over all other sciences. Beginning with the Renaissance and continuing through the Enlightenment and the modern world (including modern science), however, the queen has been dethroned and confined to her own chambers. She ceases to exercise any meaningful influence over the other sciences. The method of acquiring knowledge has shifted profoundly, and for the most part, the queen has refused to recognize the legitimacy of the new methodology. Thus her exile from the throne can be seen in part as self-imposed. She still on occasion makes dogmatic pronouncements, but nobody listens.

The queen must regain her rightful place, but in reascending the throne, she must disavow her imperial pretensions and become a servant queen who learns from her subjects as well as teaches them. With such an attitude, she will be able to incorporate all the truth God has revealed, from any and every source, into her discipline while retaining the flexibility of a learner.

C. THE THEOLOGIAN AS CONTEXTUALIZER

1. The Origins of Contextualization

Perhaps the most controversial aspect of the theologian's job description is as contextualizer. *Contextualization* is a term that comes to theology via missiology. It refers to "the translation of the unchanging gospel of the kingdom into verbal forms meaningful to peoples in their separate cultures and within their particular existential situation,"[53] that is, "the articulation of the biblical message in terms and language and thought forms of a particular culture or ethnic group."[54]

Contextualization is to some degree an integral part of any communication process, but especially in missiology, contextualization has come to be understood as not optional but essential, not only in cross-cultural communication in general, but also in biblical and theological studies, which are in a very real sense involved in cross-cultural communication.

Thus the process of contextualization involves restating truth in a new form while not compromising content. It involves a critical and self-critical awareness that though we have been entrusted with the very truth of God, our own articulation of that truth is of necessity historically limited and incomplete.

> Experience shows us that no body of divinity can answer for more than its generation. Every catechism and confession of faith will in time become obsolete and powerless. Liturgies are more persistent, but even these are changed and adapted in the process of their use by successive generations. All these symbols of Christian Worship and Christian Truth remain as historical monuments and symbols, as the worn and tattered banners that our veterans or honoured sires have carried victoriously through the campaigns of the past; but they are not suited entirely for their descendants. Each age has its own peculiar work and needs, and it is not too much to say that not even the Bible could devote itself to the entire satisfaction of the wants of any particular age without thereby sacrificing its value as the book of all ages. It is sufficient that the Bible gives us the *material* for all ages and leaves to man the noble task of shaping that material so as to suit the wants of his own time.[55]

In chapter 1 I noted that the changes in weaponry through the ages I saw at the York Castle museum showed that survival depended on changing both defensive *and* offensive weapons to meet new conditions (see p. 19). In the same way, we are faced with the necessity of retooling our theology to be adequately equipped for battle in a new generation. *The task of contextualization is reexpressing the truth of Christianity in a form that is appropriate to the context in which it finds itself.*

As noted earlier, one of the problems that arises out of an authoritative statement of faith is that it is often substituted for the reality to which it points. The creed continues to be recited verbatim through the years, but the power is gone. New generations mouth the words but do not grasp the reality of which it speaks. To regain the power of the truth expressed in the theological statement, there must be a fresh struggle with its meaning, out of which arises a restatement of the creed in a form that speaks to the needs of the day. This is what contextualization is about: the restatement of the enduring content of the gospel in a form that communicates to the heart of the new generation.

2. The Roots of Contextualization

Words, phrases, sentences, and discourses have different meanings in different contexts. In the not-so-distant past, words were thought to have inherent meaning, so that if we studied the words involved in a text and came to understand their root meaning, we would be able to understand the meaning of that text with the help of grammar. Ludwig Wittgenstein, near the middle of the twentieth century, proposed the concept of "language games." He argued that to understand a text one must have an understanding of the "game" being played.[56] For example, the exclamations: "He stole first!" "We wuz robbed!" and "Murder the guy in blue!" all mean very different things in a bank than they do in a baseball park.[57] If we are to grasp the meaning of words or texts, it is essential that we know their textual and cultural context. If repeating the same words in the same culture may communicate radically different meanings depending on the context, how much more is it necessary to translate, not only words, but also ideas into thought forms that can be readily grasped in a new linguistic, historical, and cultural setting?

a. Biblical Roots

Although the process of contextualization has been formally recognized only recently, it can be observed already in the Scriptures.

> To the Jews I became like a Jew to gain the Jews. To those under the law I became like one under the law (though I myself am not under the law) to gain those under the law. To those free from the law I became like one free from the law (though I am not free from God's law but under the law of Christ) to gain those free from the law. To

> the weak I became weak in order to gain the weak. I have become all things to all people, so that by all means I may save some. (1 Cor. 9:20–22 NET Bible)

As Paul moved out of the God-ordained culture of Judaism that was prescribed by the Law, he was confronted by a world that found Judaism strange and often hated it. The trappings of piety that had meaning within the Jewish culture were at best meaningless and in some cases a detriment to communicating the gospel to those outside. Led by the Holy Spirit, Paul came to an earth-shattering conclusion with regard to his ministry: in the proclamation of the message a methodological distinction had to be made between form and content. The forms enculturated in the Jewish tradition and maintained with the rituals of circumcision, Sabbath, and feasts—the very things that identified the people of God to the world—were disposable! They were "old forms" that in fact compromised the truth of the gospel in a gentile context.[58] While God had in the past established the Jewish culture with its rituals and laws, the gospel signaled a radical break and was to be disentangled from its Jewish roots so that it could penetrate all cultures.

Peter also recognized this truth, even if inconsistently (Galatians 2). But many of the early Jewish converts, unable to separate form from substance, resisted this truth. These so-called Judaizers followed Paul on his travels and insisted that while what Paul taught was true, converts must go a step further and receive circumcision and adhere to other Jewish customs in order to maintain their relationship with God. This conflict became so heated that a council was held in Jerusalem to debate the matter. The result was recognition of the rightness of Paul's position, with some concessions to the Jewish believers on practices that were particularly offensive to Jews.[59]

b. Historical Roots

The gospel was freed from its Jewish trappings and took root in the first-century Greco-Roman world. In that world the gospel enculturated itself over the next several centuries. Theology and apologetics adopted the thought forms of Platonic and Neoplatonic philosophy to express Christian truth in a world that was unfamiliar with the Bible.

Throughout the era of the ancient church and the Middle Ages, the Bible was assumed to be a contemporary book, that is, interpreters and theologians did not try to think the thoughts of the biblical authors as being distinct from their own. They took their own thoughts to be obviously biblical. They did not recognize a change in the historical situation. "A double continuity was presumed: the material on which Christian thought was based had been provided by the biblical writers, and the tradition of the ongoing life and thought of the church bridged the historical gap separating the Bible from contemporary Christianity."[60] For example, in medieval and even in later art, biblical figures were painted in the costumes of the painter's time and set in a landscape with buildings that reflected the painter's environment. "The Bible was taken as contemporary, as an integral part of living religion."[61]

With the Renaissance and the accompanying Reformation, the notion that the biblical world was different from the contemporary world first appeared, however tentatively.[62] It was not until the Enlightenment that a full-blown historical consciousness in the modern sense of the term arose. The rise of the historical-critical method for the first time showed the Bible to have human fingerprints in a real and vital sense. Up until this point, any true humanity of the text had been swallowed up by its divine aspects. The historical-critical method, despite its destructive beginnings, forced confessional theologies as well to recognize genuine diversity within the canon of Scripture. From then on, the particular historical-cultural milieu of a biblical text came to be understood as an integral part of the text. This recognition was the legitimate beginning of the process of contextualization. Bible scholars now understood that contextualization was involved even at the starting point of the text. While exegesis recognizes contextualization at the front end of the interpretive process, in the original text, systematic theology is concerned with contextualization at the other end of the hermeneutical trajectory: the contemporary application.[63]

While the Enlightenment sought a universal knowledge that was untouched by the contingencies of history, the push of historical consciousness in the nineteenth century eventually brought forth a new discipline—that of the sociology of knowledge. (See chapter 3.C.) Arising out of the work of Emile Durkheim, Karl Mannheim, Max Weber, and Max Scheler, and based on the insights of the Marxist intellectual tradition, the sociology of knowledge recognizes the effects of sociological factors in shaping both the form and the content of human thought. While the underlying insights arose out of the work of Karl Marx, one does not need to subscribe to either dialectic materialism or historical determinism to acknowledge the basic truth in this perspective. "The calls for the contextualization of the gospel (actually the *re*contextualization) are simply based on the recognition of the need to communicate the faith in a context-specific fashion, and to make a critical assessment of the ways in which the church's or theologian's own social situation may be distorting the understanding of the message."[64]

c. Form versus Content

Several years ago, in response to the growing number of polluting gasoline-powered vehicles that were clogging the freeways, the state of California passed a law that required automobile manufacturers to produce electric cars and that a certain percentage of automobile sales in California would have to be electric cars. In late April of 1996, Daimler-Benz announced it had perfected a hydrogen-powered engine and that it would be on the market within four years.

The situation that prompted the California law was air pollution. The legislature mandated a solution to the problem. However, they didn't foresee the possibility of new technology offering an even better solution. At this writing, there is the ludicrous possibility that even if Daimler-Chrysler's invention should be perfected and adopted by all automakers, in California automakers would still have to produce electric cars to meet the legislative mandate.

Here we have an example of how a law is made to address a specific historical-cultural situation. But when the situation changes, other means may be more appropriate to solve the specific problem that prompted the original legislation. Yet the genre of law does not allow flexibility to use other, possibly more appropriate, means to achieve the same end in a new situation. Here we have a nontheological example of the need for contextualization.

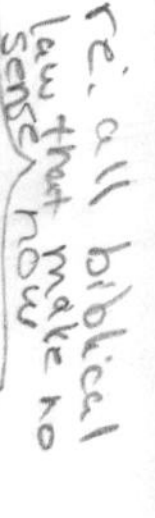

We can illustrate this underlying issue in contextualization by making the clear distinction of *form* versus *substance*. In the world of linguistics, translators speak of *surface structure* and *deep structure* in language. Surface structure includes all the facets of language a person observes—vocabulary, grammar, pronunciation, and anything else that goes into making a language a language. It is through surface structure that meaning is communicated.

But the meaning is not locked up in the surface structure of a language. Were this the case, it would never be possible to translate any text from one language to another. Translation bears witness to the fact that meaning is not *in* the surface structure but is conveyed *through* that structure. Beneath the surface structure lies a meaning that is universal, transcultural, and translinguistic. The universal meaning (meaning) may be conveyed in many different languages (form) or even in other words in the same language (form). While the deep structure does not exist without its expression in a particular form, grasping the deep structure (content) is nevertheless the whole purpose of the communication process.[65]

For the theologian to insist that meaning cannot be expressed in another form or language would mean that all Christians would have to become Hebrew and Greek scholars in order to approach the biblical text.

Contextualization

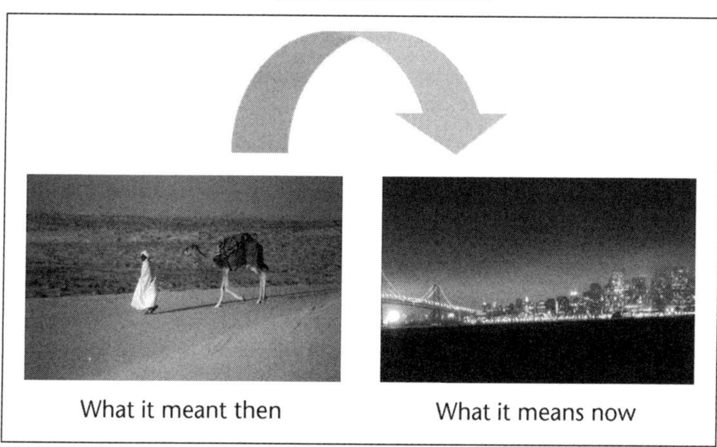

FIGURE 2.2.

The theologian is called to be a *translator*—a translator of ideas. The title of John Stott's volume on preaching, *Between Two Worlds*, recognizes that a preacher stands between the world of the Bible and the world inhabited by modern humans. It is often said that a preacher must read with the Bible in one hand and a newspaper in the other. A significant aspect of the theologian's job is to take this process one step further by dealing not only with isolated passages preached week by week but also on the comprehensive scale of the totality of biblical revelation. The job is one of "contemporary address," translating the truth revealed in the Bible into a comprehensible form for the contemporary world.

The job of the exegete and the biblical theologian[66] is to ascertain what the text meant to its first hearers. The systematic theologian's main job is to tell the current generation what the Bible means now. Biblical theology is frozen in time. It is a descriptive historical discipline that stands at one end of the continuum of contextualization. The exegete or the biblical theologian is not concerned with what Paul's teaching on principalities and powers may imply for multinational corporations or how Paul's teaching may correlate with the Jungian theory of archetypes, but this is precisely the world in which the systematic theologian is called to live and work.[67]

To accomplish this task, the theologian must be able to exegete contemporary culture as well as Scripture. The theologian must discern meaning below the surface and grasp the underlying meaning that is being communicated in the context-specific form, translate this form into an equivalent form in the contemporary culture, and apply it in a situation that is often very different from the original situation. Consider the Old Testament command, "Do not muzzle an ox while it is treading out the grain" (Deut. 25:4). This is a highly context-specific command. But Paul looked below the surface and understood that there was an underlying transcultural truth that supported this specific command and contextualized the command by applying it to just payment for laborers of the gospel (1 Cor. 9:8–10).

3. Objections to Contextualization

A natural reticence, and even resistance, accompanies the concept of contextualization. Perhaps the most obvious resistance comes from the Roman Catholic tradition. From the time of the Council of Trent, worship in the Roman Catholic tradition was conducted in Latin. When I was in high school, many of my Catholic classmates enrolled in high school Latin class so that they could understand the Mass! Within the fundamentalist Protestant tradition, there exists to this day a sizable "King James only" contingent that anathematizes any who would dare to use a translation other than the "inspired" King James Version. Even among evangelicals who tend more toward the theological center, there is resistance to contextualizing the faith in order to communicate to a postmodern world.

In the early 1990s, one review of Alister McGrath's brief popular monograph *Justification by Faith* took McGrath to task because he dared to use Martin Buber's dialogical personalism as a means of explaining the doctrine of justification by faith.[68] McGrath was essentially charged with betraying the Reformed faith and the Bible because he used a category other than the forensic declaration of righteousness to communicate the meaning of the Pauline doctrine. The reviewer denied the legitimacy of contextualization in any theology and asserted that the Reformers simply used the categories of Scripture. Ironically, in defending the Reformed doctrine, the reviewer condemned in McGrath some of the very ideas that Calvin himself had used to explain justification; specifically, Calvin stated that justification means nothing more than that we are accepted by God!

Still, the process of contextualization raises fear among many. Is it not inherently dangerous? Does not the entire process involve the danger of syncretism? Liberalism has turned into a syncretism of Christianity and contemporary culture, what H. Richard Niebuhr would call the "Christ of culture."[69] In such a situation, the church merely ends up promoting the cultural agenda rather than confronting the culture with the truth of the gospel. True as this may be, conservatives are often blind to the fact that they too have amalgamated the gospel with cultural values.

While the danger of the "heresy of innovation" is real, the danger of the "heresy of irrelevance" is just as real. In truth, systematic theology has always been a contextual enterprise. Thus it is not the *fact* of contextualization that is new; it is the *methodological self-consciousness* of the process that is new. It is far better to recognize what one is doing, and thus be able to set up critical checks on the process, than to do it subconsciously and uncritically.

4. Implications of Contextualization

A central core of the Christian faith that remains from age to age is reflected in the church's ancient creedal statements. This core lays out the parameters of what it is to be Christian. It functions as the banks of a wide river between which a variety of practices, beliefs, and emphases flow—the various enculturations of the gospel. In each age and at each place the core of the faith remains the same, but the theology that is developed in each environment looks different. It grows up facing different issues, and the church and its theology take on different forms as they respond to those issues. A well-rounded and nuanced theology may develop, but these full-blown theological understandings will become passé as conditions change. As the church moves into a new place or into a new era, the process will begin again and the theology will be expressed in the thought forms of the new cultural situation.

a. A Call for Creativity and Innovation[70]

Evangelical Protestant theology has always tended to be conservative in form as well as in content. During most of the twentieth century, the theologies written from that conservative Protestant perspective have continued to rehearse the received doctrines in their received forms, with minimal interaction with contemporary issues and developments. The late Carl Henry, elder statesman of evangelicalism, observed:

> Evangelical theology is heretical if it is only creative, and unworthy if it is only repetitious.... One often hears that non-evangelical theology seems to speak more directly to the dilemmas of the age but that its message forfeits the timeless biblical heritage. Evangelical theology on the other hand, while preserving the Judeo-Christian verities, all too often fails to project engagingly upon present-day perplexities.[71]

The idea of creativity and innovation seems, on some level, to be inherently dangerous, for as we look at the many "modern theologies" that have been creative, we see mostly one continual challenge to historic Christianity after another. In the name of creativity, numerous ancient heresies have been recycled. Despite this reality, the fact remains that simply repeating the words and categories of the past demonstrably leads to theological and spiritual stagnation. Theology is a discipline that requires that the truth of God be taken up into the life of the church and of the theologian in each generation. Once the truth is embraced, it can be reexpressed in new categories appropriate to the thought forms of the age and thus address the issues the contemporary age presents. This creativity is not a creating of content, but a creative expression of the unchanging content of the gospel with all its implications in a new form appropriate for a new situation.

b. Integrating the Academic and Practical Theological Disciplines

Within the theological disciplines, one often finds a sharp divide between the academic and the practical. This is due to an inadequate grasp of the theological task combined with an overemphasis on the preservation of truth. Theology must by its very nature be oriented toward the issues that face the church. A key part of the job is "systematic reflection on Scripture and the contemporary context of ministry in mutual relation, with Scripture as the norm."[72] This concept forges a link between systematic theology and ministry, allowing neither a purely pragmatic nor a purely theoretical approach.

c. Understanding the Sources of Theology

Traditionally theology has been constructed on the model of the pyramid. Background studies and languages form the base, and exegesis is the next level, followed by biblical theology and historical theology. The capstone discipline is systematics, the queen science. Philosophy too is historically recognized as playing a part in theological method. In the contemporary world, the secondary sources of theology must be expanded to include the hard sciences as well as the social sciences, including psychology, sociology, sociology of knowledge, cross-cultural anthropology, linguistics, and communications theory. Contemporary evangelical theologians can no longer ignore these disciplines but must see them as supplementing the traditional concerns for philosophy and natural theology. Any theological-hermeneutical method must account for the data that arise from the sciences, both hard and soft.

d. Rethinking the Nature of the Authority of the Scriptures

Evangelicals standing in the stream of the heritage left by the Reformation have always adhered to the Reformation cry *sola scriptura*: Scripture alone as the Word of God is the final and binding authority for the Christian and the church. In honoring the authority of the Scriptures, the Protestant scholastic tradition that emerged immediately after the first-generation Reformers and the more recent evangelical tradition have often treated the text as if it had fallen from heaven and its teachings were absolute. It was God's Word, and any true human aspects faded into the background. The implications for theology were profound. Scripture was treated as a lode from which dogmatic propositions could be mined and set in order.

The late-twentieth-century debate over the inerrancy of Scripture reflects these same tensions. Theologians generally agree that inerrancy is a doctrine that is deduced from the nature of biblical inspiration. But once the doctrine is established, what does it mean? Some have argued that the text of Scripture must meet contemporary standards of precision in order for its statements to qualify as true. Operating under this assumption, elaborate defenses of the truth of the biblical text have been set forth demonstrating the scientific precision of the text.[73] Others have found evidence for the findings of modern science in the poetic statements of the Old Testament (see chapter 6). Still others argue that because the Bible is the Word of God, believers are bound by apostolic practice as well as apostolic precept. They insist, for example, that first-century practices such as head coverings for women speaking in worship services are binding on contemporary believers.[74]

In recent years, there has been a growing recognition that the revelation of God was given in historically concrete circumstances, and that because of this, the text in its particulars is not absolutely binding in the same sense that it had been previously understood to be. Additionally, the literary nature of the text is now generally recognized, and questions of modern scientific precision have faded into the background. Yet another realization has contributed to the change in understanding as to how biblical authority functions. That change is the realization that the New Testament text is "task oriented"[75] and at least some of the documents are ad hoc, written to answer particular, concrete issues as opposed to establishing timeless theology.[76] These realizations shed new light on the nature of scriptural authority and have serious implications for its legitimate use.

To draw this out a bit further, the principle of contextualization recognizes that all human communication, including Scripture, occurs in specific cultural contexts and forms, and that understanding the meaning of a text includes understanding the significance of the forms employed to communicate.

e. Rethinking Denominational and Ecumenical Relations

The realization that divine revelation was given in historically concrete circumstances that must be studied to grasp the full implications of the truth communicated, and the fact that the theologian is located in a particular historical context with a distinct worldview and presuppositions, open up the reality of a variety of theological perspectives falling under the rubric of "orthodox," that is, theologies that have as their basic presupposition the final authority of Scripture as opposed to an insistence that one's own perspective is absolute. A recognition of the historical and cultural context in which one's own theological tradition emerged and developed opens the door to acknowledging other traditions as authentically Christian.[77] We may reject some aspects of another tradition as inadequate or defective without considering that tradition heretical. What is popularly labeled "heretical" may in fact be a perspective that does not violate the core of Christianity but only one or more of its particular enculturations. Recognition of this can strengthen the church by promoting better interdenominational relationships and thus publicly demonstrating the true unity of the body of Christ.

5. Evangelical Contextualization in the Contemporary World

During the 1990s, noted evangelical scholars were very public in their recognition of the vital need to contextualize the truth of Christianity if it was to be heard in contemporary society. John F. Kilner, director of the Bannockburn Institute for Christianity and Contemporary Culture in Bannockburn, Illinois, has deftly explored the problems facing evangelicals who want to influence public policy. He says:

> There is a tremendous reluctance to go the second intellectual mile. Many people exhaust themselves developing explicitly biblical positions on issues. They stop short of taking the next step of developing arguments for those positions in language that society is willing to consider. Others, anticipating the difficult challenge of developing socially persuasive arguments, simply skip the first step of formulating an explicitly biblical account. The first group is not likely to engage the society with their thoroughly biblical concerns. The second group is not likely to have thoroughly biblical concerns with which to engage society.[78]

Likewise, there have been some bold evangelical attempts to contextualize the message of the gospel in the thought forms of the postmodern world. In the theological community, the work of the late Stanley Grenz stands at the forefront of this attempt. His *Theology for the Community of God* is self-consciously arranged and presented with the concerns of the postmodern mind in view. Even the title reflects the postmodern quest for relationship.[79]

On another front, the evangelical publication *Mars Hill Review* has embraced the postmodern ethos. It actively uses those perspectives and categories to communicate the truth of Christianity to a generation that the church has largely been unable to touch because of its reticence to become involved with contemporary culture on anything more than a surface level. In adopting this stance, they have moved far beyond the evangelical and fundamentalist comfort zone and focused on deep underlying issues of life and meaning, rather than merely repeating the meaning of the faith in received forms. This stance has caused great concern and even alarm among those whose faith is subconsciously wedded to the thought forms and piety of an older generation.

D. CONCLUSION

The theologian's job is complex. Each element of the job pulls in some sense against the other elements. There is inherent tension as we seek to preserve the eternal truth revealed in Scripture while seeking new truth, tension as we seek to reexpress the received truth of the church in thought forms of the contemporary world without compromising the meaning, tension in discovering new truth and incorporating it into a contemporary context. The theologian's task is in some sense impossible, yet it must not be shunned if the church is to fulfill its commission of making disciples of all nations and of bringing all things under the lordship of Jesus Christ.

Operating within a received framework of interpretation is a double-edged sword for theologians. They respect the collective wisdom of their tradition, and the tradition may serve as a hedge against the temptation to reintroduce old heresies. But that same tradition may also keep them from discovering new insights, whether biblical or extrabiblical, that have a direct bearing on theological understanding.

BIBLIOGRAPHY

Allison, C. FitzSimons. *The Cruelty of Heresy.* Harrisburg, PA: Morehouse, 1994. • **Boers, Hendrikus.** *What Is New Testament Theology?* Philadelphia: Fortress, 1979. • **Davis, John Jefferson.** *The Essentials of Evangelical Theology.* Grand Rapids: Baker, 1984. • **Davis, John Jefferson**, ed. *The Necessity of Evangelical Theology.* Grand Rapids: Baker, 1978. • **Gerrish, B. A.** *Saving and Secular Faith.* Minneapolis: Fortress, 1999. • **Hesselgrave, David**, and **Edward Rommen**. *Contextualization.* Grand Rapids: Baker, 1989. • **Kuyper, Abraham.** *Principles of Sacred Theology.* Grand Rapids: Baker, 1980. • **Silva, Moisés**, ed. *Foundations of Contemporary Interpretation.* Grand Rapids: Zondervan, 1996. • **Webb, William.** *Slaves, Women and Homosexuals.* Downers Grove, IL: InterVarsity Press, 2000.

NOTES

[1]William Ames, *The Marrow of Theology* (Boston: Pilgrim, 1968), 77.

[2]R. J. Rushdooney, *The Necessity for Systematic Theology* (Vallicito, CA: Ross House, 1979), 57.

[3]John Jefferson Davis, *The Foundations of Evangelical Theology* (Grand Rapids: Baker, 1984), 47.

[4]J. I. Packer, "An Introduction to Systematic Spirituality," *Crux* 26, no. 1 (March 1990): 6. Cited by Alister McGrath, "Evangelical Theological Method," *Evangelical Futures*, ed. John Stackhouse Jr. (Grand Rapids: Baker, 2000), 23.

[5]The following discussion is summarized from B. A. Gerrish, *Saving and Secular Faith* (Minneapolis: Fortress, 1999), 2–14.

[6]It is for this reason that faith is seen by Thomas as meritorious. There is no merit in believing a self-evident truth. Merit comes only if the will moves the intellect to believe in divine truth apart from conclusive evidence. See Gerrish, *Saving and Secular Faith*, 6.

[7]Gerrish, *Saving and Secular Faith*, 7.

[8]Martin Luther, *A Brief Explanation of the Ten Commandments, the Creed, and the Lord's Prayer (1520), WA* 7.215.1–8. Cited by Gerrish, *Saving and Secular Faith*, 9.

[9]Ibid.

[10]John Calvin, *Institutes of the Christian Religion*, 3.2.13, in Library of Christian Classics, vol. 20, trans. Ford Lewis Battles (Philadelphia: Westminster, 1977).

[11]Ibid., 3.2.17.

[12]Ibid., 3.2.2. Italics added.

[13]Press Release, The Barna Group. *www.barna.org/cgi-bin/PagePressRelease.asp?PressReleaseID=6* (accessed July 1999, no longer available).

[14]The following argument is summarized from C. FitzSimons Allison, *The Cruelty of Heresy* (Harrisburg, PA: Morehouse, 1994), 17–23.

[15]Ibid., 17.

[16]Ibid.

[17]Ibid., 18.

[18]Ibid., 20.

[19]Lesslie Newbigin, *The Gospel in a Pluralistic Society* (Grand Rapids: Eerdmans, 1989), 22.

[20]Middle voice of αἱρεω (*hairo*), to take.

[21]Jeremy Taylor. Cited by Allison, *Cruelty of Heresy*, 23.

[22]Samuel Taylor Coleridge. Cited in ibid.

[23]Kenneth Scott Latourette, *A History of the Expansion of Christianity* (New York: Harper and Brothers, 1945), 4:428.

[24]The functional position of the doctrine of the inerrancy of Scripture is symptomatic of this mentality. When Scripture was stripped of any interpretive tradition, any threat that arose with reference to the Bible's utter truthfulness ultimately became a threat to Christianity itself.

[25]See the *Christianity Today* interview with Thomas Oden, "Back to the Fathers," September 24, 1990, for the story of his spiritual/theological journey.

[26]Thomas Oden, *The Transforming Power of Grace* (Nashville: Abingdon, 1993), 25–27.

[27]This second-century doctrinal summary was an expansion of the apostolic church's baptismal formula and became the basis for the Apostles' Creed.

[28]R. P. C. Hanson, *Tradition of the Early Church* (Philadelphia: Westminster, 1962), 238.

[29]I am speaking in broad brushstrokes here. Liberal Christianity has departed historic orthodoxy at every major point and adopted many of the ancient heresies concerning the persons of God and Christ. Also, some conservative Protestant groups, such as "Jesus Only" Pentecostals, insist on the deity of Christ while asserting the ancient modalistic heresy.

[30]Abraham Kuyper, *Principles of Sacred Theology*, reprint (Grand Rapids: Baker, 1980), 624.

[31]This phrase is not associated with American fundamentalism but was employed early in the twentieth century with reference to the theology of the ecumenical creeds of the first four centuries of the church.

[32]As of this writing, there is still a hard core of believers trying to demonstrate that the cold fusion phenomenon is genuine even though it seemingly contradicts accepted contemporary scientific models.

[33]This will not necessarily lead to agreement, but it will help focus any disagreement on the underlying theological issues rather than on distracting issues, such as accusations of "bad faith" or improper methodology on the part of the theologian.

[34]Despite the static nature of the ancient languages, our grasp of the meanings of the vocabulary and syntax has grown tremendously over the last century due to the discovery of the papyri.

[35]See chap. 3, "How Do We Know?" for a fuller discussion of Baconian inductivism as employed by Scottish Common Sense philosophy.

[36]Thomas Kuhn, *The Structure of Scientific Revolutions*, 2nd ed. enlarged (Chicago: University of Chicago Press, 1970). Kuhn's work has become a standard in historiography of science and is generally recognized as having implications for several other disciplines as well.

[37]University of California, Berkeley, Museum of Paleontology, "Alfred Wegener (1880–1930)," no date. *www.ucmp.berkeley.edu/history/wegener.html* (accessed Sept. 2005).

[38]The definition of *paradigm* in *Merriam-Webster's Collegiate Dictionary* (10th ed.) reflects this first use: "A philosophical and theoretical framework of a scientific school or discipline within which theories, laws, and generalizations and the experiments formed in them are formulated."

[39]This third sense is reflected in the broader definition of *paradigm* in the *American Heritage Dictionary* (4th ed.): "A set of assumptions, concepts, values, and practices that constitutes a way of viewing reality for the community that shares them, especially in an intellectual discipline."

[40]Cf. Vern Poythress, "Science and Hermeneutics," in Moisés Silva, ed., *Foundations of Contemporary Interpretation* (Grand Rapids: Zondervan, 1996), 477.

[41]Sue Patterson, *Realist Christian Theology in a Postmodern Age* (Cambridge: Cambridge University Press, 1999), 6.

[42]These changes in paradigms are not as universal or far-reaching as the changes in scientific paradigms, since the older perspectives still remain and exercise some influence. Nevertheless, the parallel to scientific paradigm shifts is striking. Poythress suggests that it is more fruitful to think of these changes in terms of communities revolutionized by the change rather than whole disciplines (Vern Poythress, *Science and Hermeneutics* [Grand Rapids: Zondervan, 1988], 476).

[43]Debate centers on whether Thomas's synthesis should be considered a true revolution or whether it was in fact a modification on the Augustinian synthesis. Nonetheless, even if not considered a first-order paradigm shift, it did bring about a lower-level shift in the way theology was perceived and done on a practical level.

[44]Paul vividly describes the darkening process of sin in Romans 1:18–32.

[45]F. Kerr, *Theology after Wittgenstein* (Oxford: Blackwell, 1986), 3.

[46]By virtue of the way God created us, we begin existence with a parochial view of reality that we imbibe from our parents and immediate family context as infants and children. As we grow, our world expands, but we still gravitate toward our own familiar social and cultural structures and view these as "right" and normal. Outsiders are different and wrong. If we break outside of our own preconceptions and seek to comprehend the larger world, we will be confronted by competing understandings that will confront and challenge what previously has been held as reality. This is the crisis of pluralism, and it will affect our own world unless by failure of nerve we draw back into our cocoon and assert that we alone are right, possessing the whole truth, while everyone else is wrong.

[47]An extreme example of this perspective is seen in the Muslim rationale given for the destruction of what was left of the Alexandrian library in the seventh century: "Whatever agrees with the Qur'an is superfluous and can be destroyed, whatever disagrees with it is pernicious and must be destroyed."

[48]See above, section B.1.b.

[49]Allen Emerson, "A Disorienting Look at God's Creation," *Christianity Today*, February 1, 1985, 18–24; Emerson, "Scientific Showdown," op. cit., 24–26; Carl Henry, "A Conversation with Carl Henry," op. cit., 26–28.

[50]Cliff Springer, letter to the editor, *Christianity Today*, April 5, 1985, 11.

[51]Glenn Hawkinson, letter to the editor, *Christianity Today*, April 5, 1985, 11.

[52]Emerson, "Disorienting Look," 19.

[53]Bruce J. Nichols, "Theological Education and Evangelization," in *Let the Earth Hear His Voice*, ed. J. D. Douglas (Minneapolis: World Wide, 1975), 647.

[54]J. J. Davis, *Foundations of Evangelical Theology* (Grand Rapids: Baker, 1984), 61.

[55]Charles A. Briggs, *General Introduction to the Study of Holy Scripture* (New York: Scribner, 1899), 35. Italics in original.

[56]Wittgenstein develops this language theory in his *Philosophical Investigations* (Englewood Cliffs, NJ: Prentice Hall, 1958).

[57]David Hesselgrave and Edward Rommen, *Contextualization* (Grand Rapids: Baker, 1989), 148.

[58]This is the whole point of the book of Galatians.

[59]Acts 15 gives this account of the Council of Jerusalem.

[60]Hendrikus Boers, *What Is New Testament Theology?* (Philadelphia: Fortress, 1979), 16.

[61]Ibid., 17.

[62]See chap. 11 for a fuller discussion of this issue.

[63]See John Jefferson Davis, ed., *The Necessity of Systematic Theology* (Grand Rapids: Baker, 1978), 170–73.

[64]Ibid., 172.

[65]This illustration ignores for the sake of discussion the problems involved in translation due to the highly contextualized nature of meaning in its original context. See chap. 3 for this discussion.

[66]The term "biblical theologian" is a technical one referring to the discipline of biblical theology that arose in the nineteenth century with the rise of historical consciousness.

[67]John Jefferson Davis, "Contextualization and the Nature of Theology," in Davis, ed., *Necessity of Systematic Theology*, 177.

[68]Ken Sarles, Review of *Justification by Faith*, *Bibliotheca Sacra* 586 (April 1990): 238–39.

[69]H. Richard Niebuhr, *Christ and Culture* (New York: Harper & Row, 1956).

[70]These five implications are drawn from Davis, "Contextualization and the Nature of Theology," 184–85.

[71]Carl Henry, *God, Revelation and Authority* (Waco: Word, 1976), 1:9–10.

[72]Davis, "Contextualization and the Nature of Theology," 182.

[73]Harold Lindsell's *The Battle for the Bible*, the work that was the catalyst for the twentieth-century inerrancy debate, is but one prominent example of this approach.

[74]See, e.g., Robertson McQuilkin's article in *Hermeneutics and Inerrancy* (Grand Rapids: Zondervan, 1980), 219–40. Alan Johnson's response in the same volume provides an incisive critique of McQuilkin's thesis and argumentation (pp. 257–82).

[75]Davis, "Contextualization and the Nature of Theology," 184.

[76]Gordon Fee, "Reflections on Church Order in the Pastoral Epistles, with Further Reflection on the Hermeneutics of Ad Hoc Documents," *Journal of the Evangelical Theological Society* 28, no. 2 (June 1985): 141–51, esp. 150–51.

[77]This is one of the thrusts of Vern Poythress's brief work, *Symphonic Theology* (Grand Rapids: Zondervan, 1978), 147.

[78]John F. Kilner, quoted by John Woodbridge, "Culture War Casualties," *Christianity Today*, March 5, 1995, 26.

[79]Grenz has been criticized by some for failing to interact with true postmodern theologians in trying to present a theology for the postmodern world. While there may be some justification to this observation, postmodernism is still in its infancy and in the process of truly defining itself.

OUTLINE OF CHAPTER 3

A. **The Death of the Commonsense World**

B. **The Modern Understanding of Truth and Reality**
   1. Descartes and the Enlightenment Project
   2. John Locke and the Rise of Empiricism
   3. David Hume and the Challenge of Skepticism
   4. Immanuel Kant and Phenomenalism
   5. Thomas Reid and Common Sense Realism
   6. Søren Kierkegaard and Existentialism

C. **The Postmodern Challenge to Enlightenment Certainty**
   1. The Dogmatism of Doubt
   2. The Skill of Knowing
   3. Doomed to Relativism?

D. **Preunderstandings and Theological Formulations**

E. **The Problem of History: How History and Truth Relate**

F. **Theology as Truth: How True Is Our Truth?**

CHAPTER 3

HOW DO WE KNOW? EPISTEMOLOGY, HISTORY, AND TRUTH

More than a century ago, Charles Hodge observed that every theology is in some measure a philosophy. Yet the study of theology among American students has included only the most superficial acquaintance with philosophy. A common theme among some conservative Bible teachers, which has found its way into the popular evangelical mind-set, echoes Paul's admonition to the Colossians: "See to it that no one takes you captive through hollow and deceptive philosophy, which depends on human tradition and the basic principles of this world rather than on Christ" (2:8). This is interpreted as a blanket condemnation of the discipline as a whole.[1] There has been virtually no recognition of the fact that *all* individuals and groups—including Bible teachers and theologians—operate from a philosophical worldview. Whether consciously or subconsciously, philosophy and worldview shape our understanding of God and the Bible.

Thus philosophy has a profound impact on the way a theological system is constructed, on how the system approaches questions, and, most fundamentally, on the understanding of the nature of truth that is used in the system. Huston Smith, expert on world religions, observes:

> The dominant assumptions of an age color the thoughts, beliefs, expectations, and images of the men and women who live within it. Being always with us, these assumptions usually pass unnoticed—like the pair of glasses which, because they are so often on the wearer's nose, simply stop being observed. But this doesn't mean they have no effect. Ultimately, assumptions which underlie our outlooks on life refract the world in ways that condition our art and our institutions: the kinds of

homes we live in, our sense of right and wrong, our criteria of success, what we conceive our duty to be, what we think it means to be a man or woman, how we worship our God or whether, indeed, we have a God to worship.[2]

A crucial task of philosophy is to expose these hidden assumptions and bring them into the light for examination and critique. Philosophy may suggest improvements, refinements, or even replacements of inadequate thought forms that have crept in over succeeding generations. In a very real sense, philosophy deals with the tools that theologians use in their task, which is thinking. It also provides the categories in which the theologian thinks and expresses his or her ideas. It provides *structure* or *form* as opposed to *content*, which for the theologian is drawn from revelation.[3]

In the early 1980s, Bernard Ramm, in an appendix to his book *After Fundamentalism*,[4] compared the education and influence of two twentieth-century theologians, one continental, Karl Barth, the other American, Lewis Sperry Chafer. He looked especially at their knowledge of intellectual and philosophical history. Ramm focused particularly on Barth's mastery of the nineteenth century and his interaction with the major currents of thought. Turning to Chafer, Ramm pointed out his lack of training in this area and his naive biblicism. American evangelical theologians protested that the comparison was unfair since Chafer lived and taught in a very different environment than Barth. While this is undeniably true, Ramm's point was nonetheless accurate.[5] Contemporary conservative American theology by and large does not understand the world in which we live from a philosophical perspective.

This lack of philosophical sophistication has relegated evangelicals to the sidelines in contemporary theological discussion, or it has isolated them in an evangelical ghetto where they speak only with one another. And because they lack the background to grasp the content of the conversation, they condemn as beyond the pale those on the outside as well as those on the inside who venture out to explore.

The passage of time since Ramm's comparison has not brought improvement. While the study of philosophy by evangelicals is at an all-time high and evangelical philosophers are on the forefront of contemporary thinking, many evangelical seminaries have dropped even a prerequisite survey of philosophy as an entrance requirement.

As a beginning theologian, you *must* have some sense of philosophical issues and approaches if you are to understand theology and theologians. You (as a particular individual within a specific tradition) also must have critical awareness of how the way you do theology fits into the larger picture, a picture that includes not only biblical exegesis and specific doctrinal formulations, but also philosophical/epistemological and historical underpinnings.

This chapter looks at epistemology (how we know what we know), particularly as it impacts the theological disciplines. These questions involve philosophy, history, and sociology, and are often left unaddressed as we enter the theological process. Yet they demand attention if each of us is to be a student who "correctly handles the word of truth" (2 Tim. 2:15).

A. THE DEATH OF THE COMMONSENSE WORLD

Until the time of the Renaissance, Westerners relied on the five senses and on a series of assumptions about creation drawn from Scripture and Aristotle for their view of the world and reality.[6] The advent of the printing press, however, made the dissemination of knowledge possible in a way scarcely dreamed of before. At about the time the printing press was invented, new understandings of reality emerged that challenged the status quo that had endured for centuries.[7] Up to that point the Western intellectual tradition had understood that the earth was the center of reality and that the whole cosmos revolved around it. At the center of the earth was Jerusalem, the holy city, the place chosen by God himself as his dwelling place on earth in the Old Testament and predicted to be the center of the earth once again after the return of Christ.

The Psalter Map, a thirteenth-century world map with Jerusalem at the center

The geocentric view of the world and of reality received its death blow at the hands of Copernicus and Galileo. Galileo's astronomical discovery confirmed Copernicus's predictions, but in the process, he demonstrated that "sense experience was capable of fraud on a grand scale."[8] The demise of geocentricism also caused a profound crisis of faith with reference to humankind's place in the universe. If the earth was not the center and was not the special place prepared for humans by God at the focal point of creation, what was humankind's place? These findings were enough to cause a person to lose his or her existential equilibrium.[9] As one historian noted, "Such a change does not necessarily involve the dethronement of man from his proud position as the summit of creation, but it certainly suggests doubts of the validity of that belief."[10]

In addition to discoveries on a macro scale, discoveries on a micro scale also challenged the established parameters of reality. The invention of the microscope with the revelations it brought about the world proved as troubling as Galileo's observations regarding the heavens. Placed under a microscope, everyday objects were seen to be of a very different nature than the unaided eye would lead the observer to conclude. Galileo himself had inferred that the basic constituents of matter possessed no color, taste, or smell. He believed that these were things our five senses added. His resulting conclusion was that the origin of the texture of creation was from within man.[11]

While these advances in technology extended our ability to probe the nature of the physical universe, they had the profoundly ironic effect of destroying the story of reality that our senses had told us up to that point. The destruction of this story precipitated a revolution in human knowledge from which emerged a radically different view of reality, a view that prevails to this day. But this new understanding came at a high price. No longer could we simply trust our five senses to discover the true state of affairs. Neither could authority—particularly claims of the church or pretended claims to divine revelation—be trusted. Europe was embroiled in the Thirty Years' War (1618–48), a religious war between Catholics and Protestants, both of whom claimed to have *the* truth. But this truth came in two versions that were so different that they plunged Europe into a horrendous, bloody conflict. This helped to give rise to the perceived necessity of grounding human knowledge in something other than simple sense perception or claimed revelation. If we can't trust our senses and we can't trust claims of revelation, how can we know? And how can we know for certain? Can we have knowledge that we know to be true with *absolute certainty*?

B. THE MODERN UNDERSTANDING OF TRUTH AND REALITY

1. Descartes and the Enlightenment Project

René Descartes (1596–1650), who is regarded as the father of the Enlightenment, was profoundly troubled by the question of knowledge. He

René Descartes

enthusiastically adopted the Copernican understanding of the solar system but quickly realized that this discovery posed a profound problem for the status of all human knowledge. If even the most foundational source of human knowledge (sensory perception) is not capable of giving humans the true nature of reality, even the human senses must henceforth be treated with suspicion. But Descartes was not content to live in a state of uncertainty. His work was an attempt to discover a means by which human beings can arrive at certain knowledge, an unshakable foundation on which knowledge can be built. To that end he set out on a project of programmatic doubt. He resolved to doubt everything until he found something that could not be doubted. He in effect established a "faith-free zone" for knowledge.[12] Descartes reasoned that it was precisely because people had believed on the basis of authority rather than of critical examination that they now found themselves in an epistemological crisis. Knowledge could no longer be naively accepted on the basis of authority alone but must somehow be tested.

FIGURE 3.1

One winter day, Descartes was prevented from going outside because of the cold. Alone in thought, he discovered one fact that he could not doubt: the fact that he doubted. From this discovery came his famous *Cogito ergo sum* ("I think therefore I am"). Descartes became the father of epistemological *rationalism*—the idea that the mind is capable of obtaining knowledge apart from experience. It must be remembered that Descartes' programmatic doubt was not designed to destroy knowledge but rather to establish it by founding it on a sure, necessary, and self-evident foundation.

As a mathematician, Descartes brought to his quest a mathematician's desire for necessary and self-evident truth, truth that is universal, true under every circumstance, unconditioned by the vagaries of created existence. He contended that "those who are seeking the strict way of truth should not trouble themselves about any object concerning which they cannot have a certainty equal to arithmetical or geometrical demonstration."[13] This insistence drove a wedge between faith and knowledge, a wedge that has characterized all post-Enlightenment thought and has held unchallenged sway until the recent emergence of postmodernism.

This view of truth led logically to the conclusion that it was possible to gain a "God's-eye view" of reality, lifted above the stream of history. Knowledge could be apprehended in something like a cosmic spectators' gallery. This was a direct denial of the fact that human knowledge must be bound to a specific perspective. The rigorous application of the principle of doubt would allow one to reach the spectators' gallery and be lifted above the ebb and flow of perceptions by establishing one's knowledge on an unshakable and indubitable foundation.

All modern philosophy has flowed from the work of Descartes. One of the characteristics of the modern world has been epistemological *foundationalism*, accompanied by a commitment to the idea that if one could not be absolutely sure of something, he or she could not be certain of anything at all, hence the necessity to prove all knowledge apart from a prior faith commitment.

Since the time of the Enlightenment, foundationalism and the absolute universality of truth have become hallmarks of modern human thinking about truth and knowledge, both from conservative and from liberal perspectives.

2. John Locke and the Rise of Empiricism

In contrast to Descartes and his inward-looking rationalism, John Locke in Britain asserted that there are actually three types of knowledge rather than just the one Descartes postulated. The first is knowledge gained from empirical science—knowledge founded on ideas arising from sensory experience. The second type is Descartes' indubitable knowledge based on deductive reasoning. Mathematics in general and geometry in particular are examples of this type of knowledge. The third type of knowledge is founded on divine revelation. Locke appealed to the revelation of Scripture as a basis of theological knowledge. For him the messiahship of Jesus fell into this category, but not such doctrines as the Trinity or predestination.

Locke's work had profound implications for the development of theology. Science now stood properly outside the realm of theology and vice versa. They existed as two structures of knowledge beside one another. Science was built on the foundation of sensory observation, theology on the foundation of revealed Scripture. But there was a problem. Since there was no clear justification as to why the Bible should be treated as privileged over and against other claims of revelation, what was it that grounded the Bible on the bedrock of indubitable human knowledge? The task of apologists from Locke's day to the present has been to prove beyond all doubt that the Bible is revelation. The great Princeton theologian B. B. Warfield contended that the task of the theologian/apologist is not the defense but the *establishment* of the faith.[14] From Locke's day forward, the appeal to miracles has been a key pillar in the foundationalists' proof that the Bible's claim to be revelation did not arise from the interior experience of the prophet alone but was also rooted in history (the same realm as science). In short, there had to be some sort of rational proof of God and his existence and activity in the world to buttress the claim of revelation.

John Locke

But Locke went further in his epistemological investigations, delving into the question of *how* we know things. He argued that in the strictest sense we "see" things in the world according to the perspective we adopt. And the thing we "see" is not identical to the thing itself but is in reality a representation of the thing produced by our brain as a result of incoming sensory stimuli. The representations we "see" will vary according to our closeness to an object, the angle from which it is viewed, and the like. All the while the thing itself remains unchanged. In everyday experience, we never break down the process of knowing to think about its various components, but we must admit that this is in fact the way it works.

The problem comes when we realize that it is theoretically possible for the thing we "see" to pass out of existence before we perceive it. On the scale of the created world around us, this may appear silly. But all we have to do is look up at the night sky and see light that has been traveling untold numbers of light-years to see that this realization has a very real immediate application. We are perceiving light from stars that may no longer exist!

On a more mundane level, even our sensory experience is indirect. As I touch the keyboard of my computer and feel the keys, I am not in reality feeling the keys themselves. I am feeling the result of electromagnetic interactions between the keys and my fingers; these are carried through my sensory system to my brain and interpreted so that "feeling" results. If my nerves were stimulated in the same way by another object or even the proper set of electrical impulses, I would "feel" the same thing. Evidence of this can be seen in recent amputees who continue to "feel" sensation in a now absent limb.

Locke's observation about the inferred nature of reality/truth had profound implications. Admitting a gap between our knowledge and the world "out there" opened a Pandora's box concerning the relationship between the two spheres, the world "out there" and one's perception of it. If we have no direct access to the world, how do we know that our perception is in fact accurate? Locke followed Galileo, asserting that the mind supplies many of the qualities that are normally ascribed to objects. The implications of this uncomfortable realization were expressed by Alfred North Whitehead:

> Thus the bodies are perceived as with qualities which in fact are purely the offspring of the mind. Thus nature gets credit which in truth should be reserved for ourselves: the rose for its scent; the nightingale for his song; and the sun for his radiance. The poets are entirely mistaken. They should address their lyrics to themselves and should turn them into odes of self-congratulation on the excellency of the human mind. Nature is a dull affair, soundless, scentless, colourless; merely the hurrying of material endlessly, meaninglessly.[15]

As radical as some of these conclusions were, even more radical conclusions were to follow.

3. David Hume and the Challenge of Skepticism

David Hume took Locke's musings about the nature of human knowledge and pushed them to their logical conclusions. If in fact our knowledge of the world is only indirect, we do not actually *know* the world but only *representations* of it arising from our own minds. We can never be sure that the representations we experience accurately reflect the world "out there." We have no means of knowing or verifying our experience. We do not have the capacity to compare the copy against the original. While Descartes appealed to reason to escape this type of trap, Hume (along with Locke) was convinced that knowledge arose outside the human mind, not from within. There are no innate ideas or eternal truths resident to start with. The mind is a *tabula rasa* (blank slate) on which sense per-

David Hume

ceptions are written and from which knowledge arises. Hume's relentless logic concluded that in the final analysis we could know nothing at all of the world "out there." All the mind knows is its own contents with ideas arising from sensory experience.

In such a construction, the question of truth becomes problematic. For if truth is defined as correspondence with reality[16]—that is, that a true thought or statement corresponds to the way things are in the world "out there," which is the most common definition—but we have no way to check the way things really are, how do we know there is a real world out there? We are trapped within our solipsistic world and our own subjectivity. As Hart says, "We are left with the lurking fear that 'reality as we know it' or as it appears to us may be no more than a breathtaking virtual reality game fashioned by the computer of our minds."[17]

In such a situation there is no room for truth, and each perspective is as valid as any other. Truth cannot be thought of in terms of correspondence with reality; at most it can be thought of in terms of coherence within a well-ordered system within our own minds.

4. Immanuel Kant and Phenomenalism

Into this epistemological crisis stepped the Prussian philosopher Immanuel Kant, whose answer to the dilemma would literally change the way people think. So revolutionary was his solution that philosophers still refer to "Kant's Copernican revolution." Kant himself confessed that it was Hume who awakened him from his "dogmatic slumbers" about his perception of reality. He became the greatest of the Enlightenment philosophers, but also the last. Before Kant there were two parallel streams of epistemological thought: rationalism and empiricism. In his genius, Kant fused insights from each stream into a new epistemological synthesis that gave birth to the modern mind.

While the empiricists insisted that the mind was a *tabula rasa* on which sensory perceptions were recorded, Kant insisted, with Descartes and the rationalist tradition, that the mind possesses an inherent structure. This structure is to be found in the form of categories by which the mind processes incoming sensory data and turns it into knowledge. These categories in and of themselves produce no knowledge but provide the framework for organizing, arranging, and interpreting data. We might liken the mind to a supercomputer and the categories to a powerful operating system. To press the analogy, in the *empiricist* understanding, the mind was the computer and sensory perceptions were the raw data that the mind organized and edited into true knowledge. In the *rationalist* understanding, the mind was the computer that came preprogrammed with all potential knowledge contained implicitly therein.

While Kant rejected the extravagant rationalist claims, he adopted an understanding of a preexisting structure in the mind that produced knowledge. Kant answered the empiricist dilemma of the senses deceiving the mind: the mind's categorical structure guarded against such deception. But in contrast to Descartes' skepticism, Kant accepted that the world as ordinarily perceived has a high degree of correspondence with the way it actually is, and the senses are a generally reliable guide to the nature of reality. While there is a need for critical testing of first appearances, it is the exception rather than the rule that the critical testing will overthrow first impressions.

In Kant's construct, the mind exists in potentiality. It is the interaction of the incoming sensory data with the innate categories that produces knowledge. Human knowledge arises from the interplay of incoming sensory data (absorbed through the five senses) and innate categories built into the mind itself, which process that data and in turn make it "knowledge."

Kant further held that reality is to be divided into two realms, the *phenomenal* (the created order in which we live and that is open for us to experience) and the *noumenal* (spiritual, metaphysical reality). As noted, Kant held that the human mind is divided into categories. These include *quantity* (unity, plurality, totality), *quality* (reality, limitation, negation), *relation* (inherence and subsistence, causality and dependence, community), and *modality* (possibility-impossibility, existence-nonexistence, necessity-contingency). These are the *only* categories possessed by the mind and thus the only categories by which to interpret data.

Significantly, in Kant's system, there are no categories through which to receive data from the noumenal (spiritual) world. In this way, humanity is like the blind man. He has no organ to receive the light that surrounds him. He believes that light as well as things to be seen exist, but he has no faculty by which to directly perceive them. Since humans are blind to noumenal reality of all types, they cannot know "the thing in itself." All that can be known is things as they are experienced.

Part of the Enlightenment project included the attempt to know God as he is in himself by "reasoning up" to him. This task was, according to Kant, a vain attempt doomed from the outset. God inhabited the noumenal realm and thus could not be experienced by humans. Kant did not entertain the possibility that God could or would break into the realm of history (the phenomenal realm) and reveal himself.

Yet Kant was not an atheist. He postulated the existence of God but denied the possibility of any cognitive knowledge of him. It is the human conscience that testifies to God's existence, and God is to be known through the realm of morality. Kant published another work, *Religion within the Limits of Reason Alone*, which set forth his conception that religion is to be reduced to the sphere of morality. For Kant this meant living by the *categorical imperative*, which he summarized in two maxims:

1. Act only on that maxim whereby you can at the same time will that it should become a universal law.
2. Act as if the maxim of your action were to become by your will a universal law of nature.

In other words, every action of humanity should be regulated in such a way that it would be morally profitable for humanity if it were elevated to the status of law. In one sense, this can be seen as a secularization of the Golden Rule.

An important contribution Kant made here was the concept that the mind edits sensory experience. Sensory experience is not an independent source of information. *Knowledge* is a composite of the raw data and the order imposed on it by the mind. The fact that all human minds have the same inherent categorical structure means that from an objective perspective all humans experience the external world in basically the same way. Hart notes of Kant's contribution, "Even if I am, in effect, participating in a vast virtual reality package, then, just so long as everyone else is participating in the same game and playing by the precise same rules, the notion of truth and falsity can be reintroduced with impunity. Truth is more than a matter of 'the way things seem from where I stand,' "[18] because in fact everyone else is standing in the same place.

The modern mind and modern theology evolved from the implications of the work of Kant, who represented the major response to Hume's skepticism. This modern mind emerged first on the Continent, particularly in Germany. Kant's work effectively cut the human mind off from immediate knowledge of God. Henceforth, modern theology sought its foundation not in knowledge but in experience. Friedrich Schleiermacher made the starting point of theology feeling (*Gefühl*), that is, the feeling of absolute dependence on God, or God-consciousness.

5. Thomas Reid and Common Sense Realism

As noted above, when we speak of the modern mind, we immediately think of the post-Enlightenment tradition that finds Kant as the springboard for its understanding. That is in large measure accurate. But what is not often recognized is that a second stream flowed out of the Enlightenment from Thomas Reid, the founder of Scottish Common Sense philosophy. What makes this approach more difficult to recognize as Enlightenment thought is that the theology associated with it is conservative, historic, orthodox Christianity and that the worldview it represents is decidedly nonphilosophical and nonspeculative. In surveys of philosophy, Common Sense, or Scottish Common Sense, is given little attention, despite the fact that it was the dominant philosophy that held together the very fabric of American society for nearly a century.

Church historian Sidney Ahlstrom has noted that Common Sense is no longer "in good repute despite its proud reign in another day. Indeed, few, if any, schools of philosophy have been given such disdainful treatment by historians as Common Sense Realism."[19] Scottish Common Sense Realism was popularized in America by John Witherspoon, the sixth president of Princeton University, where he used it as a weapon to vanquish the continuing influence of the idealism of Jonathan Edwards.[20] From Princeton the philosophy spread swiftly throughout the land through the higher education system. The swiftness of its acceptance was due to the fact that Scottish Realism "contained an immediate conviction of right and wrong, of the reality of the external world, freedom ... about which there was no need or warrant for debate or doubt, while its discussion of association, will, and feeling was lucidity itself, and fitted for our practical country."[21]

Several key assumptions were involved in Common Sense Realism. One was the objective tangibility of the world as understood by Newtonian physics. Thomas Reid himself had contended that without this key assumption, humans were cut off from certain knowledge that could be gained by the inductive method.[22] The ultimate result of this severance would be hopeless skepticism. Second, Common Sense posited the reliability of the senses in perceiving reality.[23] By means of one's senses, one was able to know "the thing in itself." Third, there was a strict subject-object dichotomy. From this distinction flowed the characteristic methodology of Common Sense, empiricism. Truth was to be discovered strictly through the inductive method. While empiricism (and the scientific method) is today commonly associated with a materialistic view of reality, such was not the case with Common Sense. Indeed Scottish Common Sense saw the universe ruled by natural law, a law that included moral precepts.[24] The method assumed that there is truth available to humanity and that such truth is unchanging.[25]

While in other matters Reid was Locke's successor, Reid reacted to Hume's explicit skepticism, which had been implicit in Locke. In this sense, Reid and

Reid's Epistemological Principles

A summary of Reid's epistemological principles shows to what extent we still view many of these principles as self-evident rather than as philosophical assumptions.

A. Principles of Common Sense Relating to Contingent Truth

1. The existence of every thing of which I am conscious.
2. The thoughts of which I am conscious are the thoughts of a being, which I call myself, my mind, my person.
3. Those things did really happen which I distinctly remember.
4. Our own personal identity and continued existence as far back as we remember distinctly.
5. Those things do really exist which we distinctly perceive by our senses, and are what we perceive them to be.
6. We have some degree of power over our actions and the determinations of our wills.
7. The natural faculties by which we distinguish truth from error are not fallacious.
8. There is life and intelligence in our fellow men with whom we converse.
9. That certain features of the countenance, sounds of the voice, and gestures of the body, indicate certain thoughts and dispositions of the mind.
10. There is a certain regard due to human testimony in matters of fact, and even to human authority in matters of opinion.
11. There are many events depending on the will of man in which there is a self-evident probability, greater or less according to circumstances.
12. In the phenomena of nature, what is to be will probably be like to what has been in similar circumstances.

B. Principles Relating to Necessary Truths

1. Grammatical; as, that every adjective in a sentence must belong to some substantive expressed or understood.
2. Logical axioms; such as, any contexture of words which does not make a proposition is neither true nor false.
3. Mathematical axioms.
4. Axioms in matters of taste.
5. First Principles in Morals; as, that an unjust action has more demerit than an ungenerous one.
6. Metaphysical; as that,
    a. The qualities which we perceive by our senses must have a subject, which we call body; and that the thoughts we are conscious of must have a subject, which we call mind.
    b. Whatever begins to exist must have a cause which produced it.
    c. Design and intelligence in the cause may be inferred with certainty from marks or signs of it in the effect.[26]

FIGURE 3.2.

Kant were involved in the same project, refuting the skepticism of Hume. But Reid's refutation took an entirely different direction than Kant's. Rather than build on the philosophical debate between rationalism and empiricism as Kant had done, Reid went behind Hume and back to Locke to take issue with the disjuncture between objects and perceptions of objects. Building on a Newtonian worldview, he proceeded to lay the foundation for knowledge that was sensory and immediate.[27]

It is not hard to grasp the radical difference between Reid's and Kant's solutions to the epistemological crisis precipitated by Hume. Reality is not created in the mind but exists objectively outside of it and can be discovered via the empirical method (understood in terms of Baconian inductivism).[28] Here, as we look at the history of theology, we see how conservative American theologians adopted this epistemology wholesale. At Princeton most did not view this as philosophy but simply the perspective of the Bible itself, although there were a few who recognized that they were employing what has come to be called Common Sense. But even these few saw Common Sense as endorsed by Scripture itself.[29]

The inductive theological methodology of Common Sense can be seen in the works of Charles Hodge, A. A. Hodge, and B. B. Warfield as well as in those of Baptist theologian A. H. Strong. Lockean empirical foundationalism, the necessity of proof of the existence of God, and the objective nature of the "facts" of divine revelation that serve as the foundation of all theology point unmistakably to a system built on the epistemology of Thomas Reid.

This theological edifice stood for nearly a century, but the epistemological foundations were not able to bear the discoveries of modern science that defied "common sense" (such as relativity and quantum physics) and the development of higher critical methodologies that were used to challenge the assumptions of the totally divine nature of Scripture—a proposition that conservative evangelical theology took for granted. While this Common Sense epistemology has persisted among much of conservative lay Christianity to this day, within the conservative theological academy a more sophisticated form of realism, critical realism, has largely replaced Common Sense Realism. This realistic epistemological tradition has developed a "hard" philosophical/epistemological foundationalism to defend the received truth of divine revelation.[30] This hard foundationalism, rather than being a part of historic Protestant orthodoxy, has its roots deeply embedded in the Enlightenment.

Realism, either Common Sense or critical, has become so identified with conservative evangelical theology that there are many who would deny that one can in fact be evangelical and at the same time reject epistemological realism.[31]

6. Søren Kierkegaard and Existentialism

While the Enlightenment period was formally brought to a close with the work of Kant, the effects of the Enlightenment continued. One more epistemological innovation in philosophy in reaction against the continuing legacy of the Enlightenment had profound implications for theology. That was the existentialism pioneered by Søren Kierkegaard, the "melancholy Dane."

Existentialism was a revolt against the rationalism of the Enlightenment project. It is an "antiphilosophy philosophy" in that it rejects the whole notion of the systematization of truth as both impossible and unnecessary. Truth, rather than being grasped intellectually, must be experienced. An existential perspective contends that rationalism and rationalistic philosophies are abstract, theoretical, and unrelated to life, and that such philosophical systems ignore the real needs of humanity. Kierkegaard rejected the whole idea of objective truth. Rather, he said, truth is something to be discovered within, but only after long and tortuous self-analysis.

Søren Kierkegaard

In contrast to a comprehensive system of knowing, recurring *themes* run through existential thought, including *angst* (anxiety, dread, and fear of death), *being and existence*, *intentionality*, *absurdity*, and *individual choice.* Existentialism magnifies the concept of freedom and proclaims that "existence precedes essence."

In the existentialist perspective, anxiety is a key experience of human existence. When human beings think about matters of life and death, they are overcome by feelings of dread and the amazement of being. Feelings of meaninglessness and the experience of suffering in life in particular evoke feelings of *angst*. This anxiety is general and unfocused. It is part of the human condition with which each person must come to terms. Existentialism, in contrast to other philosophies, contends that questions of being and existence cannot be neatly put into categories, yet such questions are at the core of the existential perspective.

Existentialism is concerned with the question of being and with the way the individual exists in the world. It seeks a way to transform "inauthentic existence," an existence characterized by fear, dread, and anxiety, into "authentic existence."

Existentialism focuses on inner human experience, emotions and will, beliefs and intentions. The key to knowledge is in understanding the inner life of the person. This stands in stark contrast to other philosophies that focus on what is "out there" in the external world. The world "out there" is pointless. Meaning is to be created by the *choices* the person makes.

Choice then becomes the center of human existence. One becomes truly human through the exercise of choice. Refusal to choose condemns one to continued inauthentic existence, while the act of choosing moves one into the realm of authentic existence. It is not the *object* of choice but the *fact* of choice that is in view here. Existentialism insists that the truly authentic human being exercises choice and in so doing takes responsibility for his or her own existence.

But choice is something more even than an agent in the creation of one's humanity. Choice is exercised in the realm of *absurdity*. While other philosophies try to demonstrate meaning in life and creation, existentialism denies that meaning can be found either in any one thing or in all things put together. Life is absurd, and it is in the face of absurdity that choices must be made.

As originally formulated by Kierkegaard, existentialism was a challenge to the then reigning Hegelian philosophy and later to the comfortable, self-satisfied Danish Lutheran Church. Kierkegaard's perspective was profoundly Christian and began with the presupposition of the existence of God and the incarnation of Jesus Christ as the most important facts of human existence. God's existence was beyond the capacity of reason to prove. He could be known only by faith, not as a theoretical commitment to a set of facts but by a radical commitment that turns one's whole being into discipleship.

Later philosophers, beginning with Nietzsche, turned Kierkegaard's perspective on its head and asserted an atheistic version of existentialism, a perspective carried into the mid-twentieth century by Sartre, Camus, and numerous others.

Existentialism in theology has taken various forms. Rudolf Bultmann, relying on the work of Martin Heidegger, used existential ideas and categories to express his theology and in so doing divorced theology from history while insisting on the necessity of faith. It would be a mistake, however, to see Bultmann as strictly existential in his views. He employed a neo-Kantian framework in his view of God. Others, such as Paul Tillich, used existential categories in thinking about questions of ontology and in doing so effectively turned Christianity into a philosophy. Others, less radical in their approach and without rejecting the historical basis of Christianity, have focused on the faith from the perspective of its relation to the individual.

Among the neoorthodox (see chap. 15), we see the epistemological indebtedness to existentialism in the disavowal of propositional truth and in holding instead that truth is personal and existential and is experienced in encounter. Karl Barth was profoundly affected in his early years by the existentialism of Kierkegaard. His concept that the Bible *becomes* the Word of God in a moment of existential encounter reveals that indebtedness. While the early Barth was heavily existential in his perspective, the later Barth self-consciously distanced himself from his earlier dependence on existentialism. Emil Brunner also constructed his theology from an existential perspective. In Brunner's case, the dialogical personalism of Martin Buber, who saw truth expressed in the I-Thou encounter, became foundational.

C. THE POSTMODERN CHALLENGE TO ENLIGHTENMENT CERTAINTY

While the Enlightenment project was envisioned as a *faith-free* project that admitted only knowledge that was certain, the reality was far different.

> At its core the Enlightenment held to a bedrock *faith* in the ability of the self to discover universal, binding truths of science, politics, and morality. Since it conceived of human nature as essentially rational, the Enlightenment could claim that every free individual would reach similar conclusions about the most crucial matters of civic, moral, and intellectual life.[32]

The emergence of postmodernism in the late-twentieth century has called into question the whole Enlightenment project of establishing objective knowledge and rational certainty, raising the disturbing specters of skepticism and relativism. The postmodern critique of the project of modernity has been scathing and insightful. It also has profoundly disturbing implications for theology. These implications are, however, only *logical* as opposed to *necessary* conclusions of the critiques. A number of theologians and philosophers have admitted the validity of the postmodern *critique* but have challenged the postmodern *solution*.

The modern mind has been built on a rationalistic understanding of the universe and an assumption of the ability of the human mind to fully understand

and master the created order. The postmodern critique has challenged this understanding directly by attacking the very foundations on which the modern mind has been constructed. Postmodernism recognizes that cultures, societies, and peoples are held together by *stories* that embody the identity of people. A story that is globalized and given universal standing attains the status of *metanarrative*, or myth.[33]

The myth or metanarrative of the modern world is that of *progress.* It has been summarized by John Dewey, who says that modern humans are no longer occupied with the supernatural but delight in the this-worldly natural and secular order. In contrast to the medieval submission to the authority of the church, "there is a growing belief in the power of individual minds guided by methods of observation, experience and reflection to attain the truths needed for the guidance of life." This is combined with a view toward the future: "The future rather than the past dominates the imagination. The Golden Age lies ahead of us not behind us." Add to this the work of science, which through the patient and experimental study of nature bears fruit in inventions that control nature and subdue nature's forces for society's use. This is the method by which progress is made.[34] Humans are autonomous and omnicompetent. They will undertake and build a modern tower of Babel that touches the heavens. They will demonstrate their own greatness for all creation to view. The power of autonomous humankind belongs not to a lone modern Prometheus who stormed the heavens and stole the fire, but to all people.

The postmodern critique of modernity has proceeded on several fronts. First came the attack on the myth of progress itself. The vision based on this myth is European, largely Protestant, and almost exclusively male. The majority of the world is marginalized and oppressed in the fulfilling of this vision.[35] The second, and for purposes of this chapter more pointed, critique is the denial of the whole idea of objective knowledge as naive and impossible. There is no way to gain what American philosopher Thomas Nagel has termed "a view from nowhere."[36] There is no such thing as objective truth available for all to see.

In recent decades, there has been a profound revolution in the understanding of knowledge. The rise of the discipline of the sociology of knowledge[37] has demonstrated that knowledge arises within a community and is passed on within that community. As long ago as the seventeenth century, French mathematician Blaise Pascal observed that what was true north of the Pyrenees was not necessarily true south of them. Put in postmodern terms, knowledge arises out of the local narratives of a given community.

At this point, the specter of relativism raises its ugly head. If truth is determined by the community, and there are innumerable communities, then there can be no one absolute objective truth to which one can appeal, only community standards.

1. The Dogmatism of Doubt

A consequence of the Enlightenment quest for certainty was the perception that if you didn't know something for certain, you didn't know anything at all.[38] Or, put another way, it is more appropriate to doubt than to accept anything on faith. This mentality is the legacy of Descartes' *Cogito ergo sum*, and it has a smothering effect. Skepticism is more intellectually respectable than trust in *unproven* claims. The "open mind" is valued over "dogmatism."

The idea is that the person who employs the principle of doubt, allowing only the proven facts of public knowledge, will not be deceived by "mere belief." This position, when rigorously applied, leads to radical skepticism and prides itself in holding no knowledge rather than naively trusting dubious claims.

This whole program is logically fallacious, for as scientist and philosopher Michael Polanyi has shown, doubt and faith, contradiction and affirmation, manifest a logical equivalence. To doubt one thing is at the same time to believe something else.

> The skeptical statement "I doubt P" can be restated in a positive form: either "I believe not P" or "I believe P is not proven." But these statements provoke the question, "On what basis do you believe this?"[39]

The answer to this question reveals a *framework of belief* that cannot be doubted while at the same time doubting P. This framework provides the conditions of doubt, but the framework itself is not doubted. If it were doubted, the ground for doubting P would be removed.

> Thus every doubt has a fiduciary structure and is rooted in a set of faith commitments which for so long as they support the doubt, cannot themselves be doubted. The branch upon which every doubt sits is a belief. To insist on chopping this branch off in the misguided attempt to assume a wholly uncommitted position can only result in self-referential destruction, as the initial doubt itself falls to the floor.[40]

Shifting the focus of our doubt means shifting the focus of our faith commitments. The whole enterprise of doubt rests on an *uncritical* acceptance of and reliance on a whole framework of meaning. Thus *doubt is not an objective process.* Rather, it is highly subjective and rooted in all sorts of commitments beyond the awareness of the doubter. The act of doubting, then, is not avoidance of unproven beliefs. The doubt itself rests on unproven belief. If we commit ourselves to the principle of doubt, we must ultimately either be reduced to silence, since nothing at all can be proved, or be willing to move from one belief structure to another so that we may avoid permanently associating ourselves with any other unproven beliefs. "Philosophic doubt is thus kept on the leash and prevented from calling in question anything that the skeptic believes in, or from approving of any doubt that he does not share."[41] The skeptic in effect says that his own chosen beliefs are neutral and objective and that we could accept the way he sees things if only we would accept rational beliefs like his own. As Polanyi has observed, "a dogmatic orthodoxy can be kept in check both internally and externally, while a creed inverted into a science is both blind and deceptive."[42]

2. The Skill of Knowing

The myth of scientific objectivity and of the ability of science to deliver truth is communicated in the image of the dispassionate scientist carefully engaging in experiments and patiently awaiting the results. The experiments are carried out and the facts gathered under carefully controlled conditions. Since the scientist deals with hard data, there is no room for deception or manipulation of the facts through personal prejudice or privately held convictions. The scientist is only a functionary in the process with no personal responsibility for the results. He or she constructs a descriptive story of the kind of place the world is. The story can then be verified by agreed upon methods.

Surely this is the Enlightenment ideal: the facts are merely "out there" to be collected, arranged, comprehended, and used, regardless of what our personal background, training, or beliefs happen to be. Facts are facts, prereflective raw data, unencumbered by any theory of interpretation and universally recognizable by experience. In reality, however, *the assumption that facts are simply "given" is strictly an Enlightenment construction.*

No one—not even the scientist—is ever in a position to be totally neutral or just a passive receptor of pure data. This is not the way reality comes to us. Our responsibility toward knowledge is much more than merely preserving it unspoiled. The reality is that every act of knowing is an action that *requires skill.* To know, we must make use of various linguistic, conceptual, and physical tools. The process often requires us to make judgments and to commit ourselves to procedures and suppositions and previous results. The success of the knowing process is not guaranteed but is dependent on the knower's own contribution to the process.

Moreover, the success of the scientific method depends on the *personal vision* of the scientist. Rather than being strictly objective, the process hinges throughout on the scientist's ability to discern patterns that further experiments will either confirm or disprove. And it is to a large extent the personal vision of the scientist that determines what he or she will see—or not see.

For a theory to stand, it must have *predictive powers* that guide further researchers to new insights into the nature of reality. Once a theory fails to provide further insight, it is in danger of being replaced by a vision of reality that will yield more insight. The point here is that the scientific process, far from being objective, dispassionate, and absolutely certain is founded on the subjective vision and hope of the researcher.

Once a theory has been formulated, it undergoes testing for verification of its truth or falsity. Note that a theory can never be proven true in the absolute sense, although it can be falsified. Any data that contradict a theory will show the theory to be false, but positive data will only logically *support* the theory rather than *prove* it. The very nature of the inductive method leads only to probability as opposed to certainty. Certainty can be achieved only in deductive mathematics, since what is proved there is already implicit in the propositions.

In the process of testing a theory, the activity of the scientist is not dispassionate and uninvolved. At every point, the scientist must make judgments and act accordingly, must use skill and training to gather and interpret data, and must know what tools to use and when to use them. The process of knowing is a highly complex process that actively involves the knower. As Polanyi says, "Even the most strictly mechanized procedure leaves something to personal skill in the exercise of which an individual bias may enter."[43]

To take this a step further, some aspects of the knowing process must be "caught rather than taught." These we might call the "tricks of the trade." Practitioners can only pass this knowledge on through a "discipleship," or master-apprentice, relationship. Some things even the best texts cannot teach.

So, contrary to the Enlightenment model, knowing is never an impersonal or passive transaction with the world. We bring existing frameworks of interpretation to even the most straightforward acts of knowing. These frameworks are not universal but rather a product of participation in our specific human community.

An example, on a most basic level, can be seen in a real-life situation. People raised in the cultural tradition of the modern Western industrialized world are accustomed to seeing many types of images and pictures: movies, videotapes, color photographs, black and white images, line drawings. When confronted with these, they immediately and intuitively understand and interpret the symbols they see. However, when Wycliffe Bible Translators prepare translations for indigenous populations that are largely or completely untouched by Western society, an astounding phenomenon occurs. For many of these indigenous people who only know a three-dimensional world, a two-dimensional representation—some form of picture—is abstract and, in some tribal contexts, nothing but meaningless lines or colors. In other cases, line art can be recognized, but drawings with shades of gray or color photographs or art are incomprehensible.[44]

We "see" by virtue of the mental categories we bring to the sensory data we apprehend. In this Kant was partially right: the mind is active in providing categories. These categories are not innate, however, but learned from the community we inhabit. Likewise, our memories act as filters to strain out much of the sensory data we experience. When we think of "facts," we do not include the profusion of minutiae we constantly experience. Rather, we strain out what is not, and retain what is, significant for us. This, too, involves subjective judgment: we do not all see the same, identical "objective facts." Thus the question, "What are the facts?" involves knowing the relevant questions to ask of "reality" in order to sift the wheat from the chaff.

"Facts, like telescopes and wigs for gentlemen, were a seventeenth-century invention."

—ALASDAIR MACINTYRE

The upshot of all this is that facts are not pretheoretical, value-free units of pure information that is publicly available for all rational humans to see. Straightforward facts do not exist. Alasdair MacIntyre says, "Facts, like telescopes and wigs for gentlemen, were a seventeenth-century invention."[45] Trevor Hart concludes, "Real facts are already theory-laden, quarried from the mass of our experience via a complex process of interpretation, in reliance upon tools to which we entrust ourselves and through the exercise of skills upon the performance of which the success of our quest for knowledge depends."[46] These facts cannot be understood as neutral; they are in reality statements of belief. There is no *absolute* certainty available in the Enlightenment sense, since every fact rests on a bedrock of uncritically accepted preunderstandings. *Truth, then, is the external pole of belief. If you destroy belief, you destroy truth.*[47]

> Truth is the external pole of belief. If you destroy belief, you destroy truth.

3. Doomed to Relativism?

Are we then doomed to relativism, as the implication of the preceding discussion would seem to be? Nonrational precommitment (faith or belief) involves, as Polanyi insists, in fact a precommitment to all rational activity. But that activity does not occur in a vacuum; it occurs in the context of an intellectual tradition. Indeed, all rational activity is rooted in a set of principles or fundamental beliefs. This makes the quest for truth inescapably culture bound, both historically and socially. So the answer to the Enlightenment question, "What is true?" or "What is rational?" must be, "It depends on who you are and in what intellectual tradition you find yourself." Rationalities and truths are inescapably context specific.

We begin thinking within an intellectual tradition, but by the questions we ask, our tradition is carried forward and transformed. The inherited tradition with its "unproven assumptions" forms the basis for inquiry. To critically examine these assumptions, we must step out of our own tradition and into another tradition. There is no neutral territory.

Human beings have an amazing ability for self-transcendence. We desire to know, to be sure. But the only sort of self-transcendence available to us comes from other intellectual traditions. It is not the "God's-eye view" sought by the Enlightenment. Self-transcendence is about making progress in the quest for truth. To the relativist and the skeptic, this quest is irrelevant and nonsensical, since one truth is as good (or as bad) as another.

We must admit that there is a world external to ourselves. The quest for knowledge consists of exploring that world and incorporating its complexity into our understanding, recognizing that the world in all its complexity is more than our finite minds can comprehend. Nevertheless, we are compelled to try to grasp its complexity. Thus we can have real knowledge, even though it is always partial and incomplete and open to further clarification. Our knowledge can never be certain in the Enlightenment sense of the term.

Consider the three umpires having a drink after a baseball game. The first ump says, "There are balls and there are strikes, and I call 'em the way they are." The second responds, "There are balls and there are strikes, and I call 'em the way I see 'em. The third says, "There are balls and there are strikes, and they ain't nothin' till I call 'em."[48]

Here we have three fundamental epistemologies at work. The first is that of a naive realism (like Scottish Common Sense). The second umpire is a critical realist. He is a perspectivalist.[49] He recognizes that there is a reality, but he also recognizes his fallible part in the interpretation of that reality. The third ump is a radical postmodernist (either relativist or skeptic) who sees his task as creating reality. He has no notion of trying to make his judgments correspond with reality. His words define reality. For the theist, the first alternative must be rejected in light of the advances in understanding the knowing process. The third is self-evidently to be rejected. This leaves the second option, *perspectivalism* or *moderate constructivism*,[50] as the legitimate option for the serious student.

The legitimacy of "hard" epistemological foundationalism arising out of the Enlightenment project can no longer be maintained. To continue to do so in light of the destruction of the whole project out of which it was born is fundamentally wrongheaded. There is no objective or privileged position from which to view reality; there is no "view from nowhere." All our knowledge involves a faith commitment.

D. PREUNDERSTANDINGS AND THEOLOGICAL FORMULATIONS

As we have seen, there is no such thing as the objective neutral observer. Preunderstandings are always at work. This reality has often not been recognized by theologians. For example, Charles Hodge saw all theologies in some respect as a reflection of an underlying philosophy—except his own theology.[51] His theology was simply pure theology drawn from the text of Scripture itself. For Warfield in particular, the Westminster Confession represented the pinnacle of all theological understanding, to which no new insight could be admitted; all traditions that failed to attain to the Westminster standards were open to criticism as inadequate or false.

This same phenomenon could be multiplied innumerable times, especially among conservative theologians. The fortress walls, however, are showing cracks as evangelicals become critically aware of their own traditions. For example, Stanley Gundry, in his presidential address to the Evangelical Theological Society in 1979, stated:

> I wonder if we recognize that all theology represents a contextualization, even our own theology? We speak of Latin American libera-

> tion theology, black theology, or feminist theology; but without the slightest second thought we will assume that our own theology is simply theology, undoubted in its purest form. Do we recognize that the versions of evangelical theology held to by most of the people in this room are in fact North American, white and male and that they reflect and/or address those values and concerns?[52]

Likewise, John Jefferson Davis has observed that

> if systematic theology is essentially a "biblical theology" that merely repeats and arranges the statements and categories of Scripture, then which biblical theology is the really biblical one? The Lutheran? The Reformed? The Wesleyan? The dispensational? The very variety of theological systems within the evangelical tradition alone, all claiming an equally high regard for the authority of Scripture, is in itself an indication that there are factors beyond the text itself which shape the gestalt of the system. In no case does the exegete or theologian come to the text completely free of presuppositions. We can to a degree become more critically aware of our presuppositions, but we cannot eliminate them entirely. There is an inescapable element of personal judgment which shapes the theologian's vision, just as it does the artist's or scientist's.[53]

In the late 1980s, Vern Poythress of Westminster Theological Seminary published *Symphonic Theology: The Validity of Multiple Perspectives in Theology.* Rather than being a theological textbook, this slim volume outlined the perspectival nature of all human understanding and demonstrated the implications of this linguistic understanding for the practice of the theological disciplines. Drawing on the work of Thomas Kuhn, Max Black, and Mary Hesse, he contended that even in the "objective" hard sciences (as opposed to the soft sciences, which are universally recognized as having a large subjective element involved) all knowledge and discovery are tied directly to the perspective of the researcher.[54]

Poythress listed "twelve maxims of symphonic theology." The first is "Language is not transparent to the world." While we think of language as simply giving us an accurate and adequate means to communicate with others our experience of the world, the actual process is much more complex than we normally realize.

> Natural human languages are not simply perfect, invisible glass windows that have no influence on what we see in the world. Nor is there

> a perfect language available that would be such a perfect window. In particular, no language will enable us to state facts without making any assumptions or without the statements being related to who we are as persons. No special language can free us from having to make crucial judgments on the basis of partial analogies or similarities. No special language can immediately make visible to us the ultimate structure of categories of the universe.
>
> Positively, natural languages are adequate vehicles for human communication and for communication between God and human beings. Some of the features that might be supposed to be imperfections are in fact positive assets. In the Bible, God uses ordinary human language rather than a technically precise jargon. He does not include all the technical, pedantic details that would interest a scholar. By doing so, he speaks clearly to ordinary people, not merely to scholars with advanced technical knowledge.[55]

The nature of language as the means to communicate accurately and adequately has in the past half century been brought to the forefront in philosophical investigation. Wittgenstein's statement about the inability of language to communicate the smell of a cup of coffee powerfully illustrates that language is at best an imperfect vehicle for communication. Wittgenstein further advanced our understanding of the working of language in the communication process with his observations about "language games." While early in his career he had taught a "picture theory of meaning," contending that language always relates to the world in the same way, later in his career he repudiated this understanding[56] and instead argued that the use of language is different in different contexts. In each context, whether it be building a house, learning to paint, worshiping, playing football, or some other activity, language is shared by a specific community of speakers. He observed that the appropriate understanding of any particular utterance is only to be discovered when one understands the "game" in which that utterance was made.

E. THE PROBLEM OF HISTORY: HOW HISTORY AND TRUTH RELATE

The Enlightenment heritage identified truth with that which is absolute and noncontingent. In other words, for something to be considered truth, it has to be true at all times for all people in all places. The Enlightenment project involved, as it were, distilling away all contingencies from any so-called truth until only what is universal and absolute is left. In practice such a method relegated history to the level of a problem rather than being a source of truth.

The philosopher Gotthold Lessing encapsulated the Enlightenment understanding in his maxim, "The accidental truths of history can never become the proof of the necessary truths of reason."[57] Lessing was, like Descartes, a mathematician who sought absolute certainty in the mathematical sense. Since history could not provide first-order certainty, it could not provide the basis of any systematic thought. Lessing contended that between the certainty of mathematical formulation and the certainty of historical formulations, there was an "ugly, broad, ditch" across which he (and supposedly others) could not jump.[58] The implication for traditional Christianity, as based on the person and work of Jesus Christ in history, was devastating. But for Enlightenment thinkers, the truth of religion (Christianity in particular) was to be found in its *moral teaching*, which reason adjudges to be true and can be experienced immediately, rather than in history, from which it arose.

In recent years, the whole Enlightenment approach to history has been challenged on several levels, especially with reference to the nature of historical knowledge as opposed to the "necessary truths of reason." Key in this challenge is the emergence of the discipline of the sociology of knowledge—that is, "the study of the way in which the production of knowledge is shaped by the social context of thinkers."[59] While not spoken in precisely these terms, there has long been an implicit recognition of the legitimacy of this concept in the historical disciplines. The question, "Do the times make the man or does the man make the times?" reflects at least an awareness of the larger social context out of which great individuals arise. The theological disciplines have been far slower in recognizing the validity of these insights, but as the observations of Stanley Gundry and J. J. Davis cited above demonstrate, even among evangelicals this awareness is growing. Alister McGrath adds:

> The exegete brings to the text questions which he or she has been conditioned to ask through his or her experience, social position, political conviction, gender, and so forth. The recognition that human thought—whether sociology, theology, ethics, or metaphysics—arises in a specific social context is of fundamental importance to the sociology of knowledge. All social movements, whether religious or secular, including the literature which they produce, involve implicit or explicit ideological perspectives and strategies by which personal experience and social reality may be interpreted and collective needs and interests may be defined and legitimated.[60]

These observations leave haunting questions about the certainty of our knowledge, and if pressed, we ask in frustration, "How can anyone know anything at all?" Alister McGrath, Trevor Hart, and Nancey Murphy[61] have all addressed the question of relativism and certainty of knowledge, each focusing on different aspects of the question.

From the perspective of the philosophy of history, McGrath has addressed the issue of radical historicism, which is thoroughly relativistic, demonstrating the impossibility of its claims. The answer is not, however, to abandon the legitimate insights of historicism altogether. Rather, the legitimacy of three key insights must be granted.

1. All thought is historically located.
2. Historical thought is essential to self-understanding.
3. A flight from history is improper and impossible.[62]

The primary target of historicism is the tradition of Descartes and Kant with its attempt to transcend all limitations of time and space by eliminating historical contingencies. In fact, the incongruity of building theology on these presuppositions becomes immediately obvious, since the very offense of the Christian faith is the historical rootedness of its very core. The fact that God would privilege one people (the Jews), one place (Palestine), one time (the early first century); incarnate himself in one historic person (Jesus Christ); and designate one key historical event (the crucifixion-resurrection) as the standard of all human history flies in the face of the whole Enlightenment mentality.

Ideas and theories, including Christian doctrines, must be placed in their proper historical contexts *prior* to analyzing and evaluating them.[63] The historical background and community out of which teachings arose must not be treated as the disposable trappings of timeless truths. From the perspective of theology, the fact that doctrine arises in history opens it up to historical investigation. However, this recognition does not give justification for relativizing the core idea involved in a doctrine. Still, the entire process *seems* to subject the search for truth to radical relativization. Peter Berger has identified the central question for the theologian:

> When everything has been subsumed under the relativizing categories in question (those of history, of sociology of knowledge, or what have you), the question of truth reasserts itself with almost pristine simplicity. Once we know that all human affirmations are subject to scientifically graspable socio-historical processes, *which affirmations are true and which ones are false?*[64]

One cannot assert that all beliefs are equally true (the claim of the radical relativist) nor that all beliefs are equally false (the claim of the radical skeptic). In the case of the former, one need only ask, "What about beliefs that contradict one another?" In the case of the latter, the very assertion that all beliefs are false must in and of itself also be false!

Another problem in judging what is true and false is that the judge—whether sociologist, theologian, psychologist, or historian—is not in a privileged position of neutral objectivity. What is "obviously true" depends on the presuppositions of the one doing the analyzing. Every discipline—even that of sociology of knowledge—has developed its own commonsense presuppositions by which it judges truth and falsity. This fact leads to the uncomfortable conclusion that both the observed and the observer are socially conditioned, but there is no way to appeal to a neutral objective observer.

This would seem to lock humanity into hopeless cultural relativism, as the radical postmodernist would claim. But it does not. Rather, it obligates us to acknowledge the difficulty in communication between human beings, not only of different cultures but even within the same culture. It also demands that we abandon any thought of a universal framework of rationality that is independent of time and place. Our understanding of the past (and indeed of other cultures' present) will of necessity be partial. The beliefs of the past are not invalid simply because they are past; rather, the past framework of belief must be carefully interrogated as to its plausibility.

The key to answering the problem is found in the *search for grounds of plausibility of belief.* What factors led or lead to a belief becoming credible? Why did and why do people believe *that*? The question for theology is, Why did a particular belief arise? "It is necessary to identify the constraints under which they were formulated as much as the factors which led to their plausibility in the first place. It is necessary to ask, not merely *why* anyone should believe *that*, but *how* that belief came to be expressed, articulated or conceptualized in the specific form which it assumes."[65]

F. THEOLOGY AS TRUTH: HOW TRUE IS OUR TRUTH?

The previous discussions leave the uncomfortable suspicion of relativism in the back of our minds and the feeling that there is no absolute to which we can appeal. If we follow the logic of the preceding, even the Bible itself—verbally inspired, inerrant, divine revelation—is locked into the historical process and thus relative to us. If this is the case, how can we know anything for sure? Are we to base our faith on nothing more than a hunch or preference?

Thus we are still left with the problem of "How can I know?" It is at this point that Thomas Oden has done us a great service. In his systematic theology, he has attempted to say, like the writer of Ecclesiastes, "nothing new." Rather, he has sought to set forth the historical consensus of the church following the fourth-century Vincentian Canon, *Quod ubique, quod semper, quod ab omnibus creditum est* ("that which has always, everywhere, and by all Christians been believed [about God's self-disclosure]").[66]

The strength of Oden's project is perhaps a bit different than he perceives it to be. If we are conditioned by our historical circumstances, as I believe we are,[67] and if the goal of a totally objective truth is beyond our grasp, as I am convinced it is, then all our knowledge is by definition finite, limited, and warped to some degree by the presuppositions that we subconsciously employ. This presents us with a problem: How much of our knowledge arises out of our presuppositions and how much from the data itself? The answer to this dilemma is found at least in part in conversation with the past. While we all make mistakes, we do not all make the same mistakes. If our spiritual predecessors, beginning in their own concrete historical situations with their own worldviews and presuppositions, have looked at the same data we have, and if they have come up with conclusions similar to our own, we can have a high degree of assurance that our reading of the data is not hopelessly skewed due to our preconceptions.

Levels of Truth
TRUTH God alone is absolute TRUTH.
Truth Scripture is simple Truth, historically conditioned/concretized.
truth Theology is truth insofar as it accurately reexpresses the historically concrete Truth of Scripture in categories understood by contemporary hearers.
Truth and **truth** can approach **TRUTH**—but only at points. As frameworks of understanding, all theological systems fall under the category of **truth**.

FIGURE 3.3.

The Christian by definition must admit that absolute truth exists. This follows necessarily from the nature of creation by God. But there is a hook here. We affirm that there is absolute truth from an ontological perspective, but we can never achieve the "God's-eye view." This was the hubris of the Enlightenment. We are, as McGrath has observed, "condemned to history" with no way to lift ourselves above it. We cannot get out of the box and admire "the view from nowhere." That is the prerogative and ability of God alone.

We also recognize that God has broken into history and given us his revelation, which has been preserved for us in Scripture. While we affirm the complete and utter truthfulness of Scripture, it is one thing to say that Scripture is absolutely true yet quite another to say that it is absolute truth. A. A. Hodge and B. B. Warfield themselves observed that Scripture does not give us absolute truth; it gives us simple truth.[68] The truth of God comes mediated in human garb and in the contingent historical process.

Theology—that is, systematic theological understanding—is another step removed from that absolute truth, since it takes one historically concrete form of revelation and infers, systematizes, and reexpresses it in another form in a context foreign to the one in which it was given. Vern Poythress has drawn the crucial distinction between *absolute truth* and *relative knowledge.*

> Among theists, at least, I suppose that no one would deny that human knowledge is relative in these respects. (Some people might not want to use the term "relative," for fear of compromising their conviction that truth is not relative, but I think most would agree with the substance of this section.) Nevertheless, I do not think that we have always appreciated the consequences of this relativity of our knowledge. We know that truth is absolute—in particular, the truths of the Bible. We allow ourselves, however, to slip over into excessive presumption with regard to our human knowledge. We do not reckon with the fact that our interpretation of the Bible is always fallible. Or if we know a piece of truth, we may erroneously suppose that we know it precisely and exhaustively. The Pharisees doubtless thought that they understood the Sabbath commandment exactly. Therefore they knew that Jesus was breaking the Sabbath. The Pharisees were drawing their boundaries very precisely. They knew, for example, exactly how far they could travel on a Sabbath day without "taking a journey" (i.e., working). But at this point the Pharisees were overconfident and presumptuous. They did not really understand the Old Testament.

> But let us apply this example to ourselves. We may erroneously suppose that we, in our knowledge, do not really need a background of other, related truths in order to make sense of a certain teaching. We make one truth the basis for a long chain of syllogisms, without considering its context. For instance, we ignore the context in which the Sabbath laws are given. At this point, it seems to me, the absoluteness of truth has been confused with the questionable idea that we can isolate and dissect any one bit of truth. Individual true statements are not self-existent in this way.[69]

The idea of truth is not as simple as we commonly think. We intuitively long for certainty, TRUTH in our understanding. While there is absolute truth, human understanding of that truth is always partial and perspectively bound. As one wag observed, "The man with a watch knows what time it is. The man with two watches is never sure." The human knower is limited in space and time and culture. We might liken truth to a flawless diamond that refracts the light from each of its many facets. However, we can only view the light from a single facet at one time. We recognize truth as it is refracted through the facet at which we gaze, but we err if we globalize that refracted ray of light from one facet in such a way that we deny the validity of the refraction from other facets.

BIBLIOGRAPHY

Brown, Colin. *Philosophy and the Christian Faith.* Downers Grove, IL: InterVarsity Press, 1968. • **Greer, Robert C**. *Mapping Postmodernism.* Downers Grove, IL: InterVarsity Press, 2003. • **Grenz, Stanley**. *A Primer on Postmodernism.* Grand Rapids: Eerdmans, 1996. • **Hart, Trevor**. *Faith Thinking.* Downers Grove, IL: InterVarsity Press, 1995. • **McGrath, Alister**. *The Genesis of Doctrine.* Oxford: Blackwell, 1990. • **Middleton, J. Richard**, and **Brian J. Walsh**. *Truth Is Stranger Than It Used to Be.* Downers Grove, IL: InterVarsity Press, 1995. • **Murphy, Nancey**. *Anglo-American Postmodernity.* Boulder, CO: Westview, 1997. • ———. *Beyond Liberalism and Fundamentalism.* Valley Forge, PA: Trinity Press International, 1996. • **Poythress, Vern**. *Symphonic Theology.* Grand Rapids: Zondervan, 1987.

NOTES

[1]The reference here in Colossians is not a blanket condemnation of philosophy as a discipline, but rather a condemnation of the Colossian heresy that undermined the basic tenets of the gospel and Christ. By extension the warning would apply to all philosophies that seek to exercise hegemony over the truth of the gospel, the person and work of Jesus Christ, and divine revelation.

[2]Huston Smith, *Beyond the Post-Modern Mind*, 2nd ed. (Wheaton: Theosophical Publishing House/Quest Books, 1989), 3–4.

[3]The distinction between structure and content is at this point oversimplified. In reality the two overlap.

[4]Bernard Ramm, *After Fundamentalism* (San Francisco: Harper & Row, 1983).

[5]Despite the accuracy of the comparison, Ramm's motivation behind it was perceived to be his unfortunate and bitter experiences at the hands of former colleagues. These fundamentalists did not and could not understand the things he was saying as he moved away from his fundamentalist heritage and into a larger theological orbit. As a result, they regularly denounced him as having become liberal. The comparison between Barth and Chafer was interpreted as a "cheap shot" directed at his former colleagues.

[6]The Psalter Map (p. 73) gives a visual understanding of how the medieval individual viewed the world. " 'The Psalter Map' is so called because it accompanied a thirteenth-century copy of the Book of Psalms. It is one of the earliest maps with Jerusalem at the center, reflecting the medieval worldview. Although tiny (15 cm. x 10 cm.), it contains a wealth of information. It is the earliest surviving map to symbolize Christ's power as overseer of the world and one of the earliest maps to depict biblical events—e.g., Moses crossing the Red Sea (the large red expanse, top right); and the earliest to display the 'monstrous' races in Africa (the strange figures, some without heads, depicted on the right-hand edge). The map shows the world with an encircling sea and three important waterways: the rivers Dan and Nile and the Mediterranean. They divide the land into three continents with Asia at the top, Africa at bottom right, and Europe in the bottom left quarter. The map has east at the top; just below Christ is a depiction of Adam and Eve in the Garden of Eden. If the map is rotated so that north is at the top, it becomes much easier to understand" ("The Earth and the Heavens: the art of the mapmaker," British Library Online Gallery, *www.bl.uk/onlinegallery/features/mapmaker.html* [accessed Sept. 2005]).

[7]Much of the following discussion is drawn from Trevor Hart, *Faith Thinking* (Downers Grove, IL: InterVarsity Press, 1995), 23–47.

[8]Ibid., 26.

[9]Ibid.

[10]W. Dampier, *A History of Science and Its Relations with Philosophy and Religion* (Cambridge: Cambridge University Press, 1946), 123.

[11]Ibid., 27.

[12]Hart, *Faith Thinking*, 29. Later John Locke (1632–1704), standing in this Enlightenment tradition, would define faith as "a persuasion that falls short of knowledge."

[13]From *Rules for the Direction of the Understanding*. Cited in *Dictionary of Philosophy*, s.v. "Descartes" (London: Pan, 1979), 89.

[14]B. B. Warfield, *Studies in Theology* (Grand Rapids: Baker, 1981), 3.

[15]A. N. Whitehead, *Science in the Modern World*. Cited in Cyril E. Joad, *Guide to Philosophy*, reprint (New York: Dover, 1985), 40.

[16]Numerous definitions of truth have been put forth. The two most common are called the correspondence theory of truth and the coherence theory of truth.

[17]Hart, *Faith Thinking*, 40.

[18]Ibid., 42.

[19]S. Ahlstrom, "The Scottish Philosophy and American Theology," *Church History* 24 (1955): 257.

[20]Stephen Douglas Bennett, "Thomas Reid and the Scottish School of Common Sense Philosophy: Historically and Philosophically Considered" (Th.M. thesis, Dallas Theological Seminary, 1980), 47–50.

[21]G. Stanley Hall, "On the History of American College Textbooks and Teaching in Logic, Ethics, Psychology and Allied Subjects," *Proceedings of the American Antiquarian Society*, n.s., 9 (1893–94): 158. Quoted in Martin Terrance, *The Instructed Vision: Scottish Common Sense Philosophy and the Origins of American Fiction* (Bloomington: Indiana University Press, 1961), 3.

[22]See Thomas Reid, *Essays on the Intellectual Powers of Man* (London: Macmillan, 1941), 389–91.

[23]Ibid., 186.

[24]Reid balanced his empiricism with an emphasis on intuition, which gave his epistemology a dualistic bent. In addition, he was adamant about the limits of empirical inquiry; induction could not answer ultimate questions concerning first causes (Bennett, "Thomas Reid," 62. Cf. Reid, *Essays*, 399–400).

[25]Reid, *Essays*, 338–39; 384–86. Cf. Daryl G. Hart, "The Princeton Mind in the Modern World," *Westminster Theological Journal* 46 (1984): 4.

[26]See James McCosh, "The Scottish Philosophy," 201–2, an article excerpted from his massive *The Scottish Philosophy* and included in the *Internet Encyclopedia of Philosophy* (*http://socserv2.socsci.mcmaster.ca/~econ/ugcm/3113/mccosh/scottishphilosophy.pdf* [accessed Oct. 2005]).

[27]Ibid. (accessed Oct. 2005).

[28]Baconian inductivism saw knowledge or absorption of knowledge arising from mere repeated experience. It was precritical in that it did not seek falsification of an experiment/experience.

[29]At the inauguration of William Henry Green to his professorship in Biblical and Oriental Literature at Princeton, the charge was given: "Amid the ceaseless mutations of philosophical systems, there is one system which remains unchanged; and that system is the only one which the Bible recognizes as true,—the philosophy of Common Sense" (Samuel Bach Jones, "A Charge to the Professor," *Discourses at the Inauguration*

of the Rev. William Henry Green ... [Philadelphia: C. Sherman, 1851], 26–27. Cited by C. R. Jeschke in "The Briggs Case: The Focus of a Study in Nineteenth-Century Presbyterian History" (Ph.D. diss., University of Chicago, 1966), 107.

[30]The writings of Carl F. H. Henry, Norman Geisler, John Warwick Montgomery, Josh McDowell, and John Gerstner serve as contemporary popular examples of this hard foundationalism.

[31]Much of the debate within historic evangelicalism at the turn of the millennium has this issue at the very center of the discussion. Postmodernism with the specter of radical skepticism has provoked an epistemological crisis. Some within the evangelical community have declared war on postmodern thought, while others are willing to accept the postmodern critique and adjust their understandings in light of the *legitimate* aspects of that critique.

[32]Roger Lundin, *The Culture of Interpretation* (Grand Rapids: Eerdmans, 1993), 85.

[33]The term *myth* is not used in the sense of a fairy tale, but in the sense of a story that embodies the collective history, goals, and identity of a people.

[34]J. Richard Middleton and Brian J. Walsh, *Truth Is Stranger Than It Used to Be* (Downers Grove, IL: InterVarsity Press, 1995), 14.

[35]For a full discussion of this attack on modernity, see ibid., 11–79.

[36]Thomas Nagel, *The View from Nowhere* (New York: Oxford University Press, 1986).

[37]See Peter Berger and Thomas Luckmann, *The Social Construction of Reality* (Garden City, NY: Doubleday, 1967).

[38]The substance of the following discussion is drawn from Hart, *Faith Thinking*, 49–70, and from Michael Polanyi, *Personal Knowledge* (Chicago: University of Chicago Press, 1962).

[39]Hart, *Faith Thinking*, 57.

[40]Ibid., 58.

[41]Polanyi, *Personal Knowledge*, 297.

[42]Ibid., 268.

[43]Ibid., 19.

[44]Conversation with Kirby O'Brien, Wycliffe Bible Translators, Dallas, July 1998. O'Brien's job is to prepare the graphics for inclusion in various tribal translations. He must work closely with translators to discern what types of artwork and illustrations will be understood by a particular tribal group.

[45]Alasdair MacIntyre, *Whose Rationality? Which Justice?* (Notre Dame, IN: University of Notre Dame Press,1988), 357.

[46]Hart, *Faith Thinking*, 56.

[47]Polanyi, *Personal Knowledge*, 286.

[48]Walter Truett Anderson, *Reality Isn't What It Used to Be* (San Francisco: HarperSanFrancisco, 1990), 75.

[49]The second ump could also be interpreted as a moderate postmodernist who accepts the truth of the social construction of reality based on the insights of sociology of knowledge. There is a significant overlap between the perspectivalism of the critical

realist and the constructivism of the moderate postmodernist. They occupy the same epistemological ground and espouse similar conclusions about reality while starting from different presuppositions.

[50]The moderate constructivist understands the "social construction of reality," while the realist may insist on the objective nature of the world "out there" in an Enlightenment fashion.

[51]M. James Sawyer, *Charles Augustus Briggs and Tensions in Late Nineteenth-Century American Theology* (Lewiston, NY: Mellen University Press, 1994), 29. Cf. Hart, "Princeton Mind."

[52]Stanley N. Gundry, "Evangelical Theology: Where Should We Be Going?" *Journal of the Evangelical Theological Society* 22, no. 1 (1979): 11.

[53]John Jefferson Davis, "Contextualization and the Nature of Theology," in John Jefferson Davis, ed., *Necessity of Systematic Theology*, 2nd ed. (Grand Rapids: Baker, 1978), 177.

[54]Shortly thereafter Poythress published *Science and Hermeneutics* (Grand Rapids: Zondervan, 1988), developing at length and much more technically the survey insights he had put forth in *Symphonic Theology.* Poythress unravels the implications of Kuhn's insights into the structure of scientific revolution for hermeneutics, and I would argue by extension for theological study generally.

[55]Vern Poythress, *Symphonic Theology* (Grand Rapids: Zondervan, 1987), 69–70.

[56]With reference to the concept of language games, Wittgenstein "argued that if one actually looks to see how language is used, the variety of linguistic usage becomes clear. Words are like tools, and just as tools serve different functions, so linguistic expressions serve many functions. Although some propositions are used to picture facts, others are used to command, question, pray, thank, curse, and so on. This recognition of linguistic flexibility and variety led to Wittgenstein's concept of a language game and to the conclusion that people play different language games. The scientist, e.g., is involved in a different language game than the theologian. Moreover, the meaning of a proposition must be understood in terms of its context, that is, in terms of the rules of the game of which that proposition is a part. The key to the resolution of philosophical puzzles is the therapeutic process of examining and describing language in use" ("Wittgenstein, Ludwig Josef Johann," *Microsoft Encarta. http://encarta.msn.com/encyclopedia_761565894_2/Wittgenstein.html* [accessed Sept. 2005]).

[57]Gotthold Ephraim Lessing, *Theological Writings*, trans. H. Chadwick (Stanford, CA: Stanford University Press, 1957), 53.

[58]Ibid., 55.

[59]"Sociology of Knowledge," Sociological Concentrations, University of Texas at San Antonio. *http://colfa.utsa.edu/Sociology/masters/topics.htm* (accessed Sept. 2005).

[60]Alister McGrath, *The Genesis of Doctrine* (Oxford: Blackwell, 1990), 89–90.

[61]Nancey Murphy has contributed to the discussion from the perspectives of philosophy of science and the nature of postmodernism. See her book *Beyond Liberalism and Fundamentalism* (Valley Forge, PA: Trinity Press International, 1996).

[62]McGrath, *Genesis of Doctrine*, 92.

[63]The following discussion is drawn from ibid., 90–102.

[64]Peter Berger, *Rumor of Angels* (Garden City, NY: Doubleday, 1969), 57. Quoted by McGrath in *Genesis of Doctrine*, 93–94. Italics in the original.

[65]McGrath, *Genesis of Doctrine*, 101.

[66]Thomas Oden, *The Living God* (San Francisco: Harper & Row, 1987), xvi.

[67]See here McGrath's *Genesis of Doctrine*, chaps. 4–6, esp. chap. 4.

[68]By this Hodge and Warfield meant that Scripture communicates contingent historical reality rather than the absolute uncontingent and absolute truth sought by the Enlightenment.

[69]Poythress, *Symphonic Theology*, 46–47.

OUTLINE OF CHAPTER 4

A. Theological Method

1. The Wesleyan Quadrilateral
   a. Scripture
   b. Reason
   c. Tradition
   d. Experience
2. The Lutheran Trilateral
3. The Reformed *Sola Scriptura*
   a. The Place of the Creeds in Reformed Theology
   b. *Sola Scriptura* and the Briggs Case
   c. Charles Briggs's Proposal: The Bible, the Church, and the Reason

B. Sources and Authorities

1. The Bible
2. Church and/or Tradition
3. Reason and/or Experience
   a. Life Experience and Categories of Understanding
   b. Reason and Rationalism

C. Factors Involved in the Gestalt of Doctrine

1. The Four Dimensions of Doctrine/Theology
2. The Epistemological Substructure

D. Relating the Authorities

1. Revelation
2. Special Revelation: The Bible
3. General Revelation
   a. Wisdom and Wisdom Literature
   b. Human Ability to Discover Truth
   c. Tension between Fallenness and Ability
   d. General Revelation and Grasping Reality
   e. The Value of General Revelation

CHAPTER 4

SOURCES AND AUTHORITY IN THEOLOGY

The sixteenth-century Reformation saw a recovery of Scripture from its enslavement to the official, authorized interpretation of the medieval Roman Catholic Church with all the hubris that had developed along with it. Indeed, Protestantism became known by the great *solas* of the Reformation: *sola fide*—salvation is obtained through faith alone apart from works*; sola gratia*—salvation is only by free grace of God in Jesus Christ apart from human works of righteousness; *sola christus*—Christ alone is the source of salvation; and *sola scriptura*—the Scripture alone, as the Word of God, is the infallible, final, and binding authority upon the believer as opposed to popes and councils.

At the very beginning of the Reformation, Luther challenged the authority of the established church. At the Diet of Worms, when ordered to recant his views, he replied: "Unless I am convicted by Scripture and plain reason—I do not accept the authority of popes and councils, for they have contradicted each other—my conscience is captive to the Word of God. I cannot and will not recant anything, for to go against conscience is neither right nor safe. God help me. Amen."[1]

Protestants elevated the Scriptures to the place of primacy in the church: the sermon replaced the Mass as the central point of the service, and an open Bible replaced the altar in the churches. Yet Protestants did see value in other authorities. In Puritan Massachusetts there was regular and, by contemporary standards, lengthy exposition of the Word by the preacher. While the Puritans believed in the perspicuity of Scripture—that is, that the central message of Scripture is plain enough for a child to grasp—they also believed that its depths could not be plumbed by the most mature saint. Since this was the case, the Puritans deplored the "dumb reading" of Scripture in worship, insisting that the Word be explained and interpreted to the congregation.

The beginnings of a significant shift in attitude could be seen around the time of the Second Great Awakening. With the birth of new denominations and the rise of the democratic mind-set, there was among conservative evangelical believers a reassertion of the unique, sole, and final authority of the Bible in a way heretofore unknown. The Stonites—followers of Barton Stone, one of the founders of the Disciples of Christ (Christian Church)—insisted that they had "no creed but the Bible." This same attitude was later seen in such groups as the Baptists. Whereas during the Puritan period the Baptists had been responsible for such theological masterpieces as The New Hampshire Confession, they too adopted what I would call a "primitivist mentality," ignoring more than eighteen centuries of history and tradition when they attempted to anchor all understanding directly in the Scriptures. Other groups adopted this attitude as well. Among the smaller but highly influential groups that adopted the "Bible alone" mentality with an accompanying "plain sense of the text" hermeneutic and a disdain for scholarship was the Plymouth Brethren, whose influence spread through its dispensational perspective throughout American evangelicalism. As this attitude took root, the Reformation doctrine of the perspicuity of Scripture became the doctrine that the Bible's meaning is plain for all. For example, R. A. Torrey insisted that "in ninety-nine out of one hundred cases the meaning the plain man gets out of the Bible is the correct one."[2]

Among contemporary denominations, we find statements such as that of the Christian and Missionary Alliance, which in its licensing and ordination questionnaire asks candidates if they agree that the Bible is "the *only and infallible* rule of faith and practice" for the believer (italics added).

The Reformation doctrine of *sola scriptura* has become a mere slogan. Among much of popular evangelicalism *sola scriptura* has become *nuda scriptura*, "bare" Scripture open for anyone to interpret apart from any tradition or even a competent hermeneutic.[3] This has unwittingly let in through the back door the Enlightenment view of knowledge as objective, unconditioned, and universal, and applied these qualities to the text of Scripture. When we look beneath the surface of the words that are used and examine the Protestant traditions, we find that despite the rhetoric, there is always more than Scripture that has gone into the theological equation. While the "more" has varied somewhat in the ways it has been expressed, there has been a remarkable consistency from a conceptual perspective.

A. THEOLOGICAL METHOD

In previous generations, there was often an assumed equation of theology with *truth* and that truth was viewed as simply a systematization of biblical revelation. In recent years, however, several factors have come to the fore that make it clear that such a facile equation is no longer possible. Theologians now speak freely of the Wesleyan quadrilateral and the Lutheran trilateral (see below). Alister McGrath has suggested four factors that come together to determine the "gestalt" of doctrine.[4] With the passing of modernity, the vision of simple, unvarnished, universal truth, untouched by the contingencies of the historical processes, has also died. Even in the sciences researchers are recognized as active participants rather than passive observers: their involvement in the process of the discovery of knowledge shapes that knowledge by virtue of the questions they ask and experiments they devise. As Middleton and Walsh have observed, "Truth is stranger than it used to be."[5]

These realizations have injected an uncomfortable subjectivity into the discipline of theology. In the late nineteenth century, Charles Hodge could confidently assert that theology is the arrangement and display of the facts of Scripture.[6] We, however, can no longer think of theology as simply the objective rearrangement of the propositions of the Bible. The theologian is not and cannot be a disinterested observer. Rather, like every other person, the theologian comes to the task with precommitments and preunderstandings that affect the work.

More than two decades ago, John Jefferson Davis challenged the evangelical understanding of the nature of theology:

> If systematic theology is essentially a "biblical theology" which merely repeats and arranges the statements and categories of scripture, then which "biblical theology" is the really biblical one? The Lutheran? The Reformed? The Wesleyan? The dispensational? The very variety of theological systems within the evangelical tradition alone, all claiming an equally high regard for the authority of scripture, is itself an indication that there are factors beyond the text itself which shape the gestalt of the system.[7]

What are these factors? And how are we to coordinate them? Proposals such as the Wesleyan quadrilateral and the Lutheran trilateral have been put forth. Over a century ago, Charles A. Briggs proposed "the Bible, the Church, and the Reason." Even the Reformed tradition, which loudly asserts *sola scriptura*, manifestly employs other authorities, both implicitly and explicitly, in the theological task.

1. The Wesleyan Quadrilateral

For many years John Wesley was viewed as a preacher and not as a major theologian. In recent decades this evaluation has changed radically as a result of the study of Wesley's writings. He is now regarded as a major theologian with a specific theological method and perspective. Albert Outler called Wesley's method the "Wesleyan quadrilateral," referring to the four sources to which Wesley appealed for authority in doing theology: Scripture, reason, tradition, and experience. In appealing to four sources, Wesley interpreted the Reformation principle of *sola scriptura* in typical Anglican fashion, making the Bible the primary authority and the other three essential in the formulation of doctrine and its application to life.

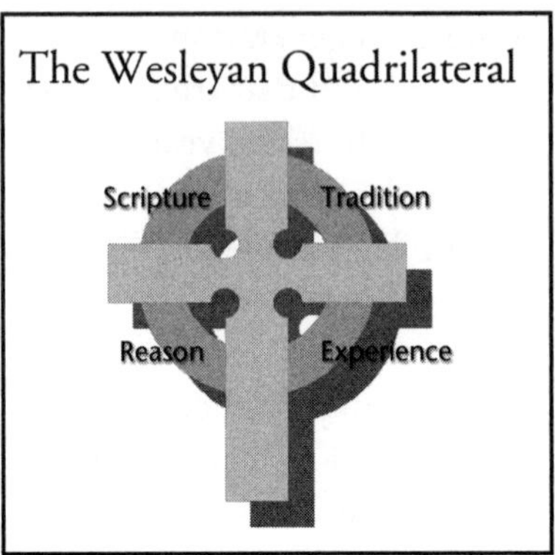

FIGURE 4.1

a. Scripture

For Wesley Scripture was the primary, rather than the only, authority for the Christian. However, he saw the Bible as the final authority for the Christian in determining faith and practice. At times he even went so far as to declare Scripture the only or the sole authority.[8] The authority of Scripture spreads over every area of life. "You are in danger ... every hour, if you depart ever so little from Scripture; yea, or from the plain literal meaning of any text, taken in connection with the context."[9]

Yet Wesley did not promote a naive biblicism; he was aware of contemporary exegesis. Hermeneutically Wesley was committed to the plain literal meaning of the text as opposed to allegorism. If two texts appeared to contradict one another, the clearer was to shed light on the more ambiguous one. Likewise, context, or macroexegesis, was to have priority in the understanding of Scripture. Wesley was committed to the principle of "analogy of faith," that is, Scripture interprets Scripture. He did stress, however, the importance of reason, experience, and tradition for interpreting Scripture and defining theology.

Wesley saw the Bible as "a solid & precious system of Divine Truth,"[10] and he argued that no one could be a good theologian without a thoroughgoing knowledge of the text. He often objected to his opponents' exegesis, noting that it contradicted "the whole tenor of and scope of Scripture."[11]

b. Reason

Wesley frequently coupled reason with Scripture. He believed that human reason was an aspect of the divine image stamped on every person, including sinners. Thus he had great confidence in people's ability to think about spiritual matters. He rejected both antirational enthusiasm and Enlightenment antisupernaturalism. He tried to steer a course between the two extremes, but he often seemed more concerned about the possibility of devaluing reason than about the other extreme of exalting it. Reason is not a primary source of knowledge but a processor that organizes and draws inferences from the knowledge of experience. Wesley explicitly denied the Enlightenment position of a natural theology that could lead to God apart from special revelation. He was adamant that reason could not take away the veil and disclose God. It is thus improper in his scheme to polarize reason and revelation as being opposed to one another. Rather, reason enables the individual to respond to revelation.

To decry reason as the mystics do is utterly unscriptural. Thus Wesley pleads, "It is a fundamental principle with us [the Methodists] that to renounce reason is to renounce religion, that religion and reason go hand in hand, and that all irrational religion is false religion."[12] Reason is essential in spiritual service, both in laying the foundation of true religion, under the guidance of the Spirit of God, and in raising the superstructure. It is the "candle of the Lord" given to aid in comprehending revelation and putting it into practice.

c. Tradition

For the twenty-first-century evangelical, *tradition* often evokes images of Catholicism and the elevation of tradition to a status equal with Scripture. Wesley, however, viewed the authority of tradition in a different sense than Catholicism does. Rather than being independent of Scripture, he saw tradition as founded on Scripture and explaining it. Randy Maddox describes Wesley's understanding of tradition as a "normed norm"—a norm that is itself derived from and dependent on a higher norm—that helps to enlighten and apply Scripture.[13] Of particular value and authority is the early church during the period when it was still young and close to its sources, before the Council of Nicea (A.D. 325), and before the legalization of Christianity by Constantine brought wealth and spiritual laxity to the church.

Wesley held that a *new* doctrine must be wrong. The old religion is the only true one. No doctrine can be right unless it is the same as it was from the beginning. These assertions arose from his conviction that the early church had advantages that the modern church does not enjoy. They lived in close historical proximity to the biblical authors; the patristic writers tended to be of sterling moral/spiritual character; and a special work of the Holy Spirit was upon them in that age.[14] Wesley recognized that the period of the early church was not a golden age, and he did not adopt the perspective of some groups that sought to restore the primitive church. He was aware of the problems but still saw the age as instructive both from a positive and negative perspective. Tradition could not legitimately go against Scripture, but it could go beyond it. It could explicate the general sense of scriptural principles by giving specific examples of how these were concretely worked out in the life of the church. Thus Scripture and tradition existed in a reciprocal relationship.

d. Experience

The final element of the quadrilateral is the authority of experience. In today's theological climate, spiritual experience is either stressed, as is the case in Pentecostalism, or downplayed to such an extent that it has no practical importance in theological formulation. Wesley picked up on vital Reformed themes seen particularly in John Calvin, developed them, and then formally integrated them into his theological method. Wesley particularly advocated and further developed Calvin's doctrine of the witness of the Spirit in the heart of the believer. He insisted with Calvin that the witness of the Spirit is a personal experience *prior to* rational reflection.

The witness of the Spirit functions in two areas. First, as assurance of salvation, the Spirit speaks directly to the human heart, giving guaranty that the individual is in fact adopted into God's family. The second area of the witness of the Spirit is in the ongoing relationship the believer has with God, especially at the moment of entire sanctification. This is not just an initial, momentary emotional feeling; it is a genuine ongoing personal relationship. Wesley says that faith is a divine, supernatural evidence or conviction of things not seen, not discoverable by our bodily senses. In this experience, the Spirit takes truth that is known rationally and makes it personal. For example, to the question "How do you know that you are sanctified, saved from your inbred corruption?" Wesley answers, "We know it by the witness and fruit of the Spirit. First, by the witness, for, when we were justified, the Spirit witnessed to our spirit that our sins had been forgiven; even so, when we were sanctified He witnessed that we had been washed ... the latter witness of the Spirit is just as clear and firm as the former."[15]

While the witness of the Spirit is an internal experience, Wesley denied that it is mystic because it retains the subject-object relationship. There is no melding of the human personality with the divine; rather, the individual is touched by God the Spirit in such a way as to give assurance of his or her personal relationship with God.

The key issue that arises is how experience and Scripture interrelate. Wesley always viewed religious experience with skepticism. He was particularly wary of visions, dreams, and the like, and he insisted that Scripture must have priority in judging the validity of such personal experiences. Experience cannot stand in opposition to the Bible. On the other hand, he recognized that experience can and does confirm Scripture. But even here he drew the distinction between an emotional feeling and a settled conviction. Emotions can wax and wane, but heart-settled convictions will not waver. In practice Wesley did not use experience as an independent authority to confirm the truth of Scripture but as a test of the viability of various proposed interpretations of scriptural passages. He also recognized that the Spirit deals in different ways with different people. When appealing to experience, Wesley often appealed to the corporate experience of the church and thus balanced the stress on individual personal experience.

2. The Lutheran Trilateral

While perhaps not discussed as much as the Wesleyan quadrilateral, the Lutherans also have reflected on their theological method and formally recognize what can be called the Lutheran trilateral,[16] that is, a threefold authority structure in theological method: Scripture as the primary authority, with reason and experience functioning as secondary authorities. Despite the *sola scriptura* slogan, we can see in Luther himself a multiplicity of authorities that mirror this trilateral.

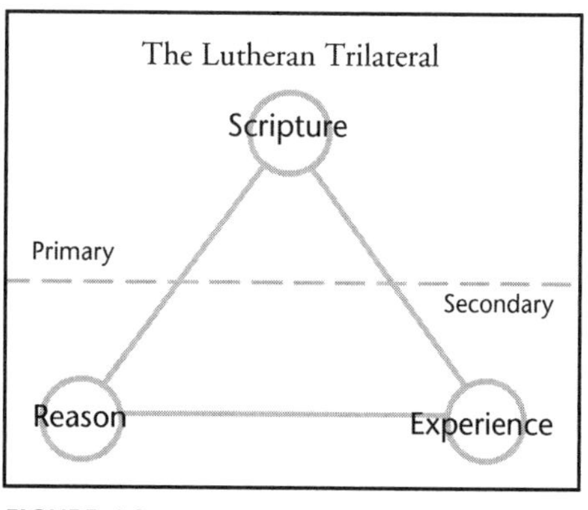

FIGURE 4.2

In the Lutheran explanation, Scripture has the primary position as God's inspired, infallible revelation to humanity concerning the human spiritual condition and the means of salvation. It is the legal authority of the church. But God has also spoken in the larger created order.

Under the rubric of reason, the larger created order is addressed. Reason gives the processing facilities to arrive at truth, that is, logic. But reason also goes beyond internal thought processes and provides material from what is usually referred to as general revelation. The material available to the theologian includes the physical sciences, life sciences, social sciences, and reflective sciences.

The third sphere of authority is experience. Under this rubric fall both personal experience and the corporate experience of the believing community as expressed in its tradition.

3. The Reformed *Sola Scriptura*

a. The Place of the Creeds in Reformed Theology

The *sola scriptura* assertion receives its clearest articulation within the Reformed tradition. This assertion was made in the context of Catholicism's raising unwritten tradition to a level of authority equal with and independent of Scripture and claiming that the church by divine right was the guardian of the true interpretation of Scripture. In this structure, Scripture could not sit in judgment on the church. Instead, the church sat in judgment on the meaning of Scripture. It was against this hegemony that the Reformers rebelled, freeing Scripture from the iron grip of the medieval Catholic establishment. They cut through the centuries of tradition and scholastic interpretation and went *ad fontes* (back to the sources) in true humanist fashion.[17] But even in this move, the Reformers did not break with tradition. When we read Calvin, we are struck by his knowledge of patristics, especially of Augustine, and his awareness that he is operating within the framework of the early patristic consensus.

Creeds play a central role in defining the theological norms of the Reformed tradition. The Westminster Confession, the Canons of Dort, the Heidelberg Catechism, and the Second Helvetic Confession all serve as doctrinal touchstones. Within American Presbyterianism as represented by Princeton, there was an unyielding allegiance to the Westminster Confession. To the Princetonians generally, and to B. B. Warfield particularly, it was evident that Westminster represented the apex of theological achievement. No new or different theological insight could be advanced. Far from appealing to Scripture alone, the norm in English-speaking congregations was the Westminster Confession. However, it was not the confession only but a particular interpretation of the confession that was elevated to authoritative status, as can be seen in the Briggs case.

b. Sola Scriptura *and the Briggs Case*[18]

In the latter decades of the nineteenth century, the Northern Presbyterian Church subscribed to a particular interpretation of the Westminster Confession—specifically, one that included the doctrine of inerrancy. Until the Portland Deliverance (a theological resolution made by the General Assembly in 1892) formalized the doctrine, the interpretation of the confession requiring inerrancy was held by consensus. Charles A. Briggs, professor at Union Seminary in New York, denied that such an interpretation was legitimate, much less legally binding on the members of the ministry. Even A. A. Hodge, professor of theology at Princeton, admitted to Briggs that the question of *errorlessness* in the modern scientific sense of the term was not before the minds of the Westminster divines, and that while the language as a whole in Hodge's opinion favored errorlessness, it did "not explicitly and in terms exclude the other view—so that the view which admits errors cannot be proved to be excluded from the Confession."[19] Nevertheless, the Portland Deliverance made the doctrine of inerrancy the explicit dogma of the Presbyterian Church (USA).[20] By denying inerrancy, Briggs was unquestionably out of step with his Presbyterian brethren.

It was in this atmosphere that the Bible came to be elevated as the *sole* source of religious knowledge. The stress on inerrancy led the conservative forces within the denomination to deny that God spoke through any means other than the Scriptures. This elevation of the Bible to the position of sole source of religious/theological knowledge was not common to all branches of Reformed theology on the Continent or in England. The doctrine of the witness of the Spirit, as a subjective element in theology, was repudiated by Princeton, but it was evident in the Dutch Calvinism of the late nineteenth century. Abraham Kuyper insisted that the "mysticism of the Spirit is necessary for the theologian."[21] He rejected the narrow conception that Scripture alone was the divine authority in the construction of theology, noting, "Coordinated under one head, one might say that the Holy Spirit guarantees this organic articulation through the agencies of the Holy Scripture, the Church, and the personal enlightenment of the theologian."[22] This concept bears a startling resemblance to Briggs's "the Bible, the Church, and the Reason" as the sources of divine authority. While Briggs undeniably pushed far beyond Kuyper's position, it is noteworthy that in moving outside the realm of a theology dominated by Common Sense philosophy, he found an emphasis on the subjective and personal work of the Spirit that the conservative American Presbyterian formulations denied.

c. Charles Briggs's Proposal: The Bible, the Church, and the Reason

The common Presbyterian position held that the Bible was the sole authority in matters of faith and practice.[23] Briggs, however, took the Westminster Confession literally—that is, the Bible was the "only *infallible* rule of faith and practice" for the believer. This, he contended, did not exclude the possibility of God speaking through other means, so long as those means were not elevated to the position of an infallible norm.

Briggs's assertion of three fountains of divine authority brought an immediate response from his opponents, who charged that Briggs had equated the authority of the church and the Reason with that of the Bible.[24] In an attempt to clarify his position, he penned *The Bible, the Church and the Reason*. In that work he laid out his understanding of the nature of the authority of each "fountain."[25]

To Briggs's opponents, the terms "fountain" and "authority" spoke of objective, ultimate courts of appeal. To Briggs, however, the concept of a fountain, or source, of divine authority spoke of the *medium* of authority rather than of the authority itself. "The seat of authority is not the authority itself any more than the throne is the monarch seated on the throne." The "term 'fountain of divine authority' ought not to be obscure, for no one can reasonably confuse the fountain with the living water which flows through it."[26] To Briggs's adversaries, any "divine authority" had of necessity to be infallible. Thus, if one were to assert another authority beside the Bible, the Bible would of necessity lose its unique authority. Briggs, however, saw these three "fountains" as functioning in a complementary manner,[27] even though he, as one in the Reformed tradition, heartily endorsed the fact that the Bible is the Word of God and the locus of salvific revelation.

In terms of the church, Briggs had a decidedly "high church" perspective. He was convinced that the *visible* church was the true and legitimate guardian of the Scriptures and the visible dispensary of divine grace in the world. Additionally, Briggs followed the Reformers in ascribing grace in the administrations of the sacraments, both baptism and the Eucharist. If, in fact, the Holy Spirit thereby conferred grace, was that not evidence that a genuine divine authority was resident within the church?[28] The nature of the church's authority lay in four areas: the public proclamation of the Word of God, the ministrations of the sacraments, the administration of ecclesiastical discipline, and the defining of dogma.

As for "the Reason," Briggs used the term in a much broader sense than the strict rational powers of the human mind. It included both the "conscience and the religious feeling." It would not be too much to say that for Briggs the Reason represented the *imago dei* (image of God) in humans.[29] He was not suggesting that humans had the ability to reason their way to God based on their own innate rational capacity.[30] He drew a careful distinction between *the Reason* and human reasoning, conception, and imagination, all of which he declared were merely human, having nothing certain in them and being often extremely fallible.[31] Additionally, he was adamant in his support of the Westminster doctrine of the total depravity of the human soul and agreed that natural revelation is insufficient for salvation.[32]

Instead, the Reason was an independent channel by which God spoke to the individual. The voice of God was heard immediately in the soul *apart from rational reflection*, giving an indisputable sense of oughtness to issues with which it was confronted. As such the Reason was not alien to the authority of the church or the Scriptures. Rather, without this capacity of human nature, church and Scripture could not accomplish their purpose.[33]

Practically speaking, the three fountains in Briggs's proposition functioned in much the same manner as the three branches of the United States government. The Bible became the legislative principle of divine authority. As such, it was the "only *infallible* rule of faith and practice." The church was the executive principle, making no rules, but interpreting and applying the apostolic teaching. The Reason became the judicial principle within the person. Ideally, the three worked in harmony. But if disagreement arose, two could usually be used for verification of the third.[34]

For Briggs there was ultimately only one authority, God himself, who had revealed himself to humankind through the Bible, the church, and the Reason. When these three were used properly, they would "always speak the divine message and lead to the same throne of divine grace. When men [were] cut off from any one, or any two of them, they may use the third, and it will give them divine testimony."[35] These three found their unity in "Christ the everlasting Logos."[36]

B. SOURCES AND AUTHORITIES

As we reflect on the proposals that have been made in relation to authority, it is clear that they revolve around a common core, even though they differ in emphasis.

1. The Bible

The Bible stands at the heart of Christianity as its final source of authority and norm. The authority of Scripture is recognized by Christians of all traditions. Even Catholicism, which at the Council of Trent in 1546 posited tradition as being a source of authority equal with Scripture, returned at Vatican II to the older position that tradition interprets Scripture rather than being equal to and independent of it. Today the Bible defines Christianity and Christian theology. McGrath has succinctly noted, "While the theologian may feel free to explore other sources of potential interest, doctrine is historically linked with Scripture."[37]

In speaking of the Bible as an authority, three areas come into focus: *inspiration*, the *perspicuity* of Scripture, and the question of *normativeness.*

1. The early church inherited from Judaism its concept of *inspiration*, and as the New Testament books were progressively recognized as canonical, they too were recognized as being the inspired Word of God. However, any formal theory of inspiration developed only gradually, and recognition of the human element in Scripture was slow in coming.

2. The doctrine of the *perspicuity* of Scripture arose during the Reformation in opposition to the Roman Catholic teachings that locked the understanding of the Bible into the interpretive grid of the church. The Reformers contended that the central salvific message of the Bible was simple and clear enough for even a child to grasp. This did not mean that the Reformers gave up on scholarship. Quite the opposite: they insisted that the meaning of Scripture was so deep that even the greatest saint or most learned scholar could not plumb its depth.

3. The *normativeness* of Scripture has always been asserted by the church. The Bible is the touchstone of faith revealing God and his salvation for all people at all times. The very fact that we still study the Scriptures and appeal to them as the ultimate authority is testimony to their normative nature as that which defines the community of faith. As a community of faith, we further believe that the Scriptures embody a divine revelation that is in a very real sense true for all people at all times. Yet we all recognize that the message of Scripture comes clothed in concrete historical circumstances and that while the Scripture is the inspired revelation of God, not all of it is meant for all people at all times *in the same way*.

Proper understanding of normativeness has to do with *continuity* and *discontinuity*. To the extent that the text in its historical concreteness expresses the universal human condition and the divine answer to that condition, it is normative. To the extent that the answer to the human situation is clothed in concrete cultural garb, we must recognize a surface discontinuity; but the very fact that humans in the twenty-first century recognize the centrality of the Bible speaks to an implicit recognition of normativeness. (See chapter 7.A.3 for a fuller discussion of this point.)

2. Church and/or Tradition

It can hardly be doubted that the church and/or tradition operates as a de facto authority in the theological process. J. I. Packer, one of the great contemporary Reformed theologians, has noted of the nature of tradition:

> All Christians are at once beneficiaries and victims of tradition—beneficiaries who receive nurturing truth and wisdom from God's faithfulness in past generations; victims who now take for granted things that need to be questioned, thus treating as divine absolute patterns of belief and behavior that should be seen as human, provisional and relative. We are all the beneficiaries of good, wise and sound tradition and victims of poor, unwise and unsound tradition.[38]

In the same vein he notes:

> Nobody can claim to be detached from traditions; in fact, one sure way to be swallowed up by traditionalism is to think that one is immune to it. . . . The question is not, then, whether we have traditions, but whether our traditions conflict with the only absolute standard in these matters: Holy Scripture.[39]

John Jefferson Davis has observed:

> The problem in rejecting all church history and tradition is that the reflections of less gifted minds tend to be substituted for the wisdom of the spiritual and theological giants of the past. . . . It merely substitutes new traditions—those of the denominational leader and his followers—for older ones. Anti-creedal and anti-traditional attitudes can lead, theologically and ecclesiastically, to counter-productive efforts that merely "reinvent the wheel."[40]

All three proposals we have examined—the Lutheran, Reformed, and Wesleyan—understand that the church and/or tradition acts as an authority in theology. This should in no way be construed as being in continuity with the Tridentine (= of [the Council of] Trent) position that there are two equal and independent sources of authority: Scripture and tradition.[41] Early in the development of the church the concept of a "traditional" interpretation of the Scriptures arose in opposition to the fanciful and bizarre interpretations of Gnosticism. Irenaeus argued that there was a living stream of interpretative tradition going back to the apostles themselves. In fact, this was precisely the position of the Reformers. The idea of private judgment elevated over the corporate understanding of the church came not from the Reformers themselves but from the Radical Reformation.[42]

How are we as Protestants to view the authority of the church, particularly in light of the Reformation dictum *sola scriptura*? Interestingly, Richard Muller has argued that, far from being a call to reject all authority but the Bible, *sola scriptura* is implicitly "as much a mandate to study the history of the church as is the Roman Catholic emphasis on tradition. In fact, Protestant theology in general needs to be more conscious, in a functional and constructive sense, of the importance of the tradition in mediating both Scripture and fundamental understanding of Scripture to the present."[43]

In understanding the authority of the church and/or tradition, we begin with the presupposition that the Holy Spirit is active in the church and does teach. We must listen to the believers who have gone before us. As noted above, we are looking at an interpretive tradition arising out of Scripture, not an independent, equal source of authority. This authority is not absolute; it is relative. We must take the consensus of our spiritual ancestors. If we are to depart from their understanding, it ought not be for less than overwhelming and compelling reasons.

3. Reason and/or Experience

Reason and/or experience is another commonly agreed upon authority. As we reflect on the proposals, we see that there is some overlap of corporate experience and the authority of the church and/or tradition. Nevertheless, some areas are peculiar to this category.

a. Life Experience and Categories of Understanding

The term *experience* is used in several senses. In a general sense, experience is that which is gained while traveling through life: an accumulated knowledge based on a firsthand encounter with life. As used in a religious sense, however, the focus of the term is more restricted. It has come to be correlated with the inner life of the individual, and as such it is by definition subjective. William James, in 1902, was among the first to formally study this aspect of religion in general and Christianity in particular in his *Varieties of Religious Experience.* Christianity is not simply about facts and truths that are "out there," but rather about the transformation of the inner life of the person. Thus Christianity has an existential dimension. It is to this aspect of Christianity that Kierkegaard appealed in his protest against the cultural Lutheranism of the Danish church. And it is this area that is perhaps the most controversial. Yet it seems necessary to acknowledge that experience is in some sense used as an authority in theological reflection.

Those of the more rationalistic side of the evangelical tradition are often loath to acknowledge the crucial role of experience in our theological understanding and even its formulation. Jack Deere of the Vineyard movement has directly challenged conservative evangelicalism on this very point. In his book *Surprised by the Power of the Spirit,*[44] Deere surveys and critiques his own former understanding regarding the cessation of the charismata. In a chapter entitled "The Myth of Pure Biblical Objectivity," he insightfully shows how the claim of the "Bible Church" tradition to live by the Word of God rather than by experience is in fact founded on experience, or in this case the lack of an experience. Specifically within the cessationist tradition the interpreter's lack of a personal experience of the charismata is raised to a level of presuppositional authority in defining the possibility of the continuation of the sign gifts of the Holy Spirit.

> There is one basic reason why Bible-believing Christians do not believe in the miraculous gifts of the Spirit today. It is simply this: *they have not seen them.* Their tradition, of course, supports their lack of belief, but their tradition would have no chance of success if it were not coupled with their lack of *experience* of the miraculous. Let me repeat: Christians do not disbelieve in the miraculous gifts of the Spirit because the Scriptures teach these gifts have passed away. Rather they disbelieve in the miraculous gifts of the Spirit because they have not experienced them.
>
> No cessationist writer that I am aware of tries to make his case on Scripture alone. All of these writers appeal both to Scripture and to either present or past history to support their case. It often goes unnoticed that this appeal to history either past or present is actually an argument from experience, or better, an argument from the lack of experience.[45]

On another level, Don Richardson, in his now famous book *Peace Child* (Regal, 1975), relates his attempts to bring the gospel to the Sawi people of Irian Jaya. These headhunters had one supreme "virtue": treachery. As Richardson tried to relate the gospel, the hero was not Jesus, but Judas! He made no headway in ministry until he discovered the Sawi practice of the peace child, a child of one tribe given to another as a peace offering. As long as the child lives, there will be peace between the two tribes. Richardson then was able to explain the gospel to the Sawi in terms of Jesus being God's peace child, at which point the Sawi understood the message. The corporate experience of the Sawi culture and the personal experience of the individual Sawi people gave them insight into the gospel through what we would consider unusual means. But in their case, the usual Western portrayal was ineffective because their experience had poisoned the idea of sacrifice.

While the community's experience of God shapes the individual's understanding and provides the categories by which he or she interprets personal experience, the reverse can also happen. The spiritual experience of an individual leader may be canonized as normative for a community. Numerous examples of this phenomenon could be given, but one will suffice here. The Christian and Missionary Alliance, founded by A. B. Simpson in the late nineteenth century, has two distinctive doctrines: postconversion crisis sanctification and healing as part of the atonement. A. B. Simpson was a Canadian Presbyterian who pastored in the United States during the late nineteenth century. In the post–Civil War era, he involved himself with pastors from other denominational traditions in cooperative revival efforts that propounded Holiness perspectives. During this period when the Holiness movement was gaining ascendancy, Simpson himself had an experience that he identified as "crisis sanctification," which moved him immediately into a state of "entire sanctification." Several years later he experienced healing from lifelong physical ills. Simpson himself was broadly evangelical, not insisting on these experiences for others, but his followers latched on to these distinctive teachings arising out of Simpson's experience and made them normative in the denomination to this day. The denomination's articulation of the fourfold gospel is: Jesus Christ as Savior, Sanctifier, Healer, and Coming King.

The fact that experience functions as an authority in theology cannot be denied. The question becomes, "How are we to explain the role of experience?" Donald Bloesch has noted, "Experience is not an independent source of theology but a dependent medium, which nevertheless shapes theological explication.... [E]xperience is indeed a medium of revelation, but it should never determine the interpretation of revelation, for revelation contains within itself its own interpretation."[46] In a similar vein P. T. Forsyth tells us that

> [prayer] is to the theologian what original research is to the scientist. It is that whereby we put ourselves in touch with the reality to be known. Without it, or without the divine activity which it craves, the various media of the Christian's knowing of God remain opaque. Our knowing terminates on the textual, verbal, fleshly and other created realities of church life. But when God is active in making himself known, these same media assume a transparent aspect, serving as tools through which it is granted us to extend ourselves into the world and lay hold of (or more properly to be laid hold of by) the reality of God himself, Father, Son and Holy Spirit.[47]

This perspective seems to reflect the teaching of the apostle Paul in 2 Corinthians 3.

Forsyth has contended that it is not the *fact of our experience*, but the *fact which we experience* that shapes and determines Christian faith.[48] "We have not two certitudes about these supreme matters, produced by authority and experience, but one, produced by authority in experience; not a certitude produced by authority and then corroborated by experience, but one produced by an authority active only in experience and especially the corporate experience of the Church."[49] Taking this a step further, it is not too much to say that the authority of experience in this sense is grounded in a relationship with the infinite, personal God through the dynamic activity of the Holy Spirit. And that experience, as well as church and/or tradition and reason and even the Scriptures themselves, points beyond itself to God in Christ. As Forsyth has said, "The final authority is not only external or other in its action, but personal. It is a relation of persons in holy love."[50]

- - -

The contentions of Bloesch and Forsyth are not new, nor are they simply "existential" or "neoorthodox." I noted earlier that the Dutch Calvinist Abraham Kuyper insisted on the necessity of the "mysticism of the Spirit." This emphasis was consistent with the Reformers' doctrine of the "witness of the Spirit." Perhaps one of the most comprehensive proposals of the place that the subjective and personal element plays in the theological process came from the nineteenth-century German theologian Isaac August Dorner.

A student of F. C. Baur at Tübingen, Dorner was deeply influenced by Friedrich Schleiermacher, G. W. F. Hegel, and Immanuel Kant. In his labors he used their philosophical insights to set forth his own theology in an evangelical and historic fashion.[51] Regarded as leader of the "mediating school," he sought to reestablish the "objective" doctrines of the historic faith, focusing particularly on the personality of God, the Trinity, and Christology.[52] In contrast to Schleiermacher, he held that all three terms—*Christian*, *doctrine*, and *faith*—must be regarded as equally important.[53] Dorner called his view *pisteology*, the meaning of which is best derived from the essay entitled "The Doctrine of Faith as the Postulate in Cognition of Christianity as Truth, or Pisteology" that prefaced his *System of Christian Doctrine*.[54] To Dorner religion has to be balanced in its objective and its subjective apprehension. It is a living, reciprocal relationship between God and man. Subjectively, religion consists of absolute humility before God and involves absolute dependence on him. Objectively, it is the self-manifestation of God to man in his majesty, power, and will. This mutual interrelationship functions empirically within the context of covenant.

Dorner stridently affirmed, like the supernaturalists, that the Scriptures could be proved to be historically true and therefore historically reliable. However, in contrast to a "biblical supernaturalism,"[55] he drew a sharp distinction between the certain knowledge of religious truth and all other truth. All other truths may be apprehended as "facts" external to the person. Religious truth, however, makes a demand on the soul if certainty is to be attained.[56] Thus certainty and assurance of religious truth are of a qualitatively different nature than certainty of all other knowledge.[57]

While facts concerning the historical reality of the faith and the revelation contained in the Scriptures may be known objectively, God is apprehended subjectively and directly by the soul. In this Dorner was careful to reject any mystical interpretation, maintaining that there remains a strict subject-object distinction between God and the individual. In faith we do not lose ourselves in the "absolute." Rather, God as a person reaches out directly to touch our souls individually and to give certain knowledge of himself. In this divine touch that engenders faith, a true albeit limited knowledge is imparted. It remains for faith to be nurtured by objective truth.[58]

Given this stress on the primacy of faith, Dorner eschewed any attempt to offer rational proofs for the formal authority of the Scriptures. The proof of the truth of the Scriptures is to be deduced from their contents and from their "coherence with what is objectively certain in faith."[59] It follows, therefore, that the doctrine of inspiration is appropriate *within* a system of doctrine rather than as a proof of the truth of a system.

Dorner saw his pisteology as a faithful reflection of the Reformers' stress on the witness of the Spirit in matters of faith. Yet his understanding did place his perspective at odds with the biblical rationalists (the fundamentalist approach) and the religious empiricists (the liberal approach).

b. Reason and Rationalism

All the proposals surveyed in this chapter explicitly or implicitly use reason as an authority in the process of theological reflection. Conservative nineteenth-century Presbyterian theologian William G. T. Shedd went so far as to speak of human reason as an "unwritten revelation."

> Human knowledge, then, considered from this point of view, *is an unwritten revelation* because it is not aboriginal and self-subsistent, but derived. It issues ultimately from a higher source than the finite intelligence. Human reason has the *ground of its authority in the Supreme Reason.* This is seen particularly in that form of reason which Kant denominates "practical" and whose judgments are given in con-

> science. This faculty has for man an authority for man that cannot be accounted for, except by its being the voice of God. If conscience were entirely isolated from the Deity, and were independent of Him, it could not make the solemn and sometimes terrible impression it does. No man would be afraid of himself if the self were not connected with a higher being than the self. Of judgments on conscience, it may be said literally that God reveals His own holy judgment through them.... General or unwritten revelation, though trustworthy, is not infallible. This differentiates it from special or written revelation.
>
> 1. In the first place the ethical and religious teaching of God through the structure of the human mind is vitiated more or less by human depravity.... 2. Secondly, infallibility cannot be attributed to unwritten revelation, because of the limitations of the finite mind.[60]

In asserting reason as an authority, we recognize that its authority is not independent and separate from Scripture, or church and/or tradition, or experience. Reason is an aspect of the *imago dei.* Its authority is both critical and corrective in function. While we do take seriously the received traditions, they are not received mindlessly. There must be a critical reflection on both the Scriptures and tradition. The mind, as Shedd has noted, is an unwritten revelation reflecting the divine mind. Yet the mind is both finite and fallen and so is liable to error and therefore not absolute.

Within the realm of "reason" in the broad sense is also the area of the conscience. Bloesch has observed that the

> inner light of conscience also reflects the indissoluble mystery of the divine in the human. Conscience is both the voice of God and the superego. Only a conscience that is captive to the Word of God (Luther) is absolutely normative for the Christian. Conscience is not so much a criterion as a clarification of the truth of faith (Ellul). Moreover, conscience can be lost with the demise of faith (1 Tim 1:19–20 NIV). Like the church it can be seared and maimed (1 Tim 4:2), but so long as the believer is linked with Christ in the mystery of faith, conscience will always be somewhat of a guide on the pilgrimage of faith.[61]

More recently there has been a recognition of the "creative imagination" as an aspect of reason and as a vehicle for discerning truth. Garrett Green, in his *Imagining God,*[62] has gone so far as to suggest that it is the imagination that is in fact the image of God in man. The imagination unquestionably acts as a source in theological study even as it does in the sciences. It is the imagination that conceptualizes and gives framework and interpretative coherence to the data with which the theologian deals.

C. FACTORS INVOLVED IN THE GESTALT OF DOCTRINE

As noted earlier, we have in the past tended to think of theology as simply *truth*. Or perhaps more accurately as TRUTH (see figure 3.3. on p. 100). We have on a cognitive level succumbed on the one hand to a kind of reductionism and on the other hand to the Enlightenment hubris that espouses truth as a "view from nowhere,"[63] absolute and unconditioned. McGrath has observed that doctrine/theology is primarily an integrative concept, bringing together a number of elements to form a greater whole. He has argued that attempts to describe and/or define doctrine/theology have been subject to reductionistic approaches that have surrendered significant parts of that which is essential to Christianity.[64]

The divergence between confessional Lutheranism and Pietism in the seventeenth century provides an illustration. Pietists were willing to admit that Orthodoxy was true but objected that it had become irrelevant to everyday life. Doctrine/theology must also be related to worship; otherwise it becomes isolated from the community to which it relates and that it supports. We must be cognizant of the fact that doctrine preserves for us a glimpse of reality, even a transcendent reality, however limited that glimpse may be.

1. The Four Dimensions of Doctrine/Theology

We are not discussing the question of what doctrine/theology *ought* to be but, rather, what it *is*. McGrath suggests that there are four major dimensions to doctrine/theology:[65]

1. Doctrine functions as a social demarcator.
2. Doctrine is generated by, and subsequently interprets, the Christian narrative.
3. Doctrine interprets experience.
4. Doctrine makes truth claims.

A fifth element underlies these four—the element of epistemology/philosophy.

2. The Epistemological Substructure

Charles Hodge himself acknowledged that every theology reflects an underlying philosophy. He recognized in his *Systematic Theology* that every theology was in some measure a philosophical undertaking. Throughout the ages various theological systems have been built employing either consciously or subconsciously the epistemology of the reigning philosophical system and using that system's categories to express the truth of Christianity to their contemporaries. Some of these philosophies and epistemologies include

- Realism, both naive and critical
- Idealism, both Platonic and Hegelian
- Existentialism

The proper role of philosophy in the theological enterprise is to provide categories of understanding that will help contextualize the content of the message for the target audience. Every age is characterized by a particular philosophy and an accompanying vision of reality. The theologian must employ that philosophy critically, using it to provide categories of understanding while not allowing that philosophy to exercise hegemony over divine revelation and pass judgment as to what can and cannot be true. For example, we might contrast the use of Platonism by Origen and Augustine. Origen, as a convinced Platonist, allowed his philosophical categories to determine his exegesis and his theological conclusions. Augustine, on the other hand, while thoroughly Neoplatonic in his perspective, rejected aspects of Platonism when the conclusions disagreed with the teaching of Scripture.

The evangelical tradition has historically been characterized by some form of epistemological realism, either naive or critical. Some evangelical theologians assert that for one to be an evangelical one must subscribe to some form of philosophical/epistemological realism. If one does not, then one will deny some key facet of evangelical understanding. Others argue that such a tight wedding of evangelical understanding to a particular epistemology is improper, since evangelicalism has been formally defined by a set of theological commitments and an agenda that surround personal faith in Christ rather than a particular epistemology.

D. RELATING THE AUTHORITIES

We have looked at how different traditions and theologians have perceived the theological task in relation to the question of authority, and how theology/doctrine is much more than simply the arrangement and display of the facts of Scripture. However we slice the question, it seems clear that there are in practice several authorities in the theological enterprise. Some suggestions as to how we relate these authorities have been made in the foregoing material. We might say that in a sense there is only one authority, God himself.

At that point, we must ask how he has made himself known. The answer, of course, is revelation.

1. Revelation

Theologians have generally divided revelation into two broad categories, general and special revelation. While Richard Muller questions the adequacy of the traditional categories of revelation[66] and gives some good reasons for doing so, we will nevertheless use these categories, for they are the ones the student will most likely encounter in further study. At the same time, we recognize that for the present discussion we need a more nuanced understanding.

It is a given that revelation is the source of theology. Yet the issue is more complex than simply asserting that Scripture unfolds for us the full nature of reality or simply making a facile identification of Scripture with the totality of divine revelation. The Reformers themselves recognized two books of revelation—the book of nature and the book of Scripture. Both of these books spoke divine revelation and could not contradict each other. (See chapter 6 for a fuller discussion of this point with reference to science.) In general discussions, one often finds the distinction that general revelation is addressed to man as man and is thus nonredemptive, while special revelation, the Bible, is addressed to man as sinner, its goal being salvific. This distinction is helpful, but what does it really mean?

2. Special Revelation: The Bible

The Bible is God's special revelation; it is the final and ultimate authority for and source of theology. On this the major Protestant theological traditions are united.[67] Untold volumes have been written on the inspiration, inerrancy, and authority of Scripture. For our purposes here, the ultimate and final authority of the Scriptures is taken as a given. It would be beyond the scope of the present discussion to attempt to explore the nature and implications of biblical inspiration. In affirming the final authority of Scripture, however, we must be careful to draw a sharp distinction between Scripture itself and our particular understanding of Scripture. Historically there has been a consistent temptation to equate our understanding of the Bible with the Bible itself. One needs only to look at the example of Galileo to see this happen. While that particular instance involved the Roman Catholic Church, the present-day insistence of many evangelicals on a six-day recent creation as the only biblical position is but one contemporary example of this phenomenon.

In this vein, we would do well to remember the observation made by A. A. Hodge and B. B. Warfield, the architects of the modern doctrine of inerrancy, over a century ago in their definitive article "Inspiration" that the Bible is not *absolute* truth, it is *simple* truth.[68] The truth of the Bible is contingent historical truth; it does not belong to the realm of the philosophical absolute. The historical nature of Christianity is precisely the cause of offense to the intellectual world of Enlightenment and post-Enlightenment philosophy. As historical truth, it bears the marks of historical contingency and time-boundedness. We might say that the Bible, while absolutely true, is not absolute truth.

3. General Revelation

Several years ago one of my colleagues and I were discussing the place of the Bible in the authority structure and belief structure in the church. In the course of the conversation, he advanced what I considered to be some rather extreme positions. So I asked him if he believed in general revelation. His response was, "All Scripture is given by inspiration of God and is profitable for doctrine, for reproof, for instruction, for training in righteousness, that the man of God may be thoroughly equipped...." In short, he did not even have a category in his understanding that would allow him to process the question. He held something close to an all-or-nothing perspective. That is, if we admit any extrabiblical truth into our equation, we have compromised the unique authority of the Scriptures. Yet the Scriptures were given in a larger context, a context that comprises also general revelation.

The term *general revelation* is used in two senses. The narrow sense refers to what can be discovered *about God* in creation. The second and broader sense subsumes under the rubric of *general revelation* not only the former, narrower sense but also extends the category to encompass the entirety of what can be discerned of the nature of the created order. In this broader sense, *general revelation provides the context into which special revelation is given.*

While Scripture explicitly declares its purpose in passages such as 2 Timothy 3:15–17, it is also abundantly clear that Scripture did not intend to give to humanity an exhaustive exposition of the nature and complexities of the created order into which God placed humankind. In fact, the command to "have dominion" seems to imply that God had left to humanity the discovery and ordering of the creation. Thus the work of studying the world and the yielding up of its secrets is a legitimate God-ordained activity for humanity. This human ability to use reason to discern truth is taken for granted by the biblical authors and even by our Lord himself.

a. Wisdom and Wisdom Literature

The Scripture recognizes the legitimate wisdom embodied in the culture and perspectives of the surrounding idolatrous nations, specifically the wisdom of the Egyptians, the Phoenicians, the Persians, and the Babylonians. The achievements of human wisdom are acknowledged in Job 28:1–11, and human technological advancements and artistic achievements are recognized as early as Genesis 4. While condemning the arrogant pride often accompanying this wisdom, Scripture acknowledges the legitimacy of the wisdom itself. It has long been recognized that the wisdom literature of Israel parallels that of Egypt and Mesopotamia. Some have argued that the pagan nations borrowed insights from Israelite wisdom, for example, from the canonical proverbs, but it is demonstrable that some of this material predates the origin of the material in the Hebrew Scriptures. This would indicate that the truth stated in this material is available to any careful observer of the world and of human behavior.

While Scripture recognizes that God is the *source* of wisdom, it also suggests that that wisdom may be *mediated* through the created order. For example, the wisdom of horticulture, planting, cultivating, and harvesting is said by Isaiah to come from God (28:23–29), but this does not imply a special revelation. The farmer learns the traditional methods from his community, and he experiments with various techniques that may allow him to refine and improve on the tradition he has received. To take this a step further, the farmer exercises faith in the received tradition, empirical observation, and creative insight in developing this wisdom that comes from God.

The concept of wisdom reminds us that

> man's creatureliness is an abiding feature of him, and one of positive significance. Man is not just "lost" and the world just the sphere of Satan's activity. Man in the world is given life by God and called to live in accordance with his nature as God's creature, with the nature of the world as God's creation, and with the nature of his experience as God's gift. The wisdom tradition assumes that, living in and confronted by God's world, man as man is in the presence of and confronted by God himself. Inanimate nature, worldly experience, human reasoning, all reveal something of the truth of God in regard to man and the world.[69]

The nature of the wisdom literature also opens the door to an additional insight. The wisdom literature is by and large not directly theological in its focus. Its insights arise out of daily life and experience that are not directly touched on by Torah or the prophets. Derek Kidner has noted that one finds in wisdom "details of character small enough to escape the mesh of the law and the broadsides of the prophets, and yet decisive in personal dealings."[70] Wisdom literature deals particularly with character (a topic subsumed in the New Testament teaching on sanctification) and grounds that teaching in the authority that God has placed in the created order as opposed to the law. This insight opens the door to continue to receive insight into the nature of the created reality in which God placed humans and into humans themselves.

b. Human Ability to Discover Truth

We find in Scripture the assumption that people are able to discover truth by reflecting on the world. The Bible never gives any direct theological justification for this assumption; rather, it seems to be implicit in man's creation in the image of God. Scripture presents a desacralized (secular) creation in the sense that the world is neither inhabited by nor controlled by nature deities. The world is a creation of God, and dominion over that creation is given to humans. Walter Kaiser has gone so far as to suggest that the desire to discover the secrets of the working of the creation are in fact rooted in the image of God borne by humankind. There exists

> a deep-seated desire, a compulsive drive, because man is made in the image of God to appreciate the beauty of the world (on an aesthetic level); to know the character, composition and meaning of the world (on an academic and philosophical level); and to discern its purpose and destiny (on a theological level).... Man has an inborn inquisitiveness and capacity to learn how everything in his experience can be integrated to make a whole.[71]

God has not revealed *directly* to humankind the makeup of the cosmos, or the characteristics of bacteria and their effects, or the psychological effects of child abuse, or the nature of linguistics. He has however *mediately* revealed these things in that he has given to humankind the pieces and the ability to put those pieces together into a coherent whole.

c. Tension between Fallenness and Ability

The ability of humanity to discover some measure of truth has generally been admitted by most theological traditions, although various explanations of this phenomenon have been given. Nevertheless, this recognition has not always made its way into the popular piety of some traditions. In the popular versions of some traditions of Holiness background, the "world" is rejected along with all "worldly wisdom." Likewise, some branches of the Reformed tradition have forsaken their heritage and have, together with other parts of the evangelical tradition, made a sharp distinction between, for example, "biblical counseling" and "secular humanist psychology." Implicit in these dichotomies is a lack of recognition that there is legitimate truth on a plethora of topics that can be discovered by humans even apart from the Scriptures.

The Reformed tradition especially has emphasized the depravity and fallenness of the human condition and the fact that that fallenness affects not only the will, as the Thomists held, but the perceptive faculties as well. The Reformed tradition has insisted that humanity is able to contribute nothing to salvation, but even Calvin, the father of Reformed theology, recognized and endorsed the fact that people can and do learn truth through the study of the works of nonbelievers.

> Whenever we come upon these matters in secular writers, let that admirable light of truth shining in them teach us that the mind of man, though fallen and perverted from its wholeness, is nevertheless clothed and ornamented with God's excellent gifts. If we regard the Spirit of God as the sole fountain of truth, we shall neither reject the truth itself, nor despise it wherever it shall appear, unless we wish to dishonor the Spirit of God. For by holding the gifts of the Spirit in slight esteem, we condemn and reproach the Spirit himself. What then? Shall we deny that the truth shone upon the ancient jurists who established civic order and discipline with such great equity? Shall we say that the philosophers were blind in their fine observation and artful description of nature? Shall we say that those men were devoid of understanding who conceived the art of disputation and taught us to speak reasonably?... Those men whom Scripture [1 Cor. 2:14] calls "natural men" were, indeed, sharp and penetrating in their investigation of inferior things. Let us, accordingly, learn by their example how many gifts the Lord left to human nature even after it was despoiled of its true good.[72]

Calvin explicitly condemns those who refuse to learn from non-Christian authors. Commenting on Titus 1:12 he notes:

> From this passage we may infer that those persons are superstitious, who do not venture to borrow anything from heathen authors. All truth is from God; and consequently, if wicked men have said anything that is true and just, we ought not to reject it; for it has come

> from God. Besides, all things are of God; and, therefore, why should it not be lawful to dedicate to his glory everything that can properly be employed for such a purpose?[73]

d. General Revelation and Grasping Reality

Prior to the Enlightenment, the prevailing understanding was that people were to accept truth on the basis of authority, either the authority of the church or of revelation. The Enlightenment fostered a rebellion against all forms of claimed authority and submitted all truth claims before the bar of reason. For all the legitimate, negative evaluations of the Enlightenment that have emerged in the postmodern critique of modernity, we must recognize that the Enlightenment also made significant contributions to the world.

First was the demonstration that the capacity of the human mind to discover truth was far greater than had heretofore been imagined. In contrast to the medieval and Reformation notion of the capacity of the mind, Shapiro has noted, "Christendom was obliged to deal with the dangerous notion that man was competent, by reason of his senses, to discover his own truth, and again and again that truth appeared to contradict Holy Writ."[74] Out of this Enlightenment mentality arose the scientific method that opened up the physical universe to human understanding in ways unimaginable. The dark side was that the method was reductionistic in that it was able to deal only with the physical universe. The method was analytical and saw the whole as merely a sum of the parts. It lacked the ability to look beyond the physical and empirical. The ultimate result was logical positivism, which argued that any truth claim must be empirically verifiable.

The second contribution flowing from the Enlightenment was the emphasis on critical thinking with its insistence on proper logic applied to evidence. Conclusions in all areas of intellectual endeavor, including theological studies, had to be based on evidence. This caused tension in biblical and theological studies where the habit had been to rely on tradition rather than to subject that tradition to rigorous scrutiny. However, due to the methodological requirements flowing from the rationalistic modern mind-set, even conservative theologians and interpreters became more careful in reaching conclusions. Those who refused to apply more critical methods of knowledge were relegated to the sidelines in biblical and theological discussions.

e. The Value of General Revelation

Greater ambiguity exists in general revelation than in special revelation. Interpretation of special revelation involves linguistics, culture, history, and philosophy as well as the hard and soft sciences. These disciplines all fall within the realm of general revelation and set the context for special revelation. Even such biblical concepts as redemption, covenant, and sacrifice derive their significance from the cultures into which the special revelation was given. Thus general revelation has a legitimate role in interpreting the special revelation of Scripture. But the ambiguity of general revelation itself speaks to the danger of dogmatic conclusions.

General revelation also gives us information about which the Bible says little but which still bears on daily life in significant ways. From another perspective, general revelation may be seen as supplemental to special revelation. In numerous cases, the Bible speaks to issues in broad brushstrokes or only obliquely. Careful attention to general revelation in these areas can supplement and clarify and even provide structures within which sometimes enigmatic references become clear.

- - -

The authorities are mediums or channels of the authority of God. None are independent or autonomous, nor can there be real contradiction between them.

Donald Bloesch, in discussing the relationship of the authorities in theology, has observed:

> Jesus Christ is the light, the Bible is the lamp and the church is the household of light. The inner light is the eyes of faith, or the eyeglasses that enable us to perceive the light correctly. We can therefore say that the church is under the Bible, and the Bible is under the gospel. The authorities for faith are not equal, but they are all of decisive importance. Religious experience is the medium by which we discern the light and truth of Christ, but it is not the source or norm for this light and truth. Religious experience is dependent on the Bible for its truth, but the Bible is in turn dependent on religious experience for its efficacy.[75]

BIBLIOGRAPHY

Bainton, Roland. *Here I Stand.* Nashville: Abingdon, 1950. • **Bloesch, Donald.** *A Theology of Word and Spirit.* Downers Grove, IL: InterVarsity Press, 1992. • **Briggs, Charles Augustus.** *The Bible, the Church and the Reason.* New York: Scribner, 1892. • **Davis, John Jefferson.** *Foundations of Evangelical Theology.*

Grand Rapids: Baker, 1984. • ———. *The Necessity of Systematic Theology.* Grand Rapids: Baker, 1978. • **Deere, Jack.** *Surprised by the Power of the Spirit.* Grand Rapids: Zondervan, 1993. • **Erickson, Millard.** *Christian Theology.* 2nd ed. Grand Rapids: Baker, 1998. • **Hart, Trevor.** *Faith Thinking.* Downers Grove, IL: InterVarsity Press, 1995. • **Hodge, Charles.** *Systematic Theology.* Grand Rapids: Eerdmans, 1975. • **Kuhn, Thomas.** *The Structure of Scientific Revolutions.* 2nd ed. Chicago: University of Chicago Press, 1970. • **McGrath, Alister.** *Christian Theology: An Introduction.* 2nd ed. Cambridge, MA: Blackwell, 1997. • ———. *The Genesis of Doctrine.* Oxford: Blackwell, 1990. • **Sawyer, M. James.** *Charles Augustus Briggs and Tensions in Late Nineteenth-Century American Theology.* Lewiston, NY: Mellen University Press, 1994. • **Sire, James.** *The Universe Next Door.* 2nd ed. Downers Grove, IL: InterVarsity Press, 1988. • **Thorson, Donald A. D.** *The Wesleyan Quadrilateral.* Grand Rapids: Zondervan, 1990.

NOTES

[1]Quoted in Roland Bainton, *Here I Stand* (Nashville: Abingdon, 1950), 185.

[2]*Blackwell Encyclopedia of Modern Christian Thought*, ed. Alister McGrath, s.v. "Dispensationalism" (Oxford: Blackwell, 1993).

[3]The term *nuda scriptura* comes from Donald Bloesch, *A Theology of Word and Spirit* (Downers Grove, IL: InterVarsity Press, 1992), 193. In this section, I have sought to illustrate, not prove, popular contemporary evangelical attitudes toward the concept of *sola scriptura.*

[4]Alister McGrath, *The Genesis of Doctrine* (Oxford: Blackwell, 1990). This work is the publication of the 1990 Bampton Lectures at Oxford. McGrath's theses are summarized in chap. 5, "Doctrinal Taxonomy: Are All Doctrines of Equal Importance?"

[5]J. Richard Middleton and Brian J. Walsh, *Truth Is Stranger Than It Used to Be* (Downers Grove, IL: InterVarsity Press, 1995).

[6]See Charles Hodge, *Systematic Theology*, reprint (Grand Rapids: Eerdmans, 1975), 1:17, 19.

[7]John Jefferson Davis, "Contextualization and the Nature of Theology," in John Jefferson Davis, ed., *The Necessity of Systematic Theology* (Grand Rapids: Baker, 1978), 177. Davis continues, "In no case does the exegete or theologian come to the text completely free of presuppositions. We can to a degree become critically aware of our presuppositions, but we cannot eliminate them entirely. There is an inescapable element of personal judgment which shapes the theologian's vision, just as it does the artist's or the scientist's."

[8]Randy L. Maddox, *Responsible Grace* (Nashville: Kingswood, 1994), 36. While on the surface it sounds contradictory to say that the Bible is the only source and that there are other sources, the answer to this dilemma is found in the way Wesley wove these authorities together in practice. His first and final commitment was to the text

of Scripture as the Word of God; the other three factors become hermeneutical in applying Scripture to life and formulating doctrine.

[9]John Wesley, "A Plain Account of Christian Perfection," in *The Complete Works of John Wesley*, The Master Christian Library 7.0 (Rio, WI: Ages Software, 1999), 11:502.

[10]John Wesley, *Explanatory Notes upon the New Testament*, preface, in *The Complete Works of John Wesley*, The Master Christian Library 7.0 (Rio, WI: Ages Software, 1999), 11:5.

[11]Maddox, *Responsible Grace*, 38.

[12]John Wesley, *Letters*, in *The Complete Works of John Wesley*, The Master Christian Library 7.0 (Rio, WI: Ages Software, 1999), 14:475.

[13]Maddox, *Responsible Grace*, 44. In this respect, Thomas Oden can be seen as a true contemporary heir of Wesley. He made a significant contribution with his theology by endeavoring merely to reproduce the consensus of the Christian tradition, in accordance with the Vincentian Canon (see chap. 5.C.1).

[14]Other evangelical traditions take exception to this contention, arguing that it was the apostolic age rather than the age of the early church that saw the special work of the Spirit. Wesley's contention seems to afford the pre-Nicene ancient period a revelatory status in the formation of explicit doctrine.

[15]Wesley, "A Plain Account of Christian Perfection," 492.

[16]See Duane W. H. Arnold, *The Way, the Truth and the Life: An Introduction to Lutheran Christianity* (Grand Rapids: Baker, 1982), 41–49.

[17]The term *humanist* is decried regularly among the popular evangelical establishment. As used in the Renaissance and Reformation, however, the term had reference to both a method and a field of study (the humanities as opposed to canon law) rather than an anti-Christian ideology. See Alister McGrath, *The Intellectual Origins of the European Reformation* (Oxford: Blackwell, 1987), 32–68.

[18]The following discussion is drawn from M. James Sawyer, *Charles Augustus Briggs and Tensions in Late Nineteenth-Century American Theology* (Lewiston, NY: Mellen University Press, 1994), 45–55, 113–76.

[19]Briggs Transcripts, A. A. Hodge to CAB, 6:18. Located at Union Seminary Library, New York.

[20]Charles Hodge himself had argued against the legitimacy of tightening the terms of subscription to the Confession by means of a deliverance as illegal and a violation of the basic tenets of Presbyterian government. If the terms of subscription were to be changed, the creed itself had to be changed (Charles Hodge, *The Rights of Presbyteries Not to Be Annulled* [New York: Anson D. F. Randall, 1896]).

[21]Abraham Kuyper, *Principles of Sacred Theology*, reprint (Grand Rapids: Baker, 1980), 624.

[22]Ibid.

[23]The Westminster Confession actually stated that the Bible was the "*only infallible* rule of faith and practice" (italics added) rather than the *only* rule. Nevertheless, the first four of the heresy charges brought against Briggs stemmed from this interpretation that divine authority was mediated exclusively through Scripture.

[24]E.g., T. W. Chambers, "The Inaugural Address of Professor Briggs," *The Presbyterian and Reformed Review* 2 (1891): 481–92.

[25]The subject of authority was one that underwent maturation in Briggs's thinking from the early 1890s until the time he published *Church Unity* in 1909. The position he took early developed considerably during the ensuing years, but he never retracted his basic premise, that divine authority was mediated through other channels than the Bible alone.

[26]Charles Briggs, *The Bible, the Church and the Reason* (New York: Scribner, 1892), 58–59. Note the similarity here with Isaac A. Dorner's concept of looking past the form of Scripture to the God who spoke through it. The subtlety of this implied distinction was lost to Briggs's hearers.

[27]Donald Bloesch compares Briggs to Wesley in his *Theology of Word and Spirit*, 210–11. Bloesch, however, has not studied the breadth of Briggs's thinking and caricatures Briggs's thought to some extent.

[28]Briggs, *The Bible, the Church and the Reason*, 14–16.

[29]This is reminiscent of the position espoused by Wesley, noted above.

[30]Briggs, *The Bible, the Church and the Reason*, 32, 69. Cf. I. A. Dorner, *A System of Christian Doctrine*, trans. Alfred Cave and J. S. Banks (Edinburgh: T. & T. Clark, 1881), 1:135–36.

[31]Ibid., 69.

[32]Ibid., 33.

[33]Briggs, *The Bible, the Church and the Reason*, 35–39. Briggs's definition and illustration of the Reason is confusing at times. It moves back and forth between the conscience, the religious feeling, the soul itself, and the rational processes. His proof of the authority of the Reason included examples from all of these areas, yet he defined the Reason as existing prior to reasoning and conscience.

[34]Charles Briggs, *Church Unity* (London: Longmans, Green, 1910), 244.

[35]Briggs, *The Bible, the Church and the Reason*, 53.

[36]Ibid., 85.

[37]McGrath, *Genesis of Doctrine*, 55.

[38]J. I. Packer, "The Comfort of Conservatism," in *Power Religion*, ed. Michael Horton (Chicago: Moody Press, 1992), 290.

[39]Ibid., 289.

[40]John Jefferson Davis, *The Foundations of Evangelical Theology* (Grand Rapids: Baker, 1984), 239.

[41]Trent insisted that tradition was a separate and distinct source of revelation in addition to Scripture, filling in the gaps where Scripture was silent. In this manner, Trent justified its teaching of doctrines not rooted in Scripture (Alister McGrath, *Christian Theology: An Introduction*, 2nd ed. [Oxford: Blackwell, 1996], 220–21).

[42]Ibid., 219, 221–22.

[43]Richard Muller, *The Study of Theology*, in Foundations of Contemporary Interpretation series (Grand Rapids: Zondervan, 1991), 602.

[44]Jack Deere, *Surprised by the Power of the Spirit* (Grand Rapids: Zondervan, 1993).

[45]Ibid., 55–56.

[46]Bloesch, *Theology of Word and Spirit*, 198–99.

[47]Summarized by Trevor Hart, *Faith Thinking* (Downers Grove, IL: InterVarsity Press, 1995), 229.

[48]Bloesch, *Theology of Word and Spirit*, 203.

[49]P. T. Forsyth, *The Principle of Authority* (London: Independent Press, 1952), 55. Quoted by Bloesch in *Theology of Word and Spirit*, 203.

[50]Ibid., 328. Quoted by Bloesch in *Theology of Word and Spirit*, 204.

[51]Karl Barth, *Protestant Theology in the Nineteenth Century* (Valley Forge, PA: Judson Press, 1973), 575. Cf. Ian Sellers, "Dorner, Isaac August," in *New International Dictionary of the Christian Church*, ed. J. D. Douglas (Grand Rapids: Zondervan, 1978).

[52]Claude Welch, ed., *God and Incarnation in Mid-Nineteenth-Century German Theology* (New York: Oxford University Press, 1965), 105.

[53]Barth, *Protestant Theology*, 578.

[54]I. A. Dorner's *System der christlichen Glaubenslehre* first appeared in 1879–80; the authorized English translation, *A System of Christian Doctrine*, by Alfred Cave and J. S. Banks appeared in 1881 (Edinburgh: T. & T. Clark). Dorner, like Briggs, was not a towering figure in the history of theology, but again like Briggs, he played a significant role in the theological debates of his day, which are still relevant today. The term *pisteology*, coined by Dorner, never gained wide acceptance.

[55]He used this term to describe a "fundamentalist-rationalist" type of approach to the Scriptures found commonly among conservatives in the German church. He did not name Princeton in this group, but their attempts to build certainty on rational evidence correspond to the attempts of one segment of the German evangelicals.

[56]Dorner, *System of Christian Doctrine*, 75.

[57]Ibid., 72.

[58]Ibid., 179. Additionally, this faith included in itself a knowledge on the part of the individual that he or she stood in need of atonement and that God had met that need himself.

[59]Ibid., 175. Dorner saw Scripture as inspired only in a mediate sense. Humans, he contended, had been inspired; Scriptures became the memorial to that which had been originally revealed (2:186). Faith, rather than looking at the external form of the Scriptures, pressed toward the goal, the knowledge of God that was mediated therein. Thus criticism actually offered a service to the faith by warning the believer not to be sidetracked from the core of Scripture, the knowledge of Jesus Christ, into relatively unimportant matters (1:149). Inspired humans might err when treating matters not "in essential connection with Spiritual truth" (2:196). These errors did not, however, affect the author's purpose in writing. It was sufficient that the authors transmit without "adulteration the unerring spiritual truth, *of which they are constituted witnesses*, leaving it to the inherent force of this truth to bear witness concerning itself" (ibid., 197; italics added).

In so saying, Dorner posited a division between form and substance in Scripture. Errors in the form might actually be beneficial in that they would keep people from trusting in it instead of God who gave it. Faith, as he had defined it in the introduction, would be able to determine the substance of truth and cling to it.

[60]Shedd, William G. T., *Dogmatic Theology,* 3 vols. (New York: Scribner, 1888–94), 1:64–65.

[61]Bloesch, *Theology of Word and Spirit,* 201.

[62]Garrett Green, *Imagining God* (Grand Rapids: Eerdmans, 1989).

[63]See Hart, *Faith Thinking,* 48–70, quoting Thomas Nagel (chap. 3.C).

[64]McGrath, *Genesis of Doctrine,* 36.

[65]For a fuller discussion of these four dimensions, see chap. 5.B.

[66]Muller, *Study of Theology,* 633.

[67]Fringe groups, such as the Schwenkfelders, the Quakers, and other inner-light groups have elevated mystical experience or inner light to a normative status. But these groups do not represent mainstream Protestantism.

[68]A. A. Hodge and B. B. Warfield, *Inspiration,* reprint (Grand Rapids: Baker, 1979), 44.

[69]John Goldingay, "The 'Salvation History' Perspective and the 'Wisdom Perspective' within the Context of Biblical Theology," *Evangelical Quarterly* 51 (1979): 202.

[70]Derek Kidner, *Proverbs,* Tyndale Old Testament Commentary (Downers Grove, IL: InterVarsity Press, 1964), 13.

[71]Walter Kaiser, *Ecclesiastes: Total Life* (Chicago: Moody Press, 1979), 66.

[72]John Calvin, *Institutes of the Christian Religion,* 2.2.15, in Library of Christian Classics, vol. 20, trans. Ford Lewis Battles (Philadelphia: Westminster, 1977).

[73]John Calvin, *Commentary on the Epistle to Titus,* The Comprehensive Calvin Collection (Albany, OR: Ages Software, 1998), 1:12.

[74]Gary Shapiro, "God and Science." Quoted by Edward M. Curtis, *Transformed Thinking* (Franklin, TN: JKO Publishing, 1996), 148.

[75]Bloesch, *Theology of Word and Spirit,* 204.

OUTLINE OF CHAPTER 5

A. The Problem

1. Two Examples
   a. Inerrancy
   b. Eschatology
2. Scholastic Maximalism
3. The Content of the Christian Faith: The Apostolic Proclamation
4. Degrees and Ranking of Authority

B. The Components of Doctrine/Theology

1. Doctrine as That Which Defines the Community
2. Doctrine as Interpretation of Narrative
3. Doctrine as an Interpretation of Experience
4. Doctrine as Truth Claim

C. The Necessity of Establishing a Doctrinal Taxonomy

1. Establishing a Doctrinal Taxonomy Historically
   a. Trinitarianism
   b. The Two Natures of Christ
   c. The Nature of Divine Grace
   d. The Canon of the New Testament
2. Establishing a Doctrinal Taxonomy Exegetically

D. A Theology of Minimums?

E. Ranking Noncore Issues

CHAPTER 5

DOCTRINAL TAXONOMY: ARE ALL DOCTRINES OF EQUAL IMPORTANCE?

A. THE PROBLEM

As the world in which the church found itself changed over the centuries, the church was confronted with challenges to the doctrinal commitments it held as divine truth. These challenges provoked reactions in the church in which different doctrines were raised to a new level of prominence. The changing situations did not necessarily bring about any further development of doctrine; rather, to meet a current challenge, doctrines that had up to this time been considered less important were in some cases raised in importance.

An example of this can be seen in the status of the doctrine of the virgin birth of Christ and the doctrine of the inerrancy of the Scriptures during the fundamentalist-modernist controversy of the early twentieth century. With the rise of liberalism, historic-orthodox Christianity took a defensive posture and militantly reasserted the "fundamentals" of the faith. However, these "fundamentals" were not simply a restatement of the content of the historic ecumenical creeds. They were often boiled down to five propositions.

1. The inerrancy of Scripture
2. The deity of Jesus Christ
3. The virgin birth
4. The bodily resurrection of Christ
5. The personal return of Christ

Note that two of these five "fundamentals," the virgin birth and the inerrancy of Scripture, are not echoes of the *core* of the historic faith; instead, they demonstrate a raising of historically more minor doctrines to a primary level of importance to fulfill an apologetic need. The doctrine of the virgin birth had always been contained in the church's understanding and creedal affirmation as the means of the incarnation. But during the fundamentalist-modernist controversy, the doctrine was elevated to "touchstone" status. It became a litmus test as to whether one believed in the supernatural activity of God in the world. The modernists denied the possibility of miracles in the sense of God breaking into history and "violating" the "laws of nature." The apologetic rationale of the fundamentalists was that if one would admit the reality of the virgin birth, he or she would not have a problem affirming the reality of "lesser" miracles.[1]

1. Two Examples

a. Inerrancy

The church had always affirmed the utter truthfulness of the Scriptures. As early as Augustine we find affirmations of the inerrancy of the Scriptures. Catholicism always held the truthfulness of Scripture, but throughout the medieval period, tradition was progressively elevated as a separate and equally valid source of revelation and authority. This position was formally adopted as part of the creeds at the Catholic Counter-Reformation Council of Trent. Protestants responded with the doctrine of *sola scriptura.*

During the period of Protestant scholasticism, the doctrine and understanding of divine inspiration were developed in new, more refined ways. Some of the Protestant scholastic theologians even held that the vowel points in the Hebrew text were inspired.[2] The authority of Scripture was consciously raised during the Reformation and the immediate post-Reformation period in direct opposition to the Roman Catholic claims of the authority of tradition and the authority of the pope. But even in the great Protestant confessions of the sixteenth and seventeenth centuries, the doctrine of inerrancy is not explicit.

The nineteenth century saw the rise of higher-critical theories that attacked the literary and historical integrity of the Scriptures. It was in response to this attack that conservative representatives of historic Protestantism asserted the doctrine of the inerrancy of the Scriptures. While the concept of inerrancy goes back at least to Augustine, the nineteenth-century response to the literary criticism of the sacred text involved a refinement, sharpening, and extension of the older concept of scriptural infallibility/inerrancy. This sharpening took place in the heat of controversy and became an apologetic tool to defend the veracity of the Bible—and with it the historic Christian faith. Inerrancy became a touchstone doctrine for fundamentalists and their successors, evangelicals.

Inerrancy has remained a touchstone for conservative evangelicalism to this day,[3] with the doctrine functioning as the basis of scholarly societies such as the Evangelical Theological Society and also as a foundational doctrine for numerous evangelical seminaries and Bible colleges. In fact, from a practical perspective, the doctrine is often deemed as more critical than matters of Christology or understandings of the person of God. (Please note that the point here is neither to attack nor defend the doctrine of inerrancy, but merely to show how and why it historically achieved its central position among American evangelicals.)

b. Eschatology

Another recent example illustrates this same tendency to elevate to a primary level doctrines that were historically never seen as primary. Throughout the early- and mid-twentieth century, heated and acrimonious debates raged between covenant theologians who adopted an amillennial eschatology and dispensational theologians who adopted a futurist or premillennial eschatology. At issue was a doctrine that had never been agreed on by the consensus of the church. Yet within dispensationalism, a particular eschatological understanding had on a practical level been raised to a fundamental of the faith. In the eyes of many dispensational teachers, a denial of their particular understanding of the details surrounding the return of Christ and the establishment of the kingdom was (and is) a denial of the faith.

2. Scholastic Maximalism

The distinction between absolute TRUTH and a human grasp of truth is crucial in any discussion of a relative hierarchy of significance and importance of doctrines (see chart "Degrees of Authority" on p. 149).

The very nature of Christian theology demands from its practitioners and adherents a commitment to the fact that truth exists and that it can in some measure be grasped. However, virtually all recognize intuitively that issues of church government, for example, are of a qualitatively different nature than issues surrounding the person of God or of Christ. Yet despite this implicit recognition, there is still in many quarters a mind-set that insists that since truth is of God, *all* truth must be defended with *equal* vigor. Many are willing to "go to the wall" for fine points of eschatology or ecclesiology or even finely developed and nuanced points of doctrine concerning core issues. These tend to be "theological maximalists," that is, they believe that we must discover and systematize *all* truth and commit ourselves absolutely to those maximums. They believe that to admit degrees of importance of truth is somehow an affront to the whole concept of truth.

This approach can be traced to the period after the Reformation that saw the rise of Protestant (Reformed) scholasticism, which viewed the systematized whole of Christian doctrine as TRUTH. The scholastic method sees *all* truth as being on the same level and sees a denial of *any part* of the system as a denial of the *whole* system.

This mentality was promoted by the scholastic practice of building frameworks and then deducing within those frameworks what must be true from that which is known. Scholastic methodology was from one vantage point a magnificent achievement. The method allowed theologians to build "cathedrals of the mind," magnificent structures that attempted to incorporate all theological knowledge into one comprehensive system, showing the place of each part and the interrelationships of all the various parts. The down side was that the system tended to become an end in itself rather than a means to an end, and there was a leveling of the relative importance of truth. The interrelatedness of doctrines led to the conclusion that to deny anything in the system was to deny the whole body of Christian doctrine and therefore the faith itself.

This methodology very naturally leads to a rigid doctrinaire mentality that sees, for example, fine points of eschatology as being on the same level of importance as the doctrine of the Trinity or the hypostatic union of the humanity and deity in the incarnate person of Jesus Christ. It further leads to the charge of heresy against anyone who does not hold the exact same formulation of doctrine as oneself. This mentality has over the centuries filtered its way down from the level of the theologians to the educated layperson in the pew, where it is not so much a matter of knowledge or understanding as a matter of mind-set.

Another negative side effect of the scholastic methodology and mind-set is that it tends to foster an intellectual dishonesty because it places off limits any study that might threaten an existing systemic conclusion.

Perhaps the best example of this mentality is seen in B. B. Warfield, who has been called the greatest theologian in America after Jonathan Edwards. Yet he never produced a systematic theology of his own because he believed that the Westminster Confession presented the apex of theology and that Charles Hodge's exposition of Reformed theology could not be improved upon. Any theological conclusion that challenged or threatened a conclusion of Westminster had to be discredited. Warfield's collected works fill ten sizable volumes. The quality is superb, but the perspective is always critical and analytical, not creative and probing. He took his stand on Westminster and never wavered. In fact, his position at Princeton Seminary at the end of his life was Professor of Polemic Theology!

3. The Content of the Christian Faith: The Apostolic Proclamation

Scripture clearly indicates that belief is important and that the content of the Christian faith is to be jealously guarded. An individual or group cannot take "the faith that was once for all entrusted to the saints" (Jude 3) and modify it by addition or deletion, or by twisting the received truth. Paul admonishes Timothy, "The things you have heard me say in the presence of many witnesses entrust to reliable men who will also be qualified to teach others" (2 Tim. 2:2).

The concept of a Christian *tradition* emerged out of the church's encounter with Gnosticism in the second century. Gnosticism somewhat resembled a second-century New Age movement that appeared, on the surface at least, to be very similar to Christianity. It formed the first major theological challenge to the young church. It was in the context of this confrontation that the concept of tradition arose. *Tradition* means literally "that which has been handed down or handed over" and echoes Paul's admonition to Timothy in 2 Timothy 2:2. The early church leaders argued that the content of the apostolic *kerygma* (the essential Christian message or proclamation) had been faithfully preserved by the leadership of the church and that the apostolic proclamation of that message was also preserved in the emerging canon of the New Testament. This stood in contrast to the Gnostics who claimed to have a secret knowledge that had been handed down from the apostles outside the church (and that was thus not part of the *kerygma*), but in fact merely invented their teachings while claiming they were Christian.

Within the evangelical fold there is a precommitment to Scripture and a desire to base all doctrines on Scripture through solid exegesis. However, it must be recognized that from a historical perspective the church's theology did not come directly out of the New Testament but rather out of the apostolic kerygma, a kerygma that predated the writing of the New Testament and centered around the person and work of Jesus Christ. Paul refers to this when he commands Timothy to contend earnestly for the faith. It is this focus—the person and work of Jesus Christ—that forms the heart of Christian theology.

To reiterate, in contrast to the scholastic methodology, we must recognize that theologies and doctrines are human constructions that more or less adequately encapsulate, interpret, and contextualize the apostolic kerygma and the teaching of Scripture for later generations. Philip Schaff, nineteenth-century church historian, in describing the creedal commitments of the church, observed that confessions are humankind's answer to God's Word.[4]

And even in the best case, any creed or confession is only "an approximate and relatively correct exposition of revealed truth and may be improved by the progressive knowledge of the church."[5] If we extend Schaff's observation to theology generally, the fallibility and limitedness of the human construction become more apparent, since a theological system arises out of a single mind rather than the life of the church or a collection of minds.

Extending Schaff's observations further, we must distinguish between the *form* of a doctrine and its *substance*.[6] This criterion recognizes that by virtue of the fact that we live in specific historical situations, we will conceptualize and express our understanding of the truth in concrete historical forms that arise out of our own Zeitgeist. An example may prove helpful. A building contractor in the South uses bricks to build a house while a contractor in the Northwest uses wood and a contractor in California uses stucco. These houses look different on one level, but they bear a "family resemblance" on a deeper level and all accomplish the same purpose, and we are comfortable moving from one type of house to another. The contractor uses the building material at hand rather than importing material from afar. Likewise, the church fathers used the intellectual material at hand to express the truth of the Trinity to their society rather than importing Hebrew thought into a Greek-speaking and thinking world. And it may be appropriate to reexpress the truth of a given doctrine in a form that is appropriate to the concrete historical situation in which we live. A good example of the recasting of a doctrine can be seen in Alister McGrath's recasting the doctrine of justification by faith in the categories of existentialism and personalist theology.[7]

This distinction between form and substance alerts us to the ever-present danger of placing too much emphasis on particular words and not going past the words to the meaning expressed by those words. In point of fact, doctrinal statements and creedal affirmations can easily become verbal shibboleths that obscure meaning and foster divisions over words rather than nurturing understanding and community. On the other hand, it is possible to reinterpret doctrinal statements to mean something entirely different than the creed was meant to express. W. Robertson Smith, the nineteenth-century Scottish Old Testament scholar, when told that he was accused of denying the divinity of Jesus Christ, is said to have replied, "How can they accuse me of that? I have never denied the divinity of any man, let alone Jesus."[8]

4. Degrees and Ranking of Authority

We are to contend for the truth, but all truth is not of the same order, despite the thinking of many theologians and teachers. We must recognize that there are theological truths that transcend local and temporary historical situations, while other "truths" are so affected by the Zeitgeist out of which they arise as to be idiosyncratic. An example of this idiosyncratic tendency would be the tendency of some denominations to enshrine the spiritual experience of the denomination's founder in doctrinal terms that become normative and "distinctive" of the denomination. For example, the spiritual experience of A. B. Simpson, founder of the Christian and Missionary Alliance, is reflected in the two distinctive doctrines of that denomination, healing in the atonement and postconversion crisis sanctification.[9] This leads to the conclusion that some theological truths are more important than others. But if this is the case, how are we to determine the criteria by which decisions about the importance of a truth are to be made? What are the first-order theological truths that *must* be maintained? What are the second-order truths, and so on? And how are we to recognize them?

The ranking of theological truth affects not only the historical articulation of a doctrine and the marginalization of that which is idiosyncratic, but it also involves the ranking of truths that come directly out of Scripture itself. In many cases, the scriptural material is abundantly clear and the church has always plainly affirmed certain doctrines. In other cases, the scriptural evidence is scanty or cloudy. In these cases, any conclusions that are drawn must be held with a degree of tentativeness.

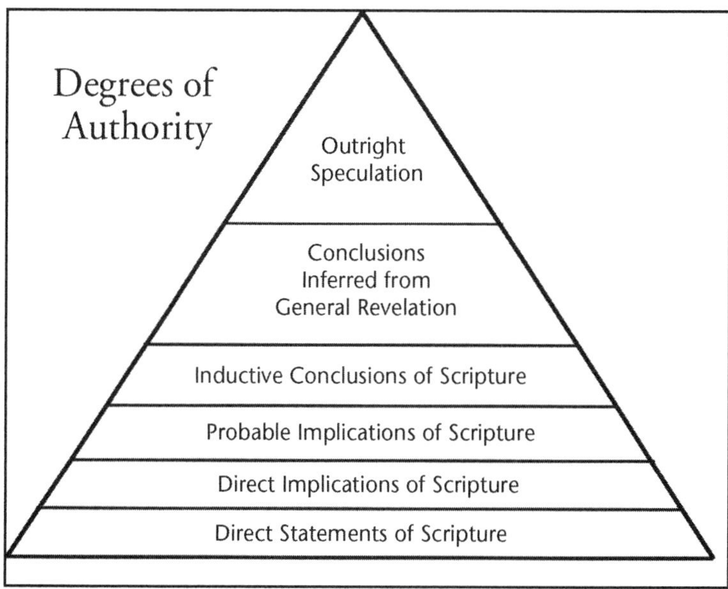

FIGURE 5.1

Millard Erickson has suggested ranking the importance and authority of theological statements as shown in figure 5.1.[10] This ranking is helpful for considering the relative certainty of the things one believes. But from the perspective of formal theological affirmation, this hierarchy of authority is not totally adequate, especially if it is lifted from a more nuanced context. For example, direct statements of Scripture that may on the surface sound absolute may be qualified or relativized by other scriptural evidence. Erickson speaks of "direct statements of Scripture." While there is no hint that Erickson intends this, one might infer a theological method whereby a teaching is supported by a verse of Scripture pulled out of its context and absolutized without reference to the larger biblical theological teaching on the subject. This was the rabbinical method of "pearl-stringing" scriptural references together without regard for their literary or historical context. This method was also adopted by the scholastic theological method and too often is seen even in contemporary popular theological method. "Direct statements" can be and are used as a theological "trump card" to clinch an argument. A direct statement of Scripture is authoritative to the extent that the statement is interpreted accurately within its literary and historical context and not erroneously made to be a contextless, abstract, and global assertion.

On the second level of authority, we must draw the distinction between *necessary* inference and *logical* inference. Erickson draws the distinction between direct implications and probable implications of Scripture, which, while helpful, is not the same as the distinction between necessary and logical inferences from Scripture. *Necessary* implications are those that either undergird an assertion that would fall without this underpinning, or they are implications that from a logical perspective are included in an assertion and need only the application of a syllogism to draw out the implicit information. A *logical* implication would be an inference that is in harmony with the statement but not necessarily drawn from it in syllogistic fashion.

Near the top of his hierarchy of authority, Erickson places inductive conclusions drawn from Scripture. Again, this level of authority/certainty needs further qualification. The scientific method is by its very nature inductive and thus can never yield absolute certainty in its conclusions. However, inductive conclusions can approach the level of practical certainty if all the data have been examined and accurately interpreted. Thus the degree of certainty of inductive conclusions depends on the thoroughness of the inductive study.

Erickson is implicitly drawing a distinction between the *teaching* of Scripture and the *phenomena* of Scripture. This type of arrangement of authority is seen particularly in discussions of biblical authority. It is generally recognized within evangelicalism that if one begins with the teaching passages of Scripture and, having established the teaching, moves to the phenomena of Scripture, he or she will ultimately emerge with a doctrine of Scripture that embraces inerrancy. Whereas, if a person begins with the phenomena of Scripture and from the phenomena proceeds to the explicit teaching passages, that person will not embrace inerrancy. It is at this point that the question of method inserts itself into the whole equation. (See the appendix.)

Erickson places conclusions from general revelation near the top of the pyramid and outright speculations at the top as having no authority. His statements with reference to the authority of general revelation need serious qualification. General revelation, taken broadly, refers to the God-created order and forms the larger context within which we must interpret the special revelation given in Scripture. The failure within more recent evangelicalism to give general revelation its proper place by allowing it to set boundaries on some issues that have scientific answers has led to all sorts of intellectual and theological mischief in making the supposedly direct statements of Scripture speak to issues far beyond the purposes for which they were given and globalizing the authority of the Bible beyond its purposes. To say that conclusions drawn from general revelation must be subject to the clearer statements of Scripture, slavishly applied, could be used to "prove" a flat earth or a geocentric universe. There must be some kind of reciprocal process by which general revelation informs special revelation and special revelation interprets general revelation.[11]

B. THE COMPONENTS OF DOCTRINE/THEOLOGY

Charles Hodge defined theology as the arrangement and display of the facts of the Bible. This simple definition is to this day still the operative cognitive definition among many evangelicals. As we have seen in previous chapters, much more goes into the construction of a doctrine or a theological system than simply the biblical text. Numerous preunderstandings of various types shape the gestalt of any theological expression. Alister McGrath, in his 1990 Bampton Lectures, focused on the elements that go into doctrinal construction and identified four elements that give shape to any articulation of doctrine.[12]

1. Doctrine as That Which Defines the Community

A couple of illustrations will demonstrate how doctrine functions to define the community. Paul argued in Scripture that the true gospel did not include works of the Jewish law such as circumcision for justification. It came by faith alone. Those who taught the necessity of works of the law in addition to faith were outside.[13] Likewise, justification by faith became the doctrine that demarcated Lutherans from Roman Catholics. Furthermore, the Lutheran understanding of the nature of the Eucharist (often referred to as *consubstantiation*) defined Lutheranism vis à vis Reformed Protestants. Even the Council of Trent focused on the self-definition of the Roman Catholic Church rather than on a definition of the heretics. Thus we can say that doctrine gives the theological justification for a group's existence and is key in its self-definition. An essential aspect of doctrinal articulation is therefore the element of social demarcation, defining who is in and who is out.

A more contemporary illustration is the doctrine and practice of glossolalia in the Pentecostal/charismatic/Third Wave traditions. At the outbreak of Pentecostalism in 1906, the defining phenomenon was the practice and doctrine of tongues. So central was the doctrine to early Pentecostal self-understanding that many insisted that the experience of tongues defined who was or was not saved. It is interesting to note that as the tradition matured and moved transdenominationally, the emphasis on tongues diminished, and at one point in the 1980s, only about 35 percent of those who identified themselves as charismatic spoke in tongues.

2. Doctrine as Interpretation of Narrative

In the modern era, the emphasis has been on the propositional nature of truth, a perspective closely aligned with the Enlightenment concept of universal truth. The advent of postmodernism has brought about a reassertion of the power of narrative and the priority of story over the didactic—a position more in harmony with the perspective of Scripture itself.

Ultimately, Christianity is about narrative, about a story—*the* story—of God's dealings with humanity culminating in the life and work of Jesus Christ. Christian community is derived from and receives its identity from the story of Jesus of Nazareth. The New Testament itself adopts this perspective. It insists that the believer's identity is found with Christ. Paul develops the concept of ἐν Χρίστῳ (*en Christo*, "in Christ"). Jesus' story becomes the believer's story; he or she has been crucified with Christ, buried with him, and become a participant in his resurrection. Jesus is the paradigm of existence.

Narratives are not universal abstractions—they are grounded in history. Even the church's sacraments are rooted in the story of Christ; they focus on his life and death. *But story is not doctrine/theology.* The two are fundamentally different. McGrath suggests that the story itself contains the fundamental structure, the implicit interpretive framework out of which doctrine is constructed.

During my first year as a college professor, I was expounding the doctrine of the Trinity to college juniors and made the comment that the church didn't have a formal doctrine of the Trinity until the Council of Nicea in A.D. 325. The hand of one of the students shot up: "What do you mean, they didn't have a doctrine of the Trinity? I open my Bible and I find it everywhere!" He failed to realize that the "self-evident truth" of the Trinity he saw in Scripture was in fact the result of the interpretive framework that had been worked out during those early centuries. McGrath rightly suggests that the generating of doctrine from narrative involves a similar process.[14] The story contains a substructure of conceptual frameworks. These implicit frameworks serve as the starting point. They are the "hints" and "signposts" that guide the reader/interpreter/theologian in making initial doctrinal affirmations. Then the text is reread in light of the initial doctrinal conclusions, and modifications and improvements to the framework are made. There is a dynamic interplay, a dialectical interplay between the text and the doctrine.

In the process of constructing doctrine, a transformation from narrative to propositional statements occurs. Narrative, because it is given as story, is not to be approached deductively but rather inferentially. The difference between the two methods of analysis is significant. All too often theologians have been guilty of treating the text as a series of premises from which conclusions could be drawn deductively. (If scriptural statement A is true and B is also true, then the conclusion we can draw from A and B *must* also be true. This generally can be expressed in the form of a syllogism.) This is a serious methodological error. Instead, it is at this transformation point that we decisively shift genres and produce doctrines that are given in a form foreign to the Scriptures and teach truths Scripture does not necessarily *explicitly* expound but that may be *inferred* from the statements of Scripture with a degree of certainty, but not with absolute certainty.

The church has always had those who could legitimately be called theological *primitivists,* those who do not wish to step beyond the text. But the whole point of doctrine/theology is that simple reiteration of the *statements* of Scripture is not enough. Thus the *doctrine* of the Trinity arose out of reflection on the nature of God as revealed in the text of Scripture in an attempt to explain how the one God could also be three. It is not metaphysical speculation based on Greek philosophy, although those early theologians used philosophy to help them explain the concept.[15] Rather, *the doctrine of the*

Trinity is an interpretation of the narrative. We may illustrate this with the concept of an acorn. The acorn is not the oak tree, but it contains the material from which a tree will grow.[16] In this sense, it is legitimate to speak of the development of doctrine. We recognize that doctrine must be ultimately linked to the text of Scripture as its primary source. As McGrath has noted, "The *sola scriptura* principle is ultimately an assertion of the primacy of the foundational scriptural narrative over any framework of conceptualities which it may generate."[17]

> While the theologian may feel at liberty to explore other sources of potential interest, doctrine is historically linked with Scripture on account of the historicity of its formulating communities. Christian communities of faith orientate and identify themselves with reference to authoritative sources which are either identical with or derived from Scripture.[18]

Scripture's primary function is not to give theological statements but to relate the story of God's dealing with humanity, especially in the person of Jesus of Nazareth. "Scripture does not articulate a set of abstract principles, but points to a lived life."[19] Whether approached directly or through a filter of creeds and traditions, Scripture constitutes the foundational documents of the Christian faith.[20] These foundational documents provide the material from which theology is inferred and constructed.

3. Doctrine as an Interpretation of Experience

When attention is turned to the third of McGrath's four components, doctrine as interpretation of experience, many within the evangelical tradition tend to get very uncomfortable. Evangelicals heartily assert that genuine Christianity involves experience, yet, at least from the time of the Princetonians, evangelicals have compartmentalized theology and life into two separate areas, not letting experience inform or shape theology, or theology necessarily inform experience. Charles Hodge insisted that experience did not make a Christian; believing a set of facts about Jesus Christ did.[21] Following in the Common Sense tradition of Hodge and Princeton, evangelicals have seen truth as absolutely separate from the knower, as something that exists "out there." (See chapter 3, pp. 78–79 for the inadequacies of this assumption.) Additionally, "experience" may bring to mind Friedrich Schleiermacher and liberalism on the one hand and the excesses of the Pentecostal tradition on the other. But McGrath's appeal to experience is looking not at private religious experience but at the communal experience of the Christian community. In particular, he notes that Christianity addresses the *human experience of alienation.* It is this experience that becomes a point of contact. Christianity "addresses such experiences in order to transform them, and to indicate what the shape of the experience of redemption through Jesus Christ might be like."[22] It is at this point, he contends, that we encounter a problem—the inadequacy of language to express experience. As an example of this unhappy phenomenon, McGrath invokes Wittgenstein's musing that words cannot communicate the aroma of a cup of coffee. But while words cannot adequately express experience, they can point to experience as signposts.

McGrath notes that while the experiential aspect of doctrine is most frequently associated with Romantic theologies such as that of Schleiermacher, we find roots and even specific explications of this concept as early as Augustine.[23] Although McGrath does not explicitly draw the conclusion, it can be inferred that at the beginning of the Christian faith, experience preceded doctrine, that is, the apostles experienced the risen Christ and that experience led them (under the inspiration of the Holy Spirit) to write as they did. The experience could not have been a prelinguistic mystic experience, but one that occurred within their existing framework of reality.[24]

The question of experience again raises the troubling question of the adequacy of human language. McGrath observes:

> Underlying the profundity of human experience and encounter lies an unresolved tension—the tension between the wish to express an experience in words, and the inability of words to capture that experience in its fullness. Everything in human experience which is precious and significant is threatened with extinction, in that it is in some sense beyond words, and yet requires to be stated in words for it to become human knowledge. It is threatened with the spectre of solipsism, in that unless an experience can be communicated to another, it remains trapped within the private experiential world of the individual. Words can point to an experience, they can begin to sketch its outlines—but the total description of that experience remains beyond words. The words of John Woolman's associate express this point: "I may tell you of it, but you cannot feel it as I do." Words point beyond themselves to something greater which eludes their grasp. Human words, and the categories they express, are stretched to their limits as they attempt to encapsulate, to communicate, something which tantalizingly refuses to be reduced to words. It is the sheer elusiveness of human experience, its obstinate refusal to be imprisoned within a verbal matrix, which underlies the need for poetry, symbolism and doctrine alike.[25]

C. S. Lewis observed a similar tension on the aesthetic level:

> The books or the music in which we thought the beauty was located will betray us if we trust to them; it was not *in* them, it only came *through* them, and what came through them was longing. These things—the beauty, the memory of our own past—are good images of what we really desire; but if they are mistaken for the thing itself, they turn into dumb idols, breaking the hearts of the worshippers. For they are not the thing in itself; they are only the scent of the flower we have not found, the echo of a tune we have not heard, news from a country we have never yet visited.[26]

McGrath endorses a suggestion made nearly two centuries ago that "the function of doctrine is to effect a decisive transition within the language of the Christian community from the poetic and rhetorical to the 'descriptive-didactic.'" This means that poetic or rhetorical language and doctrinal language are distinct but related means of communication within the believing community. In fact, it is because rhetorical and poetic language is the primary language of the community that doctrine becomes necessary for responsible communication to the community in its primary language.[27] Doctrine functions as the cognitive element within Christianity, the skeleton that supports and gives shape to the flesh of spiritual experience.

While the Enlightenment separated facts from interpretation and implicitly endorsed a view of knowledge that has been characterized as "brute empiricism," it is now generally recognized that there are no such things as bare, brute facts. Experience is not pretheoretical but is already theory laden, arising within an interpretive framework, however tentative that framework may be. Prior belief plays a vital part in interpreting experience.[28]

To sum up this most difficult point: Doctrine arises out of the poetic and rhetorical and narrative language of Scripture, language that points beyond itself to the experience of God and redemption. It gives cognitive form to the experience referenced in that language and in so doing provides a framework, a skeleton to support the life of the believing community. It does more than this however. The doctrine, the meaning, creates and restores the original experience in the life of the hearer. "Doctrine opens the way to a new experience of the experience."[29]

For the church today, experience is an inadequate foundation for doctrine. Nor does contemporary experience legitimately generate doctrine, but doctrine informs experience and thereby gives significant insight into the existential side of Christianity.

4. Doctrine as Truth Claim

From the fact that this factor is discussed last, some might infer that the truth claim of doctrine is of less than paramount importance. Nothing could be further from the truth. It is, in fact, the truth claim of doctrine that underlies its importance and its fulfilling of the other three functions. But this raises the question Pilate asked our Lord: "What is *truth*?"

Numerous definitions of truth have been propounded, but there is no universally accepted definition. Different disciplines have different criteria for truth, some explicit, some implicit, none universally agreed upon. One suggestion, traceable ultimately to Marx and Engels, is that truth is simply "correspondence with reality." Truth is that which describes things "as they actually are."

Classically there are several definitions of truth, all of which bear what Wittgenstein calls a family resemblance, despite their distinct (but related) emphases on the nature of truth.

1. The Greek term ἀλήθεια (*aletheia*) carries the interpretation of truth as the "state of discoveredness or unhiddenness." The term has primary reference to the thing itself and only secondarily to a statement about the thing. It is a description of how things are now, in the present moment.

2. The Latin *veritas* by contrast carries a sense of precision of utterance or exactness. The truth is faithful and exact without omission. It is complete. *Veritas*, as opposed to *aletheia*, has primary reference to past events and is closely associated with history, or narrative. As Cicero said, "Who does not know the first law of history to be that an author must not dare to recount anything except the truth? And its second that he must endeavor to recount the whole truth."[30]

3. The Hebrew word אֱמוּנָה (*emunah*) contains a sense of personal reference—truth related to a sense of trust. Thus the true God is not simply the only god who exists, but the God who is trustworthy and faithful to his promises. So in everyday language, the false friend is not one who is nonexistent, but one who cannot be trusted. *Emunah* therefore has a proleptic aspect as it points toward future faithfulness. *Emunah* has, like *veritas*, past reference but not simply for the sake of the past. Rather, the focus is a shaping of the present and future through predictive hope and gives a paradigm for understanding the goal of history.

Christian doctrine relates to these three ideas of truth in that it is rooted in history. Theologians speak of the "Christ-event." While the terminology is not popular among evangelicals, it does serve to call attention to the fact that Christianity is rooted in history with all its contingencies rather than in timeless truths. Emil Brunner has gone so far as to say that truth is something that *happens*. Jesus is truth (John 14:6). God is not to be identified with sterile philosophical concepts but rather with reference to Jesus: "Anyone who has seen me has seen the Father" (John 14:9). Truth is then grounded in history and reflection on historical events. Doctrine involves interpretation, as McGrath has suggested above. But in any interpretation, the question that was asked is at least as important as the answer that is given. Thus, in examining Christian doctrine, we must *not only look at the cognitive statements, but also at the questions that led to those statements.* Does Jesus Christ, the "Christ-event," precipitate the questions to which doctrines are the answer? The church has always answered this question with a resounding yes. There is an essential continuity of the core doctrines of the Christian faith throughout the ages. Doctrine has ventured beyond Christology, but we must not forget that Christ is the lens through which our understanding of other doctrines is mediated. For example, for the Christian to affirm "God is love" involves an implicit christological reference. The affirmation links a hitherto general concept, love, to its concrete demonstration in the historic person of Jesus of Nazareth, God incarnate.

The truth of doctrine also involves *internal self-consistency*. Indeed, heresy has been defined as adherence to teaching that is inconsistent with the central affirmations concerning Jesus Christ and the redemption he provides. Doctrine/theology is an integrated whole with one doctrine informing another. We may speak of a doctrine of Christ, of man, of God, or of sin, but we recognize that for these doctrines to be true, they must be internally consistent and consistent with the foundational doctrines of the faith. An intrasystemic unity of the truth must be expressed in doctrine. For example, we could show how the person of Jesus Christ controls what have been referred to as the four natural heresies of Christianity, all relating to either the need of, or the possibility of, redemption. (See chapter 6 for further discussion.)

The truth of doctrine is not simply a reflection on the past or even the "Christ-event." The truth of doctrine is not simply information. A great failure in evangelical tradition is that we have tended at least since the time of old Princeton to view all truth as being of the same type.[31] Doctrine, however, must be oriented toward faith. It cannot be simple factual information. As Dorner contended, there is a personal demand on the individual for facts to move from the realm of the abstract and theoretical to the realm of the vital. With this faith commitment arises a certainty that comes from personal encounter with the living God. This is the existential aspect of doctrine, associated with Kierkegaard but implicit within the text itself. It was at this point that confessional faith failed in the era of Protestant scholasticism. This point also relates to the authority of experience, for doctrine involves an existential imperative that demands to be appropriated personally in one's inner life.

Doctrine makes truth claims, but these claims are of necessity colored by the lenses of the theologian and the epistemology he or she employs. Therefore it is necessary to be in conversation with past generations, with the continuity of the Christian tradition. We all make mistakes, but we do not all make the same mistakes.

C. THE NECESSITY OF ESTABLISHING A DOCTRINAL TAXONOMY

As noted above, there is a general recognition that some doctrines are more important than others. Erickson deals explicitly with this in his *Christian Theology.*[32] The more important doctrines are to be given more prominence in discussion. Thus "eschatology is a major area of doctrinal investigation. Within that area, the Second Coming is a major belief. Rather less crucial (and considerably less clearly taught in Scripture) is the issue of whether the church will be removed from the world before or after the great tribulation."[33] Certain doctrines in and of themselves are major, or core, doctrines, but finer developments of those doctrines are not to be considered of first-order importance.

1. Establishing a Doctrinal Taxonomy Historically

A generation before the fundamentalist-modernist controversy, Philip Schaff published *The Creeds of Christendom*; a few years later Charles Briggs published *The Fundamental Christian Faith.* Both of these works recognize that the doctrines embodied in the creeds of the ancient church represent the theological core of the Christian faith. This perspective was also that of Vincent of Lerins in the fifth century. Vincent recognized the inadequacy in a simple appeal to the text of Scripture in that Scripture was subject to a variety of interpretations. Something more was needed. He settled on the principle of the "consensus of the faithful." In other words, a doctrine had to be universally recognized by the laity as well as the clergy. Furthermore, a doctrine could not be local or new.

> I have made earnest and diligent inquiries of men outstanding for their holiness and learning, seeking to distinguish, by some sure and, as it were, universal rule, between the truth of the catholic faith and the

falsity of heretical perversity.... The reason is ... that by its very depth the Holy Scripture is not received by all in one and the same sense, but its declarations are subject to interpretation, now in one way, now in another, so that, it would appear, we can find almost as many interpretations as there are men.... For this reason it is very necessary that, on account of so great intricacies of such varied error, the line used in the exposition of the prophets and apostles be made straight in accordance with the standard of ecclesiastical and catholic interpretation.... Likewise in the catholic church itself especial care must be taken that we hold to that which has been believed everywhere, always, and by all men. For that is truly and rightly "catholic," as the very etymology of the word shows, which includes almost all universally. This result will be reached if we follow ecumenicity, antiquity, consensus. We shall follow ecumenicity if we acknowledge as the one true faith what the whole church throughout the world confesses.[34]

Thomas Oden has brought this presupposition of universality or catholicity to his systematic theology, which is a "consensual" theology, using as his method the Vincentian Canon, focusing on what is common to all branches of Christianity.

As stated earlier, we must distinguish between the *form* and the *substance* of a doctrine. It is possible to say the same thing in a variety of ways and even in a variety of languages. This should alert us to the necessity to probe what linguists call deep structure, the universal meaning, rather than stumbling over surface structure, specific verbal articulations of theological conclusions.

Having said this, the question remains, "What specifically belongs at the core of our theological commitment?"

a. Trinitarianism

The person and work of Jesus Christ belong at the heart of any theological taxonomy. As a number of interconnected teachings and assumptions were worked out historically, the questions focused first on the relationship of the preincarnate Son to God the Father. The early church struggled with finding adequate language to express the relationship between the Father and the Son, recognizing the deity of each but without inadvertently falling into the trap of asserting two gods. Several early attempts to explain this relationship were judged to be inadequate.

The crisis that precipitated the church's formally declaring its understanding at the Council of Nicea (A.D. 325) was the teaching of Arius, a presbyter

The Council of Nicea

from Alexandria, who taught that the Son was the first created being, who became the creator of the cosmos. Arius summed up his teaching with the phrase, "There was a time when the Son was not." The church responded at Nicea in the Nicene Creed, asserting that the Son was "consubstantial with the Father." This statement was an assertion of the eternal divinity of the Son as a full participant in the deity of the Father. The Council of Nicea did not address the question of the Holy Spirit as such. The understanding of the Holy Spirit's full participation in the Godhead came as a result of the work of the three great Cappadocian fathers (Basil the Great, Gregory of Nyssa, and Gregory of Nazianzus), especially Basil, and was codified at the Council of Constantinople (A.D. 381). This statement gave explicit form to the already existing practice of recognizing Father, Son, and Holy Spirit as fully and equally divine.

As explanations of the nature of the Trinity developed, the Eastern and Western churches developed different frameworks for understanding the doctrine—frameworks that especially from the perspective of Eastern theology are incompatible. Therefore, in a taxonomy of doctrine, the fact that God exists as Trinity stands at the very core of the church's faith, while explanations, or a framework, of Trinitarian understanding would be ranked as second-level theological reflection.

b. The Two Natures of Christ

The second major theological development of the ancient period was a precise articulation of the nature of the incarnate person of Jesus Christ, specifically the doctrine of the two natures, deity and humanity, and the explanation as to how these two natures come together in one person (the hypostatic union). Since the birth of the church, there had been an implicit recognition that Jesus was uniquely both fully human and fully divine. Early on, the church had simply repeated these assertions without trying to explain the nature of the incarnation or relate the divine and human in the one historic person of Jesus Christ. As with the Arian controversy, the church's understanding of the person of Christ also arose out of controversy. But in this case, the understanding was refined in three successive controversies.

To understand the christological conclusions forged at Chalcedon (A.D. 451), we must understand the theological climate of the ancient church in the fourth and fifth centuries. The question of the person of Christ was one that occupied the Greek-speaking church, a church that was divided into two theological schools. The first school, that of Alexandria, was heavily influenced by Platonic philosophy and was interested in spiritual realities. The tendency here was to emphasize the deity of Christ, often at the expense of his humanity.

One of the staunch defenders of Nicene orthodoxy was Apollinarius, an Alexandrian theologian and friend of the great Athanasius, the architect of Trinitarian orthodoxy. Apollinarius saw that one of Arius's arguments was not properly Trinitarian but focused on the nature of the incarnation. Apollinarius responded with an explanation of the relationship of Christ's deity to his humanity, which in effect made Christ less than fully human. Apollinarius's hypothesis was that in the incarnation Jesus Christ had a human body and soul, but the spirit (rational mind) had been replaced by the divine Logos, the second person of the Trinity. The reaction against Apollinarius's teaching was swift in coming, and his position was condemned as heretical by the Council of Constantinople in A.D. 381.

Roughly a generation later, Nestorius was patriarch of Constantinople and a representative of the other major theological school in the Greek-speaking East, the Antiochean school, which was interested in the historical interpretation of Scripture and focused on the true humanity of Christ. While not denying Christ's deity, their focus was on Jesus' humanity and the example he gave to his followers. Nestorius drew, as was typical of the school of Antioch, a sharp distinction between the humanity and the deity in the incarnate person of Jesus. So sharp was the distinction that he was understood to be teaching that Jesus was in reality two separate persons inhabiting a single body, Son of Mary and Son of God. This perception was exacerbated because of Nestorius's opposition to the already popular designation of Mary as *theotokos* ("God-bearer").[35] Nestorius was himself an intractable person, and when Cyril, bishop of Alexandria, challenged Nestorius's position, he defiantly refused to back down and challenged the orthodoxy of Cyril. After a series of confrontations, the emperor convened a council that met at Ephesus in A.D. 429. This council condemned Nestorius and his doctrine of "two sons." While historical research has questioned whether Nestorius himself did in fact hold the doctrine that bears his name, Nestorianism as popularly understood undermined the doctrine of salvation with its failure to adequately integrate the two natures into the one historic person who was Jesus Christ.[36]

Twenty years later another christological crisis arose. This time the nexus of the controversy was Eutyches, a well-respected, elderly, but unimaginative and poorly trained monk in Constantinople who reacted with disfavor to the insistence of the Council of Ephesus that Christ existed in two natures after the incarnation. Heavily influenced by Alexandrian theology and spirituality, Eutyches taught that after the incarnation Jesus had but one nature, the divine. He was variously understood to be teaching that Jesus' humanity was absorbed by his deity, or that in the incarnation the two natures fused to become one that was more than human but less than divine, a *tertium quid* ("third something"). Eutyches' heresy did not violate the dictum arising out of the Apollinarian controversy ("that which he did not assume he did not heal"[37]), but he did ultimately fall into a docetic heresy and violated the antidocetic dictum "Grace never destroys nature." Eutyches' heresy destroyed the humanity of Jesus after the incarnation and also fed into the dualistic temptation to flee from the flesh. After much political maneuvering and a council that declared Eutyches orthodox (the Robbers Synod of Ephesus in A.D. 449), he was finally condemned at Chalcedon in A.D. 451.[38]

Chalcedon produced the final creed of the ancient church. Pronouncements since that time have been confessions.[39] The Creed of Chalcedon addressed particularly the understanding of the incarnate person of Jesus Christ. A careful reading of the creed, however, shows that the statements are apophatic rather than cataphatic (or kataphatic). It is a creed of negation rather than assertion. Instead of giving a precise definition of the incarnate Christ, the creed draws parameters around what is allowed within orthodox christological theologizing. As later centuries proved, there was still much room for debate and discussion about particular emphases, but the boundaries were established. In looking taxonomically at the doctrine of the incarnate person of Christ, an affirmation of the truth of the creed that came out of Chalcedon is to be considered at the heart of the Christian faith. Further refinements and frameworks built within the boundaries, which from the very beginning accommodated Alexandrian and Antiochean emphases, are of second- or third-level importance.

c. The Nature of Divine Grace

The early church recognized implicitly the necessity of divine grace for salvation. From the immediate postapostolic period, the church recognized the absolute necessity of divine grace for salvation, because left to itself, humanity could not be saved. But the theological climate of Gnosticism kept the church from reflecting on the nature of human depravity and the need of divine grace.

During the fifth century, a British monk named Pelagius came to Rome and taught a gospel of moral reformation, stressing the ability of humanity to obey God completely. At this time, Augustine had already articulated his doctrine of human depravity and the accompanying spiritual inability to please God apart from a prior application of divine grace. The ensuing debate, the Pelagian controversy, brought into bold relief the issues concerning the nature of human depravity and divine grace. The church recognized the legitimacy and necessity of the concept of human depravity as being inexorably bound up in the nexus of the doctrine of salvation. It did not, however, unequivocally endorse Augustine's doctrine of total depravity. Pelagianism was condemned at Ephesus and at a number of local synods, but it was not until the Reformation that the Augustinian doctrine was endorsed and incorporated into a formal theological matrix. Thus it would be proper to say that an understanding of human depravity is at the center of the historic faith, but the historic faith does not endorse any particular articulation of depravity, whether it be Augustinian, Reformed, semi-Augustinian, or even semi-Pelagian. The doctrine of human depravity and its correlate doctrine, the necessity of salvation being of God and by grace, belong at the center of the web of Christian proclamation; any particular articulation must be viewed at the most as a second-level truth.

d. The Canon of the New Testament

As we turn our attention to the rise of the New Testament canon, we must recognize that at this point we are not dealing with the foundational *doctrines* of the faith; we are dealing with the foundational *documents* of the faith. The early church adopted the Old Testament as its original Scripture.

Very early it recognized the canonicity of the Gospels and the Pauline Epistles. Gradually the rest of the New Testament writings were recognized as having divine imprimatur. With the text of the New Testament, however, the process is qualitatively different than with the doctrinal controversies discussed above. Here the church never made a universal formal declaration of the extent of the New Testament. The lists that arose were associated with particular bishops, for example, Athanasius in his festal letter of A.D. 369, and with local synods associated with the great Augustine in Hippo and Carthage about twenty years later.

Thus the canon of the New Testament was not imposed on the church by ecclesiastical authority. Rather, its authority arose by consensus.[40] As a result of the way the canon of the New Testament arose, it was not formally closed until the Reformation period, although from a practical perspective it was virtually closed in the sixth century. Again, due to the historic consensus of the church, the shape of the canon of the New Testament would be understood as standing at the center of the faith, albeit from an epistemological rather than a formal doctrinal perspective. Certainly there has never been a serious attempt within the church to add any more books to the received canon, and any questioning of the legitimacy of any of the books of the New Testament has focused on the "fringes" as opposed to the books that preserve the heart of the inspired apostolic proclamation of Christ and his Word.

2. Establishing a Doctrinal Taxonomy Exegetically

The theologian and exegete experience constant tension due to contradictory expectations—expectations to preserve truth on the one hand and to act on the other hand as a scientist to test the validity of truth and to act as an explorer seeking new truth or a fuller grasp of truth.[41] Along these lines, the theologian and exegete must wrestle with how we define orthodoxy and whether a simple pursuit of truth can be accomplished in light of the noetic effects of sin. Too many evangelicals do not nuance their theological convictions, nor do they hold them up to critical examination. Ironically, this does exactly what they would deny: it gives tradition an unqualified authority and is more in keeping with historic Roman Catholic methodology than having a Protestant spirit, for it regards the tradition (whatever that tradition may be) as unquestionable and undifferentiated.

If we approach the question of the certainty of doctrine from an exegetical (as opposed to a historical) perspective, the greatest certainty about doctrine comes from a two-pronged approach that is both empirical (solid exegesis, biblical theology, etc.) and pneumatological (that is, the Spirit of

God bears witness to our spirit about certain truths, thus bringing home a greater degree of certainty about more central things). A taxonomy of doctrine is the result.

To what does the Spirit bear witness? Essentially to matters pertaining to Christology and soteriology. Practically, this tells us that rationalism and the Enlightenment cannot invade the Spirit's territory; solid historical-critical exegesis cannot destroy one's faith in the resurrection of the theanthropic person because that faith, though rooted in history, is not based solely on history.

When it comes to less central issues, there needs to be a hierarchical order of certainty and a concomitant hierarchy of centrality as we develop a taxonomy of doctrine. Thus, for example, looking at issues of eschatology, the central truth of Christ's bodily return is what unites believers. First John explicitly says that the Spirit bears witness to this fact. But *when* Christ comes is left to the church to hammer out on the basis of solid exegesis. Conviction in such issues dare not be as certain as convictions about the person and work of Christ. Otherwise we succumb to the danger of "majoring in the minors," of missing the central message of the Bible, and of suppressing the witness of the Spirit on the more crucial issues.

There are, to be sure, less central issues on which we can have a very high degree of certainty—largely because any reasonable exegesis must come to such conclusions. But there are also topics on which a person *thinks* his views are Spirit-guided, yet he states his certainty of such matters more humbly. Note, for example, the language Paul uses in his view of remarriage after the death of a spouse: "But if the husband dies, she is free to marry whom she will, provided the marriage is within the Lord's fellowship. She is better off as she is; that is my opinion, and I believe that I too have the Spirit of God" (1 Cor. 7:39–40 REB). There seem to be degrees of certainty to which the Spirit bears witness. Issues of marriage and remarriage are not core doctrinal convictions but must still be worked out in terms of sapiential preference and solid exegesis. Thus, in areas outside core theological commitments, we have both the freedom and the responsibility to do tough exegetical spadework and to follow where the evidence leads us.

As those who believe that God is truth, we must commit ourselves to pursue truth in our exegesis no matter the cost, as long as it is within the bounds of taxonomically core doctrinal commitments as defined by the Spirit's witness and solid exegetical conclusions. This will by its very nature involve taking on—and maybe slaughtering—sacred cows. But it is the exegete's and the theologian's sacred responsibility to examine the text historically.

Checks and balances are in place, both theologically and exegetically, via the witness of the Spirit, solid exegesis, and the fact that the theologian's and the exegete's labors are done in community with others who can evaluate and challenge conclusions.

D. A THEOLOGY OF MINIMUMS?

In all that has been said, the question may arise, "Are we not forced to accept a theology of minimums rather than organizing and arranging truth and bringing all things under the lordship of Christ?" Not necessarily. What we are arguing is that there is a central core of truth that has established itself through the centuries and been agreed to by all who name the name of Christ, regardless of the communion or denomination of Christianity to which they belong. This core is the starting point of our theological understanding. It represents the minimum theological commitment of a Christian. But beyond that minimum there is within the theologian an inner push to organize all understanding and systematize it into a comprehensive whole. This drive, it could be argued, is an inner human need.

As explorers and scientists, we test, probe, investigate, extend our theological knowledge, and build a comprehensive understanding we believe is right. As we work, we operate within a paradigm of understanding, and we seek to extend the paradigm. As we learn, we develop a full-orbed system that tries to incorporate all truth about God and his universe from any and every source under its umbrella. But eventually, for a number of possible reasons, that paradigm cannot accommodate new data and another paradigm is proposed. That proposal is inevitably met with stiff resistance, and the charge of heresy is leveled against those who would change the status quo.

Theology deals by definition with revelation. The ultimate database from which it draws is the entirety of creation. The subset database is the Bible, special revelation. The subset of special revelation is the salvific message of redemption. It is this that composes the "theological core," the sine qua non of the faith. The theological enterprise is broader than the core; it seeks to organize and make sense first of the rest of special revelation and beyond that of the totality of general revelation. As we move beyond the core, the conclusions become more tentative and open to interpretation and debate.

But when we step back from this system we have built, a system of maximums, we must recognize that our system arose out of a particular set of assumptions and preunderstandings that, though universalized in our understanding and thought patterns, were in reality not universal. Rather, they were local and historically conditioned. That is not to say that all that understanding was wrong; it was the best that could be done at that place and time with the data and methods available.

To approach this question from another perspective, we recognize *the core of the faith as having the status of metanarrative*. It expresses universal and transcultural realities, although these realities arose out of particular historical events. When we elaborate on the core of the faith and add "second-level" doctrines, we in effect encapsulate the transcultural metanarrative within what is essentially a *local narrative*.[42] When conditions change, the local narrative may be challenged and even discarded, but this discarding is not a discarding of the metanarrative core encased in the local narrative. Rather, it is the discarding of the local understandings and interpretations that have grown up around the core metanarrative and involve even the framework in which it has been encased. The battle arises between those who have transformed the local narrative (be it Thomism, Lutheranism, Reformed theology, or whatever theology) into metanarrative and treat it as normative for all people, places, and times and those who advocate a new—and as yet untested—paradigm that does not view the theological issues involved in the same manner or with as much importance as does the old paradigm.

E. RANKING NONCORE ISSUES

The historic faith of the church expresses that which is at its core, the sine qua non of Christianity. A denial of the essential truth of any of the core doctrines places one outside the faith from the perspective of its essential proclamation and involves one in heresy. Yet there are many more doctrines and perspectives than those incorporated in the historic and ecumenical creeds of the church. The church is divided into three major communions—Orthodoxy, Roman Catholicism, and Protestantism. Within Protestantism there are numerous traditions—Lutheran, Reformed, Anglican, Anabaptist, and Arminian, as well as innumerable denominations. While Christians agree on the fundamental doctrines of the faith,[43] how are we to deal with the significant differences that exist between major communions and narrower traditions? How are we to rank the authority of theological constructions that are narrower than those embodied in the ecumenical creeds?

The first reality that must be reiterated is that all theological constructions are finite, limited approximations that re-present, re-contextualize, or re-describe the presentation of the scriptural material. Additionally, by virtue of the nature of language, there is a high degree of metaphor and figurative language in Scripture and in the concepts embodied there. Grant Osborne has discussed the metaphorical nature of theological language with reference to hermeneutics and its implications for theological construction.[44] Osborne argues rightly that theological statements are at their core metaphorical. The consequence is that "doctrinal statements are figurative representations of theoretical constructs, and the accuracy or 'truth' of their portrayal is always a moot point."[45] When added to the historical dimension, this makes for a degree of tentativeness in the degree of certainty with which we hold our assumptions.

In Christian theology, we are dealing with something analogous to what Thomas Kuhn would call "paradigm communities" in science. Those theological formulations that transcend the boundaries separating the three major Christian communions must have the highest authority. Within particular communions, those doctrines that are common to the entire communion will be ranked next in level of authority. In actuality, this principle applies particularly within Protestantism, since it, to a far higher degree than Catholicism or Orthodoxy, finds itself characterized by discrete traditions, subtraditions, and sub-subtraditions.

Within Protestantism we would look historically at doctrines such as these:

- Justification *sola fide*, by faith apart from human works. This is the doctrine out of which Protestantism was born.
- An understanding of the sacraments as testimonies and reminders as opposed to sacerdotalism, which sees the sacraments as actually infusing divine grace into the recipient.
- The centrality and the final authority of the Scriptures, which ranks as a hallmark of Protestantism as opposed to Catholicism and Orthodoxy.
- The extent of the canon as excluding the Apocrypha.

These are all examples of second-level doctrines. They are important, maybe important enough to divide over, but not a part of the fundamental core of the apostolic kerygma and hence not an *explicit* part of the historic faith.

Divisions also exist between Protestant traditions, particularly between the Reformed/Calvinist tradition and the Arminian and Wesleyan/Arminian tradition. Issues that separate these traditions focus particularly on the understanding of the nature of human depravity and spiritual ability and the nature of divine grace. The battle between these two camps has often devolved into heated and acrimonious debate over the issue of election/predestination. Often unrecognized is that in these doctrinal constructions there is a divergence in the theological methods by which the doctrines are established and defended. The Reformed camp particularly has committed itself to a scholastic theological method that John Calvin himself would find objectionable. Conversely, the Arminian camp has historically had no solid center around which to build its system and has tended to drift theologically in the direction of rationalism. While not denying that there are profound implications to the questions raised, looking taxonomically at the importance of these debates, they must be ranked as third level.

Many other issues beyond the scope of this book beg to be addressed, such as questions about organizing principles,[46] philosophical systems employed by various schools and theologians, hermeneutics and the application of hermeneutics to various genres of Scripture, and the implications for the development and articulation of doctrine. This chapter has tried to demonstrate, however, that it is a fundamental error to view all doctrines as being on the same level of importance. The doctrines fundamental to the faith are the consensus doctrines spelled out in the ancient creeds. Ironically, evangelicals don't get very upset when these doctrines are challenged—the discussions that engender the most heat and least light are about those doctrines that are historically and exegetically the least well established but have been raised to touchstone level by particular denominations and traditions in a sectarian fashion.

It is in the realm of ranking doctrine that theological politics rears its ugly head. After all, everyone believes that his or her theological construction is *the* biblical one. Very few Christians consciously recognize that factors other than the biblical text come into play in their theological belief structure. The commitment to the truth of God leads them to adopt a defensive posture and to attack those who challenge their beliefs at any point. A commitment to pursuing understanding and truth within a dogmatic or confessional community must often be accomplished quietly and without challenging the powers that be, for such a challenge could well cost the person his or her job or ministry. I have seen this happen on numerous occasions over issues as seemingly trivial as advocating dialogue with other denominations, adopting a hermeneutical principle that is perceived to threaten the existing structure, or declaring that a denomination's "denominational distinctives" are not cardinal doctrine.

There often tends to be a fundamental insecurity among those who wield the power in denominations and schools that cannot tolerate the mind that dares to ask questions. Reactions to new perspectives are often "knee-jerk" reactions. While addressing primarily the evangelical community on this point, the same intolerance is seen on the left wing of the theological spectrum. Numerous conservative students have found their theses and dissertations rejected because they did not toe the line with politically correct exegesis or ride a theological hobbyhorse of the party line at more liberal institutions.

The raising of issues that properly are fourth- or fifth-level concerns to touchstone level reveals a fundamental flaw in the way theology is approached. While we would not normally think in these terms, this mentality becomes schismatic and culpable before Christ, because it takes the focus off him and his work and introduces division into his body, the church.

As has been said elsewhere, systematic theology does not arise directly from the Bible, the claims of adherents to particular systems notwithstanding. It is a human enterprise.[47] Theological definition is a human response to God's revelation, and the organizing principles are of human, not divine, origin.[48]

While God is truth, we are not God and have only an incomplete grasp of his truth. By recognizing the relative importance of the truths we hold, we are better able to maintain the bond of unity in love.

> In essential things unity.
> In nonessential things tolerance.
> In all things charity.

BIBLIOGRAPHY

Briggs, Charles A. *Church Unity.* London: Longmans, Green, 1913. • **Erickson, Millard.** *Christian Theology.* Grand Rapids: Baker, 1984. • **McGrath, Alister.** *The Genesis of Doctrine.* Oxford: Blackwell, 1990. • ———. *Studies in Doctrine.* Grand Rapids: Zondervan, 1997. • **Osborne, Grant.** *The Hermeneutical Spiral.* Downers Grove, IL: InterVarsity Press, 1991. • **Sawyer, M. James.** *Taxonomic Charts on Theology and Biblical Study.* Grand Rapids: Zondervan, 1999. • **Schaff, Philip.** *The Creeds of Christendom.* Grand Rapids: Baker, 1977.

NOTES

[1]Millard Erickson explicitly recognizes this raising of the virgin birth to touchstone status as an apologetic ploy and says that the virgin birth is not absolutely necessary for maintaining the reality of the incarnation. It is in his understanding probably a second-level doctrine, i.e., not necessary for salvation (*Christian Theology*, 2nd ed. [Grand Rapids: Baker, 1998], 757–60, 772).

[2]These vowel points were not added until the medieval period by the Masoretes, because Hebrew had ceased to be a spoken language and there was a danger that the Jews would forget how to pronounce the text of the Hebrew scriptures.

[3]The 1970s saw a renewal of the inerrancy controversy that had raged during the late nineteenth and twentieth centuries. The inerrancy controversy of the 1970s and '80s was an in-house fight among evangelicals who asserted the characteristic essentials: "*conversionism*, the belief that lives need to be changed; *activism*, the expression of the gospel in effort; *biblicism*, a particular regard for the Bible; *crucicentrism*, a stress on the sacrifice of Christ on the cross. Together they form a quadrilateral of priorities that is the basis of Evangelicalism" (David Bebbington, *Evangelicalism in Modern Britain* [Grand Rapids: Baker, 1989], 3). Traditionalists insisted upon the adequacy and authority of the formulations made in the late nineteenth century, while the opponents raised numerous objections to the doctrine based on epistemology, linguistics, history, and the phenomena of the text.

[4]Philip Schaff, *The Creeds of Christendom* (Grand Rapids: Baker, 1977), 1:7.

[5]Ibid.

[6]Hubert Cunliffe-Jones, ed., *A History of Christian Doctrine* (Philadelphia: Fortress, 1980), 19–20.

[7]Alister McGrath, *Studies in Doctrine* (Grand Rapids: Zondervan, 1997), 408–36. McGrath is supremely concerned about the communication of doctrine to generations unfamiliar with the categories of Scripture and of the Reformation.

[8]Cited by Erickson, *Christian Theology*, 758.

[9]See also chap. 4, p. 1240. These "truths," to be sure, have been taught in other times and places, but the fact that Simpson experienced physical healing and had a crisis spiritual experience of the Holiness variety that he identified as "sanctification" led to these doctrines being elevated to touchstone status in the denomination.

[10]Erickson, *Christian Theology*, 83–84.

[11]A bit on the troubling side is that this whole presentation of levels of authority seems to be based on a Baconian/Common Sense assumption that the facts are pretheoretical and "out there" as objective information. As we saw in chapter 2, this is an inadequate conception of the reality of the situation. We are aware of the primarily narrative nature of the text and the difficulties that come in transforming narrative statements into theological assertions.

[12]Alister McGrath, *The Genesis of Doctrine* (Oxford: Blackwell, 1990), 35–80. The following is drawn from McGrath's discussion.

[13]See Romans 4–5; Galatians 3–5.

[14]McGrath, *Genesis of Doctrine*, 35–80.

[15]It is at this point particularly that we see the epistemological/philosophical substructure of the theologian affecting the gestalt of the doctrine articulated.

[16]McGrath, *Genesis of Doctrine*, 61.

[17]Ibid., 64.

[18]Ibid., 55.

[19]Ibid., 56.

[20]Ibid., 55.

[21]Charles Hodge, as representative of the Princetonian position, displayed a great antipathy toward any emphasis on the subjective nature of Christianity. At one point he said, "The idea that Christianity is a form of feeling, a life, and not a system of doctrines is contrary to the faith of all Christians. Christianity always has a creed. A man who believes certain doctrines is a Christian" ("Inspiration," *Biblical Repertory and Princeton Review* 29.4 [1857]:693).

[22]McGrath, *Genesis of Doctrine*, 66.

[23]Ibid., 66.

[24]See Sue Patterson, *Realist Christian Theology in a Post-Modern Age* (Cambridge: Cambridge University Press, 1999), 73–93. In this chapter entitled "The Anatomy of Language Riddenness," she explores the way in which language actually creates and shapes our world.

[25]McGrath, *Genesis of Doctrine*, 67–68.

[26]C. S. Lewis, *Weight of Glory and Other Addresses* (Grand Rapids: Eerdmans, 1949), 4–5.

[27]McGrath, *Genesis of Doctrine*, 69.

[28]See chap. 2.B.1.b. Thomas Kuhn's classic work, *The Structure of Scientific Revolutions*, deals at length with the interpretation of data and how it is given meaning within a framework. Only when data accumulate over a period of time that will not fit the framework do new understandings arise.

[29]McGrath, *Genesis of Doctrine*, 71.

[30]Ibid., 73.

[31]See M. James Sawyer, *Charles Augustus Briggs and Tensions in Late Nineteenth-Century American Theology* (Lewiston, NY: Mellen University Press, 1994), 27–33.

[32]Erickson, *Christian Theology*, 82–83.

[33]Ibid., 82.

[34]Vincent of Lerins, *The Commonitory*, 2:1–3, *Early Medieval Theology*, trans. and ed. George McCraken, Library of Christian Classics 9 (Philadelphia: Westminster, 1957), 37–39.

[35]See chap. 8.

[36]For an excellent discussion of the implications of Nestorianism, see C. FitzSimons Allison, *The Cruelty of Heresy* (Harrisburg, PA: Morehouse, 1994), 119–38.

[37]That is, if Christ did not assume a human mind, he could not heal that part of human nature by his incarnation and death.

[38]Allison, *Cruelty of Heresy*, 139–51.

[39]The difference between a creed and a confession is significant in that a creed is affirmed by all of Christendom, whereas a confession is limited to a particular tradition.

[40]See M. James Sawyer, "Evangelicals and the Canon of the New Testament," *Grace Journal of Theology* 11, no. 1 (1990).

[41]This section addresses the question of taxonomy from the perspective of the work of the exegete and is drawn from unpublished work done by Daniel B. Wallace. Grant Osborne also discusses this topic in *The Hermeneutical Spiral* (Downers Grove, IL: InterVarsity Press, 1991), 286–317.

[42]I am using the postmodern term "local narrative" here, not in the more conventional sense of geographically or culturally local, but in the sense of a theological system/tradition that conceptualizes Christianity in a peculiar fashion and that those within that tradition tend to globalize as the one right understanding.

[43]For the purposes of discussion, fringe groups and liberal Christianity are not in view here, since both of these groups actively deny crucial elements of the historic faith. Even noncreedal groups such as the Baptists agree with the doctrines taught by the ecumenical creeds while not generally accepting the authority of the creeds themselves.

[44]Osborne, *Hermeneutical Spiral*, 299–309.

[45]Ibid., 307.

[46]See Vern Poythress, *Symphonic Theology* (Grand Rapids: Zondervan, 1987), for an excellent discussion about issues surrounding system building and organizing principles.

[47]See Schaff, *Creeds of Christendom*, 1:3–11. Schaff's discussion focuses on the development of creeds in the life of the church. Systematic theology in this sense is a further extension of the theologizing found in the creeds of the church.

[48]See B. B Warfield, "The Idea of Systematic Theology," in *The Necessity of Systematic Theology*, ed. John Jefferson Davis (Grand Rapids: Baker, 1978), 137–67. Even as he insists on the objectivity of the facts of divine revelation, Warfield's whole argument hinges on the idea that theology is a science as are geology and other natural sciences. It is the work of humans to collect and organize the data and show the organic relationship of the data, integrating it into a concatenated whole. See also Poythress, *Symphonic Theology.* Poythress's argument is for the perspectival nature of human knowledge—a perspectivalism that extends even to biblical and theological study. Implicit in his argument is that human understanding is finite and limited; thus while there may be objective truth in the mind of God, humans cannot attain to it. Therefore no one system of theology can give us ultimate truth. All systems are incomplete.

OUTLINE OF CHAPTER 6

A. **Three Case Studies**
   1. Catholicism, Copernicus, and Galileo
   2. Warfield, the Princetonians, and the Nature of Biblical Inspiration
   3. Scientific Creationism
      a. Background
      b. The Rise of Scientific Creationism
      c. The Literal Hermeneutic
      d. Creationist Historiography
      e. The All-or-Nothing Mind-Set

B. **Implications**
   1. Knowledge, Orthodoxy, and Obscurantism
   2. Orthodoxy and Orthodoxism
   3. Extra-Confessional versus Contra-Confessional Belief

C. **Conclusion**

CHAPTER 6

HARDENING OF THE CATEGORIES: WHY THEOLOGIANS HAVE OPPOSED "NEW KNOWLEDGE"

> He told them this parable: "No one tears a patch from a new garment and sews it on an old one. If he does, he will have torn the new garment, and the patch from the new will not match the old. And no one pours new wine into old wineskins. If he does, the new wine will burst the skins, the wine will run out and the wineskins will be ruined. No, new wine must be poured into new wineskins. And no one after drinking old wine wants the new, for he says, 'The old is better.'"
>
> (Luke 5:36–39)

Jesus spoke these words with reference to his bringing God's more complete revelation of himself and to the salvation he was about to accomplish. But the final statement of the parable, "The old is better," embodies a profound truth about human nature and existence. Humanity is basically conservative in its outlook on life. Culture itself is a conservative force that keeps humans in touch with their heritage and provides a sense of identity, belonging, and stability. And when it comes to issues that involve God and things divine, especially eternal destinies, the conservative bent is all the stronger. This basic conservatism pulls against the call to bring all areas of knowledge under the lordship of Christ.

Evangelical theologian Michael Bauman has vividly described the state many (perhaps most) theologians fall into in their quest to lay hold of the whole counsel of God.

> Some theologians, however, being either unable or unwilling to pursue their quarry any further, become entrenched.... Rather than striking out in a new direction or pioneering uncharted territories in search of

> the doctrinal Northwest Passage, they hunker down and plant settlements in comfortable valleys, having decided at last that they will never reach the sea, or even continue to try. They have forgotten that, in this case, it is better to travel hopefully and never to arrive than to settle prematurely. To that extent, then, their theological settlements are a failure of nerve. Fatigue and uncertainty have made it seem more desirable to plant roots than to look around one more doctrinal bend or to climb up and peer over one more theological hill. The spirit of pioneering thus gives way to the spirit of dogmatism.
>
> Once a pioneer becomes a settler, he starts to build fences. Fences are soon replaced by walls and walls by forts. The pilgrimage has become a settlement, and those within the walls become suspicious of those without. Outsiders think differently, talk differently, act differently. To justify their suspicions, settlement theologians begin to think that they belong in doctrinal fortresses. They develop what I call the "Ebenezer doctrine." "Was it not the map of God—our Bibles—that led us here?" they ask. In one sense, of course, they are right. The Bible did in fact lead them this far. *But not the Bible only*.... Traveling mercies were exchanged for staying mercies. That is *because fortress theologians interpret the intellectual security they have erected for themselves as the blessing of God.* The perceived blessing of God becomes to them the perceived will of God. "Hitherto the Lord has led us" becomes not only their reason for staying, but also for fighting.... Those who settle elsewhere or not at all are perceived to militate against the truth of God. They must be stopped, the fortress dwellers believe.[1]

The situation described by Bauman is repeated over and over again in the history of theology. One of the three major Christian communions, Eastern Orthodoxy, is seemingly frozen in time. It has admitted no theological development since the death of John of Damascus in the eighth century. To attend an Orthodox service today is to be transported back in time nearly a millennium and a half. The liturgy is likely the same liturgy as that produced by John Chrysostom in the fifth century. In the minds of the Eastern Orthodox, "If it is new, it is heretical." There can be no such thing as doctrinal development. All that is left is to preserve the faith once delivered to the saints, and all who would advocate anything more or different are regarded as heretics.

We will look at three case studies that demonstrate the tendency for theological categories to become rigid and unyielding: The case of Galileo and the heliocentric worldview, the case of B. B. Warfield and the Princetonians in their understanding of biblical inspiration, and the case of the emergence of scientific creationism.

A. THREE CASE STUDIES

1. Catholicism, Copernicus, and Galileo

The struggles between Galileo Galilei and the Roman Catholic Church are legendary and form the foundation for the reputed hostility between theology and science. Galileo's condemnation by the church has been called the most notorious incident in the long history of the interaction between science and theology.[2]

Galileo

Italy was in turmoil during Galileo's lifetime. Rome had been sacked, the republic of Florence had collapsed, and Spain dominated most of the Italian peninsula. A majority had responded to the resulting loss of faith in the institutions by transferring their faith to the authority of the princes. During this period, the reigning theology was that of Thomas Aquinas, who had in the thirteenth century produced the great medieval synthesis, self-consciously utilizing the philosophy of Aristotle to answer the pressing questions of the day. The then dominant but decaying Augustinian synthesis was replaced by the new paradigm that incorporated elements of Augustine (with the accompanying Neoplatonism) but also employed the perspective of Aristotle to answer questions heretofore not even imagined.

The Council of Trent (1545–63) had formally adopted Thomism as the official position of the church. The newly adopted synthesis breathed life into the Counter-Reformation, which sought to meet the Protestant challenge. The Inquisition spawned by the Counter-Reformation sought to control the thought of Catholic Europe, even publishing the "Index," a list of books banned in Catholic lands. The early 1600s produced a wave of ideological condemnation. "Individuals and governors were considered subject to a single eternal system of justice based ultimately on eternal and divine law, of which the Catholic Church was the sole guardian and interpreter."[3]

In such an environment, innovation in any field was automatically suspect as being a potential threat to the system unless it could be shown to be otherwise. Galileo understood this and made every attempt to show that his discoveries were not contrary to the Scriptures or a threat to the ruling powers. Yet as the debate developed, Galileo was attacked on both scientific and theological grounds. In 1615, with trouble already brewing, Galileo wrote *A Letter to the Grand Duchess Christina*, setting forth his view of the relationship between science and theology. He had three essential points.

1. The issue had been brought before the Roman Church based on faulty premises.
2. Astronomical theories were not properly matters of faith.
3. The new cosmology was indeed in harmony with the Bible if the Bible was interpreted according to ordinary exegetical principles long employed by the church, even though these principles were at variance with Trent's literal emphasis.

Galileo insisted that his opponents argued fallaciously, appealing to the authority of the Bible but never understanding his arguments. He insisted that "The Holy Bible can never speak untruth—whenever its true meaning is understood."[4] But the meaning is not always to be found in a simple, literal surface reading of the text. The Bible uses figures of speech to communicate truth, and the Holy Spirit inspired such language "in order to accommodate them to the capacities of the common people, rude and unlearned as they are."[5] He boldly appealed to the "book of nature" as a revelation of God: "The Holy Bible and the phenomena of nature proceed alike from the Divine Word.... God is known ... by nature in His works, and by doctrine in His revealed word."[6]

Since nature is a genuine revelation of God, discussion of the physical universe ought to begin with *experience of the universe* and experiments drawn from nature, rather than with *exegetical conclusions* from Scripture. The purpose of the Bible is not scientific but salvific; therefore one would not expect the Bible to speak at length on physical or astronomical themes. Galileo's oft-quoted aphorism, "The Bible was given to teach us how to go to heaven not how the heavens go," was in fact a paraphrase of a statement by Cardinal Baronius! Galileo quoted Augustine, who warned against setting the authority of Scripture against clear and evident reason. He argued that the job of the exegete is to interpret the text of Scripture in its true sense that will ultimately be in accord with physical reality.

Concerning the language of Scripture, Galileo at one point argued that the biblical writers employ what would later be called phenomenological language. Conversely, he also argued that the scientist must provide "conclusive demonstration" of a position before the theologian must ask whether to interpret a statement of Scripture in a nonliteral fashion. But because of the different realm addressed, Scripture cannot be used against scientific statements demonstrated by the methods of science.

Despite this carefully reasoned position, Galileo's arguments were rejected. He was tried and convicted of heresy for claiming that the earth moved around the sun. The tribunal declared the Copernican system that Galileo used and the assumption that the earth moved "stupid and absurd philosophy." He was forbidden to teach the Copernican system as true.

Galileo had a brilliant and insightful mind. He tried to keep within the strictures laid on him by the church, but over the years he had accumulated numerous enemies in the academic establishment who had been stung by his conclusions. As Galileo began to publish again, his enemies took advantage of the works and twisted their meaning before the Inquisition. His later work, once approved for publication, was placed on the Index. He was again charged with heresy and eventually condemned and sentenced to prison. This sentence was in time commuted to house arrest.[7] The church had made an authoritative pronouncement on science that would haunt it for more than three hundred years.[8]

Galileo's crusade was not simply for acceptance of the Copernican system, but also to keep the church from making disputed scientific conclusions matters of faith. His goal was to keep science free from both theology and philosophy.[9]

Much more could be said here with reference to Galileo, but the point is that an interpretative community, in this case the Roman Catholic Church, had constructed a worldview that allowed no new insight.[10] That worldview, constructed in measure from Aristotelian philosophy, was wedded to divine revelation and the authority of the Bible and the church. But they did not realize what they were doing by making the theological construct simply truth to be believed and defended at all costs.

2. Warfield, the Princetonians, and the Nature of Biblical Inspiration

During the late nineteenth century, profound theological battles were waged within American Presbyterianism. For more than two hundred years, the Westminster Confession had stood as the touchstone of orthodoxy for those in the English-speaking Calvinistic/Reformed tradition. But during the last quarter of the nineteenth century there was increasing pressure to revisit the formulations of Westminster in light of the newly discovered insights into the nature of the Bible that were emerging from higher-critical methodology, as well as insights into the nature of the created order because of discoveries in the natural sciences, particularly in the biological sciences in the wake of Darwin. This impetus was met with profound opposition from the conservative forces within the Northern Presbyterian (PCUSA) denomination who were convinced that truth was one and that it was unchanging. These conservative forces were led by what is referred to as the Princetonians.

Princeton Seminary had a proud tradition as an untiring defender of historic Reformation orthodoxy, which it equated with biblical orthodoxy. At the fifty-year celebration of Charles Hodge's tenure as a professor at Princeton, Hodge made the claim that a new idea never originated at Princeton. While contemporary ears would hardly hear this claim as a ground for boasting, to the faithful within the Presbyterian tradition, it was an affirmation that Princeton held solidly to the faith with which it had been entrusted.

"To the Princeton mind, truth was objective and inviolable. There was no pressing need to discover new truths. The Princetonians saw their task not as discovering 'new truths' but as constantly applying existing truth, as elaborated in the Reformed creeds and scholastic dogmatic systems, to the specific new situations."[11]

As a result of the push for a new, simpler creed, battle lines were drawn. The conservative contingent was led by the Princetonians, particularly B. B. Warfield. For Warfield, Westminster represented the pinnacle of all theological knowledge, and all other systems of theology were inferior and threatened the truth codified by Westminster. Thus all other systems were fair targets of his criticism, whether it be the historic enemy of Reformed theology, Arminianism, or the newer, idealistic theology of Friedrich Schleiermacher and his followers, or some hybrid that attenuated the Calvinistic understanding of the nature of man and sin as did so many of the "perfectionistic" teachings on the Christian life that sprang up in the nineteenth century.

The opposition was centered at Union Seminary in New York. Union had been founded in the 1840s as a "new school" institution in response to Princeton's "old school" theology and had been theologically avant garde since its inception. Many Union professors studied in Germany, where they drank from the well of idealism and higher critical thought. It would be a mistake to think of Union Seminary as "liberal" in the formal sense of the term (as defined in chapter 14 on liberalism). They were not necessarily liberal in theology but rather in spirit and outlook. They did not hold rigidly and defensively to the Westminster Confession as the Princetonians did. They tended to be open-minded and willing to examine the flow of new theological currents and incorporate into their own perspectives what they saw as valid. Particularly, higher critical thought took root at Union Seminary, and one of its most ardent propagators was Old Testament professor Charles A. Briggs. For nearly fifteen years an uneasy truce existed between Princeton and Union.

During the 1880s, they even had a joint publication, *The Presbyterian Review*, edited by a representative from Princeton, first A. A. Hodge and finally Warfield, with Briggs as the representative from Union. While the journal had been envisioned as a means of promoting understanding between the antagonistic faculties, its history proved something very different. Early in the life of the journal, Hodge recognized that the question of biblical criticism and the doctrine of inerrancy were at the center of the denomination's theological attention. Hodge and Briggs agreed to a series of articles on the subject of biblical criticism with each article being penned alternately by a representative of the Princeton and then the Union faculty. The first article in this series, "Inspiration," was jointly written by Hodge and Warfield. This article became the foundation for the twentieth-century understanding of the doctrine of inerrancy. Briggs responded in the following issue with an article entitled "Critical Theories of Sacred Scriptures in Relation to Their Inspiration."[12]

Charles Augustus Briggs

Briggs remained a thorn in the side of the conservatives, and tensions between the two parties increased. A decade later Briggs was transferred to the newly endowed Edward Robinson Chair of Biblical Theology at Union Seminary. Briggs's inaugural address became the focal point of conservative attention and consternation. The tone of the address was what made it appear to be a declaration of war on the conservative forces, and the conservative forces responded with six charges of heresy,[13] drawn up by Warfield himself. All but one involved biblical inspiration and authority. The New York presbytery dismissed the charges. The denomination insisted Briggs be tried, and as a result, Briggs was tried for heresy and acquitted. The prosecution then appealed the verdict to the General Assembly in 1893, which convicted Briggs and defrocked him.

For the purposes of this discussion, the issue is not whether Briggs's position was heretical or not. Rather, the issue is the mind-set of the conservatives. During the controversy, significant doctrinal defining and tightening were going on within the conservative camp. As noted above, a decade before the heresy trial, A. A. Hodge, one of the architects of the modern doctrine of inerrancy, indicated that while he disagreed with Briggs's position on biblical infallibility, he recognized that Briggs's position fell within the scope of the wording of the Westminster Confession. This notwithstanding, the doctrine of inerrancy was perceived as being so central to the Christian faith and historic Reformed orthodoxy that in 1892 the PCUSA adopted the "Portland Deliverance," which became the official interpretation of the Westminster Confession's statement on biblical authority, and insisted that all ordained into the Presbyterian ministry agree to the new tighter terms of subscription.[14]

The conviction of Briggs on heresy charges was followed by the conviction of several others, while yet others, rather than stand trial, withdrew from the denomination. In the short run, it appeared that the conservative forces had staved off theological liberalism within the denomination. But the reality was something else again. The issues that drove the nontraditionalists did not go away. In 1909 the Auburn Affirmation was adopted. It was a theological manifesto by the nonconservative forces, by now far to the left theologically of those convicted of heresy in the 1890s. The demands for change were again clamoring within the denomination. Ultimately the conservative forces led by Princeton lost the battle as they were overwhelmed by the rising tide of new perspectives, and the Northern Presbyterian Church drifted from its Reformed roots.

3. Scientific Creationism

The mid-to-late twentieth century saw the rise of a controversy that in many ways parallels the Roman Catholic Church's seventeenth-century confrontation with Galileo. This time, however, the antagonist in the controversy is not a long-established tradition with official conciliar church sanction. Rather, it is a position that is out of harmony with historic Protestantism and propagated by those of an essentially fundamentalist persuasion: scientific creationism. The term as used by its adherents does not simply have reference to God as the ultimate creator of all who may have used various means to accomplish his creative activity. Rather, as they normally use it, the term refers to a literal surface reading of the text of Genesis 1 through the eyes of Baconian inductivism to conclude that the earth was created recently (on the scale of thousands of years ago) and in six literal, twenty-four-hour days, rather than in the ancient past (billions of years ago). While having no historic formal authority, those espousing the scientific creationist position have spread their doctrine as the only orthodox Christian position, so that in a majority of evangelical and fundamental churches, the average layperson has no idea that any other position is held by evangelical scholars and theologians.

a. Background

While it is common to assume that Darwin's theory of biological evolution was met with immediate and implacable hostility from the conservative Christian community, such is simply not the case. When his theory of biological evolution was put forth, many conservative evangelical Christians, including scientists, exegetes, and theologians, far from universally decrying Darwinism as simply atheism,[15] saw the hypothesis as a viable explanation of the means God may have used to accomplish his task of creation.[16]

Evangelical science during the nineteenth century followed in the footsteps of the Reformers and Puritans. It saw two books of divine revelation, the written word—the Scriptures—and the book of nature, discovered by scientific inquiry. Since God was the author of both books, it was impossible for the two to be in conflict. While the Bible provided the overarching framework for interpreting life and creation, this book of nature informed the theologians and biblical interpreters in their labors and conclusions.[17]

As early as 1812, Archibald Alexander, the first professor of Princeton Seminary, declared in his inaugural address, "Natural history, chemistry, and geology have sometimes been of important *service assisting the Biblical student to solve difficulties contained in Scripture*; or in enabling him to repel the assaults of adversaries which were made under the cover of these sciences."[18] Charles Hodge took the arguments even further in his journal, the *Biblical Repository and Princeton Review.* An 1863 article by Joseph Clark, a conservative Presbyterian, recognized the necessity for the Christian scientist to pursue inductive conclusions without precommitments to the "teachings" thought to be found in the Scriptures. Clark argued that earlier Christians had concluded that the Bible taught a "flat earth" and that this interpretation had been abandoned in light of scientific discovery.[19] Importantly, he insisted that this kind of adjustment in no way undermined the authority of Scripture or its divine inspiration.[20] While not all agreed with Clark and he received criticism even in the press, Hodge was even more adamant in a response to criticism of Clark's position.

> Nature is as truly a revelation of God as the Bible; and we only interpret the Word of God by the Word of God when we interpret the Bible by science. As this principle is undeniably true, it is admitted and acted on by those who, through inattention to the meaning of terms, in words deny it. When the Bible speaks of the foundations, or pillars of the earth, or of the solid heavens, or the motion of the sun, do not you and every other sane man, interpret this language by the facts of science?... Shall we go on to interpret the Bible so as to make it teach the falsehood that the sun moves around the earth, or shall we interpret it by science, and make the two harmonize?[21]

A host of evangelical scientists and theologians adopted the position advocated by Hodge, yet they by no means agreed with one another on specific issues. Despite heated disagreements, however, there was a common understanding that proper biblical interpretation and theology could not be done without input from the best scientific findings available.[22]

Yet with the rise of fundamentalism early in the twentieth century, the presupposition of the necessity of scientific input and assistance in proper biblical interpretation was sacrificed on the altar of biblical authority. It was within the context of fundamentalism that the Reformation credo of *sola scriptura* was transformed into *nuda scriptura*.[23]

b. The Rise of Scientific Creationism

The roots of modern creation science in America[24] are to be found in the teachings of George McCready Price, a Seventh-day Adventist who in 1923 published *The New Geology*, arguing that a simple "literal" reading of the book of Genesis revealed that God created the cosmos in six literal twenty-four-hour days between six and eight thousand years ago. The present state of the earth was to be explained by a worldwide flood in the time of Noah. This book at first had little influence outside Adventist circles. But in the early 1940s, some "flood geologists" began to promote their agenda, without measurable success.

Then, in the late 1950s, John C. Whitcomb, Old Testament professor at Grace Seminary in Winona Lake, Indiana, and Henry M. Morris, a hydraulic engineer, both reacted negatively to Bernard Ramm's landmark book *The Christian View of Science and Scripture* (Eerdmans, 1954). In this work, Ramm confronted the fundamentalists' naive Baconian hermeneutics and their failure to read the Scriptures in light of their historical and cultural background. Whitcomb and Morris joined forces to pen *The Genesis Flood* (1961), in which they adopted Price's logic and argumentation wholesale but gave it a much more sophisticated theological and scientific expression. The book was an immediate success and then spawned over the years the Creation Research Society, the Institute for Creation Research, and other organizations committed to the position in the United States and Great Britain.

c. The Literal Hermeneutic

Streams of Enlightenment Thinking

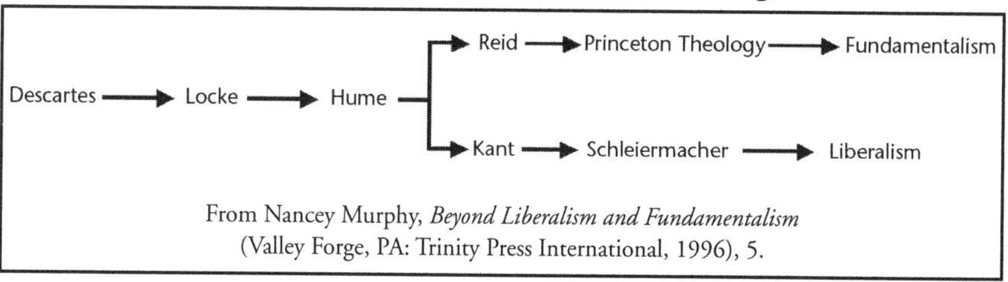

From Nancey Murphy, *Beyond Liberalism and Fundamentalism* (Valley Forge, PA: Trinity Press International, 1996), 5.

FIGURE 6.1.

Foundational to the program of conservative evangelical and fundamentalist Christianity in the nineteenth and twentieth centuries has been the commitment to the literal truth of the Bible. The particular cast of this assumption, while arising out of a rejection of the Enlightenment program, is paradoxically also itself a product of the Enlightenment, particularly the philosophical and epistemological work of Thomas Reid and Common Sense philosophy. While most analyses of the Enlightenment trace its development from Descartes down through Hume to Kant, few recognize that there was an intellectual bifurcation in the reaction to Hume's skepticism. The major stream followed Kant and his phenomenology, but another, smaller but still significant stream followed Scottish philosopher Thomas Reid, who responded to Hume with a view of reality based on a naively realistic epistemology that came to be known as Common Sense or Scottish Common Sense. It was this Common Sense understanding of reality that formed the warp and woof of the fabric of the American psyche from the late 1700s until it was overwhelmed by the changes in the world a century later. It was Common Sense that gave Americans their no-nonsense practical view of reality.

It was also Common Sense that gave nineteenth-century evangelicalism its mind-set that the Bible could be approached and known apart from historical and literary context. It was not a book for scholars but a book for the people. R. A. Torrey summed up this approach to the Scriptures: "In ninety-nine out of one hundred cases, the meaning that the plain man gets out of the Bible is the correct one."[25] Another aphorism concerning literal interpretation commonly heard stated, "If the plain sense makes sense, seek no other sense."

The presupposition of the literal truth of the Bible led to corollaries. Among the most important was the doctrine of the perspicuity of Scripture. This doctrine had arisen during the Reformation, and its sense had always been that the salvific message of the Bible is clear enough even for a child to grasp. However, coupled with this clarity was the recognition of depth of meaning within the text, a depth that could not be plumbed even by the most learned scholar. However, when applied under the influence of Common Sense, the Bible was democratized and opened for all men and women to interpret it independently of any tradition, history, scholarship, or literary context.

Thomas Reid

When it came to the issue of science, from the seventeenth century onward, Protestant Christians sought to demonstrate that science and the Bible were in harmony and that Christianity was truly scientific. As we read the nineteenth-century apologists, we find them operating under Baconian principles of induction from the "facts." Let the facts speak for themselves, apart from any speculative theory.

The explosion of scientific knowledge in the late nineteenth and early twentieth centuries, however, placed a strain on the relationship between the Bible (interpreted through Baconian lenses) and science. The harmony seen in earlier centuries was seemingly shattered. Nevertheless, many believers still held to the assumption that, contrary to prevailing opinion, science, properly done, supported the Scriptures. But this support was a one-way street. Science was only valid if it supported the received interpretation of the Scriptures. It was not an aid to comprehending and nuancing scriptural understanding. Scripture stood supreme over and against science and reason. When the two came into conflict, trust had to be placed in the Bible. Henry Morris made this clear in his 1946 work, *That You May Believe*. He asserted that he would accept the Bible "even against reason if need be."[26]

The nature of the Bible was understood to be truth, absolute divine truth that was not dependent on genre, context, or original audience. The Bible was to be interpreted in a Common Sense fashion, because it "in no way does violence to common sense and intelligence."[27] Morris, with his engineer's mind, particularly applied this Common Sense hermeneutic to the Scripture and found scientific truths that had lain hidden in the text for millennia. Such truths as "the stars cannot be numbered" and the hydrological cycle were deduced from allusions in the Psalms and put forth as evidence of the Scripture's scientific accuracy.[28]

It must be noted that the Common Sense worldview that dominated fundamentalism provided fertile soil for creation science to take root and flourish.[29] The fundamentalist heritage of American evangelicalism made the straightforward interpretation of the biblical text vis-à-vis origins an attractive option, and major evangelical seminaries and Bible colleges were increasingly found to support the particular version of origins espoused by creation science.

d. Creationist Historiography

David Livingston has observed, "The way in which any group deals with the burden of its history—whether casually dismissing it, slavishly guarding it, or capriciously manipulating it—reveals much about the way it perceives itself."[30]

Some creation scientists have dealt with opponents of their position by calling into question the legitimacy of their evangelical conviction. The treatment of Asa Gray, a nineteenth-century evangelical botanist and Harvard professor, at the hands of Bolton Davidheiser is instructive here. Davidheiser, making the standard of evangelical Christianity a rejection of evolution, observes of Gray, "It turns out that Asa Gray is a very questionable example of an evangelical Christian. But he is a good example of a person who has a Christian testimony and who is used by the evolutionists to influence other Christians to accept the theory of evolution."[31] Davidheiser dealt similarly with conservative Scottish Presbyterian theologian James Orr.

> Dr. Orr ... seems to have been convinced that the scientists had proved evolution to be true and that he had to do the best he could with it. He should not have capitulated so easily, and if he had not, he could easily have shown that the theory of evolution and the Bible are incompatible.... The espousal of the theory of evolution leads to compromises which in turn lead to liberalism, modernism and a repudiation of the gospel.[32]

Henry Morris goes further than Davidheiser and characterizes people such as Orr, Warfield, and A. H. Strong as part of a "chronicle of pervasive theological apostasy."[33] He even accuses Augustine, father of all Western theology, of representing the "old compromising types of exegesis used by the early theologians."[34]

Thus the proponents of creation science have to a greater or lesser degree successfully rewritten history to give the impression that their version of origins is the version that has always characterized evangelicalism.

e. The All-or-Nothing Mind-Set

Although this discussion has not focused on evolution, that concept represents the fear at the heart of creation science. Creation science adherents believe that the only options are (1) a six-day literal creation by the transcendent and almighty God as presented in Genesis, or (2) materialistic evolution. To admit any degree of evolution even under the direct control of God is to give away the store; no variation in understanding can be tolerated.

- - -

Again we see among the conservative mainstream an opposition to new discoveries, learning, and knowledge. These cases have been set forth as anecdotal examples of a tendency that is present in each person who studies theology. That tendency is to identify our own understanding of the truth with the truth itself and cling to the fear that reality itself will come unraveled if we change our position or open our minds to new perspectives.

B. IMPLICATIONS

1. Knowledge, Orthodoxy, and Obscurantism

Bernard Ramm, in his work *After Fundamentalism*, observed that the Enlightenment was an intellectual watershed for theology. Liberal theology capitulated to the Enlightenment and lost its message as anything distinctively Christian. In contrast to the liberal acceptance of the Enlightenment program, conservative theology rejected the Enlightenment but in that rejection became obscurantist.[35] While the issue is a bit more complex than Ramm implies,[36] the basic observation is on the whole accurate.

Obscurantism is defined as a rejection of, or opposition to, intellectual advancement. The question becomes, "Is refusal to admit new insight and perspectives in one's understanding obscurantist?" Oxford professor Charles A. Whittuck contends that obscurantism is a primary temptation for those of religious conviction if for no other reason than that it is found more in religion than anywhere else.[37] The term was used during the Renaissance of those who opposed the new learning and during the nineteenth century in

Catholicism of those who desired to preserve the medieval Roman Catholic Church unchanged. From a social perspective, some of the extremely conservative Mennonite communities, such as the Amish, could be considered obscurantist on the face of it. While not Christian, the phenomenon of Muslim fundamentalism provides a striking example of an obscurantism that militantly rejects the modern world. I could cite numerous other examples of groups whose obscurantism, while not so blatantly obvious as those just noted, casts a profoundly pervasive, intellectually smothering effect. The tongue-in-cheek adage, "I know what I believe; don't confuse me with the facts," describes in a nutshell the obscurantist mentality.

The Enlightenment brought a profound and massive shift in the understanding of the way knowledge is obtained. The model for knowledge became the scientific method with its insistence on critical examination to verify received knowledge to see if it met the requirements of public evidence (as opposed to nonpublicly verifiable knowledge based on the authority of, for example, the church or the Bible) to be accepted as truth. The emphasis on modern knowledge does not imply that the conclusions are right; rather, the focus is on a *methodology* by which knowledge is obtained and verified. Modern learning involves the scientific method and critical inquiry that looks for evidence rather than relying on tradition and/or credulity.

Obscurantism involves a denial of modern learning/critical inquiry. It is the attitude that characterizes those who believe that the modern world and its methods of knowledge as well as its conclusions threaten their beliefs. In either its secular or religious form, it is characterized by three factors:

1. It is *selective* in that the obscurantist lives in a technological society that can neither be denied nor ignored. The obscurantist must select elements that he or she accepts in order to live in the contemporary world.
2. It is *hypocritical* in that the obscurantist uses technological discoveries and inventions to promote obscurantist beliefs.
3. It is *systematic*. At any point where a contemporary understanding may undermine an obscurantist position, the modern learning is denied.[38]

The charge of obscurantism against fundamentalism and evangelicalism is perhaps given some legitimacy in that in the wake of the fundamentalist-modernist controversy early in the twentieth century, fundamentalists withdrew from the larger world of theology and separated themselves from the "spiritual apostasy" of the "liberals."[39] The literature produced by the fundamentalists and early evangelicals gained no hearing outside the evangelical-fundamentalist arena, not primarily because it espoused historic orthodox conclusions, but because it did not use critical methodology to sustain its conclusions.[40]

2. Orthodoxy and Orthodoxism

Over a century ago, Charles Briggs made a distinction between true and false orthodoxy. He gave the label *orthodoxism* to a form of orthodoxy that "assumes to know the truth and is unwilling to learn; it is haughty and arrogant assuming to itself the divine prerogatives of infallibility and inerrancy; it hates all truth that is unfamiliar to it and persecutes it to the uttermost."[41] By contrast, he contended, orthodoxy

> loves the truth. It is ever anxious to learn, for it knows how greatly the truth of God transcends human knowledge. It follows truth, as Ruth did Naomi, wherever it leads. It is meek, lowly, and reverent. It is full of charity and love. It does not recognize an infallible pope. It does not recognize an infallible theologian. It has only one teacher and master—the enthroned Savior, Jesus Christ—and expects to be guided by His Spirit into all truth.[42]

Briggs asserted that no one is totally orthodox save God alone. All human understanding involves some degree of heterodoxy.

This understanding did not, however, open the door for subjectivism, with each person determining truth for himself or herself.

> There must be some objective standard, some comprehensive statement by which the relative orthodoxy of man may be estimated and measured. The absolute standard of human orthodoxy is the sum total of truth revealed by God. God reveals truth in several spheres; in universal nature, in the constitution of mankind, in the history of our race, and in the sacred Scriptures, but above all in the person of Jesus Christ our Lord.
>
> If a man has mastered this entire revelation of the truth, all that science, philosophy, history and the sacred Scriptures and Jesus Christ can give him, then and only then, he may claim to be entirely orthodox.[43]

Until the time that such a condition might be achieved, the orthodoxy of any person will be incomplete. The refusal to learn and accept and appropriate growing understanding from all of God's revelation renders an individual heterodox, because that person has rejected truth gleaned from God's revelation.

> Any man or church that refuses to accept the discoveries of science or the truths of philosophy or the facts of history, or the new light that breaks forth from the Word of God to the devout student, on the pretense that it conflicts with his orthodoxy or the orthodoxy of the standards of his church, prefers the traditions of man to the truth of God, has become unfaithful to the calling and aims of the Christian disciple, has left the companionship of Jesus and His apostles and has joined the Pharisees, the enemies of truth.... *A traditional attitude of mind is one of the worst foes to orthodoxy.*[44]

> "No one is totally orthodox save God alone."
> —C. A. BRIGGS

It might seem easy to reject Briggs's assertions as the conclusions of a heretic, but the true picture is actually much more complex. First, Briggs's words have over the past century been echoed by numerous evangelical scholars and theologians who have no taint of heresy in their past. Second, within a decade of Briggs's conviction of heresy by the Northern Presbyterian Church, members of the prosecuting committee were hailing Briggs as a defender of the faith—a strange situation to say the least.[45] What in fact happened is that, in the decade following Briggs's conviction of heresy, the focus of theological debate shifted from the doctrine of inspiration and inerrancy to the doctrine of Christology and the virgin birth. While Briggs rejected inerrancy, he was an ardent supporter of historic Christology and regularly defended the doctrine of the virgin birth in print and in debate.

3. Extra-Confessional versus Contra-Confessional Belief

When we speak of orthodoxy and heresy, we divide all theological knowledge into two camps: that which is true and that which is false. This type of division, while common, is both simplistic and misleading and, in fact, seriously distorts the issues under discussion.

First, we must examine the nature of orthodoxy. Simply defined it means a "right belief." But right according to what standard? Therein lies the rub. If we are to use the word with any degree of integrity, *orthodoxy* must mean something broader than "What I was always taught." What is that broader meaning? Evangelicals, particularly those of a Baptist persuasion, often insist that there be no creed but the Bible. But here again we fall into the same problem: the Bible as interpreted by whom? So the standard of orthodoxy must be narrower than a general affirmation of the teachings of the Bible. We find ourselves looking at the historic faith of the church as a touchstone of what is genuinely Christian and therefore orthodox teaching, and what is not. The place where this teaching is distilled is in the historic creeds of the church.

Another issue arises here—what about a belief that has not been addressed in the historical articulation of the faith? We might call this extra-creedal or extra-confessional belief. Is it permissible for someone to hold and teach beliefs that have not been addressed in the creeds of traditional confessions? Would not such a teaching in and of itself be heretical? Not necessarily. The issue here is not the novelty of a position—that is, that the teaching has never been articulated before, or at least not in the form one now finds it. The issue is whether the teaching conflicts with the received body of truth as expressed in the consensus of the historic creeds. Under this definition much that is called heresy does not fit the formal criteria.

Another twist in this discussion is how we apply the charge of heresy. While one definition given by *Merriam-Webster's Collegiate Dictionary*—"an opinion, doctrine, or practice contrary to the truth or to generally accepted beliefs or standards"[46]—is perhaps the operative definition for most people when they invoke the charge, this definition is too general to be of any value in theological discussions. The definition relevant at this juncture is "adherence to a religious opinion contrary to church dogma."[47] To develop this a bit further, for one to be considered a heretic, one must as a member of a particular Christian communion hold a view, practice, or belief contrary to the dogma of the communion *to which one belongs*.

The case of Charles Briggs provides a good example here. Briggs was adjudged to be a heretic in the Northern Presbyterian Church for his denial of the doctrine of inerrancy. After he was expelled from that church, he joined the Episcopal Church, a communion that did not formally and officially embrace the doctrine of inerrancy. As a member of the Episcopal Church, Briggs could not be considered a heretic.

To put this another way, heresy is an internal judgment applicable to those within a communion and based on the doctrinal commitment of that particular communion. For a Protestant to accuse a Roman Catholic or an Orthodox Christian of heresy because of his or her understanding of the nature of justification is to misunderstand the nature of heresy. Roman Catholics and the Orthodox have never subscribed to the Protestant understanding of justification; nor have they ever dogmatically been subject to creedal statements that spell out the Protestant understanding of justification.

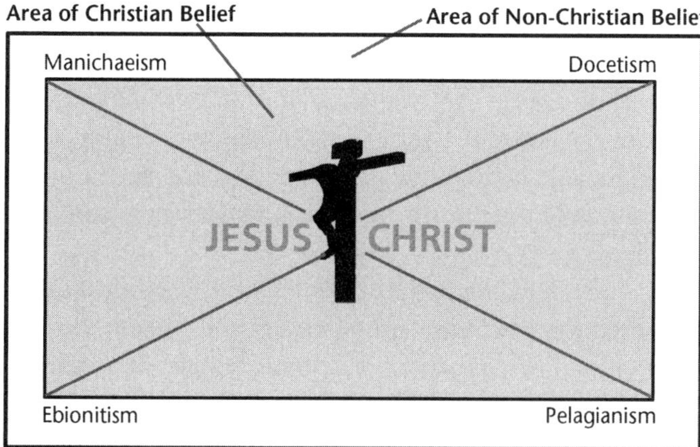

FIGURE 6.2.

Alister McGrath has suggested that ultimately heresy must involve a denial of the person and/or work of Jesus Christ.[48] The ancient heresies did just this. Christianity is centered around the redemptive work of Jesus Christ on the cross. Any teaching that compromises the integrity of the person of Jesus Christ in his deity or in his humanity, or any position that compromises the necessity or the possibility of the salvation of humanity is a fundamental error, which, if allowed to stand, would compromise the very fabric of the faith itself and reduce Christianity to little more than a philosophy rather than a faith involving divine redemption.

Jude commands that believers contend for the faith *once* delivered to the saints (v. 3). That faith, however, was not the theology of the Protestant Reformation, Lutheran or Reformed; nor was it Baptist, Roman Catholic, or Orthodox. Perhaps the earliest formal systematic expression of the faith we have is Irenaeus's *Demonstration of the Apostolic Preaching* (c. A.D. 200). A quick perusal of that work reveals how simple yet sophisticated the apostolic kerygma is. That faith was what C. S. Lewis called "mere Christianity." The *form* that that Christianity takes in a particular place and time changes, but the substance must remain. The new need not, and must not, be feared if it does not compromise the essence of the faith, a faith centered on the person and work of Jesus Christ. Orthodoxy, right belief, is based on knowledge—knowledge of God, his Word, and his creation. Orthodoxy must be progressive, adapting to meet the challenges it faces, rather than defensive, frozen in time and perspective, and no longer able to speak to the world in which it finds itself.

C. CONCLUSION

Controversy has often surrounded theological change. We have seen anecdotally that the approach to new ideas and doctrines is often one of reaction and rejection based on appeal to a traditional authority structure rather than an engagement of the issues at hand. While it is not my purpose to *prove* this cannot work, I would contend that in a world where there is public access to knowledge, it simply does not work. This approach may win the battle, but it will lose the war.

Another strategy, marketing, has been used by scientific creationists. They have interpreted the Scriptures simplistically and broken the argument for recent creationism down into an oppositional framework, admitting only two mutually exclusive extremes. This is naive at best, but I would argue that this strategy is motivated by fear and involves patent intellectual dishonesty, ad hoc argumentation, and intellectual special pleading that would never gain a hearing in any debate where the laws of logic and rules of evidence are applied.

In each case presented, there has been a precommitment to a philosophical system that has led to an unrecognized and unacknowledged contextualization of the message. In the case of Galileo, that contextualization came through the melding of the Bible and Christianity with Aristotelian philosophy. In the case of the Northern Presbyterians (in their opposition to Briggs) and the scientific creationists, that contextualization involved an uncritical acceptance of Baconian inductivism and Scottish Common Sense as the basis of their worldview. In each case an uncritical philosophical/epistemological precommitment blinded the members of the community to other possibilities and threatened the very existence of the community as it perceived itself.

A key quality that any good theologian must develop is an ability to recognize a disjuncture between truth and one's own understanding of that truth. The theologian must become self-critical and critically aware of his or her own presuppositions. The failure to recognize this simple fact has led to no end of mischief and brought great shame and dishonor on the church of Jesus Christ as battles have been waged, not over the truth itself, but over parochial understandings of truth.

BIBLIOGRAPHY

Bauman, Michael. *Pilgrim Theology*. Grand Rapids: Zondervan, 1992. • **Hummel, Charles.** *The Galileo Connection*. Downers Grove, IL: InterVarsity

Press, 1986. • **Livingston, David.** *Darwin's Forgotten Defenders.* Grand Rapids: Eerdmans, 1987. • **Marsden, George.** *Understanding Fundamentalism and Evangelicalism.* Grand Rapids: Eerdmans, 1994. • **Murphy, Nancey.** *Beyond Liberalism and Fundamentalism.* Valley Forge, PA: Trinity Press International, 1996. • **Noll, Mark.** *The Scandal of the Evangelical Mind.* Grand Rapids: Eerdmans, 1994. • **Numbers, Ronald.** *The Creationists.* Berkeley: University of California Press, 1992. • **Ramm, Bernard.** *After Fundamentalism.* San Francisco: Harper & Row, 1983. • **Sawyer, M. James.** *Charles Augustus Briggs and Tensions in Late Nineteenth-Century American Theology.* Lewiston, NY: Mellen University Press, 1994.

NOTES

[1]Michael Bauman, *Pilgrim Theology* (Grand Rapids: Zondervan, 1992), 20–21, italics added.

[2]Charles E. Hummel, *The Galileo Connection* (Downers Grove, IL: InterVarsity Press, 1986), 103. Much of the following discussion is drawn from pp. 103ff.

[3]William R. Shea, "Galileo and the Church," in David C. Lindburg and Ronald L. Numbers, eds., *God and Nature.* Quoted by Hummel, *Galileo Connection,* 104.

[4]Hummel, *Galileo Connection*, 105.

[5]Ibid.

[6]Ibid.

[7]For a good summary of the debate and the eventual condemnation of Galileo, see Hummel, *Galileo Connection*, 103–25.

[8]It was not until the 1990s that the Roman Catholic Church formally admitted the errors of Galileo's judges.

[9]The account of Galileo heroically struggling against the entrenched hierarchy has often been told in such a way as to leave the impression Galileo was simply an honest seeker of truth against the ignorant entrenched hierarchy. This view is at the very least simplistic, at worst a gross caricature of the situation. Galileo himself, although brilliant, was vain and self-seeking, wickedly mocking his opponents and alienating his supporters. The prosecution of Galileo was probably motivated more by the personal vindictiveness and hatred of his opponents than by theological conviction; nevertheless, on the formal level, the authority of the church versus the authority of the emerging scientific method was an issue. See Thomas Schirrmacher, "The Galileo Affair: History or Heroic Hagiography?" *Creation Ex Nihilo Technical Journal* 14, no. 1 (2000): 91–100, *www.geocities.com/Athens/5948/Galileo.pdf.*

[10]It would be a mistake to infer that no one in the Roman Catholic Church other than Galileo questioned or had doubts about the accepted synthesis. It has been demonstrated that many Catholics did. But as an institution, the church appealed to the authority of the dogmatized Thomistic synthesis.

[11]Kim Riddlebarger, "Fire and Water: A Princeton Apologist Still Helps Us See Why Calvinism and Arminianism Simply Don't Mix," *Modern Reformation Review* (May/June 1992): 8–10.

[12]Charles A. Briggs, "Critical Theories of Sacred Scriptures in Relation to Their Inspiration," *The Presbyterian Review* 2 (1881): 550–79.

[13]For a full account of Briggs's life, see Max Gray Rogers, "Charles Augustus Briggs: Conservative Heretic" (Ph.D. diss., Columbia University, 1965), University Microfilms.

[14]This practice had been employed at least once before, after the Civil War. At that time, Charles Hodge had vociferously objected to the illegality and immorality of the practice of after-the-fact changing of the rules of subscription. He moreover denied that a general assembly had the power to tighten the terms of subscription to the received creed (*The Rights of Presbyteries Not to Be Annulled by Any Assumed Authority of the General Assembly: Their Relations to Each Other Defined by Dr. Hodge in the Princeton Review* [New York: Anson D. F. Randolf & Co., 1896]; reprint of the original article, which appeared in the *Princeton Review* in July 1865).

[15]This was the conclusion of Charles Hodge from a philosophical perspective, but his successors at Princeton, particularly B. B. Warfield, the architect of the modern doctrine of inerrancy, disagreed and saw evolution as a means by which God had brought creation to its present state.

[16]David Livingston's *Darwin's Forgotten Defenders* (Grand Rapids: Eerdmans, 1987) is an admirable study documenting the support for Darwin's theory among even the Princetonians.

[17]Mark Noll, *The Scandal of the Evangelical Mind* (Grand Rapids: Eerdmans, 1994), 182.

[18]Ibid., italics added.

[19]In point of fact, the "flat earth" understanding was never widely held by Christians. This was a caricature propagated by the opponents of Christianity in favor of the emerging science (Jeffrey Burton Russell, "The Myth of the Flat Earth," for the American Scientific Affiliation Conference, August 4, 1997, at Westmont College [*id-www.ucsb.edu/fscf/library/RUSSELL/FlatEarth.html*]). The fact that as early as 1863 this myth was accepted as true in the conservative Christian community is very telling as to how rapidly it made its way into the popular psyche.

[20]Hodge defended the position taken by Clark, saying that it was all but self-evident that the tested conclusions of the scientific enterprise should be brought to bear in the interpretation of Scripture.

[21]Charles Hodge, "The Bible and Science," *New York Observer*, March 26, 1863, 98–99. Quoted in Noll, *Scandal*, 183–84.

[22]Ibid., 185.

[23]*Sola scriptura* had from its inception meant that the Bible was the final authority in matters of faith and practice. Fundamentalism, sometimes implicitly, sometimes explicitly, made Scripture the only authority. And in some cases, it taught that the Bible was over and against *all* human authorities and wisdom, especially the pronouncements of science.

[24]Christians have held a literal understanding of the Genesis account for centuries. While there were in Britain "scriptural geologists" who held a version of what might be termed "scientific creationism" in the early nineteenth century, the twentieth-century adoption of this position has not been tied to the earlier British understanding.

[25]Cited by George Marsden in *Understanding Fundamentalism and Evangelicalism* (Grand Rapids: Eerdmans, 1991), 165.

[26]Henry M. Morris, *That You Might Believe* (Chicago: Good Books, 1946), 4. Quoted by George Marsden in *Understanding Fundamentalism and Evangelicalism*, 163.

[27]Ibid.

[28]In some Islamic circles, similar arguments are used to prove that the Qur'an is divinely inspired and scientifically accurate. These include, among others, arguments in the areas of human embryonic development, the origin of the universe, and the cerebrum. Reading these arguments in support of the Qur'an makes us aware to what extent this approach (Muslim as well as Christian) smuggles in all kinds of precommitments and assumptions without which the arguments simply fail to convince or prove the intended point. This information can be found in *A Brief Illustrated Guide to Understanding Islam*, a seventy-six-page book that can be purchased or downloaded free of charge at *www.islam-guide.com*.

[29]See Noll, *Scandal*, 123–45, for an excellent description of the intellectual character of evangelicalism.

[30]David N. Livingston, *Darwin's Forgotten Defenders* (Grand Rapids: Eerdmans, 1987), 170. Much of the following discussion is drawn from Livingston.

[31]Bolton Davidheiser, *Evolution and the Christian Faith* (Nutley, N.J.: Presbyterian and Reformed, 1969), 80.

[32]Ibid., 38–39.

[33]Henry Morris, *History of Modern Creationism* (San Diego: Master Book, 1984), 39.

[34]Ibid., 37.

[35]As the intellectual ethos of society has moved into the postmodern era, the Enlightenment has become an intellectual whipping boy in much the same manner as the medieval era was for the Renaissance. Yet, for all the faults and hubris of the Enlightenment agenda, its program also advanced human knowledge of the world in a manner heretofore unimagined. The Enlightenment agenda set the stage for the modern world, and even the advent of postmodernism has not nullified its legitimate insights.

[36]Nancey Murphy has observed that there was a split in the Enlightenment tradition following David Hume. The major portion of intellectual development followed Immanuel Kant's phenomenology, while a significant but smaller stream followed Thomas Reid's Common Sense. So from an epistemological perspective, conservative theology also fell under the influence of Enlightenment ways of thought (*Beyond Liberalism and Fundamentalism*, 4–7).

[37]Charles A. Whittuck, "Obscurantism," *Hastings Encyclopedia of Religion and Ethics*, 9:442–43. Cited in Bernard Ramm, *After Fundamentalism* (San Francisco: HarperSanFrancisco, 1983), 19.

[38]Ramm, *After Fundamentalism*, 19.

[39]These terms are in quotation marks here because the situation was actually much more complex than the fundamentalist theologians and preachers perceived. There was in fact a large contingent of theologians who accepted the critical methodology flowing out of the Enlightenment but remained essentially conservative and orthodox in the broader historical sense in their theological outlook. The fundamentalists saw this group as simply liberal, since they rejected (on supposed evidence) the traditional definition of biblical authority arising out of Protestant scholasticism.

[40]Mark Noll chronicles the evangelical abandonment of serious intellectual work in his *Scandal of the Evangelical Mind.* Here Noll laments the fact that evangelicalism excused itself from the world of intellectual pursuits and abandoned that world to the liberal and secular communities. The fundamentalist and evangelical communities adopted wholesale an anti-intellectual mind-set that still characterizes it as a movement (see particularly 122–45).

[41]Charles Augustus Briggs, *Whither?* (New York: Scribner, 1889), 7.

[42]Ibid., 7.

[43]Ibid., 8.

[44]Ibid., 9, italics added.

[45]See M. James Sawyer, *Charles Augustus Briggs and Tensions in Late Nineteenth-Century American Theology* (Lewiston, NY: Mellen University Press, 1994), 179.

[46]*Merriam-Webster's Collegiate Dictionary*, 10th ed., s.v. "heresy," 2b.

[47]Ibid., 1a.

[48]See Alister McGrath, *Studies in Doctrine* (Grand Rapids: Zondervan, 1997), 467–72.

OUTLINE OF CHAPTER 11

A. Biblical Theology

1. The Nature of Biblical Theology
2. Biblical Theology and Other Theological Disciplines
   a. Exegesis
   b. Critical Studies
   c. Historical Theology
   d. Systematic Theology
3. The Origin and Necessity of Biblical Theology as a Discipline
   a. Continuity and Discontinuity between the Reader and the Biblical Text
   b. The Medieval Answer: Living Tradition
   c. The Reformation Wedge
   d. The Enlightenment: The Overthrow of the Scholastic Method
4. Biblical Theology Movement
5. Divisions of Biblical Theology
   a. Old Testament Theology
   b. New Testament Theology
6. Issues in Biblical Theology
   a. Unity and Diversity
   b. The Issue of Method

B. Historical Theology

1. The Nature of Historical Theology and the History of Doctrine
2. The Development of Historical Theology
3. History of Dogma or History of Doctrine?
   a. Dogma
   b. Doctrine

C. Systematic Theology

1. A Joint Venture with Philosophy
2. Organizing Point
3. The Question of Questions/Issues
4. The Development of Systematic Theology
   a. The Ancient Church
   b. The Medieval Period
   c. The Reformation
   d. Post-Reformation Protestant Scholasticism

D. Modern Theology

1. The Liberal Impulse
2. The Mediating School
3. Reformed Theology
4. Neoorthodoxy
5. Other Twentieth-Century Theologians

CHAPTER 7

THE DIVISIONS OF THEOLOGICAL STUDY

The term *theology* is broad in scope. In its broadest usage, it is applied to any topic that is somehow related to God and things divine. We may hear of a "theology of Christian education," a "theology of urban ministry," or even a "theology of church architecture." In each case, the discipline in question is trying in some way to apply scriptural principles to a particular area of life. In a more formal sense, we speak of all areas of study that have to do with Scripture, its interpretation, and its application as being the realm of theological studies.

For our purposes, we are assuming that the formal theological disciplines (biblical theology, historical theology, and systematic theology) build on the foundation laid by the disciplines of the biblical languages, Bible backgrounds, archaeology, and exegesis. The theological process begins with *biblical theology*,

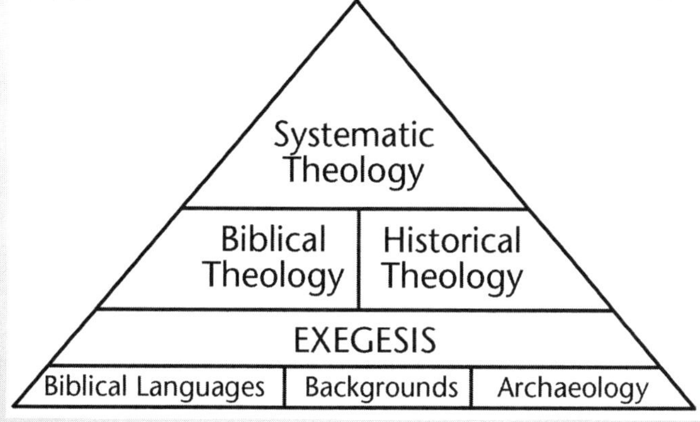

FIGURE 7.1.

which synthesizes and summarizes the comprehensive results of the exegetical process into a coherent whole. The next step in the process from a logical perspective is *historical theology*, which involves the study of the development of theological understanding throughout the history of the church. The capstone of the process is *systematic theology*, which synthesizes the results of the entire process into a coherent whole and contextualizes the truth of God in language, categories, and thought forms that are comprehensible to the current generation. As we have seen in the preceding chapters, the task of theology is never done, because the contemporary situation is different from age to age and culture to culture.

Each of the formal theological disciplines has a different focus, history, and method that must be understood if one is to enter intelligently into the discipline.

A. BIBLICAL THEOLOGY

> **Biblical theology** is the division of theological studies that attempts to present the progressive unfolding of the teaching of the various eras and authors of the Bible in their own thought forms, categories, and historical context, rather than imposing upon the biblical text the divisions of systematic theology. As a discipline, it is descriptive and synthetic rather than analytic.

Before discussing biblical theology, it is important to realize that the term *biblical theology* is used in two different senses: a "technical" sense, as in the above definition, and a popular sense.

Biblical theology in the popular sense is often used by preachers, teachers, and earnest Christians to speak of a doctrine or system of doctrines supported only by texts drawn from the Scriptures. Evangelical Protestants particularly insist that their theology must be biblical. Thus Reformed Christians, Wesleyans, Lutherans, dispensationalists, and Pentecostals all claim to have a pure biblical theology. But although they agree on the basics, these "biblical theologies" are at odds with one another on significant points. They all claim the Bible as their ultimate source and authority, but the differences show that other factors enter in to shape the doctrines and the conclusions of these systems.

In past generations, this method of theological study has been called *biblical dogmatics.* Biblical dogmatics is a method that is part of the discipline of systematic theology (rather than of biblical theology in the technical sense) as it has been in past centuries. As a method, biblical dogmatics is a priori and deductive rather than inductive and exegetical. Biblical dogmatics deduces dogmas from the Scriptures and then arranges them in an a priori system that is humanly devised. Thus, unlike biblical theology, biblical dogmatics does not present the thought forms presented in Scripture itself.

While claiming to be a "biblical theology," such a system in fact draws its categories and arrangement from philosophy and church tradition. "Biblical theology" in the more specific sense we are using the term cannot properly step beyond the Bible itself for its sources, including the source of categories and its arrangement. It is *inductive* and *exegetical* in its methodology. In its *ideal form*, it is a high-level synthesis of the exegetical process, so that biblical theology deals only with the actual teaching of the biblical authors in their own conceptual categories and does not extend even to the legitimate logical implications of that teaching. When we approach the text, we cannot assume that the author or his readers thought through all the implications of his statements or intuitively recognized them—and thus, strictly speaking, we cannot make these implications part of biblical theology. But this assertion in no way denies that the faith and practice of the people of God in any generation in which Scripture was given was broader than the information presented to us in the text. Biblical theology by its very nature will give us a *theology of the minimums* of any author or period rather than a *theology of maximums.*[1] But we must remember that this minimum theology is the inspired authority to which alone we can definitively appeal.

The only implications with which biblical theology deals are those that were developed historically by later biblical writers in the progress of revelation, and even here we must be careful not to read later revelation and conclusions back into the mind and teaching of earlier authors and texts.

To those who would claim to use only Scripture as the source of their theology under the guise of the slogan *sola scriptura*,[2] this caveat was given over a century ago:

> That system of theology which would anxiously confine itself to supposed biblical material, to the neglect of material presented by philosophy, science, literature, art, comparative religion, history of doctrine, the symbols, the liturgies, and the life of the Church, and the pious religious consciousness of the individual or the Christian society must be extremely defective and unscientific and cannot make up for its defects by an appeal to the Scriptures and a claim to be biblical. None of the great systematic theologians, from the most ancient times, has ever proposed such a course. It has been the resort of the feebler Pietists in Germany, and of the narrower Evangelicalism of

Great Britain and America, doomed to defeat and destruction, for working in such contracted lines.[3]

1. The Nature of Biblical Theology

Biblical theology as a discipline is concerned with "what the Bible *meant*" to its first hearers. It is not concerned with the normative question of "what the Bible *means* now" to twenty-first-century hearers.[4] That is the domain of systematic theology. Biblical theology is thus by its nature *descriptive* and *historical*. Its goal is to arrange and present the teaching of the Bible in the categories used by the biblical authors as opposed to systematic theology, which arranges the biblical material in categories that may appear to us to be logical and even necessary but are not the thought forms of Scripture.

Biblical theology stands above the exegetical process, which deals with the details of a text in all its particulars. It synthesizes the results of exegesis into a comprehensive tapestry, giving us a picture of the revelation of God in its original setting. It has long been recognized that biblical theology stands as a regulative discipline between exegesis and systematics (systematic theology), insuring that the systematician does not take the results of a single passage or of a group of passages as normative while ignoring the larger context of biblical perspectives and the contextualized nature of the biblical revelation.

2. Biblical Theology and Other Theological Disciplines

Biblical theology stands in the midst of the other theological disciplines. As a discipline, it is *synthetic*, bringing together the results of the exegesis of all of the biblical material. As a synthesis of preliminary analytical study, it takes the various strands of biblical teaching and unifies those strands into overarching themes that can be traced throughout the biblical text without forcing an artificial unity of perspective onto the diverse biblical material. It stands as the intermediate discipline between exegesis and systematics and alongside historical theology.

a. Exegesis

Princeton theologian and dogmatician B. B. Warfield noted, "The task of biblical theology ... is the task of coordinating the scattered results of continuous exegesis into a concatenated whole, with reference to a single book of Scripture or to a body of related books or to the whole scriptural fabric."[5] Exegesis is absolutely vital and is the major foundation of all other theological disciplines. It is by nature *analytic* and *detailed*. It is concerned with details and the meaning of the details. Exegesis done rightly should cause the exegete to "lose the forest for the trees." Thus, methodologically exegesis as exegesis is not concerned with broader perspectives. The details with which exegesis works are vitally important but do not give a vision of the whole; that comes later, in biblical theology and systematics, where the details are fit into the larger whole. Properly done, exegesis is not antithetical to synthesis; rather, it involves a reassembling of the details of the passage in light of the exegetical insights gained.

In this sense the exegete passes off the results of his work to the biblical theologian, whose task it is to place the exegetical findings in their proper place on the larger biblical-theological map. While this description of the relationship focuses on the distinctions between the disciplines of exegesis and biblical theology, in practice the exegete often will wear two hats, that of exegete and that of biblical theologian. Depending on the level of the exegete's competency and interest, the exegete will allow biblical theology to inform his or her exegesis and will often correlate the results of his or her study into the larger whole.

b. Critical Studies

During the past two centuries, the critical study of the text has reigned paramount in nonconservative circles. Questions of authorship, sources, redactors, and the like have occupied critical scholars. In this process, the message of the Bible has often been lost. The relationship of biblical theology to critical studies is tangential, for biblical theology is concerned with the text as it has come down to us. In this sense, biblical theology is canonical in its outlook as opposed to critical, that is, it takes the canonical text as given rather than trying to go behind the text to questions about its formation and development.

c. Historical Theology

Like biblical theology, historical theology is a *descriptive* discipline; but whereas biblical theology deals directly with divine revelation as given in the Scriptures, historical theology describes the progressive appropriation of that revelation by the church. From a methodological perspective, historical theology involves the descriptive task of telling how previous generations took the biblical material and appropriated it within their own historical context.

d. Systematic Theology

B. B. Warfield recognized the vital role biblical theology played in the theological process. While one often hears in some quarters that systematic theology must be grounded (directly) in exegesis, Warfield observed:

> The relation of biblical theology to systematic theology is based on a true view of its function. Systematic theology is not founded on

> the direct and primary results of the exegetical process; it is founded on the final and complete results of exegesis as exhibited in biblical theology. Not exegesis itself, then, but biblical theology, provides the material for systematics.... Biblical theology is not, then, a rival of systematics; it is not even a parallel product of the same body of facts, provided by exegesis; it is the basis and source of systematics. Systematic theology ... uses the individual data furnished by exegesis, in a word, not crudely, not independently for itself, but only after these data have been worked up into biblical theology and have received from it their final coloring and subtlest shades of meaning—in other words, only in their true sense, and after exegetics has said its last word upon them. Just as we shall attain our finest and truest conception of the person and work of Christ, not by crudely trying to combine the scattered details of His life and teaching as given in our four Gospels into one patchwork life and account of His teaching; but far more rationally and far more successfully by first catching Matthew's full conception of Jesus, and then Mark's, and then Luke's, and then John's, and combining these four conceptions into one rounded whole: so we gain our truest systematics not by at once working together the separate dogmatic statements in the Scriptures, but by combining them in their due order and proportion as they stand in the various theologies of the Scriptures.[6]

3. The Origin and Necessity of Biblical Theology as a Discipline

a. Continuity and Discontinuity between the Reader and the Biblical Text

The nature of the biblical material is ad hoc—that is, it was written largely to fulfill specific needs of the community of faith. The only New Testament author who comes close to presenting what is normally thought of as theology is Paul. He argues his case, trying to persuade by reasoning that calls on the reader to recognize the validity of what is presented rather than simply presenting his material in aphoristic fashion. Nevertheless, Paul's letters are also ad hoc; they do not present a fully developed, coherent system of thought. Even in his most "theological" book, Romans, Paul's concerns are immediate and pastoral rather than reflective.

b. The Medieval Answer: Living Tradition

Theology as a discipline did not arise directly from the Scriptures. In fact, it did not take formal shape until the emergence of scholasticism in the High

Middle Ages. The emergence of theology as a discipline came through the influence of Greek philosophy. The Bible, to be sure, provided the *material* for reflection, but the principles of disciplined thought, the *means and manner of reflection*, were derived from philosophy. With the emergence of theology in the Middle Ages, theologians did not consciously try to "think God's thoughts after him" as distinct from their own thoughts. This would not happen until later centuries. Rather, they thought their own thoughts, assuming they were the thoughts of the Scriptures and their authors. The reason for this assumption was that these theologians assumed a double continuity between themselves and the biblical writers: a *continuity of material* in the form of the Scriptures and a *continuity of living tradition* that connected the medieval theologian directly with the world of the Bible.

Medieval Christianity did not recognize the historical distance between itself and the world of the Bible. This lack of distance can be seen graphically in medieval art, which pictures biblical scenes in contemporary medieval settings and dress, and at times they even picture contemporary people mingling with characters from the Bible. The Bible and its stories were well known and formed an integral part of the living religion of the time.[7]

c. *The Reformation Wedge*

The Reformers insisted on the Scriptures as the sole basis and norm for Christian life and thought as opposed to the authority of the living traditions of the contemporary Roman Catholic Church. Failure to subject tradition to the Scriptures had given rise to intolerable abuses in the life of the church. Scripture alone could judge, correct, purify, and renew the life of the church. But this insistence broke the continuity of the living tradition that was assumed to be in continuity with the Bible. The Reformers recognized the Bible as historically distant and not contemporaneous with the present life of the church. Theologians could no longer think their own thoughts and assume that they were in continuity with the Bible. They had to self-consciously think the thoughts of the biblical writers and then interpret the Scriptures for the daily life of the believer. Both John Calvin and Martin Luther accomplished this task with great skill in their commentaries, and Calvin did so systematically in his *Institutes of the Christian Religion*. This process of interpretation attempted to reestablish a sense of immediacy with the Bible that had been lost in the destruction of the continuity of tradition.

The Protestant insistence that theology must not only be *founded upon* the Bible as its source but also *grounded in* it conceptually produced a crisis in theological methodology. By its very nature the Bible could not provide the formal categories of thought on which a theological system could be built, so philosophy as a discipline could not be surrendered in favor of the Bible. But the discipline itself was alien to the biblical perspective. This crisis affected Catholicism as well as Protestantism. By this time, Catholicism, although it rejected the *sola scriptura* of the Reformation, agreed with Protestantism in asserting that theology must be grounded in the Bible. This was the time of system building. Protestants and Catholics both produced theologies that were eminently "biblical," that is, the pronouncements were supported by biblical texts. In producing these "biblically based" theologies, however, the Bible was treated as an *ahistorical* book that dropped down from heaven, expressing the timeless truth of God, which could be understood by the trained student. The theologian's job, therefore, was to treat the Bible as his sourcebook of facts. Since God was the author of the facts, there was naturally a harmony among all parts of the Scripture. These facts were to be arranged and displayed in some systematic form.

While the formal categories could not be biblically based, many theologians insisted that their theologies were simply derived from the natural arrangement of the biblical material. From these *systems* of doctrine, deduced from the Scripture, other truths were also deduced. Methodologically, the Protestant scholastics inverted the practice of the first generation of Reformers and retreated into the scholastic methodology of the medieval church. Very importantly, the text was not viewed as literature with various genres or as being historically conditioned by the times in which it was given. The system reigned supreme, and frequently all truths were seen to be on the same level of importance. To deny even one truth of the system was seen by some as a denial of the whole system since the truths were understood to be inexorably interlocked. Consequently, as the dogmaticians built their systems, they often had little to no regard for the literary context and the historical situation into which a text as originally given was speaking.

We should also note that pietism, which arose as a reaction to the dry, heady Lutheran scholasticism, opposed the work of the dogmaticians. Philipp Jakob Spener decried the fact that while Luther had thrown scholasticism out the front door, his orthodox successors let it back in the back door.

The recognition that theology could not be completely *grounded* in the Bible as long as the discipline was in some sense derived from philosophy served as an impetus to the critical study of the Bible as a historical document and the rise of the formal discipline of biblical theology. The rise of critical thinking did not, however, take place in a vacuum.

d. The Enlightenment: The Overthrow of the Scholastic Method

The devastation of the European religious wars of the early 1600s, fought by principals who each claimed divine authority, provided a context and the felt need to have some ultimate court of appeal other than a church-mediated and church-interpreted revelation. Out of this felt need was born the Enlightenment. Rationalism had already been reigning by virtue of the scholastic methodology. It was but a short step to turn reason from a tool for the organization and display of truth into a judge and arbiter of the truth.

The beginnings of the critical study[8] of the Bible arose from the labor of a Catholic priest, Richard Simon (1638–1712), who pioneered the work of literary criticism in the New Testament, showing that the titles of the Gospels were not part of the text, that the "long ending of Mark" (16:9–20) and the passage of the woman taken in adultery (John 7:53–8:11) were not included in the earliest manuscripts. These insights, accepted by nearly all today, whether conservative or liberal, were rejected in his day by Protestant and Catholic alike. Nevertheless, Simon became the father of the critical investigation of the text of Scripture. He worked out one particular implication of the phrase "*sola scriptura*," the slogan that had placed the Bible over and against contemporary thought as a means of renewing the church. This separation, however, also made it possible to make the Bible itself an object of investigation, thus giving rise to historical criticism.

Biblical theology as a discipline arose in Germany out of the battle between rationalism and supernaturalism.[9] The battleground for the two parties was the Scripture, and each side sought to present the Bible from its own perspective. In this context, it became vital to distinguish the Scripture's own teaching from the interpretations imposed on it by the various contending parties. Among the *supernaturalists* there was a move to compare the teaching of the Scriptures themselves with the received doctrines of the church, with the goal of correcting and purifying the church's doctrine. The result was a theology that recognized an advancing economy of redemption but failed to see the Scriptures as having developed organically. Among the *rationalists*, biblical theologies were also written but from the perspective of antisupernaturalism.

The origin of biblical theology as a separate discipline is ultimately linked to the foundational distinction first made in 1787 by Johann Philipp Gabler. Gabler insisted that the *historical principle* distinguished biblical theology from dogmatics. His program was founded on two premises: (1) there is a distinction between the word of God as revealed in Scripture and the words of Scripture themselves, and (2) biblical theology is not to be found in the biblical writings but to be derived from them. In proposing these foundational principles, he formally separated the discipline of biblical theology from that of dogmatic/systematic theology and made it independent. His goal was to reassert the Bible as the basis of all theology, while dogmatics, as biblically based, would become the apex and final achievement of the theological process.

Gabler saw that the Bible presented the student with a religion, a divine teaching handed down in writing, rather than a theology. Religion was simple while theology was highly developed and subtle. As such the two stood over and against each other, yet theology was to be based on religion. Gabler based his method on three considerations:

1. Inspiration was to be left out of the equation due to the fact that the Spirit of God did not destroy in the authors of Scripture their own ability to understand and their natural insight into things. The important factor is not divine authority but the perspective of the author.
2. The task of biblical theology recognizes that the authors of Scripture present more than a single perspective, so the perspectives of the various authors must be carefully arranged, related to general concepts, and compared with one another.
3. Since biblical theology is a historical discipline, it is by definition obligated to "distinguish between the several periods of the old and new religion" and in so doing investigate which of the ideas are applicable today and which are without validity for our time.[10]

The task of biblical theology was to mediate between the religion presented in the text of Scripture on the one hand and the task of dogmatics on the other by becoming the basis for the latter. It was to transform biblical religion into a theological system that provided the basis for dogmatics.

New Testament studies diverged from Old Testament studies in the early nineteenth century, and under the influence of Georg Lorenz Bauer, New Testament theology as a formal discipline arose. "Biblical theology is to be a development—pure and purged of all extraneous concepts—of the religious theory of the Jews prior to Christ and of Jesus and his apostles, a development traced from the writings of the sacred authors and presented in terms of the various periods and the various viewpoints and levels of understanding they reflect."[11]Bauer was a thoroughgoing practitioner of the historical-critical method, and the discipline, as it developed after him, presupposed the method.

New Testament theology as a discipline reached its fully developed form under F. C. Baur, whose influence raised the Tübingen (Germany) school to prominence in New Testament studies. In addition to insisting on the historical method, Baur operated from the perspective of the Hegelian dialectic as applied to history. He saw early Christianity as engaged in a struggle between Jewish Christianity, represented by Peter, and gentile Christianity, represented by Paul. The synthesis that emerged was early Catholicism.[12] This period was a fertile one for the development of New Testament studies. Numerous New Testament theologies appeared, written from various perspectives—critical, liberal, mediating, and conservative.

While most advances in the development of biblical theology came from critical scholarship, several significant conservative scholars also made contributions. Among these were Johann A. Bengel, Johann T. Beck, and Johann C. K. von Hofmann, who pioneered the concept of *Heilsgeschichte* (salvation history). Von Hofmann's contribution has been called "the most fruitful theological development of the nineteenth century."[13] The premier conservative representative of biblical theology of this period was Adolf Schlatter, generally recognized as being in the same class as the dominant liberal biblical scholars Baur, Wilhelm Wrede, Wilhelm Bousset, and Rudolf Bultmann. Schlatter is associated with the *Heilsgeschichte* perspective in biblical theology and argues that the inherent atheism of the historical-critical method is illegitimate. Further, he argues that the method is inadequate to establish New Testament theology: the theologian and historian cannot be neutral objective observers, because the message confronts people as a message to be believed. In these matters, Schlatter anticipated the debate between Old Testament scholars Otto Eissfeldt and Walter Eichrodt in the 1920s. What Schlatter rejected was not history as such but rather the naturalistic assumption of modern historiography with its presupposition of a "closed system" universe and the liberal assumption of radical immanentism that denies divine transcendence.

In stark contrast to Schlatter's approach was that of Wilhelm Wrede, who stood as a representative of the history of religion school; by the end of the nineteenth century, the entire discipline had been swallowed up by the history of religion approach.

During the twentieth century, one name dominated New Testament theology and New Testament studies generally: Rudolf Bultmann, who presented a synthesis of numerous major emphases.

- He adopted the purely historical research from the history of religions school.
- He followed a "consistent eschatology."

- He was committed to the historical-critical method.
- He presupposed the existentialism of Martin Heidegger.
- He attempted to "demythologize" the New Testament for the modern world. Adopting the presupposition that modern man can no longer accept the "myths" found in the New Testament, he attempted to reinterpret that myth existentially for the contemporary hearer.[14]

Since Bultmann's death in 1976, a "post-Bultmannian school" of New Testament studies has emerged.

4. Biblical Theology Movement

The challenge by Karl Barth and neoorthodoxy to the dominant liberal theology spawned a new interest in the Bible and theology. This reaction in turn gave rise to the so-called biblical theology movement,[15] a movement that has been identified with such concerns as making a distinction between Greek and Hebrew thought, viewing the Bible within its culture, and attempting to identify the unifying thread of the Bible. As a movement, it flourished concurrently with neoorthodoxy and finally declined as a force in American theology in the 1960s. Gerhard Hasel contends that the failure of the movement was that it arose out of liberalism and amounted to an attempt to correct liberalism from within. Its failure was the result of its basic captivity to modes, patterns of thought, and methods of liberal theology.[16]

5. Divisions of Biblical Theology

We are painting with broad brushstrokes in this discussion, recognizing that the reality is more complicated than this cursory survey.

a. Old Testament Theology

The overarching goal of Old Testament theology is to trace the progressive revelation of God in Scripture from its earliest period, demonstrating how the content of understanding grew throughout the centuries. Old Testament theology traces themes and motifs over the centuries, noting repetition of concepts as well as growth of understanding, showing how God has progressively added to revelation throughout history. During the twentieth century, a plethora of Old Testament theologies appeared, seeking to explain the whole of the Old Testament through a single unifying theme. Just as systematic theologians seek to present their material around central organizing motifs, so also Old Testament theologians have sought to organize the biblical material around themes such as covenant or kingdom. But as noted earlier, these themes are not superimposed on the data; they arise from the data themselves. The fact that so many theologians have proposed different centers or organizing principles witnesses to the difficulty of discovering an overarching center.

b. New Testament Theology

New Testament theology proceeds from the perspectives of the various authors of the New Testament books and the uniqueness of each. A key factor here is the recognition that the New Testament is not "flat" in its perspective; rather, each author looks at his subject matter from a unique perspective. We might liken the perspectives of the various authors to the facets of a diamond, each of which refracts the light of divine revelation in a slightly different way but in that different refraction gives depth and color to the various perspectives. Thus, for example, while Paul presents salvation in legal categories, such as adoption, justification, and reconciliation, John looks at salvation as life and explains the truth from that perspective. Therefore a full-orbed New Testament theology will include such perspectives as Pauline theology, Johannine theology, Petrine theology, the theology of the Synoptic Gospels, and so on.

6. Issues in Biblical Theology

a. Unity and Diversity

A central problem in doing biblical theology is the tension of unity and diversity within the biblical material. Critical antisupernaturalist scholars view the text simply as a collection of religious and historical material that documents the evolving religious conceptions of Israel and the church. They usually deny any fundamental unity in the biblical material, interpreting diversity of perspective as contradiction. Those who view the text as divine revelation find this option unacceptable, and while recognizing diversity within the text, they insist that there must be an overarching unity in the biblical material. God is the source of all the material and the author of all truth. They assert the presupposition that ultimately truth cannot contradict truth.

b. The Issue of Method

While the goal of biblical theology is simple, the means to reach that goal have proved to be anything but. Specifically, there has been no universally recognized and accepted method. Instead, numerous methods have been employed by various biblical theologians. These include the synthetic, analytical, history of religions, diachronic and tradition-critical, christological, confessional, and multiplex.[17]

B. HISTORICAL THEOLOGY

> **Historical theology** as a discipline investigates the progressive realization of Christianity and of the truth of divine revelation in the lives, hearts, worship, and thought of humanity. As with biblical theology, its task is descriptive in that it deals with the past as the past and answers the question, "What did previous generations understand and teach with reference to the Christian faith, and why did they understand and teach these things as they did?"

1. The Nature of Historical Theology and the History of Doctrine

The study of the history of doctrine shares a recent beginning with the related fields of Old and New Testament theology. All trace their beginnings to the late seventeenth century and the rise of modern historiography and historical consciousness.

Johann S. Semler, German church historian and biblical critic, demonstrated in 1762 that the history of doctrine should be separated from ecclesiastical history. Before Semler, doctrines had been perceived as static by both Protestants and Catholics, but Semler proposed that history was a moving, steadily changing element:

> The essence of dogma is only restless change. History for [Semler] is governed by the arbitrary powers of subjectivity.... His work represents the first critical examination of primitive Christianity and the development of dogma. It is based upon the presupposition that Christianity can be regarded only as an historical phenomenon to be studied historically and without dogmatic presuppositions, and its historical manifestation must be analyzed in the context of its historical milieu.[18]

It was particularly during the nineteenth century with the rise of the romantic movement and Hegelian philosophy that history and theological thought were envisioned as dynamic. *Enwicklung* ("development") became the watchword of the nineteenth-century German mind-set and has continued to exercise influence over all theological studies since that time. Prior to this, both Roman Catholic and Protestant theologians viewed their theological systems as static, as if they had emerged directly from the New Testament even as Minerva was seen to have emerged from the head of Zeus fully grown and armed for battle. Particularly influential in popularizing the concept of the development of doctrine was Cardinal John Henry Newman.[19]

Historical theology is a hybrid discipline that draws from both theology and history. This hybrid recognizes that both historical and sociological forces are involved in the way questions are asked and answers given, but it does not subsume the answers under the sociological. Rather, while recognizing the contingent factors involved, historical theology is vitally concerned with the content of the beliefs put forward as intrinsically Christian. According to Hubert Cunliffe-Jones, "The ideal historian of Christian theology would be grounded deep in the truth of the Gospel and in Christian churchmanship, equally at home in the fields of history and philosophy, and endowed with the powerful gifts of exposition."[20] Furthermore, "the historian of Christian theology should be aware of the cultural context of the theologians and their propositions which he is investigating and recording. All theology is formulated in a cultural background. Cultural factors have influenced the theology of theologians of the past in ways in which the theologians themselves have not always been aware."[21]

2. The Development of Historical Theology

Wilhelm Muenscher, a disciple of Semler and theologian of the Enlightenment, has been called "the father of modern history of dogma."[22] As with biblical theology, the task of historical theology is descriptive, not critical. The church has given its faith a fixed form in dogma. However, from the Protestant perspective at least, the fallibility of dogma must be recognized as axiomatic. The dogma of the church as well as the doctrines propounded by various schools and teachers must be subjected to the final authority of the Scriptures.

> To prove the harmony or disharmony of Dogma [or doctrine] with these courts of appeal is not the office of History of Doctrines, but rather that of Dogmatics and Practical Theology. The History of Doctrines can only be required to present the arguments which have been adduced by the original advocates of a given dogma. History is not historical criticism.
>
> Additionally we must realize that there is no Divine Dogma. Dogma/doctrine is the human response in faith to divine revelation. As a human response there is ever the possibility of admixture with error. "Upon this principle, it may be possible for one to recognize the Christian and Biblical character of the ideas maintained by the Councils of Nicea and Chalcedon ... while unable to approve all the terminology employed by them."[23]

Another name prominent in the development of the discipline is that of Ferdinand Christian Baur. While best remembered as a New Testament scholar, Baur also produced a five-volume history of dogma, in which he saw the task of the history of dogma as twofold: (1) to discern the facts in their actual settings as ascertained through credible witnesses and (2) to interpret these facts according to their inner unfolding.

As with his work in New Testament criticism, Baur applied the Hegelian dialectic of progress to the data. But the idea of development grew beyond its Hegelian roots.

The greatest historian of doctrine or dogma was Adolf von Harnack (d. 1932). His *History of Dogma* still stands as the giant in the field of history of doctrine. It was he who introduced the idea that dogma originated with the infusion of Hellenism into the early church. The field of history of doctrine has been dominated, not surprisingly, by German scholarship. Of those translated into English the following are particularly useful:

Karl Rudolf Hagenbach, *A History of Christian Doctrines* (English translation, 1881)
Adolf von Harnack, *History of Dogma* (English translation, 1897–1900)
Johann August Wilhelm Neander, *History of Christian Dogmatics* (English translation, 1858)
Reinhold Seeberg, *The History of Doctrines* (1896, 1898)

Among American works, six are outstanding:

George Park Fischer, *History of Christian Doctrine* (1886)
Otto W. Heick, *A History of Christian Thought* (1965)
Arthur Cushman McGiffert, *History of Christian Thought* (1932, 1933)
Jaroslav Pelikan, *A History of Christian Thought* (5 vols., 1971–89)
Willian G. T. Shedd, *History of Christian Dogma* (1889)
H. C. Sheldon, *History of Christian Doctrine* (1886)

3. History of Dogma or History of Doctrine?

a. Dogma

While the terms *dogma* and *doctrine* are often used interchangeably, in the strict sense, the terms are not synonymous. The term *dogma* is derived from the Greek δοκέο (*dokeo*, "it seems"). Even within the New Testament itself, the term became attached to the findings of an ecclesiastical body (Acts 16:4, *dogmata*). Seeberg says:

> The theological term, Dogma, designates either an ecclesiastical doctrine, or the entire structure of such doctrines, i.e., the doctrinal system of the church. As Dogma is the formal expression of the truth held by the church at large, or by a particular church, the church expects the acknowledgment of it by her members, and . . . of her recognized teachers. We apply the term, Dogma, . . . only to such propositions as have attained ecclesiastical character. . . . Although the form of Dogma is the work of theology, its content is derived from the common faith of the church.[24]

Heick likewise observed, "The name dogma is applied to the crystallized statements of the church."[25]

Using the technical sense of the term, *dogma* refers to the study of creedal and confessional statements. It is the study of the gradual development of theological thought from its beginnings in the immediate postapostolic age and the time of the apostolic fathers until its final creedal formulation. Most recognize that there is a fundamental core of dogmatic statements recognized by all Christian traditions. This core of statements arises out of the first four ecumenical councils of the church, beginning with Nicea (325) and running through Chalcedon (451). By tradition the Apostles' Creed and the Athanasian Creed are also revered, but these two do not bear the formal imprimatur of the ancient church's doctrinal consensus. Beyond these basic creeds, different communions trace their creedal commitments in a sectarian fashion, with final formulation varying according to the particular communion.

Among the Eastern Orthodox, dogmatics culminates with the second Council of Nicea in A.D. 787. Orthodox theology has admitted no further development or clarification since that time. Of all Christian communions, its theology is the most ancient in the sense that it preserves unchanged the theology and liturgy of the ancient church.

Unlike Orthodoxy, Roman Catholic dogmatics continues to develop through the centuries, and while its most recent statement is embodied in the pronouncements of Vatican II (1963–65), the development of doctrine within Catholicism is an ongoing process and has not in principle been halted.

Within Lutheranism, dogmatics ends with the Formula of Concord (1580). Since that time, there has been much theological discussion, but no alteration of its creeds.

Reformed dogmatics finds classic expression in the findings of the Synod of Dort (1519), which was called to answer the Remonstrance put forth by the growing Arminian party. This was the only international synod of the Reformed churches and is thus the only truly universally recognized creed to come out of the Reformed tradition. The English-speaking churches in the Reformed traditions look to the Westminster Confession (1649) as authoritative; they also hold other confessions, such as the Second Helvetic Confession, in high regard. But in the strictest sense, these latter two documents ought not be regarded as dogmatic statements, since they are not formally recognized by the entire Reformed tradition.

Pelikan has observed that "a doctrine, once formulated [does not] stop developing and become fixed; not even the dogma of the Trinity has stood perfectly still since its adoption and clarification."[26] Since this is so, we must look beyond dogmatic formulations in our study and examine not just the creedal statements, but also the doctrinal formulations that have developed since the creedal pronouncements.

b. Doctrine

The term *doctrine* (*didaskalia*, 1 Tim. 4:16) is almost universally translated "teaching" in the New Testament. It is broader in meaning than dogma. Doctrine reflects the idea of that which is taught, held, or put forth as true, or supported by a teacher, a school of thought, or group. Dogma, by contrast, includes only teachings contained in the confessions of the church. Doctrines are therefore much more diverse and may be much more detailed than dogmatic statements.

A very visible example of the difference between the terms *dogma* and *doctrine* is that the confessional churches (Reformed, Lutheran, Roman Catholic) have dogma, while Baptists, independent churches, and those of the Free Church traditions generally do not recognize dogma but assert doctrines. Many in the nonliturgical tradition will not formally recognize the authority of the ancient ecumenical creeds, while they do affirm the theology contained therein. Instead, they formally recognize only the Bible as authoritative.

C. SYSTEMATIC THEOLOGY

> **Systematic theology** is "the branch of theological study which follows a *humanly devised* scheme or order of doctrinal development/presentation and which attempts to incorporate into its system all the truth about God and his universe from any and every source" (B. B. Warfield, italics added).

We have already observed much about the nature of systematic theology by looking at the theologian's job description in chapter 2. Rather than repeat much of that material here, we will "fill in the cracks" with a few more details and observations. As noted in chapter 2, there are different conceptions of the theological task. Commonly that task has been envisioned in one of three ways—*sapientia, scientia*, or *orthopraxis*.[27] One's vision of the theological task will shape the gestalt of the theology produced.

A theology that has *scientia* as its basic vision will attempt to produce a comprehensive understanding of reality. This comprehensive understanding, while perhaps not being a "cathedral of the mind" in the sense that scholastic systems bear that description, will nevertheless produce a paradigm of reality that will consciously attempt to integrate knowledge from Scripture, history, the created order, the hard and soft sciences, tradition, and experience to give a comprehensive vision of a theocentric reality. One contemporary theologian in this category is Wolfhart Pannenberg, whose theology falls under the rubric "revelation as history."

If, however, theology is conceived in the *sapientia* mode (whether consciously or subconsciously), the focus will be on living in the presence of God. A contemporary example of this mode of theological conception is *narrative theology*, which seeks to bring the reader into the biblical paradigm of reality through the biblical story, as opposed to entering via the route of a more traditional theological system.

The Comprehensive Nature of Systematic Theology

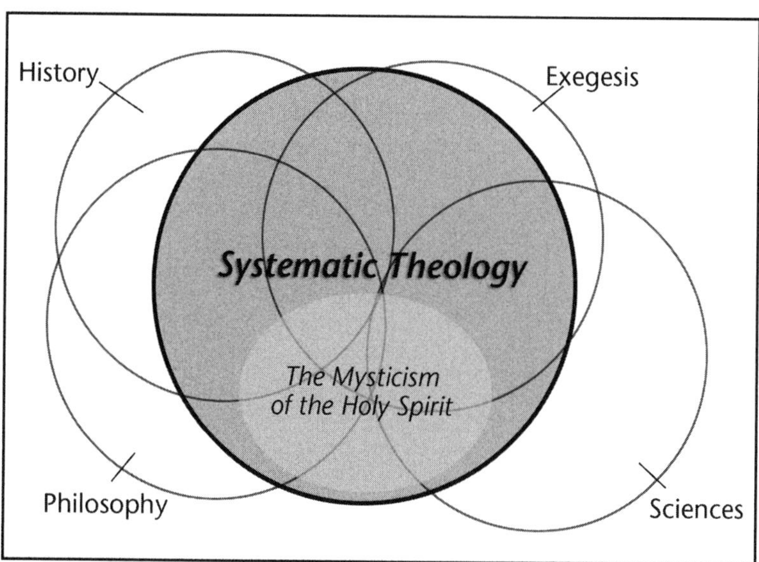

FIGURE 7.2.

In the theological pyramid in figure 7.1 (p. 203), we placed systematic theology at the top and all other theological disciplines in foundational levels, their conclusions flowing up into systematics. Although accurate, the pyramid does not give the whole picture. Systematics is a comprehensive discipline in that it seeks to incorporate to some degree all knowledge of God and his universe into its purview. While special revelation as found in Scripture is its focus and primary source, it must also have at the very least a passing acquaintance with other disciplines. All of this must be coupled with faith and the mysticism of the Spirit.[28]

1. A Joint Venture with Philosophy

Ever since the second century, theologians have recognized that systematic theology is a joint venture with philosophy. Even Charles Hodge, the great Princeton theologian, whose formal definition of theology saw it simply as the arrangement and display of the facts of Scripture, recognized in his systematic theology that every theology was in some measure a philosophical undertaking.[29] In the ancient church, Origen and Augustine self-consciously used versions of Platonic philosophy. Thomas Aquinas and the schoolmen as well as the Protestant scholastics employed Aristotle. Nineteenth-century liberalism used Hegelian idealism and Kantian phenomenalism, while Princeton used Common Sense Realism. Neoorthodoxy has used to a greater or lesser degree existentialism, as has Paul Tillich. Pannenberg employs neo-Hegelianism. While Scripture provides the primary data of theology, philosophy brings categories and forms of thought to be employed by the theologian in his labors. It is not possible for a theology to be philosophically neutral, because the theologian knowingly or unknowingly views the world through a particular philosophical grid, usually the grid of the culture in which he or she was raised.

2. Organizing Point

Most students, when first exposed to theology, probably have no idea that theology or doctrine is an organic whole. As a youth, I was introduced to various doctrines, which I identified as "my theology." In college I learned of the broader concept of systematic theology and even purchased several weighty tomes. At this point in my life, my notion of systematic theology was that it was a comprehensive and detailed study: the term *systematic* carried the idea of all-inclusiveness. It was not until years later that I grasped the fact that the term *systematic* referred not primarily to comprehensiveness but to the organic nature of theology as a whole in which everything is conceived and organized around a central idea or principle. Furthermore, conclusions in one area of study affect conclusions in other areas.

As the discipline of systematic theology has matured, theologians have generally used a central theme or motif as the organizing principle and integrating factor. Thus, in Lutheranism the doctrine of justification by faith is the overarching principle and central doctrine, the lens through which everything else is viewed. In the Reformed tradition, the organizing principle is divine sovereignty or predestination. In classic Arminianism, the principle is human freedom, and in Wesleyan Arminianism, it is scriptural holiness/sanctification. Individual theologians operating within a particular framework can also adopt a particular motif that guides them in their task. In such cases, the theologian's motif is subsumed under the larger organizing principle of the tradition within which he or she is operating.

3. The Question of Questions/Issues

As discussed in chapter 2, a major part of the theologian's job is contextualizing the message. One method proposed to accomplish this is that of Paul Tillich.[30] Tillich recognizes that each age has its own issues and problems with which it must deal. The theological method at this point is dialectic: it moves between two poles, the pole of theological authority (in the case of the evangelical this would be the Bible and the historic faith of the church) and the pole of contemporary culture or the "situation." This situation is the human condition as it is experienced and expressed by the contemporary generation. In one sense, the human condition never changes, but the "presenting problem" does change. That presenting problem is found in the Zeitgeist (the spirit and "mood" of the times) as expressed in art, music, literature, and politics. A study of these leads the theologian to an understanding of the age, of the questions being asked, either explicitly or implicitly, and of the underlying assumptions about reality.

> The task is not to get society to ask the questions for which we have ready-made answers, but to address the questions that are being asked.

The probing of the Zeitgeist is primarily the task of philosophy. The theologian takes the questions and crafts his answers from the authority of Scripture but casts them in a form that will address contemporary concerns. Tillich calls this method "correlation." Failure to understand one's own culture leads to what has been described as the "heresy of irrelevance." This is not to say that biblical truth is ever truly irrelevant; rather, its relevance is severely compromised when it fails to touch the perceived needs of the audience. This method must be applied in the statement of theological content as well as in apologetics. The task is not to get society to ask the questions for which we have ready-made answers, but to address the questions that are being asked, which today include issues raised by postmodernism, pluralism, and relativism.

4. The Development of Systematic Theology

The following discussion provides a thumbnail sketch of the development of the discipline of systematic theology. It is by no means meant to be a complete exposition.

a. The Ancient Church

The discipline of systematic theology has its roots in the early church and arose out of its life. As noted in chapter 1, the primary model of the theology of this period is *sapientia*, wisdom. The theological works written during this period were occasional and pastoral. The idea of theology being conducted in the academy as an intellectual exercise would have been incomprehensible to the early church. Nevertheless, several of the Fathers did leave us important theological works. (See chapter 17 for biographies of the early church fathers.)

Irenaeus. Irenaeus (d. 203?), bishop of Lyons (in France) and disciple of Polycarp, is remembered as the premier apologist against Gnosticism in the late second and very early third centuries. His five books refuting Valentinian Gnosticism *(Adversus Haereses, Against Heresies)* were a massive contribution and stand as the greatest source on the Gnosticism of that era. But he also composed another work, *The Demonstration of the Apostolic Preaching,* as a handbook for ordinary Christians. It is an abstract of the theology he presented and defended in *Adversus Haereses.* Irenaeus is not speculative, theoretical, or philosophical. His perspective is profoundly biblical, although he does step beyond the words of Scripture to explain the concepts of sin and redemption against the backdrop of Gnosticism.

> No more than other Christian authors of his era does Irenaeus write out of an interest in the problems of theology for their own sake. His work is in the strictest sense, occasional, motivated out of pastoral rather than purely intellectual concerns. In consequence what he has

to say and the way in which he says it are jointly determined by the concrete situation to which he addressed himself.[31]

Irenaeus's work had a profound influence on the development of theology, particularly in the East. Some within the Orthodox tradition see all further development after Irenaeus as merely footnotes to his contributions. But even his profoundly biblical perspective is shaped by the crisis of Gnosticism, and we see in his work what may appear to be speculative aspects concerning redemption, such as the Adam-Christ and Eve-Mary parallels. This construct answers the then-current situation and is presented as an alternative to the Gnostic doctrines.

Origen. A younger contemporary of Irenaeus, Origen lived and worked in a very different environment. A child prodigy of Christian parents, Origen took over the leadership of the catechetical school of Alexandria at the age of eighteen. Like his mentor, Clement of Alexandria, he was a speculative thinker, and he tried to synthesize Neoplatonic philosophy and biblical teaching into a grand scheme of Christian thought. He was an apologist, philosopher, textual scholar, commentator, and theologian. He produced over eight hundred works during his lifetime. His systematic theology, *On First Principles* (Gk. Περί Αρχων, *Peri archôn*, Lat. *De Principiis*), reveals some of the factors associated with the formal discipline of theology we see emerging in the medieval period.

Origen's life was surrounded by controversy. As a youth, he sought to follow his father into martyrdom but was prevented when his mother hid his clothing. He was the originator of the allegorical interpretation of the Bible, yet he took Jesus' statements regarding becoming eunuchs for the sake of the kingdom literally. This caused him great problems later in his career, since in the eyes of the church it made him unworthy of ordination. He was eventually ordained in Caesarea, but the bishop of his native Alexandria was outraged by the action and caused so much trouble for Origen that he eventually moved from his native Alexandria to Caesarea. His teachings, like his life, were also surrounded by controversy, and although he died as a result of torture received in the Decian persecution, he was never canonized as a saint. He was posthumously condemned as a heretic by a general council in A.D. 553 for teaching the preexistence of souls (which indeed he did) and advocating that ultimately all including Satan would be reconciled to God (whether he did indeed teach this is uncertain).

Origen cast a long shadow over Alexandrine theology, providing it with the categories in which it expressed its thought. After Origen, Alexandrine theology was universally Origenistic. The question became whether one was a left-wing Origenist or a right-wing Origenist. Athanasius and the Cappadocians (Basil the Great, Gregory of Nyssa, and Gregory of Nazianzus) of the fourth century were profoundly indebted to Origen.

Origen's *On First Principles* may be called a philosophical theology, in which he reflected on the nature of God and the Logos as well as on many other doctrinal topics. This work may rightly be seen as the first true systematic theology. In it we see a self-conscious adoption of Neoplatonic categories used to express the truth of Christianity. We also find, however, what appears to be a captivity to the thought forms of Platonism insofar as his philosophical presuppositions became a Procrustean bed when it came to his interpretation of the Scriptures. Wherever the Scripture's literal sense offended Origen's Neoplatonic sensibilities, he had a penchant to allegorize the text of Scripture.

Origen tried to be a loyal son of the church. He adamantly asserted the authority of Scripture, the apostolic tradition, and the reality of the incarnation, and he made significant contributions to Trinitarian discussions. His concept of salvation reflected the Eastern idea of *theosis*, or deification, a category that continues to be the dominant salvific motif in Eastern theology (see chapter 8, "Orthodoxy"). But the theological system Origen produced was so overcontextualized that it compromised some points of the faith.

Augustine. In Augustine we find ourselves in the presence of a spirit very different from that of Origen. Unquestionably the greatest theologian of the ancient church, Augustine became the father of all Western theology, Roman Catholic as well as Protestant. Like Origen, Augustine was a Neoplatonist and used philosophy as a tool that provided categories in which to express and defend Christianity. But unlike Origen, Augustine gave biblical authority precedence over the philosophical perspectives whenever Neoplatonic perspectives contradicted Scripture.

Like so many others throughout the history of theological thinking, Augustine's writings are mostly occasional. He wrote extensively against Pelagius and his followers as well as against the Donatists. Even his magnum opus, *The City of God*, the first true Christian philosophy of history, was occasional in nature in that it was an apologetic defending Christianity against the charge that it was responsible for the demise of the empire. He did, however, produce one theological volume that is in some sense in continuity with the concept of a systematic theology—the *Enchiridion* (*Handbook*), a brief doctrinal handbook for believers.

Augustine uses as his organizational principle the Pauline triad of faith, hope, and love. Under the first heading, he discusses the main articles of

Christian doctrine; under the second, the concepts of prayer following the order laid out in the Lord's Prayer; and under the rubric of love, he addresses moral issues.

Augustine's great theological contribution was in the area of sin and grace. And in these areas his contributions had a unique twist. While many other doctrines in the history of the church were worked out in the heat of controversy, Augustine's understanding of sin and grace arose out of his personal spiritual struggles. He had reached his basic conclusions before Pelagius ever appeared on the scene. His anti-Pelagian writings reveal a sharpening of thought and the application of already existent conclusions.

Another lesser known work of Augustine, *Retractions*, was published late in his life. This volume was a reflection on positions he had earlier taken a stand on but about which he later changed his mind after further reflection and growth. This volume gives us insight into the necessity of theologians remaining teachable and continuing to think and probe even after they have publicly committed themselves on an issue. Augustine personally revealed a consistently growing body of theological convictions that he was willing to adjust and even change after reflecting on and examining the implications of a doctrine or upon seeing how an opponent might misuse what he taught. Therefore, when studying Augustine's writings, we must ask whether it is the early or later Augustine who is speaking.

John of Damascus. John of Damascus represents the final form of Eastern theology. His work *An Accurate Exposition of the Orthodox Faith* is the definitive form of Eastern theology. As such it is both speculative and ecclesiastical. John divides his work into four parts: (1) God and the Trinity; (2) creation and the nature of man; (3) Christ's incarnation, death, and descent into Hades; and (4) the resurrection and reign of Christ.

Subsumed under the final topic are such topics as faith, baptism, icons, and the like. The work is conservative and reflects the sum of Eastern theology.

b. The Medieval Period

During the early medieval period, learning all but died out in Europe as the Dark Ages extinguished the intellectual light of the Roman Empire in which the early church had been born and flourished. After many centuries, there was a rebirth of learning and particularly a devotion to the study of theology. This devotion reached its height in the eleventh through thirteenth centuries, the so-called High Middle Ages. This period saw the birth of the modern university system coupled with the rise of scholasticism. Scholasticism was an attempt to deal with the received biblical truth using a systematic method. Scholasticism did not presume to prove truth but rather to demonstrate its rationality. During this period, theology became more self-consciously dependent on philosophy, both in its dialectical method and in the questions and problems it pursued. The line between philosophy and theology blurred significantly, and the dominant philosophical assumptions were derived predominantly from Platonism, Aristotelianism, and nominalism.[32]

Anselm of Canterbury

Anselm of Canterbury. While Anselm never produced a comprehensive systematic theology, he stands as a pivotal influence in the development of theological study. Of his works, *Proslogion* (which is a deductive argument for God's existence), *Monologion* (an inductive argument for the existence of God), and *Cur Deus Homo?* ("Why Did God Become Man?") have continued to have an influence on theologians down to the twentieth century.

Peter Lombard. The most important systematic theology of the period was Peter Lombard's *Sentences*, covering the whole field of theology. This work was comprised of four books, dealing with (1) the Trinity, (2) the creation, (3) Christ and redemption, and (4) the sacraments and last things. *Sentences* provides a synthesis of patris and for centuries was the standard handbook of theology. In many quarters, it was regarded as the authoritative exposition of the truth.

Aquinas. Thomas Aquinas ("The angelic doctor") is generally regarded as the greatest of the scholastic theologians, although as a student he was nicknamed the "Dumb Ox" by his classmates. His teacher Albertus Magnus ("The universal doctor") responded to this characterization of Thomas by declaring, "This Ox shall shake the world." To better understand Thomas's contribution, we must observe that since the late ancient period, the theological world had relied on Augustine and the underlying Platonic philosophy. With the profound changes that were occurring in the world during Thomas's day, however, the Augustinian synthesis was thrown into crisis. It could no longer meet the challenges it faced. The work of Aristotle, lost for many centuries to the West, had recently been introduced to Europe by the Arabic scholar Averroes, who translated the Arabic version of Aristotle into Latin.[33] Thomas employed the categories and perspectives of the newly discovered Aristotelian philosophy for the formal structure of his theological presentation while retaining the essence of Augustinian understanding. Thomas's work met stiff opposition, particularly from Duns Scotus, but was officially endorsed as Roman Catholic dogma at the Council of Trent.

Thomas's *Summa Theologia* covers in three volumes the whole field of systematics. It is divided into (1) God and his works, (2) man as the image of God, and (3) Christ and the means of grace. Thomas marks the high point of scholasticism. After his work, there were several centuries of decline in theological studies.

c. The Reformation

The Reformation marks the next great contribution to systematic theology, with contributions from both the Lutheran and the Reformed camps.

Melanchthon. Philip Melanchthon, Luther's younger associate, produced the first dogmatic handbook of the Reformation, *Loci Communes.* (Luther himself, unlike his Reformed counterpart Calvin, was not a systematic theologian by temperament.) The organization principle is Paul's epistle to the Romans. In the various editions of the work, we see the development of Melanchthon's thought. In the first edition, he is entirely at one with Luther. Subsequently we see the growing influence of Erasmus as Melanchthon backs away from the unconditional predestination taught by Luther and endorses a doctrine of free will. Later editions of the *Loci* also displayed a shift toward the work of Calvin, particularly with reference to the Lord's Supper and Christology.

Calvin. At the fountainhead of all Protestant systematic theologies stands John Calvin's *Institutes of the Christian Religion.* Originally a brief handbook published when Calvin was only twenty-seven years old, the *Institutes* went through three editions. The final edition is the definitive statement of Calvin's thought. Methodologically he followed the common humanistic[34] methodology. He was exegetical and inductive. In contrast to later Reformed/Calvinistic theology, Calvin himself displayed a reluctance to speculate beyond the limits of Scripture. While earlier generations argued that Calvin's organizing principle was the absolute sovereignty of God or predestination, a number of contemporary theologians object that this amounts to reading Calvin through the lens of later Reformed orthodoxy. Systematic theology as it is normally understood smacked of medieval scholasticism and was contrary to Calvin's thought processes. McGrath insists, "At no point is there any evidence to suggest that a leading principle, axiom or doctrine—save that of clarity of presentation—has governed the form or the substance of the work."[35] McGrath insists that it is anachronistic to speak of a "hard core" or "central premise" in Calvin's theology; this came only later to be seen as an essential part of the theological task. In fact, he identifies this trend in theology as associated with the Enlightenment mentality.[36]

The organization of the *Institutes* is basically Trinitarian, with the first three books focusing on the members of the Godhead, while the final book turns its attention to the church.

Book 1: The Knowledge of God the Creator
Book 2: The Knowledge of God the Redeemer
Book 3: The Way We Receive the Grace of Christ
Book 4: The Means of Grace: Holy Catholic Church

As a humanist who was concerned with clarity of communication, Calvin admirably accomplished his task, creating the exposition of Protestantism by which all later works would be judged.

d. Post-Reformation Protestant Scholasticism

Lutherans. After the death of Luther, Lutheranism and Lutheran theology divided into two camps—the Lutherans, who rigidly followed Martin Luther, and the Philipists, who followed in the more moderate tradition of Philip Melanchthon. After a period of internecine theological conflict, the Lutheran party emerged victorious. There were several other theological controversies during this period, but the reigning theology was an exposition of the theology contained in the Lutheran *Formula of Concord.* The most significant theologian of the period was Martin Chemnitz. In fact, Lutherans often speak of "the two Martins," Luther and Chemnitz.[37]

The Reformed tradition. Theodore Beza, while not actually producing a great systematic theology himself, had more influence on the development of Reformed theology than any other individual. Upon Calvin's death, the mantle of leadership of the Swiss Reformed Church fell to Beza. While he preserved the substance of Calvin's theology, he introduced subtle changes that had profound consequences. Whereas Calvin had clearly taught predestination with reference to salvation as a prerogative of God, his discussion of the topic was in conjunction with the doctrine of salvation and followed his discussion of justification. Beza moved the discussion of the topic and placed it in the context of the divine attributes. This had the effect of giving the doctrine more prominence than Calvin had given it in the *Institutes.*

Beza also represents a significant methodological shift from Calvin. Whereas Calvin eschewed scholastic methodology and was inductive and exegetical, Beza returned to the medieval methodology of scholasticism with its penchant for system building. This method gave rise to the question of the divine decree and the logical ordering therein. He adopted a rigidly supralapsarian perspective that became dominant during the period of Reformed scholasticism. These factors combined to give Reformed theology its rigid and at times deterministic cast.

Covenant/Federal theology. Although the covenant idea had been implicit in Reformed theology from the days of Ulrich Zwingli, the development of the idea did not come until the mid-1600s. The rigid supralapsarian mind-set that dominated much of the Reformed world elevated God and his power, majesty, and sovereignty but in the process, reduced the place of man virtually to that of a pawn. Against this background, German theologian Johannes Cocceius, a student of the English Puritan William Ames, developed the idea of covenant and made it central in his theological presentation. Whereas Reformed orthodoxy had been preeminently philosophical, it now became biblical in its emphasis.

Cocceius's system presented the relationship between God and man as one of covenant. In Eden God instituted the *covenant of works*, promising life for obedience and death for disobedience. After the fall, God introduced a new covenant, the *covenant of grace*, offering salvation as a divine gift to be received through faith. The covenant of grace has governed divine-human relationships ever since. Later the concept of the *covenant of redemption* was adopted by some in the Reformed tradition. This covenant was understood as an eternal covenant between the Father and the Son whereby the Father would give to the Son the elect, and the Son would become incarnate to pay the price for their salvation. The effect of the covenant of redemption was that the radical role of divine sovereignty as propounded by Beza was reestablished, thus subverting Cocceius's intent. Covenant theology has become synonymous with the Reformed tradition.

Remonstrants. In response to the rigid supralapsarian cast of Reformed theology in the period of Reformed scholasticism, a reactionary movement developed from the work of James Arminius. The two names of note here are Episcopius, who gives a clear and comprehensive exposition of Arminian theology, and the Dutch jurist Hugo Grotius. Grotius developed the governmental theory of the atonement that was adopted later, during the period of degeneration of New England Calvinism following the death of Jonathan Edwards.

D. MODERN THEOLOGY

1. The Liberal Impulse

Out of the ashes of the Enlightenment arose a new theological tradition intended to be both modern and Christian. This tradition was founded by Friedrich Schleiermacher with Albrecht Ritschl as its second major inspiration. Schleiermacher's systematic theology, *The Christian Faith*, is an amalgamation of Enlightenment rationalism, pietism, romanticism, incipient idealism, and a type of supernaturalism that begins with *religious experience* as the foundational authority for theology. This "experience" is the feeling of absolute creaturely dependence of which all theology is merely an explication. Jesus Christ is the one human individual who was in a state of perfect God consciousness and thus provides the perfect example.

Schleiermacher marked a radical departure from traditional theology. Before him all theology had the Word of God as its foundation and highest source of authority. Schleiermacher turned theological method on its head and substituted subjective experience for objective revelation. The tradition of Albrecht Ritschl is radically empirical and finds its greatest exponent in Adolf von Harnack and his seven-volume *History of Dogma*. More concise is his *What Is Christianity?* transcribed lectures given in Berlin in 1900. This slim volume is the outstanding exposition of the fundamental principles of liberalism as a coherent system. (See chapter 14 for a discussion of liberalism as a system.)

2. The Mediating School

During the mid-nineteenth century, the mediating school of theology emerged in Germany. This school sought to mediate between the theology of Schleiermacher and historic orthodoxy, as well as between the Lutheran and Reformed traditions. The mediating theologians were orthodox in their theology but decried the cold creedal state into which theology and Christianity had fallen. They saw in Schleiermacher a helpful corrective in that he placed his emphasis on the heart rather than just the head. The two leading lights of this school were Isaac August Dorner, who contributed *A History of the Doctrine of the Person of Christ* as well as his *System of Christian Doctrine*, and Julius Müller, whose greatest contribution was a monograph on the doctrine of sin. Much of the material produced by the mediating school has never been translated into English from the original German.

3. Reformed Theology

Beginning in the late nineteenth century, there was a "late flowering" of Calvinism in the Netherlands that also affected the United States. Among those who deserve mention are Abraham Kuyper, Herman Bavinck, and G. C. Berkouwer. American theologians arising out of this tradition include Louis Berkhof and Cornelius Van Til.

Among the American theologians of the nineteenth century, the Princetonians Charles Hodge, A. A. Hodge, and B. B. Warfield stand as paramount. The Southern Presbyterians James Henley Thornwell and R. L. Dabney are also significant. Henry Boynton Smith of Union Seminary, New York, and his more famous colleague William G. T. Shedd also produced significant works. Additionally, the Calvinist Baptist theologian A. H. Strong also produced a significant contribution.

4. Neoorthodoxy

The twentieth century saw the demise of classic nineteenth-century liberalism largely at the hands of Karl Barth, the father of Neoorthodoxy. Barth produced massive amounts of theological scholarship, the most significant of which was his *Church Dogmatics*. His *Dogmatics in Outline* and *Evangelical Theology* provide more accessible entrances into his thought. Standing with Barth at the fountainhead of neoorthodoxy is Emil Brunner, also a Swiss. His three-volume *Dogmatics* is far more accessible than Barth's, and Brunner had more early influence than Barth in the English-speaking world. (See chapter 15 for a discussion of the neoorthodox perspective and method.)

5. Other Twentieth-Century Theologians

Paul Tillich, a contemporary of Barth and Brunner, had a long career in Germany before emigrating to the United States, where he produced many works on contemporary theology. Tillich's three-volume *Systematic Theology* is written from the perspective of existential philosophy and reads more like a philosophy than a traditional theology.

During the later half of the twentieth century, two men emerged as leading theologians, Wolfhart Pannenberg and Jürgen Moltmann. Pannenberg's *Systematic Theology* has been translated into English. His foundational theme is "revelation as history." Moltmann's perspective has been termed "theology of hope," and he is often regarded as the theological and intellectual father of liberation theology, black theology, and feminist theology.

BIBLIOGRAPHY

Boers, Hendrikus. *What Is New Testament Theology?* Philadelphia: Fortress, 1979. • **Cunliffe-Jones, Hubert.** *A History of Christian Doctrine.* Philadelphia:

Fortress, 1978. • **Davis, John Jefferson**. *The Necessity of Evangelical Theology.* Grand Rapids: Baker, 1978. • **Harrisville, Roy**, and **Walter Sundberg**. *The Bible in Modern Culture*. Grand Rapids: Eerdmans, 1995. • **Hasel, Gerhard.** *New Testament Theology: Issues in the Current Debate*. Grand Rapids: Baker, 1978, rev. 1991. • **Kummel, Werner G.** *The New Testament.* Translated by S. McClean Gilmour and Howard C. Kee. Nashville: Abingdon, 1972. • **Pelikan, Jaroslav.** *The Christian Tradition.* 5 volumes. Chicago: University of Chicago Press, 1971–89.

NOTES

[1]See chap. 5.

[2]As noted elsewhere, this interpretation of *sola scriptura* is not faithful to the Reformation cry and is in fact what Donald Bloesch has labeled *nuda scriptura* (Donald Bloesch, *Theology of Word and Spirit* [Downers Grove, IL: InterVarsity Press, 1992], 193).

[3]Charles Augustus Briggs, *The Study of Holy Scripture* (New York: Scribner, 1899), 596.

[4]Krister Stendahl made this point in distinguishing biblical from systematic theology in his classic article, "Biblical Theology, Contemporary," in *Interpreter's Bible Dictionary*, ed. Keith R. Crim and George A. Buttrick (Nashville: Abingdon, 1981), 1:419.

[5]B. B. Warfield, "The Idea of Systematic Theology," in John Jefferson Davis, ed., *The Necessity of Systematic Theology* (Grand Rapids: Baker, 1978), 144.

[6]Ibid., 145–46.

[7]See Hendrikus Boers, *What Is New Testament Theology?* (Philadelphia: Fortress, 1979), 15–18.

[8]An excellent history of the historical-critical method is found in Roy A. Harrisville and Walter Sundberg, *The Bible in Modern Culture* (Grand Rapids: Eerdmans, 1995).

[9]A detailed survey of the development of biblical theology has been done by Gerhard Hasel and can be found in his *Old Testament Theology: Basic Issues in the Current Debate*, rev. ed. (Grand Rapids: Eerdmans, 1991), and *New Testament Theology: Basic Issues in the Current Debate* (Grand Rapids: Eerdmans, 1978). These works form the basis of the following summary.

[10]Hasel, *New Testament Theology*, 23.

[11]Georg Lorenz Bauer, *Biblische Theologie des Neuen Testaments*, 2 vols. (Leipzig: 1800–1802). Cited in Werner G. Kummel, *The New Testament: A History of the Investigation of Its Problems*, trans. S. McClean Gilmour and Howard C. Kee (Nashville: Abingdon, 1972), 105.

[12]This early Catholicism is not to be identified with Roman Catholicism, which did not emerge until the early medieval period.

[13]Hasel, *New Testament Theology*, 37.

[14]Ibid., 55.

[15]See chap. 15, "Neoorthodoxy."

[16]G. Hasel, "Biblical Theology Movement," in Walter Elwell, ed., *Evangelical Dictionary of Theology* (Grand Rapids: Baker, 1984), 152.

[17]See Hasel, *New Testament Theology*, 72–139, for a discussion of these various methods.

[18]Hubert Cunliffe-Jones, ed., *A History of Christian Doctrine* (Philadelphia: Fortress, 1978), 6.

[19]See chap. 9, "Roman Catholicism," for a discussion of Newman's contribution. While Newman's perspective was aimed at explaining change within Catholicism, the underlying idea that doctrine is dynamic and develops over time is recognized by virtually all in the field.

[20]Cunliffe-Jones, *History of Christian Doctrine*, 17.

[21]Ibid.

[22]J. L. Neve and O. W. Heick, *A History of Christian Thought* (Philadelphia: United Lutheran Publication House, 1943), 1:6. Muenscher wrote *Handbuch der christlichen Dogmengeschichte* (4 vols.) from 1797 to 1809 and *Lehrbuch der christlichen Dogmengeschichte* in 1811.

[23]Reinhold Seeberg, *Text-Book of the History of Doctrines*, trans. Charles E. Hays (Grand Rapids: Baker, 1952), 20–21.

[24]Ibid., 19.

[25]Neve and Heick, *History*, 1:3.

[26]Jaroslav Pelikan, *The Christian Tradition: A History of the Development of Doctrine* (Chicago: University of Chicago Press, 1971–89), 1:5.

[27]See figure 2.1 on p. 26.

[28]See chap. 4, p. 117.

[29]However, this ascription was apparently reserved for competing theologies only. While other systems were influenced by philosophy, Princeton perceived itself as philosophically neutral, preserving the unalloyed Reformation doctrine (Daryl G. Hart, "The Princeton Mind in the Modern World," *Westminster Theological Journal* 46 [1984]: 4). This perception notwithstanding, there were some even at Princeton who were conscious of the close relationship Princeton maintained with Scottish Common Sense. At the inauguration of William Henry Green to his professorship in biblical and Oriental literature at Princeton, the charge was given: "Amid the ceaseless mutations of philosophical systems, there is one system which remains unchanged; and that system is the only one which the Bible recognizes as true—the philosophy of Common Sense" (Francis Landy Patton, "Princeton Seminary and the Faith," *Centennial of Princeton Seminary* [Princeton: At the Seminary, 1912], 349–50).

[30]Paul Tillich, *Systematic Theology* (Chicago: University of Chicago Press, 1956), 1:1–8.

[31]R. A. Norris, *God and the World in Early Christian Theology: A Study in Justin Martyr, Irenaeus, Tertullian and Origen* (New York: Seabury, 1965), 72.

[32]E.g., Anselm worked within the Augustinian synthesis, which was at its base Neoplatonic (realism) and asserted the reality of universals. Aquinas became the

author of a new synthesis that incorporated elements of Aristotelianism and Platonism and was called "moderate realism" or "conceptualism," which denied the objective character of universals but saw instead universals as being abstracted from particulars. William of Occam became the father of nominalism, a philosophical perspective that denied philosophical universals altogether.

[33]Averroes's actual name was Faylasuf Abu al-Walid Ahmad ibn Rushd, which is why he is also known as Ibn-Rushd. He lived during the Spanish renaissance in the twelfth century. His "rationalistic thought influenced such Jewish and Christian philosophers as Maimonides, Thomas Aquinas, and Albert the Great [Albertus Magnus]" (Karen Armstrong, *Islam: A Short History* [New York: Modern Library, 2000], 83–84). Averroes was a devout Muslim and an expert in Shariah law but was thought to give insufficient primacy to the Qur'an, and in 1195 he was exiled, the study of Greek books was banned, and his books were burned. He died three years later in Morocco.

[34]While the term *humanism* became pejorative in the late twentieth century, it originally described a method and course of study. It was founded on the humanities as opposed to the study of canon law. McGrath deals extensively with humanism as a method of study in his *Intellectual Origins of the European Reformation* (Oxford: Blackwell, 1987), 32–68.

[35]Alister McGrath, *A Life of John Calvin* (Oxford: Blackwell, 1990), 148.

[36]Ibid., 149.

[37]For an accessible survey of scholastic Lutheranism, see Justo Gonzalez, *History of Christian Thought* (Nashville: Abingdon, 1975), 3:226–41.

PART 2

THEOLOGICAL SYSTEMS

OUTLINE OF CHAPTER 8

A. A Brief History of Orthodoxy

B. The Mystery of God
   1. Apophatic Theology
   2. The Trinity
   3. The Filioque and the Procession of the Holy Spirit

C. Images
   1. Christ the Image of the Father
   2. Icons

D. Deification (Theosis)

E. Scripture, Tradition, and the Witness of the Spirit

F. Observations and Critique

CHAPTER 8

ORTHODOXY

The Eastern Orthodox tradition is viewed by many Western Protestants as an Eastern version of the Roman Catholic Church, except that its priests can wear beards and marry and that it does not recognize the pope. This, however, is a serious misunderstanding. Eastern Orthodoxy developed along radically different lines than Western Christianity and faced very different struggles. From both a historical and a theological perspective, the key to the differences between them is found in the role Augustine plays in each.

In the West all theology has been shaped by the massive influence of Augustine: both Protestantism and Catholicism look to the thought of Augustine as a touchstone. In the East, however, Augustine holds no such definitive position in the development of theology. He is not even regarded as a saint but is merely "the blessed Augustine." In contrast to the Western Augustinian perspective, the East looks to the Greek fathers, particularly Athanasius and the Cappadocians (Basil the Great, Gregory of Nazianzus, and Gregory of Nyssa) for the cast of its theology. This is why Orthodoxy has a very different "feel" than Western theology. In the West, the heritage of the Roman legal system and a legal mentality have prevailed from the time of Tertullian, whereas in the East, the perspective has been philosophical, mystical, and personalistic.

A. A BRIEF HISTORY OF ORTHODOXY

On June 16, 1054, Cardinal Humbert, representing Pope Leo IX, entered the cathedral of Hagia Sophia (Holy Wisdom) in Constantinople at the beginning of the celebration of the Holy Eucharist. Humbert approached the altar and placed on it a sentence of excommunication against Michael Cerularius, patriarch of Constantinople, and all who stood with him. This act, which was followed shortly by a reciprocal excommunication pronounced by Cerularius against Humbert, served to seal the separation of the Eastern and Western churches for centuries to come.

This separation between the Eastern Orthodox and the Western Catholic branches of Christianity in 1054 became known as the Great Schism. The roots of this schism, however, are to be found much earlier in the history of the church. The underlying issues that had provoked earlier rifts (in 476–519 and 867) had never truly been resolved, and by the eleventh century, the churches of East and West had been heading in very different directions for so long that the Great Schism merely made official what had already become a fact.

The reasons for the distinct characters of, and deep differences between, the two parts of what had always been seen as one Holy Church are manifold. As in all human institutions, lack of goodwill and understanding were manifest on both sides, as seen especially in the confrontation between Humbert and Cerularius. Both sides, however, saw the issues that were in dispute as being of supreme importance to the integrity of the faith, that is, to the preservation of the inheritance of doctrine and practice that defined what it meant to be a Christian.

Some of the stated reasons were

- The addition in the West of the phrase "and the Son" (*filioque*) to the Nicene Creed
- The controversy over statues (in the West) and the use of icons in worship (in the East)
- The use of unleavened bread in the Eucharist (West)
- The primacy of the pope (West)[1]
- The subordination of the church to the state (East)
- The enforced celibacy of priests (West)
- The issue of priests having beards (East)

Of the theological issues, the most serious one concerned the *filioque*. While the addition of a single word to a creed may seem trivial, the insertion of that word by the West turned the Eastern understanding of both God and the church (as reflecting the unity of the Trinity) on its head (see below, p. 244).

Still other issues drove a wedge between East and West.

- The two parts of the church spoke different languages (Latin in the West, Greek in the East), so that by the early Middle Ages they could no longer readily understand each other.
- They lived in very different political environments—the West had lived through the dissolution of the Roman Empire and the incursion

of barbarian tribes, whereas the East enjoyed the continuation and relative stability of the Byzantine Empire.

- In the West, the pagan tribes were Christianized and incorporated (sometimes violently) into the prevailing Christian culture. In the East, the Byzantine Empire decreased in size as it was walled in on the east and south by the expansion of Islamic culture and religion.
- In the West, the church and its leaders (bishops and pope) often exercised dominant political leadership. In the East, the church was closely allied with a dominant emperor and state.

The nature and methodology of theological thought also differed greatly between East and West:

- In the West, thinking took a turn toward a *pragmatic* and *legal* understanding and application of doctrine. In the East, theology moved in a more *personalistic* and *mystical* direction, reflecting the heritage of the Greek fathers.
- The West often tended toward *innovation* and *adaptation* to changing circumstances. The East maintained a more *traditional*, stable, and conservative approach to liturgy and doctrine.
- The West struggled with a *plurality of local and regional cultures* and their varying influences on liturgical practices and doctrinal interpretation. The East was far more *homogeneous* in culture and customs.
- The concern of Western theology tended more and more to the destiny of the individual believer *in the next world*, whereas the East maintained a strong element of belief in the deification *(theosis)* of the person *in this life* (see below, p. 248).[2]

The eventual hardening of the differences between the church in the East and the church in the West that culminated in the Great Schism seemed historically inevitable, despite belief on both sides in the unity of the Christian faith and of the church that proclaimed and protected that faith. From the eleventh century on, the two parts of the church largely went their own way. In the East, Orthodoxy was continually challenged by the presence of Islam and the success of the Islamic expansion. In 1453 Constantinople fell to the Muslim Turks. The center of gravity in the Orthodox church moved north, into the Slavic nations and especially into Russia. After the fall of Constantinople, Moscow was declared "the Third Rome." Since the tenth century, Slavic and Russian character have been profoundly formed and marked by Orthodox Christianity. Reciprocally, the Slavic and Russian experience has left deep marks on Orthodox Christianity.

In the West, the path the church followed led to the definition of Roman Catholicism, to the delineation of papal authority, and to the many attempts to realize an earthly kingdom that would manifest Christendom. The Eastern church had a progressively smaller influence on the West until the beginning of the Protestant Reformation in the sixteenth century. Lutheran and especially Anglican reformers once more turned to the patristic sources that formed the foundation of the Eastern theological tradition. Orthodoxy, by virtue of its inherent conservatism, preserved liturgical continuity with, and traces of the traditions of, the ancient church. It also reflected a theological rootedness—in the Fathers and the councils—that was lost in the Roman Catholic tradition. Orthodoxy also provided a historically relevant critique of the universal claims of Roman Catholicism. The traditions and theology of the Eastern church reached over and beyond Roman Catholic southern Europe to influence the development of a northern European reformation of the church—a contribution that is often underestimated or overlooked altogether.

In recent decades, the rise of ecumenism in the West has led to numerous attempts to bridge the gap between East and West. Various Protestant groups have made strides in this direction, especially the Anglican Communion. However, the Roman Catholic Church has not been entirely absent from these attempts. In 1965 a joint declaration by Pope Paul VI and Patriarch Athenagoras stated that both sides "deplore the disturbing precedents and subsequent events which, under the influence of various factors, including a failure to understand and mutual distrust, finally led to the effective schism in communion." The pope and patriarch pledged themselves and their respective churches to repentance and to a commitment to pursue a path that would perhaps lead to restoration of "a common understanding and expression of the apostolic faith and its demands." Perhaps the possibility exists for a future healing of the Great Schism and a closer relationship between the Eastern and Western church. The events of recent years that resulted in the end of the Cold War and greater access to Russia and Eastern Europe will keep Eastern Orthodox Christianity within sight of the rest of the world, including the Western church, both Catholic and Protestant. It is clear that Orthodox Christianity will play a crucial role in the development of Russia and the countries of the former Soviet Union in the twenty-first century.

B. THE MYSTERY OF GOD

1. Apophatic Theology

One of the central tenets of Orthodox theology is that God in himself is absolutely transcendent and rationally unknowable. Thus he can be described only in the *apophatic*[3] language of negation—that is, we can describe what he is *not* like rather than make positive assertions about what he *is* like, for example, "God is not finite" rather than "God is infinite." However, God can be known experientially and mystically, not in his *essence* but in his divine *energies* (his dynamic working). The emphasis in Orthodoxy is on the limitations inherent in the finiteness of the human mind, which make it impossible for us to grasp the infinite greatness of the holy Creator. "We can say that the negative way of the knowledge of God is an intellectual experience of the mind's failure when confronted with something beyond the conceivable."[4] This position asserts that the mystical and personal path to the knowledge of God is superior to the intellectual. While nearly all branches of Christian theology contain apophatic elements, in Orthodoxy it has become a predominant theme.

Orthodoxy does not deny the value of *cataphatic*[5] (positive) statements about God, for example, that he is holy, just, good, and so on. But these are true in a relative sense and cannot adequately grasp God *as he is in his essence*. According to John of Damascus, positive statements about God tell us "not the nature but the things around nature. That there is a God is clear, but what he is by essence and nature, this is altogether beyond our comprehension and knowledge."[6]

In asserting that God is absolutely transcendent, the Orthodox do not deny his immanence. Rather, they assert that God exists within his creation by virtue of his divine energies. By this is meant that God himself *works* intimately and immanently in the created order while in his essence he remains apart and separate from creation. It could be said that God works in and is known and experienced through his work in creation, but personally he is totally separate from that creation. Thus arises the paradox that God is a God who hides himself while being at the same time a God who acts and who through his actions reveals himself.

This work of God in his divine energies does not imply that God in his workings is an impersonal force; he is profoundly personal. His personal nature is God's triunity. When God is apprehended in his workings, he is apprehended face-to-face and experienced as a personal being.

2. The Trinity

Eastern theology is profoundly Trinitarian. The Orthodox contend that God made man in his own image. The Christian understands that God is in his innermost being a trinity,[7] and it is only by properly understanding God as a trinity that we can understand ourselves and who God intends us to become. Orthodoxy, unlike Western theology, views the doctrine of the Trinity not as a theoretical theological abstraction, but rather as a truth of profound practical importance for every believer. A proper understanding of self, personal relationships, and the structure of the church and its effect on society have their foundations in the understanding of God as a trinity.

Twentieth-century Orthodox thinker Vladimir Lossky states that the sole theological/dogmatic ground that separates East and West is the understanding of the doctrine of the Trinity.[8] While both East and West assert the truth of the Trinity as foundational to the beliefs of anyone who claims the name Christian, the two have taken different approaches to their explanations of the doctrine. The East, following in the tradition of the Cappadocian fathers, has begun with the presupposition of diversity (three persons) and worked toward unity (one essence/being/*ousia).* The West, following Augustine, has begun with the concept of unity and worked toward the assertion of three persons.

Eastern explanations of God as a trinity have focused on the divine community that is inhabited by three coequal persons, each of whom is fully and completely deity and whose divine fellowship is so complete that each member fully "indwells" the other *(perichoresis)* in the perpetual movement of divine love. God in his fullness is thus *both unity and union.* It is from this interpersonal relationship that the church is to reflect the mystery of the Trinity.[9]

3. The Filioque and the Procession of the Holy Spirit

The actual dogmatic division between East and West occurred over the issue of the *filioque* (Lat. "and the Son") clause. The Council of Nicea (A.D. 381) had declared that the Holy Spirit proceeds from the Father (see John 15:26). This was an ecumenical pronouncement, agreed upon by the entire church. During the early medieval period, the Council of Toledo (A.D. 589) added the word *filioque* to the Nicene Creed, so that it now said that the Holy Spirit proceeds from the Father *and the Son.* The East objected on two counts. The first was ecclesiastical and political: the addition was made without authority and without the consent of the East, which was illegitimate in light of the ecumenical nature of the creed. The second objection was theological: the implications of the *filioque* are heretical.

Eastern theology has always held the Father to be the source of the Godhead and the Unbegotten One. The Son's relationship to the Father was seen in his begottenness (see John 3:16), whereas the Spirit's relationship to the Father was seen in his procession from the Father. Eastern theologians objected that the concept of the double procession of the Spirit from both Father and

Son introduced *two* ultimate sources of being into the Godhead and destroyed the unity of the Trinity. Eastern theology understands there to be a *mon*archy within the Trinity. God the Father *in his person* is the source of all. Irenaeus spoke of the Son and the Spirit as the two hands of God.[10]

The *filioque* has had the further effect of subordinating the Holy Spirit to the Son so that in effect the Spirit becomes the ignored member of the Godhead. His role in the life of the church has been diminished, and the church has taken on an institutional character rather than being an expression and reflection of the divine life that indwells it. This in turn has led to the overemphasis on unity that has ultimately resulted in the solidification of ecclesiastical power in the papacy.

C. IMAGES

1. Christ the Image of the Father

The Orthodox Church, along with Western Christianity, asserts that in the Old Testament God reveals himself to be utterly transcendent relative to any and every image that might make his nature known.[11] Protestantism, particularly Reformed Protestantism, has understood the Old Testament injunctions against images to imply that the use of any image in worship is to be regarded as idolatrous. This understanding came in reaction to the abuse of images, the cult of the saints, and the Mariolatry that had characterized medieval Catholicism. When Protestants are exposed to the icons of the Orthodox Church, they generally have a negative reaction that has its roots in the Reformation struggles.

Gregory of Nyssa

However, the Eastern Orthodox use of icons and the Roman Catholic veneration of saints are very different theologically and rest on very different foundations. Central to Orthodox theology is the notion that Christ is the image (Gk. εἰκών, *eikon*) of the Father. Gregory of Nyssa asserted, "The Son is in the Father as the beauty of the image resides in archetypal form.... The Father is in the Son as the archetypal beauty remaining in its image,... and we must think both these things simultaneously." Patristic theology introduced the distinction of *hypostasis* and *essence* into Christian Trinitarian understanding. This distinction asserted that while Christ was divine, he was distinct from the Father. He was the Son and *image* of his Father, one who existed in personal relationship with the Father. This image manifests not the person but the *nature* of the Father. It is from this Trinitarian theology of *image* that a derivative theology of *images* was developed. When the incarnation was considered with these Trinitarian distinctions in the background, the incarnation of Christ was thought to manifest to creation the image of the Father.

The image of Christ, the visible image of the invisible God, is near the core of Eastern Orthodox theological understanding.[12] Athanasius asked, "How was the Son, who is by nature impassable and immortal, to suffer death on our behalf so that we might be liberated from the sentence of death that stands against us?"[13] The answer of course is the incarnation, which becomes the means to "achieve the destiny designed for mankind ... perceived as the deification and immortalization of humanity."[14] Athanasius asks again, "What was the use of man having been originally made in God's image?"

> The plain fact, with which all deniers of Christ's deity must be faced, is that "a creature could never be saved by a creature, any more than creatures were created by a creature." ... And so, "the Word of God came in his own person, so that, being himself the Image of the Father, he might be able to create man afresh after the image. None was sufficient for this need, save the Image of the Father."[15]

Yet, while the image is central to Orthodoxy, it is but a footnote in Western theology. Modern Protestant writers have developed their theology along different lines. Several, including Karl Barth, Emil Brunner, and Anders Nygren, deny that it is a scriptural representation and assert that it is a Platonic category imported into the biblical material, or that it is not an important biblical category.[16] Nevertheless, if we are to understand the heart of Orthodoxy, we must come to grips with the theology of the image and its implications.

The fact that the second person of the Trinity would take on human flesh and become a part of the created order became a bold assertion of the created goodness of the material order. This in turn gave rise to a theology of creation that embraced all of the senses in the worship experience. Whereas churches of the Reformed tradition appear stark and cold, reflecting an understanding that worship is a matter of the spirit, the Orthodox churches are a sensual feast, exulting in beauty.

2. Icons

Within Orthodoxy there is a *philokalia*, a love of the beautiful. Orthodox theology is consciously displayed in the architecture and ornamentation of the churches. The icons that are so prominent in Orthodox worship also reflect this and bring the aesthetic into the service of the sacred.

For the Eastern Orthodox, the theology of the image is celebrated and understood by their use of icons. Whereas Western theology has been taught in terms of ideas, Orthodoxy theology is communicated in terms of concrete images. The Orthodox assert that "seeing is better than hearing."[17]

The use of icons was the subject of controversy during the eighth and ninth centuries to the point that for nearly a century their use was alternately banned and approved. At issue was not merely the place of Christian art but deeper theological issues, including the nature of Christ's humanity, the Christian perspective on the material creation, and the true meaning of redemption. The legitimacy of icons as aids in worship was upheld by the seventh and last ecumenical council at Nicea (787).

When an Orthodox Christian prostrates himself before icons, kisses them, or burns candles in front of them, the Protestant sees this as acts of idolatry. The Orthodox insist, however, that icons are not idols but symbols. The veneration is not directed toward the material object but toward that which is represented. Furthermore, the Orthodox insist that they do not *worship* icons, but *venerate* them. Worship is due God alone.

Icons are viewed as "opened books to remind us of God,"[18] and they are used as a means of instruction. By teaching the meaning of the symbols, the Orthodox claim to teach the whole body of Christian truth in pictorial and symbolic form. Leonard of Neapolis (c. A.D. 650) declared, "We do not make obeisance to the nature of wood, but we revere and do obeisance to Him who was crucified on the Cross.... When the two beams are joined together I adore the figure because of Christ who was crucified on the Cross, but if the beams are separated, I throw them away and burn them."[19]

The theological significance of icons is seen as being rooted in the doctrine of the incarnation. God the Father cannot be represented by any material image. Yet the fact of the incarnation made religious art possible, because in the incarnation God took on human flesh. John of Damascus argues that material representations can be made of Christ because he took on a material body.

> Of old God the incorporeal and uncircumscribed was not depicted at all. But now that God has appeared in the flesh and lived among men, I make an image of the God who can be seen. I do not worship matter, but I worship the Creator of matter, who for my sake became material and deigned to dwell in matter, who through matter effected my salvation. I will not cease from worshipping the matter though my salvation has been effected."[20]

The Orthodox Church argues that in denying the legitimacy of icons the iconoclasts have fallen into a dualism that fails to do justice to the incarnation. They argue that God took on a material body *to prove that matter can be redeemed.* Thus the doctrine of icons is ultimately bound up in the doctrine of creation and the recognition that the whole of creation will ultimately be redeemed and glorified. John of Damascus argued, "The icon is a song of triumph, and a revelation, and an enduring monument to the victory of the saints and the disgrace of the demons."[21]

Protestants also have typically viewed icons as an accommodation to popular piety or even as the remnants of paganism. The Orthodox disagree, saying that while images were forbidden in the Old Testament, it is appropriate to use icons as aids in worship now because of the New Testament focus on the incarnation. The icons do not represent God in his spiritual nature; they represent Christ as he appeared in the flesh and the saints who have believed in him and labored for him.

Related to this is another Orthodox practice with which Protestants disagree: prayer to the saints. Again, the Orthodox Church rejects the Roman concepts of the cult of the saints and a treasury of merit. Rather, they see the concept of prayer to the saints as akin to asking fellow believers to intercede for them in prayer. The Orthodox see a unity in the church that allows the departed saints who are in the presence of Christ to pray for their brothers and sisters in the same way that the living pray for one another.

Reflecting the Orthodox affirmation of the goodness of all that God has made, the use of icons has shaped their understanding of anthropology and humankind's ultimate destiny in the transformation into the image of Christ. On this issue, the East and West are theologically close to being in agreement, yet the expressions of the idea are quite distinct. Whereas the West writes about it in books on dogmatic theology, the East meditates on it in liturgical prose, poetry, and music. Both assert the same understanding but employ radically different means of expression.

D. DEIFICATION (THEOSIS)

Whereas in the West the categories used to describe salvation have been legal categories such as forgiveness, reconciliation, adoption, and justification, the controlling metaphors in Orthodox soteriology have been personalistic and mystical. The overriding category for salvation is that of *deification* or *theosis.* Athanasius declared that Christ became man that we should become god (that is, participants in the divine nature). Maximus the Confessor declared, "All that God is, except for an identity in nature, one becomes when one is deified by grace."

Behind the concept of deification lies Jesus Christ's prayer for believers in John 17:21, "May [they all] be one, Father, just as you are in me and I am in you. May they also be in us." Saved humanity is called to dwell in the Trinitarian fullness. Maximus the Confessor declared that the saints are those who express the Holy Trinity in themselves. This is a recurring theme in John's gospel as well as for Paul, who sees salvation in terms of life "in Christ," and Peter, who declared, "Through [Jesus' own glory and goodness] he has given us his very great and precious promises, so that through them you may participate in the divine nature" (2 Peter 1:4).

The means of deification is the Holy Spirit who is dynamically indwelling the church. He is the agent who accomplishes salvation. The Father conceived of salvation, the Son realized it in time, and the Spirit finalizes, completes, and perfects it in the life of his people in the sphere of the church, the mystical body of Christ. Basil writes, "From the Holy Spirit there are the foreknowledge of the future, the comprehension of the mysteries, the understanding of hidden things, the distribution of the graces, the heavenly way of life, association with angels, unending happiness, residence in God, the likeness of God, and the highest of all things to be desired to become God."[22] The Orthodox declare that the Holy Spirit is "both divine and divinizing."[23]

To the Western mind, this concept seems to lead to an expression of pantheism, whereby the created is joined in essence to the uncreated divine nature. This is an implication the Orthodox soundly reject. As noted above, the Orthodox make a distinction between God in his essence, which is totally transcendent, and his energies, which are immanent. The union with God is understood to be a union with his energies rather than his essence. While deification involves a true union of the human and the divine, it is to be distinguished from any Eastern notion of monism and fusion with the one. In the process of deification, the human being always retains his or her full personal integrity, distinct but not separate from God. Deified human beings then reflect the unity *in diversity* of the Trinity. The process of deification does not change a human into the essence of deity. As Lossky explains, "We remain creatures while becoming god by grace, as Christ remained God when becoming man by the Incarnation."[24] The human becomes a "created god" or "a god by grace or by status."[25]

Despite the lack of image terminology in Protestant theology, there is an innate recognition that the believer is to incarnate in some sense the presence of Christ to the world in which he or she lives. This concept finds expression in the oft-misunderstood words of Athanasius, "He became man in order that we might be made god." This may remind contemporary Protestant Christians of Mormonism, but that is an incorrect conclusion to draw. Reformed theologian Philip Hughes observes:

> It is true that Athanasius did not always pause to clarify what he intended by his conception of the deification of man, but there are places where he took the trouble to do so, and from these, as well as from the whole tenor of his theology, it is obvious that he was not thinking in terms of an ontological change, but of the reintegration of the divine image of man's creation through the sanctifying work of the Holy Spirit conforming the redeemed into the likeness of Christ, and also of the believer's transition from mortality to immortality so that he is enabled to participate in the eternal bliss and glory of the kingdom of God.[26]

When Athanasius said that the Word of God became incarnate that we might be deified, he was speaking of the redemptive purpose of the Son's coming, which was not only to set us free from the guilt and power of sin and to reconcile us to the Father, but also to exalt us in himself to the glorious perfection of God's everlasting kingdom and to eternal life. In short, he was referring to the attainment of the resplendent harmony with our Creator that was intended for us from the beginning. Athanasius was not speaking of the obliteration of the ontological distinction between Creator and creature; he was speaking of the establishment at last of intimate and uninterrupted personal communion between them.[27]

Athanasius

This deification involves not just the soul but the body as well; however, this final deification must await the glorification of the resurrection. The conviction that both the soul *and* the body will be deified has led the Orthodox to venerate the relics of the saints. Ware asserts that this veneration is not done out of ignorance or superstition; rather, it arises out of a highly developed theology of the body.[28]

Deification is intended for all—it is the goal of every Christian. Deification is, in the Orthodox understanding, a process that is begun in this life and in which the Christian grows progressively. It is very much akin to the concept of progressive sanctification among Protestants, although it does not begin with a legal change in standing due to the declarative act of justification. The deified person does not lose consciousness of sin; rather, he or she remains in a continual state of repentance. The means of deification mirror in measure the traditional Protestant means of grace. They include church attendance, reception of the sacraments, reading of the Gospels (in community worship), obedience to the commandments, and prayer in spirit and in truth. Deification is not just an individual process, it has a social dimension involving loving one's neighbors in practical ways, such as ministering to the hungry, the sick, and the poor. Finally, deification presupposes that the church will participate together in common spiritual life and receiving of the sacraments.

The stress on the necessity of good works may give the appearance that these good works are believed to save and unite one to God. This is expressly denied. The place of good works is a means to, not a ground of, salvation. "The purpose of the Christian life is not good works.... They do not of themselves grant *theosis*."[29] Works are the outward manifestation of an inward spiritual reality.

According to some, the term *theosis* is technically applicable only to the final stages of holiness in this life, when the saint has reached a level whereby he or she mystically enters into the presence of God (we might compare this to Wesley's doctrine of entire sanctification). However, the term has more often been applied to the entire Orthodox conception of the process of salvation.

E. SCRIPTURE, TRADITION, AND THE WITNESS OF THE SPIRIT

Whereas the West locates authority in the objective written Word of God, in the East authority is viewed as internal and pneumatic. These two different conceptions of authority, one pneumatic and internal, the other dogmatic and external, constitute the "ultimate difference" between Eastern and Western confessions of faith.[30] Fr. John Myendorf noted, "This lack in Orthodox ecclesiology of a clearly defined, precise, and permanent criterion of Truth besides God Himself, Christ, and the Holy Spirit, is certainly one of the major contrasts between Orthodoxy and all classical Western ecclesiologies."[31] While to Western ears this sounds like abject subjectivism that allows no sure, objective ground to stand on, the Eastern theologians had to wrestle with heretics who made use of Scripture to establish their points. "Heretics showed that they could be as painstaking in their use of the Scripture as the saints. The fact soon became obvious to any intelligent thinker that the principle of 'the Bible and the Bible only' provides no automatically secure basis for a religion that is to be genuinely Christian."[32] It was this problem that caused Orthodoxy to find ultimate authority beyond the text of Scripture. Irenaeus claimed that the heretics' use of Scripture was like taking a beautifully crafted mosaic of a king and rearranging the pieces into a dog or a fox and then claiming that the rearrangement was the authentic mosaic because it contained all the original material.[33]

While Orthodoxy places a premium on tradition, it recognizes that all tradition is not of equal worth or importance. It therefore ranks tradition in a hierarchy in which some traditions are seen as primary and others as secondary. Of primary importance outside of Scripture is the authority of the first seven ecumenical councils.[34] The Scriptures must not be approached apart from the historic witness of the Fathers. While any one Father individually might hold an errant opinion, the consensus interpretation, particularly of the first four centuries, is to be trusted.

The idea of novelty is anathema to Orthodoxy. "Devising new formulas" or "making up new terms according to our own ideas is presumptuous, deranged and heretical."[35] For the Orthodox, any appeal to tradition, be it Scripture, councils, Fathers, or liturgy, is in itself insufficient. It would mean accepting a theological truth on the basis of external authority, and no external authority can guarantee truth. As important as the councils are to Orthodoxy, even councils are seen as fallible "charismatic events" rather than as "canonical institutions." Ultimately it is only the "internal witness of the promised Holy Spirit that keeps the church in truth."[36]

F. OBSERVATIONS AND CRITIQUE

While Orthodox theology is basically an expression of the ancient and early medieval period, it has not lacked for thinkers who have interacted with culture and contemporary theological and philosophical developments. They have not, however, advanced theology in the Protestant sense. Orthodox theology remains rooted in the patristic period and faithful to the seven ecumenical councils as the definitive expression of its doctrine.

A critique of the Eastern Orthodox tradition is difficult for two reasons. First, the theology is truly representative of a very ancient and orthodox form of the faith. As such there is little on a formal theological level with which one could take issue. Second, its different developmental history made the thought of Athanasius and the Cappadocians the foundation of Orthodox theology, rather than the thought of Augustine, which makes the "look and feel" of Orthodoxy very different from both Protestantism and Catholicism. It has adopted different motifs and organizing principles as central to its articulation of the faith. Thus, evaluating Orthodoxy by Western standards involves a "comparing of apples with oranges." We must keep in mind that what is different from and unfamiliar to us is not necessarily wrong or bad. To criticize Orthodoxy on the basis of later developments in the Western tradition is somewhat problematic. Nevertheless, a few matters deserve comment.

1. Frozen in time. The Eastern church's greatest strength is also its greatest weakness. It has faithfully preserved the form and content of the ancient faith and steadfastly refused any temptation to modernize or innovate or accommodate to modern thought. The theology and worship are virtually identical to that of the late ancient period. However, as was argued in chapter 2, a key part of the theological task is contextualization. In its refusal to contextualize, Orthodoxy has bypassed one of the great responsibilities of the church: the confrontation and transformation of culture. Scripture itself provides ample examples of the necessity of contextualization.

Recitation of the truth in liturgy, even though it is worship in that God's person and works are rehearsed and praised, does not necessarily transform the heart, as the phrase "dead orthodoxy," used of Protestant liturgical churches, indicates. The failure to grasp meaning afresh, to take it in, and to reexpress it can become a practical heresy. In making this criticism, I am by no means downplaying the necessity for the mystical communion that is inherent in Eastern Orthodox thought, for this is a positive and vital element often bypassed in the Western, rational approach to the faith.

2. Exclusivity. Orthodoxy exhibits a rigid exclusivity in its claim to be *the* true church. It rejects the legitimacy of other communions. Within the United States a major evangelistic thrust appears to be the attack on other communions, particularly Protestant denominations, as not being the true church, with the clear implication that one's eternal salvation is linked to membership in an Orthodox church. To be sure, Catholics and Protestants have at times made similar claims, but this does not obviate the point at hand.

3. Veneration of icons. During the Protestant Reformation, the question of the use of statues and icons in worship was addressed. John Calvin in particular had much to say on the subject. While it is recognized that the Orthodox have a fully developed theology surrounding the use of icons in worship, we must still ask whether the distinction between veneration and worship is too subtle to be of practical value—that is, can one in truth venerate an icon without slipping inadvertently into idolatry?

BIBLIOGRAPHY

Clendenin, Daniel. *Eastern Orthodox Christianity: A Western Perspective.* Grand Rapids: Baker, 1994. • **Clendenin, Daniel**, ed. *Eastern Orthodox Theology: A Contemporary Reader.* Grand Rapids: Baker, 1995. • **Lossky, Vladimir.** *The Mystical Theology of the Eastern Church.* London: J. Clarke, 1957. • **Pelikan, Jaroslav.** *Spirit of Eastern Christendom.* Chicago: University of Chicago Press, 1974. • **Schemann, Alexander.** *For the Life of the World: Introduction to Liturgical Theology.* Crestwood, NY: St. Vladimir's Seminary Press, 1986. • **Ware, Timothy.** *The Orthodox Church.* New York: Penguin, 1993.

NOTES

[1]From the fourth to the eighth century, tension already existed in the church between East and West over the true significance of the Roman primacy. The latent tension only came to the surface in the ninth century, when it developed into open hostility.

[2]The Eastern understanding of *deification* derives from Peter's statement that we have become participants in the divine nature (2 Peter 1:4). This is the central point for understanding Orthodox soteriology.

[3]From αποφάσις (*apophasis*), "denial."

[4]Vladimir Lossky, "Apophasis and Trinitarian Theology," in *Eastern Orthodox Theology: A Contemporary Reader*, ed. Daniel Clendenin (Grand Rapids: Baker, 1995), 149.

[5]From καταφάσις (*kataphasis*), "affirmation."

[6]John of Damascus, *Exposition of the Orthodox Faith*, The Master Christian Library 7.0 (Rio, WI: Ages Software, 1999), 1:4.

[7]While it is true that, e.g., Jesus Only Pentecostals and Liberals deny the Trinity, the assertion of the Trinity is the most basic theological assertion for Christianity.

[8]Vladimir Lossky, "The Procession of the Spirit in Orthodox Trinitarian Theology," in *Eastern Orthodox Theology: A Contemporary Reader*, ed. Daniel Clendenin (Grand Rapids: Baker, 1995), 163.

[9]Timothy Ware, *The Orthodox Church*, rev. ed. (New York: Penguin, 1993), 209.

[10]Western theology, in order to avoid ditheism (two gods) and semi-Sabellianism (the persons are mere outward manifestations of the one divine essence), has been forced to retreat to the concept of unity being founded on the common essence shared by the three persons of the Godhead. This, object the Orthodox, has had the effect of depersonalizing God in Western theology and turning him into an abstract idea to be contemplated theoretically rather than a person whom one is to encounter in relationship.

[11]Vladimir Lossky, *In the Image and Likeness of God* (New York: St. Vladimir's Seminary Press, 1985), 131.

[12]The basic position comes from a Chalcedonian understanding of the person of Christ and steers a clear course between the twin rocks of docetism and Apollinarianism.

[13]Philip E. Hughes, *The True Image* (Grand Rapids: Eerdmans, 1989), 279.

[14]Ibid., 282.

[15]Ibid., 278.

[16]Lossky, *In the Image and Likeness of God*, 127.

[17]Daniel Clendenin, *Eastern Orthodox Christianity: A Western Perspective* (Grand Rapids: Baker, 1994), 75.

[18]Ware, *The Orthodox Church*, 40.

[19]Leonard of Neapolis, quoted by Ware in *The Orthodox Church*, 40.

[20]John of Damascus, *On Icons*, 1:6. See John of Damascus, *The Orthodox Faith*, in *St. John of Damascus: Writings*, trans. F. H. Chase Jr., Patristic Series (1958; repr., Baltimore: Catholic University of America Press, 1999).

[21]Ibid., 11:11.

[22]Quoted by Christophorus Stavoropoulos, "Partakers of the Divine Nature," in *Eastern Orthodox Theology: A Contemporary Reader*, ed. Daniel Clendenin (Grand Rapids: Baker, 1995), 189.

[23]Ibid.

[24]Vladimir Lossky, *Mystical Theology of the Eastern Church* (London: J. Clarke, 1957), 87.

[25]Timothy Ware, *The Orthodox Church* (London: Penguin, 1963), 232.

[26]Hughes, *True Image*, 281.

[27]Ibid., 286.

[28]Ware, *The Orthodox Church*, 239.

[29]Stavoropoulos, "Partakers of the Divine Nature," 190.

[30]Clendenin, *Eastern Orthodox Christianity*, 98. This concept of the internal authority of the Holy Spirit is at least as old as Irenaeus, the late-second-century Father and biblical theologian: "Where the Church is, there is the Spirit of God, and where the Spirit of God is, there is the Church, and every kind of grace; but the Spirit is Truth" (*Against Heresies*, 3.24.1).

[31]John Myendorf, *Living Tradition*. Cited by Clendenin in *Eastern Orthodox Christianity*, 107.

[32]George L. Prestiege, *Fathers and Heretics* (London: SPCK, 1984), 14–15.

[33]Irenaeus, *Against Heresies*, 1.8.1.

[34]Clendenin, *Eastern Orthodox Christianity*, 114.

[35]Maximus the Confessor, *Theological and Polemical Opuscula*, 9, 19. Cited by Jaroslav Pelikan, *Spirit of Eastern Christendom* (Chicago: University of Chicago Press, 1974), 20.

[36]Clendenin, *Eastern Orthodox Christianity*, 116.

OUTLINE OF CHAPTER 9

A. **History**
   1. The Emergence of the Catholic Consensus
   2. The Rise of the Papacy
   3. The Great Schism: The Split with Orthodoxy
   4. Scholasticism
   5. Late Medieval Decadence
   6. Reform and Self-Definition at Trent
   7. The Church Since Vatican II
      a. Vatican II
      b. The Results of Vatican II

B. **Theology**
   1. God Is Transcendent
   2. Historic Rootedness
   3. John Henry Newman and the Dynamic Development of Doctrine
   4. Justification by Faith vis-à-vis Protestantism
   5. Sacramentalism and Sacerdotalism
      a. The Sacraments
      b. Sacramentals
   6. Ecclesiology

C. **The Papacy**
   1. Biblical Basis
   2. Historical Elevation
   3. Infallibility

D. **Status of Mary (The Cult of the Blessed Virgin)**

E. **Observations and Critique**

CHAPTER 9

ROMAN CATHOLICISM

The term *Roman Catholicism* arose in the sixteenth century during the Protestant Reformation. Roman Catholics understand themselves to be members of the church catholic, founded by Jesus Christ, which is presided over by the bishop of Rome, the pope, who is the legitimate heir to the supreme spiritual authority of the apostle Peter as the vicar (representative) of Christ.

The American colonies were founded as self-consciously Protestant, and all but two of the original thirteen colonies were consciously anti-Catholic. Catholicism emerged as a major force in American religion and culture due in large part to the number of Catholics that entered the United States in the waves of immigration of the nineteenth and early twentieth century from predominantly Catholic portions of Europe, particularly Ireland and Southern and Eastern Europe. Also, the Catholic Church, by virtue of its organization, was able to speak with a unified voice on moral and spiritual issues affecting the life of those under its care. Protestants, by contrast, were fractured. The mainline denominations had fallen under the spell of theological liberalism, and the conservative denominations tended to withdraw from the world and adopt a defensive position that did not allow an effective pulpit from which to address larger issues.

Many conservative Protestants remain woefully ignorant of the largest group of professing Christians in the United States, the Catholics. One commonly hears rhetoric accusing the Roman Catholic Church of being a cult or of being heretical. The Reformation rhetoric of the pope as the Antichrist is still propagated in some conservative evangelical circles. Others try to prove that the Catholic Church is not and never has been a legitimate representative of Christianity, but that the true church is to be traced outside Catholicism, through a "silver line of grace" or a "trail of blood," traced in part through fringe groups like the Albigenses and the Montanists. Moreover, some missions are working to convert Catholics to "Christianity." Many evangelicals have only a vague and distorted idea of the nature and teachings of Catholicism. Thus they often think Catholicism teaches that a person is saved by good works. This perception cries out for correction, for the heritage of the Roman Catholic Church is the common heritage of Protestants also. And despite the fact that contemporary evangelicals rally around the slogan "*sola scriptura*," the Reformers themselves never sought to sweep away one and a half millennia of Catholic darkness. They built on the patristic consensus, particularly on the work of Augustine, and what they sought to correct were the late-medieval abuses and the biblical illiteracy that characterized sixteenth-century Catholicism.

A. HISTORY

1. The Emergence of the Catholic Consensus

Whereas the New Testament hints at a plurality of leadership in the early church, even within the local churches, by the turn of the second century, there was a concerted push toward institutionalism and the concentration of authority in a single monarchical bishop. Ignatius, the early-second-century bishop of Antioch whose life ended in martyrdom, stridently insisted on the authority of the bishop and on obedience to him. This trend continued so that by the late second century there was little hint of the freedom of the Spirit that had characterized the apostolic church. Several challenges arose in response to this institutionalization. The most significant for this discussion was Montanism, a charismatic and ascetic movement founded in the late second century that stressed the dynamic of the Holy Spirit as opposed to the institutionalism of the Roman Catholic Church. The church rejected Montanism as heretical, due in measure to its apocalyptic prophetic visions that failed to materialize and to its claims for authority of the sect's leader, Montanus, whom his followers regarded as the *paraclete.*

The concept of *apostolic succession* arose in response to the claims of Gnosticism, a second- and third-century rival sect claiming that salvation came through secret knowledge. The Gnostics saw Jesus as a revelation of God, but they held that Jesus had not entrusted the heart of his teaching to the masses (as expressed in the church) but rather had told the deep truths to secret followers, who had in turn entrusted it to others. Irenaeus, bishop of Lyons in Gaul, countered this claim by insisting that the ones to whom Jesus would have entrusted himself and his teaching were the apostles, whom he had personally chosen to be with him, rather than an unknown group of followers. The apostles then were the guardians of the true teaching of Christ, and they in turn entrusted this true doctrine to their successors. Following this logic, a true church was one that could demonstrate a link with the apostles through a direct succession of authority via the bishops. The issue here was not spiritual authority as centered in the bishop of Rome, but purity of doctrine.

As the church passed into the Nicene period in the fourth century, Christianity's place in the world shifted dramatically. It was no longer persecuted but was legalized by the Roman emperor Constantine, and late in the fourth century, it became the official religion of the Roman Empire. During this period, five churches rose to a level of supreme prominence. These were the church in Jerusalem, the mother church of all Christianity; the churches of Antioch and Alexandria, whose origins were rooted in the first century; the church of Constantinople, the capital of the Eastern empire; and the church at Rome, which had roots in the first century and also a long-revered history as the place where both Peter and Paul were martyred.

Rome was very early given a position of honor, more or less as a "first among equals" among the five chief episcopal sees. These sees exercised authority not only over their immediate cities, but also over the surrounding areas. In the theological controversies that raged during these centuries, Rome acquired a reputation for orthodoxy as it emerged on the victorious side of every theological controversy, while the other major episcopal sees were touched by heresy. This reputation for orthodoxy raised the status of the bishop of Rome in the eyes of the rest of the church. Among the five prominent churches, the only Western (Latin-speaking) church was that of Rome.

The catholic consensus was expressed in the theological statements arising out of the early church councils: Nicea (Nicene Creed), Constantinople (affirmed Nicea and further elaborated the place of the Holy Spirit in the Trinity), Ephesus (condemned the Nestorian heresy), and Chalcedon (defined the human and the divine natures in Christ). This consensus lies at the heart of the historic faith and is shared by all major Christian traditions (Orthodox, Roman Catholic, and Protestant).

2. The Rise of the Papacy

The rise of the authority of the bishop of Rome to the position of pope is intimately tied to political and cultural factors as well as to theological history. When Constantine split the Roman Empire into East and West, he established Constantinople as the new Rome and capital of the Eastern empire.

Over the next centuries, the West, particularly the Italian peninsula and the city of Rome, was subject to repeated sacks by barbarian tribes. During this time, the political authority of Rome broke down, and it fell to the bishop of Rome to use his influence to save the city. It was in this context that the bishop of Rome took on political authority that had heretofore belonged to the Roman civil authorities. The bishop of Rome assumed the role of pontiff, a title formerly applied to the emperor. Additionally, the bishop of Rome, as the only bishop of a chief episcopal see in the Latin-speaking world, gradually extended his episcopal care throughout the entire West.

During the papacy of Gregory I (the Great) (c. A.D. 600), the structure, administration, and worship of the Western church were unified, and the church took on the character that is identified with the medieval Roman Catholic Church.

3. The Great Schism: The Split with Orthodoxy

In theory the church was still one, but the split in the empire between the Latin West and the Greek East, as well as the demise of the relatively easy communication enjoyed during the heyday of the Roman Empire led to the practical emergence of two separate churches. Each church had its own peculiar language, customs, liturgy, and theological emphases. During the seventh and eighth centuries, repeated clashes took place between the bishop of Rome and the patriarch of Constantinople (who had by this time achieved supremacy in the Eastern church) over questions of theology and the final authority in the church. During this period, a theological controversy arose that would finally split the church in 1054. The Synod of Toledo (A.D. 589) inserted the phrase *filioque* ("and the Son") into the Nicene Creed with reference to the relationship of the Holy Spirit to the Father and the Son. (For a discussion of the significance of this addition, see chapter 8.B.3.)

This arbitrary addition of the *filioque* to a received ecumenical (universal) creed was viewed by the Eastern church as both illegal and heretical. The impropriety of the addition arose from the fact that one section of the church had no right to unilaterally alter the universally received faith. The *filioque* struck at the very center of the Eastern church's theological integration. Tensions between the two sides continued to simmer. Things finally came to a head in 1054 with the decision by Pope Leo IX to excommunicate the patriarch of Constantinople who, in turn, excommunicated the pope and the Western church later that same year. This schism remains unhealed to this day, although in 1965 Pope Paul VI and Patriarch Athenagoras lifted the mutual excommunication.

4. Scholasticism

The rise of scholasticism was due to several factors, including the rediscovery of Aristotelian philosophy, a crisis of authority in the church, and the desire to dialogue with reasonable people of other religions about matters of ultimate truth. The medieval Roman Catholic Church claimed to be the guardian of an unbroken tradition dating back to the apostles and universally witnessed by the church fathers. The early scholastic thinker Peter Abelard composed the work *Sic et Non* (Yes and No), in which he gathered patristic quotations on numerous subjects and placed the quotations in juxtaposition to one another, demonstrating that the so-called universal agreement of the Fathers on all theological issues was a myth. The Fathers, in fact, held a variety of irreconcilable opinions on most questions. This study of sources led to a crisis in authority, since the church's claim of a universal tradition had been demonstrated to be in error. The faith could no longer be accepted solely on the ground of the church's claim to consensus. Thus scholastic methodology sought to demonstrate the truth of the church's faith claims by means of reason. Significantly, the scholastics did not use reason as a method of finding new truth; rather, they demonstrated and defended by means of reason the truth already taught by the church.

5. Late Medieval Decadence

After the political prominence the church enjoyed under Innocent III and the zenith of scholastic thought under Anselm, Albertus Magnus, Thomas Aquinas, and the other scholastic luminaries, the late medieval period was characterized by moral, spiritual, political, and theological decay. Within a century of Innocent's hegemony over the kings of Europe and his claim that he ultimately wielded the swords of spiritual power and temporal authority, the papacy under Boniface VIII reached its political nadir. This was followed by the "Babylonian Captivity" of the church, a nearly seventy-year period (1309–1377) during which the papacy fell under the domination of the French king and was moved from Rome to Avignon, France. As the papacy was moved back to Rome, a period followed known as the Great Papal Schism (1378–1417) during which papal authority was split and there were first two and then three rival popes.

During this time, the church was beset by all kinds of vices. Priests were often uneducated and exercised little or no pastoral care over their flocks. The practice of simony (the buying and selling of church offices) was rampant. Priests commonly kept concubines in violation of their oaths of celibacy.

As the Renaissance dawned, the moral and spiritual life of the papacy reached new lows. Sexual immorality, the appointment of illegitimate children of high church officials to church offices, as well as the raising of armies and leading them into battle brought disrepute to the entire authority structure of the church. A preoccupation with the arts and raising money to pay for the magnificent Renaissance projects of Michelangelo, Raphael, and other artists drained the papal treasury. To raise money for these projects, the church sold indulgences. Popular respect for the papacy and the church fell to an all-time low.

In the theological arena, Aquinas's theology and his synthesis were seriously challenged and did not immediately find universal support in the church. The rise of the *via moderna* (the modern way to do theology, that is, nominalism; see chap. 18) provided a serious threat to the place of reason in theology. The church was split into competing schools of theology with competing theological methods.

The center of power in the church during this period vacillated between the pope and church councils. At one time the councils held authority over the pope, while at other times the pope reigned supreme even over the authority of the councils.

6. Reform and Self-Definition at Trent

The decadence in the church was directly responsible for the rise of the Protestant Reformation. As protests arose, the Roman Catholic Church at first responded defensively by excommunicating the heretic Martin Luther. But as Protestantism became a serious threat to the future of the church, a new council was called—the Council of Trent (1545–63). While one might have expected the council to focus on the Protestant threat, such was not the case. The primary focus of the council was reform of the abuses that led to the Protestant Reformation and a self-definition of the church's own theology. Trent did define its doctrines with reference to Protestantism, most significantly its doctrine of justification. But it also went much further. It officially adopted the theology of Thomas Aquinas and his synthesis of Aristotle and Scripture. This became official Catholic theology for the next four hundred years. Trent gave birth to the modern Roman Catholic Church.

Particularly important was the council's formal identification of the two sources of authority within the church, a view that had emerged during the fourteenth and fifteenth centuries. It held that God had given two separate and distinct revelations—the Bible and unwritten tradition *(dual-source* or *two-source* theory*)*. Tradition filled in the gaps on issues and practices about which the Bible was silent but that had been passed down from the apostles themselves. Trent dogmatized this understanding, declaring, "All saving truths and rules of conduct ... are contained in the written books and the unwritten traditions, received from the mouth of Christ himself or from the apostles themselves."

This explanation allowed the church to defend practices and doctrines that had no explicit warrant in the Bible. It also led to an institutionalizing of scholastic methodology with its highly legalistic cast and mind-set. This institutionalization gave the church a monolithic structure that allowed it to withstand the onslaughts of rationalism and liberalism that attacked Protestantism during the seventeenth through nineteenth centuries. It also continued the paternalistic perspective that maintained the index of books forbidden to Catholics and a wholesale rejection of the emerging Western liberal democratic ideal, which was thought to threaten the monarchical authority established by Christ in the church.

Also during this time, the papacy went into ascendancy over the authority of councils. This ascendancy is seen particularly in Vatican I, which in 1869 formalized the doctrine of papal infallibility. The doctrine had been widely asserted since the Middle Ages but never formally recognized by the church.

7. The Church Since Vatican II

a. Vatican II

Despite the monolithic structure of the Tridentine church (i.e., the church after Trent), the tide of modern learning and philosophy and critical methodology could not be stemmed forever. The late nineteenth and early twentieth centuries saw cracks in the universal consensus. Catholic biblical scholars and theologians began questioning the church's position on a variety of issues. With a recognition of the changes that had taken place in the world and the church, in 1962 Pope John XXIII called the twenty-first council in the Roman Catholic Church's history. The Second Vatican Council (Vatican II) would become the most significant assembly of the Catholic Church since the Council of Trent. Pope John XXIII died during the early part of the council,

Pope John XXIII

which was continued under the papacy of Paul VI. The goal of Vatican II was not to define doctrine, as had been the case with Vatican I. Its agenda was twofold: to promote renewal and to redefine traditional dogma.

John XXIII's agenda was for a council of healing rather than condemnation. Pope John himself was progressive and wanted to break down the walls between the various sects of Christendom that had been erected during the Reformation and post-Reformation periods. John's successor was a theological conservative who inherited a council he didn't want. Nevertheless, John's vision of a true ecumenical spirit was taken seriously by many delegates, and the council polarized between two conflicting parties: the traditional conservatives, who felt that change was unnecessary, and the radical (liberal) priests and scholars. The assembly consisted of about 2,300 delegates (plus Protestant observers) and spanned the years 1962–65.

b. The Results of Vatican II

The outcome of Vatican II was stated in sixteen major pronouncements. Some of these key decisions have had and continue to have a profound impact.

The church. Vatican II reaffirmed the doctrine of papal infallibility but also extended the limits of authority to the bishops: "The infallibility promised to the Church resides also in the body of bishops when that body exercises supreme teaching authority with the successor of Peter."[1] Another important shift involved the role of the laity. Trent had reaffirmed that only the ordained clergy constitute the church. The practical outworking of this position was the marginalization of the laity. Vatican II formally recognized "that these faithful [i.e., the laity] are by baptism made one body with Christ and are established among the People of God. They are in their own way made sharers in the priestly, prophetic and kingly functions of Christ."[2] This shift even affected the position of evangelism and missions that had heretofore been the province of the clergy.

Revelation and the authority of tradition. In its "Declaration on the Relationship of the Church to Non-Christian Religions," the council declared that "God, his providence, his manifestation of goodness, and his saving designs extend to all men against that day when the elect will be united in that Holy City ablaze with the splendor of God, where the nations will walk in his light."[3] This statement signaled a shift away from the rationalist Thomistic approach toward the knowledge of God to one that is more immediate and intuitive. The shift away from propositionalism has great affinities with the neoorthodox perspective (see chapter 15).

Hand in hand with this shift in the understanding of revelation was a corresponding shift in the position of the authority of tradition. The Council of Trent had declared that there were two equal and independent sources of revelation and authority: Scripture and tradition. These two sources were understood as separate, parallel, and of equal weight.[4] Vatican II backed away from this position and returned to the older *single-source* theory in which tradition refers to the traditional way of interpreting Scripture. The 1994 Catechism of the Roman Catholic Church holds:

> In keeping with the Lord's command, the Gospel was handed on in two ways:
>
> —orally, by the apostles who handed on, by the spoken word of their preaching, by the example they gave, by the institutions they established, what they themselves had received—whether from the lips of Christ, from his way of life and his works, or whether they had learned it at the prompting of the Holy Spirit.
>
> —in writing, by those apostles and other men associated with the apostles who, under the inspiration of the same Holy Spirit, committed the message of salvation to writing.
>
> In order that the full and living Gospel might always be preserved in the Church, the apostles left bishops as their successors. They gave them their own position of teaching authority. Indeed, the apostolic teaching, which is expressed in a special way in the inspired books, was to be preserved in a continuous line of succession until the end of time. This living transmission, accomplished in the Holy Spirit is called Tradition, since it is distinct from Sacred Scripture, though closely connected to it. Through Tradition, the Church, in her doctrine, life, and worship perpetuates and transmits to every generation all that she herself is, all that she believes.... The Father's self-communication made through his Word in the Holy Spirit remains present and active in the Church.

The change from the Tridentine two-source theory is significant. Tradition is an active process of passing on the faith from generation to generation as opposed to a separate and static source of authority and revelation separate from Scripture.

Non-Catholics. The perspective adopted by Vatican II toward non-Catholics was nothing short of revolutionary. The Council of Trent anathematized Protestants and said that all outside the church were destined for hell. While the language of the documents retained a traditional form, it radically reinterpreted the concepts. The documents continue to proclaim the church's role as the sole mediator of salvation, while placing beside these traditional statements declarations on universalism. Protestants are no longer anathematized but treated as "separated brethren," who "have by no means been deprived of significance and importance in the mystery of salvation."[5] Orthodox Christians are recognized as direct descendants of the apostolic church, and future relations between either Protestants or Orthodox and Catholics were not seen as necessarily tied to reunion with Rome.

With reference to those outside of the bounds of Christianity, the council stated:

> From ancient times down to the present, there has existed among diverse peoples a certain perception of that hidden power which hovers over the course of things and over the events of human life; at times, indeed, recognition can be found of a Supreme Divinity and of a Supreme Father, too. Such a perception ... instills the lives of these people with a profound religious sense. Religions bound up with cultural advancement have struggled to reply to these same questions with more refined concepts and in more highly developed language.
>
> Thus in Hinduism men ... seek release from the anguish of our condition through ascetical practices or deep meditation or a loving, trusting flight toward God.[6]

Moral theology. Traditionally, moral theology had been based on the concept of immutable natural law, which was the foundation for universal moral principles and then coupled it with the positive moral obligations based on the moral law of the church. As moral theology developed, it became a heavy legalistic burden akin to the pharisaical traditions against which Jesus railed.

The post–Vatican II situation marks a radical break with the legalistic framework and casuistry[7] of the past. Pre–Vatican II moral theology was heavily legalistic and dependent on a framework of detailed case law. It served primarily as a manual for confessors. Vatican II reasserted the primacy of Scripture in moral theology, and the law was reinterpreted as the life-giving law of the Spirit in Christ and the need for personal conversion. Coupled with this was a call to perfection (maturity) of all Christians, not just the clergy and monks. In the present circumstance, law has become secondary to relationship to Christ. There are significant continuities with the past, but a whole new spirit and reasoning in the field of moral theology exists within Catholicism.

Liberation theology. Liberation theology is a major theological movement, Roman Catholic in origin and heavily Catholic in its continuing character. It was born out of the South American context of extreme poverty and oppression. Roman Catholic priests have been at the forefront of the movement, which has overtly political and revolutionary goals. The church has responded to the challenge of liberation theology with two statements recognizing several forms of liberation. They recognize that the most basic form of liberation needed is from radical sin and its consequent slavery. They also endorse identification with the poor and oppressed. The church is critical, however, of the practice of raising the exodus to the level of a primary model and condemns political liberation pursued for its own sake. (See chapter 16 for more on liberation theology.)

B. THEOLOGY

1. God Is Transcendent

Whereas in Eastern Orthodoxy the overarching understanding of the person of God is profoundly Trinitarian, relational, and mystical, and embraces a healthy view of divine immanence, in Roman Catholicism the stress is on the transcendence of God and his distance from humanity. God is understood as high and holy and separated from all that is sinful. Humanity itself is as nothing in the sight of the majesty of God. Even the architecture of the medieval cathedrals bespeaks this exalted but distant conception of God. This God is holy and governs his relationship to humanity by law. His authority on earth is delegated to a structure, the church, which mediates his presence.

2. Historic Rootedness

Like the Eastern Orthodox Church, Roman Catholicism is deeply rooted in history, so much so that it claims an unbroken line of succession of spiritual authority leading back to the apostle Peter, to whom Jesus entrusted the "keys to the kingdom."

Major creeds. The theology of Roman Catholicism is founded on the ecumenical pronouncements of the ancient church. They particularly venerate the Nicene Creed, the Apostles' Creed, the Athanasian Creed, and the christological definition of the Council of Chalcedon, as well as the rest of the first seven ecumenical conciliar decisions.

Major theologians. The theology of the Western church has been heavily influenced by two massive figures, Augustine and Thomas Aquinas. Augustine of Hippo set in the fourth and early fifth centuries

Augustine of Hippo

Thomas Aquinas

the theological agenda for Western Christianity for the next millennium. It is not too much to say that Augustine is the single most influential force in the development of Western theology (both Catholic and Protestant) and that his contribution is the single greatest factor in distinguishing Western Christianity from Eastern Christianity.

Augustine's theological synthesis held sway from the fifth until the thirteenth century, at which time Thomas Aquinas put forth a new synthesis incorporating the newly introduced Aristotelian philosophy into his formulations. It would be a mistake to say that Aquinas overthrew Augustine. Rather, the Augustinian synthesis of the fifth century proved to be inadequate for the questions of the thirteenth century. Aquinas built on Augustine but added the philosophical insights of Aristotle to produce his new synthesis. Aquinas's theology did not gain immediate adherence and met with opposition for several centuries, both from the older, strict Augustinianism and from the newer nominalism propounded by William of Occam. The Council of Trent codified Aquinas's perspective as the official Roman Catholic position, a perspective that was reinforced by Vatican I (1879).

3. John Henry Newman and the Dynamic Development of Doctrine

The status of doctrine within Catholicism has changed dramatically over the last century and a half. Following the Council of Trent, the truth of Catholic doctrine was seen to have emerged fully developed from the earliest times and perpetuated and protected by the church. However, with the advent of modern historiography and the philosophical and epistemological idealism of the nineteenth century as popularized by Hegel, a different model, one of doctrinal development over the centuries, was proposed. Central in proposing this radical change was Cardinal John Henry Newman, a former evangelical Anglican priest who converted to Catholicism during the height of the Oxford movement.

Newman argued that in history there is a progressive realization of the truth revealed in the Scriptures. The analogy might be made with the tiny acorn and the mighty oak tree. There is continuity between the two, and within the acorn is the genetic blueprint for the full-grown oak. The oak is the faithful and perfect development of the acorn, although the oak does not resemble the acorn. Newman suggested that just as a new convert grows in his or her understanding of the faith, grasping at first only the basic and broad truths of the faith and slowly learning the more advanced concepts, so too the church at first grasped only the basics of the truth and grew slowly into a full understanding.

Newman saw seven principles, or "tests of true development," being worked out in the development of doctrine that distinguished development from corruption.[8] Whatever one may say about Newman's seven tests of true development, he did make the greatest English contribution to theological thought since William of Occam. His thought developed independently of the work going on at the Tübingen school of Germany, which embraced the idealistic and romantic spirit of the day, asserting that while doctrine is unchanging in its essence, the form is adaptable to meet the needs of successive generations.

Newman's proposals met with stiff resistance from the entrenched Catholic establishment during the nineteenth century. In the twentieth century, however, his thought pointed the way as Catholic scholars wrestled with the concept of the development of doctrine. This new understanding of the nature of doctrine made its way into the Vatican II deliberations and signaled a break with the Tridentine mentality.

John Henry Newman

While the doctrine of the church after Trent was viewed as static, the past century has given way to an evolutionary view of doctrine. Doctrine is understood to develop, much as Newman suggested in the mid-nineteenth century. Catholicism recognizes that its teachings and doctrine go beyond the biblical mandate but, unlike conservative Protestantism, doesn't consider this problematic. Contemporary Catholic scholars and theologians claim that the tradition of the church develops and grows the seed of doctrine, the "trajectory of images," found in the New Testament. That is, postbiblical tradition develops the thrust of the images found in the New Testament and develops them to their natural conclusion, all the while remaining consistent with the truth conveyed in the New Testament.

In this postbiblical development, the outward appearance of a doctrine may change, but the essence of the doctrine remains consistent. Pope John XXIII appealed to the principle of contextualization, stating, "The substance of a doctrine is one thing.... The way it is presented is another." (See chapter 2 for a discussion of contextualization.)

4. Justification by Faith vis-à-vis Protestantism

While a plethora of issues separate Roman Catholicism from Protestantism, the primary issue is the understanding of the doctrine of justification by faith. Of the great *solas* of the Reformation,[9] two overriding issues emerge. The first is that of authority. Martin Luther's oft-quoted declaration before the Diet of Worms reflects the authority issue addressed in *sola scriptura.*[10] The other three *solas* speak to different aspects of the doctrine of justification by faith alone (see chapter 10).

What separated Protestantism and Catholicism was in part a misunderstanding of what is implied in the use of the term "justification by faith." The Catholic understanding of justification was built on the explanation of Augustine, who, relying on the etymology of the Latin *iustafacare* ("to *make* righteous"), taught that justification is a process by which the believer is progressively made righteous in character. This righteousness becomes the basis of one's final salvation.

The Protestant Reformers Philip Melanchthon and John Calvin insisted that the church's understanding of justification as a process was in error. They argued that the Greek term δικαιοσύνη (*dikaiosune*) clearly reveals that justification is a legal declaration of "not guilty," pronounced by God on the basis of the alien righteousness of Christ, imputed to the believer's credit. As such, in the Protestant understanding, justification involved a synthetic[11] judgment of God. Because the believer is accepted on the basis of Christ's righteousness, one can have assurance of one's standing before and acceptance by God. The Protestants objected that the Catholic doctrine amounted to salvation by human works rather than salvation based on the grace of God. To put it another way, the Protestants separated salvation into two parts: initial justification as a legal forensic act, and progressive sanctification, a growth in holiness that is distinct from but emerging from the legal pronouncement.

Catholicism responded to the Protestant challenge. When the Catholics heard the Protestants insisting on justification apart from works, they understood the Protestants to be saying that good works played no part in a believer's salvation. This perceived divorce of salvation from personal holiness horrified them. They could not grasp the Reformers' insistence that justification was an act of free grace, coupled with a sanctification process that must arise out of the newly established relationship the believer enjoys with God.

The Catholics responded by insisting on the traditional Augustinian understanding of justification as a process of regeneration and renewal of human nature.[12] In this process, the believer is infused with the grace of God and is progressively filled up with righteousness. This infusion of grace is both sacramental and also by the performance of good works. In the formal theological understanding, works are not understood as acts done to earn divine favor; they are acts done in and through the power of the Holy Spirit and are thus produced by the grace of God working in and through the life of the believer.[13] But these works and the holiness produced in one's life become the basis for final acceptance or rejection by God. Thus, in the Roman Catholic understanding, there can be no assurance of final salvation, because the last chapter of life has not yet been written. Justification in the Catholic understanding involves an analytic judgment based on the believer's existential holiness. The grace that produces this state of renewal is mediated through the church in its sacramental system.[14]

5. Sacramentalism and Sacerdotalism

a. The Sacraments

The Roman Catholic Church's ministry of the grace of Christ to the faithful is sacramental. The grace of God is dispensed to the faithful through the seven sacraments of the church — baptism, confirmation, Eucharist, penance, anointing the sick (formerly called extreme unction), holy orders, and matrimony. These seven were declared by Trent to have been instituted by Christ himself. By participating in them, the faithful strengthen their spiritual lives and their actual level of holiness. The sacraments have been described by Pope Paul VI as "a reality imbued with the hidden presence of God." Their purpose is to infuse the church with the grace of Christ.

The conception of the efficacy of the sacraments has changed over time. The Council of Trent, in response to the Reformation, insisted that the sacraments are causes of grace that can be received independent of the merit of the recipient (*ex opere operato*, "from the work done"). Vatican II has made more explicit the understanding that the sacrament has no efficacy if the person partaking does not have faith.

Baptism. The first sacrament experienced by Roman Catholics is baptism. Since the patristic period, baptism has been understood as the initiation rite into the Christian community that remits original sin and thus is absolutely necessary for salvation. To this day, the practice of infant baptism is seen in Catholicism as rescuing the newborn from the possibility of damnation, because baptism remits original sin. In fact, during the early fifth century,

Augustine appealed to the then already ancient practice of infant baptism as proof of the doctrine of original sin. He argued that if original sin were not remitted by baptism, then the practice of infant baptism made no sense. In this rite particularly, the concept of the sacrament operating *ex opere operato* can be seen.

In the case of an adult convert, baptism is also understood to remit all personal sins committed before baptism. It was for this reason that adult converts in the ancient church sometimes postponed baptism until near the end of life or even until their deathbed. If baptism remitted both original sin and personal sins, it would be theoretically possible to die in a state of sinlessness. This condition would assure salvation and immediate entrance into the presence of God without any time spent in purgatory.

Not all baptism is sacramental. Besides water baptism, Catholicism also recognizes a "baptism of blood," that is, a baptism of martyrdom received by dying for Christ (for example, the innocents, Matt. 2:16–18). Additionally, a "baptism of desire" is reckoned to those who explicitly or implicitly desire a sacramental baptism but for some reason are not able to undergo the rite. "Even those who ... do not know Christ may be counted as anonymous Christians if their striving to lead a good life is in fact a response to his grace, which is given in sufficient measure to all."[15]

Confirmation. The theology undergirding the sacrament of confirmation was developed in the medieval period and was understood as a gift of the Holy Spirit for the strengthening of faith. The Council of Trent ratified the sacrament, at which time it was administered sometime after baptism by the bishop. Today confirmation is often administered at the same time as baptism, emphasizing the initiatory aspect of the sacrament.

Eucharist. The term *Eucharist* comes from εὐχαριστέω (*eucharisteo*), to give thanks. From the ancient period there was debate over the nature of the Lord's Supper (also called Communion or Eucharist and celebrated in the Mass). Although there was general agreement that a profound spiritual reality was occurring, there was no general agreement as to the nature of that reality. From the late ancient through the medieval period, the concept of transubstantiation gradually gained favor until this understanding of the nature of the Lord's Supper was dogmatized by the Fourth Lateran Council (A.D. 1215). This doctrine holds that the Mass is an unbloody sacrifice of Christ in which the bread and the wine are transubstantiated in their substance (not appearance)[16] into the very body and blood of Christ. The efficacy of the sacrifice performed in the Mass is the same as the bloody sacrifice of the cross. Due to the holiness of the consecrated elements, the practice arose of giving Communion in one kind (the bread not the wine), because to spill the blood of Christ would be the greatest of sacrileges. Giving Communion in one kind rather than two was an issue that fostered demands for reformation.

During the Reformation, the nature of the Mass as transubstantiation became a major point of contention between Protestants and Catholics, and it remains so to this day. Catholics view the sacrifice of the Mass as being in ontological continuity with the Holy Thursday Mass of Jesus (the crucifixion). Many Protestants regard the sacrament as ultimately idolatrous because the elements involved in the sacrament are worshiped in the same sense that Christ is worshiped.

Penance. The sacrament of penance, popularly called *confession*, has its roots in the ancient church. Scripture (James 5:16) and the *Didache* (14:1) hint that confession may have been public in earliest times, but the practice soon fell into disfavor. Public confession was exchanged for a private confession to the bishop. Those guilty of serious public sins (adultery, idolatry, murder) were required to do long periods of public penance during which they wore sackcloth and ashes and were barred from Communion. They also performed deeds of penance (fasting, prayer, and other, more severe, punishments) in the hope that the discipline would change them. When penance was completed, penitents were reconciled to the church on the Thursday before Easter. Those whose sins were less serious did not undergo a prolonged period of public discipline but were expected to fast, pray, and give alms to gain forgiveness.

The practice of personal confession began in the eighth century with the Irish monks, who in turn reflected an ancient Eastern custom. The newly introduced practice granted absolution of sin immediately and left penitential acts for later. This is the pattern still in use today. During the Middle Ages, penance slowly evolved to the place where it was elevated to the status of a sacrament. The Council of Trent confirmed the status of penance as a sacrament and required all Christians to confess their mortal sins to a priest by type and number. By the time of Trent, penance was seen to have four components: *satisfaction* (the act of doing penance), *confession* (verbal acknowledgment of sin), *contrition* (an attitude of sorrow), and *absolution* (the declaration of forgiveness by a priest). Following Trent the dominant conception of penance was a restoration of a relationship with God. Vatican II brought a new emphasis, that of penance bringing reconciliation with the church. Contrition is thought to restore the sinner's relationship with God, but since the sinner's actions have compromised the church's mission, forgiveness must be sought through the priest so that the church may be recognized as a holy people.

Anointing the sick (called extreme unction or last rites before Vatican II). During the medieval period, the rite of anointing the sick was increasingly reserved for the dying, from which arose the phrase *extrema unctio* ("last anointing"). Vatican II restored the original emphasis of the sacrament, stating that the rite is not only for those who are at the point of death. Thus the rite is now performed on both the sick and the dying. The biblical basis for the sacrament of healing is James 5:14–15.

Matrimony. In Catholicism marriage has been seen as a sacrament, which makes it an indissoluble union. This position was declared by the Council of Florence and reaffirmed by the Council of Trent. The church takes seriously the biblical injunction, "What God has joined together, let man not separate" (Matt. 19:6). The sacramental character of marriage has caused the Roman Catholic Church to oppose divorce stridently. As a matter of course, divorce is forbidden, but on occasion an annulment (a declaration that the marriage was never a valid marriage) may be granted.

Holy orders. While the church has historically defined itself by the ordained clergy, since Vatican II the church has recognized that all Christians are in some sense priests. Nevertheless, a distinction still exists between the priesthood confirmed by baptism and the priesthood conferred by ordination. Catholicism recognizes three levels of ordination—bishops, priests, and deacons.

b. Sacramentals

In addition to the sacraments that are held to arise from the authority of the Scripture and the apostolic church, Roman Catholicism also recognizes numerous sacramentals. In contrast to the sacraments that operate *ex opere operato*, the sacramentals operate *ex opere operantis* ("by the work of the worker"). The sacramentals cause grace through the faith and devotion of the worshiper. They include holy oil, baptismal water, candles, holy ashes, crucifixes, and statues.

6. Ecclesiology

The key to understanding Roman Catholicism is its ecclesiology. It sees itself as the divinely commissioned representative of God on earth. It is thus a top-down church, reflecting in many ways the feudal worldview out of which it arose. The authority structure is vertical, hierarchical, and authoritarian. The church self-consciously mediates God's presence on earth, with the pope acting as the "vicar of Christ on earth." The episcopal structure is monarchical, and historically its teaching has held that there is no salvation outside the church.[17] The characteristics of the church as the true representative of Christ are unity, holiness, catholicity, and apostolicity.

Catholicism views the mission of the church as fourfold: (1) proclamation of the gospel, (2) celebration of the sacraments, (3) witnessing to the gospel, and (4) service to all in need.

C. THE PAPACY

1. Biblical Basis

The theological and biblical justification for the papacy is rooted in Matthew 16:17–19 and John 21:15–19. In Matthew 16:17–19 the office is solemnly promised to the apostle Peter. In response to Peter's profession of faith in the divine nature of his Master, Christ thus addresses him: "Blessed are you, Simon son of Jonah, for this was not revealed to you by man, but by my Father in heaven. And I tell you that you are Peter, and on this rock I will build my church, and the gates of Hades will not overcome it. I will give you the keys of the kingdom of heaven; whatever you bind on earth will be bound in heaven, and whatever you loose on earth will be loosed in heaven." Catholicism is insistent that this passage establishes the fact that the church is to be built on Peter himself rather than on his confession of Christ as Protestants hold.

The role of the pope is described under four prominent metaphors—universal shepherd of the flock of Christ, elder, rock (referring to Peter's confession), and fisherman (referring to Peter's occupation).

2. Historical Elevation

Theological authority. In the early centuries, the elevation of the bishop of Rome to the position of primacy in the church reflected the fact that the Roman Church was untainted by the stain of heresy that had besmirched the reputations of the other four "mother churches" of the ancient Mediterranean basin (Jerusalem, Antioch, Alexandria, Constantinople). The position and prestige of the Roman Church naturally rose as the defender of orthodox doctrine, and Rome became the court of appeal in complex theological questions. Since the polity of the church was monarchical and episcopal, the church was identified with the bishop, and consequently the status of the bishop of Rome was elevated.

Political authority. With the collapse of the Western empire and the invasion of the Germanic tribes (Vandals, Huns, Goths, Ostrogoths, Visigoths, and others), the social order in Italy was threatened repeatedly. Into this social vacuum stepped the bishop of Rome, trying to preserve peace and order. On numerous occasions, the pope was able to avert catastrophe. This enhanced the prestige and reputation of the papacy, and the title *pontiff*, a term formerly used of the emperor, was applied to the pope.

Temporal authority. Out of this chaos the papacy gained temporal authority over the "papal states," a number of city-states in Italy that looked to the pope as their king. This temporal authority continued until the nineteenth century with the rise of the modern, unified nation state of Italy under Garibaldi.

Feudalism and authority. With the rise of feudalism, a relationship was established between the feudal kings and the pope. This relationship was especially strong between the Frankish kings and the church. The kings looked to Rome for spiritual leadership, and Rome looked to the kings for political support. It was out of this symbiotic relationship that the Holy Roman Empire arose under Charlemagne. As king of the Franks, Charlemagne had supported the pope and rescued him from his enemies in Italy. On Christmas Day, A.D. 800, the pope crowned Charlemagne emperor of the Holy Roman Empire. This revival of the Roman Empire signaled the supremacy of the papacy over the majority of Europe. Over the next several centuries, there was incessant conflict between the pope and the holy Roman emperor as to who had ultimate supremacy.

Early in this period, the theory of the Two Swords arose, a political theory that stated that the pope wielded ultimate spiritual authority over the entire earth, while the emperor yielded ultimate temporal authority. While in theory there was a clear division of authority, in practice it did not turn out to be so. By the time of Innocent III (1198–1215), the most powerful of the medieval popes, the pope was thought to wield ultimate spiritual and temporal authority over the entire earth. Innocent challenged kings and forced them to do his will under penalty of excommunication and loss of their kingdoms.

Supremacy over councils. With such authority the pope also became supreme over councils of the church. During the High Middle Ages, the conciliar movement arose to reform the church from the decadence into which it had fallen. Councils were declared to be of higher authority than the pope, and they could depose the pope. The claims of conciliarism, however, could not be sustained, and the papacy ultimately regained supreme authority in the church.

3. Infallibility

While the authority of the papacy has been held from ancient times, it was during the medieval period that the pope first began to be considered infallible. This doctrine was commonly held for centuries but only officially adopted at Vatican I in 1870. The infallibility of the pope is severely restricted. The only time he is said to be able to speak infallibly is when he makes a pronouncement fulfilling his office as the teacher of the church. This is called speaking *ex cathedra*, that is, "from the [papal] chair." Since being officially granted this privilege, only one pope has spoken *ex cathedra*, and that was in 1950 when the pope declared the assumption of Mary into heaven to be official dogma of the Roman Catholic Church.

The papacy continues to be a defining concept of the Roman Catholic Church. Vatican II declared the office to be the "perpetual and visible source and foundation of the unity of the bishops and of the multitude of the faithful."

D. STATUS OF MARY (THE CULT OF THE BLESSED VIRGIN)

In the early fifth century, the church was embroiled in the christological controversies that ultimately defined the parameters of the church's understanding of the incarnate person of Christ, in a manner that corresponded to the way the Council of Nicea defined the church's understanding of the Trinity.[18] In the early fifth century, the term *theotokos* ("God-bearer") was regularly applied to Mary. Some, particularly from the school of Antioch, objected to this title. Nestorius, patriarch of Constantinople, was in the forefront of this opposition. He preferred the term *Christotokos* ("Christ-bearer") to describe the role of Mary. He believed that the use of *theotokos* confused the human and the divine in Christ. Nestorius was charged with heresy and condemned for failing to properly maintain the unity of the incarnate person of Christ. The use of the term *theotokos* with reference to Mary was endorsed, and those who denied the validity of the term with reference to Mary were anathematized.[19]

The Chalcedonian definition of Christology (A.D. 451) gave an impetus to Marian devotion so that within two centuries four annual feasts were observed in her honor—the feasts of annunciation, purification, assumption, and the nativity of Mary. During the High Middle Ages, the renowned monk Bernard of Clairvaux taught that while Christ is our mediator, he is also our judge. Therefore humans need a mediator between them and the Mediator. Mary was put in this position as the merciful mother who then was contrasted with the fierce Christ. From the eleventh to the fifteenth centuries, Marian devotion blossomed, the rosary developed, and prayers began to be directed to Mary. In 1854 Pope Pius IX declared the doctrine of the immaculate conception—that Mary herself was conceived without sin. Then in 1950 the doctrine of the assumption of Mary[20] into heaven—which had been a widespread belief from the ancient period—was declared to be official Catholic dogma.

The turn of the millennium was marked by a growth in popular Marian devotion. For many years the popular piety of the church has spoken of Mary as co-redemptrix with Christ. Pope John Paul II, himself a devotee of the cult of Mary, on numerous occasions publicly referred to Mary as co-redemptrix, yet resisted great popular and ecclesiastical pressure to formally declare this role as part of binding Catholic theology.

E. OBSERVATIONS AND CRITIQUE

Nature of grace. *Sacramentalism.* For the Protestant, the Catholic conception of the nature of grace is problematic. Unlike the Protestant understanding of grace as the unmerited favor of God whereby he establishes and maintains a relationship with sinful human beings, Catholicism sees grace as a spiritual substance, "stuff" that is transferred to the believer via the sacraments. The sacraments become vehicles by which to receive grace in the most literal sense. The Protestant usage of the term *means of grace* with reference to sacraments, prayer, preaching, Bible study, and fellowship with other believers is metaphoric, symbolizing the means by which spiritual growth is aided. Catholicism, in contrast, by its *ex opere operato* understanding of the sacraments, makes the sacraments means by which God's favor is more fully attained. This goes hand in hand with the Catholic understanding of justification as an analytic judgment[21] as opposed to a synthetic judgment (see n. 11). The sacraments actually pour righteousness into the believer. This concept is unacceptable to Protestants.

Captivity of grace to the priesthood. Hand in hand with the previous critique is the fact that within the hierarchy of the Roman Catholic Church, grace is held captive by the priesthood. The priesthood is the officially sanctioned means to transfer God's grace to believers; therefore, if the sacraments are not celebrated by a priest, the believer is cut off from the reception of grace. Historically this was a powerful weapon wielded by the papacy to influence political leaders to do the pope's will. Since Vatican II a decidedly more open stance has been taken on the dispensing of divine grace, but the church's message is still confusing.

Mary and the cult of the saints. The status of Mary within Catholicism is more problematic than it is within Eastern Orthodoxy. Catholicism has de facto raised the status of Mary from a position of honor to virtual deity. Her status in popular piety as co-redemptrix is unacceptable to Protestants on several counts. First, there is no scriptural justification for the elevation. It seems to have arisen from an improperly understood Christology, whereby the Savior's love and mercy were lost in the popular understanding, and only judgment was found in his eyes. This was precisely the situation with which Martin Luther was confronted and which drove him to despair before he discovered the grace of God in the Scriptures.

A corollary of the cult of (devotion to) Mary is the cult of the saints. The cult of the saints within Catholicism is markedly different than the veneration of the saints within Orthodoxy and far more problematic. Within Catholicism the concept slowly arose that some believers were especially holy—holy enough to merit the title *saint.* The good works done by these saints were more than was necessary for their salvation. These works of supererogation were deposited in a treasury of merit from which the church could dispense credit to less holy Christians through the medium of indulgences. These indulgences were sold at a price to shorten the time spent in purgatory by believers who died while having sins on their ledger. The abuse of this system was one of the factors that gave birth to the Protestant Reformation. Although the blatant abuse of the system has disappeared, the concept of indulgences is still part of the official church teaching and practice. From the Protestant perspective, the whole notion of a treasury of merit undermines the concept of the finished work of Christ.

Appropriation of salvation. The issue of the appropriation of salvation is the one with which Protestants have the most serious problems. In recent years, there has been some rapprochement between Protestants and Roman Catholics, as seen in the historic document *Evangelicals and Catholics Together*[22] and in the fact that several controversial but high-profile Catholic theologians have publicly proclaimed their conviction that Luther's theological criticism of the church was right. Nevertheless, the idea of participating in the sacramental system as the means of receiving grace remains problematic to Protestants. Despite movement within American and Northern European Catholicism, the church as a whole remains committed to a paradigm of the doctrine of salvation that is incompatible with the basic historic Protestant model. While the anti-Catholic rhetoric of previous centuries has cooled considerably, many Protestant theologians contend that the clarity of the proclamation of the gospel of grace within the Catholic structure is muddy.

Nature of authority. In the Catholic understanding, the church is the visible representative of Christ on earth and the mediator of the divine presence. A problem of authority is inherent within the structure. This has at numerous times led to a lack of accountability of the magisterium and allowed for flagrant abuses of power and authority. Likewise, since the church is the official interpreter of Scripture, there is no independent witness with access to legitimate authority to challenge the church's position on issues. Various times the church has tried to make councils superior to the papacy, but every attempt has been short lived and ultimate authority has reverted to the papacy.

Superstition in popular piety. Whereas official Catholic theology has much in common with other historic forms of Christianity, the popular piety of Catholicism is often characterized by deeply rooted superstition and, in many parts of the world, an outright syncretism. This syncretism is tolerated by the authority structure of the church with its claim to visibly represent Christ on earth and mediate his presence.

Lack of direct study of the Scripture. Historically the Bible has been guarded by the church, and laypeople have not been encouraged to study—or have been actively discouraged from studying—the Scripture for themselves apart from the authoritative interpretation of the church. Since Vatican II this situation has changed somewhat as the status of the lay Catholic has been elevated. And the church has officially sanctioned the study of Scripture by the laity. Still, lay Catholics complain of biblical ignorance. The Bible is read in the service but is not really known by the individual.

The tension of changing unchangeable doctrine. Many positive changes have been made in the church since Vatican II, including the move toward a more direct confrontation with Scripture, the celebration of Mass in the vernacular, and the recognition of other branches of Christianity as legitimate representatives of the faith. Nevertheless, the church still finds itself unable to recognize that theological and practical errors have been made in the past. Rather than simply admitting previous understanding as wrong, the Roman Catholic Church has adopted the practice of radical reinterpretation of previous positions. The concentration in the authority of the magisterium has trapped the Roman Catholic Church in an untenable position that makes it almost impossible to alter doctrine. Again, the doctrine of the infallibility of the church and the pope (when speaking *ex cathedra*) is problematic.

BIBLIOGRAPHY

Abbott, Walter M., ed. *The Documents of Vatican II.* Translated by Joseph Gallagher. Piscataway, NJ: New Century, 1966. • ***Catechism of the Catholic Church.*** New York: Doubleday, 1995. • **McBrien, Richard P.** *Catholicism.* San Francisco: Harper, 1970. • **Newman, John Henry.** *An Essay on the Development of Christian Doctrine.* New York: Longmans, Green, 1949. • **Ott, Ludwig.** *Fundamentals of Catholic Dogma.* Rockford, IL: Tan Books, 1955. • **Pelikan, Jaroslav.** *The Riddle of Roman Catholicism.* Nashville: Abingdon, 1959. • **Schrotenboer, Paul G.** *Roman Catholicism, a Contemporary Evangelical Perspective.* Grand Rapids: Baker, 1987.

NOTES

[1]Walter M. Abbott, ed., *The Documents of Vatican II,* trans. Joseph Gallagher (Piscataway, NJ: New Century Publishers, 1966), 49.

[2]Ibid., 57.

[3]Ibid., 661.

[4]Trent insisted that tradition was a separate and distinct source of revelation in addition to Scripture, filling in the gaps where Scripture was silent. In this manner, Trent justified its teaching of doctrines not rooted in Scripture. Alister McGrath, *Christian Theology: An Introduction,* 2nd ed. (Oxford: Blackwell, 1996), 220–21.

[5]Abbott, *Documents of Vatican II,* 346.

[6]Ibid., 661–62.

[7]Casuistry (Lat. *casus,* case) refers to the practice of applying abstract moral principles to concrete specific historical circumstances. While abstract principles can be readily understood, it is often difficult to apply them to specific complex situations of life. Casuistry seeks to bridge the gap between abstract norm and concrete act.

[8]The seven tests are:

1. *The preservation of the idea or type.* If the essence or core values of a philosophical or political system continue in the context of meeting new and changing situations, the system is said to be true to its founding principles or ideals; otherwise it becomes corrupt. Thus, doctrinal development involves the reappropriation of the original revelation in new historical contexts not foreseen in the context of the original revelation. Failure to reappropriate the type signals corruption. E.g., if the members of a monastic community abandon their vows, the institution of monasticism has failed to preserve the type.
2. *The continuity of principles.* This test is akin to the first. "When we talk of the spirit of a people being lost, we do not mean that this or that act has been committed, or measure carried, but that certain lines of thought or conduct by which it has grown great are abandoned."

3. *The power of assimilation.* Newman also proposed the test of "assimilation," likening the system of thought to a natural organism. If the organism is to survive, it must assimilate itself into its environment. Unless it takes food and water from the environment it will die. A living system demonstrates its viability by its ability to assimilate into itself new material.
4. *Early anticipation.* "Although vague and isolated, anticipation of later large developments occur in the histories of nations and movements. E.g., in the very early history of monasticism, which had as an essential feature manual labor, there are indications that the monks will spend their times in literary pursuits. And, fulfilling this anticipation, much academic scholarship has come from the monastic communities in modern times—such as the Benedictines of Paris who edited the works of the Fathers."
5. *Logical sequence.* Newman here contended not that the historical development of doctrine is a conscious reasoning from premises to conclusions, but that on examination, the unfolding of an idea or doctrine will produce developments that are logically related to the initial concept.
6. *Preservative additions.* A true development may be described as one that is conservative of the course of development that went before it. Which is that development and something beside; it is an addition which illustrates, not obscures, corroborates, not corrupts, the body of thought from which it proceeds; and this is its characteristic as contrasted with a corruption.
7. *Chronic continuance.* While decay is a long, slow process, corruption is characterized by energetic action. Corruption is distinguished from development by its transitory, "flash in the pan" nature. True development in doctrine has a staying power that carries it through adversities while heresies quickly fade away.

Source: Peter Toon, *The Development of Doctrine in the Church* (Grand Rapids: Eerdmans, 1979), 11–12.

[9]*Sola scriptura* (Scripture alone as the authority over and against popes and councils), *sola fide* (salvation is by faith alone apart from human works done to merit divine favor), *sola gratia* (salvation is by divine grace alone, apart from any human merit), *sola christus* (salvation is based on the finished atoning work of Christ alone). See chap. 10.C.1.

[10]"Since your Majesty and your lordships desire a simple reply, I will answer without horns and without teeth. Unless I am convicted by Scripture and plain reason—I do not accept the authority of popes or councils, for they have contradicted each other—my conscience is captive to the Word of God. I cannot and will not recant anything, for to go against conscience is neither right nor safe. God help me, Amen" (Martin Luther, quoted in Roland Bainton, *Here I Stand* [Nashville: Abingdon, 1950], 185).

[11]*Synthetic* as used in logic and philosophy refers to a proposition "that attributes to a subject [in this case the believer] a predicate [righteousness] not inherent in the subject and that does not result in a contradiction if negated."

[12]Alister McGrath, *Reformation Thought: An Introduction*, 2nd ed. (Cambridge, MA: Blackwell, 1993), 113.

[13]"The single formal cause (of justification) is the righteousness of God—not the righteousness by which he himself is righteous, but the righteousness by which he makes us righteous, so that, when we are endowed with it, we are 'renewed in the spirit of our mind' (Ephesians 4:23), and are not only counted as righteous, but are called, and are in reality, righteous.... Nobody can be righteous except God communicates the merits of the passion of our Lord Jesus Christ to him or her, and this takes place in the justification of the sinner" (*The Decrees of the Council of Trent,* chap. 7).

[14]See Alister McGrath's fine discussion of this question on an introductory level in *Studies in Doctrine* (Grand Rapids: Zondervan, 1997), 376–405.

[15]Walter Elwell, ed., *Evangelical Dictionary of Theology* (Grand Rapids: Baker, 1984), 957.

[16]The philosophical justification for this doctrine of the changing of the substance (inner reality) as opposed to the accidents (outward appearance) found its basis in Aristotelian metaphysics and is difficult for the modern mind to grasp. See also "Eucharist" and "transubstantiation" in chap. 18.

[17]As noted above, this claim has been radically reinterpreted as a result of Vatican II so that the church no longer condemns any who are outside its visible bounds. Vatican II even went so far as to introduce universalistic strains into its understanding of salvation.

[18]The final definition of Trinitarian theology came at Constantinople in A.D. 381. That statement expanded the original Nicene definition by including a fuller explication of the person of the Spirit.

[19]Some contemporary Protestants who consider the Catholic elevation of Mary to go too far have an aversion to the term *theotokos* and even sympathy for Nestorius. Yet Protestant theologians from Calvin, Zwingli, and Luther to Barth and Tom Oden have all maintained the theological necessity of understanding Mary as *theotokos*. See, e.g., Thomas Oden, *The Word of Life* (San Francisco: Harper Collins, 1989), 157.

[20]E.g., Mary was taken bodily into heaven after she died. "The fact of her death is almost generally accepted by the Fathers and Theologians, and is expressly affirmed in the Liturgy of the Church.... for Mary, death, in consequence of her freedom from original sin and from personal sin, was not a consequence of punishment of sin. However, it seems fitting that Mary's body, which was by nature mortal, should be, in conformity with that of her Divine Son, subject to the general law of death" (Ludwig Ott, *Fundamentals of Catholic Dogma* [Rockford, IL: Tan Books, 1955], Bk. III, Sec. 2, Pt. 3, Ch. 2, §6, 207–8).

[21]See Alister McGrath, *Justification by Faith* in *Studies in Doctrine* (Grand Rapids: Zondervan, 1997), 396, 402, for a discussion of the distinction between justification by faith as a *synthetic judgment* of God and an *analytic judgment* of God. The Catholic concept of justification as an analytic judgment has to do with God analyzing the individual life of the believer with reference to righteousness.

[22]The twenty-five-page statement *Evangelicals and Catholics Together: The Christian Mission in the Third Millennium* was produced in the spring of 1994 by thirty-nine scholars and church leaders as a result of consultations that began in September 1992.

OUTLINE OF CHAPTER 10

A. The Medieval Background: Precursors to Reformation

1. Humanism
2. Scholasticism

B. The Reformation

1. Martin Luther
2. Philip Melanchthon

C. Theological Tenets of Lutheranism

1. Confessional Lutheranism and the Four Solas
2. Theology of the Cross
3. Ecclesiology
4. The Sacraments as Means of Grace
   a. Baptism
   b. The Eucharist
5. Other Elements of Lutheran Theology

D. Observations and Critique

1. Baptism
2. The Eucharist
3. *Simul iustus et peccator*

CHAPTER 10

LUTHERANISM

A. THE MEDIEVAL BACKGROUND: PRECURSORS TO REFORMATION

For at least 125 years prior to the formal beginning of the Reformation, the fires of theological and spiritual discontent with the medieval Roman Catholic synthesis had been simmering. In the fourteenth century, John Wycliffe, "the Morning Star of the Reformation," had challenged the assumptions of the Roman Catholic Church regarding its temporal and spiritual authority. The medieval conception of authority, reinforced by Innocent III, the most powerful pope of the High Middle Ages, held that the pope, as the visible representative of Christ on earth, had supreme authority over all earthly affairs of humans, whether temporal or spiritual.

During the fourteenth century, the papacy, which was then occupied by a series of weak and corrupt popes, had fallen to new spiritual lows. Wycliffe challenged the Roman see's claim to dominion over civil governments. He published two treatises, *On Divine Dominion* and *On Civil Lordship*, which challenged the prevailing theory and proposed that churchmen who live in sin forfeit their rights as stewards of God. Upon the church's condemnation of his views, Wycliffe adopted more radical views, attacking all ceremony not mentioned in Scripture. He denied transubstantiation, the sacramental power of the priests, and the effectiveness of the Mass, and he contended that the whole ceremonial structure of the church interfered with the true worship of God. During this period, he became convinced of Augustine's teaching that salvation comes by divine grace rather than by human effort, and of the need to get the Bible into the hands of ordinary believers. In this he anticipated Luther's doctrine of justification by faith alone and his translation of the Bible into the vernacular. Although placed under house arrest, Wycliffe's teaching received a broad hearing, both in England and on the Continent.

Wycliffe's message was incorporated into the preaching of Jan Hus (John Huss), a faculty lecturer and priest in Prague. Hus emphasized that Christ, not the pope, was head of the church. Hus became a nationalist leader as well as a spiritual figure. The pope placed Bohemia under the interdict because of Hus's teachings, and he was summoned under a promise of safe conduct to appear at the Council of Constance. There he was condemned as a heretic and burned at the stake under the pretense that a promise to a heretic is not binding.

Besides individuals like Wycliffe and Hus, who took the lead, other forces were stirring that paved the way for the Reformation. Among these were the rise of humanism and a dethroning of scholasticism.

1. Humanism

To the modern ear the term *humanism* speaks of a philosophy and worldview that places humanity at the center and discounts all thought of God or of divine revelation, as reflected in the well-known term *secular humanism.* This was not always the case, however. As it first emerged at the beginning of the Renaissance, humanism was a course of study that emphasized the humanities (poetry, grammar, and rhetoric) as opposed to canon law. It was also a method of study. The cry was *"Ad fontes!"*—"Back to the sources!" In Italy this involved a return to the classic Greek and Roman roots of Western civilization. In the North the focus was on a return to the primacy of Scripture as given in its original languages and its authority over the theologians and the reigning scholasticism. In short, humanism was not a philosophy nor a common body of beliefs; it was a methodology that sought for *clarity of thought and eloquence of expression* based on the original source material.[1]

Desiderius Erasmus

Each country in Northern Europe produced humanists, but they came in many flavors. The French produced a legal emphasis that argued for a return to Roman law (i.e., the law of the Roman Empire). Swiss humanism tended to be strongly moralistic. English humanism was far from indigenous; its spirit can be traced to the Italian Renaissance. The prince of the humanists was Desiderius Erasmus[2] of Rotterdam (1466–1536). Although he was from the Low Countries, Erasmus lived and labored all over Europe. He held a Lady Margaret lectureship at Cambridge and worked at Oxford and on the

Continent. His great contribution to the Reformation was a printed edition of the Greek New Testament, which made available to the scholarly community the New Testament in its original, pure form, unvarnished and unfiltered by translation or commentary.

2. Scholasticism

The reigning theological method of the late medieval period was *scholasticism*. As a theological method, it sought to organize all knowledge around an integrating idea and then to fill in the gaps of knowledge through logical deduction. Popular disdain for scholasticism is seen in the caricature of scholastic theologians debating how many angels can dance on the head of a pin. This image reveals the popular attitude toward scholasticism as a method that through theoretical speculation made theology abstract, pointless, and unrelated to life. Scholasticism, like humanism, was not a system of belief, but a method of accomplishing the theological task and organizing its results. As a system, it sought to show the rationality of Christianity. The systems produced by scholasticism at its height have been described as "cathedrals of the mind."

By the late medieval period, the philosophical realism of Anselm and the moderate realism of Thomas Aquinas had in large measure been replaced with nominalism.[3] Luther was schooled in the theology of the nominalist tradition, particularly that of the *via moderna*, which set the stage for Luther's personal spiritual battles in trying to find acceptance before God. Popular discontent with the state of the church, the decay of scholasticism, and the rise of humanism prepared the fire of the Reformation that Luther lit.

B. THE REFORMATION

As noted, the Reformation did not occur in a vacuum. It is often argued that if Luther had not taken up the task, someone else would have, for the times were ripe. While this is undoubtedly true, Luther did take up the task and became the father, not only of Lutheranism, but ultimately of all Protestantism.

1. Martin Luther

As is the case with most theological systems, Lutheranism cannot be understood apart from the spiritual struggles of its founder, Martin Luther (1483–1546).[4] Luther was born to a peasant family and named in honor of St. Martin, the patron saint of his birthday. He endured a harsh upbringing at the hands of both his father and mother. He relates, "My mother once beat me with a cane for stealing a nut, until the blood came. Such strict discipline drove me to the monastery, though she meant it well." His father also flogged him for infractions. Despite their harsh discipline, his parents were honest, pious, and hardworking. They taught young Martin to pray and to revere the church.

Luther attended the University of Erfurt, where he attained a B.A. in 1502 and an M.A. in Law in 1505. That same year, Luther had a personal crisis—a close friend was tragically killed. Two weeks later, he had another crisis experience. Roland Bainton writes:

> On a sultry day in July of the year 1505 a lonely traveler was trudging over a parched road on the outskirts of the Saxon village of Stotternheim. He was a young man, short but sturdy, and wore the dress of a student. As he approached the village, the sky became overcast. Suddenly there was a crashing storm. A bolt of lightening rived the gloom and knocked the man to the ground. Struggling to rise, he cried in terror, "Saint Anne, help me! I will become a monk."[5]

True to his word, Luther entered the Augustinian monastery at Erfurt. There he threw himself into his obligations. He earnestly searched for God through rigorous self-discipline, pious exercises, and his theological studies. During this period, he even engaged in self-flagellation and extreme ascetic practices. He recounts, "If anyone could have earned heaven by the life of a monk, it was I." But he could find no peace for his troubled soul. His conscience was wracked with guilt, and he felt God, not as the loving Father, but as an unrelenting, righteous judge, under whose condemnation he fell. He spent long hours confessing his sins to his abbot, who at one point in exasperation told Luther to do something worthy of confession but not to bother him with all his peccadilloes.

Luther entered the priesthood in 1507. At his first Mass, he was so overcome by the terror of the Holy God that he tried to run from the altar. How could a sinner approach the high and holy God who stood in judgment of even the slightest transgression? He was overwhelmed by both his finitude and sinfulness in the presence of the infinite, holy, and omnipotent God.

Luther's abbot, Staupitz, saw the troubled soul of his brilliant young monk and concluded that he would send him off to get more schooling, keeping him so busy that he would not have time for introspection. Obeying Staupitz's directive, Luther returned to study and received his doctorate in 1511. Throughout the following years, he held the chair of biblical studies at the young University of Wittenberg. He lectured on Psalms (1513–15), Romans (1515–16), and Galatians (1516–17). During this period, he wrestled with the concept of justification. As a faithful student of the *via moderna*, he accepted the notion that God would accept people on the condition that they first fulfill certain demands. These demands were summarized in the Latin phrase *facere quod in se est* (lit., "doing what lies within you" or "doing your best"). When people met this precondition, God was obliged to accept them. The noted late-medieval theologian Gabriel Biel, whose writings influenced Luther, explained that "doing your best" meant rejecting evil and trying to do good.[6]

Martin Luther

But this concept gave Luther irreconcilable difficulties with the concept of the righteousness of God. Divine righteousness, prominent in both Psalms and Romans, was understood early in Luther's lectures as an impartial attribute of God.[7]

Luther testifies of the threat the idea of the righteousness of God was to him, how it brought not comfort but condemnation. Sometime during his study and lecturing on the book of Romans, Luther had his theological breakthrough.

> I had certainly wanted to understand Paul in his letter to the Romans. But what prevented me from doing so was not so much cold feet as that one phrase in the first chapter: "the righteousness of God is revealed in it" (Romans 1:17). For I hated that phrase, "the righteousness of God," which I had been taught to understand as the righteousness by which God is righteous and punishes unrighteous sinners.
>
> Although I lived a blameless life as a monk, I felt that I was a sinner with an uneasy conscience before God. I also could not believe that I had pleased him with my works. Far from loving that righteous God who punished sinners, I actually hated him.... I was in desperation to know what Paul meant in this passage. At last, as I meditated day and night on the relation of the words "the righteousness of God is revealed in it, as it is written the righteous person shall live by faith," I began to understand that "righteousness of God" as that by which the righteous person lives by the gift of God (faith); and this sentence, "the righteousness of God is revealed," to refer to passive righteousness, by which the merciful God justifies us by faith, as it is written, "the righteous person lives by faith." This immediately made

me feel as though I had been born again, and as though I had entered through open gates unto paradise itself. From that moment, I saw the whole face of Scripture in a new light.... And now, where I had once hated the phrase, "the righteousness of God," I began to love and extol it as the sweetest of phrases, so that this passage in Paul became the gate of paradise to me.[8]

It was only when Luther understood righteousness as a God-imparted gift rather than punishment that his heart was calmed. This was Luther's *tower experience*, a fundamental change in his understanding of the foundation of man's relationship to God. The insight that God's righteousness is not a punishing righteousness but a righteousness that imparts faith set the agenda for the Lutheran Reformation.

2. Philip Melanchthon

The second major figure of the Lutheran Reformation was Philip Melanchthon (1497–1560).[9] A child prodigy, he ascended to the position of professor of New Testament at Wittenberg at a mere twenty years of age. Luther was impressed with Melanchthon from the start, and they became friends and colaborers. In 1521 Melanchthon published *Loci Communes*, the first systematic treatment of Lutheran theology. To this day it ranks as one of the great theologies to come out of the Reformation, second in quality and influence only to John Calvin's *Institutes*. He also wrote the Augsburg Confession and worked with Luther to author the other major Lutheran confessions.[10]

Whereas Luther had the title the "*Reformer* of Germany," Melanchthon was known as the "*Teacher* of Germany." Theologically he mediated between the position of Luther and that of Calvin in Switzerland. As a humanist scholar, Melanchthon was second only to Erasmus and in some areas surpassed him.[11] Unlike Luther, he did not undergo any violent spiritual struggles; rather, he was raised in a pious atmosphere, revered the church, and continually studied the Scriptures. He was the most humanistic of the Lutheran Reformers. He was a man of mild spirit, always interested in reconciliation with Rome.

Philip Melanchthon

Melanchthon was never ordained and never a pastor, yet his fame as a teacher spread over Europe to the extent that he had offers from Tübingen, Nuremberg, and Heidelberg, as well as from England, France, and Denmark. He preferred, however, to stay at Wittenberg.

Luther and Melanchthon were opposites in temperament; each made up for the lack in the other. Melanchthon looked up to Luther as a father figure; Luther, on the other hand, was captivated by Melanchthon's scholarship. In fact, Luther testified, "I prefer the books of Master Philippus to my own."[12] Luther recognized the gentleness of his younger colleague, stating: "I am rough, boisterous and altogether warlike. I am born to fight against innumerable monsters and devils. I must remove stumps and stones, cut away thistles and thorns, and clear the wild forest; but Master Philippus comes along softly and gently, sowing and watering with joy, according to the gifts which God has abundantly bestowed upon him."[13] While Luther was the creative genius, Melanchthon was the profound and untiring scholar. He was the balancing force who restrained Luther.

C. THEOLOGICAL TENETS OF LUTHERANISM

1. Confessional Lutheranism and the Four Solas

Unlike American evangelicalism, which tends to be theologically diverse, amorphous, and hard to define, the perspective of Lutherans is confessional. Lutherans of all stripes, if asked what they believe, will articulate similar answers—answers built on the accepted confessions of faith that were gathered together into the *Book of Concord* in 1580. These include the ecumenical creeds—the Apostles' Creed, the Nicene Creed, and the Athanasian Creed—and the Formula of Concord.

As a movement, Lutheranism has always been theologically conservative. Rome's break with Luther was over a fundamental teaching of Scripture. To this day, Lutherans maintain that they simply teach what the Bible teaches and what Christians through the ages have believed. The Lutheran mind-set is both catholic (universal) and evangelical (insisting on a personal relationship with Jesus Christ)[14] with the gospel at its core. Lutheranism stands firmly on the Trinitarian and christological tradition of the fourth and fifth centuries, coupled with an Augustinian understanding of sin and its effects. It is out of the Lutheran Reformation that the *solas* of the Reformation arose:

Sola gratia: Justification and salvation are by God's grace alone. Lutheranism denies that man has any claim on God.

Sola fide: Faith alone is the means of appropriating God's gracious salvation.

Sola scriptura: Scripture is the sole source, rule, and norm of faith. It is the means by which humans come to know God and his will and is the foundation of theological understanding.

Solus Christus: Christ's redemptive act is the central message of Scripture. Communion with Christ is the central fact of the Christian life.

2. Theology of the Cross

Luther's great conceptual contribution to theology is his *theology of the cross.* Scholastic theologians had speculated on the nature of Christ and the nature of the Trinity from an abstract and detached perspective. Luther labeled this method a "theology of glory" and derided it as "sophistic." The theologians of glory were "enemies of the cross" (Phil. 3:18) because their goal was to find God and to observe God as he can be seen in his works, rather than in the humiliation and suffering of the cross. The theology of glory was a theology of pride because it puffed up the theologian, who claimed to see God as he actually is. Paul condemns this type of theology in Romans 1:22: "Although they claimed to be wise, they became fools." True theology does not seek God as he is in himself; it is content to find God as he has given himself to us, in the suffering and revelation of the cross.

Luther develops this theme by positing two types of knowledge of God, legal and evangelical. Legal knowledge of God is that which is available to man from reason and general revelation. This is the knowledge of the philosophers. The method of attaining such a knowledge of God is like the method used to attain to any other knowledge. It treats God as an object of investigation and forgets the biblical warning "No man shall see God and live." True knowledge of God comes through the paradox of God's hiddenness. Luther charges that those who seek to know God apart from this hiddenness are like those who would ascend to heaven without ladders (the Word). Luther rejects both moralism and rationalism as means of knowing God.

Scholasticism had based its method on philosophy. Both Thomism and nominalism were in his estimation seeking for a "naked," "unveiled," and "absolute" God rather than seeking the hidden God of the Scriptures. A key issue here is the problem of reason. Whereas Thomism saw the mind as unfallen, Luther understood it as radically fallen and only able to serve its proper function when it was redeemed. This is not to say that Luther or Lutheranism after him discounted reason. On the contrary, it has been highly regarded, but it must be used with caution and within its proper limits.

While Luther had respect for the mystics, he saw them falling into the same error as the scholastics, that of trying to view God unveiled. Thus Luther also placed the mystics under the rubric of the theology of glory rather than the theology of the cross.

3. Ecclesiology

Lutherans understand the church to be spiritual Israel, and as a tradition, Lutheranism has never committed itself to any particular church polity. Lutheran churches have existed under various governmental systems. In Germany and Scandinavia, where Lutheranism took root early, the church existed as the established state church. This close tie with the state may well be one factor that has kept Lutheranism from having the wide influence that has been characteristic of Reformed theology. As Lutheranism spread to the American continent and elsewhere, the preference in polity was for local autonomy under the authority of the Word of God.

4. The Sacraments as Means of Grace

While Lutherans acknowledge that the term *sacrament* is not found in the Scriptures, they insist that the concept is. The term itself is linked to Tertullian (c. 160–c. 220), who used the Latin term *sacramentum* to translate μυστήριον (*mysterion*). The Latin term had reference to an "oath of allegiance" or a promise. Augustine defined a sacrament as "a visible form of invisible grace."[15] Over the centuries, the number of sacraments in the Roman Catholic Church had grown to seven: baptism, Eucharist, penance, confirmation, matrimony, holy orders (ordination to the priesthood), and extreme unction (see chapter 9.B.5.a).

Luther struggled with the Catholic concept of the sacraments. His main target was the sacrament of holy orders, since it had become the cornerstone of the medieval Catholic establishment. At the opening of his work *The Babylonian Captivity of the Church*, he wrote: "I deny that there are seven sacraments, and for the present maintain that there are only three: baptism, penance and the bread. All three have been subjected to a miserable captivity by the Roman authorities, and the church has been robbed of her freedom."

Luther's struggle continued, even as he wrote this treatise, so that by the end of the work he asserted: "Hence, strictly speaking, there are only two sacraments in the church of God—baptism and the bread. For only in these two do we find the divinely instituted sign and the promise of the forgiveness of sins."[16] He concluded that baptism alone contained the unconditional promises of God to forgive sins; similarly, the Lord's Supper was instituted by Christ himself as a source of strength and a bridge to the new life to be fully realized after death.[17]

Eventually Lutheranism, together with the Anglican and Reformed traditions, asserted that legitimate sacraments must (1) have been instituted by

Christ, (2) rest on his command, and (3) be derived from his Word. With this assertion, the Protestant churches independently returned to the most ancient tradition of only two sacraments, nullifying the multiplication of sacraments that had occurred within Catholicism during the previous millennium.[18]

With reference to the concept of sacrament, Lutheranism moved between a dialectic of promise and faith. The sacrament is a visible demonstration of God's work in specifically ordained rites in which people participate by faith alone apart from any human merit. According to the Large Catechism of 1529, sacraments have three basic features:

1. A sacrament is "a holy divine thing and sign," instituted by a word promising salvation independent of human merit.[19]
2. Its purpose is to save man from sin, death, and the devil, and to establish man's eternal fellowship with the resurrected Christ.[20]
3. The saving power of the sacrament is mediated by faith in the external word and sign.[21]

So the whole of the Christian life is clothed in the garment of baptism—a penitential struggle between good and evil.[22]

a. Baptism

Unlike Catholicism, which sees baptism as washing away the stain of original sin, and unlike the Reformed tradition, which equates baptism with the Old Testament covenantal rite of circumcision, the Lutheran tradition insists that baptism is a regenerating sacrament linked to faith.

> Through water God touches a weak and vulnerable crown of his creation and says Yes!
> "You are incorporated into Christ, and into his body, the church.
> "You are initiated, adopted into my covenant people.
> "You are called! Chosen! Saved! Born again!
> "You are forgiven—free to live without excuses.
> "You are ordained, set aside to be a minister.
> "You are marked with the cross of Christ forever.
> "You are given the gift of the Holy Spirit."
>
> DANIEL ERLANDER†

†Daniel Erlander, *Baptized We Live* (Holden Village: Chelan Washington, 1981), 7.

"Baptism is the means whereby the little one is regenerated. From the moment of baptism the child has life in God."[23] The efficacy of baptism in effecting regeneration is vividly pictured by Lutheran writers as actually effecting salvation. They are careful, however, to distinguish their position from that of a sacrament that works *ex opere operato* in the manner of the Roman Catholic understanding. Lutherans link baptism decisively with faith. The manner in which this faith operates is variously explained. Luther himself early held that the infant was saved by the faith of the parents, sponsor, or pastor. Later in his ministry he changed his position, insisting that the infant was able to exercise faith and believe when the Word was pronounced over the water at baptism. Operating from this assumption, Lutheran theologians insist that pedobaptism (infant baptism) is actually "believer's baptism." Luther himself said, "We say and conclude thus: In baptism children themselves believe and have faith of their own."[24]

But baptism does more than bring salvation; it is also an ordination into priesthood. On this Luther said, "Whoever comes out of the waters of baptism can boast that he is already a consecrated priest, bishop and pope."[25] In so saying, Luther tied the rite of baptism to the Lutheran (and Protestant) doctrine of the priesthood of all believers.

Yet it is precisely at the point of baptism that Lutherans differ from others of the Protestant and evangelical tradition. The evangelical terms *born again* and *conversion experience* are strange and even incomprehensible within the Lutheran framework. For the Lutheran, baptism as an infant points to his or her introduction to the faith.

b. The Eucharist

Luther and his followers broke decisively with the Roman Catholic doctrine of transubstantiation. The Roman Catholic doctrine as it had developed over many centuries came to hold that the Mass was an unbloody sacrifice in which the priest who performed the rite actually changed the substance of the bread and wine into the body and blood of Christ (transubstantiation) while their physical appearance (the "accidents") remained unchanged.[26] To Luther the doctrine seemed absurd and an attempt to rationalize a divine mystery. He agreed that Christ was really present in the sacrament, but that to delve into the manner of the mystery of his presence was to fall victim to the subtlety of scholastic rationalism. Likewise, Luther rejected as unscriptural the concept that the priest made an offering or sacrifice on behalf of the people.

Luther and Lutheranism after him have insisted on a "real presence" of Christ at the Communion table. The Lutheran doctrine of the presence of

Christ at Communion has been termed *consubstantiation*.[27] This doctrine denies that there is a physical transmutation of the elements as in the Catholic doctrine, yet it insists that the risen Christ is under, with, and in the elements of the table in a special way. The eucharistic table is God's gift to his people by which they are nourished spiritually as the Word is taken in a visible form.

This doctrine became the defining doctrine of Lutheranism vis-à-vis the Reformed churches, even as justification by faith alone had become the defining doctrine of Lutheranism (and the rest of the Protestant community) vis-à-vis Roman Catholicism. As the Reformation progressed, leaders such as Philip of Hesse, Martin Bucer, and others sensed the urgency for the Protestant churches to unify. The political threat from the Roman Catholic princes was increasing, and there was a new spirit of goodwill between Germany and Switzerland. Looking toward the possibility of a unified front against the Catholics, the Marburg Colloquy was convened.[28] Protestant leaders from both camps, Lutheran and Reformed, were present, most notably Luther, Melanchthon, and Zwingli. The agenda consisted of fifteen items that separated the two communions, and all were resolved except the nature of the Lord's presence at the Communion table. Luther insisted that the words "this is my body" had to be taken literally. Zwingli, on the other hand, understood that the "is" in the context of Matthew 26:26 ought to be understood as "signifies." It was a figure of speech. The interpretation of the word "is" in Matthew 26:26 kept the Reformation communions apart. Years later, after reading Calvin's explanation of the nature of the supper, Luther commented that he thought the differences between them could be settled in about a half hour.

Luther's interpretation of the nature of the supper was ultimately rooted in Christology. There are two divergent emphases in the understanding of Christology as defined at Chalcedon (A.D. 451), one emphasizing his divinity (the Alexandrine school), the other clearly differentiating his deity and humanity (the Antiochene school). Luther insisted on the "ubiquity of the body of Christ"—that is, the risen incarnate Christ is present everywhere.[29] This is an Alexandrian emphasis, whereas the rest of Protestantism holds an essentially Antiochene view, making it difficult for non-Lutheran Protestants to understand the Lutheran view of the Eucharist. Despite this difficulty, some general comments offered by Lutheran theologians do help in illuminating their understanding:

> In 1577 the Formula of Concord tried to settle the controversy over the Lord's Supper by using the formula "under, with and in

the bread."... Neither "transubstantiation" nor "consubstantiation" ... are true Lutheran options. Christ is present *both* spiritually and bodily.... This happens whenever Christ's command is obeyed in the liturgy of the Lord's Supper.... The "sacramentarians" are wrong when they claim that Christ is present only internally, by faith, and that those who do not believe do not receive him. "Oral eating"... and "sacramental eating by the unworthy" ... are essential parts of the Lutheran doctrine of the Lord's Supper since they affirm the efficacy of the word.... "It is not our faith which makes the sacrament, but solely the Word and institution of our almighty God and Savior, Jesus Christ, which always remain efficacious in Christendom and which are neither abrogated nor rendered impotent by either the worthiness or unworthiness of the minister or the unbelief of him who receives the sacrament."[30]

5. Other Elements of Lutheran Theology

Election. Like the Reformed tradition (Calvinism), Lutheranism affirms a doctrine of election/predestination. But unlike the Reformed doctrine of double predestination, Lutheranism affirms only a predestination unto salvation.

The medieval doctrine of predestination was rooted in God's absolute divine sovereignty as Lord of all creation. It did not give comfort to the faithful; instead, it instilled terror and revulsion. Luther wrote of his own wrestling with the medieval doctrine:

> Admittedly, it gives the greatest possible offense to common sense or natural reason that God by his own sheer will should abandon, harden, and damn men as if he enjoyed the sins and the vast, eternal torments of his wretched creatures, when he is preached as a God of such great mercy and goodness, etc. It has been regarded as unjust, as cruel, as intolerable, to entertain such an idea about God, and this is what has offended so many great men during so many centuries. And who would not be offended? I myself was offended more than once, and brought to the very depth and abyss of despair, so that I wished I had never been created a man, before I realized how salutary despair was, and how near to grace.[31]

He reacted strongly to the syllogistic scholastic logic that attempted to probe the mysteries and resolve the tension between the God who is hidden in himself and the God who is revealed in the gospel.

> The eternal election of God or God's predestination to salvation does not extend over both the godly and the ungodly, but only over the children of God, who have been elected and predestined to eternal life "before the foundation of the world was laid," as St. Paul says, "Even as he chose us in him, he destined us in love to be his sons through Jesus Christ" (Eph. 1:4, 5).[32]

These fell under the rubric of "theology of glory." Moreover, for Luther, the certainty of salvation for the believer is not rooted in signs that one is elect, nor in good works, as was taught by Calvinistic Puritanism, but in the promise of God as found in the gospel. But the fact is, Luther did not ultimately try to resolve the question of predestination, because he felt that was speculation that goes beyond the Scriptures.[33] The Formula of Concord clearly states that if anyone hears the gospel and does not repent and believe, the fault lies with the individual alone and cannot be blamed on any hidden purpose of God.[34]

> Hence if anyone so sets forth this teaching concerning God's gracious election that sorrowing Christians can find no comfort in it but are driven to despair, or when impenitent sinners are strengthened in their malice, then it is clearly evident that this teaching is not being set forth according to the Word and will of God but according to reason and the suggestion of the wicked devil.[35]

With reference to the question of human freedom, Lutherans admit that even the doctrine of justification implies a doctrine of predestination. They argue that the language of justification is "passive voice" language with reference to humans. When that language is transformed into "active voice" language with reference to God, one finds the language of predestination.[36] Questions as to whether predestination denies human freedom are seen to revolve around what sort of understanding one has of God and what one means by human freedom. Ultimately, "alarm at predestination is simply alarm at having to deal seriously with God."[37]

Providence. God sustains his creation. He directs and guides all creatures to fulfill the purpose of their existence. In so doing, he is working out his eternal purpose in the lives of individuals and nations. That purpose finds its center in the church.

Anthropology. Luther himself adopted a strong Augustinian position on the spiritual condition of humanity. Erasmus attacked Luther's doctrine of man's condition in *Diatribe on the Freedom of the Will*, which was met by a vigorous response from Luther in *The Bondage of the Will*, in which he argued that the will of man is totally dead with reference to spiritual goodness, and apart from the sovereign work of the Spirit, man is damned.

In traditional Lutheran understanding, man is described as a duality or a dichotomy, that is, composed of two parts, the material and the immaterial. The origin of each soul is understood to be traduced from the parents of the person as opposed to being individually created by God. The image of God in humanity is understood as *original righteousness*, "that is, in true knowledge of God and in true righteousness and holiness and endowed with a truly scientific knowledge of nature."[38]

Hamartiology. Following in the Augustinian tradition, Lutherans believe "that all men are sinners already by birth, dead in sins, inclined to all evil, and subject to the wrath of God." The correlate doctrine is one of *total depravity* with an accompanying *total inability* in spiritual matters. People are simply unable, through any efforts of their own or by the aid of "culture and science," to reconcile themselves to God and thus conquer death and damnation.[39] This is not to say that Lutherans see either individuals or humanity as a whole as utterly evil. Rather, they recognize two types of righteousness. The first is external, "civil righteousness," as seen in good deeds done by humans. However, these acts of civil righteousness are not motivated by a heart of love and obedience to God and are thus not acts of "spiritual righteousness," (internal and arising out of a relationship with God).

Atonement. Christ, by his perfect obedience, satisfied divine justice in man's stead, turning God's wrath to grace. Christ's death was penal, substitutionary, and universal, made on behalf of all humanity in an objective sense.[40]

Soteriology. The heart of Lutheran soteriology is the doctrine of justification by faith, the juridical declaration of God by which sinners are pronounced not guilty when they exercise faith in Jesus Christ. This faith comes by means of the grace of God through his Word, which in turn teaches sinners to lament their sin. This divine grace is universal and the efficient cause of conversion, but it is also resistible. Both irresistible grace and synergism are strongly denied.

Progressive sanctification. Lutherans understand a dialectic in the Christian life and eschew any form of perfectionism. The life of the Christian is characterized by a dual state, as caught in Luther's description of the saved sinner as *simul iustus et peccator* (at once justified and sinner). This condition is never escaped in this life. Lutherans hold that the moral life of the individual is a life lived *coram dei* (before or in the presence of God). That which is good is that which is done in faith, or out of a relationship with God. Good works are never done to curry favor with God. The dynamic and existential encounter and relationship with God in the ambiguity of life on earth is always morally accountable but never perfect.

While Lutheranism is insistent that justification is by faith alone, it likewise contends that conversion effects a genuine change in the heart. True justification cannot exist without sanctification. Good works are a necessary consequence of regeneration. "If good works do not follow, our faith is false and not true."[41] The life of the believer is to be Christ to one's neighbor, embodying the relationship of God to humanity. This is not a "good work" by which one earns favor with God.

Lutheranism eschews any type of legalistic ethics; rather, it holds to a type of what could be called "situation ethics." It "implies the use of reason when faith is active in love."[42] Lutherans recognize an ethical dialectic between reason and faith. The employment of reason can produce civil righteousness but not spiritual righteousness, for spiritual righteousness must arise out of faith.

Salvation is always and only from God. The one who perseveres does so in faith. But it is possible to fall away from the faith and finally apostatize. This situation is wholly the responsibility of the person involved and is not the fault of God.

D. OBSERVATIONS AND CRITIQUE

1. Baptism

In recent years, even some Lutheran theologians have questioned the historic Lutheran stand on infant baptism. As Friedrich Mildenberger points out, "The problem is that the church's practice of infant baptism makes it impossible for us to see God working in the unified process of giving and receiving."[43] Lutheranism has emphasized the sacrament as an example of salvation being totally a work of God. Some object, however: "This argument is not convincing because it does not provide the necessary context to describe the fact that [the child] must still at some point appropriate this baptism."[44] Mildenberger argues that the church's practice is truly at odds with its more basic theological assertions with reference to promise and faith. He notes that in practice the insistence that infants must be baptized to attain salvation comes dangerously close to, if it does not cross the line into, an *ex opere operato* view, that is, the sacrament is efficacious apart from the faith or spiritual condition of the recipient and thus accomplishes salvation and correspondingly makes the church the mediator of salvation in a sense directly comparable to Roman Catholic practice, and God's freedom in salvation is nullified. This whole model, he argues, is "inconsistent with the gospel." There must be a correlation between gospel and faith in the sacrament.[45]

2. The Eucharist

The Lutheran explanation of the Eucharist has been problematic for most Protestants. As noted above, non-Lutherans refer to this position as *consubstantiation* and see the explanation as only a half step away from the Catholic doctrine of transubstantiation; Lutherans refer to their view as *spiritual presence.* The language of a physical presence "under, with, and in" the elements while the elements themselves are not transubstantiated sounds confusing at best to non-Lutheran ears.

The underlying theological issue revolves around the ancient question of the *communicatio idiomatum* (the communion of attributes between the two natures of the incarnate and now glorified Christ). While all orthodox Christologies assert the *communicatio idiomatum* either explicitly or implicitly, the way it is explained and applied within the Lutheran tradition would appear to view aspects of Christ's human nature as being divinized by the union of the two natures. It is to this that non-Lutheran Protestants object.

3. *Simul iustus et peccator*

The Lutheran doctrine of sanctification ("at once justified and sinner") proceeds from the dialectal perspective that embraces the continuing problem of sin even in the life of the believer despite the fact that he or she has been declared righteous when faith was placed in the work of Christ. As such the framework for interpreting the Christian life is considerably different than either the gradual transformation taught in the Reformed tradition or the perfectionism taught in the Wesleyan and Keswick traditions. The Lutheran perspective provides a healthy corrective especially for the perfectionistic traditions by taking seriously the problem of sin, and by focusing on relationship rather than action.

BIBLIOGRAPHY

Althaus, Paul. *The Theology of Martin Luther*. Philadelphia: Fortress, 1966. • **Arnold, Duane W. H.**, and **C. George Fry**. *The Way, the Truth, and the Life*. Grand Rapids: Baker, 1982. • **Bainton, Roland**. *Here I Stand.* Nashville: Abingdon, 1950. • **Erlander, Daniel**. *Baptized We Live*. Chelan, WA: Holden Village, 1981. • **Gritch, Eric W.**, and **Robert W. Jensen**, *Lutheranism.* Philadelphia: Fortress, 1976. • **McGrath, Alister**. *Intellectual Origins of the*

European Reformation. Oxford: Blackwell, 1987. • ———. *Luther's Theology of the Cross*. New York: Blackwell, 1985. • ———. *Reformation Thought*. Oxford: Blackwell, 1993. • **Mildenberger, Friedrich**. *Theology of the Lutheran Confessions*. Philadelphia: Fortress, 1986. • **Plass, Ewald M.**, ed. *What Luther Says*. St. Louis: Concordia, 1959. • **Schaff, Philip**. *A History of the Christian Church*. Vol. 7. Grand Rapids: Eerdmans, 1977.

NOTES

[1]For a discussion of humanism and the current scholarly assessment of the movement with reference to its effect on the Reformation, see Alister McGrath's *Reformation Thought* (Oxford: Blackwell, 1993), 40–66, and his *Intellectual Origins of the European Reformation* (Oxford: Blackwell, 1987), 32–68.

[2]For a fine biography of Erasmus, see Roland Bainton's *Erasmus of Christendom* (New York: Crossroad, 1982).

[3]Philosophical realism focused on the universals, while nominalism denied the universals and focused instead on the particulars. This debate had no direct theological relevance but had a great indirect effect on the way theology was done. The nominalism of the late medieval period was subdivided into two groups, one optimistic about the possibility of humanity establishing a relationship with God (essentially Pelagian) and the other pessimistic (essentially Augustinian).

[4]See also Luther's biography in chap. 17.

[5]Roland Bainton, *Here I Stand* (Nashville: Abingdon, 1950), 21. Bainton's work is an excellent account of Luther's life. Additionally, the film *Martin Luther*, produced in the early 1950s, is a historically accurate and moving portrayal of Luther from his entrance into the monastery through the early Reformation period.

[6]Ibid., 76. McGrath describes at great length the theological sophistication of the *via moderna* in trying to escape the charge of Pelagianism.

[7]McGrath, *Reformation Thought*, 92.

[8]Quoted in ibid., 95.

[9]See also Melanchthon's biography in chap. 17.

[10]The sole exception is the Formula of Concord, which was composed after Luther's death.

[11]Philip Schaff, *A History of the Christian Church* (Grand Rapids: Eerdmans, 1977), 7:187.

[12]Ibid., 7:193.

[13]Ibid.

[14]I am speaking theologically here. On the lay level the liturgical nature of Lutheranism has often led to a creedal orthodoxy as opposed to a vital personal faith.

[15]Duane W. H. Arnold and C. George Fry, *The Way, the Truth and the Life* (Grand Rapids: Baker, 1982), 141.

[16]Eric W. Gritch and Robert W. Jensen, *Lutheranism* (Philadelphia: Fortress, 1976), 71.

[17] *The Babylonian Captivity of the Church* (1520), esp. 2.50.

[18] Arnold and Fry, *The Way, the Truth and the Life*, 141.

[19] Large Catechism, 4.3–22.

[20] Ibid., 4.23–31.

[21] Ibid., 4.32–36.

[22] Ibid., 4.84.

[23] O. Hallesby, *Infant Baptism and Adult Conversion* (Minneapolis: Augsburg, 1924), 60.

[24] Ewald M. Plass, ed., *What Luther Says* (St. Louis: Concordia, 1959), 53.

[25] Martin Luther, "Address to the Christian Nobility of the German Nation," *Luther's Works*, 44:129.

[26] This distinction arises out of an Aristotelian philosophical construct. A substance was something essential in nature, while accidents have to do with outward appearances only (McGrath, *Reformation Thought*, 169).

[27] Lutheran scholars and theologians disavow the propriety of this term to accurately describe their doctrine, preferring the simple "real presence" (Arnold and Fry, *The Way, the Truth and the Life*, 148).

[28] Bainton, *Here I Stand*, 318–19.

[29] At its root is a peculiar understanding of the ancient doctrine of the *communicatio idiomatum* (communion of attributes in the incarnate Christ). Thus, it was possible for the risen Christ to be truly present at the supper, since the communion of divine and human attributes gave to Christ's glorified humanity the divine quality of omnipresence.

[30] Gritch and Jensen, *Lutheranism*, 79–80.

[31] *Luther's Works*, ed. H. T. Lehmann (Philadelphia: Fortress, 1955), 33:190.

[32] *Formula of Concord*, Solid Declaration 11:5.

[33] Ibid., 11:7, 85.

[34] Ibid., 11:78.

[35] Ibid., 11:91.

[36] Gritch and Jensen, *Lutheranism*, 158.

[37] Ibid.

[38] "Of Man and Sin" (St. Louis: Concordia, n.d.), [adopted 1932] Lutheran Church Missouri Synod. *www.lcms.org/pages/internal.asp?NavID=567* (accessed Sept. 2005).

[39] Ibid.

[40] "Of Redemption." *www.lcms.org/pages/internal.asp?NavID=567* (accessed Sept. 2005).

[41] Schmalkaldic Articles, 3:13:3.

[42] Gritch and Jensen, *Lutheranism*, 141.

[43] Friedrich Mildenberger, *Theology of the Lutheran Confessions* (Philadelphia: Fortress, 1986), 108.

[44] Ibid.

[45] Ibid., 109.

OUTLINE OF CHAPTER 11

A. John Calvin and Reformed Theology
1. Influences on Calvin's Theology
    a. Humanism
    b. Patristics
    c. Luther
2. Major Tenets of Calvin's Theology
    a. Knowledge of God
    b. Humanity
    c. Salvation
    d. Predestination
    e. The Doctrine of the Church
    f. The Sacraments

B. Protestant Scholasticism
1. Theodore Beza
2. The Reaction of Jacob Arminius
3. The Synod of Dort, Five-Point Calvinism, and TULIP
4. Francis Turretin
5. Four-Point Calvinism (Amyraldism)

C. Covenant Theology

D. The Puritans
1. The Westminster Confession and Catechism
2. Emphasis on Conversion
3. The Sabbath

E. Princeton Theology
1. Scripture
2. Reformed Confessionalism
3. Scottish Common Sense

F. Dutch Calvinism
1. Abraham Kuyper (1827–1920)
2. Herman Bavinck (1854–1921)
3. Louis Berkhof (1873–1957)

G. Observations and Critique

CHAPTER 11

REFORMED THEOLOGY (CALVINISM)

The term *Reformed theology* (or *Calvinism* as it is more popularly called) refers to the theological tradition associated with two movements: the French-Swiss Reformation in Geneva led by John Calvin and the German-Swiss Reformation that was born under the ministry of Ulrich Zwingli and matured under Heinrich Bullinger. In its essential theological affirmations, Reformed theology did not differ substantially from the theology of Luther. But whereas Lutheranism proved to be tightly wedded to the political structure of Germany, Reformed thinking spread widely and rapidly beyond its native Switzerland. Its ethos spread and developed a character that made it recognizably distinct from Lutheranism.

> The term *Reformed,* with reference to the distinctive Swiss theology, arose from the observation of Queen Elizabeth I of England, who commented on the more radical tone of these non-Lutheran Protestants, referring to them as "more reformed" and thus labeling this movement as the *Reformed* wing of Protestantism. In this context, a key and visible distinction between the Lutherans and the Reformed is evident.

Luther's approach to reform was to purge the church of anything Scripture forbids, while the Swiss Reformers wanted to purge the church of everything Scripture does not warrant. Everything in the practice of the church required biblical warrant. For instance, Luther's approach to worship was to welcome different kinds of musical instruments and music because Scripture does not forbid this. The Swiss, on the other hand, limited their hymnody to the singing of the Psalms and forbade musical accompaniment because Scripture does not warrant anything else.

While the Swiss Reformation was born under Zwingli, his contribution to the development of Reformed theology has been overshadowed, due in part to his untimely death at the battle of Cappel (Kappel) at the age of forty-seven, and more significantly because of the emergence of John Calvin in Geneva as *the* greatest theologian of the era.[1] Calvin wrote the definitive work of Reformed theology, the *Institutes of the Christian Religion*. Calvin's *Institutes*, numerous commentaries, *Geneva Psalter* revision, worship reform, and volumes of correspondence attest to the reality that he, more than any other person, shaped Reformed theology.

Despite Calvin's massive influence and genius, however, the shape of contemporary Reformed theology often bears a different ambiance and emphasis than that of the Geneva Reformer. As historical circumstances changed and new challenges arose, theologians interpreted Calvin and subtly changed his emphases. The careful student will observe that the Reformed theology of today ("Calvinism"), although differing in a variety of ways from the thought of its founder, maintains a homogeneity of thought that binds the various strands of Reformed theology together despite their differences.

A. JOHN CALVIN AND REFORMED THEOLOGY

Although John Calvin spent his working life in Geneva, he had been born, and forever remained, a Frenchman. He was born into a Catholic family in Noyon on July 10, 1509. His father initially wanted his son to study theology and thus sent him to the University of Paris. Relentless study ultimately led to a breakdown in his health, and from that time forward, he was weak and sickly, suffering from numerous bodily ailments. In about 1527, Calvin's father had a change of mind and sent his son to Orléans to study law. Calvin graduated with a degree in law in 1531 but with no plans to practice as a jurist. At Orléans he had drunk deeply from the well of humanism and directed his pursuits toward a career as a man of letters and eloquence. Shortly after his graduation from Orléans he published a commentary on Seneca's *De Clementia* at his own expense. But the work proved a disappointment to the budding scholar and did not bring the fame for which he had hoped.

The only testimony from Calvin concerning his conversion is found in his commentary on the Psalms. In the preface to the commentary, Calvin describes a sudden conversion during which he felt singled out by God and called to something specific. What we know about Calvin's conversion is the series of events that took place around that time. Calvin was associated with

Nicolas Cop, an advocate of reform in the very traditional and conservative city of Paris. Cop was a doctor of medicine and rector of his department at the university. For his 1534 rectorial address, Cop preached a sermon on the Beatitudes. The address stirred so much opposition that Cop immediately fled to Basel.

John Calvin

Cop had delivered the address, but many in authority suspected that the twenty-five-year-old John Calvin was the true author of the sermon. He too was forced to flee for his life and spent the next year in exile, wandering from city to city under an assumed name. Meanwhile, in Paris, Calvin's room was searched and his papers confiscated by the authorities. For a portion of this time, Calvin stayed with his friend Louis de Tillet. Calvin used Tillet's excellent personal library, and it is thought that during this time he began his work on the *Institutes* and wrote some sermons. As things worsened in Paris, some evangelical sympathizers were arrested and executed. Finally, Calvin, along with his friend de Tillet, set off for Basel, arriving in January of 1535, where he lived under the pseudonym Martinus Lucianus. This marked the beginning of his break with the Roman Catholic Church.[2] By 1535 Calvin's evangelical sympathies became clearer as he began work on the first edition of the *Institutes*, an apologia addressed to Francis I of France and to those who were comparing the French evangelicals to the Anabaptists, and published it at the age of twenty-seven.[3]

Intending to relocate in Strasbourg and to begin a quiet life of scholarship, Calvin was unable to take the direct route because of troop movements in the war between Francis I and the Holy Roman emperor, Charles V. He was forced to take a detour that was to take him to Geneva for a single night. What happened there would change the course of his life—indeed, the course of history. As Calvin passed through Geneva on that day in 1536, he was met by the fiery Reformer Guillaume Farel, who zealously urged him to stay. Later Calvin described the encounter:

> Guillaume Farel kept me at Geneva, not so much by advice and argument, as by a dreadful curse, as if God had laid his hand upon me from heaven to stop me.... And after having heard that I had several private studies for which I wished to keep myself free, and finding that he got

> nowhere with his requests, he gave vent to an imprecation, that it might please God to curse my leisure and the peace for study that I was looking for, if I went away and refused to give them support and help in the situation of such great need. These words so shocked and moved me, that I gave up the journey I had intended to make.[4]

Farel's words, along with his passion for the gospel, so terrified Calvin that he remained in Geneva. Apart from a two-year exile in Strasbourg, Calvin spent the rest of his life changing that small city into what Scotsman John Knox later called "the most perfect school of Christ since the Apostles."[5]

1. Influences on Calvin's Theology

No theological system arises in a vacuum. It is the result of cultural, religious, social, and personal influences. So it is with Calvin and Calvinism. Three major influences on Calvin were Renaissance humanism with its stress on original source material, the study of patristics (particularly the direct study of Augustine, bypassing the medieval interpretations of his writings), and the German Reformation and writings of Martin Luther.

a. Humanism

Not to be confused with today's "secular humanism," the humanism[6] of the sixteenth century was a revival of learning sparked during the Renaissance. "Humanism was the scholarly study of Latin and Greek classics and the ancient Church fathers both for their own sake and in the hope of a rebirth of ancient norms and values."[7] This renewed study of rhetoric (theory of communication) and of the power of language involved analyzing the writings of antiquity in an attempt to learn the skills of persuasion. Humanistic study cared deeply about the author's intent, context, and parallel passages that gave meaning. All such study was undertaken only in the original languages. Calvin's works demonstrate an unfailing devotion to the humanistic method as he applied it faithfully to the text of Scripture and the construction of his theological understanding. This humanistic method is what gave Calvin's exegesis, theology, and preaching power. He was devoted to the sources and their exposition as well as to the principle of not moving beyond the text into speculation.

Whereas the Renaissance in Italy looked back to the glory of its classical Greek and Roman heritage, in Northern Europe the sources became the original text of the Scriptures. Humanistic studies became focused on religious reform. This can be seen in the quintessential humanist of the North, Erasmus. Erasmus produced critical editions of both the New Testament and the church fathers. His faith was a simple piety focused on the imitation of Jesus. It was this kind of humanism that led many to challenge the worldly and decadent Roman Catholic Church of that era.[8] In fact, many of the early enthusiasts for reform were humanists. Not until the radical nature of Luther's reform program became clear did most begin to oppose the Reformation. The humanists generally wanted a reform in church life, but they were not prepared for a reform in underlying doctrine and practice.[9]

Virtually all of the Reformers were humanists in their approach to truth. They were committed to the inductive study of the original biblical texts, and their hermeneutics were informed by classical rhetoric. As historian William Bouwsma says of Calvin, "He applied the general principles of humanistic hermeneutics in his own scholarship."[10]

b. Patristics

One of the key questions addressed by the Reformation was how to interpret Augustine. The Reformation was not only about the interpretation of Scripture, but equally about "the continuation of a debate over the status, and supremely the interpretation, of Augustine, inherited from the late medieval period."[11] New translations of Augustine and new evaluations were appearing. Both the German and Swiss Reformers leaned heavily on Augustine for their understanding of the doctrines of man and grace, downplaying his views of the church, while the Catholics built on his understanding of the church and softened his teaching on sin and grace. Calvin himself was an erudite student of Augustine and acknowledged a heavy dependence on him.[12]

Alister McGrath has suggested three reasons for the Reformers' preference for the writings of the early church fathers over those of the medieval scholastics.[13] First, the humanist training of the Reformers attracted them to the superior Latin style of the Fathers as opposed to the vulgar medieval ecclesiastical Latin. Second, the Reformers were attracted to the simplicity of the Fathers' theological expression. Third, the Reformers found it significant that the Fathers lived and wrote so close to New Testament times.

c. Luther

It almost goes without saying that John Calvin was influenced by Martin Luther, the father of the Reformation, but the depth of this influence is open to debate.[14] Significantly, Luther's ideas had gained a large audience at the University of Paris while Calvin was a student there. It would have been nearly impossible for Calvin to have been ignorant of the radical heresy being promoted by the Wittenberg Reformer. Nevertheless, even though Calvin was dependent on Luther in his writing of the *Institutes*, he still remained a critic of Luther and his scholarship.[15]

2. Major Tenets of Calvin's Theology

To understand Reformed theology as a system, one must begin with the major emphases of Calvin himself.

a. Knowledge of God

Calvin's first concern in his *Institutes* is the knowledge of God, and he approaches the subject from two angles: the natural knowledge of God and the supernatural revelation of God in the Word. First, Calvin notes that every human being has a natural awareness of God, as seen in the universal human tendency toward idolatry. This awareness of God does little else than to make every person inexcusable in the presence of God, for human evil prevents people from having a true knowledge of him. True knowledge of God comes only from divine revelation in the Word of God.

Calvin understood the Word of God as presenting itself to humanity in two distinct forms. First, God accommodates himself to humanity in the incarnation of Jesus Christ, the true Word. The second form of the Word of God is Scripture, as attested through the inner witness of God's Spirit. Calvin practiced what he preached; his whole ministry revolved around the written Word of God. In spite of all the influences on his life and theology, Calvin "can be fully understood only when we comprehend also the constraint in which he found himself under the Word of God; for it was his experience of the Word, and his interpretation of it, which determined what he attempted and achieved."[16] This is reflected in his preaching regimen. He preached systematically on New Testament books each Sunday morning and afternoon, and he preached on an Old Testament book each weekday morning.

b. Humanity

The image of God in man, in Calvin's thinking, is located primarily in the soul, although he admitted that the image is also reflected in our physical form. But that image was distorted in the fall. Man's supernatural abilities, such as faith, disappeared, and the natural abilities, such as the intellect and will, were defaced. Calvin asserts that every aspect of our humanity has been affected by the first sin.[17]

Because of the fall, all human beings have inherited the sin of Adam. "Not only has the punishment fallen upon us from Adam, but a contagion imparted by him resides in us, which justly deserves punishment."[18] Simply put, since we are Adam's children, we too are sinful. Therefore humans are completely bound by sin and incapable, even undesirous, of righteousness.

c. Salvation

Calvin is thoroughly Augustinian in his evaluation of the condition of humanity: due to the crippling effects of sin, there is no way for a person to come to God; therefore, if man is to be rescued from his desperate plight, God must initiate the action. This was the purpose of the incarnation of Jesus Christ. He understands the work of Christ on the cross to be a satisfaction of God's judgment.[19] That sacrifice of Christ opens the door for our salvation. Yet no one can or will enter that door unless the Holy Spirit gives that person the faith necessary to do so. In other words, since faith was destroyed at the fall, faith must be re-created in a person for him or her to come to Christ. It follows, then, that the justification that results from such a gift of faith is not based on any inherent goodness in the person but is based solely on the righteousness of Christ. Therefore a person cannot be considered to be objectively righteous (in the moral sense). Despite a person's sinfulness, God declares the person to be righteous on the basis of Christ's atoning sacrifice—that is, Christ's righteousness is *imputed* to the believer.[20] Like Luther, Calvin asserts justification by faith, not by works.[21]

d. Predestination

While the doctrine of *predestination*, or *election*, has become the hallmark of Reformed theology, it did not occupy such a preeminent place in Calvin's teaching. He introduced the subject only *after* discussing the doctrine of salvation. Predestination is neither central, nor key, to Calvin's theological system. He does not develop the idea of predestination until the end of book 3 of the *Institutes* (which has four books), and he even warned against making too much of the doctrine. "To seek any other knowledge of predestination than what the Word of God discloses is not less insane than if one should purpose to walk in a pathless waste or to see in the darkness."[22]

With that in mind, observe Calvin's definition of predestination: "We call predestination God's eternal decree, by which he determined with himself what he willed to become of each man."[23] Calvin is equally clear that God did not decide the eternal fate of each person based on his foreknowledge of how that person would respond to his offer of grace. Predestination is God's decision about each human's eternal fate. Calvin followed Augustine, who understood predestination to effect not only God's choice of who would receive eternal life but who would be forever damned. Sometimes called *double predestination,* it is a doctrine Calvin held with the greatest awe and respect. Unlike many of his followers, Calvin refused to speculate as to the reason God predestines some to life and others to destruction: "For we should be no wiser than it becomes us to be."[24]

e. The Doctrine of the Church

With reference to the church, Calvin declared that there are two distinct marks that allow us to differentiate a true church from a false church: "Wherever we see the Word of God purely preached and heard, and the sacraments administered according to Christ's institution, there, it is not to be doubted, a church of God exists."[25] He held that the Roman Catholic Church was not a true church on the grounds that it did not *truly* preach the Word or administer the sacraments. He rejected the Roman Catholic doctrine of apostolic succession, the belief that the authority of Christ had been passed down to the original apostles, who then passed on that same authority through the succession of bishops. While Rome uses this doctrine to justify the authority of the papacy, Calvin held that "true apostolicity is derived not from the laying on of hands, but from the preaching of the doctrine of the apostles."[26]

Calvin gave church organization more attention than did the other Reformers, saying that the true church must hold to the New Testament pattern of organization, which included four biblical offices. The *pastor* is charged with ministering the Word of God, delivering the sacraments, and exercising discipline. The *teacher* is charged with scriptural interpretation in the church but is not charged with the other duties of the pastor. Also serving the church are *elders* charged with oversight and discipline; they, along with the pastor, are to guard the morals of church members. Finally, the church is served by *deacons* who care for the poor and distribute alms.

f. The Sacraments

Along with the other Reformers, Calvin held that there are only two sacraments: baptism and the Lord's Supper. Concerning the Lord's Supper, however, Calvin disagreed with both Luther, who taught a doctrine that has been termed *consubstantiation,*[27] and Zwingli, who reduced the supper to mere memorial. The debate revolved around how Christ is present during the supper. At issue was the interpretation of Christ's statement, "This is my body." On the one hand, Luther took the phrase more literally and said the body of Christ is metaphysically present in the bread and wine. How, Calvin asked, is that possible if the body of Christ is in heaven? On the other hand,

Calvin also rejected Zwingli's assertion that the supper is nothing more than a memorial. Calvin believed that the elements of bread and wine are indeed efficacious because of the inner work of the Spirit commensurate with the supper. To Calvin the Lord's Supper is a way through which God's Spirit works to fortify the faith of those who accept his work by faith.

On baptism, Calvin parted company with both Luther and Rome. He held that the rite neither saves nor converts the person being baptized. Like the supper, baptism serves to fortify one's faith, but the truth baptism conveys is more significant than the act itself. The significance is found in how the believer responds to the work of the Spirit. Like the other Reformers, however, Calvin believed that not only believers should be baptized, but also the children of believers, as a sign of God's grace to his people. The Reformed wing of the Reformation held that infant baptism is to be understood as a covenant sign and likened it to circumcision in the Old Testament. As circumcision did not save, neither does baptism. Rather, it brings the child within the covenant community and signifies a commitment of the community to the child, that he or she be raised in the fear and admonition of the Lord. Historically, the debate over the sacraments was what divided the Swiss Reformers from their German counterparts. The two Swiss groups, the Zwinglians and Calvinists, met and produced the Zurich Consensus of 1549, which, in effect, joined the two Swiss strands together.

The significance of Calvin's theology can be likened to an earthquake deep within the sea. Like a tremor in the ocean bed that produces wave after wave crashing against the shore, Calvin's thought quickly resulted in numerous theological waves that crashed onto the shores of Christendom. Indeed, Calvin's theology is so powerful that even today those waves keep hitting as contemporary scholars interpret and rework his theology. It is crucial to remember, however, that these "aftershock" theological waves are not the earthquake itself; they are other theologians' interpretations of the earth-shaking thought of Calvin.

B. PROTESTANT SCHOLASTICISM

These waves began crashing onto the shore immediately following Calvin's death in 1564 at the age of fifty-five, as his mantle was passed to Theodore Beza, the director of the academy in Geneva. Although a close associate and trusted colleague of Calvin, Beza's theological method marked a retreat from that of the Geneva Reformer. Whereas Calvin followed a humanistic and inductive method, Beza fell back into the deductive Aristotelian method that had characterized medieval scholasticism. The theology produced by Reformed scholasticism did not differ greatly in content from that of Calvin, but the feel and the freshness of Calvin's work were lost. Theology now focused on systematization and propositions, and attempted to extend theological knowledge into fine details, but in the process, the intimate relationship of theology to life was again obscured. This was the era of Protestant scholasticism.

John Leith, in his excellent study *An Introduction to the Reformed Tradition*, suggests three reasons why, after Calvin's death, Calvin's doctrine was altered.[28] First, the theological atmosphere required a greater refinement and precision of definition. Second, certain pressures developed between the different Protestant communities that led to intricate controversies. Third, the original enthusiasm for reform had disappeared, and it became obvious that the whole world would not be won over. This resulted in a tendency to build walls around the various Protestant camps and turn the focus inward.

"Scholasticism is a type of theology that places a great emphasis upon precision of definition and upon logical, coherent, consistent statements."[29] Historian Brian Armstrong suggests four tendencies of scholasticism.[30] First, scholasticism employs a deductive form of reasoning as opposed to Calvin's inductive approach. From first principles, or assumptions, the scholastic theologian works out a logical belief system. Second, reason is elevated to such a level that it could even threaten the authority of divine revelation. Third, scholasticism stands on the assumption that Scripture contains a whole and rational theology that can, with some effort, be distilled into a comprehensive statement. Such a statement may then be applied in an effort to judge the orthodoxy of another position. Fourth, scholasticism is interested in a kind of abstract and speculative thinking, the kind that Calvin wanted nothing to do with. In fact, this whole new approach was something Calvin would not have recognized.

This new outlook represents a profound divergence from the humanistically oriented faith of John Calvin and most of the early Reformers. The strongly biblical and experientially based theology of Calvin and Luther had been overcome by the metaphysics and deductive logic of a restored Aristotelianism.[31]

1. Theodore Beza

As noted above, the man most directly responsible for this shift in thinking was none other than the heir to Calvin's position in Geneva, Theodore Beza.[32] He was converted after a serious illness and later became professor of Greek at the Academy of Lausanne. He was invited by Calvin to become the first rector and professor at the new academy in Geneva.

While Beza's theology was heavily dependent on Calvin and held to the main core of Calvin's doctrine, his theology differed in subtle ways. One such difference was the emphasis Beza placed on predestination. Although Beza claimed to be a proponent of Calvin's view, he changed Calvin's emphasis by moving the discussion of predestination from the doctrine of salvation, where it acted as a "check valve" to remind the believer that salvation is ultimately a work of God, and placed it under the doctrine of divine knowledge, which gave it a new place of prominence. Predestination became the integration point of doctrine, occupying a place of central importance to Beza in contrast to Calvin, who, as noted, refused to give this mysterious doctrine such a central position. This shift also made God an arbitrary and capricious distant deity rather than the loving Father Calvin described. Henceforth, Reformed theology, or Calvinism, emphasized absolute divine sovereignty and related doctrines.

Theodore Beza

Alongside Beza's emphasis on predestination was his development of a theological position called *supralapsarianism* (from Lat. *supra lapsum*, "above the fall," hence "before the fall"). It refers to the concept that God's decree to elect some and reprobate others stood logically before the decree permitting the fall of Adam and Eve. The opposing view, *infralapsarianism*, understood the decree of God concerning election to come in logical sequence *after* the decree permitting the fall. Although this subtle distinction may seem trivial and purposeless to the modern mind, it is an example of scholasticism's relentless pursuit of precision.

In short, supralapsarianism understands God to have first decreed that some would be elect and some would not. Second, God decreed to create the elect and the reprobate. Third, God decreed to permit the fall. Finally, God decreed to permit salvation for the elect. Infralapsarianism, by contrast, posited that God's first decree was to create. His second was to allow the fall. His third was to elect some to salvation. Fourth, God decreed to allow those not elected to receive their just condemnation. And fifth, God decreed to provide a redeemer. The infralapsarian order softens the harshness of the scholastic doctrine of predestination as opposed to supralapsarianism, which makes God absolutely arbitrary.

The Order of the Decrees†	
SUPRALAPSARIANISM	**INFRALAPSARIANISM**
1. Elect some, reprobate others	1. Decree to create all humans
2. Create both elect and nonelect	2. Permission of the fall
3. Permission of the fall	3. Provision of salvation for humans
4. Provision of salvation of the elect	4. Election of some, passive reprobation of others
5. Application of salvation of the elect	5. Application of salvation to the elect, that is, those who will believe

FIGURE 11.1.

Finally, Beza formally developed the doctrine of the *limited atonement.*[33] The doctrine of limited atonement asserted that what Christ achieved on the cross was only *intended* to redeem the elect. The case can be stated the opposite way: Christ did not ransom those whom God has not elected. The doctrine is logically based on the prior doctrine of election. If God decreed to elect some and not others, then it follows that his decree to provide redemption through Christ was only for the elect. To conclude otherwise would be to assert that God the Son was working at cross-purposes with the Father. The doctrine of limited atonement serves as an illustration of the pressing of logical conclusions by the scholastic methodology. Scholastic procedure took Calvin's doctrines to their logical, rational, conclusion, beyond the conclusions Calvin himself was willing to draw. The most that can be said is that the doctrine of a limited atonement is one "that can be drawn from some of Calvin's premises, but that Calvin himself refused to draw."[34]

2. The Reaction of Jacob Arminius

One of Beza's students in Geneva was Jacob Arminius, a native of the Netherlands. After his study in Geneva, Arminius returned home to pastor a church for fifteen years. During that time, Arminius had a radical change of theological opinion, for he began to question the conclusions of Reformed scholasticism. He came to the troubling conclusion that scholasticism logi-

†In speaking of supralapsarianism, infralapsarianism, and sublapsarianism, one finds universal agreement on the order of the decrees only within a supralapsarian framework, but there is no consistency in nomenclature and in the ordering within the infralapsarian and sublapsarian frameworks. The logical order is what one would adopt with an unlimited atonement interpretation, whereas the order presented here is logically consistent with a limited atonement view, the position that has historically characterized the Reformed tradition. See Millard Erickson, *Christian Theology* (Grand Rapids: Baker, 1984), 2:826.

cally made God the author of sin. (A fuller study of his theology is found in chapter 12.) His doctrine was eventually formalized by his followers, who came to be known as "Arminians." In 1610 the Arminians met and drafted an appeal for tolerance of their viewpoints. Their Remonstrance was a shortened version of five of their major doctrines. In this statement, the Arminians modified the doctrine of unconditional election, which asserts that God elects a person to salvation based solely on his grace. The Arminians argued that the elect are chosen based on their foreseen faith. Faith then becomes a condition to election. The Arminians also rejected the idea of a limited atonement, believing that Christ died for all humanity.

3. The Synod of Dort, Five-Point Calvinism, and TULIP

The orthodox Calvinists responded to the Remonstrance with a statement they called the "Counter-Remonstrance." The Dutch government then stepped in to try and settle the controversy but to no avail. The situation worsened until a synod was called to settle the issues at hand.

The Synod of Dort

Calvinists from all over Europe attended the 1618 synod held in the city of Dort in Holland; it became the first general synod of Reformed Protestantism. Dutch theologian Simon Episcopius (Simon Biscop) represented the Arminians. As a result of the synod, Arminianism was soundly rejected, and in their response to the Arminians, the Calvinists offered five statements that came to be known as the Canons of Dort. In the first place, the Calvinists responded that humans are totally unable to save themselves because they are wholly depraved by sin.[35] Second, the Calvinists held that God elects people unconditionally. In other words, election is not based on something found in the person elected; nor is it based on faith that God foresees the individual will exercise. Third, while the death of Christ was sufficient for all of humanity, the benefits of Christ's death are designed only for the elect. Fourth, God works irresistibly to draw the elect to himself in salvation. The elect cannot resist the power of God's drawing them to faith.[36] And fifth, those who are regenerated and justified will persevere in the faith until the end. All of these statements are logically connected and interdependent. Popularly, these points are known as the five points of Calvinism and are remembered with the acrostic TULIP.

TULIP acrostic spelling out the five points of Calvinism

Calvinism's TULIP
• **T**otal Depravity • **U**nconditional Election • **L**imited Atonement • **I**rresistible Grace • **P**erseverance of the Saints

FIGURE 11.2.

These five points (TULIP) were not intended to be a full exposition of Calvinism. Furthermore, they represent some shifts in Calvin's theology. They can be understood properly only against their historical backdrop.

4. Francis Turretin

One more theologian in Reformed scholasticism deserves consideration: Francis Turretin (1623–87). Turretin was born in Geneva, where he pastored an Italian congregation. His comprehensive three-volume work, *Theological Institutions*, is the most important Calvinist work since the *Institutes*. In fact, Turretin has been called "the most important systematic theologian of Calvinist orthodoxy on the continent."[37]

Turretin was a typical scholastic. His efforts demonstrated a commitment to finding subtle distinctions, making rigid outlines, and formulating syllogistic rationales. His theology has several important aspects. One is his concern with the doctrine of Scripture. His treatment of Scripture represents a shift, characteristic of scholasticism, in which the inspiration of Scripture receives a great amount of detailed attention. Moving from concerns over the inspiration of the Septuagint to the reliability of the various manuscripts, Turretin gives a great deal of attention to defining the inerrancy of Scripture. To be sure, this would become characteristic of later Calvinism, but such an interest is not found in Calvin himself. Turretin's thought reemerged later in the halls of the newly formed Princeton Theological Seminary, where scholastic Calvinism was to find a vehicle to spread its particular nuances throughout the new world.

5. Four-Point Calvinism (Amyraldism)

"It is a well-known fact that French Protestantism never accepted the strict Calvinistic orthodoxy of the seventeenth century."[38] Nowhere was this belief more prominent than at the most illustrious of the French Reformed schools, the Academy of Saumur. The academy was dominated by two figures, John Cameron and his student and successor, Moise Amyraut (1596–1664). Cameron laid the foundation for his theology by asserting that his doctrinal position was truly faithful to John Calvin, but it was Amyraut who articulated the distinctiveness of the school of Saumur in contradistinction to the Reformed scholastics, and the theology that emerged from Saumur has been labeled Amyraldism.

Moise Amyraut studied law but was encouraged by his pastor to turn his attention toward theology. He undertook a thorough study of Calvin's *Institutes.* He then served the Reformed church in Saumur and at the same time taught at the academy there. His life was often in turmoil, for his theology was continually refuted and he was charged with heresy at three national synods, although never convicted. His influence continued to grow so that by the end of the seventeenth century, most French pastors and theologians were Amyraldists.[39]

Moise Amyraut developed a theology that was both frustrating and irritating to the reigning scholastics, because "his whole theological program [was] at odds with the orientation of scholasticism."[40] In his understanding, God was awesome and mysterious and desired that we remain ignorant of certain things. In fact, Amyraut warned against too much curiosity and believed that reason could actually keep us from the truth of divine revelation, which may be beyond, and even contradictory to, reason. As this theological position developed, two areas of Amyraut's theology diverged from the theology of the Reformed scholastics.

The central issue of Amyraut's theology in contradistinction to the common Reformed consensus revolved around the doctrine of predestination. Amyraut rejected the popular Reformed elevation of the doctrine to the integrating point of theological understanding. Instead, in a manner reminiscent of Calvin, Amyraut placed the doctrine after the theology of salvation as a means of explaining why some believe the gospel and others do not. He argued that the crux of the issue revolved around the dichotomy between God's secret will and his revealed will. On the one hand, God's revealed will is that he desires all to come to salvation. On the other hand, God's secret will is to elect only some to participate in Christ's benefits. Amyraut frequently pointed out that Calvin is the one who made such a distinction between these two wills of God.[41] He further explained this distinction, noting that there are two ways of willing something: by making the will, or desire, known and by the determination to make that will take place. Another way this may be explained is that God has a "wish-will," which simply expresses his desire, and a "will-will," which determines that something is going to take place. Therefore God wishes/desires that all come to salvation, but he wills that only certain people be given the faith to do so.

Moïse Amyraut

It follows then that Amyraut's doctrine of the atonement is affected by his doctrine of predestination. Indeed, he challenged the commonly held doctrine of limited atonement by asserting that Christ died for everyone. Christ came to redeem every person, but the benefits of his death are applied only to those who believe. Amyraut believed that Christ's death was universal in its *design* but particular in *application*. It is true to say, on the one hand, that salvation is intentionally offered to all, but it is equally true to say that it is effective only for those who believe. "These words, 'God wills the salvation of all men,' necessarily meet with this limitation, 'provided that they believe.'"[42] In line with Calvin, Amyraut believed that election is unconditional and that faith is created in a person to enable that person to respond to God's offer of salvation.

Although Amyraut's theology took hold among the French clergy and professorate, his theology was never embraced elsewhere on the Continent. The general course of history demonstrates that scholastic Calvinism, not Amyraldism, prevailed throughout Reformed circles.

C. COVENANT THEOLOGY

One of the unique contributions of Reformed theology is the understanding that the essence of God's dealings with humanity has been through divine covenants. "A covenant is an unchangeable, divinely imposed legal agreement between God and man that stipulates the conditions of their relationship."[43] The covenant idea is seen at the very outset of the Swiss Reformation in the writings of Ulrich Zwingli and his successor, Heinrich Bullinger, and it is also implicit in Calvin. But the idea faded with the advent of scholastic methodology. As supralapsarian Calvinism gained ascendancy in the Reformed community, the conception of God as omnipotent and arbitrary came to dominate. Against this background the covenant idea was again brought to the fore, this time by the Dutch theologian Johannes Cocceius (1603–69).

Although the Reformed theologians became uniform in their emphasis of the centrality of covenant in the story of redemption, they had varying opinions on how many covenants there were. Theologian Edward Dowey notes three stages of development in the Reformed understanding of the biblical covenant. First, in Calvin's writings, *covenant* described God's relationship to the patriarchs, Israel, and the church. Second, after the time of Calvin, the concept of covenant was understood to go back further in time to include the demands of obedience God placed upon Adam. Third, still later Reformed thinkers extended the concept beyond time constraints and held that a covenant was made between the three members of the Trinity, who agreed to provide redemption and to predestine each human.[44]

Johannes Cocceius is the name most commonly associated with covenant theology. He avoided the prevalent scholasticism and held that one should attempt to read the Scriptures without presuppositions. Emphasizing the concept that all theological truth should come from Scripture alone, Cocceius developed a covenant understanding of biblical redemption in his work *Doctrine of the Covenant and Testaments of God* (1648). He held to three periods of God's covenant dealings with humanity: the covenant of works with Adam, the covenant of grace with Moses, and the new covenant of Jesus Christ. This emphasis on the centrality of covenant in God's dealings with humanity was later revived by the Puritans and brought to center stage in their Westminster Confession.

D. THE PURITANS

The Puritans have been called "the most consistent embodiment of the Reformed perspective subsequent to the Continental Reformation."[45] The Puritans cannot, however, be understood apart from their historical context. Compared with the continental expressions of the Reformation, the Reformation in England was long, complex, and unique in its development. While the continental Reformation was theological in its impetus, the English Reformation was politically motivated, born out of the desire of Henry VIII to divorce Catherine of Aragon, a divorce the pope would not sanction. To achieve his objective of a legitimate divorce, Henry made a break with the Roman Catholic Church. A second feature of the English Reformation was that no one figure dominated its development. During the reign of Elizabeth I, Protestantism was established with the Elizabethan Settlement, and the church was conceived as a *via media* broad enough to encompass both Catholics and the stridently Reformed under one umbrella. The resultant form of Anglicanism was something between Catholicism and the Protestant Reformation on the Continent. The Elizabethan Settlement displeased a significant portion of the English Protestants whose sympathies lay with the Reformed. This party demanded that the worship forms be purified of vestiges of Catholicism (e.g., clerical vestments) as well as liturgy. This desire to purify the worship of the church begat the label *Puritan* for this party. The Puritans were greatly influenced by the continental Reformers and the English theologians John Wycliffe and William Tyndale.

J. I. Packer calls Puritanism a movement of revival, noting that spiritual revival is what the Puritans professed to be seeking.[46] It was the subject matter of much of their devotional literature, and the ministry of Puritan pastors brought about revival. Like all other movements within the Reformed tradition of Protestantism, Puritanism made unique contributions to the rest of Christendom.

1. The Westminster Confession and Catechism

During much of the seventeenth century, Puritans dominated the English Parliament. In 1643 Parliament ordered a confession written. The task was undertaken by 121 clergymen and 30 members of Parliament and was completed two years later. The resultant Westminster Confession, with the associated Longer and Shorter Catechisms, became the standard confessional statements in the English-speaking world.

In line with the Reformed scholastics, the decrees of God were made prominent. Early in the third chapter, the doctrine of predestination is introduced and developed. The doctrines of Christ and salvation follow predestination, and the doctrine of faith does not come into focus until chapter 7. This, once again, represents a shift in theology from that of John Calvin, who moved from a discussion of faith (*Institutes* 3.2) to predestination (*Institutes* 3.21). Again, in keeping with the tenor of popular scholasticism, Westminster seems to favor a limited atonement, although it is not expressly stated. Nevertheless, the wording betrays this underlying assumption in Puritan theology: Christ's death was "for all those whom the Father hath given unto him."[47] Finally, covenant theology enjoys a central role in the theological system, as it dominates the discussion of chapter 7. Here the writers speak of both a covenant of works and of grace.

2. Emphasis on Conversion

"The distinctive contribution of the Puritans on the subject of human salvation was their emphasis on conversion."[48] Much of their theological writing concerns this subject. Furthermore, the Puritans created evangelistic tracts aimed at the conversion of the masses. The Puritan understanding of and emphasis on conversion is not the same as that embodied in the revivalist preachers of the nineteenth century, for the Puritan's theology was a Reformed theology that saw a person's turning to God to be, in reality, an act of God turning a person to himself. Furthermore, some of these conversions were sudden and some were not. Some were dramatic and some were not. All of this was in line with their doctrine of predestination and their conviction that conversion is an act of God, not an act of the individual human subject. The evangelist was more like a midwife whose job was to help during the conversion process but could do nothing to bring it about.

3. The Sabbath

Although a strict, consistent view of Sabbath observance never caught on in continental Europe, the Puritans established a Christian Sabbath (Sunday) during which Christians must "not only observe an holy rest, all the day, from their own works, words, and thoughts about their worldly employments and recreations, but also are taken up, the whole time, in the public and private exercises of [God's] worship, and in the duties of necessity and mercy."[49] The Puritans saw this Sabbath as binding and honored it with the utmost seriousness. In fact, they believed so strongly in Sabbath adherence that they thought natural disasters resulted from a lack of obedience.

The Puritan Sabbath was significant because it differed from common practices and beliefs. In English society, for instance, Sunday was a day for loud play, gambling, and drunkenness. Where Puritan Sabbath observance took root, society began to change. Packer notes that as a result of Richard Baxter's pastoral work at Kidderminster, there was soon no disorder but only families singing psalms and repeating sermons.[50] When Puritanism spread to the shores of New England in the early seventeenth century, recreational pursuits were altogether banned on Sundays. Sixteen-year-old Nathaniel Mather wrote that one of the many sins of his youth that was worse than the others was whittling wood on the Sabbath.[51] Contrary to this rather stiff understanding of the Sabbath, Calvin saw the Sabbath as fulfilled by Christ, who gives us rest from having to work for our salvation.[52] The furthest Calvin seems to take the Sabbath and apply it to New Testament Christians is to suggest that the principle of a Sabbath is a good idea, and each believer should try to take one day in seven as a day of rest.

E. PRINCETON THEOLOGY

As Reformed thought took root in America, it took on a distinctive form reflecting the milieu from which it arose. Puritanism flourished in New England but fell into decline in the latter eighteenth century and ultimately gave birth to American theological liberalism in the mid-nineteenth century. Princeton Seminary became the bastion of Reformed theology. Theology there reflected several streams that were synthesized and proclaimed and defended by the then dominant American epistemology, Scottish Common Sense. While the Princetonians claimed to merely preserve and maintain the pure theology of the Reformation, the theology arising out of Princeton did have a specific form that can be isolated vis-à-vis other strains of Reformed thought. The influence of the theology propagated by Princeton cannot be overemphasized. For nearly 120 years (1812–1929)—until it was reorganized and the last remnants of the Old Princeton tradition left to form Westminster Seminary—Princeton theology became the standard of historic Reformed orthodoxy in North America.

The architect of Princeton theology was Archibald Alexander[53] (1772–1851), founding professor of the seminary. Upon arriving at Princeton, Alexander was unable to find a theology textbook in English that he considered adequate to instruct the handful of entering seminary students. After much searching, Alexander found Turretin's massive three-volume work in Latin, *Institutio theologiae elencticae*.[54] This choice of texts set the direction of the Princeton theology as both Reformed and scholastic. Turretin's theology and Alexander's theological method were adopted and propagated by his student and successor, Charles Hodge,[55] who continued to use Turretin's text until the publication of his own systematic theology in 1872. Hodge's

Systematic Theology represented a departure from Turretin at several points. First, his theology was written in English whereas Turretin had never been translated from the Latin. Second, Hodge interacted with then current theological trends. Third, he espoused Scottish Common Sense philosophy, the Baconian inductivism of the emerging scientific method, and the then dominant Newtonian worldview.[56] Hodge was succeeded in the chair of systematic and polemic theology by his son, A. A. Hodge.[57] A. A. Hodge in turn was succeeded by the great and indefatigable B. B. (Benjamin Breckinridge) Warfield.[58] Together these men provided more than one hundred years of stability in American theological thought.

Charles Hodge

Princetonian theologians attempted to preserve the legacy of orthodoxy they had received from the Reformers. Their task was to preserve rather than innovate. At the celebration of Charles Hodge's fiftieth anniversary as a professor at Princeton Seminary, Hodge boasted that a new idea had never arisen at Princeton.[59] This self-proclaimed perspective has received negative critical evaluation by a number of historians and theologians. Presbyterian historian Lefferts Loetscher has noted, "The so-called *Princeton Theology* seemed to offer an almost mathematical demonstration of an unchanged and unchangeable religious outlook."[60] American religion historian Sidney Ahlstrom observed that several elements had come together to give Princeton theology its gestalt, including "an almost absolutely rigidified Biblicism," "a reliance on the Common Sense Realists of Scotland," and the Reformed confessions.[61]

The Princetonians stood squarely in the Reformed tradition yet were in touch with the scientific and philosophical movements of the day, often without discerning the compatibility of these movements with the received theology. In the end, however, one could discern several themes that tied Princeton thought together and made it an identifiable entity.

1. Scripture

As noted above, Princeton's heavy emphasis on Scripture led to the charge of a "rigidified biblicism." While this is an overstatement, it does reflect the Princetonian presupposition that it was the Bible that defined the Christian faith. The Bible provided the backbone necessary to defend against the rising tide of rationalism (seen in the form of higher criticism) and mysticism (seen in the theology of Friedrich Schleiermacher). So great was Princeton's commitment to the authority of Scripture that they progressively gave more and more precise definitions of the nature of biblical inspiration and inerrancy. The quintessential definition was a collaborative work between A. A. Hodge and Warfield in the *Princeton Review* in 1882. This article became the defining document in all subsequent discussion of the inspiration and inerrancy of Scripture. Warfield further defined and defended this definition in numerous articles throughout his lifetime. The Princetonians gave great attention to detailed polemics on the authority and inerrancy of Scripture because they saw the Scriptures as the foundation of all theological study and authority. If the foundation were eroded, Christians would be left without a sure and objective foundation for their faith. In keeping with the scholastic methodology, inerrancy was defended by logic, history, and detailed evidences.

2. Reformed Confessionalism

Princeton theology was characterized by its commitment to the Reformed confessions, especially the Westminster Confession. Warfield put it best: "Calvinism is just religion in its purity. We have only, therefore, to conceive of religion in its purity, and that is Calvinism."[62] It follows then that to a large extent the Princetonians simply repeated the major Calvinist doctrines. The Princetonians did not recognize the various strains of Reformed theology that simultaneously existed in the Reformed tradition. For them the Reformed tradition spoke with one united voice, in much the same manner as the Roman Catholic perception of the unanimity of the church fathers on certain issues. In fact, their particular understanding of Calvinism reflects the influence of Francis Turretin.

The major themes of Reformed theology emphasized by the Princetonians included (1) a good creation by a good God; (2) the reality of the fall, by which humankind fell under the wrath of a holy God; (3) the imputation of Adam's sin to the entire race and the subsequent depravity and spiritual inability of humankind to accomplish any spiritual good; (4) the just condemnation of humankind for sin; (5) the inability of sinners to turn to God apart from the sovereign mercy of God drawing them; (6) God's love expressed in the covenants of grace and redemption that brought salvation to the elect; (7) the continuing effects of sin, even upon the redeemed, but the ability to work for the furtherance of the kingdom of God despite the effects of the fall.

Princeton theology's reliance on Turretin reflected the response to the Arminians on the freedom of the will, to Amyraut on the extent of the atonement, to the Lutherans on the nature of the sacraments, and to the Roman Catholics and rationalists on the nature of biblical authority.

3. Scottish Common Sense

The Princetonians were influenced by the epistemology called Scottish Common Sense (or Scottish Realism, or Common Sense Realism), which had arisen in reaction to the skepticism of David Hume, who suggested that the human mind cannot know reality immediately. The best that one can hope for is to have ideas of what reality is; one cannot know reality directly. Thomas Reid, the founder of Scottish Common Sense, believed that, indeed, one *can* know immediately, because God has given us all common sense. Scottish Common Sense was brought to America by John Witherspoon, who became president of Princeton College and taught the men who would become Princeton Seminary's early professors. It was an approach to truth that was at once empirical, inductive, and scientific. Such a philosophical approach tends to see reason and empirical research as having no presuppositions and thus as able to prove anything.

From Princeton University the philosophy spread rapidly across the country through the higher educational system. The swiftness of its acceptance was due to the fact that Scottish Realism "contained an immediate conviction of right and wrong, of the reality of the external world, freedom,... about which there was no need or warrant for debate or doubt, while its discussion of association, will, and feeling, was lucidity itself, and fitted for our practical country."[63]

Princeton Seminary was theologically committed to the theology of the Reformation as it had been codified in the Westminster Confession and by Francis Turretin, and also to the view that truth was "objective and invariable."[64] In light of this fact, Charles Hodge's boast that a new idea never originated at Princeton takes on added significance. Because the sixteenth-century Reformers had discovered theological truth and the Reformed scholastics had given the truth its fullest expression, there was no need to change. Thus Princeton could by definition make no other contribution to the cause of orthodoxy than a defense of the faith.[65]

Since Common Sense and Princeton both held truth in the same esteem, realistic philosophy became a natural ally in defending the truth. Methodologically, Princeton shared four key assumptions with Common Sense.[66]

1. The first was a *stress on the objective, external nature of revelation*. This can be seen as a by-product of Scottish realism's stress on the empirical nature of knowledge.

2. The second area of agreement was the *common use of the inductive method.* According to Hodge, "the true method of theology is ... the inductive, which assumes that the Bible contains all the facts or truths which form the contents of theology, just as the facts of nature are the contents of the natural sciences."[67] Since this was the case, the theologian had to consider himself a scientist who assumed the trustworthiness of his senses to ascertain facts. He also assumed the trustworthiness of his mental faculties. The theologian, like the scientist, had to "take for granted that he can perceive, compare, combine, remember, and infer; and that he can safely rely on these mental faculties in their legitimate exercise."[68] In addition, he assumed the certainty of those truths not gained from experience but "given in the constitution of our nature."[69] The "givens" included such innate abilities as the perception of cause and effect.

B. B. Warfield

3. The third area was the *conviction that all knowledge is of the same type.* A rigorous inductivism implied the same subject-object distinction in the study of theology as in any other scientific discipline. "Knowledge," contended Hodge, "is the persuasion of what is truth, on adequate evidence."[70] When applied to the knowledge of God, this implied that "natural knowledge of God and spiritual knowledge of God, differ only in degree, not in kind."[71] God was to be known through external objective revelation rather than through an "inner" experience that was in contrast to all other experiences that were "outer."[72]

4. This in turn suggests the fourth area of correspondence between Common Sense and Princeton theology—*a common disdain for any "mystic" tendencies.* C. W. Hodge disparaged a mysticism that bypasses experience and seeks direct contact with God.[73]

Hodge did not rule out the place of "experience" in knowledge. "That 'experience' is important for knowledge goes without saying. Indeed in a certain sense it is true that knowledge grows out of experience, or that experience furnishes the raw material for thought; it is not meant that knowledge grows out of bare feeling.... In a word, feelings do not produce ideas."[74]

Apologetics was the area in which Princeton relied most heavily on realistic epistemology, as can be seen in the writings of B. B. Warfield. He viewed the primary task of apologetics, not as "the defense, not even the vindication, but the *establishment* ... of that knowledge of God which Christianity professes to embody and seeks to make efficient in the world."[75]

Warfield's perspective on apologetics revealed his understanding of reason and faith. It followed in the realistic tradition, which saw faith as arising from sufficient evidences. "Though faith is the gift of God, it does not in the least follow that the faith which God gives is an irrational faith, that is, a faith without cognizable ground in right reason.... The action of the Holy Spirit in giving faith is not apart from evidence, but along with evidence."[76] Faith had to be grounded in "right reason"; it had to conform to objective reality.

This teaching had profound implications for the authority of Scripture. The authority of Scripture became not a premise, but a conclusion of the whole apologetic process. Before we can trust the Scriptures, we must have been convinced on sufficient evidence that Scripture contains the knowledge of God.

Finally, the Princeton apologetic saw revelation as rationally received. Knowledge of God was seen as being of the same order as any other truth. The Princetonians allowed no bifurcation between scientific and religious truth. Such a distinction was irrational to them.[77]

Because of its assertion of the immediate and certain knowledge of truth with no other theoretical base than what humans could commonly perceive, Common Sense philosophy proved a boon to Princeton in defending the truth of Christianity. As an epistemology, it gave coherence to the whole outlook of America in the early nineteenth century. It could not, however, withstand the onslaughts of scientific discoveries that shook the Newtonian foundations of the system. Although Princeton continued to employ Common Sense epistemology, it was increasingly perceived as irrelevant to a world that had become conditioned to the concept of change and in which new scientific discoveries challenged the received understandings of Scripture.

F. DUTCH CALVINISM

On the other side of the Atlantic, as Princeton theology was developing and spreading, Dutch Calvinists were busy creating a vision of Reformed theology all their own. It too would be profoundly influential on Reformed theology worldwide and on the Netherlands as a nation.

1. Abraham Kuyper (1827–1920)

The dominant figure of Reformed theology in the Netherlands was Abraham Kuyper.[78] Early in his pastoral career, Kuyper was devoted to the agenda of liberalism, but as he saw its bankruptcy, he turned to the historic evangelical answers that had their roots in the theology of the Reformed tradition. He was convinced that Christians should recognize God's lordship over all areas of life. He wrote on a great many subjects, founded two newspapers, and became a member of Parliament after he helped form a new political party, the Anti-Revolutionary Party, for which he wrote the manifesto. In 1880 Kuyper founded the Free University of Amsterdam, and some years later he led a movement to break free from the state church and create the Reformed Church (*Gereformeerde Kerk*).[79] In 1890 his party took power, and Kuyper became the prime minister of the Netherlands until 1905.

Kuyper was a Calvinist in all things. He said, "In Calvinism, my heart has found rest."[80] Furthermore, his conviction that Christ should be Lord over all aspects of life was a Calvinist conviction. Calvinism "is such an all-embracing system of principles, and, rooted in the past, is able to strengthen us in the present and to fill us with confidence for the future."[81] Kuyper stressed this principle to his followers. "They had to recognize the Lordship of Christ over all areas of life, which meant that they could neither dismiss various fields (art, science, politics) as inherently 'worldly' nor participate in these simply with and as non-Christians, but must bring into each a distinctively Christian commitment and program."[82]

Abraham Kuyper

Theologically speaking, Kuyper and the church he led stood in the rich tradition of the three confessional statements that provided the theological context: the Belgic Confession (1561), the Heidelberg Catechism (1563), and the Canons of Dort (1619).

Beyond the Dutch belief in Calvinism as a life system, a comparison of their theology with their cousins in the New World, the Princetonians, shows another interesting difference. The Dutch felt that the Princeton theologians minimized the profound effects of sin on both humanity in general as well as each particular human being. With the American belief in Common Sense, the Princetonians believed that almost anyone could understand and come to believe in Christianity. Further, they believed it was possible to rationally demonstrate a coherent system of belief that anyone could understand, so that apologetics became the greatest task of the theologian. The Dutch, by contrast, standing firmly on the conviction that humanity is totally depraved, thought that their American counterparts overestimated human reasoning abilities. Kuyper and the Dutch held that everyone's reasoning capacities are hindered by sin. In fact, the only way one can know truth is through the inner witness of the Spirit. Apologetics then becomes the *last* work of the theologian.

2. Herman Bavinck (1854–1921)

Although it can be demonstrated that Abraham Kuyper was an idealist and Herman Bavinck a realist, after Kuyper, Bavinck was the leading theologian of Dutch Calvinism. After a short pastorate, Bavinck became professor of systematic theology at the seminary in Kampen and later at the Free University of Amsterdam (1902–20).

Herman Bavinck

Bavinck had a great grasp of philosophy and wrote on a variety of topics; he was most interested, however, in applying the tools of modern scholarship to the study of Reformed scholasticism. His major contribution to theology was his four-volume *Reformed Dogmatics*, published between 1895 and 1901.[83] This work was significant, among other reasons, because of its profound influence on the theology of Louis Berkhof.

3. Louis Berkhof (1873–1957)

For American students, the influence of Louis Berkhof is more directly felt than that of either Kuyper or Bavinck. At the age of eight, after moving from the Netherlands with his family, Berkhof became immersed in the Christian Reformed Church. After receiving degrees from Calvin College and Seminary, Berkhof served as a pastor before earning the Bachelor of Divinity at Princeton Theological Seminary. Thirty-eight years of his professional career were spent serving Calvin Theological Seminary.

"Louis Berkhof was not a creative and imaginative theologian."[84] Theology was to him essentially a scientific endeavor. His view was that Scripture is supremely authoritative, but its facts and ideas are not presented logically. The task of the theologian, then, is to analyze and organize these facts into a comprehensive system.

Berkhof's greatest influence was through his writing, which he continued for years after his retirement in 1944. His magnum opus was the collection of his class notes, which were originally published in two volumes called *Dogmatic Theology* (1932). This work represents in many ways an abridgement of Bavinck's *Reformed Dogmatics.* "Berkhof's theology was essentially the theology of Herman Bavinck."[85]

Berkhof's writings covered a variety of different concerns, including his firm conviction that the gospel is the greatest force in the world and should be directly applied to social ills. Although Berkhof was humble and hated discord, his convictions were powerfully felt. He publicly objected to premillennialism, and under his leadership, the Christian Reformed Church "purged itself of premillennialism."[86] At about the same time, Berkhof's influence also helped rid the Christian Reformed Church of any belief in infralapsarianism.

G. OBSERVATIONS AND CRITIQUE

While Calvin's influence can be pictured as an earthquake deep within the sea that has initiated wave after wave crashing against the shore, it has not been uncommon for those waves to claim to be the truest embodiment of the earthquake itself. The various forms of Calvinism have each laid claim to being the truest manifestation of Calvin's thought.

Scholasticism. One must look with a critical eye at the scholastic approach, which came to the fore shortly after Calvin's death, seeking to fine-tune and popularize Calvinism. Of concern is whether it is possible to shape so precise a theology. Indeed, would not Calvin himself take the exacting nature of scholasticism to task? As we have seen, the theology of John Calvin was anything but precisionist. He had a literary approach to the text, seeing the Scriptures as "a rhetorical document and a work of inspiration."[87] Looking to the text in an attempt to extract a precise dogmatic theology that answered all the questions was foreign to Calvin. For instance, Calvin showed no interest in the details of biblical inerrancy, angelology, or the doctrine of double predestination. These doctrines are simply not given much attention in Scripture, and Calvin chose to do the same. He did not seek precision the way later scholastics did.

Rationalism. Akin to scholasticism was the rationalistic mind-set of so many of Calvin's followers, for whom theology was the attempt to reduce everything to propositional truth. The rationalistic approach was deductive as opposed to Calvin's humanistic inductivism. Indeed, for Calvin, Christian theology was to be found in Scripture, not in dogmatics. Calvin's followers, however, attempted to take first principles and, using a syllogistic methodology, create carefully reasoned truths. The problem here is that such carefully reasoned arguments may be logically coherent yet remain exegetically unsupportable. Scholasticism stands on the presupposition that Scripture contains one whole, rational theology. This assumption is undergirded by an unspoken assumption that the divine revelation is flat and one-dimensional. The discipline of biblical theology has demonstrated the variegated nature of and multiple perspectives encountered in the text of Scripture. Moreover, the rationalistic methodology does not deal adequately with the literary features of the text, such as genre and figures of speech. Such an approach is directly opposed to the inductive and biblical approach of John Calvin, whose effort was always to plumb the depths of the text in order to let it yield its fruits.

Reducing Calvinism to TULIP. Many beginning students of theology equate Calvinism, and therefore Reformed theology, with the seventeenth-century acrostic TULIP. This is both inaccurate and unfortunate, because the theological system that Calvin launched cannot be reduced to this post-Calvin acrostic. There are two significant reasons why this is important. First, one is hard put to sustain the notion that Calvin himself held to all of the five points. Yes, Calvin articulated a clear understanding of the total depravity of humanity. Yes, Calvin believed that God's divine election unto eternal life was not a decision based on anything inherent in the object of his grace. But, as we have seen, the case cannot be clearly made as to whether Calvin believed in a limited atonement. Calvin himself simply never addressed this question unequivocally. Reducing the essence of Reformed theology to the five points of the TULIP misses the point that Calvinism is a worldview that encompasses all of life. To reduce Calvin's theology, or Calvinism as a system, to a concise array of theological propositions is to overlook the greater part of it. It is important to recognize that in the *Institutes* alone, Calvin goes well beyond that which is covered by the TULIP acrostic. There he deals with the sacraments, civil ceremonies, the government, prayer, and sanctification. This whole-life system is perhaps best seen in the classic work *Lectures on Calvinism*[88] by the Dutch Calvinist and exemplar of whole-life Calvinism, Abraham Kuyper.

Covenant theology. The concept of covenant has become central in the articulation of Reformed theology. As originally formulated, Cocceius's exposition of the covenant notion intended to reintroduce the concept of the relationship between God and man that had become obscured in the supralapsarian emphasis of the decrees of God. God had been exalted, but man had been reduced to the level of a puppet and denied any real responsibility and personal accountability before God. The covenant scheme denoting the covenant of works and the subsequent covenant of grace had emphasized divine grace and human responsibility. The later introduction of the covenant of redemption into the schema let in through the back door a reassertion of the very type of sovereignty that the covenant concept was intended to obviate.

The challenge of practical theology. A recurrent issue in the Calvinistic tradition is one of practical theology. As the Protestant tradition with the most developed and precise theology, it has had, particularly in America, a tendency to focus on correct doctrine and obedience to that doctrine as the answer to spiritual issues. Many of those who are rigidly committed to the tradition stress the doctrines of divine sovereignty, election, and predestination to a degree that obscures human responsibility for evangelism.

Concurrent with this problem is the issue of practical assurance of salvation. This question may take the form, "How can I know I am one of the elect?" or "How can I know that I am saved?" Much popular Calvinistic teaching stresses a position that is popularly known as "Lordship salvation."

Several recent studies have traced the development of Calvinism among English-speaking people and noted that in both the Puritan and Scottish traditions, the doctrine of faith underwent a startling evolution, beginning with Beza and continuing into the early seventeenth century, at which point the doctrine was virtually indistinguishable from the doctrine of faith espoused by Arminius.[89] Whereas Calvin spoke of initial saving faith as being a passive knowledge of God,[90] in the later theologians, faith became activistic and voluntaristic, a matter of the will rather than a matter of the heart, commitment rather than trust.[91]

Calvin saw the doctrine of justification as the "principal hinge by which religion is supported."[92] It was this rediscovery of the judicial/forensic nature of justification that gave birth to Protestantism and delivered the church from the Augustinian–Roman Catholic concept of justification as infused righteousness. As important as the doctrine was to the first generation of Reformers, in succeeding generations, the debate with Catholicism continued on a variety of topics,[93] and justification ceased to occupy the central place of preeminence in Reformed circles particularly. While there was a theoretical commitment to the primacy of the doctrine, theological structures were erected that obscured the vital function of the doctrine of justification by faith alone in the ongoing Christian life.[94] Particularly, as English-speaking Calvinists progressively embraced a version of the covenant system that obscured the emphasis of the Reformers and radically changed the concept of saving faith from one of passive knowledge to a voluntaristic act of the will,[95] justification ceased to function as the balm for the troubled soul.[96]

The dynamic of assurance espoused by proponents of Lordship salvation has its roots deep in the tradition of the Puritans and the Scottish Calvinists. The Scots referred to this process as the *practical syllogism*. The Puritans called it the *reflex action*.[97] By whatever name, the process is the same. The believer is denied direct access to the Savior for assurance. Instead, he or she must look inside and complete the following syllogism: "The Scripture tells me that he who believes shall be saved. If upon examining myself I find fruits of righteousness in my life, I may then complete the syllogism 'But I believe, therefore I shall be saved.' "[98] However, such a doctrine lays the ground of assurance solely within ourselves, "causing the believer to rely more on his own works for assurance, than on the work of Christ on our behalf."[99] The ultimate result of such teaching is uncertainty.

This position is what Berkhof has labeled "pietistic nomism" which is in opposition to the Reformers and the apostles. Berkhof has noted that the Reformers in opposition to Rome sometimes stressed assurance as the *most important element* of faith. Both Calvin and the Heidelberg catechism saw assurance as belonging to the essence of faith, whereas

> Pietistic Nomism asserted that assurance does not belong to the very being, but only the well-being of faith; and that it can be secured, except by special revelation, only by continuous and conscious introspection. All kinds of "marks of the spiritual life" derived not from Scripture but from the lives of approved Christians became the standard of self-examination. The outcome proved, however, that this method was not calculated to produce assurance, but rather to lead to everlasting doubt, confusion and uncertainty.[100]

Calvin similarly observed that "*faith implies certainty.*" [101] He observed of those who deny this truth:

> Also there are very many who so conceive of God's mercy that they receive almost no consolation from it. They are constrained with miserable anxiety at the same time as they are in doubt with whether he will be merciful to them because they confine that very kindness of which they seem utterly persuaded within too narrow limits. For among themselves they ponder that it is indeed great and abundant, shed upon many, available and ready for all; but uncertain whether it will ever come to them, or rather they will come to it.... Therefore it does not so much strengthen the spirit in secure tranquility as

trouble it with uneasy doubting. But there is a far different feeling of full assurance that in the Scriptures is always attributed to faith. It is this which puts beyond doubt God's goodness clearly manifested for us [Col. 2:2; 1 Thess. 1:5; cf. Heb. 6:11 and 10:22]. But this cannot happen without our *truly feeling its sweetness and experiencing it* ourselves. For this reason, the apostle derives confidence from faith and from confidence, in turn, boldness. For he states: "Through Christ we have boldness and access with confidence which is through faith in him." ... By these words he obviously shows that there is no right faith except when we dare with tranquil hearts to stand in God's sight. This boldness arises only out of a sure confidence in the divine benevolence and salvation. This is so true that the word faith is often used for confidence.[102]

The contemporary advocates of Lordship salvation, by following the Puritan teaching regarding sanctification and assurance, are unwittingly compromising the cardinal Reformed and Protestant doctrine of justification by faith alone by suspending assurance of salvation at the time of belief, and are in practice basing assurance of salvation on works.

BIBLIOGRAPHY

Calvin, John. *Institutes of the Christian Religion.* Translated by Ford Lewis Battles. Philadelphia: Westminster, 1977. • **Dowey, Edward A.** *A Commentary on the Confession of 1967 and an Introduction to "The Book of Confessions."* Philadelphia: Westminster, 1967. • **Hesselink, I. John.** *On Being Reformed.* 2nd ed. New York: Reformed Church Press, 1988. • **Kuyper, Abraham.** *Lectures on Calvinism.* Grand Rapids: Eerdmans, 1961. • **Leith, John H.** *Introduction to the Reformed Tradition.* Atlanta: John Knox, 1981. • **McGrath, Alister.** *The Intellectual Origins of the European Reformation.* Oxford: Blackwell, 1987. • ———. *A Life of John Calvin.* Oxford: Blackwell, 1990. • **Noll, Mark.** *The Princeton Theology.* Grand Rapids: Baker, 1989. • **Parker, T. H. L.** *John Calvin: A Biography.* Philadelphia: Westminster, 1975. • **Wallace, Ronald S.** *Calvin, Geneva and the Reformation.* Grand Rapids: Baker, 1990. • **Wells, David,** ed. *Dutch Reformed Theology.* Grand Rapids: Baker, 1989.

NOTES

[1]Many would see Calvin as one of the four or five greatest theologians in the history of the church.

[2]Alister McGrath, *A Life of John Calvin* (Oxford: Blackwell, 1990), 70.

[3]The story of John Calvin's life is detailed in T. H. L. Parker, *John Calvin: A Biography* (Philadelphia: Westminster, 1975).

[4]Cited in McGrath, *Life of John Calvin*, 95.

[5]Ronald S. Wallace, *Calvin, Geneva and the Reformation* (Grand Rapids: Baker, 1990), vii.

[6]See also the discussion of humanism in chap. 10.A.1.

[7]Donald Kagan, Steven Ozmet, and Frank M. Turner, *The Western Heritage* (New York: Macmillan, 1979), 340.

[8]E.g., Erasmus's *Julius Excluded from Heaven* is a scathing satirical piece aimed at the "warrior pope."

[9]Kagan et al., *Western Heritage*, 366.

[10]William J. Bouwsma, *John Calvin: A Sixteenth-Century Portrait* (New York: Oxford University Press, 1988), 118.

[11]Alister McGrath, *The Intellectual Origins of the European Reformation* (Oxford: Blackwell, 1987), 179.

[12]See John Calvin, *Institutes of the Christian Religion*, 3.22.8, in Library of Christian Classics, vol. 20, trans. Ford Lewis Battles (Philadelphia: Westminster, 1977).

[13]McGrath, *Intellectual Origins of the European Reformation*, 181.

[14]See Alexandre Ganoczy, *The Young Calvin* (Philadelphia: Westminster, 1987), 137.

[15]See Bouwsma, *John Calvin*, 18.

[16]Ibid., vii.

[17]Calvin, *Institutes*, 2.1.8.

[18]Ibid.

[19]Ibid., 2.17.4.

[20]Ibid., 3.11.2.

[21]Calvin develops the concept of the believer's incorporation into Christ, reflecting the apostle Paul's teaching that the believer is "in Christ" as foundational to his doctrine of justification. Thus this is not a "legal fiction" as some have charged. By virtue of incorporation into Christ, Christ's merit covers the believer's demerit.

[22]*Institutes*, 3.21.2.

[23]Ibid., 3.21.5.

[24]Ibid., 3.24.13.

[25]Ibid., 4.1.9.

[26]Justo L. Gonzalez, *A History of Christian Thought* (Nashville: Abingdon, 1975), 3:162–63.

[27]Lutheran scholars deny that the term is an accurate description of their eucharistic doctrine. See chap. 10.C.4.b.

[28]John H. Leith, *An Introduction to the Reformed Tradition* (Atlanta: John Knox, 1981), 117–18.

[29]Ibid., 118.

[30]Brian G. Armstrong, *Calvinism and the Amyraut Heresy* (Madison: University of Wisconsin Press, 1969), 32.

[31]Ibid.

[32]See also the biographical sketch of Beza in chap. 17.

[33]Calvin himself made some statements that seem to lead naturally to the doctrine of a limited atonement. At other times, however, particularly in his commentaries, he made statements that cannot be reconciled with the limited atonement understanding. Since Calvin never directly addressed this issue, trying to claim him for either side of the debate is historically anachronistic.

[34]Gonzalez, *History of Christian Thought*, 3:271.

[35]The doctrine of total depravity is commonly understood to subsume the corollary doctrine of the total inability of humanity to turn to God apart from a prior work of the Holy Spirit.

[36]In irresistible grace, God is understood to work in the human will to make it willing to come to him. He does not force himself upon the unwilling.

[37]Gonzalez, *History of Christian Thought*, 3:271. Turretin's theology was the required systematic theological text at Princeton until the publication of Charles Hodge's text in the early 1870s.

[38]Ibid., 3:288.

[39]Armstrong, *Calvinism and the Amyraut Heresy*, xviii.

[40]Ibid., 37.

[41]See John Calvin, *Commentary on 2 Peter*, The Comprehensive Calvin Collection (Albany, OR: Ages Software, 1998), 2:9.

[42]Amyraut, quoted by Armstrong in *Calvinism and the Amyraut Heresy*, 169.

[43]Wayne Grudem, *Systematic Theology* (Grand Rapids: Zondervan, 1994), 515.

[44]Edward A. Dowey, *A Commentary on the Confession of 1967 and an Introduction to "The Book of Confessions"* (Philadelphia: Westminster, 1967), 243.

[45]Edward LeRoy Long Jr., "Ministry and Scholarship in the Reformed Tradition," in *Scholarship, Sacraments and Service: Historical Studies in Protestant Tradition*, D. B. Clendenin and W. B. Buschart, eds. (Lewiston, NY: Edwin Mellen, 1990), 4.

[46]J. I. Packer, *A Quest for Godliness* (Wheaton: Crossway, 1990), 37.

[47]Westminster Confession 8.5.

[48]*Eerdmans' Handbook to Christianity in America*, ed. Mark Noll et al. (Grand Rapids: Eerdmans, 1983), 22.

[49]Westminster Confession 21.8.

[50]Packer, *Quest for Godliness*, 236.

[51]Leland Ryken, *Worldly Saints* (Grand Rapids: Zondervan, 1981), 192.

[52]Calvin, *Institutes*, 2.8.34.

[53]See also the brief biographical sketch of Archibald Alexander in chap. 17.

[54]Turretin's theology was not translated into English until the early 1990s.

[55]See also the brief biographical sketch of Charles Hodge in chap. 17.

[56]Throughout his career, Charles Hodge was a polemicist who fought relentlessly for the truth of Princeton theology. He was as well the most feared and respected theological mind of the mid-nineteenth century. See Mark Noll, *The Princeton Theology* (Grand Rapids: Baker, 1983), 22–24.

[57]The younger Hodge lacked his father's theological brilliance but had the gift of clear thought and communication. He published several works on Reformed (Princeton) theology that were widely disseminated. See also A. A. Hodge's biographical sketch in chap. 17.

[58]One observer has noted that Warfield had the theological mind of a Charles Hodge and a William G. T. Shedd rolled into one. Yet Warfield produced no systematic theology of his own. He believed that Hodge's *Systematic Theology* couldn't be improved upon. Thus he contented himself with defending the received faith against the threats of the day. Warfield was a prodigious writer. His collected works encompass ten volumes and remain in print to this day. See also Warfield's biographical sketch in chap. 17.

[59]A. A. Hodge, *The Life of Charles Hodge* (New York: Scribner, 1881), 521.

[60]Lefferts Loetscher, *The Broadening Church* (Philadelphia: University of Pennsylvania Press, 1957), 21.

[61]Sydney Ahlstrom, "The Scottish Philosophy and American Theology," *Church History* 24 (1955): 257.

[62]Cited in Noll, *Princeton Theology*, 27.

[63]G. Stanley Hall, "On the History of American College Textbooks and Teaching in Logic, Ethics, Psychology and Allied Subjects," *Proceedings of the American Antiquarian Society* n.s., no. 9 (1893–94): 158, quoted by Terrance Martin in *The Instructed Vision, Scottish Common Sense Philosophy and the Origins of American Fiction* (Bloomington: Indiana University Press, 1961), 3. For further discussion of Common Sense Realism, see chap. 3.B.5.

[64]Darryl G. Hart, "The Princeton Mind in the Modern World and the Common Sense of J. Gresham Machen," *Westminster Journal of Theology* 46:1 (Spring 1984): 4. Cf. George Marsden, "J. Gresham Machen, History, and Truth," *Westminster Journal of Theology* 42:1 (1979): 142.

[65]Hart, "Princeton Mind," 4.

[66]Stephen Douglas Bennett, "Thomas Reid" (Th.M. thesis, Dallas Theological Seminary, 1980), 68–73.

[67]Charles Hodge, *Systematic Theology*, reprint (Grand Rapids: Eerdmans, 1975), 1:17.

[68]Ibid., 9.

[69]Ibid. These "givens" corresponded to Reid's intuition.

[70]Ibid., 1.

[71]Bennett, "Thomas Reid," 69.

[72]C. W. Hodge argued that all experience was "inner," contending that the distinction between "inner" and "outer" related only to the object of knowledge, not to the way in which it was known ("Christian Experience and Dogmatic Theology," *The Princeton Review* 8 [1910]: 8–9).

[73]See ibid., 13. See also M. James Sawyer, *Charles Augustus Briggs and Tensions in Late Nineteenth-Century American Theology* (Lewiston, N.Y: Mellen University Press, 1994), 29–30. While to twenty-first century ears C. W. Hodge's statement may on the surface sound a bit confusing, the Princetonians saw all experience as of the same

kind and involving the intellect. They refused to distinguish "inner" and "outer" experience. Additionally, if we use Martin Buber's terminology, we can say that they saw knowledge of all things (including God) in terms of an "I-it" encounter as opposed to an "I-Thou" personal encounter. In their understanding, mysticism bypassed the intellect and thus did not involve knowledge.

[74]Ibid., 16.

[75]B. B. Warfield, "Apologetics," in *Studies in Theology* (Grand Rapids: Baker, 1981), 3 (italics added).

[76]Ibid., 15.

[77]Hart, "Princeton Mind," 9.

[78]See also Kuyper's biography in chap. 17.

[79]The state church was the Dutch Reformed Church (*Nederlands Hervormde Kerk*). (Both *Hervormd* and *Gereformeerd* mean reformed, but the former name is of Germanic, the latter of Romance origin.) Especially since the 1950s there has been a pull toward the left in the *Gereformeerde Kerk*, and in 2003 the two denominations merged to form the Protestant Church of the Netherlands. Many of the more conservative members and congregations left before the merger.

[80]Abraham Kuyper, *Lectures on Calvinism* (Grand Rapids: Eerdmans, 1983), 12.

[81]Ibid., 19.

[82]David F. Wells, *Dutch Reformed Theology* (Grand Rapids: Baker, 1989), 21.

[83]This seminal work is being published in English at last. The first volume was published in 2003. Herman Bavinck, *Reformed Dogmatics*, vol. 1, *Prolegomena*, ed. John Bolt, trans. John Vriend (Grand Rapids: Baker, 2003).

[84]Wells, *Dutch Reformed Theology*, 48.

[85]Ibid., 49.

[86]Ibid., 45.

[87]Bouwsma, *John Calvin*, 121.

[88]These lectures were delivered at Princeton Theological Seminary in 1898.

[89]M. Charles Bell, *Calvin and Scottish Theology* (Edinburgh: The Handsel Press, 1985), 11; R. T. Kendall, *Calvin and English Calvinism to 1649* (Oxford: Oxford University Press, 1979), 142–50, cf. 65.

[90]Kendall synthesizes Calvin's understanding of faith: "The position which Calvin wants pre-eminently to establish (and fundamentally assumes) is that faith is *knowledge*. Calvin notes some biblical synonyms for faith, all simple nouns such as 'recognition' (*agnito*) and 'knowledge' (*scientia*). He describes faith as illumination (*illuminatio*), knowledge as opposed to the submission of our feeling (*cognitio, non sensus nostri submissio*), certainty (*certitudino*), a firm conviction (*solida persuasio*), assurance (*securitas*), firm assurance (*solida securitas*) and full assurance (*plena securitas*)" (19).

[91]Bell, *Calvin and Scottish Theology*, 8.

[92]Calvin, *Institutes*, 3.11.1.

[93]E.g., transubstantiation, marks of the church, authority of the Scriptures.

[94]See Bell, *Calvin and Scottish Theology*; Kendall, *Calvin and English Calvinism to 1649*; Brian G. Armstrong, *Calvinism and the Amyraut Heresy* (Madison: University of Wisconsin Press, 1969).

[95]"Scottish theology ... gradually came to teach that faith is primarily active, centred in the will or heart, and that assurance is *not* of the essence of faith, but is a fruit of faith, and is to be gathered through self-examination and syllogistic deduction, thereby placing the grounds of assurance *intra nos*, within ourselves.... Calvin's view is eclipsed to such a degree, that it is actually viewed as nothing other than a part of the Antinomian heresy.... The national Church of Scotland officially condemned the view that assurance is of the essence of faith" (Bell, *Calvin and Scottish Theology*, 8). My response: "I do not mean to imply that there is no active element to faith. Rather that the later expositions were persistently one-sided stressing the activity of the will. While a creedal commitment to the doctrine of faith as a gift of God was affirmed, the excessive stress of the human aspect of faith had the effect of obscuring the grace aspect of faith" (M. James Sawyer, "Some Thoughts on Lordship Salvation," a paper delivered at the Evangelical Theological Society Annual Meeting, Kansas City, 1991, 12). *www.bible.org/page.asp?page_id=347* (accessed Sept. 2005).

[96]See Bell, *Calvin and Scottish Theology*, 7–11. In fact, in several instances theologians who rediscovered Calvin's emphasis on the unconventionality of God's grace were regarded as antinomian and on occasion were convicted as heretics, e.g., John Cotton and John McCleod Campbell.

[97]Contrast this with Calvin, who states unequivocally that we *know* that we are saved by a direct act of faith rather than a reflex act—e.g., *Concerning the Eternal Predestination of God* (London: James Clark, 1961), 130–31.

[98]Bell, *Calvin and Scottish Theology*, 82.

[99]Ibid., 98.

[100]Lewis Berkhof, *Systematic Theology* (Grand Rapids: Eerdmans, 1979), 508. With reference to special revelation as a basis of assurance, Ken Sarles, in a debate with Bob Wilkin at Dallas Seminary in April 1990, said that the only way anyone could be absolutely certain of their salvation (prior to death or the rapture) was if the Bible clearly and irrefutably indicated that they specifically had eternal life. No general reference to believers in Christ having eternal life would provide such certainty, because it is impossible, he argued, to know with certainty that one is a believer. He argued that since no one alive today can find his or her name in Scriptures, absolute certainty of salvation is no longer possible (Robert Wilkin, "Assurance: That You Know," a paper presented at the Evangelical Theological Society Annual Meeting, New Orleans, Nov. 1990, 2). Compare this with Calvin concerning the alleged uncertainty as to whether we will persevere to the end: "Not content to undermine the firmness of faith in one way alone, they assail it from another quarter. Thus they say that even though according to our present state of righteousness we can judge our possession of the grace of God, *the knowledge of final perseverance remains in suspense.* A fine confidence of salvation is left to us, if by moral conjecture we judge that at the present moment we are in grace, but we know not what will become of us tomorrow! The apostle speaks far otherwise: 'I am surely convinced that neither angels, nor powers ... will separate us from the love by which the Lord embraces us in Christ' [Rom 8:38–39]. They try to escape with the trifling solution, *prating that the apostle had his assurance from a special revelation.* But they are held too tightly to escape. For there he is discuss-

ing those benefits which come to all believers in common faith, not from those things he exclusively experiences" (Calvin, *Institutes*, 3.2.40; italics added).

[101]Calvin, *Institutes*, 3.2.15.

[102]Ibid., italics added. Significantly, this is exactly the trap into which those who claimed the name of Calvin fell. With their emphasis on limited atonement, they could never be sure that Christ had died for them; hence they were forced to look inside rather than rely on the promises of Scripture. But even here there was no peace, because the doctrine of temporary faith which developed stole the hope of assurance by injecting the question of one's election into the equation. "Perhaps the 'fruit' I see in my life is not that of regeneration but the pre-regenerate work of the Spirit, from which I may fall away." In San Diego in 1989, Dr. John MacArthur was asked when a believer could be assured of his salvation; his reply was that such assurance could be had only after death.

OUTLINE OF CHAPTER 12

A. The Development of Arminianism
1. The Hardening of Reformed Theology
2. Jacobus Arminius and Arminianism
3. The Remonstrant Defense of Arminianism
4. Arminianism in England
5. Later Developments in Arminianism

B. John Wesley and Wesleyanism
1. Family Background
2. Before Aldersgate
3. Aldersgate
4. Distinctive Doctrine of Sanctification

C. Methodism and the Holiness Movement
1. The Move Away from Wesley's Theology
2. A Synthesis of Wesleyanism and Arminianism
3. Pentecostalism

D. Wesleyan-Arminian Theology
1. Theology Proper
2. Anthropology
3. Transmission and State of Sin
4. Salvation
5. Sanctification

E. Observations and Critique

CHAPTER 12

WESLEYAN-ARMINIAN THEOLOGY

Arminianism and its more common American manifestation, Wesleyan-Arminianism, belong to the tradition of the Reformation. They represent a reaction against the perceived harshness of scholastic Reformed/Calvinistic theology. While they share many assumptions and perspectives, Arminianism and Wesleyan-Arminianism arose in response to different concerns and have two very different emphases. Arminianism emphasizes unlimited atonement and human freedom, whereas Wesleyanism, though agreeing with classic Arminianism, emphasizes the nature of justification and sanctification as crisis experiences.

These ideas were first espoused by Jacobus Arminius at the turn of the seventeenth century and were advanced by his followers throughout Europe, especially in England, after the Synod of Dort declared Arminianism's tenets to be heretical aberrations from the dominant scholastic Calvinism.

A. THE DEVELOPMENT OF ARMINIANISM

1. The Hardening of Reformed Theology

John Calvin was trained as a humanist and used an inductive method of study that looked to the original sources rather than a deductive method that tried to deduce truth from first principles. As a result of induction, Calvin's method was rooted in an exegesis of the text that gave his theology a freshness and life that stood in stark contrast to the allegorizing and spiritualizing methods of the scholasticism that had preceded him.

Upon Calvin's death, his mantle fell to Theodore Beza, who made a shift in theological method from Calvin's induction to logical deduction. This led Beza to make predestination the logical starting point of his system.[1] He also explicitly taught the doctrine of supralapsarianism[2] with reference to the eternal decrees of God. This concept (not explicitly taught by Calvin), coupled with the stress on divine sovereignty in predestination and the doctrine of an atonement designed only to purchase the salvation of the elect, had given the Reformed tradition a harsh and arbitrary edge not present in Calvin's synthesis.

This shift in theological method from induction to deduction caused Protestant theology, both Reformed/Calvinist and Lutheran, to retreat to the scholastic methodology of the late Middle Ages. This was the age of theological system building, in which Protestant orthodoxy saw as its goal the articulation of truth. During this age, the vital personal faith taught by the Reformers went into eclipse, and emphasis on God's sovereignty made him seem distant, concealed, and uncaring. Faith was often reduced to assent to the creedal affirmations of the church rather than a vital living faith in which one personally encountered Jesus Christ. It was in this atmosphere of the late sixteenth century that Jacobus Arminius labored.

2. Jacobus Arminius and Arminianism

Jacobus (James) Arminius (1560–1609) was educated in the Calvinistic tradition, studying at Leyden, Geneva, and Basel. At Geneva (1582, 1584–86) he studied under Beza but found that he had an increasing aversion to the scholastic theology based on Aristotelian deductive logic. This contributed to his eventual rejection of Beza's system and its underlying method. After completing his education, Arminius returned to his native Netherlands, where he pastored in Leyden for fifteen years (1588–1603).

Jacobus Arminius

During Arminius's pastorate, he was called upon by the church court to refute the "libertine" (Anabaptist) views of Dirck Koornheert (Coornheert) (1522–90). Koornheert attacked austere Calvinism, especially the teaching of double predestination. Arminius undertook the task, but in the process of his study, he came to doubt several of the cardinal tenets of scholastic Calvinism.

Methodologically Arminius sought to return to the original analytical and inductive method of Calvin as opposed to Beza's method of synthesis and deduction of theological principles that led to such conclusions as limited atonement. He stressed the supremacy of the Scriptures over systems in matters relating to doctrine. While the logical system of second-generation Calvinists led to a view of limited atonement, Arminius's inductive approach, asserting the supremacy of Scriptures over system, led him to conclude that the plain teaching of the Bible was unlimited atonement: Christ's atoning death was universal (not just for the elect) and yielded prevenient benefits for all humankind, enabling them to respond to God.

Arminius held with the Reformers that justification is by grace alone and that faith is not meritorious (that is, does not earn favor with God). Arminius held to a view of human depravity. He saw that humankind is utterly unable, apart from the grace of God, to respond to God. In this he was much closer to his Reformed predecessors than to his Arminian followers. He became convinced that Reformed scholasticism had developed into a system that obscured God's love and grace for all people. Particularly, he came to believe that the Reformed scholastic emphasis on supralapsarianism and unconditional predestination ultimately made God both arbitrary and the author of sin. He opted instead for an understanding of God that saw salvation as a result of God's pity on all humankind. Humans retain a free will (as opposed to the Calvinistic doctrine of total depravity/inability), and those who respond in faith to the call of the Holy Spirit are the elect. Predestination is therefore conditional, since the basis of election is God's *prescience* (passive foreknowledge) as to whether one will freely trust or reject Christ.

Also arising out of the concept of human freedom was the teaching that a person may forfeit salvation by choosing to deny the faith and reject God's grace. In other words, if one were free to choose salvation, one would be free at a subsequent date to reject salvation. While not tied systemically to his thought but related methodologically, Arminius also argued for toleration and freedom of conscience for the Christian, a notion that contributed to the spread of democratic thought in Europe.

3. The Remonstrant Defense of Arminianism

The new theological views of Arminius aroused much attention and provoked debate and controversy. The Synod of Dort (1618–19), which rejected Arminianism, showed to what extent not only theological motivations but also political, social, and personal ones play a role in the direction theology takes.

The provinces of Holland had for many years struggled to be free of the king of Spain, who ruled the Low Countries. The provinces had adopted

Reformation theology, perhaps in part to establish an identity apart from the king, who was Roman Catholic. In 1584 Prince William of Orange, the "founder" of the Republic of Holland, was assassinated, probably on orders of the Spanish.

However, the Low Countries were not uniformly Calvinistic. There were also Lutherans, Zwinglians, and Anabaptists. But the Calvinists had managed to get by far the most power, economically as well as politically. In order to hold any kind of public office, one had to be a Calvinist. The state also paid the salaries of the pastors. There were, however, two kinds of Calvinist: the "precise" or strict group and the "stretchable" or flexible (*rekkelijke*) group. Thus the struggle was not only between Arminians and Calvinists, but also between orthodox and more liberal Calvinists.

Franz Gomarus (1563–1641), a strict Calvinist professor of theology at Leyden and colleague of Arminius, considered Arminius to be dangerous as a trainer of new ministers. The situation between the two became so tense that church authorities called upon Arminius and Gomarus to debate the issue in front of eight other ministers. In the end, the church leaders advocated mutual tolerance. Gomarus, however, condemned Arminius throughout the country. After four or five years of persecution, misunderstanding, and physical suffering, Arminius died at the age of forty-nine in 1609.

Arminius's cause was taken up by a group led by, among others, John Oldenbarneveldt, leader of the province of Holland, and Hugo Grotius (1583–1645), a statesman and theologian. In an attempt to reconcile the two views, Oldenbarneveldt in 1610 asked the followers of Arminius to prepare a declaration of their faith to be presented to the government in order to obtain tolerance for their position. The Arminian ideas were compiled by John Uytenbogaert, chaplain to Prince Maurice, in a document that came to be known as the Remonstrance, a five-point distillation of Arminius's teaching. (After the Synod of Dort, this document was given systematic elaboration by a disciple of Arminius's, Simon Episcopius.)

When the Remonstrance was presented, the States General decided that the issues could be debated—but not from the pulpit. There were riots and a general mood of unrest. Churches were closed and pastors removed from their pulpits. Oldenbarneveldt realized that the unrest could divide the still fragile republic and lead to civil war. He proposed that no synod be held (since this would only sharpen the divisions) and that each city could put militiamen on retainer to keep order when necessary. This suggestion, which reflected Oldenbarneveldt's republican instincts, greatly offended Prince Maurice because it gave a measure of power to the cities and thus went counter to his monarchical aspirations of absolute power.

Prince Maurice, who understood little about the theological issues and "did not know whether predestination was blue or green,"[3] decided to support the Gomarists, the orthodox Calvinist group that represented the greater political and economic power. Maurice put Oldenbarneveldt in jail *before* the Synod of Dort was called in 1618, along with Hugo Grotius. At issue was not theology but power. Oldenbarneveldt was convicted on a trumped-up charge of treason and beheaded before the synod was over.[4] Grotius was sentenced to life in prison in a castle near Amsterdam but managed to escape thanks to the ingenuity of his wife, who sent a crate with his books to the castle and had him carried out in the same crate.

The Synod of Dort (1618–19) was assembled to consider the points of the Remonstrance. The scholastic Reformed majority at the synod answered with the Counter-Remonstrance, out of which arose the "five points of Calvinism," remembered by the acronym TULIP (see figure 12.1). The synod declared Arminianism heretical, and Arminians who would not accept the decisions of the synod were exiled (they were allowed to return after the death of Maurice in 1625, six years after the synod concluded).

This experience of persecution has made Arminians historically tolerant of those who have chosen to explore intellectually variant theological schemes.

Remonstrance and Counter-Remonstrance	
The Five Points of the Remonstrance	**The Five Points of Calvinism**
Depravity of the sinner is in extent but not degree, so that the Holy Spirit must help men to do things that are truly good (like having faith in Christ for salvation).	**T**otal depravity
The decree of salvation applies to all who believe in Christ and who persevere in obedience and faith.	**U**nconditional election
Christ died for all persons.	**L**imited atonement
God's grace is not irresistible.	**I**rresistible grace
It is possible for Christians to renounce their faith and be lost eternally.	**P**erseverance of the saints

FIGURE 12.1.

4. Arminianism in England

Prior to the Synod of Dort, theologian and apologist Richard Hooker (1553–1600) laid the groundwork for the acceptance of Arminian ideas in the Church of England. While insisting that justification is a divine act made possible through the merits of Jesus Christ, he advocated the personal responsibility of the believer. Hooker insisted that "the validity of man's election to justification does depend on his own consent; his will is consulted, and nothing is given him except by his own deliberate advice and choice."[5]

John Hales (1584–1656), a prominent clergyman and professor of Greek at Oxford, was sent to the Synod of Dort by King James I. There Hales was converted to the Arminian position, and he returned to his homeland a proponent of Arminianism.

In 1622 William Laud (1573–1645), archbishop of Canterbury and adviser to King Charles I, argued for an interpretation of salvific faith that made humans cooperative agents with God in the work of their salvation. Much later, in 1699, Bishop Gilbert Burnet (1643–1715) gave a new impulse to Arminian tendencies when in the publication of his *Exposition of the Thirty-nine Articles* (of the Church of England) he interpreted Article XVII, on predestination, from an Arminian perspective.

As the Anglican Church struggled for a position mediating between the Roman Catholic and Protestant concepts of salvation, a synthesis began to emerge around Arminian themes of grace and faith as a human work. These views became foundational to the Arminian understanding of soteriology, which is *synergistic* in that it requires acts of both God and man—that is, the call to salvation is initiated by God to man, but man is free to accept or reject it.

This notion of a synergistic soteriology became widespread among clergy in the eighteenth century. While the *Thirty-nine Articles of Religion* were primarily Calvinistic, the Anglican clergy by and large held Arminian ideas about atonement, election, and justification.

5. Later Developments in Arminianism

Although Arminianism had widespread influence, it did not prove to be in a stable position. Because Arminianism was developed under the threat of persecution, the Arminians were averse to strict doctrinal tests. They were advocates of toleration and were inclined to reduce the requirements for orthodoxy to a minimum. Thus there was a broad spectrum of opinion, and many joined them because they found an atmosphere of theological freedom congenial. Many, however, went much further than Arminius in the denial of supralapsarianism. In Holland Arminianism became allied with liberalizing tendencies, including Socinianism, rationalism, and universalism. Unfortunately, these alliances drew the movement away from traditional historic Christianity. In England Arminianism also developed a strong affinity with Socinianism in its Christology and took on a decidedly Pelagian view of man. Out of Arminianism emerged the Latitudinarians, who embraced Greek philosophy and natural religion. For others Arminianism became a repudiation of Calvinism rather than a fully developed doctrinal system. In America the Arminian spirit manifested itself in the advocating of freedom of thought and toleration.

B. JOHN WESLEY AND WESLEYANISM

Perhaps the most influential preacher and theologian of the eighteenth century was John Benjamin Wesley (1703–91). Through Wesley's tireless preaching, the evangelical revival in England and the First Great Awakening in America were born. Out of these awakenings came the Methodist movement and the emergence of a type of theology akin to the perspectives of Arminius but synthesized from very different sources. Wesley was influenced by Arminian ideas, especially in his understanding of universal atonement and the effort of man. Nevertheless, the center of Wesley's theology was not Arminian soteriology, but sanctification. His greatest influence on Christian thought was his emphasis on the crisis experiences of regeneration and sanctification. He is usually remembered as an Arminian and in fact edited a journal called

John Wesley

the *Arminian Magazine*, but his use of the term included virtually anyone who did not fit the supralapsarian Reformed position.

1. Family Background

John Wesley was born into a fourth-generation family of Anglican preachers. His father was educated at Oxford, and his mother, Susanna, was of intellectual, devout, nonconformist ancestry. Both of his parents belonged to the school of thought called "English Arminianism," which rejected the doctrine of supralapsarianism and held that humankind was justified by both faith and works. Thus John and his eighteen siblings were reared in a pious home where doing God's will was emphasized. The key event in Wesley's spiritual biography and theological journey was his conversion experience at Aldersgate in 1738.

2. Before Aldersgate

Prior to Wesley's evangelical awaking at Aldersgate in 1738, he sought God through intellectualism at Oxford, the ritualism of the church ordinances, legalism and social service, the piety of abstaining, and missionary service at home and in America.

John and his younger brother Charles were both educated at Oxford. To understand key themes in John Wesley, one must look beyond the immediate context of the Calvinistic/Arminian debate to his early life experiences. While at Oxford, Wesley participated in the general revival of patristic studies within Anglicanism. He was particularly influenced by the early Greek fathers and absorbed key concepts of Eastern Orthodoxy, placing them in a Western context.

Anglican Puritanism also profoundly influenced Wesley's developing theology. At age twenty-two, he read Jeremy Taylor's *Rules and Exercises of Holy Living and Holy Dying*, resulting in his understanding the importance of purity of intention, service, and obedience. This piece greatly influenced his final decision to go into ministry. In the same year, he read *The Imitation of Christ* by Thomas à Kempis, soon followed by William Law's *Christian Perfection* and *A Serious Call to a Devout and Holy Life*.[6] These works steered Wesley toward the notion that perfecting the faith consisted in obedience and performance of duty, which overshadowed the joy of loving God.

While at Oxford, John and Charles formed a group called the Holy Club, the purpose of which was to promote a strict sense of self-denial and a regimented schedule of prayers, readings, and meditations. It was this methodical way of practicing his religion that earned the derisive epithet *Methodism*.

After ten years of pietistic living, Wesley was dissatisfied with his understanding of the Christian faith. He then became a missionary in the Colonies, in Georgia, with the hope that he would somehow learn the true sense of Christianity by preaching it to the heathen. Thus, at this point prior to his conversion at Aldersgate, the basic principle of Wesley's theological understanding was that he should be right with God through piety, moral goodness, universal obedience, and rigid fulfillment of all the commandments of God.

3. Aldersgate

Wesley first came into contact with the Moravians while traveling on a ship to Georgia as a missionary. In a fearsome storm and in the face of death, the Moravians demonstrated a serenity of faith that was unknown to Wesley. He always acknowledged his debt to their influence on his life. After failure as a missionary in Georgia, Wesley returned to London, where he met another Moravian, Peter Bohler, who encouraged him to preach faith until he experienced it. While in London he attended a Moravian Bible study at a house on Aldersgate Street on May 24, 1738. That night the preface to Luther's *Epistle to the Romans* was being read aloud, and Wesley later wrote, "I felt my heart strangely warmed. I felt I did trust Christ, Christ alone, for salvation; and assurance was given me that he had taken away my sins, even mine and saved me from the law of sin and death."

Wesley's persistent lack of assurance, which had expressed itself in the form of uncertainty, doubt, and fear; his failure to find peace through his missionary efforts to Georgia; and the Pietist (Moravian) influence that stressed that faith is not a rational belief in a way of life—all of these now became the backdrop for Wesley's theology. Albert Outler says of Wesley's Aldersgate experience: "The unique mixture of theological notions thus far accumulated was now melted and forged into an integral and dynamic theology in which Eastern notions of synthesis (dynamic interaction between God's will and man's) were fused with the classical Protestant *sola fida* (faith alone) and *sola Scriptura* (Scripture alone), and with the Moravian stress upon 'inner feeling.'"[7]

In 1739, after spending a few months in Germany with the Moravians, Wesley moved back to Bristol, England. While in Bristol, Wesley began open-air preaching, and revival broke out. As more and more people trusted Christ, Wesley began to organize local "societies" and "class meetings" (groups of twelve), which sustained the revival for his fifty years of ministry. He remained a loyal member of the Church of England, and Methodism did not become a separate denomination in England until after his death.

4. Distinctive Doctrine of Sanctification

One of the distinctive doctrines developed by Wesley was *Christian perfection.* By this he meant the sanctifying work of the Holy Spirit in a believer's life in which the heart is cleansed from sin so that the person can live in perfect love toward Christ—in an unbroken relationship with the Savior. Love becomes the sole principle of action. "[Perfection] is nothing higher and nothing lower than this: The pure love of God and man, the loving God with all our heart and soul, and our neighbor as ourselves. It is love governing the heart and life, running through all our tempers, words, and actions ... this we confess ... we expect to love God with all our heart, and our neighbor as ourselves."[8]

Wesley was careful to distinguish this teaching from absolute perfection, in which a person completely ceases from sinning, making errors in judgment, and committing involuntary transgressions out of ignorance. He was not referring to absolutely sinless living; rather, his emphasis was on a purified love toward God. "It is not *absolute.* Absolute perfection belongs not to man, nor to angels, but to God alone. It does not make a man *infallible*: none is infallible while he remains in the body."[9] While Wesley's view of the nature and extent of sanctification was modified later in his life to accommodate both the instantaneous and gradual aspect of sanctification, his brother Charles "became increasingly convinced that it could be attained only at death."[10] Nevertheless, Wesley was convinced that entire sanctification, or as he often called it, *perfection,* was both a goal and possibility in this life. Like justification, sanctification is wrought through a means of God's grace and human response. Moreover, he emphasized that at a moment of crisis in the soul over sinful tendencies, there is a resignation to the will and grace of God that purifies the heart, removing sinful tendencies and replacing them with the fullness and power of the Holy Spirit. Wesleyan theologian Randy Maddox summarizes his understanding of Wesley's doctrine of perfection as it finally matured: "His clear concern was to preserve a dynamic tension that could celebrate whatever God's *grace* has already made possible in our lives, without relinquishing our *responsibility* to put that grace to work in the new areas that God continually brings to our attention."[11]

C. METHODISM AND THE HOLINESS MOVEMENT

Methodism was established formally in America when Francis Asbury was ordained and then appointed as the general superintendent of the Methodist Episcopal Church in 1784. The new church adopted a liturgy based on the *Book of Common Prayer* and the *Twenty-five Articles of Religion* provided by

Wesley and adapted from the *Thirty-nine Articles* of the Church of England. The Americanization of Methodist theology involved subtle shifts, among them from revelation to reason, from sinful man to natural man, and from free grace to free will.

Methodism grew rapidly after Wesley's death, but his distinctive theology was progressively ignored. The latter half of the nineteenth century in American Methodism saw the slavery controversy, religious fanaticism in the name of "perfection," increased participation in secret societies, and abuse of the autocratic nature of the Methodist episcopacy, all of which contributed to a decline in the spiritual fervor of the Methodist Episcopal Church in America. From both the pulpit and the pew there was a declining emphasis on and understanding of Wesley's original doctrine of sanctification, especially of the crisis experience.

The Holiness movement in America arose in the mid-nineteenth century as a protest against the forsaking of Wesley's teaching on sanctification and holiness by the Methodist Church as a denomination. The movement emphasized two crisis experiences—conversion and sanctification—and defined holiness in terms of the avoidance of any activities, dress, or associations that appeared "worldly." Holiness theology sought to revitalize in the churches the Wesleyan teaching on sanctification. Out of this movement came several new denominations, such as the Wesleyan Methodists, Pilgrim Holiness Churches, Nazarenes, Church of God (Anderson, Indiana), and Free Methodists. While claiming Wesley as their inspiration and theological founder, the leaders of the movement had neither Wesley's grasp of theology nor of history. Furthermore, they labored in a very different historical-cultural setting, so that in applying their understanding of Wesley, the resulting doctrine differed from his emphases in significant ways.

1. The Move Away from Wesley's Theology

The early Holiness groups moved away from Wesley's teaching when they followed Adam Clarke's view of entire sanctification as *instantaneous.* Clarke, a younger contemporary of Wesley, viewed the doctrine of sanctification as *only* instantaneous, while Wesley allowed for both gradual and instantaneous sanctification.[12]

Wesleyan theologian Colin Williams writes, "Both the spontaneous and the gradual are essential to Wesley's doctrine [of perfectionism]."[13] Clarke, on the other hand, says, "In no part of the Scripture are we directed to seek holiness *gradatim.* We are to come to God as well for an instantaneous and complete purification from all sin as for an instantaneous pardon."[14] Thus "the Holiness Movement understood Clarke's view [instantaneous sanctification only] to be scriptural, instead of Wesley's."[15]

This departure from Wesley's view was due in part to Wesley's omission of a statement on entire sanctification from the *Articles of Religion* he prepared for American Methodism. This caused some churches to settle for a position of gradual sanctification or to deemphasize sanctification altogether. The reaction against worldliness in other churches sparked the effort to return to Wesleyan-Holiness roots. When such denominations broke from the Methodist Episcopal Church to return to pure Wesleyanism, they needed to define and articulate the Holiness doctrine. In their zeal to emphasize holiness, early leaders were satisfied with a more limited reading of Wesley. The outcome was a doctrine and a movement that taught against gradual and progressive sanctification.

For example, in 1860 at the organizing conference of the Free Methodist Church, a mild debate arose as to how to best describe Wesley's position on sanctification. Was it instantaneous, or could it accommodate gradualism? In the end, the instantaneous view prevailed and a motion allowing for interpretations of gradualism along with the instantaneous was rejected.[16] The Free Methodists and other Holiness groups tended toward what Wesley had called "high strained" perfectionism. As a reaction against "worldliness," Holiness denominations developed standards for church membership that defined norms of holy living. Thus the Holiness movement tended toward legalism and an absolutizing of cultural mores, defining holiness in terms of activity and abstention from activity rather than, as it had been for Wesley, as perfect love.

For Wesley there was continual tension between crisis and process aspects of sanctification. Some Holiness theologians have attempted to resolve this tension by suggesting a distinction between sanctification and maturity. Entire sanctification is instantaneous and purifies, while maturation is gradual. Nazarene theologian Orton Wiley explains: "Purity is the result of cleansing from the pollution of sin; maturity is due to growth in grace. Purity is accomplished by an instantaneous act; maturity is gradual and progressive, and is always indefinite and relative."[17] Again, this position contravenes Wesley, who never did make an explicit distinction between sanctification as *only* instantaneous and maturity as *only* gradual. Rather, he spoke of sanctification in both instantaneous and gradual terms.

2. A Synthesis of Wesleyanism and Arminianism

While in theory espousing Wesley's theology, many of these groups synthesized his theology with the soteriological positions of Arminianism after the Remonstrant period, adopting the position that prevenient grace provides for the ability of humans to respond to God and that salvation is conditional. While some have argued that American Arminianism became avowedly semi-Pelagian with regard to soteriology, evangelical Wesleyan-Arminianism has consistently rejected Pelagian tendencies. The semi-Pelagian view suggests a level of inherent human power and human initiative. But this semi-Pelagian Arminianism has liberal tendencies and often slips into a full-blown Pelagianism and ultimately into universalism, by which human depravity is denied and salvation is understood as human monergism (by human initiative alone). However, the evangelical Arminian view holds to a view of human depravity that is akin to Calvinism—that apart from God's initiative, humankind is unable to respond without a prior work of grace.[18] While Reformed theology asserts that this grace is extended only to the elect and is irresistible, evangelical Arminianism holds that prevenient grace is extended to the entire human race and is resistible. Prevenient grace is initiated by God and restores humanity's ability to respond to him. It has emphasized the doctrines of unlimited atonement, free will, and justification by grace through faith alone.[19]

Holiness also tended to be identified with ascetic self-denial and even denial of the believer's personality. There has as well been a tendency to reject all secular culture and shun involvement in society. Holiness often sees God's presence as confined to "religious experience." Many times there is an overemphasis on "feeling" and an eagerness to claim "the leading of the Holy Spirit" even when the so-called leading is in ways directly contrary to biblical mandates. While Wesley emphasized the experiential aspect of conversion and sanctification, he warned against fanaticism: "Beware of that daughter of pride, *enthusiasm!* ... give no place to a heated imagination. Do not easily suppose dreams, voices, impressions, visions, or revelations to be from God."[20]

3. Pentecostalism

Pentecostalism is an offshoot of Wesleyan-Holiness theology. Holiness doctrine explained that entire sanctification was a "second blessing" of grace consummated by the baptism with the Holy Spirit. In 1900 a Methodist minister, Charles Fox Parham, formulated a doctrine that the initial evidence of the baptism of the Holy Spirit is glossolalia, speaking in tongues. While Wesley did not use the term "baptism with the Holy Spirit," the term was used by a contemporary of his, John Fletcher, and by subsequent American Holiness teachers such as Phoebe Palmer and John Inskip. Parham taught that entire sanctification was the "second blessing" and glossolalia the "third blessing." Others began to deemphasize sanctification and stressed only a second blessing of "instant power" and signs and wonders.[21]

The revival that began in 1906 on Azusa Street in Los Angeles marked the beginning of the Pentecostal movement in America. While many Holiness leaders rejected glossolalia and began to distance themselves from the Pentecostals, other denominations began to form around the distinctive Pentecostal doctrine, the first of which was the Assemblies of God. Its founder, William Durham, taught that sanctification was a progressive work of the Holy Spirit that began at conversion. The baptism of the Holy Spirit was a second blessing, evidenced by speaking in tongues. This became the doctrine of other Pentecostal denominations as well.

D. WESLEYAN-ARMINIAN THEOLOGY

Wesleyan-Arminian theology is most easily understood in its distinctives vis-à-vis Reformed theology. Reformed theology is motivated by *theocentricity*—the sovereign activity of God, who glorifies himself by sending Jesus Christ to redeem his elect. Hence, Reformed theology views God as Lord. In contrast, the motivating factor in Arminian theology is *anthropocentric*—God is viewed primarily as love. "God, in Christ, extends His love to all men and ... each man must accept personal responsibility for his attitude toward that love."[22] Pure Wesleyanism does not have either of these foci at its center; the motivating factor behind Wesleyanism is "scriptural holiness," or sanctification. Wesleyanism seeks to establish justification by faith as the gateway to sanctification. Salvation becomes a return to original righteousness via the Holy Spirit. Evangelical Wesleyan-Arminianism has as its center the merger of both Wesley's concept of holiness and Arminianism's emphasis on synergistic soteriology.

1. Theology Proper

Election/predestination. As a theological system, Wesleyanism retains the concepts of predestination and election, noting that they are explicitly taught in Scripture. In stark contrast to the unconditionality of these concepts as explained in Reformed theology, however, Wesleyan-Arminian theology sees them through the lens of God as loving Father rather than as sovereign monarch. Thus predestination is God's general and gracious plan of saving people by adopting them as children through Christ, based on their response.

Whereas in Reformed theology the terms *election* and *predestination* are used interchangeably, in the Wesleyan-Arminian tradition, these terms are distinct. Predestination is understood as being based on God's passive foreknowledge (prescience), whereby God, on the basis of foreknown faith, chose in Christ individuals to be heirs of eternal life. In contrast, election has to do with vocation, one's calling in life. In the Arminian understanding, predestination is conditional, dependent on the personal acceptance of the universal call to salvation. "It is not an arbitrary, indiscriminate act of God intended to secure the salvation of so many and no more. It includes provisionally, all men in its scope, and is conditioned solely in faith in Jesus Christ."[23] Contemporary Wesleyan theologian Thomas Oden summarizes the orthodox Wesleyan view: "Every human being, even if twisted by pride and sensuality, by grace is given from time to time some capacity for contrition. When that gift is given, it must be exercised to the utmost; otherwise, the opportunity will wither and fade."[24] The *effectual call*, Oden explains, is resistible.

Decrees. Wesley denies an order of decrees that leads logically to double predestination. "If you ask, 'Why then are not all men saved?' the whole law and the testimony answer, First, Not [*sic*] because of any decree of God."[25] Arminius taught a set of divine decrees different from the Reformed articulation and set them in logical order: (1) God decreed salvation through Jesus Christ; (2) God decreed that those who repent and believe would find favor; (3) God decreed prevenient grace—enabling grace so that everyone is able to repent and believe; and (4) God decreed who would be saved or damned based on foreknowledge of the way in which they would freely respond to his gracious offer.[26] (See also chapter 11.B.1.)

Providence. Wesleyanism teaches that God conserves, cares for, and governs his world. He exerts influence on humans but also honors human freedom and responsibility. God is gracious and acts preveniently in and on his creation, working graciously in the hearts of humans, wooing them by the Spirit (rather than the perceived coercive work understood to be taught by Reformed theology) in such a way so as not to violate their freedom of choice.

Oden has developed a threefold construct of providence: (1) *preservation*, or upholding providence, which conserves the laws of nature; (2) *concurrence*, or allowing providence, in which God's permissive will cooperates with human and natural circumstances; and (3) *governance*, or guiding providence, in which God guides all things through fitting means toward ends appropriate to his larger purpose in creation.[27]

2. Anthropology

Wesley and Arminius both argued for a non-Pelagian view of human freedom. Both believed profoundly in original sin; and thus that, unaided by prevenient grace, humans are incapable of choosing righteousness. Both understood human freedom in the context of salvation. Grider summarizes, "We can either accept Christ or reject Him—and our eternal destiny depends upon our free response to God's offer of salvation."[28]

3. Transmission and State of Sin

Transmission of sin. Most Wesleyan-Arminians hold that depravity is inherited. While Wesley himself alluded to a form of federalism in which all people are guilty of Adam's sin,[29] contemporary Wesleyan theologians differ in their description of the transmission of Adamic depravity. Grider argues that both Wesley and Arminius held a position consistent with the federalist/representative theory.[30] Later Wesleyan-Arminian theologians articulated a genetic view, in which sin is transmitted from parent to offspring in the same manner physical characteristics are passed on genetically.[31] Some attempted to combine both representative and genetic views (that humankind is not guilty of Adam's sin but suffers the effects of that sin).[32] In his later years, Wesley modified his view, saying that the guilt inherited from original sin was canceled by the work of Christ on the cross.[33]

Original sin. As opposed to the Reformed concept of original sin as the immediate imputation of the sin of Adam, the Wesleyan-Arminian tradition defines original sin as the corruption of the human nature, with death as its universal penalty. Wiley explains, "We believe that original sin, or depravity, is the corruption of the nature of all of the offspring of Adam, by reason of which every one is very far gone from original righteousness, . . . is averse to God, is without spiritual life, and is inclined to evil, and that continually."[34]

Inherited depravity. Following Augustine and Calvin, Wesley strongly asserted that the entire human race is totally depraved. In convincing language, he said that all religions but Christianity are "wholly ignorant of the entire depravation of the whole human nature, of every man born into the world, in every faculty of his soul, not so much by those particular vices which reign in particular persons, as by the general flood of atheism and idolatry, of pride, self will, and love of the world."[35] Wesley understood that as the Great Physician, Jesus Christ came to heal the soul diseased by sin and "restore human nature, totally corrupted in all its faculties."[36]

Prevenient grace. Wesley used the term *prevenient grace* (that is, God's grace comes before [from Lat. *prevenire*] any human action) to describe the activity of God that restores human ability to respond to the offer of salvation. His doctrine was influenced little by Arminius, who advocated a similar position; rather, it arose primarily from his Anglican tradition and paralleled the Orthodox tradition of *uncreated grace.*[37] Speaking of the sin nature, Arminius originally said that the free will of the lost is "not only wounded, maimed, infirm, bent, and weakened; but it is also imprisoned, destroyed, and lost. And its powers are not only debilitated and useless unless they be assisted by grace, but it has no powers whatever except such as are excited by divine grace."[38] Some of Arminius's followers, however, drifted into the position of Pelagianism. Wesley expressly rejected the position developed by his contemporary liberal Arminians, as well as the Roman Catholic position, which asserted that there is still some possibility within humanity to respond to God (that is, depravity is not total). Wesley held that no freedom is left in the fallen nature; humankind is enslaved to sin. The grace of God intervenes to restore what has been forfeited by the fall, enabling humans to respond to God. While the effect in this view is the same as that in the liberal Arminian, Catholic, and Orthodox understandings, there is a significant difference, for the ability to respond to God comes not from any native ability within man but from God's gracious loving activity.

The term *prevenient grace* is used in two distinct senses. In one sense, there is an affinity between the Wesleyan doctrine of prevenient grace and the Reformed doctrine of efficacious grace, but with a crucial difference. Whereas the Reformed saw in efficacious grace an inevitable and irresistible moving of the Spirit in working salvation in the elect, Wesley saw the Spirit's activity as enabling all humanity to respond to this grace without rendering this response as automatic. This usage reflected the Calvinist/Arminian debates of his era. In a wider sense, he saw prevenient grace as influencing every activity of humanity from the first stirring of faith to the highest level of sanctification. Maddox concludes that Wesley's understanding of grace had three dimensions—the removal of guilt by virtue of Christ's work on the cross; the healing of the human spirit, which is sufficient for one to respond to God; and God's specific offer inviting the work of sanctification.[39]

Oden developed a five-step concept of prevenient grace. Each aspect of grace is preceded by and is subsequent to grace, which culminates in consummating grace.[40] (See chart on next page).

4. Salvation

Synergism. Between the Pelagian view that salvation is of man alone and the Augustinian/Reformed view that it is of God alone stands the Wesleyan-Arminian view that salvation is *synergistic*, initiated by God and responded to by humans. Individuals must cooperate with God's gracious but resistible

The Concept of Prevenient Grace				
GRACE				
Heals the Soul	Moves the Will	Enables Salutary Action	Perseveres in Resolve	Consum-mates in Glory
prevenient → subsequent ↓				
	prevenient → subsequent ↓			
		prevenient → subsequent ↓		
			prevenient → subsequent	

FIGURE 12.2.

call to salvation. Prevenient grace is the initiative God takes to restore the depraved nature of the entire human race so that all are capable of response. God's work is grace, which gives man the capacity to respond; man's response is faith.

Evangelical Wesleyan soteriology is careful to reject any form of Pelagianism or semi-Pelagianism that denies or minimizes the fall and inherent sin or that exalts Jesus as an example over Jesus as Redeemer. Grider concludes, "The free will to accept Christ could not be exercised apart from God's help, so there is no merit whatever in our acceptance of the first work of grace."[41] He further clarifies the non-Pelagian perspective of evangelical Wesleyan-Arminians: "This view [of anthropology] means that we will not say to a congregation in an evangelistic service, 'You do your part and God will do His part.' Unregenerate people cannot do any such thing until God first does His part of extending prevenient grace to them."[42] Synergism is human response to the work of prevenient grace, which leads to justifying faith.

Assurance of salvation. For Wesley assurance of salvation was critical. Prior to his Aldersgate experience, Wesley understood that "if we can never have any certainty of our being in a state of salvation, good reason it is that every moment should be spent, not in joy, but fear and trembling."[43] Early he saw the answer as assent to faith. Ultimately he found the basis of faith in the inner witness of man's spirit with the Holy Spirit. To Wesley, justifying faith is a personal divine assurance of the provision of Christ. Thus abiding saving faith grows out of and includes the justifying act of faith that precedes it. He says, "The testimony of the Spirit is an inward impression on the soul, whereby the Spirit of God directly witnesses to my spirit, that I am a child of God; that Jesus Christ hath loved me, and given Himself for me; and that all my sins are blotted out, and I, even I, am reconciled to God."[44]

Justification by faith. Wesley is firm that justification is by faith alone. Yet the fruit of justification leads to personal transformation. "We are doubtless justified by faith. This is the cornerstone of the whole Christian building.... But [the works of the Law] are an immediate fruit of that faith whereby we are justified. So that if good works do not follow our faith, even all inward and outward holiness, it is plain our faith is worth nothing; we are yet in our sins."[45] Yet in Wesley and the Holiness tradition, one finds clear statements that make justification conditional on obedience and progress in sanctification as opposed to the declarative act of God based on the finished work of Christ.

Holiness proponent Phoebe Palmer said, for example: "As I ascended the heavenly way, clearer light shone upon my mind, revealing higher duties, requiring more of the spirit of sacrifice, and furnishing yet stronger tests of obedience. But with increasing light, increasing strength was given, enabling me to be answerable to these higher duties: for I had not *learned how to retain justification* while under condemnation at the same time for neglecting known duties."[46] Elsewhere she contends, "I saw I could not; I must either make the necessary sacrifices, or I must sin, and by my sin forfeit my state of justification. And here *my justification would have ended* with me had *I refused* to be holy."[47] Such statements reveal at best inconsistency and an unclear understanding of the Protestant teaching of justification by faith alone.

5. Sanctification

Conversion/regeneration/initial sanctification. Conversion has temporal priority in Wesleyan soteriology. The order is understood to begin with prevenient grace, followed by conviction, regret, and repentance. Repentance leads immediately to saving faith and justification. Regeneration logically follows justification and adoption into God's family. While the Reformed limit justification to *righteousness imputed*, Wesleyans include *righteousness imparted.* Accordingly, initial sanctification occurs, enabling the new believer to "break away from the previous life of sin."[48]

Entire sanctification. The doctrine of entire sanctification represents the distinctive feature of Wesleyan theology. Sanctification from the Wesleyan perspective is distinguished from other traditions that emphasize either *positional* sanctification or *final* sanctification. While aberrations and extremes have occurred within its circles, the prevailing emphasis of the Wesleyan tradition has been *experiential* sanctification, the present, ongoing response of faith to God's grace in which a believer can have the mind of Christ Jesus. Thomas Oden describes sanctification from a consensual Wesleyan perspective as "Those in Whom Grace Is Working Optimally."[49]

Sanctification is the present continual deliverance from the plague of sin, not just from its penalty. At the moment of justification, initial sanctification occurs. Newborn Christians are purified in that they are freed from the necessity of committing any outward sins. In the Wesleyan tradition, Christians are *perfected*, or sanctified, in that they experience a significant encounter with grace so that they are able to "perfectly love" God. Wesley emphasized the significance of a postconversion crisis experience (a second work of grace) whereby the heart is cleansed from significant sin.

Wesleyans from within the Holiness denominations emphasize that entire sanctification is an instantaneous, one-time experience, while others hold to a more original understanding of sanctification as a crisis-process experience. Some extreme Holiness teachings suggest that at the moment of entire sanctification, the Adamic nature is so cleansed from sin that it becomes no longer possible for a believer to sin consciously. On the other hand, consensual Wesleyan teaching stresses that sanctification merely makes it possible for a believer to experience victory over sin. Neither Wesley nor mainline Wesleyans conceived of sanctification as sinless perfection or freedom from finitude, ignorance, involuntary transgressions, or antinomian license. Nevertheless, the distinguishing factor of a Wesleyan view of sanctification is that it is a profound work of sanctifying grace, found possible to experience subsequent to salvation, experienced prior to death, and received and retained by faith. Sanctification is a work of grace raising one from a carnal state to that of heightened spirituality. It is preceded by a gradual work that leads to a defining moment—often at a point of crisis—in which the Holy Spirit so fills the heart that one will continue in maturity at a much more rapid rate. Oden summarizes the doctrine of sanctification as a "sustained, radical, responsiveness to grace."[50]

Perseverance. Wesleyans believe that those who persevere are the elect. But perseverance is not a result of absolute decrees and unconditional election. By logical extension of a synergistic soteriology, a rejection of absolute predestination and emphasis on human freedom, subsequent to the moment one has trusted Jesus Christ, there is a possibility, however unlikely, that a person may resist grace, abandon faith in the sufficiency of Christ, refuse to repent, and die in a state of final apostasy. While Wesley did not develop this thought, Arminius held that human freedom to resist salvific grace does not cease after justification. Observe the Arminian expression in the summary of the Remonstrance: "That they who are united to Christ by faith are thereby furnished with abundant strength and succor sufficient to enable them to triumph over the seductions of Satan, and the allurements of sin; nevertheless they may, by the neglect of these succors, fall from grace, and dying in such a state, may finally perish. This point was started at first doubtfully, but afterward positively as a settled doctrine."[51]

Beyond anything Wesley or Arminius expressed, many early leaders of Holiness denominations advanced the position of falling from grace to teach that when a person commits sin, he or she "loses both justification and sanctification ... and no longer is a saint; he becames [*sic*] a sinner. If he gets back to God, he must come confessing like any other sinner."[52] Most evangelical Wesleyan-Arminians reject such an extreme view of falling from grace but do retain the cooperative and conditional nature of election and allow for the possibility of final apostasy through willful rejection of salvific grace.

E. OBSERVATIONS AND CRITIQUE

Arminianism as a theological system proved to be unstable, primarily because it lacked a solid theological center. It was born as a *reaction* to scholastic Calvinism and never truly had a distinct, positive tenet as an anchor. As a movement, Arminianism rapidly drifted into Socinianism, unitarianism, and moralism. As it did so, it reflected a "cultural Christianity" but gave up the life-transforming dynamic of a gospel of divine salvation.

This theological drift also belies an underlying rationalism associated with the Enlightenment. The healthy corrective emphasis of Arminius to Reformed scholasticism with reference to theological method was not continued by his successors. They imbibed the rationalism of the era and progressively eschewed the supernaturalness of Christianity for a theology and religion that were palatable to cultured Enlightenment minds.

Underlying this theological drifting has been a perennial temptation to flirt with Pelagianism. This has been encouraged by Enlightenment rationalism as well as by the anthropological moral optimism of the nineteenth and twentieth centuries and has contributed to the emphasis of liberal understandings of inspiration, Christology, and soteriology. While some evangelical Wesleyan-Arminian denominations remain today, mainline Methodism has abandoned orthodoxy for the exaltation of the goodness of man.[53]

Wesleyan-Arminianism is a synthesis of a theological movement born in later stages of the Reformation as a reaction against rigid Calvinism with a revival movement born in the spiritual experience of a theologian whose heart was set free from legalistic piety. Unlike Arminianism itself, Wesleyanism had a solid center, sanctification, which acted as a tether to keep it from drifting as far as had Arminianism.

The Wesleyan-Arminian tradition is unlike other traditions that have more developed systematic and monolithic theologies. It has as a movement focused on more practical as opposed to scholastic system building. While Wesley was a competent theologian, his greatest contribution to theology was perhaps his quadrilateral, a hermeneutical method for doing theology based on the four sources to which he appealed for authority—Scripture, tradition, reason, and experience.

Several aspects of the distinctive doctrine of the Wesleyan-Holiness tradition, entire sanctification, are problematic. While the doctrine of sanctification is universally accepted by orthodox evangelicals, its understanding in Wesleyan-Holiness terms is rejected by other traditions on several counts. First, the concept of sin as defined by Wesley as a *conscious act of willful disobedience to known law* is understood by non-Wesleyan theologians as falling far short of the biblical picture and is seen to treat sin as isolated acts rather than as a condition of radical fallenness.[54] This is unfortunate, because the doctrine is often misunderstood because of semantics and the misguided teaching and poor exegesis of some theologically untrained preachers of the Holiness movement. While Wesley's concept of perfection as such is problematic, his concept has often been distorted to mean that a Christian who is sanctified never sins. When combined with a skewed doctrine of falling from grace, it has often led to emotionally devastated people torn between guilt and acceptance. These people can be seen weekly at the altar seeking to be "saved again" because they have sinned.

Furthermore, the Holiness teaching of the late nineteenth and early twentieth centuries gravitated to a rigid legalism, attempting to define holiness, or "sanctified living," in terms of outward adornment, temperance, and extreme piety. Later in his life, Wesley warned against a definition of perfection that meant that one never sinned. Perfection, according to Wesley, was a heart that was oriented consistently toward love of God.

The idea of the instantaneous nature of entire sanctification is a Wesleyan distinctive and is actively rejected by non-Wesleyan evangelicals. Even within Wesleyan circles, debate has raged regarding the instantaneous versus gradual nature of sanctification. Oden suggests a mediating position that even some in the Reformed tradition would affirm. "Yet even though there is a process of growth required for every believer, there still may be moments when such grace for growing is incomparably given. It is rash to rule out the possibility that the Holy Spirit may flood the soul with sufficient grace that the trajectory of continued walking in the way of holiness is firmly set, even if not irreversibly determined."[55]

Another area of critique involves Wesley's teaching on the assurance of salvation. Despite Wesley's acknowledgment that assurance was necessary and that it was to be found in justification as a juridical act of God, we see in his own life a battle over assurance of his own salvation. In his journal, we find at various times throughout his life a denial of his own salvation, since he could not find within himself love for God. He recorded:

> October 14, 1738, "I cannot find in myself the love of God, or of Christ. Hence my deadness and wanderings in public prayer.... Again: I find I have not that joy in the Holy Ghost."[56]
>
> On January 4, 1739, "My friends affirm I am mad, because I said I was not a Christian a year ago. I affirm, I am not a Christian now. Indeed, what I might have been I know not.... Though I have constantly used all the means of grace for twenty years, I am not a Christian."[57]
>
> On June 27, 1766, to Charles Wesley, "... and yet (this is the mystery) I do not love God. I never did. Therefore I never believed in the Christian sense of the word. Therefore I am only an honest heathen."[58]

Wesley himself seems to embody the problem inherent in the tradition that bears his name, specifically looking inward for assurance of salvation as opposed to looking to Christ. This is a procedure that has plagued all varieties of Pietism (even in the Reformed tradition), the dangers of which Calvin warned against centuries earlier.[59]

BIBLIOGRAPHY

Cannon, William B. *The Theology of John Wesley*. Nashville: Abingdon-Cokesbury, 1946. • **Grider, J. Kenneth.** *A Wesleyan-Holiness Theology*. Kansas City: Beacon Hill, 1994. • **Maddox, Randy L.** *Responsible Grace: John Wesley's Practical Theology*. Nashville: Kingswood, 1994. • **Oden, Thomas.** *The Transforming Power of Grace*. Nashville: Abingdon, 1993. • **Outler, Albert C.** *John Wesley*. New York: Oxford University Press, 1980. • **Wesley, John.** *The Complete Works of John Wesley*. 14 vols. The Master Christian Library 7.0. Rio, WI: Ages Software, 1999. • **Williams, Colin W.** *John Wesley's Theology Today*. Nashville: Abingdon, 1990. • ***The Writings of Arminius.*** Edited and translated by James Nichols and W. R. Bagnall. Grand Rapids: Baker, 1956. • **Wynkoop, Mildred.** *Foundations of Wesleyan-Arminian Theology*. Kansas City: Beacon Hill, 1977.

NOTES

[1]Alister McGrath, Intellectual Origins of the European Reformation (Oxford: Blackwell, 1987), 192.

[2]See "supralapsarianism" in the dictionary. The logic of double predestination—that God predestined some to be lost—became especially offensive to Arminius.

[3]John T. McNeill, *The History and Character of Calvinism* (New York: Oxford University Press, 1954), 264–65.

[4]The Dutch monarchs have always been Reformed. The funeral of the former Queen of the Netherlands, Juliana, in 2004 was for the first time in history conducted by a Remonstrant pastor, who is also a woman. This was seen by some as an implicit condemnation of the murder of Oldenbarneveldt in 1619.

[5]William B. Cannon, *The Theology of John Wesley* (Nashville: Abingdon-Cokesbury, 1946), 35.

[6]Wesley documents the influence these readings had on his theological development in the opening pages of his famous publication *A Plain Account of Christian Perfection.*

[7]Albert C. Outler, *John Wesley* (New York: Oxford University Press, 1980), 14.

[8]John Wesley, "A Plain Account of Christian Perfection," in *The Complete Works of John Wesley*, The Master Christian Library 7.0 (Rio, WI: Ages Software, 1999), 11:464.

[9]Ibid., 518. Italics added.

[10]Randy L. Maddox, *Responsible Grace: John Wesley's Practical Theology* (Nashville: Kingswood, 1994), 186.

[11]Ibid., 190. Italics in original.

[12]John Wesley, "Plain Account of Christian Perfection," 470, 519.

[13]Colin W. Williams, *John Wesley's Theology Today* (Nashville: Abingdon, 1990), 187.

[14]Adam Clarke, *Entire Sanctification* (Louisville: Pentecostal Publishing, n.d.), 38.

[15]J. Kenneth Grider, *A Wesleyan-Holiness Theology* (Kansas City: Beacon Hill, 1994), 399.

[16]Leslie R. Marston, *From Age to Age a Living Witness* (Winona Lake, IN: Light and Life, 1960), 257–59.

[17]H. Orton Wiley, *Christian Theology* (Kansas City: Beacon Hill, 1952), 2:506.

[18]One of the clearest recent expositions of the Wesleyan-Arminian position on soteriology is Thomas Oden's *The Transforming Power of Grace* (Nashville: Abingdon, 1993).

[19]J. Kenneth Grider, "Arminianism," in Walter A. Elwell, ed., *Evangelical Dictionary of Theology* (Grand Rapids: Baker, 1984), 79–81.

[20]Wesley, "Plain Account of Christian Perfection," 361.

[21]Grider, *Wesleyan-Holiness Theology*, 373–74; Vinson Synan, "Pentecostalism," in Walter A. Elwell, ed., *Evangelical Dictionary of Theology* (Grand Rapids: Baker, 1984), 835–39.

[22]Mildred Wynkoop, *Foundations of Wesleyan-Arminian Theology* (Kansas City: Beacon Hill, 1977), 65.

[23]Wiley, *Christian Theology*, 2:337.

[24]Oden, *Transforming Power of Grace*, 205.

[25]John Wesley, *Works*, 7:53.

[26]Grider, *Wesleyan-Holiness Theology*, 249.

[27]Thomas C. Oden, *The Living God*, vol. 1 of *Systematic Theology* (San Francisco: Harper & Row, 1987), 270–71.

[28]Grider, *Wesleyan-Holiness Theology*, 245.

[29]In his *Notes* on Romans 5:14, Wesley said that since Adam was "the federal head of mankind," he became "the fountain of sin and death to mankind by his offense" (John Wesley, *Notes upon the Whole Bible: New Testament*, in The Master Christian Library 7.0 [Rio, WI: Ages Software, 1999], 448). In "A Plain Account of Christian Perfection," Wesley said, "Sin is entailed upon me, not by immediate generation, but by my first parent. In Adam all died; by the disobedience of one, all men were made sinners; all men without exemption, who were in his loins when he ate the forbidden fruits" ("Plain Account of Christian Perfection," *The Complete Works of John Wesley*, in The Master Christian Library 11:468).

[30]Grider, *Wesleyan-Holiness Theology*, 279–80.

[31]Ibid., 281–84.

[32]Wiley, *Christian Theology*, 2:96–140; Richard S. Taylor, *Exploring Christian Holiness*, vol. 3 in *Theological Formulation* (Kansas City: Beacon Hill, 1985), 96–98.

[33]Maddox, *Responsible Grace*, 87.

[34]Wiley, *Christian Theology*, 2:121.

[35]John Wesley, "Sermon XLIV—Original Sin," in *Wesley's Standard 52 Sermons* (Salem, OH: Schmul, 1988), 456.

[36]Ibid.

[37]Maddox, *Responsible Grace*, 90.

[38]*The Writings of Arminius*, ed. and trans. James Nichols and W. R. Bagnall (Grand Rapids: Baker, 1956), 1:526. Cited in Grider, *Wesleyan-Holiness Theology*, 351.

[39]Maddox, *Responsible Grace*, 90.

[40]Oden, *Transforming Power of Grace*, 54.

[41]Grider, *Wesleyan-Holiness Theology*, 352.

[42]Ibid., 246.

[43]John Wesley, *Letters*, to Susanna Wesley (June 18, 1725). Cited in Maddox, *Responsible Grace*, 124.

[44]John Wesley, "Sermon X—Witness of the Spirit Discourse I," in *Wesley's Standard 52 Sermons*, 95.

[45]John Wesley, "Sermon XXXV—The Law Established by Faith," in *Wesley's Standard 52 Sermons*, 361.

[46]Phoebe Palmer, *The Way of Holiness* (New York: n.p., 1854), 172. Italics added.

[47]Ibid., 172–73. Italics added.

[48]Grider, *Wesleyan-Holiness Theology*, 364.

[49]Thomas C. Oden, *Life in the Spirit*, vol. 3 of *Systematic Theology* (San Francisco: HarperCollins, 1994), 228.

[50]For a full discussion, see ibid., 226–46.

[51]The fifth point of the Remonstrance, quoted by Wiley, *Christian Theology*, 2:351.

[52]B. T. Roberts, quoted in Leslie Roy Marston, *From Age to Age a Living Witness* (Winona Lake, IN: Light and Life Press, 1960), 281.

[53]Mainline Methodism has not done so formally, i.e., from a creedal perspective, but rather informally, from the perspective of its adherents in the denomination.

[54]J. I. Packer observes with reference to Wesley's concept of sin and perfection: "It was indeed confusing for Wesley to give the name *perfection* to a state which from many standpoints was one of continued imperfection. It was yet more confusing that he should define sin 'properly so called,' subjectively, as 'voluntary transgression of a known law,' rather than objectively, as failure, whether conscious or unconscious, voluntary or involuntary, to conform to God's revealed standards. It was supremely confusing when he let himself speak of sanctified people as being without sin (because they were not consciously breaking any known law) while at the same time affirming that they need the blood of Christ every moment to cover their actual shortcomings. Wesley himself insisted that by the objective standard of God's 'perfect law,' every sanctified sinner needs pardon every day; that makes it seem perverse of him also to have insisted on stating his view of the higher Christian life in terms of being perfect and not sinning (J. I. Packer, *Keep in Step with the Spirit* [Old Tappan, NJ: Revell, 1984], 138).

[55]Oden, *Life in the Spirit*, 223.

[56]John Wesley, Journal: Jan 4, 1739, in *The Complete Works of John Wesley*, The Master Christian Library 7.0 (Rio, WI: Ages Software, 1999), 11:5.

[57]Ibid., 188.

[58]John Wesley, quoted by Stephen Tomkins, *John Wesley: A Biography* (Oxford: Lion, 2003), 168.

[59]"Indeed, if we should have to judge from our works how the Lord feels toward us, for my part, I grant that we can in no way attain to it by conjecture. But since faith ought to correspond to a simple and free promise, no place for doubting is left. For with what sort of confidence will we be armed, I pray, if we reason that God is favorable to us provided our purity of life so merit it?" (John Calvin, *Institutes of the Christian Religion*, 3.2.38, in Library of Christian Classics, vol. 20, trans. Ford Lewis Battles [Philadelphia: Westminster, 1977]).

OUTLINE OF CHAPTER 13

A. **Origins and Development**
   1. Premillennial Ferment in the Nineteenth Century
   2. Formative Period
   3. Confessional or Classical Period
   4. Revised or Essentialist Period
   5. Progressive Dispensationalism

B. **Major Features Common to Dispensationalism**
   1. Authority of Scripture
   2. Divine Administrative Arrangements as Key to Understanding Scripture
   3. Uniqueness of the Church in Relation to National Israel
   4. Practical Significance of the Universal Church
   5. Significance of Biblical Prophecy
   6. Futurist Premillennialism
   7. Imminent Return of Christ
   8. A Future for National Israel

C. **Major Representatives**
   1. Denominations and Missions Organizations
   2. Institutions
   3. Individuals

D. **Issues and Tensions**
   1. Hermeneutics
   2. Historiography
   3. Sine Qua Non?
   4. Cessation of the Charismata?

E. **Contributions of Dispensationalism**

F. **A Tradition in Transition**

G. **Observations and Critique**

CHAPTER 13

DISPENSATIONALISM

Dispensationalism is a transdenominational theological movement within evangelicalism that stresses an apocalyptic understanding of history.

A. ORIGINS AND DEVELOPMENT

1. Premillennial Ferment in the Nineteenth Century

From at least the time of Augustine, the church's common understanding regarding the kingdom of God was amillennial.[1] This eschatological understanding did not shift during the Reformation with the return to Pauline perspectives on doctrines surrounding salvation. In fact, the Reformers regularly identified the Roman Catholic Church and especially the papacy with the Antichrist.[2]

In England premillennial expectations of the kingdom exploded on the scene during the English Civil War but subsided again. Then, during the mid-seventeenth century, extremist fringe groups such as the Ranters, Muggletonians, Quakers, Diggers, and Fifth Monarchists fanned the flames of radical apocalyptic expectations. But with the return of the Stuart dynasty to power, this frenzy cooled. After this rage of end-time expectations subsided, serious interpreters of Scripture adopted a more cautious approach. Nevertheless, end-time expectations continued to appeal to the Christian consciousness. Natural disasters and political upheavals were regularly seen as heralding the end times. As premillennialism became a more clearly defined understanding, there was an overriding conviction that the world was getting worse and worse and only the return of Christ could bring about a transformation.

Alongside this premillennial expectation, an optimistic postmillennialism emerged that saw the church as advancing the kingdom until the ushering in of a one-thousand-year period of peace and harmony. In fact, this postmillennial view was decidedly the predominant eschatological understanding in America from the time of the Puritans until the mid-nineteenth century.[3]

During the early nineteenth century, both in England and America, apocalyptic movements gained attention and focused expectations on the imminent return of Jesus Christ to establish his kingdom. The premillennialism of this period was characterized by historicism, that is, an attempt to correlate biblical prophecies with contemporary events. This was often accompanied by the prediction of a date for Christ's return—which always proved erroneous. The most visible example of this phenomenon was the case of William Miller and his followers. As a result of his personal study, Miller became convinced that Christ would return between March 21, 1843, and March 21, 1844. When the latter date passed without the return of Christ,

Key Terms in Dispensationalism

Church. The church is the spiritual body of Christ, the invisible or universal church of all those who since Pentecost have been regenerated by the Holy Spirit.

Dispensation. A period in history during which God administers the world in a particular manner.

Imminence. The doctrine that Jesus Christ can return at any moment. No prophetic event has to intervene before that return.

Israel. Biblically, Israel *always* refers to national Israel and ethnic Jews, never to the church or Gentiles.

Parenthesis. In classical dispensationalism, Israel's rejection of the Messiah caused God to put his prophetic clock on hold until the end of the church age, at which time his program for Israel will again start ticking. The church is thus a parenthetical period in salvation history.

Premillennialism. This is the teaching that Jesus Christ will return before the millennium and establish and reign over an earthly kingdom that will endure for one thousand years (Rev. 20:1–6).

Rapture. The being "caught up ... in the clouds" of the church to meet Christ at his return (1 Thess. 4:15–17). The rapture will, according to most, take place immediately *before* the tribulation (*pretribulational rapture*). Others view it as occurring at the midpoint of the tribulation (*midtribulational rapture*), and a small but growing number see the rapture as taking place afterward (*posttribulational rapture*).

Tribulation. A seven-year apocalyptic period of terrible divine judgment on the earth. Also called the great tribulation.

Miller declared that he had made a computational error and predicted the return of Christ by the following October 22. The failure of this prediction became known as "the great disappointment."[4] This failure of Miller and others both in America and on the Continent contributed to the discrediting of this historicism and date setting and a popular suspicion of the premillennial expectation. The rise of dispensationalism saved premillennialism by advocating a strict futurism with reference to biblical prophecy—that is, biblical prophecy is not being fulfilled today but in the future. Hence, correlating prophetic events with current happenings was improper.

2. Formative Period[5]

John Nelson Darby (1800–1882),[6] a priest in the Church of Ireland, abandoned its ranks due to the apostasy he perceived in that church. Darby then joined the movement later known as the Plymouth Brethren, in which he developed a distinctive ecclesiology. He believed that the church was not to be identified with any institution but was a spiritual fellowship. Darby's ecclesiology became the catalyst for dispensationalism as a system. He posited a radical discontinuity between the church and Israel, asserting that God had two separate peoples and two separate programs he was working out in history. This discontinuity made it incumbent to "rightly divide the Word of truth," discerning which passages were addressed to Israel and which to the church. These features, coupled with a futurist view of biblical prophecy and the doctrine of the pretribulational rapture of the church, gave coherence to incipient dispensationalism.

John Nelson Darby

The Plymouth Brethren developed the early emphasis on the responsibility of the laity and sparked an interest in personal Bible study and devotions, generating a large volume of expositional and devotional literature. Early writers included Darby, Benjamin Wills Newton, George Müller, Samuel P. Tregelles, William Kelly, and C. H. Mackintosh.[7]

As the teachings of the Brethren movement spread to North America, due to Darby's labors as an itinerant preacher as well as the writings of the Brethren leaders, they fell on fertile soil. In England the focus had been on the local church, but in America with its different religious climate, a different vision arose. Although few left their established denominational affiliations, Darby and Brethren expositors and evangelists gained a wide hearing, particularly among Presbyterians and Baptists, significant numbers of whom adopted the dispensational historiography. The vision of the universal church, i.e., the spiritual body of Christ transcending local churches and particular denominations, became the dominant theme. In 1876 a group of prominent Presbyterian and Baptist preachers and educators organized the annual Niagara Bible Conferences for prophetic study, and these continued for a quarter of a century.

C. I. Scofield

The Bible conference movement, following the pattern of the Niagara Conferences, spread dispensationalism widely. During this period, many dispensational schemes were proposed and existed side by side. It was not until C. I. (Cyrus Ingerson) Scofield published the *Scofield Reference Bible* (1909) that a single, cohesive understanding of dispensationalism emerged. The popularity of the *Scofield Reference Bible* made it the largest single force in spreading dispensational teaching, and it de facto codified Scofield's understanding as *the* way to think about dispensationalism (and for many the only right way to interpret the Bible).

3. Confessional or Classical Period

In the wake of the fundamentalist-modernist controversy of the early twentieth century, fundamentalists (most of whom were dispensationalists) found that they had lost control of their denominations and seminaries. In response, a plethora of new theological institutions dedicated to preserving orthodoxy arose. The dispensational perspective of the *Scofield Reference Bible* became the traditional framework of instruction in many of these institutions, and as such the dispensational framework and perspective of Scofield attained an informal confessional status within these institutions.

During this period, one of the most prominent features of dispensational teaching was a dualistic doctrine of redemption. In the Scriptures, God is pursuing two different purposes, one *earthly* (Israel) and the other *heavenly* (the church). God's purpose on earth was to release it from the curse of Genesis 3 and to restore to humanity a freedom from sin and death. This earthly restoration is eternal, manifest first during the millennial kingdom but continuing throughout eternity. Those entering the millennial kingdom would continue throughout final judgment and eternity without tasting death. God's heavenly people were all who had died in faith throughout the various dispensations.

Since the church was a part of God's heavenly people, the church was to adopt an attitude of disengagement from the political and social structures of the world. Salvation was interpreted individualistically. Classic dispensationalism saw the church as a *parenthesis* in the history of redemption, essentially unrelated to God's larger purpose for the earth. Dispensational theologian Lewis Sperry Chafer believed that the idea of parenthesis was not strong enough and insisted that the church was an *intercalation*.[8]

Biblical interpretation during this period was in accordance with this central dualistic perspective. While in theory a historical-grammatical approach was advocated, in practice the Bible was interpreted through the presuppositions of the system. Also, there was a widespread practice of stringing together biblical texts dealing with a common word or theme, often without regard to context.[9]

The classical dispensational view of the kingdom, articulated by C. I. Scofield, drew a distinction between the *kingdom of God* and the *kingdom of heaven*. The kingdom of God referred to the moral rule of God over the hearts

A classic dispensational understanding of God's plan for the ages, designed by Clarence Larkin.

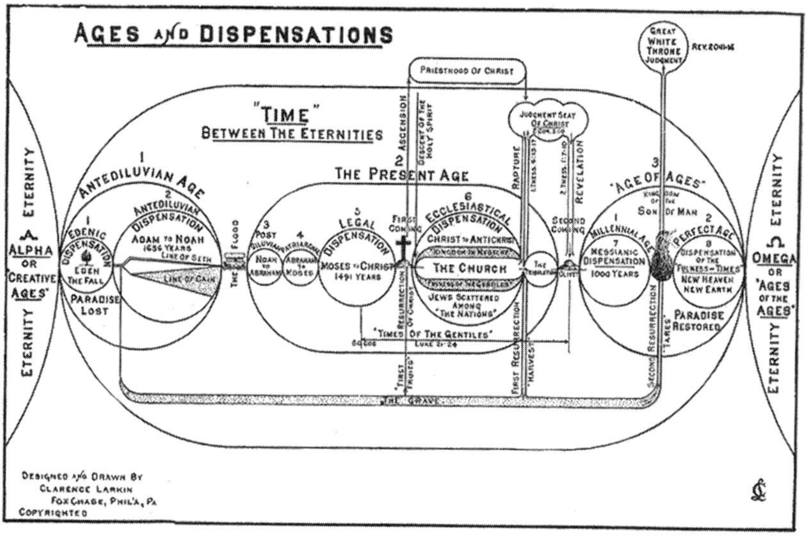

FIGURE 13.1

of humans in relation to him, while the kingdom of heaven (spoken of only by Matthew) referred to the fulfillment of the Davidic covenant for an eternal kingdom that would be inaugurated at the return of Christ.

Classic dispensationalism was characterized on a popular level by charts and graphics designed to function as a map of the progress of biblical revelation and God's purpose in history. Clarence Larkin, a mechanical engineer turned preacher, believed that the biblical interpreter "cannot intelligently do his work without a plan. He must have drawings and specifications." To that end, he wrote and illustrated *Dispensational Truth, or God's Plan and Purpose in the Ages* (1919), a 180-page book that contains ninety charts. While he admitted the charts had to be tested against the Scriptures, they were in themselves "indispensable."[10]

4. Revised or Essentialist Period

During the 1950s and '60s, there was significant development in the dispensational perspective. Two works in particular marked dispensationalism during these years: *The New Scofield Reference Bible* (1967) and Charles Ryrie's *Dispensationalism Today* (1965). The revised Scofield Bible reflected the changes in understanding that had taken place in the preceding half century, while Ryrie, also reflecting those developments, sought for the sine qua non, or essence, of dispensationalism.

During this period, the eternal dualism (Israel and the church) that was central to classical dispensationalism was abandoned. In its place came an understanding of God having two purposes in history but a single people in eternity. No longer was there to be an earthly people and a heavenly people. The eternal salvation enjoyed by the church was not essentially different from that enjoyed by Israel.

Two concepts of eternity emerged during this period. The first, advocated by Alva J. McClain, Dwight Pentecost, and Herman Hoyt, envisioned the eternal state as one of resurrection life on the "new earth." The second, proposed by John F. Walvoord and Charles Ryrie, advocated a position more closely in line with classic dispensationalism and a more platonic understanding of "heaven."

The changing conception of the church in the 1960s and '70s impacted the dispensational community. While formally retaining the concept of the church as a spiritual entity, and thus uninvolved with the world, dispensationalists were forced to recognize the community aspect of the church through the "body life" movement championed by Ray Stedman and the "building up [of] one another" teaching of Gene Getz.

Also during this period there was a shift in hermeneutical understanding. Classical dispensationalists insisted on the "literal" interpretation of the Scriptures but also indulged heavily in *typology* (a kind of spiritual hermeneutic that attempted to interpret many parts of the Old Testament, such as the tabernacle, as predictive images of New Testament truth and especially of Christ). Revised dispensationalism moved away from typology and insisted on a "literal" hermeneutic. Ryrie insisted that a *consistent* literal hermeneutic belonged to the essence of dispensationalism.[11]

The whole concept of the historical-grammatical method of interpretation broadened during the 1960s and beyond to encompass the concept of biblical theology and to extend beyond grammatical analysis to include both historical context and literary genre in meaningful ways.

Another key shift that occurred during this period was the abandonment of the distinction made by classic dispensationalists between the kingdom of heaven and the kingdom of God. While this distinction was an important feature in maintaining the dualism of the classical understanding, the insightful criticism of George Ladd from the perspective of biblical theology forcefully challenged it.[12] While not formally acknowledging Ladd's criticism, dispensational teaching about the kingdom underwent significant revision in succeeding years.

In the following decades the movement retained its apocalyptic perspective, but a historicism reminiscent of nineteenth-century Adventism modified the strict futurism of early dispensationalism in certain sections of the movement. While it should not be simply identified with dispensationalism, this historicist emphasis has been popularized through many best-selling popular works.[13] It has had its greatest impact in Pentecostal and charismatic circles, which from their inceptions have been characterized by vivid apocalyptic expectations.

5. Progressive Dispensationalism

During the 1970s and '80s, a significant development took place in dispensationalism as the implications of a more adequate and full-orbed application of the historical-grammatical hermeneutic method came to the fore. These developments came to a catalytic point in November 1986. That year at the Evangelical Theological Society's annual meeting in Atlanta, a study group in dispensationalism was founded. This group has become the think tank from which have emerged the writings of the contemporary mode of dispensationalism, known as *progressive dispensationalism*.

Earlier dispensational models had posited multiple purposes in the plan of divine redemption, but the integration of those purposes proved problematic.

Progressive dispensationalism has abandoned the dualism of classic dispensationalism as well as the view that continued in the revised scheme, which saw the church as essentially unrelated to the other redemptive purposes of God. Instead, progressive dispensationalism insists that the church is vitally involved in "*this very same plan of redemption*"[14] that applies to Israel and the Gentiles. As such, progressive dispensationalism "advocates *a holistic and unified* view of eternal salvation."[15] Likewise, the dispensations are not merely different but successive and progressive administrations of God's redemptive purpose for the fallen creation.[16]

Historically the church was seen as unrelated to God's purpose in history. It was viewed as a parenthesis or an intercalation in the outworking of the ongoing divine plan of redemption. Progressive dispensationalism rejects this classical understanding and insists that while the church is indeed a new manifestation of divine grace and a new era in the history of redemption, it is an administration of grace that is in keeping with the promises of the Old Testament concerning the new covenant, particularly as expressed in Isaiah and Jeremiah. The church does not constitute a third category of humanity alongside Jews and Gentiles or a competing nation alongside Israel. It is simply redeemed humanity (Jew and Gentile) as that body is manifest during the present dispensation.

Whereas earlier manifestations of dispensational understanding spoke of several kingdoms of God, within progressive dispensationalism only one kingdom is recognized, the eschatological kingdom promised in both testaments, whose focus is always Jesus Christ. The kingdom has both political and spiritual aspects and was inaugurated at the incarnation in the person of Jesus Christ. The progressive dispensational understanding of the kingdom has a number of features in common with the "inaugurated eschatology" popularized in the American evangelical community by former dispensationalist George E. Ladd.

B. MAJOR FEATURES COMMON TO DISPENSATIONALISM[17]

1. Authority of Scripture

From its inception with the Plymouth Brethren and throughout its development, the dispensational tradition has been characterized by a commitment to biblical exposition. The tradition has been universally committed to the Bible as the only verbal and inerrant revelation of God to his people, the church. As such, the Bible provides the sole sure foundation for Christian life and practice. The key to understanding the Scriptures is the dispensational interpretive scheme, which makes the Bible available to the ordinary believer apart from dependence on scholarly help.

The Bible conference movement of the late nineteenth and early twentieth centuries, which sought to make the Bible—as opposed to any formal organizational structure—the basis of evangelical ecumenicity, became a central vehicle in spreading dispensational understanding. This movement offered a transdenominational vision of evangelical unity based on the Pauline triad of faith, hope, and love. This vision contributed to the evangelical identity and on a practical level gave rise to transdenominational colleges, and seminaries that gave cohesion to the evangelical perspective and promoted the centrality of the Scriptures.

2. Divine Administrative Arrangements as Key to Understanding Scripture

While there is no universally agreed upon scheme of dispensations, the most commonly recognized one is that of C. I. Scofield: (1) innocence (humanity before the fall), (2) conscience (to the flood), (3) human government (until the call of Abraham), (4) promise (until Moses), (5) law (until the death of Christ), (6) church (the present post-Pentecost age), and (7) the millennium. Each of these dispensations is inaugurated by God's establishing a covenant with humanity that creates a relationship of responsibility between the covenanting parties. Normally the covenants are unconditional, based on grace, whereby God binds himself to accomplish certain purposes despite any failure on the part of covenanted humanity. The significant exception is the conditional, bilateral Mosaic covenant, which is replaced by the new covenant.

Understanding how various parts of the Bible relate to the Christian today is of particular practical significance. Dispensationalists understand that practically all of the Old Testament was given to Israel and primarily applies to that period of divine administration. However, some portions, particularly the prophetic, have reference to the future kingdom to be established. Likewise, the bulk of the New Testament has reference to the present dispensation, the church age, but as with portions of the Old Testament, it contains significant prophetic material that points to the future dispensation. Thus, when Christians read the Old Testament, they must acknowledge that the teaching and administrative arrangement are not directly related to them. The forms of worship and detailed regulations of life for national Israel were given for that time and were set aside with the establishment of the church.

While there is continuity between the dispensations in that they are established by the same God and thus reflect his character and purposes, the present age reflects new forms of worship, an equality of Jews and Gentiles, and the presence of the Holy Spirit in a way not seen in the Old Testament. Recognizing these differences enables the contemporary Christian reader of the Bible to relate to scriptural passages about other dispensations. One aphorism commonly heard is that the Bible is all written *for* us (Christians), but not all is addressed *to* us.

3. Uniqueness of the Church in Relation to National Israel

Covenant theology as expressed in the Reformed tradition has seen both testaments as speaking to one people of God, referred to as the "Old Testament church" and the "New Testament church." Historically, beginning with Darby, dispensationalism has seen a radical discontinuity between the church and Israel. The present dispensation, the church age, is distinct, new, and unanticipated in the Old Testament. The origin of the church is seen on the Day of Pentecost and is based on the death and resurrection of Christ and characterized by the blessings of the Holy Spirit.

The blessings of the present dispensation are qualitatively different than those of the Old Testament. The Spirit baptizes and indwells all believers personally. The distinction between Jew and Gentile has been erased. The political and material blessings promised to national Israel are not applicable to the church but will be fulfilled in the future kingdom age.

4. Practical Significance of the Universal Church

As noted above, a central feature of dispensationalism is its emphasis on the universal spiritual body of Christ as opposed to any particular local or denominational structure. It is this feature of dispensationalism that has provided the "glue" that has given a coherent evangelical identity. Within evangelicalism denominational distinctions are all but irrelevant as believers and even ministers move with impunity across denominational lines.

Additionally, this emphasis on the universal church has given birth to numerous parachurch ministries, evangelistic organizations, faith missions, and discipling ministries. These have arisen to accomplish tasks the local church often is not equipped to handle and as such are extensions of the church rather than in competition with it.

5. Significance of Biblical Prophecy

Whereas other theological traditions have tended to transfer the prophetic promises of Scripture from Israel to the church and to see them as being spiritually fulfilled, dispensationalism has read the prophecies in a more literal manner. Consequently, dispensationalism has consistently manifested a concept of ultimate redemption that encompasses not only the personal but also the national and political.

Despite this broad redemptive understanding of God's purposes, early forms of dispensationalism were dualistic with reference to the relationship of the church and Israel. They associated these future redemptive purposes as basically unrelated to the church, which was interpreted as having a heavenly as opposed to an earthly future. This mentality led to a fascination with biblical prophecy and even contributed to unrestrained sensationalistic popular apocalyptism.[18] Recent decades have seen a reduction of the early radical dualism as well as reaction to the excesses of popular apocalyptism.

6. Futurist Premillennialism

As a historiography, dispensationalism is a subset of premillennialism, the understanding that Christ will personally return and rule as the Davidic king over the entire earth for one thousand years. As with other premillennialists, dispensationalists hold that prior to Christ's return, God will visit a period of divine judgment upon the earth. Unlike other premillennialists, however, dispensationalists generally have held to a pretribulation rapture—that is, Christ will return and remove the church from the earth prior to pouring out his judgment. The basis for the pretribulation rapture is ultimately grounded in the dispensational ecclesiology that sees the radical disjuncture between the church and Israel. Dispensationalism has historically endorsed a strictly futurist eschatology and interpretation of biblical prophecy—that is, biblical prophecy is not being fulfilled at the current time. God's prophetic clock stopped at the birth of the church and will not begin again until the church is removed from the earth.

In recent decades, the strict futurism of earlier dispensationalism has begun to be blended with historicism. This was seen during the 1970s in the writings of Hal Lindsey (e.g., *The Late Great Planet Earth* [1970], *There's a New World Coming* [1973], and *The 1980's: Countdown to Armageddon* [1980]), but this trend has captured even more moderate dispensational scholars, such as John Walvoord (*Armageddon, Oil and the Middle East Crisis* [1974, 1990]) and Charles Ryrie (*The Living End* [1976]).

Dispensationalism's futurist perspective leads to an eschewing of the date-setting mentality that looks to Scripture to determine the date of Christ's return. A major factor in the acceptance of dispensationalism is that it rejected the sensationalism of date setting that had discredited previous futurist interpretations, such as that of William Miller and his followers in the 1840s. The late twentieth-century blurring of the lines between futurism and historicism by many within the dispensational camp runs the risk of discrediting the movement in the same way that previous movements such as the Millerites were discredited in the mid-nineteenth century.

7. Imminent Return of Christ

During the late nineteenth century, the Bible conference movement espoused a doctrine of the imminent return of Christ that was essentially a belief in premillennialism, which held that the present age would not witness a Christianizing of the world by the power of the gospel (postmillennialism) but would instead grow progressively more wicked and hostile toward God. Into this hostility and rebellion Christ would return, vanquish his enemies, and set up the millennial kingdom.

With the rise of dispensationalism, the apocalyptic sections of Daniel and Revelation were interpreted as giving a chronology of a seven-year period called the tribulation, at the end of which Christ would return. Interpreting these passages through their futurist grid, they placed the tribulation entirely in the future. Hence, the return of Christ was at least seven years away. But dispensationalists believed that Christ could come for the church at any moment and thus sharpened the understanding of imminency from a general nearness to an any-moment expectation. By the early twentieth century, imminency was defined exclusively in this "any-moment" sense. During the last decades of the twentieth century, a posttribulational understanding of the rapture, mirroring the general nearness concept of the nineteenth-century teaching, became popular in some segments of the dispensational community.

8. A Future for National Israel

Dispensationalism has been universally characterized by a belief in the future of national Israel. This belief has been manifested in support for the Zionist movement as well as in political support for the nation of Israel.

C. MAJOR REPRESENTATIVES

1. Denominations and Missions Organizations

A number of new denominations arose out of the fundamentalist-modernist debates of the early to mid-twentieth century. Nearly all of these adopted the dispensational theological perspective. These groups include the General Association of Regular Baptist Churches, the Conservative Baptist Association, the Grace Brethren, and the Independent Fundamental Churches of America. In addition the Evangelical Free Church, the Christian and Missionary Alliance, as well as many Holiness and Pentecostal denominations have been influenced by the dispensational perspective.

Numerous mission organizations have emerged from the dispensational tradition, among them Campus Crusade for Christ, Jews for Jesus, Friends of Israel, SIM (formerly Sudan Interior Mission), CAM International (formerly Central American Mission), AIM International (formerly Africa Inland Mission), Africa Evangelical Fellowship, and Baptist Mid-Missions.

2. Institutions

Moody Bible Institute (Independent): Founded in 1886 before the fundamentalist-modernist controversies, it was led from the start by dispensational leaders. The institute publishes the *Scofield Bible Correspondence Course.*

Biola University/Talbot School of Theology (Independent): Founded in 1907 as the Bible Institute of Los Angeles, it published until the 1970s the periodical *The King's Business*, successor to *The Fundamentals.*

Dallas Theological Seminary (Independent): Founded in 1924, Dallas Seminary became synonymous with dispensationalism, since its presidents and numerous faculty members published widely read volumes that championed dispensational themes. Its faculty have been major contributors to the development of dispensationalism from the older Scofieldian perspective into the contemporary era of progressive dispensationalism. *Bibliotheca Sacra*, America's oldest continuous theological journal, was acquired by the seminary in the 1930s and has functioned as the scholarly organ for the movement.

Other institutions associated in some manner with dispensationalism include Grace Theological Seminary, Western Seminary, Philadelphia School of the Bible, Denver Seminary, and Trinity Evangelical Divinity School.

3. Individuals

John Nelson Darby (1800–1882). See above and also the biographical sketch in chapter 17.

C. I. Scofield (1843–1921). Pastor and lecturer. His *Rightly Dividing the Word of Truth* set the agenda for much of American fundamentalism. Scofield's *Comprehensive Bible Correspondence Course*, first issued in 1896, became the foundational curriculum for churches and Bible institutes. His most important work, the *Scofield Reference Bible* (1909), put dispensational teaching in the hands of laypeople. Over two million copies of the Scofield Bible have been sold. A revised edition, *The New Scofield Reference Bible* was published in 1967.

Lewis Sperry Chafer

Lewis Sperry Chafer (1872–1952). First president of Dallas Theological Seminary. Chafer's eight-volume *Systematic Theology* became the standard theology of the confessional, or classical, period of dispensationalism.

Alva J. McClain (1888–1968). President of Grace Theological Seminary. He contributed *The Greatness of the Kingdom*, a major dispensational study of the kingdom.

John F. Walvoord (1910–2001). Second president of Dallas Seminary. As the author of numerous works, including *The Millennial Kingdom*, *The Blessed Hope and the Tribulation*, *Israel in Prophecy*, and commentaries on *Daniel* and *Revelation*, Walvoord was a leading spokesman for dispensational eschatology.

John F. Walvoord

J. Dwight Pentecost (1915–). Professor at Dallas Seminary. He penned *Things to Come*, a massive study of dispensational eschatology from the "Scofieldian" perspective.

Charles C. Ryrie (1925–). Professor at Dallas Seminary. A prolific writer, he made major contributions to dispensational thought in *Dispensationalism Today* (1965), which traced significant refinements in dispensational thinking since the publication of the *Scofield Reference Bible*, and the *Ryrie Study Bible*, which has replaced the Scofield Bible as the study Bible of choice among many dispensationalists. Ryrie's work marked the beginning of the attempt to define the essence of dispensational teaching and also set the direction for dispensational self-definition over the last decades of the twentieth century.

Craig Blaising (1949–). Provost of Southwestern Baptist Seminary. Blaising has been one of the key people involved in the contemporary phase of dispensational self-definition. He has, with Darrell Bock, respectively coauthored and coedited *Progressive Dispensationalism* and *Dispensationalism: Israel and the Church: A Search for Definition.* These works set the agenda for progressive dispensationalism.

Darrell Bock (1953–). Research professor of New Testament at Dallas Theological Seminary. Bock is a recognized expert on the Gospel of Luke as well as the other half of the leadership of the progressive dispensational agenda.

D. ISSUES AND TENSIONS

1. Hermeneutics

Earlier dispensationalists insisted on a consistent literal interpretation of prophecy. This insistence on a literal interpretation did not imply a denial of figurative language or symbols. Rather, the term *literal* has been employed to insist that all Scripture is to be interpreted in accordance with received linguistic conventions. The term is particularly used in opposition to the views of the older covenant theologians: (1) the denial of a literal future fulfillment of the Old Testament prophecies concerning national Israel and the messianic kingdom; (2) the spiritual appropriation of those prophecies/promises by the church; and (3) the fusion of Israel and the church into one virtually indistinguishable entity.

With their theology founded on the epistemological presuppositions of Scottish Common Sense and employing Baconian inductivism as a method, dispensationalists of the late nineteenth and early twentieth centuries approached the Bible as scientists, arranging the "facts" in a literal fashion. Operating on the assumption that the Bible teaches a single system, dispensationalism claimed to present the Bible's own view of itself.

A naive literalism, seen in such slogans as "If the plain sense makes sense, seek no other sense," often characterized the earlier movement, particularly on the popular level. Such literalism often led early dispensational writers to see sharp distinctions between concepts such as the "kingdom of God" and the "kingdom of heaven," distinctions contemporary dispensational scholars disavow. Early spokesman R. A. Torrey insisted, "In ninety-nine out of one hundred cases the meaning the plain man gets out of the Bible is the correct one." This insistence arose from the conviction that the Bible was God's message to the common man rather than to the scholar. Insistence on the "literal" meaning of the text and on commonsense interpretation opened the door for viewing the text apart from its historical context. In recent decades, the Scottish Common Sense epistemology has been supplanted by a critical realism, while the plain literal interpretation of earlier generations has been progressively supplanted by thoroughgoing historical-grammatical interpretation and coupled with increasing critical interaction and sensitivity to contemporary hermeneutical concerns, including the historical limitations of the interpreter.

2. Historiography

Prior to the nineteenth century, covenant theology had in practice denied the concept of development and progressive revelation in Scripture. The issues that gave birth to dispensationalism were the same issues that engaged higher criticism in the nineteenth century. In many respects, dispensationalism represents the mirror opposite of higher criticism, confronting the same issues but solving them on totally different bases. Whereas modernism was optimistic about the improvement of the human condition through the development of culture, dispensationalism was thoroughly pessimistic. Both focused on an understanding of the relation of the Bible to history. But while modernism viewed biblical history through the evolutionary lens of universal history, with naturalistic forces at work in the development of religion, dispensationalism contemplated human history exclusively through the lens of the Bible and answered the problem of change by appealing to divine intervention into human affairs.

Dispensational historiography views the world as a stage on which the drama of cosmic redemption is fought between divine and satanic forces. Each dispensation functions as an act in that drama. Development in the modern sense of the term may take place within dispensations but not between. Hope for improvement of the human plight is christological, posited in the return of Christ, rather than anthropological, posited in progressive human development in history. The unifying principle of history is eschatological, with God revealing his character and glory in successive dispensations.

The dispensational periodization of history has frequently been misunderstood as teaching different bases of salvation in different ages. This charge is vehemently denied. Salvation is always by grace and founded on the atonement of Christ. The content of the revelation to be trusted by the individual in the various ages is what changes, not the means or basis of salvation.

Dispensational historiography has proved to have practical political implications. Dispensationalists have had a political bias toward the nation of Israel based on God's promise to Abraham (Gen. 12:2–3). A creeping historicism has led many dispensationalists to identify the founding of the nation of Israel in 1948 as a fulfillment of prophecy. This, in turn, has led to an often uncritical support for Israel, lest one be found working against the purposes of God.

3. Sine Qua Non?

There have been many throughout the centuries who have recognized a need for the periodization of history but who cannot be considered dispensationalists. Ryrie in 1965 argued that the sine qua non (indispensable element) of dispensationalism is its distinction between the church and Israel coupled with a consistent "literal" interpretation of Scripture. As originally taught, dispensationalism posited a radical distinction between the church and Israel as two separate peoples with two radically separate destinies. The church was God's heavenly people, while Israel was God's earthly people. The hope of the church was heaven, while the hope of Israel was an eternal kingdom on the renewed earth. The radical distinction between Israel and the church has in recent decades been repudiated as most contemporary dispensational scholars argue for one eternal people of God but two distinct institutional organizations in history. Most contemporary dispensational scholars find Ryrie's sine qua non inadequate. While maintaining a distinction between the church and Israel, contemporary dispensationalists see so much continuity between Israel and the church that one critic has charged that on this issue dispensationalism and contemporary covenant theology have become virtually indistinguishable.

4. Cessation of the Charismata?

Widespread confusion exists as to the dispensational position on the charismatic renewal. Classical Pentecostalism is thoroughly dispensational, while representatives of non-Pentecostal dispensationalism have argued against the continuation of the charismata into the present. This opposition to the charismata, however, is not endemic to the dispensational system but rather reflects an affinity of non-Pentecostal dispensationalists with the Calvinistic attitudes exemplified in B. B. Warfield's *Counterfeit Miracles*.

E. CONTRIBUTIONS OF DISPENSATIONALISM

Historically, in the United States, it was a coalition of dispensational preachers, teachers, and laypeople that actively fought the onslaught of modernism on historic orthodoxy by (1) publishing works such as *The Fundamentals*, a twelve-volume paperback series mailed to more than three million pastors, missionaries, theological professors, Bible teachers, Bible college and seminary students in the English-speaking world; and (2) founding Bible institutes, colleges, and seminaries out of which contemporary American evangelicalism has arisen.

Theologically, in the United States, dispensational ecclesiology deinstitutionalized grace by its emphasis on the church as the spiritual body of Christ. This attitude played a major role in fostering an evangelical ecumenicity that spread far beyond the cooperation seen in the nineteenth-century revivals of American evangelicalism. This recognition of spiritual brotherhood deemphasized denominational loyalties and gave cohesion to the evangelical worldview. It has been suggested that the striking success of parachurch movements in the United States is due in measure to this deinstitutionalism of grace that has characterized dispensationalism.

Another major contribution of the movement lies in its insistence on an apocalyptic mind-set, not only in understanding the Scriptures, but also in accomplishing the present theological task. Ernst Käsemann has noted, "Apocalyptic . . . was the mother of all Christian theology."[19] But institutional Anglo-American theology prior to the late nineteenth century was decidedly anti-apocalyptic in its perspective. George Ladd admitted, "We must recognize our debt to Dispensationalism. . . . to all intents and purposes it revived the doctrine of the Second Advent of Christ and made it meaningful in the churches."[20]

Biblically, with its emphasis on progressive revelation and the discontinuity of the church and Israel, dispensationalism anticipated the conclusions of contemporary scholarship with reference to Paul and the law, recognizing a significant discontinuity between the Old and New Testaments in light of the Christ event. On this issue, dispensational scholarship is closer to contemporary critical conclusions than to the conclusions of covenant theology.

Practically, from the earlier advocacy of a literal hermeneutic to the contemporary insistence on historical-grammatical interpretation with its wider literary implications, dispensationalism has asserted the primacy of the Scriptures and the ability of the layperson to interpret and understand them. Its commonsense hermeneutic opened the Scriptures for the layperson and fostered comprehensive knowledge of and love for the Bible.

Due to apocalyptic expectations, a large number of early dispensationalists urged withdrawal from worldly occupations, politics, and institutions, emphasizing instead evangelism and missions, with the hope of saving as many as possible before the rapture. Thus dispensationalism provided an impetus to the explosion of missionary activity of the twentieth century. At the same time, it largely abandoned the public forum, thereby leaving it to secularism, since such involvement was viewed as "polishing brass on a sinking ship." Many contemporary dispensational theologians have rejected the narrow interpretation of salvation/redemption implicit in this mentality and its accompanying pessimism concerning the world, encouraging instead creative engagement with the social and political structures of society.

F. A TRADITION IN TRANSITION

Since the 1970s a new era of development in dispensational thought has been under way. In recent decades its scholars have moved away from the defensive posture of earlier years. Dispensational exegesis has moved beyond the naive literalism of earlier years to a more consistent application of the historical-grammatical method of interpretation. Contemporary dispensational scholars are critically reevaluating the system, and significant development is occurring, although that development is being met with outright hostility from those holding earlier forms of dispensationalism to be inviolable. Eschatologically, a significant and growing number are comfortable with an *inaugurated eschatology* as opposed to the strict futurism of previous generations, seeing the kingdom as having been already inaugurated at Pentecost but not yet fully manifested. Since the Scofield Bible has lost the confessional status it enjoyed in the last century, it is more accurate to speak of contemporary dispensationalism as a tradition bound together by shared presuppositions (futurist premillennialism, a temporal distinction between the church and Israel with an accompanying national future for Israel in fulfillment of Old Testament prophecy, and historical-grammatical interpretation) rather than a system.

G. OBSERVATIONS AND CRITIQUE

Dispensationalism as a theological system has a very different character than the other systems discussed in this volume. There are those who profess to be Calvinists, Arminians, Pentecostals, etc., who at the same time are dispensationalists.

"Literal" hermeneutic. While dispensationalism has made significant progress toward a more scholarly approach in recent decades, significant issues persist, particularly with reference to hermeneutics. Among the wider dispensational population there is still an adherence to the Common Sense view of reality that gave birth to the movement in the nineteenth century. This leads to a Common Sense hermeneutic that tends to be naive and simplistic and often pits the Bible against all other claims of understanding, particularly in the scientific realm. For example, the push for "scientific creationism" (see chapter 6.A.3) has arisen primarily within the dispensational community.

There exists among adherents an identification of dispensationalism as simply "the" literal truth of the Bible, or the Bible's own view of itself. Additionally, there is a tendency to place all "truth" on the same level.[21] This mentality can (and often does) lead to an absolutizing of idiosyncratic opinions that often will not tolerate divergent understandings.

Ignoring portions of Scripture. Many continue to use Scofield's phrase "rightly dividing the Word of Truth" to ignore in practice major areas of Scripture that were "not written to us" (e.g., the Sermon on the Mount) as opposed to seeing continuing, underlying principles that are applicable in every age.

Apocalyptic view of history. The apocalyptic vision of history continues to present two problems in the wider movement. The first problem is the temptation of historicism, that is, correlating contemporary events with biblical prophecy and then setting dates for the return of Christ. This in turn leads to "revisionist prophecy" when the correlations and predictions fail to come true. It is often unnoticed that in Scripture prophecy is recognized only in hindsight as having been fulfilled. While this mind-set has deeply influenced the fabric of twentieth and twenty-first-century American Christianity, it can obscure the redemptive core of the gospel with its focus on vivid apocalyptic imagery, as well as lead to a discrediting of the basic call to be ready for Christ's return as the dates fail. The second problem is the tendency to disengage from society. While this problem is less pronounced now than in previous generations, it still remains in many circles.

Lack of focus on the institutional church. Ironically, one of the greatest strengths in dispensationalism as a movement is also one of its greatest weaknesses. As noted earlier, dispensationalism, focusing on the universal nature of the church, has fostered an evangelical ecumenism and given rise to many parachurch organizations. Paradoxically, its lack of focus on the institutional church has downplayed the importance and the necessity of commitment to the church as a visible institution. In short, the movement suffers a decided lack of a credible ecclesiology.

BIBLIOGRAPHY

Bass, Clarence. *Backgrounds to Dispensationalism.* Reprint. Grand Rapids: Baker, 1977. • **Blaising, Craig.** "Developing Dispensationalism." *Bibliotheca Sacra* 145 (1988): 133–40, 254–80. • **Blaising, Craig**, and **Darrell Bock**. *Progressive Dispensationalism.* Wheaton: BridgePoint, 1993. • **Blaising, Craig**, and **Darrell Bock**, eds. *Dispensationalism, Israel and the Church.* Grand Rapids: Zondervan, 1992. • **Bock, Darrell.** "Evangelicals and the Use of the Old Testament in the New." *Bibliotheca Sacra* 142 (1985): 209–21, 306–19. • **Fuller, Daniel P.** *Gospel and Law.* Grand Rapids: Eerdmans, 1980. • **Kraus, C. Norman.** *Dispensationalism in America.* Richmond: John Knox, 1958. • **Marsden, George M.** *Fundamentalism and American Culture.* Oxford: Oxford University Press, 1980. • **McClain, Alva J.** *The Greatness of the Kingdom.* Chicago: Moody Press, 1968. • **Poythress, Vern.** *Understanding Dispensationalists.* Grand Rapids: Zondervan, 1987. • **Radmacher, Earl D.**

The Nature of the Church. Chicago: Moody Press, 1972. • **Ryrie, Charles C.** *Dispensationalism Today*. Chicago: Moody Press, 1965. • **Sandeen, Ernest R.** *The Roots of Fundamentalism: British and American Millenarianism, 1800–1930*. Reprint. Grand Rapids: Baker, 1978. • **Saucy, Robert.** *The Church in God's Program*. Chicago: Moody Press, 1972. • **Sauer, Erich.** *From Eternity to Eternity*. Grand Rapids: Eerdmans, 1972. • **Sheppard, Gerald.** "Pentecostals and the Hermeneutics of Dispensationalism: The Anatomy of an Uneasy Relationship." *Pneuma* 6, no. 2 (1984): 5–33. • **Weber, Timothy P.** *Living in the Shadow of the Second Coming: American Premillennialism 1875–1982*. Enlarged edition. Grand Rapids: Zondervan, 1983.

NOTES

[1]That is, there will be no literal thousand-year, earthly reign during which God's promises to Israel will be fulfilled.

[2]See Richard Kyle, *The Last Days Are Here Again* (Grand Rapids: Baker, 1998), 60–62.

[3]See Douglas W. Frank, *Less Than Conquerors* (Grand Rapids: Eerdmans, 1986), 24. See also Stanley Gundry, "Hermeneutics of Zeitgeist" *Journal of the Evangelical Theological Society* 20, no. 1 (March 1977): 47–48.

[4]Kyle, *Last Days*, 87–91.

[5]Much of the material in this section is summarized from Craig Blaising and Darrell Bock, *Progressive Dispensationalism* (Wheaton: BridgePoint, 1993), 23–56, and is used by permission of the authors.

[6]See also Darby's biography in chap. 17.

[7]The early Brethren emphasis on open assemblies of true believers soon was transformed into an exclusivist sect that stood against denominations. The Brethren as a group closed ranks and lost the early ecumenicity, splintering into factions over minor issues.

[8]L. S. Chafer, *Systematic Theology* (Dallas: Dallas Seminary Press, 1948), 4:40.

[9]Blaising and Bock, *Progressive Dispensationalism*, 28.

[10]"Enraptured with Order: How fundamentalists strove mightily to make sense of history," *Christian History and Biography*, *www.ctlibrary.com/ch/1997/Issue55/55h040.html* (accessed Sept. 2005). The chart in figure 13.1 is from Larkin's *Dispensational Truth* (Philadelphia: Clarence Larkin, 1920).

[11]Charles C. Ryrie, *Dispensationalism Today* (Chicago: Moody Press, 1965), 45–46.

[12]For a thorough discussion, see George Ladd, *Crucial Questions about the Kingdom of God* (Grand Rapids: Eerdmans, 1952).

[13]The first of these was Hal Lindsey's *Late Great Planet Earth* (1970). Recently, the phenomenal success of the Left Behind fiction series by Tim LaHaye and Jerry Jenkins (which revolves around the pretribulation rapture) underlines the appeal of popular dispensationalism. In addition, many religious films and television programs,

some focusing specifically on prophecy, continue to give this aspect of dispensationalism visibility.

[14]Blaising and Bock, *Progressive Dispensationalism*, 47. Italics in original.

[15]Ibid.

[16]The term *progressive dispensationalism* comes from the understanding of the progressive relationship between the dispensations.

[17]This section is summarized from Blaising and Bock, *Progressive Dispensationalism*, 13–21.

[18]Ibid., 19.

[19]Cited in Alister McGrath, ed., *The Blackwell Encyclopedia of Modern Christian Thought* (Oxford: Blackwell, 1993), s.v. "dispensationalism."

[20]Ibid.

[21]See chaps. 5 and 6.

OUTLINE OF CHAPTER 14

A. The Roots of Liberalism

1. The Effects of the Enlightenment
2. Immanuel Kant
3. G. W. F. Hegel

B. Liberalism in Germany

1. Friedrich Schleiermacher: Father of Liberal Theology
2. Albrecht Ritschl and Theological Agnosticism
3. Comparative Religions/History of Religions School
4. Adolf von Harnack

C. Major Theological Propositions of Liberalism

1. The Universal Fatherhood of the Immanent God
2. The Universal Brotherhood of Man and the Infinite Value of the Individual Human Soul
3. Jesus Christ Serves as the Supreme Example
4. Religious Authority, Salvation, and the Kingdom

D. Liberalism in America

1. Social Gospel
2. Modernism

E. Observations and Critique

CHAPTER 14

LIBERALISM

Liberalism is a term that is much used and little understood. It is used in the political, religious, social, and intellectual arenas, often without clear definition. Therefore many people of a conservative bent would identify a liberal simply as anyone more open-minded than they themselves are. Liberalism in the context of Christianity, however, was built on a commitment to a central set of theological and religious propositions that, when worked out, gave birth to a new form of religion that retained orthodox terminology but radically redefined those terms. For example, as quoted elsewhere, nineteenth-century Scottish Old Testament scholar and theologian W. Robertson Smith, when told that he had been accused of denying the divinity of Christ, responded by asking, "How can they accuse me of that? I've never denied the divinity of any man, let alone Jesus."[1]

Liberalism as a theological system did not arise in a vacuum, nor was its aim to destroy historic Christianity. The movement can be understood only in the historical and philosophical context out of which it came. Though often portrayed as a deliberate challenge to historic orthodox Christianity, liberalism as a system was to the contrary trying to salvage something of Christianity from the ashes of the fire of the Enlightenment. Near the turn of the century, B. B. Warfield observed of liberalism that it was rationalism, but a rationalism that was not the direct result of unbelief. Rather, it sprang from men who wanted to hold on to Christian convictions in the face of a rising onslaught of unbelief they realized they were powerless to withstand. It was a movement that came from within the church and was characterized by an effort to retain the essence of Christianity by surrendering the accretions and features that were considered no longer defensible in the modern world.[2] The rising tide of unbelief that confronted the founders of liberalism resulted from the impact of the Enlightenment.

A. THE ROOTS OF LIBERALISM

1. The Effects of the Enlightenment

The Enlightenment—also called the Age of Reason and, in Germany, the Aufklärung—was an intellectual movement during the eighteenth century that elevated human reason to near-divine status and ascribed to it the ability to discern truth of all types apart from any appeal to supernatural divine revelation. During the Enlightenment, humans believed it was possible to reason their way to God. This was the modern Tower of Babel with all the hubris that implies.[3]

The Fruit of the Enlightenment

The Enlightenment gave birth to much that we still recognize today as part of the modern mind-set:

1. The beginning of scientific history.
2. The requirement that any truth must justify itself before the bar of reason.
3. Nature as the primary source of answers to the fundamental questions of human existence.
4. The necessity of freedom to advance progress and human welfare.
5. The necessity of literary and historical criticism to determine the legitimacy of our historical legacy.
6. The need for critical philosophy.
7. Ethics as separate and independent from the authority of religion and theology.
8. A suspicion of and hostility to all truth claiming to be grounded in some kind of authority other than reason, for example, tradition or divine revelation.
9. Raising the value of science to the avenue by which man can find truth.
10. Toleration as the highest value in matters of religion.
11. A self-conscious continuation and expansion of the humanism first developed during the Renaissance.[4]

A group of scholars who have come to be known as the *neologians* (or innovators) arose during this age.[5] It was they who pioneered the work in biblical criticism, attacking the doctrine of biblical inspiration as it had been precisely articulated during the late Reformation period. The neologians assaulted traditional Protestant doctrines in general and Lutheran doctrines specifically. They attacked the supernaturalism of historic Christianity in general and such doctrines as the Trinity, the deity of Christ, the atonement, the virgin birth, the resurrection, Chalcedonian Christology, and the existence of Satan.

On another front, this age saw the rise of deism, which asserted that while God was indeed the Creator, he had created a clockwork type of universe that operated by natural law. Because God would not interfere with his creation, miracles were impossible, for they would violate the inviolable laws of nature. Works such as *Christianity as Old as Creation* appeared,[6] arguing that Christianity merely republished the revelation of God that was available to man in nature. God himself was transcendent and uninvolved in creation.

2. Immanuel Kant

Immanuel Kant is the last of the Enlightenment philosophers. His *Critique of Pure Reason* destroyed the hubris of the Enlightenment program of seeking all knowledge through the use of reason. Before Kant, philosophical epistemology had generally been divided into two camps: the rationalists who saw ultimate reality in the mind and the empiricists who saw ultimate reality in the physical universe. Enlightenment philosophers debated the status of human knowledge, empiricists arguing that all knowledge came into the brain from the outside and rationalists contending that knowledge arose out of the mind itself.

Immanuel Kant

Kant asserted that neither side of the debate was right. Instead, human knowledge arises from the interplay of incoming sensory data (absorbed through the five senses) and innate categories built into the human mind, which process those data and make it "knowledge." He further held that reality is to be divided into two realms, the phenomenal (the created order in which we live and which is open for us to experience) and the noumenal (spiritual, metaphysical reality). For Kant, there are no categories by which to receive data from the noumenal world. In this way, humanity is like the blind man. He has no organ to receive the light that surrounds him. He believes that light exists and things are there to be seen, but he has no faculty by which to perceive it. Since man is blind to noumenal reality of all types, he cannot know "the thing in itself." All that can be known is things as they are experienced.

The Enlightenment philosophers attempted to know God as he is in himself by reasoning up to him. This was, according to Kant, a vain attempt doomed from the outset. God inhabits the noumenal realm and thus cannot be experienced by man. Kant did not entertain the possibility that God can break into the realm of history (the phenomenal realm) and reveal himself.

But Kant was not an atheist. He postulated the existence of God but denied the possibility of any cognitive knowledge of him.[7] Man's conscience testifies of God's existence, and God is to be known through the realm of morality. Kant published another work, *Religion within the Limits of Reason Alone*, which set forth his idea that religion is to be reduced to the sphere of morality. For Kant this meant living by the *categorical imperative*, which he summarized in two maxims (see also chapter 3.B.4):

- Act only on that maxim whereby you can at the same time will that it should become a universal law.
- Act as if the maxim of your action were to become by your will a universal law of nature.

In other words, every action of humanity should be regulated in such a way that it would be morally profitable for humanity if it were elevated to the status of law. In a sense, this can be seen as a secularization of the Golden Rule.

3. G. W. F. Hegel

G. W. F. Hegel, a contemporary of Friedrich Schleiermacher (see below), gave the dominant shape to idealistic philosophy during the nineteenth century. A philosopher of history and religion, Hegel proposed that *all of reality is the outworking of spirit/mind (Geist).* History is the objectification of spirit; that is, spirit/mind is working itself out in the historical process, and as such, history carries its own meaning. From this it follows that there is a continual upward progress in history. History is undergoing a continual cultural and rational (although not biological) evolution, being pushed and pulled, forcing culture upward toward its final form by means of the dialectic. Hegel saw historical evolution in terms of a pendulum swing between opposites (the-

G. W. F. Hegel

sis-antithesis), which was resolved in a position that was higher than either of the opposites (synthesis). The synthesis then became a new thesis in the upward pull of the historical process.

Whereas philosophy had traditionally been occupied with the concept of *being*, Hegel substituted the process of *becoming*. Because all of history was seen as the process of the objectification of Spirit, and human beings were a part of the historical process, *all human knowledge was said to be "absolute spirit" thinking through human minds.*

Hegel's dialectic

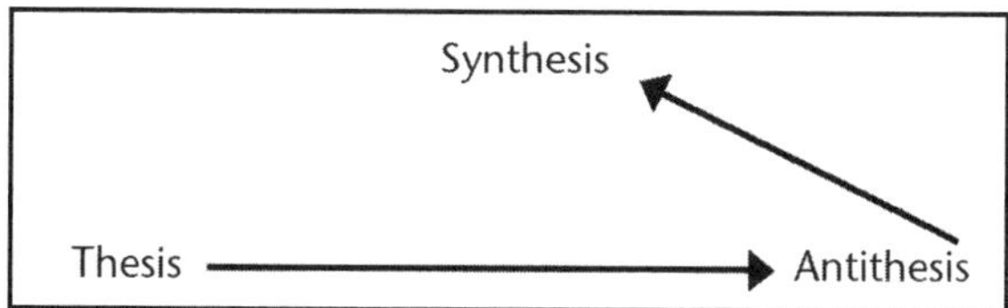

FIGURE 14.1.

An example of how Hegel saw this dialectic working itself out can be seen in his philosophy of history. The original thesis was the despotism of the ancient period. The antithesis of despotism was seen in the democracy of ancient Greece. The higher synthesis of these opposing forces was understood as aristocracy. Aristocracy in turn became the new thesis that was opposed by monarchy.

Hegel's dialectic of progress as worked out in history

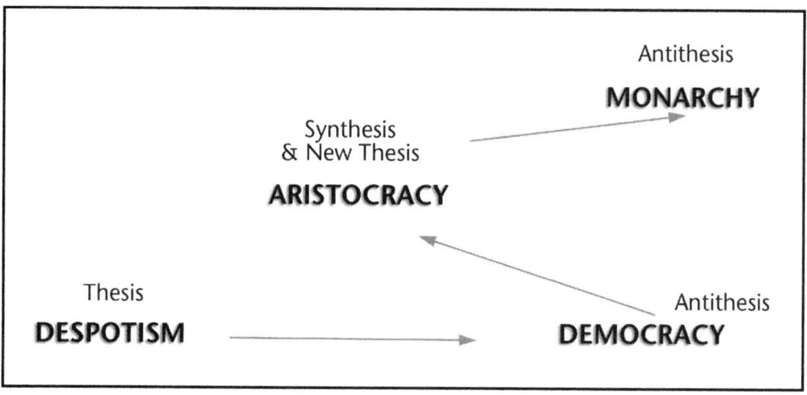

FIGURE 14.2.

Hegel's philosophy of history provided the structure adopted by the emerging schools of biblical criticism and cast an optimistic light on the entire nineteenth century, dogmatically asserting progress in history and the perfectibility of humanity. His philosophy was that of self-confidence,[8] and the slogan that characterized late-nineteenth-century liberalism, "Every day in every way we are getting better and better," reflects his optimism. Karl Barth comments, "It was precisely when [the nineteenth century] was utterly ruled and completely ruled by Hegel that the new age best understood itself, and it was then at all events that it best knew what it wanted."[9] According to Barth, Hegel held sway until the catastrophe of 1914, World War I.

B. LIBERALISM IN GERMANY

1. Friedrich Schleiermacher: Father of Liberal Theology

Friedrich Daniel Ernst Schleiermacher, the father of modern (liberal) theology and arguably the greatest theologian to live between Calvin and Barth, was born into the intellectual ferment of the Enlightenment and Kant's criticism of its program. The son of a Reformed chaplain in the Prussian army, Schleiermacher was educated in the pietism of the Moravians. From their fervent piety, with its emphasis on life in community and commitment to traditional Lutheran doctrine, he received his early religious experiences. While studying with the Moravians, he first read the neologians' critique of historic Protestant orthodoxy. He was so impressed by their arguments that he left the Moravians and enrolled at Halle, a center of neologian teaching. The young Friedrich accepted the neologians' criticism of Lutheran orthodoxy but rejected their rationalistic and moralistic substitute. About this time, he was drawn into the Romantic movement, which arose in reaction to the sterile critical and analytical rationalism of the eighteenth century. Romanticism stressed the intuitive and synthetic nature of human reason, insisting that truth was to be gained by grasping the whole rather than by an abstract analysis of the parts.

Friedrich Schleiermacher

Schleiermacher's theological program proceeded under three premises: (1) the Enlightenment criticism of dogmatic Protestant orthodoxy was valid; (2) Romantic idealistic philosophy gives a better soil in which to ground the Christian faith than the shallow moralistic rationalism of the Enlightenment; and (3) Christian theology can be interpreted in terms of Romantic idealism and thus can allow humankind to be both Christian and modern while being intellectually honest.

In viewing the neologians' critique of orthodoxy as correct and in light of Kant's perceived destruction of the possibility of a rational knowledge of God, Schleiermacher, influenced by Romanticism, found a new seat for religion and theology, one that could not be touched by Enlightenment criticism—*Gefühl* (feeling). This feeling is not to be understood as mere emotion. Rather, it is man's "God-consciousness," the deep inner sense of man that he exists in a relationship of absolute dependence on God. This is the center of religion and piety.

> §3. The piety which forms the basis of all ecclesiastical communions is, considered purely in itself, neither a knowing or a doing, but a modification of feeling, or of immediate self-consciousness.[10]
>
> §4. The common element in all howsoever diverse expressions of piety, by which these are conjointly distinguished from all other feelings, or, in other words, the self-identical essence of piety, is this: the consciousness of being absolutely dependent, or, which is the same thing, of being in relation with God.[11]

In taking this route, Schleiermacher turned the traditional theological method on its head. Rather than starting with any objective revelation, religion was seen as subjective at its core. Experience was seen as giving rise to doctrine rather than doctrine to experience. Theological statements no longer were perceived as describing objective reality, but rather as reflecting the way that the feeling of absolute dependence is related to God. This experience, rather than the objective revelation of an inerrant Scripture, is seen as the final authority in religion. He says, "Christian doctrines are accounts of the Christian religious affections set forth in speech."[12]

Despite having the potential for God-consciousness, humans are by their nature in a state of "God-forgetfulness" from which they are unable to save themselves. Redemption is found through the experience of Christ in the corporate life of the church. Redemption is "mystical," centered in the personal communion of the believer with the fully God-conscious man, Jesus Christ.

For Schleiermacher, Jesus Christ was unique—not in that he was the God-man of historic orthodoxy, but rather in that he demonstrated a perfect and uninterrupted God-consciousness. He displayed the "veritable existence of God in him." This was the redemption Jesus accomplished and brought to humankind. In this understanding, the cross is not a sacrificial atonement;

rather, it is an example of Jesus' willingness to enter into "sympathy with misery." Redemption was then the inner transformation of the individual from the state of God-forgetfulness to the state of God-consciousness. To put it another way, redemption is that state in which God-consciousness predominates over all else in life. Thus Schleiermacher's theology was utterly christocentric in that it was concerned with the example of Jesus as the perfectly God-conscious one.

2. Albrecht Ritschl and Theological Agnosticism

The second major stream in classic liberalism (which became synonymous with liberalism in its later form) was established by Albrecht Ritschl. Whereas Schleiermacher was mystic, seeing the center of religion as feeling, Ritschl was more closely tied to Kant and saw religion in terms of morality and personal effort in the establishing of the kingdom of God (a moral-ethical kingdom). According to Ritschl,

> Christianity is the monotheistic, completely spiritual and ethical religion, which, on the basis of the life of its Founder as redeeming and establishing the kingdom of God, consists in the freedom of the children of God, includes the impulse to conduct, from the motive of love, the intention of which is the moral organization of mankind, and the filial relation to God as well as in the kingdom of God lays the foundation of blessedness.[13]

Religious truth in the Ritschlian conception became different in kind from all other knowledge; it involved moral-ethical judgments that were subjectively determined by the individual. The system surrendered rational knowledge of God and things divine. In its place it substituted, as the essence of Christianity, a subjectively verified personal theism, a devotion to the man Jesus Christ as the revealer of God and his kingdom, and a subjection to his moral-ethical principles.

Employing the epistemology of Kant (as modified by the nineteenth-century philosopher and logician Rudolph Lotze) as a foundation, Ritschlianism sought to separate religion and theology from philosophy and metaphysics, founding religion strictly on phenomenological experience. Kant had asserted that the only knowledge available to humankind was that of experience, the phenomenological. The Ritschlians agreed with this proposition. "Theology without metaphysics" became the watchword of the school.[14] Following in the Kantian tradition, the Ritschlians asserted that human knowledge was strictly limited to the world of phenomena, a world that included the realm of verifiable history and the realm of personal experience. Knowledge of God as he was in himself, his essence, and attributes fell outside the possibility of human experience, so no positive assertions concerning his nature could be made. Thus Ritschlianism represented a "theological agnosticism."[15] Ritschl himself asserted (with Kant) that people could not know things "in themselves" but only in their phenomenological relations.[16] Since people had no categories by which to perceive God in the world, knowledge of him fell outside the realm of the "theoretic" (scientific/empirical). And since Ritschlianism was strictly empirical, the value of historical study was elevated as a means by which one could discover God's revelation in history: the person of Jesus Christ.[17]

Albrecht Ritschl

Revelation of God and certainty in religion for the Ritschlians took place when one was confronted with the historic person of Jesus Christ. The truth communicated in this revelation was not theoretic but religious. Such a distinction divorced faith from reason. According to the Ritschlians, the two realms had to be kept entirely separate.[18] Religious truth was no longer to be found in objective, verifiable propositions but in the realm of the subjective experience, in "value judgments." These value judgments were of a different nature than scientific knowledge. They gave no definite, objective, propositional knowledge; instead, they set forth their subjective value for the individual.[19] For example, the existence of God could not be rationally demonstrated. But man needed God, and that was proof that he existed.[20] However, nothing could be inferred concerning his nature, his attributes, or his relationship to the world.[21] The God of the Christian may be Jesus Christ, "or [the Christian] may believe in one or another kind of God. His God may not be Christian at all. It may be Jewish, as Jesus' God was. It may be neo-Platonic. It may be Stoic or Hindu. It may be Deistic."[22] One could not communicate objective truth about God from his revelation in Jesus Christ; the most one could say was that in Jesus Christ one received the impression that God was present and active before him.[23] Thus religious knowledge (in the objective sense) became the common, shared experience of God.[24]

The whole enterprise was one of religious positivism. It began with the data of the experience the individual had with the historic Christ. That experience included the freedom and deliverance Christ imparted to the person by virtue of his life and teachings. This deliverance could not be denied since it was within the realm of the person's experience. But the enterprise also ended there, for although it professed to meet Christ in the pages of Scripture, it denied any knowledge of his preexistence, atoning death, or second coming. Although Jesus was afforded the title "Son of God" and had divinity ascribed to him, these were but titles of honor, communicating no ontological reality. Such knowledge was beyond the realm of experience.[25]

> Ritschl believes Christ to be God because in Him he is conscious of a power lifting him above himself, into a new world of peace and strength. Why this should be he cannot tell, nor can he give an answer to the man who asks him for an explanation of the fact of his experience. Enough that he point to Christ as the one through whom he has received deliverance, leaving it to the other to make the test, try the experiment for himself.[26]

Since knowledge in Ritschl's system was limited to phenomena, Ritschlianism was adamantly anti-mystic. It denied the soul any direct access to God.[27] From the perspective of Ritschlianism, the aim of mysticism was "ontologically unsound in that it involve[d] getting back to the noumenal. That one may assume a noumenon back of phenomena is of course true, but that one can hold valid communion with it—that one can press back beyond phenomena and come into direct touch with it—is a delusion"[28]

God was seen as personal yet unknowable in any real sense. Knowledge of God was mediated through the person of Jesus Christ as he appeared in history.[29] Looking beyond Christ to God was a vain proposition. Communion with him involved, not mystic rapture, but moral effort on behalf of his kingdom. "To commune with God is to enter into his purposes as revealed in Christ—to make them our own and to fulfill them increasingly and to gain the inspiration and the power which come from knowing that they are God's will.... Genuine communion with God to the Christian is the conscious and glad fulfilling of God's purposes."[30]

3. Comparative Religions/History of Religions School

Another development that took place within the context of liberalism was the birth of the study of comparative religions. Two factors underlie this new discipline that proved to be another threat to the distinctiveness of Christianity. The first was Romanticism. Romantic philosophy led to a curiosity about and appreciation for other peoples' religions as authentic ways of expressing the human experience. The second factor was the increase of knowledge that came as a result of the colonization of the world by the Western European powers. Vast amounts of new knowledge about the world and competing cultures and their native religions became available. The burgeoning science of archaeology opened the past and now allowed for the Bible to be studied against its cultural milieu in a way that had not heretofore been possible.

These two factors combined to form a new area of scientific study, comparative religions. All religions were seen in their most basic form to lead to one truth (God) and to promote a common ethic of love for one's neighbor. In Germany, comparative religions took the form of the history of religions school,[31] which studied the religions of the nations surrounding Israel and concluded that Israelite religion had taken elements of the surrounding pagan beliefs and placed them within a structure of monotheism. For example, Israel's tradition of creation and the flood were said to have been borrowed from the Babylonian Genesis and the Epic of Gilgamesh.

The history of religions school was hostile to Ritschlianism because of Ritschl's lack of sensitivity to the historical background of both Christianity and Judaism. It held that biblical faith in both its Old and New Testament expressions was not distinct and a result of supernatural revelation, but represented humanity's evolving conceptions about God and religion.

4. Adolf von Harnack

Adolf von Harnack represents the apex of liberal theology. He was the greatest historian of Christianity of his generation, and his work set a standard for scholarship for the succeeding century. His *History of Dogma* has been the definitive work on the subject since its publication. Harnack operated totally within the framework of liberalism, seeing the pristine purity of the gospel as having been corrupted even within the New Testament era, transforming Christianity from the religion *of* Jesus to the religion *about* Jesus. Further corruption took place in the succeeding centuries as Christianity moved out of its Jewish context and confronted the Hellenistic world. In controversies over the Trinity and the two natures of the incarnate Christ, Hellenistic philosophy twisted the gospel message. Harnack argued that the task of the theologian was to get back to the kernel of the gospel by stripping away the husks of Hellenism to find what was real and permanent.

Specifically, the gospel was seen as having nothing to do with the person of the Son. It dealt with the Father only.[32] In this understanding, Jesus' preaching demanded "no other belief in his person and no other attachments to it than is contained in the keeping of his commandments."[33] The doctrine of the person of Christ lay not in the teachings of Christ himself, but in the modifications introduced by his followers, especially Paul.

Harnack held that it was through the work of Paul that Jesus Christ was first seen to have more than human stature. Paul introduced modifications to Christianity by which the simple gospel of Jesus was ultimately replaced by adherence to doctrines relating to the person of Christ. Moreover, Paul was seen as having been the one who first invested the death and resurrection of Christ with redemptive significance.

If redemption is to be traced to Christ's person and work, everything would seem to depend on a right understanding of this person together with what he accomplished. *"The formation of a correct theory of and about Christ threatens to assume the position of chief importance and to pervert the majesty and simplicity of the Gospel."*[34]

C. MAJOR THEOLOGICAL PROPOSITIONS OF LIBERALISM

In his brief but important work *What Is Christianity?* Harnack distilled the essence of Christianity as (1) the universal fatherhood of God, (2) the universal brotherhood of man, and (3) the infinite value of the individual human soul. Additionally, Jesus Christ serves as the supreme example, the man who was perfectly God-conscious at all times, in whom God was perfectly immanent.

1. The Universal Fatherhood of the Immanent God

God is the loving, immanent Father in constant communion with his creation and working within it rather than upon it to bring it to the perfection for which it is destined. God is the loving Father who corrects his children but is not retributive in his punishment. "The idea of an immanent God, which is the God of evolution, is infinitely grander than the occasional wonder-worker who is the God of an old theology."[35] Such a position breached the traditional barrier between the natural and the supernatural. "Miracle is only the religious name for an event. Every event, even the most natural and common, is a miracle if it lends itself to a controllingly religious interpretation. To me all is miracle."[36]

2. The Universal Brotherhood of Man and the Infinite Value of the Individual Human Soul

No longer was man seen as radically sinful and in need of redemption. Rather, he was in communion with God. There was no infinite qualitative distinction between God and man. God was even to be known in measure and by analogy through study of the human personality. Emphasis was placed on human freedom and ability to do all that God required, and eternity was interpreted as immortality of the spirit rather than the resurrection of the body.

3. Jesus Christ Serves as the Supreme Example

Liberal Protestantism rediscovered the humanity of Christ, a truth that had in practice been ignored in previous generations. But liberalism went beyond a rediscovery of Christ's humanity to a denial of his ontological deity. Instead of the incarnate God-man, Jesus Christ became the perfect man, who attained divine status because of his perfect piety (God-consciousness). Jesus is the supreme example of God indwelling man. There is no qualitative distinction between Jesus and the rest of humanity. The distinction is quantitative; he is more full of God than other humans. He lived out in his life the perfect example of that which we all may become. However, he lived his life by a "higher righteousness" governed by the law of love, independent of religious worship and technical observance of religious ritual.

4. Religious Authority, Salvation, and the Kingdom

A number of corollaries follow from the guiding principles listed above.

Religious authority. Whereas previous generations had seen the Bible as the ultimate practical authority for the Christian, liberalism made authority wholly subjective, based on individual spiritual experience. Ultimate authority was not to be found in any external source—Bible, church, or tradition—but on the individual's reason, conscience, and intuition. The Bible became the record of man's evolving religious conceptions.[37] The New Testament was normative only in the teachings of Jesus. The rest of the New Testament fell victim to changing the focus of the gospel from the religion *of* Jesus to a religion *about* Jesus.

Salvation. Man is confronted with salvation in the person of Jesus. By following his teachings and the example of his life, one enters into communion with him.

The kingdom. God's kingdom is a moral kingdom with God ruling in the hearts of humans. The kingdom is also manifested in society by the establishment of justice and righteousness in the political sphere. It finally will be established as God works through people in the historical process.

D. LIBERALISM IN AMERICA

1. Social Gospel

The social gospel was the liberal Protestant attempt to apply biblical principles to the problems associated with emerging urbanization. Key is that it saw the kingdom as a social and political entity.

Late nineteenth-century America underwent profound social upheaval. The industrial revolution had thrust the problems of urban society upon a nation that had heretofore been primarily rural. As the problems of dynamic social revolution manifested themselves in the slums and workhouses, the individualistic gospel of revivalism had little to say to the problems that faced the urban dwellers every day. Walter Rauschenbusch spent eleven years in the Hell's Kitchen area of New York City ministering among the German-speaking immigrants. The poverty, injustice, and oppression he saw led him to rethink the implications of the gospel and articulate "a theology for the social gospel" in a work by that name. His premise was that

> the social gospel is the old message of salvation, but enlarged and intensified. The individualistic gospel has taught us to see the sinfulness of every human heart and has inspired us with faith in the willingness and power of God to save every soul that comes to him. But it has not given us an adequate understanding of the sinfulness of the social order and its share in the sins of all individuals within it. It has not evoked faith in the will and power of God to redeem the permanent institutions of human society from their inherited guilt of oppression and extortion. Both our sense of sin and our faith in salvation have fallen short of the realities under its teaching. The social gospel seeks to bring men under repentance for their collective sins and to create a more sensitive and more modern conscience. It calls for the faith of the old prophets who believed in the salvation of nations.[38]

While Rauschenbusch was relatively conservative in his theological outlook, those who took up his mantle saw the message of the gospel and the task of the church solely as working to end human suffering and establish social justice.

2. Modernism

The term *modernism* was first used of a movement within Roman Catholicism and pointed to a mentality that was similar to liberal Protestantism. In the United States, however, the term came to be applied to the radical edge of liberal theology (beginning c. 1910). Whereas earlier liberalism was a kind of salvage movement trying to save the essence of Christianity from the ashes of the Enlightenment, modernism posed a direct challenge to evangelical Protestantism and fostered a full-scale response in the form of fundamentalism. In the early decades of the twentieth century, the American religious scene was wracked with the fundamentalist-modernist controversy. Progressively effected were Congregationalism, Episcopalianism, and the Northern Presbyterian, Methodist, and Baptist bodies, so that by about 1930 many of these bodies were seen as having been "taken over" by liberals. This pitted the defenders of historic Christianity against the rising tide of a new "theology" that rejected the normative status of the Bible and even of Jesus Christ. In this, modernism took a step beyond liberalism.

As a movement, modernism embraced the Enlightenment and an optimistic view of history based on the radical immanence of God, which saw the Holy Spirit as operative within and perfecting both nature and culture. This concept marked a direct dependence on Hegel's philosophy of history. The division between secular culture and the sacred were seen as invalid because the Holy Spirit was seen as operative in both realms, making "the kingdoms of this world become the kingdom of our Lord Jesus Christ."

Modernism emphasized autonomous human reason, focusing on humanity's freedom and self-determination, and it gave a religious authorization to modern efforts of man to improve his lot by relying on his own inherent goodness. The radical power of sin and evil were minimized to the level of inconvenience. Truth was seen in the latest findings of science rather than in any supernatural revelation or in any historic person. In this, too, modernism represented a step beyond liberalism.

In the United States, modernism as a movement received its impetus from Shailer Matthews and the "Chicago School" that originated at the University of Chicago. Matthews used a sociohistorical approach to religion, arguing that religion is functional in that it helps people to make sense of the environment in which they find themselves and that theology is "transcendentalized politics" arising out of the church's interaction with its particular culture. This meant that Christianity had to be "modernized" in every age in order to remain a live option for each new generation. As a movement, modernism went into decline in the 1930s under the attacks of neoorthodoxy, but key ideas found revival during the radicalism of the 1960s.

E. OBSERVATIONS AND CRITIQUE

Immanentism. Christianity had historically asserted the doctrine of God's omnipresence—that is, that he was present everywhere in the created order while remaining separate from it. The new stress on divine immanence in the world did not represent a return to the classical doctrine of omnipresence. As it had been traditionally understood, omnipresence emphasized the distinction between God and the world, whereas immanence implied an "intimate relationship, that the universe and God are in some sense truly one."[39] Thus a thoroughgoing doctrine of immanence led to a denial of the supernatural as traditionally understood. There were not two realms—a natural and a supernatural—but one. Nor were there miracles in the sense of God breaking into the natural order, for God was not perceived as being "out there" to break in; rather, all was miraculous, for God was in all.

Lack of a doctrine of sin. Coupled with this loss of divine transcendence was the elevation of man's position. No longer was he viewed as depraved and separated from God. Rather, there was a blending of the distinction between God and man, a blending that emphasized not human sinfulness but human perfectibility. It was a view of man that J. Gresham Machen called "essentially *pagan*."[40]

The catch phrase of liberalism, "Every day in every way we are getting better and better," gives clear evidence that the doctrine of man propounded by liberalism was a return to fourth-century Pelagianism. Sin was treated as a minor peccadillo rather than a radical evil that necessitated the incarnation and atonement.

Lack of need for conversion/moralistic salvation. Liberalism saw redemption as mystical communion with Christ in the community of the church or in the establishment of the kingdom of God on earth.

Rise of biblical criticism. The rise of biblical criticism in the mid- to late nineteenth century represented a wholesale attack on the *sola scriptura* foundation of the Protestant faith and the theology of the post-Reformation period, which had articulated a precisely defined doctrine of inerrancy. In some of these explanations, the doctrine of inspiration and inerrancy was extended even to the vowel pointing of the Hebrew text. The biblical critics blasted such doctrines. The rise of textual criticism shook the confidence of many in the accurate transmission and preservation of the text. Literary (or higher) criticism applied to the Bible the methods of literary analysis used for secular documents. Critics looked at the books of the Bible and concluded from antisupernaturalistic presuppositions, for example, that Moses did not write the Pentateuch. In the field of New Testament studies, the works of David F. Strauss, F. C. Baur, and others purported to demonstrate that much of the New Testament was to be dated from the second century rather than having been written by the apostles as Jesus' representatives. Such criticism served to undermine the unique character and authority of the Bible both in the scholarly as well as in the worshiping community. No longer was it possible to proclaim "Thus saith the Lord." As a result, the possibility of the rational certainty of the faith was undermined.

> "A God without wrath led men without sin into a kingdom without judgment through the ministrations of a Christ without a cross."
>
> —*H. Richard Niebuhr*

Loss of the uniqueness of Christ and the quest for the historical (merely human) Jesus. The identity and status of Jesus during the nineteenth century underwent continual revision. Strauss first attacked the supernatural in the New Testament as mere myth. This launched the nineteenth-century quest for the historical Jesus, which has been described as liberalism looking back through nineteen centuries of Catholic darkness and seeing only the reflection of a liberal Protestant face at the bottom of a deep well.[41]

The Jesus of liberalism bore little resemblance to the church's historic understanding of Jesus Christ as having both human and divine natures joined in one person. This was largely due to the radical empiricism that the liberal school applied to the area of religious truth. This empiricism eliminated all but phenomenological data from any truth claim. As this method was applied to christological doctrine, a great reduction transpired. Rather than affirm the historic formulations, a "form of the dynamic Monarchianism of Paul of Samosata [was] revived by Harnack and his followers."[42]

Any metaphysical speculation about the two natures of Christ was seen as nonsense. A history of christological doctrine could not rid one "of the impression that the whole fabric of ecclesiastical Christology [was] a thing absolutely outside the concrete personality of Jesus Christ."[43] The starting place had to be the historical Christ, the "person" Jesus.[44] Any assertion that Jesus was not limited by his cultural milieu and environment as any other person was would be to assert that he was a "specter."[45] In the liberal view, to be a human implied a complete human body, soul, and human personality.[46] That Jesus was *fully* human but *only* human became the sine qua non on which the Ritschlian understanding of Christ was built. This man Jesus was the one who was to be found in the pages of the Gospels.

Jesus became the great example. He was the founder of a religion who embodied in his own life what he taught concerning God.[47] In contrast to the majority of humankind, who came to a knowledge of God through some sort of crisis experience, this God-knowledge was in Jesus from the beginning, flowing naturally from him "as though it could not do otherwise, like a spring from the depths of the earth, clear and unchecked in its flow."[48] The means by which Jesus achieved this God-consciousness and his resulting mission to spread the kingdom of God among humankind was beyond human comprehension; it was "his secret, and no psychology will ever fathom it."[49]

> "Knowledge of God" ... marks the sphere of Divine Sonship. It is in this knowledge that he came to know the sacred Being who rules the heaven and earth as Father, as *his* Father. The consciousness which he possessed of being *the Son of God* is, therefore, nothing but the practical consequence of knowing God as the Father and as *his* Father. Rightly understood, the name of Son means nothing but the knowledge of God.[50]

In Jesus' own understanding, his God-knowledge was unique. He knew God "in a way in which no one ever knew Him before."[51] It was this unique God-knowledge that constituted him *the* Son of God. It was also from this knowledge that his vocation flowed. Jesus knew that it was "his vocation to communicate this knowledge of God to others by word and by deed—and with it the knowledge that men are God's children."[52]

> Whether we shall call Christ divine depends on what we mean by God. If God is substance then Christ is not divine for there is no evidence of divine substance in him. If God is purpose then this does make Christ divine for there is nothing higher than his purpose. Christ's divinity is a conclusion not a presupposition. Yet it is not immaterial whether we call him divine or not. Such an interpretation has importance as showing our conception of God. It does not hurt Christ to not be called divine. If we recognize his supremacy that is enough. But if we do not call him divine it is because we have another and unchristian idea of God. We seek in God something not found in Christ. We get God elsewhere than from Christ. This procedure is due to the unfortunate fact that our theology is not christianized.[53]

Society-centered activity. As liberalism developed in America, it took on a decidedly activist cast. The social gospel sought to right social injustice but at the expense of a recognition of personal sin and emphasis on personal piety. The church was the Public Church, but it ignored the personal aspects of the gospel and faith. This led to a natural blending of the church's message with the agenda of secularly dominated political systems, making the agendas often indistinguishable.

BIBLIOGRAPHY

Averill, Lloyd J. *American Theology in the Liberal Tradition.* Philadelphia: Westminster, 1967. • **Brown, Colin.** *Philosophy and the Christian Faith.* Chicago: InterVarsity Press, 1969. • **Cauthen, Kenneth.** *The Impact of American Religious Liberalism.* New York: Harper & Row, 1962. • **Dillenberger, John,** and **Claude Welch,** *Protestant Christianity Interpreted through Its Development.* New York: Macmillan, 1988. • **Harnack, Adolf von.** *What Is Christianity?* New York: Harper & Row, 1957. • **Hutchison, William R.** *The Modernist Impulse in American Protestantism.* Cambridge: Harvard, 1976. • **Miller, Donald E.** *The Case for Liberal Christianity.* San Francisco: Harper & Row, 1981.

NOTES

[1]Quoted by Millard Erickson, *Christian Theology* (Grand Rapids: Baker, 1984), 2:740.

[2]B. B. Warfield, "The Latest Phase of Historical Rationalism," in *Studies in Theology* (Grand Rapids: Baker, 1981), 591.

[3]Indeed, Peter Gay has termed the Enlightenment "modern paganism" in *The Enlightenment: The Rise of Modern Paganism* (New York: W. W. Norton, 1977). See also chap. 3 for a fuller discussion of the Enlightenment.

[4]Bernard Ramm, *After Fundamentalism* (New York: Harper & Row, 1983), 4–5.

[5]See Roy A. Harrisville and Walter Sundberg, *The Bible in Modern Culture* (Grand Rapids: Eerdmans, 1995), for a thorough survey of the work of the neologians.

[6]Matthew Tindal, *Christianity as Old as the Creation: or, The Gospel, a Republication of the Religion of Nature* (Newburgh, NY: David Denniston, 1798).

[7]Kant as a philosopher made no claims to being a Christian. Throughout his adult life he was never known to utter the name of Jesus Christ, nor would he enter a Christian church. When called upon to attend academic functions at the chapel of the University of Koenigsberg where he taught, he would march in his academic robes to the door of the chapel, then slip out of line and go home rather than enter the church.

[8]Karl Barth, *Protestant Theology in the Nineteenth Century* (Valley Forge, PA: Judson Press, 1972), 391.

[9]Ibid., 386.

[10]Friedrich Schleiermacher, *The Christian Faith*, English trans., ed. H. R. Mackintosh and J. S. Stewart (Edinburgh: T. & T. Clark, 1986), 5.

[11]Ibid., 12.

[12]Ibid., 76.

[13]Albrecht Ritschl, *The Christian Doctrine of Justification and Reconciliation*, English trans., ed. H. C. Mackintosh and A. B. Macaulay (Edinburgh: T. & T. Clark, 1900), 3:13.

[14]James Orr, *The Ritschlian Theology and the Evangelical Faith* (New York: Thomas Whittaker, n.d.), 57.

[15]A. B. Bruce noted that this agnosticism was not absolute, but a severe restriction of the knowledge of God attainable to man ("Theological Agnosticism," *American Journal of Theology* 1 [1897]: 1–2). Cf. Hutchison, *The Modernist Impulse in American Protestantism* (New York: Oxford University Press, 1976), 122–32.

[16]Albrecht Ritschl, *Christian Doctrine*, 3:18–20.

[17]It is not without significance that both Adolf von Harnack, widely regarded as the greatest of the classic liberal theologians, and his American disciple A.C. McGiffert, were primarily historians, who undertook to clear away the accretions of Greek metaphysical speculations from Christianity in order to discover the pristine gospel taught by Christ apart from philosophical considerations.

[18]Ritschl, *Christian Doctrine*, 3:207.

[19]Ibid., 207, 225.

[20]J. H. W. Stuckenberg, "The Theology of Albrecht Ritschl," *American Journal of Theology* 2 (1899): 276.

[21]Bruce, "Theological Agnosticism," 4.

[22]A. C. McGiffert, *Christianity as History and Faith* (New York: Scribner, 1934), 145.

[23]William Adams Brown, *The Essence of Christianity* (New York: Scribner, 1902), 257.

[24]James Orr, *Ritschlianism: Expository and Critical Essays* (London: Hodder and Stoughton, 1903), 8.

[25]Adolf von Harnack, *What Is Christianity?* (New York: Putnam, 1902), 131.

[26]Brown, *Essence of Christianity*, 260–61.

[27]Orr, *Expository Essays*, 63.

[28]McGiffert, *Christianity as History and Faith*, 176.

[29]The restriction of religious knowledge to the person of Jesus Christ was arbitrary. No attempt was made to show how or why Jesus had received a special knowledge of God. Rather, it was an a priori assumption (Stuckenberg, "The Theology of Ritschl," 276–77).

[30]McGiffert, *Christianity as History and Faith*, 177–78.

[31]The German term for "history of religions," *Religionsgeschichte*, is also frequently used.

[32]Ibid., 147.

[33]Ibid., 129. Cf. McGiffert, *Christianity as History and Faith*, 120. "But again when we assert our faith in the Lordship of Jesus, we declare that his moral standards and principles are the highest known to us, and we believe that they are the moral standards and principles of God himself.... This was Jesus' ethical message to the world: 'Ye are all brethren,' 'Thou shalt love thy neighbor as thyself.' "

[34]Harnack, *What Is Christianity?* 186. Italics in original.

[35]Henry Drummond, *Ascent of Man* (New York: James Pott, 1894), 334.

[36]Friedrich Schleiermacher, *On Religion* (London: Paul, Trench, Trübner, 1893), 88.

[37]Nancey Murphy incisively compares the question of religious authority in liberalism and fundamentalism in her *Beyond Liberalism and Fundamentalism* (Valley Forge, PA: Trinity Press International, 1996), 11–35.

[38]Walter Rauschenbusch, *A Theology for the Social Gospel* (New York: Macmillan, 1917), 5.

[39]Ibid., 202. This insistence on the unity of God and creation led to a panentheism, which at times became out and out pantheism (Bernard Ramm, "The Fortunes of Theology from Schleiermacher to Barth," in *Tensions in Contemporary Theology*, ed. Stanley N. Gundry and Alan F. Johnson [Grand Rapids: Baker, 1976], 19).

[40]J. Gresham Machen, *Christianity and Liberalism*, reprint (Grand Rapids: Eerdmans, 1977), 65. Obviously Machen used *pagan* in the broad sense of *nonreligious*, not in the sense in which it has come to be used in recent decades to refer to a religious approach with a specific content (also referred to as neopaganism).

[41]This image was originally used to describe the work of Harnack. It has been extended by usage to the method of nineteenth-century liberalism and has attained the status of a virtual aphorism. See George Tyrrell, *Christianity at the Crossroads* (London: Longmans, Green, 1909), 44.

[42]Charles A. Briggs, *The Fundamental Christian Faith* (New York: Scribner, 1913), 267.

[43]Adolf von Harnack, *What Is Christianity?* (New York: Putnam, 1902), 234.

[44]A. C. McGiffert, *Christianity as History and Faith*, 107.

[45]Harnack, *What Is Christianity?* 12.

[46]Ibid.

[47]Ibid., 11.

[48]Ibid., 34.

[49]Ibid., 132. McGiffert asserted of Jesus' kingdom mission: "The secret of Christ's permanent hold upon the world is largely this, that he saw visions loftier, more compelling and more enduring than those seen by other men before or since.... Jesus brought the vision of a divine Father who careth even for the meanest" (McGiffert, *Christianity as History and Faith*, 235).

[50]Harnack, *What Is Christianity?* 131. Italics in original.

[51]Ibid., 131.

[52]Ibid. Cf. McGiffert, *Christianity as History and Faith*, 118, 306–7.

[53]McGiffert, *Christianity as History and Faith*, 111.

OUTLINE OF CHAPTER 15

A. The Background of Neoorthodoxy

1. The Post-Kantian Environment
   a. The Untenable Liberal Optimism
   b. The Marginalization of the Bible
2. Theology at Loggerheads: Liberalism and Fundamentalism

B. Neoorthodoxy: A Reaction against Liberalism

1. Karl Barth
   a. Education
   b. Pastorate (1911–21)
   c. *Der Römerbrief* (1918, 1922)
   d. Break with Liberalism
   e. Christian Dogmatics in Outline (1927)
   f. Church Dogmatics (1932–68)
   g. Anselm's Influence
   h. Conflict with Natural Theology
2. Emil Brunner
3. Reinhold Niebuhr
4. Dietrich Bonhoeffer

C. The Neoorthodox Theological Perspective

1. Theological Method: Dialectic
2. God: The Wholly Other
3. Revelation and Encounter
4. Rejection of Natural Theology
5. Christology
6. Biblical Realism
7. The Biblical Theology Movement
8. Revelation in History

D. Observations and Critique

1. Contributions of Neoorthodoxy
2. Critique

CHAPTER 15

NEOORTHODOXY

A. THE BACKGROUND OF NEOORTHODOXY

The theological movement known most popularly as neoorthodoxy arose in the 1920s as a reaction to liberalism. While not a cohesive system, it has been a powerful corrective to the liberal theology ultimately grounded in the Enlightenment. Certain major themes have been embraced by all who fall within the neoorthodox camp, such as the radical transcendence of God, innate human sinfulness, christocentricity, the supernatural character of salvation, and God's Word as the source and center of true theology.

1. The Post-Kantian Environment

As seen in chapter 14, a radical shift in worldview and thinking took place in the wake of Kant, whose thought cut humans off from any rational knowledge of God. Until then, theology had been centered around the rational. Now, following in the steps of Friedrich Schleiermacher, the center became the affect/feeling, and the task became an exposition of man's religious experience.

a. The Untenable Liberal Optimism

Liberalism was engulfed in optimism about life and the future. Hegel's dialectic had worked its way into both the popular and the scholarly mind, and the notion of progress was the order of the day. Humanity had advanced beyond the barbarism and immorality that had characterized the past. "Every day in every way we are getting better and better" had become the watchword of the nineteenth and early twentieth centuries. Humans were no longer encumbered by such ideas as an Augustinian understanding of depravity. On the contrary, they were perfectible, since God was working himself out in history. Humanity was not perfect—not yet. But given the influence of the immanent God in creation and the birth of modern science as a means to truth, perfection was within humanity's grasp.

b. The Marginalization of the Bible

In the nineteenth century, a curious phenomenon arose with reference to the Bible. It became the object of intense study in a way never seen before. The Enlightenment had loosened the ties between Scripture and revelation and freed it from the hands of the theologians as a sourcebook of dogmatic proof texts. Yet because it was now viewed as a historic document like any other, the Bible was open to criticism and verification. Thus the nineteenth century saw a radical reinterpretation of the history of the Bible at the hands of antisupernaturalistic critics. The Old Testament was subjected to critical study that concluded, among other things, that Moses did not write the Pentateuch. Rather, it was redacted late in Israel's history from earlier documents whose contents (and existence) were posited largely by analysis of which divine name was used in a particular section of text to refer to God (the "Documentary Hypothesis" or the "JEDP theory").[1] Likewise, Isaiah had been written by at least two authors, the book of Daniel was intertestamental in origin, and so on.

In the New Testament, critical study gave birth to numerous successive "lives of Jesus" that sought to get back to the historical man Jesus who lay behind the presentation of the gospel texts. F. C. Baur applied the Hegelian dialectic to the New Testament and concluded that there was a *thesis*, Petrine Christianity; an *antithesis*, Pauline Christianity; and a *synthesis*, Johannine Christianity, which became dominant in the postapostolic church. Baur also concluded that many of Paul's epistles were not written by the apostle himself but were in fact written by the apostle's followers, with some epistles originating late in the second century. The text of Scripture was studied closely and avidly but as a historical document rather than as the Word of God. As a historical document, it lacked divine authority. It represented the evolving religious thinking of the Jews and the early church and thus provided no normative basis for theology.

Normativeness was posited in the person of Jesus and his teachings. This is seen on a popular level in the rise of the red-letter editions of the Bible. These editions were motivated by the belief that only the words of Jesus, the perfectly God-conscious man, had continuing authority.

Within this context, the Bible was lost to the theologians, and nineteenth-century theology was reduced to philosophy and anthropology. Theologians did not even take serious note of Scripture. It became foreign territory to them. Following in the wake of Kant, moralism became the watchword.

2. Theology at Loggerheads: Liberalism and Fundamentalism

During the Enlightenment, profound changes in thinking took root. Descartes is generally regarded as the father of the Enlightenment, but it is often not recognized that a profound split took place epistemologically in the wake of David Hume's skepticism. It is well remembered that Kant's epistemology of phenomenalism was developed in reaction to Hume (Hume awakened Kant "from his dogmatic slumbers"), but what is not generally remembered is that another stream also flowed in reaction to Hume, that of Thomas Reid and Scottish Common Sense. While modern theology (liberalism) had its epistemological basis in the Enlightenment epistemology of Kant, historic orthodoxy found a home in a different branch of the Enlightenment, that of Scottish Common Sense. (See figure 6.1 on page 187.)

Whereas liberalism reformulated the historic doctrines of the faith and became profoundly anthropocentric, the effect on orthodox theology, particularly in America, was much more subtle but nevertheless profound. Conservative Protestant orthodoxy did not reformulate doctrines in the sense that liberalism did and thus orthodoxy stood in explicit continuity with its heritage. However, the cast and mind-set of the theology that was done and even its theological method, especially the theology that came out of Princeton, took on a rationalistic and apologetic tone heretofore unknown in orthodox theology. While reacting against the Enlightenment, orthodoxy (particularly American orthodoxy) became captive to Enlightenment presuppositions of truth and reality. This bifurcation had a profound impact on the development of theological thought since these two models were built on two mutually exclusive paradigms of reality.

B. NEOORTHODOXY: A REACTION AGAINST LIBERALISM

The devastation of World War I quenched the naive optimism that had dominated the preceding generations. With millions dead in the trenches, the mantra of the "goodness of man" rang hollow. It was out of this context that protest against the theological climate of nineteenth-century Europe arose.

At the leading edge of this protest stood Karl Barth, a theologian who was thoroughly trained in philosophy and contemporary German theology, and who saw the impact that the Enlightenment had had on the modern world, both for good and for evil. Whereas liberal theology had capitulated to the Enlightenment mentality and lost the distinctive historic Christian proclamation, and fundamentalism had rejected the Enlightenment and had in large measure become obscurantist, Barth pioneered a third way. Barth neither rejected the Enlightenment outright nor accepted it wholesale. Rather, he probed the conclusions and utilized what he found to be valid, while rejecting what did not stand up under scrutiny.[2] Barth, together with Emil Brunner, pioneered a new theological movement called variously *dialectical theology*, *theology of crisis*, *neoorthodoxy*, or *Barthianism*, which served as a "wrecking crew" that demolished the reigning theological liberalism.[3]

Besides Barth and Brunner, there were significant representatives of a neoorthodox type of thought in the United States, most significantly Reinhold Niebuhr. Dietrich Bonhoeffer, a German, is often also placed within the matrix of this theological movement. Neoorthodoxy has its roots in the concrete political, social, and spiritual realities of the first half of the twentieth century, and it is for this reason that it is helpful to take a somewhat extended look at the life and thought of the four main theologians of the movement, especially Barth.

1. Karl Barth

a. Education

Karl Barth[4] is identified with the neoorthodoxy movement as well as being considered one of the greatest theologians in the history of the church with Augustine, Thomas Aquinas, John Calvin, Martin Luther, and Friedrich Schleiermacher. Some regard him as a modern church father, for his thought dominated the twentieth century. His prophetic voice went against the tide of a century of liberal Protestant theology and challenged the prevailing assumptions.

Karl Barth was born in Basel, Switzerland, in May 1886, the eldest son of a pastor in the Swiss Reformed Church who later taught at the University of Bern. The young Karl had an unusual intellect combined with seriousness of purpose, appreciation for the arts, and a developed sense of humor. His roots go deep into the Calvinistic wing of the Swiss Reformation. Both his grandfathers had been pastors in the Swiss Reformed Church. His brother Peter became the editor of Calvin's works, and two of his sons also went on to distinguished theological careers.

Barth's university studies followed a peripatetic path. He studied under his father at Bern, and there he became acquainted with the philosophy of Kant and the theology of Schleiermacher. He then wanted to go to Marburg to study under Wilhelm Herrmann, the leading neo-Kantian theologian of the day. However, his father's desire for more conservative training led him to Berlin, where he studied under the greatest of the liberal theologian-historians, Adolf von Harnack. He also studied at Tübingen for a semester under the conservative Swiss biblical theologian Adolf Schlatter. Finally, in 1908 he moved on to Marburg, where he spent three semesters studying under Herrmann, the professor he regarded as "the theological teacher of my student years."

In all this, Barth was thoroughly exposed to the reigning liberal theology and historical-critical methodology, but from his youth, he felt that these were unsatisfactory because they did not grapple with the subject matter of the text. In 1909, at age twenty-three, he completed his education and was ordained for ministry, serving for the next two years as an intern pastor in Geneva. He never pursued doctoral studies.

Karl Barth

Also in 1909, Barth published his first article in which he observed that the graduates of the liberal university faculties were more averse to pastoral ministries than the graduates of the more orthodox conservative and pietistic faculties. He attributed this phenomenon to two factors. First, the radical individualism of liberalism led to a rejection of all norms; and second, the "historical relativism" of the reigning historicism led to a denial of absolutes and of revelation. The net effect was that the Bible was stripped of any normative quality. Of the liberal approach, he observed, "Religion knows only individual values; history knows only general truths."[5] Already ten years before his epoch-making *Römerbrief*, one sees the questioning of the liberalism in which he had been trained.

b. Pastorate (1911–21)

From 1911 to 1921 Barth was the pastor of a small church in the village of Safenwil, Switzerland, near the French and German borders. He found that as he preached from week to week, he increasingly had nothing to say to his congregation. Within earshot of the big guns, talk of the goodness of man rang hollow. He was forced back to the Bible, where he found a "strange new world," one that his theology professors had never told him about. He discovered a God who was transcendent over creation as opposed to the anthropotheism he had learned in his theological training.

During these years, through the influence of his friend Eduard Thurneysen, he studied the eschatological theology of the German pietistic pastor

Johann Christoph Blumhardt. Blumhardt's theology focused on the in-breaking of the kingdom of God into history and the victory over the forces of darkness and evil. This theology had social implications, and both Barth and Thurneysen became Christian socialists, noting that socialism was a parallel concept to the kingdom of God.

Also during these years, liberalism came under a cloud when ninety-three German intellectuals, including several of Barth's former professors, signed a document endorsing the war policy of the kaiser. As World War I raged on, Barth became convinced of the bankruptcy of liberal theology and turned to the Bible.

> It is not the right human thoughts about God which form the content of the Bible, but the right divine thoughts about men. The Bible tells us not how we should talk with God but what he says to us; not how we find the way to him, but how he has sought and found the way to us; not the right relation in which we must place ourselves to him, but the covenant which he has made with all who are Abraham's spiritual children and which he has sealed once and for all in Jesus Christ. It is this, which is within the Bible. The world of God is within the Bible.[6]

It was while in Safenwil that Barth formulated what was to become the great theological revolution of the early twentieth century. Under the demands of pastoral ministry, he came face-to-face with "the need and the promise of Christian preaching." In 1922 he addressed a group of pastors and described the context of his personal theological revolution.

> For twelve years I was a minister, as all of you are. I had my theology. It was not really mine, to be sure, but that of my unforgotten teacher, Wilhelm Herrmann [*sic*], grafted on principles I had learned, less consciously than unconsciously, in my native home—princes of those Reformed Churches which today I represent and am honored to represent in an official capacity. Once in the ministry, I found myself growing away from those theological habits of thought and being forced back at every point more and more upon the specific *minister's* problem, the *sermon*. I sought to find my way between the problem of human life on the one hand and the content of the Bible on the other. As a minister I wanted to speak to the *people* in the infinite contradiction of their life, but to speak no less the message of the *Bible*, which was as much of a riddle as life.[7]

c. Der Römerbrief *(1918, 1922)*

In 1918 Barth completed a commentary on the book of Romans, the first edition of his famous *Der Römerbrief.* After some difficulty he finally found a small publisher who printed one thousand copies. Barth acknowledged the validity of the historical-critical method but at the same time affirmed that the traditional Protestant understanding of inspiration operated at a level that sought to understand the meaning of the text. In this he broke with liberal methodology, which focused on philology and historical study, to look "beyond history into the spirit of the Bible, which is the Eternal Spirit."[8]

While this first edition signaled in fact a revolution in theological thinking, the revolution was not yet complete. Barth was still heavily influenced by Platonic and idealistic forms. But when a second edition of *Der Römerbrief* appeared four years later, it "fell like a bomb on the playground of the theologians."[9] By this time Barth was teaching Reformed theology at Göttingen, Germany. He was becoming more convinced of the eschatological nature of Christianity, was studying more of Plato, was introduced to Fyodor Dostoevsky's works, and perhaps most important, came under the influence of Søren Kierkegaard. From Kierkegaard Barth obtained his characteristic theological methodology: the dialectic, the paradox, decision, and crisis. Barth noted:

> If I have a system, it is limited to a recognition of what Kierkegaard called the "infinite qualitative distinction" between time and eternity, and to my regarding this as possessing negative as well as positive significance: "God is in heaven and thou art on earth." The relation between such a God and such a man, and the relation between such a man and such a God, is for me the theme of the Bible and the essence of philosophy. Philosophers name this *krisis* of human perception—the Prime Cause: the Bible beholds at the same crossroads—the figure of Jesus Christ.[10]

Thus, by the time the second edition was published, Barth's personal theological revolution was complete. All traces of the liberal continuity between God and man had disappeared.

What Barth represents at this point is a return to the Augustinian heritage of traditional Reformation theology. While Kierkegaard introduced him to dialectical methodology, Barth ultimately became convinced that this was the method of the Reformers and of Paul. By now he had become convinced that all theology was in a manner of speaking a dialogue between God and man, speech and response, question and answer. The ultimate source of the dialectic was to be found in the incarnation, the God-man, Jesus Christ. He also came to recognize that all theology is fragmentary and fuzzy. Theology is a human activity, a human word. And no human word can with fullness of fidelity express divine truth. Only God himself can accomplish this task.

d. Break with Liberalism

Beginning in 1922, the now maturing Barth could confidently disavow the liberalism in which he had been trained. With reference to Schleiermacher (whose portrait, along with that of Mozart, hung on the wall of his study throughout his life), he could say: "With all due respect to the genius shown in his work, I cannot consider Schleiermacher a good teacher in the realm of theology, because, so far as I can see, he is disastrously dim-sighted in regard to the fact that man as man is not only in need but beyond all hope of saving himself."[11]

While the phrase "theology of crisis" is one of the epithets used for neo-orthodoxy, Barth himself noted that "theology could not and ought not to be a 'theology of crisis' for longer than a moment."

During the next several years, Barth and several other young theologians of like mind established a journal called *Zwischen den Zeiten* (*Between the Times*) to provide a forum for the exposition of biblical theology and to oppose the liberal version of the gospel. The journal continued until 1933, the year of Hitler's rise to power. Being in Germany but of Swiss nationality, he experienced relative freedom to speak. Originally Barth believed that national Socialism was irrelevant to the Christian as long as the freedom of the gospel was maintained. Later he rejected this view, seeing that neutrality was not possible, and he began to speak out vigorously against Nazism. Barth and Bonhoeffer were the major contributors to the Barmen Declaration of 1934, written for the Confessing Church. The Confessing Church (*Bekennende Kirche*) consisted of Christians who were opposed to Nazism, unlike the majority of the church, who as German Christians (*Bewegung Deutsche Christen*) supported Hitler and national Socialism. When Barth refused to take an oath of allegiance to the Führer, he was removed from his position. He returned to Basel, where he taught theology from 1935 until his retirement in 1962. These years were filled with the anxiety of the constant preparation of daily lectures. During this time, Barth mastered the Reformed tradition and gained a new appreciation for its richness. The discovery of Heinrich Heppe's *Reformed Dogmatics* transformed his earlier negative evaluation of Reformed scholasticism.

> I read, I studied, I reflected; and found that I was rewarded with the discovery that here at last I was in the atmosphere which the road, by way of the Reformers to Holy Scriptures, was a more sensible and natural one to tread than the atmosphere, now only all too familiar to me, of the theological literature determined by Schleiermacher and Ritschl. I found a dogmatic which had both form and substance, oriented upon the central indication of the Biblical evidences for revelation, which it also managed to follow out in detail with astonishing richness.[12]

e. Christian Dogmatics in Outline (1927)

In 1927 Barth produced his *Christian Dogmatics in Outline*, in which he took a position opposed to both Roman Catholicism and liberalism, because both of these allowed for the possibility of natural theology. He also rejected any metaphysics or philosophy as the starting point for theological method. He insisted that theology must be grounded in the Word of God alone, as addressed to man. At this early stage of the dogmatics, he conceived of the Word in its threefold form: the revealed (incarnate) Word, the written Word, and the proclaimed Word. He was adamant that the Word of God could never be domesticated under human control, for it is not a human possession. Theology is not grounded in Schleiermacher's *Gefühl* but in the Word of God; nor is it an exposition of human experience of faith. Rather, it has priority over human faith. Revelation comes through Jesus Christ alone as the revealed Word of God. But to apprehend the objective Word of God, what is required is the Spirit, the subjective possibility of revelation. Barth conceives of the Trinity as the framework that opposes all natural and anthropocentric theology. If anyone espouses a natural theology, he or she must show that this theology is in fact Trinitarian, for it is in Trinitarian fullness that God reveals himself.

When it comes to the human reception of the Word, Barth was less than clear. It appears that his concern was to assert that it is God the Holy Spirit who enables people to hear and respond to the Word when they encounter it. In this volume of prolegomena, he still spoke existentially about man's hearing the Word.

f. Church Dogmatics (1932–68)

Upon reflection Barth concluded that the *Christian Dogmatics* he had begun needed to be scrapped because it was too heavily existential. He began anew under the title of *Church Dogmatics*, the project that would occupy him for the rest of his life. As he reworked the first volume, he "cut out in this second issue of the book everything that in the first issue might give the slightest appearance of giving to theology a basis, support, or even a mere justification in the way of existential philosophy."[13] By so doing, he sought to avoid the trap of existentialism while escaping from the anthropocentrism of liberal idealism.

Barth recognized that all theologians come to their task with a worldview and presuppositions. He was not opposed to philosophy or its use in theological study. The issue was how it was used. In particular he pointed out the danger of theologians ceasing to be aware of the manner in which the philosophy they use affects their interpretation of the gospel. Because of this danger, Barth consciously tried to minimize the dangers that arise from a rigid adherence to any particular worldview by adopting the biblical thought form or perspective. In so doing he attempted to reproduce the thought form of the apostles and prophets. For him the controlling factor in all thinking and speaking must be the Word of God. If the Word dominates, then all other elements, including philosophy, will be subservient to the rightful center of theology, the Word of God. In this he eschewed and rejected an apologetic approach that assumed that God could be somehow known without beginning with God. This leads to a confessional methodology and in fact is reflected in the very title *Church Dogmatics.* With reference to philosophy, Barth noted, "All things are lawful for me, but nothing [save the Word of God] shall take me captive."[14]

Another aspect of Barth's thought that deserves notice is his christocentrism. This emphasis grew increasingly over the decades. Volume 2 of the *Dogmatics* reveals the increased christological focus in his thinking. In fact, his detractors at times accused him of christomonism.

g. Anselm's Influence

Another influence on Barth during these years was the work of Anselm of Canterbury. In 1930 Barth gave a seminar titled *Cur Deus Homo?* (*Why Did God Become Man?*) a study that precipitated an examination of Anselm's theological method. This investigation resulted in a book, *Anselm: Fides Quaerens Intellectum* (*Faith Seeking Understanding*). Of this study he observed late in life:

> The deepening [of my theological position] consisted in this: in these years I have had to rid myself of the last remnants of a philosophical, i.e., anthropological (in America one says "humanistic" or "naturalistic") foundation and exposition of Christian doctrine. The real docu-

> ment of this farewell is in truth, not the much read ... *Nein*, directed against Brunner in 1934, but rather the book about the evidence for God of Anselm of Canterbury which appeared in 1931. Among all my books I regard this as the one written with the greatest satisfaction. And yet in America it is doubtless not read at all and in Europe it certainly is the least read of any of my works.[15]

Anselm provided what he considered to be an adequate theological method. As David Mueller says in his biography of Barth, "Anselm taught Barth how theology should be done."[16] The crucial question for Barth here is "How can we move from faith to theology?" Anselm held that the very nature of faith sought understanding, and faith in fact summons one to knowledge. But this faith is not the existential "incipient doubt."

> Faith is the right act of the will if it is that which is owed to God and demanded by God, and bound together with a saving "experience"; that is, in so far as it is faith in God, in so far as it believes that which is true. Faith comes from hearing, and hearing comes from preaching. Faith is related to the "Word of Christ" and it is not faith if it is not the reception, that is, knowledge and acknowledgment of the "Word of Christ."[17]

Reflecting Anselm, Barth explains that at the initial level faith does comprehend a certain level of intellectual knowledge, a knowledge to which even the unbeliever may attain. But it does not stop here. Faith moves beyond this to a second level, affirming the reality behind the words. Thus faith stands at the beginning and the end of the quest, from faith to faith, but in such a manner that the quest for understanding is a quest for sight, which ultimately will be revealed eschatologically.

Anselm's influence over Barth was profound. It signaled an oft-overlooked shift away from the radical dialectic that characterized his earlier statements to a recognition that theology could be based on analogy. That is, human knowledge of God (coming through faith) is in some measure, however incomplete, conformable to God by divine grace.

h. Conflict with Natural Theology

Another aspect of Barth's thought that needs to be noted is his rejection of natural theology. The confrontation between Barth and his colleague and friend Emil Brunner over this issue is legendary. Brunner acknowledged the possibility of a natural revelation and hence a natural theology based on that revelation. To place this exchange in context, one must understand that it was at the time of the rise of Nazism. Barth feared that to allow any place for natural theology was to allow place for the program of the "German Christians" (with their liberal theological agenda that had identified God with the social program of the German state) and to compromise the supremacy of the final revelation of God in Jesus Christ. Barth's response to Brunner was entitled *Nein!* So emphatic was it that it severed their heretofore close friendship. This breach remained unhealed till near the end of their lives.

- - -

A year and a half before Barth's death, in the preface to the final fragment of his *Dogmatics*, "Baptism as the Foundation of the Christian Life," he wrote:

> Today there is much ready talk (too much and too ready) about the world which is supposed to have come of age in relation to God. However that may be, my own concern is rather with man who ought to come of age in relation to God and the age of the world, i.e., the mature Christian and mature Christianity, its thought, speed and action in responsibility to God, in living hope in Him, in service to the world, in free confession and unceasing prayer.[18]

Upon Barth's passing, Thomas Torrance summed up Barth's life: "God took him home to his rest in the early hours of December 10, 1968, the great Church Father of Evangelical Christendom, the one genuine Doctor of the Evangelical Church the Modern era has known."

2. Emil Brunner

Born in December 1889 near Zurich, Emil Brunner was educated at the University of Zurich and thereafter in Berlin, where he received his Ph.D. in 1913. He embarked on a career as a pastor and served a small congregation in the mountain village of Obstalden. After three years, he took off a year for advanced studies at Union Seminary, New York, after which he resumed his pastoral duties. In 1924 he was called to the chair of systematic and practical theology at the University of Zurich. He made frequent lecture tours on the Continent, in England, and in the United States. During 1939–40 he was visiting professor at Princeton. He continued at Zurich until 1953 when he spent two years in Japan aiding in the establishment of the International Christian University in Tokyo. On his return journey from Japan, he suffered a cerebral hemorrhage that left him permanently impaired. Despite physical handicaps, he continued to write for another eleven years until his death in 1965.

Brunner's thought developed independently of Karl Barth's but along a similar trajectory. His lineage had deep roots in the Reformation heritage, going back through "an unbroken line of farmers" to the era of the Reformation. He imbibed deeply of the Swiss democratic tradition as well as of his Reformation heritage. During his formative years, the Socialist movement arrived in Switzerland from Germany and gave Brunner a sensitivity for the industrial masses.

It was under the influence of Blumhardt that Brunner was shaped in his christocentric socialistic perspective and the dialectical method that characterized his thought throughout his life. Brunner became convinced that dialectical theology had its origin in the reality of the Holy Spirit as opposed to any philosophical or theological system of thought. The basic direction of Brunner's thought was already established before he ever encountered Karl Barth. In fact, he considered Barth's *Römerbrief* a confirmation of his own thinking.

Emil Brunner

Brunner, Barth, and their mutual friend and fellow Swiss theologian Eduard Thurneysen all began a study of Luther, which he described as "incredible joy and enthusiasm."[19] Later these three focused on the works of Calvin "with less joy but equal reverence." What is significant is that this small group agreed that the essential insights of the biblical message had been recovered ever so briefly by the first-generation Reformers, but that this message had again been at least blurred, if not actually lost, in subsequent generations. Brunner continued to have great admiration for the Reformers, and their perspectives can be seen underpinning and running beneath the surface of his theology. However, he was not an uncritical fan of Calvin and Luther, and he saw any authority that they possessed as contingent on their faithfulness to biblical revelation.

Two other important factors influenced Brunner. The first was the Oxford Group Movement (later known as Moral Rearmament), which revitalized the church and theology. While cautious of the excesses of the group, he felt that they had recovered an aspect of the New Testament church that had been lost for the majority of the church's history. He observed that for the first time he was aware of "the close connection between spiritual reality and fellowship or communion."[20] The second factor was the "I-Thou" philosophy associated with the name of the German-Jewish religious philosopher Martin Buber. Buber's thought was in turn based on Kierkegaard and, in Brunner's understanding, on the Scriptures themselves. It was the "I-Thou" category that allowed Brunner to express his anthropology from a new perspective rather than being trapped in the traditional subject-object (I-it) relationship. Expressing his anthropological insights in the context of relationship, of man as a responsible being before God, he extended these insights to the realm of truth itself. He concluded that the biblical concept of truth involved encounter. He particularly insisted that one could not understand the gospel apart from an "I-Thou" encounter with God. It was out of this understanding that his characteristic "truth as encounter" arose. This concept became the "lodestone" of his theological thinking from 1938 onward.

In Brunner's publication of *Nature and Grace: A Discussion with Karl Barth* and Barth's heated reply—*Nein!*—Brunner would allow for natural theology and the continuance of the image of God in fallen humanity whereas Barth would not. This falling-out with Barth in fact served to broaden Brunner's influence as he reached out to new contexts, focusing on the spiritual rather than the institutional nature of the church founded firmly on the biblical witness rather than the anthropotheism of liberal theology.

Brunner's thought, like Barth's, evinced a high Christology, but with this difference: Brunner's emphasis was on the personal encounter with Jesus as the centerpiece of the Christian faith. Flowing from this was an ethical perspective that attempted to retain the tension between individual liberty and life in community. To this was added the concept of the church as a dynamic fellowship based on individual existence in Christ rather than on the external organization. Brunner's greatest and most lasting contribution has been his insistence that God can be known only through personal encounter. Truth about Christ is not to be discovered in discussions about his nature but in the living encounter with him.

Brunner also restated for the twentieth century the doctrines of sin, the incarnation, and the resurrection, insisting on the centrality of Jesus Christ and the necessity of personal relationship with him. Furthermore, he was instrumental in helping to reestablish Scripture as normative for faith and practice in the church.

Brunner's literary output, like Barth's, was prolific. Brunner was more moderate and had a clarity and preciseness of style that eluded Barth. It was Brunner who first introduced neoorthodoxy to the English-speaking world, where he spent far more time than did Barth. He wrote a total of 396 books and scholarly articles, many of which remain in print to this day.

3. Reinhold Niebuhr

During the early to mid-twentieth century, the most influential American theologian was arguably Reinhold Niebuhr (1893–1971). Although he considered himself primarily an ethicist rather than a formal theologian, his work had a profound influence in America, challenging the reigning optimistic liberal theology with its doctrine of the innate goodness of man.

Niebuhr was born in 1893. The son of an immigrant minister of a German-speaking Lutheran church, he was influenced by his father's example to enter the ministry. After attending Eden Theological Seminary, he went on to Yale Divinity School for further study. He drank deeply of the liberal theology of the day. Rather than pursuing doctoral studies, he accepted a call to a pastoral ministry in Detroit, where he served for thirteen years. Although a successful pastor who saw his congregation grow from thirteen families to a membership of over eight hundred, he found the liberal theology in which he had been trained impotent to meet the challenges that confronted him in pastoral ministry. He developed an overwhelming concern for social and political ethics, particularly in the context of the newly emerging automobile industry.

Reinhold Niebuhr

In 1928 Niebuhr left the pastoral ministry to become a professor at Union Seminary in New York City. He was deeply influenced by both Kierkegaard and Barth but decried the failure of both men to deal adequately with ethical questions. His first major work, *Moral Man in an Immoral Society*, appeared in 1932.[21] This was followed by *The Nature and Destiny of Man* (The Gifford Lectures at Edinburgh of 1939, published in 1941 and 1943). Other works followed later, but it was *The Nature and Destiny of Man* that was his theological magnum opus.

Although raised in the cradle of liberal theology, brought up on the writings of Harnack at home, and nurtured in the liberalism of Yale, what he discovered in the pastorate and saw of the working conditions of his parishioners caused him to disavow liberalism as a theological system. He became an advocate of what came to be known as *Christian realism*. He repudiated his former commitment to the goodness of man, arguing instead that man and social groups were inherently self-serving. The overriding question in Niebuhr's thinking was, "How shall man think of himself?" His methodology in addressing this topic was dialectical, reflecting the influence of Barth and Brunner. Humanity was free and bound, both limited and limitless. Man was sinner and saint, subject to the social forces of history yet shaper of those forces, creature of the Creator yet potential lord of creation. In typical neo-orthodox fashion, the cross became the greatest of paradoxes, the place where powerlessness was transformed into power, where love operating in justice overcame the sinful forces of the world.

As stated above, *The Nature and Destiny of Man* is Niebuhr's magnum opus. In it he states for the American community his Christian vision of humanity. He compares his vision—a vision based on Scripture, Augustine, and the Reformers—with competing visions of humanity. He holds that man is a problem even to himself. Non-Christian views are problematic, since their viewpoints are limited in that they tend to define humanity reductionistically. In so doing, they ignore major aspects of human existence. When man is seen as basically *mind* or *rationality*, his involvement with nature is neglected. When viewed only as a creature, his self-consciousness and self-transcendence are neglected. Niebuhr argues that Scripture sees man as a unity of body and spirit, of freedom and creatureliness.

Again in opposition to liberalism, Niebuhr posited the radical evil in humanity. He decried the "easy conscience of modern man." He asserted the inherent contradiction of man as existing in the image of God yet being a radical sinner. His explanation is Augustinian at its core, seeing the image as the self-consciousness and self-transcendence of the whole self. Thus man as the image is finite and free. It is the fact that he is the image of God that tempts him to "play God" and make himself the center of all things.[22] Following in the Protestant tradition, Niebuhr asserted that even in a regenerated state, man continues to display sinful and egotistical behavior.

His doctrine was in a sense a synthesis of the Renaissance and Reformation understanding of man. Speaking existentially, he held that man in history stands before the ever-new possibilities of good and evil. This reflected the Renaissance optimism, yet the power of sin was ever present to infect even the best of human endeavors. This synthesis led him to the twin conclusions of tolerance and social justice as core values for society. He argued that man could have truth without ultimate Truth. As an ethicist, he argued that humankind can achieve a valid society of law and justice while recognizing that the achievement of these true virtues always falls short of the kingdom of God.

4. Dietrich Bonhoeffer

Dietrich Bonhoeffer is associated with many streams of thought in twentieth-century theology; and in the eyes of many, he stands as a modern martyr for the cause of Christ. Born in 1906, Bonhoeffer was the son of a prominent psychiatrist and neurologist. He studied philosophy and theology at both Berlin and Tübingen. Schooled in the tradition of nineteenth-century liberal theology, Bonhoeffer was a student of Harnack, Deissmann, and Seeberg. However, he rejected the immanentism of liberalism and espoused many themes similar to Karl Barth. After his graduation from university, he was ordained a Lutheran pastor and served a congregation in Barcelona. After this he also spent time as a student at Union Seminary in New York City. Unimpressed by American (liberal) theology, he returned to Germany and accepted an appointment as professor of theology at Berlin.

Dietrich Bonhoeffer

Early in his career, Bonhoeffer became increasingly alarmed at the nazification of the church in Germany. He cooperated with Barth in composing the Barmen Declaration (1934) and became a leader of the Confessing Church. The Confessing Church was that portion of the (Lutheran) state church that opposed both the Nazi program and the "German Christians" who had acquiesced in the Aryan Clauses that imposed Nazi ideology (including anti-Semitism) on the German church. In 1936 Bonhoeffer was ousted from his position in Berlin and pastored for two years in London. He returned to Germany to oversee an underground seminary for the Confessing Church. During a lecture tour of the United States, Bonhoeffer was invited to join the faculty of Union Seminary, but after wrestling with God in prayer over the decision, he believed that his call was to return to Germany and resist the evil of Nazism and Hitler. He expressed his heart in a letter to Reinhold Niebuhr.

> It was a mistake for me to come to America. I have to live through this difficult period in our nation's history with Christians in Germany. Will have no right to participate in the reconstruction of Christian life in Germany after the war if I do not share the tribulations of this time with my people.... Christians in Germany are faced with the fearful alternatives either of willing their country's defeat so that Christian civilization may survive, or willing its victory and destroying our civilization. I know which of the two alternatives I have to choose, but I cannot make the choice from a position of safety.[23]

Bonhoeffer's conviction of the evil of Nazism led him to become involved in a plot to assassinate Hitler. This plot was uncovered, and Bonhoeffer was arrested. At the age of thirty-nine, just days before the fall of the Third Reich, Bonhoeffer was hanged for treason. He stands as a genuine modern martyr for the Christian faith.

Bonhoeffer's thought and contribution to theology have been controversial and much debated. He was not a systematic thinker. Rather, he was characterized by a creative and critical mind. Many of the radical theologies claim him as their inspiration. Bonhoeffer is seen by some as the fountainhead of the secular theologies and the radical movements of the 1960s, and even as the inspiration for the "death of God" movement. Often he would put forth an idea and speculate about it, then leave it without ever having worked through the implications. His death at such an early age cut short any potential development of the enigmatic themes and also potential long-term theological contributions. "Cheap grace," "worldly Christianity," and "religionless Christianity" in "a world come of age" are phrases that echo Bonhoeffer and have taken on a life of their own. His provocative thought has fired the imaginations of others to provoke such movements as ecumenism, death of God theology, liberation theology, and Christian resistance to political oppression.

In continuity with Barth, Bonhoeffer had no use for "religion" as such. He regarded traditional religion as idolatrous. Bonhoeffer's thought centered around the reality of the transcendent God in Jesus Christ and the fact that the church became a continuing presence of the revelation of God in the world insofar as it is the vehicle for revealing Jesus Christ to the world. What is important is a personal encounter with God in Jesus Christ.

C. THE NEOORTHODOX THEOLOGICAL PERSPECTIVE

1. Theological Method: Dialectic

The theological method associated with neoorthodoxy is the dialectic. Both Barth and Brunner arrived at this methodology independently of each other and ultimately grounded the method in Scripture itself. The method assumes that an infinite qualitative difference exists between God and humanity and that truth cannot be stated in a merely analogical manner. Rather, it must be posed in a series of apparently paradoxical statements. Out of this opposition, truth is derived. Dialectical methodology is not new. It goes back ultimately to Socrates and was employed in the scholastic era by Peter Abelard in his *Sic et Non.* In the nineteenth century, Kierkegaard had employed the dialectic, believing that propositional truth was inadequate in the study of God. He insisted that truth about God was paradoxical and that opposite truths had to be held in tension.

Neoorthodoxy identified a number of paradoxes: God's absolute transcendence and his self-disclosure; Christ as the God-man; faith as a gift yet an act; humans as sinful yet free; and eternity entering time. The resolution of these paradoxes must not skirt the issues and avoid a crisis in faith. It is only as the crisis is faced head-on that faith rises above the paradox in a way that transcends rational explanation.

2. God: The Wholly Other

In radical contrast to the theological immanentism that characterized nineteenth-century liberal theology, the neoorthodox responded with a loud "No! Let God be God." Barth reportedly said, "You cannot speak about God by speaking about man in a loud voice." The neoorthodox insisted that God was wholly other, absolutely transcendent. For Barth in particular there was no point of contact within the created order. Here we find the "infinite qualitative distinction between God and man" reminiscent of Kierkegaard.[24] This emphasis on transcendence was a reaction to and a pendulum swing away from the anthropotheism of the nineteenth century. God cannot be captured by man or manipulated by him. God is free in himself, and even in his self-revelation, he does not cease to be free. Revelation comes only at divine discretion.

3. Revelation and Encounter

While neoorthodoxy rejected the liberal paradigm and affirmed the main tenets of historic orthodoxy, all neoorthodox theologians also rejected the fundamentalist and Reformed scholastic doctrine of the verbal inspiration of Scripture and its corollary, inerrancy. Scripture was the locus of divine revelation, not revelation itself. Coupled with this rejection of verbal inspiration was a rejection of the concept that revelation was propositional. One phrase often employed is that the Bible is "witness to revelation" rather than revelation itself. God revealed himself to the authors of Scripture, who in turn wrote about their encounter with God. As an individual reads the Scripture, God uses the text to reveal himself to the reader, at which point the text becomes the Word of God for the reader. In fact, this concept of revelation is very close to the traditional Protestant concept of illumination.

For Barth particularly and the neoorthodox theologians generally, the Bible was a thoroughly human book; it bore all the markings of humanity. It was human, fallible, and historically conditioned and was thus the legitimate object of critical study. But once critical study was done, the text still communicated a divine witness. Critical study of the provenance of the text could not destroy the divine witness.

To assert that the Bible was inerrant was to fall prey to a docetic bibliology that denied the essential humanity of the Scriptures. On this point, Barth was adamant. The first volume of the *Dogmatics* is dedicated to the proposition that the Bible is a fallible human book fully capable of error. Yet despite this starting point, Barth seldom if ever accused the Bible of actual error! So despite the theoretical foundation he laid, he treated the Bible as if it were verbally inspired, at least with reference to salvific issues.

Barth noted, "It is impossible that there should be a direct identity between the human word of Scripture and the word of God."[25] Such a view he labeled as docetic. Rather, "the prophets and apostles ... [are] real and therefore fallible men, even in their office, even when they speak and write God's revelation."[26] They are thus prone to error and even fall into error in writing Scripture. In spite of this fact, God condescends to speak through the text of the human fallible Scripture. The Bible becomes the word of God to the individual reading it in a moment of "crisis," that is, an existential encounter when he meets God in the pages of Scripture.

> Real revelation puts man in God's presence.... It is the revelation, which is attested to ourselves.... An objective revelation as such, a revelation which exists statically only in its sign-giving, in the objectivity of Scripture, preaching and sacrament, a revelation which does not penetrate to man: a revelation of this kind is an idol like all the rest, and perhaps the worst of idols.[27]

The identification between revelation and the text of Scripture is indirect rather than direct. God is free and sovereign even over the objective text of Scripture. "The Bible is God's Word to the extent God causes it to be His Word, to the extent he speaks through it."[28] God's Word is God himself communicating himself. It is not a communication of facts, mere information, but a self-communication of God.

Barth particularly rejected the idea of inerrancy, objecting that it set up a paper pope in place of the Roman papacy. He asserted, rather, that the text of Scripture is a medium through which God's voice is heard. Brunner used the illustration of the old RCA Victor trademark that pictured the dog tilting his head at the cone of the Victrola. Under the trademark was the phrase "His Master's Voice." Brunner's point was that despite the scratches, warps, dust, and imperfections of the record, the dog still recognized "his master's voice," and Christians too clearly recognize the voice of God in the text of Scripture despite the imperfections and even errors of the text.

Another illustration sees the Bible as a light bulb, while the Word of God is the light. The light (the Word of God) shines through the bulb (the Bible). The bulb is necessary; however, it is not the light; it is the medium for the light.

The neoorthodox understanding of the authority of Scripture steered a course between viewing the text as a totally human account of man's evolving religious convictions (liberalism) and a view of the nature of Scripture that denied the Bible any essential humanity (Reformed scholasticism and fundamentalism). In so doing, it came in for harsh criticism from both traditions, each of which accuses neoorthodoxy of being a crypto-representative of the opposing tradition.

4. Rejection of Natural Theology

The entire neoorthodox tradition rejected the concept of natural theology, whether it came under the guise of Thomistic Catholicism or liberalism. Instead, the Word of God was embraced as the source and norm of all theology. The radical transcendence of God as wholly other and absolutely free, coupled with the understanding that revelation is by definition redemptive, made the idea of general revelation impossible for Barth. To know God was to know him in his Trinitarian and redemptive fullness. Barth was the most extreme on this position. Brunner entertained the possibility that one could have a rudimentary, imperfect but real, knowledge of God that was not salvific. Brunner saw the existence of some indications of God (for example, the image of God in man) as remnants and reminders of God. Later in life Barth backed away from his original insistence that there was no possibility of general revelation, recognizing instead that while Jesus Christ was the Word of God and revelation par excellence, there were other "lesser lights" within the created order that pointed to God. Significantly, Barth refused to call these "lesser lights" revelation.

5. Christology

In its Christology, neoorthodoxy falls within the bounds of historic Chalcedonian orthodoxy: Jesus Christ, the God-man, fully human and fully divine. Barth affirms the virgin birth and titles the section on the incarnation "The Miracle of Christmas."

Barth maintains that the doctrine of the atoning death of Christ is objective: by his death, Jesus actually secured reconciliation of all humanity to God. So radically objective is Barth's view of the atonement that it contains the seeds of universalism. This position is one that Barth himself refused to affirm but that seemed to follow as a logical consequence from his presuppositions. Barth was, however, a dialectic theologian and was skeptical of the adequacy of traditional logic in arriving at truth.

Much debate and misunderstanding has surrounded the issue of whether the neoorthodox hold to the bodily resurrection of Christ. This question came from the use of the terms *Historie* and *Geschichte*[29] with reference to the resurrection. Both words mean "history," but *Historie* is the external aspect of history that involves the sequence of dates and events verifiable by modern antisupernaturalistic historiography, whereas *Geschichte* is the inner aspect, the meaning and significance of *Historie.* Early on, when confronted with this terminology, evangelicals concluded that Barth saw the resurrection in spiritual terms only. This, however, was a serious misreading of the case. Barth, as one schooled in historical criticism and modern historiography, knew that the canons of historical criticism ruled out the possibility of the resurrection since the canons of historical criticism rejected the possibility of miracles. An event was only properly considered "historical" *(Historie)* if it could be verified by the canons of historical criticism. As such, the resurrection fell outside the realm of the "historical." This did not mean that it did not happen in space and time. Barth was especially adamant about this fact.[30]

6. Biblical Realism

As noted above, in the United States the teaching of Reinhold Niebuhr was known as biblical realism. This realism represented a rejection of the liberal denial of sin and a reassertion of the radical nature of human sinfulness in a way that had not been seen since the Reformation.

The reigning presupposition of liberalism was that God and man stood in some sort of continuity. It was this assumption that Barth, Brunner, and Niebuhr all challenged with a vengeance. Rather than being innately good and ultimately perfectible, man stands in a state of rebellion and radical separation from his creator. He is in a state of helplessness and cannot save himself. In short, neoorthodoxy reaffirmed Augustinianism.

While evangelical theologians were content to reproduce the terminology and thought of previous generations, and had in many cases focused on sin as acts rather than as a heart issue, the neoorthodox made significant contributions to the doctrine of sin and its radical reality in the individual and in contemporary society.

7. The Biblical Theology Movement

The rise of the biblical theology movement in both America and Europe was fostered by and concurrent with the rise of neoorthodoxy and its reaction to liberalism. As such it shared the major presuppositions of neoorthodoxy. These included an understanding of revelation as centered in the person of Jesus Christ and the Bible as witness to that concrete historical revelation. As a movement, it was opposed to both classic liberalism and fundamentalism.

Barth was foundational in beginning the revolution in biblical studies with the publication of *Der Römerbrief.* By the 1930s several significant works appeared, including Walther Eichrodt's *Theology of the Old Testament* and Wilhelm Vischer's *The Witness of the Old Testament to Christ.* In the English-speaking world, the names of H. Wheeler Robinson and C. H. Dodd were among the most prominent early on.

Key to the biblical theology program was the understanding that the Bible must be understood "in its own categories" or "from within the world of the Bible" (see chapter 7). Consequently, worldview became vital, particularly the contrast between Hebrew and Greek thought. The movement also saw that although the Bible was written in Greek and Hebrew, the Hebrew worldview dominated both testaments. Out of this conviction arose myriad studies that showed that Hebrew thought patterns were reflected in the words of the Hebrew language and that Hebraic thought was also communicated through the koine Greek of the New Testament.

In contrast to the history of religions movement of liberalism that saw radical continuity between the ancient Hebrew cultures and the surrounding pagan cultures of the ancient Near East, the biblical theology movement emphasized the uniqueness of the biblical world. While there were some borrowings and similarities between Israel and its neighbors, the differences and uniqueness of Hebrew culture are far more remarkable than incidental points of contact. These differences were not posited on the basis of the faith of the theologians but on the basis of hard scientific historiography. The Bible's uniqueness was demonstrated by historical study and subjected to its norms.

8. Revelation in History

The key the biblical theology movement used to "unlock the Bible for a modern generation" and at the same time understand it theologically was "revelation in history." The Bible was seen as a unity, but that unity was not in allegory, typology, or even Christology. The unity was a unity in diversity, not a facile surface unity as had been presupposed by conservatives in the past. It was described variously as a "higher unity," a "kerygmatic unity," the unity of covenant relationship, or even the fundamental unity of history. H. H. Rowley described it as a "unity of divine revelation given in the context of history and through the medium of human personality."[31] This unity was held together by a revelation that occurred in history. This concept pitted the biblical theology movement on the one hand against fundamentalism, which held the Bible to be in essence a historical textbook of eternal truths and a deposit of true doctrine, and against liberalism on the other hand, which saw the Bible as containing only the human evolution of religious understanding. The concept of revelation as history also shifted the focus of revelation away from a propositional understanding and toward the neo-orthodox understanding of revelation as encounter without propositional content.

The biblical theology movement grew in influence in tandem with neoorthodoxy, reaching its height in the postwar years from 1945 to 1965. While the movement broke with the presuppositions of liberalism and insisted on the reality of a revelation in history, methodologically it still employed the tools of the historical-critical method popularized by liberal scholarship. Brevard Childs has noted the difficulty: "The historical-critical method is an inadequate method of studying the Bible as the Scriptures of the church," for it sets up "an iron curtain between the past and the present."[32]

Practitioners of the biblical theology movement recognized this problem. They were not interested in purely historical study for its own sake but maintained a vital interest in the theology of the text. They acknowledged, however, that the discipline was by its very nature descriptive. Krister Stendahl proposed a crucial distinction between "what the text meant" and "what it means" to the contemporary person.[33] This distinction has been widely adopted, but Gerhard Hasel has argued that this distinction struck a blow at the very heart of what the movement was trying to accomplish.[34]

Although the origins of the biblical theology movement are found in the work of Barth, and several significant assumptions are shared with neoorthodoxy, significant diversity existed among those who became associated with the movement. Many of these individuals could not legitimately be viewed as associated with neoorthodoxy. They include Rudolf Bultmann, Gerhard von Rad, Oscar Cullmann, Joachim Jeremias, H. H. Rowley, Alan Richardson, G. Ernest Wright, and John Bright, among others.

The biblical theology movement produced much material considered essential today in exegetical work. The most significant is the ten-volume *Theological Dictionary of the New Testament*, edited by Gerhard Kittel. In addition, the journal *Interpretation* and the *Biblical Commentary on the Old Testament* series launched in 1954 find their roots in the movement.

Today the biblical theology movement is dead, but biblical theology as a discipline is recognized as an essential part of the historical, linguistic, and literary study of Bible scholars from the conservative end of the scale to the liberal.

D. OBSERVATIONS AND CRITIQUE

1. Contributions of Neoorthodoxy

Reassertion of the centrality of Scripture. After a century of theological neglect and nearly two centuries of subjecting Scripture to the historical-critical method—a method that had from its inception been designed to strip Scripture of any revelational and therefore authoritative claim—the neoorthodox took the message of Scripture seriously.[35] In fact, Barth's *Church Dogmatics* contains more exegesis than any other systematic theology in church history. God was again to be heard in the pages of Scripture.

Reassertion of the transcendence of God. During the nineteenth century, the reigning concept of God had been one of radical immanence that had at many points crossed the line into panentheism and occasionally into full-blown pantheism. The neoorthodox assertion was a healthy corrective to the domestication of the historical process and to the equating of God with the progress of the German state. God was again rightly recognized as the transcendent sovereign Lord of creation who was holy and wholly other, not dependent on his creation in any way.

Reassertion of the reality and depth of sin. In contrast to the naive optimism of liberal theology, neoorthodoxy reasserted radical human depravity and sinfulness in such a stark way that it more faithfully reproduced the biblical, Augustinian, and Reformed witness than did even American evangelicalism, which claimed the Reformation as its heritage in opposition to liberalism.

Reassertion of the centrality of Christ. Whereas liberalism had viewed Christ as the perfectly God-conscious man, without any hint of ontological deity, the neoorthodox reasserted the historic doctrine of Jesus Christ as the

God-man of Chalcedonian orthodoxy. The incarnation became the central focus of neoorthodox thought, and the person and work of Christ became the unifying vision.

2. Critique

Radical transcendence. The great strength of the reassertion of divine transcendence also became a weakness. Neoorthodoxy was in part a reactionary movement, and as such it was subject to overstatement. Barth particularly, in his absolute disavowal of natural revelation, went beyond the biblical witness. It has been quipped that, for Barth, God got lost in outer space!

A truncated understanding of revelation. Particularly Barth, but also Brunner, disavowed the historic Protestant position of revelation as propositional, opting instead for a version of existentialism that viewed revelation as a personal encounter in which God communicates himself rather than information. A false dichotomy is operative here—revelation as personal *or* propositional. As noted above, although Barth argued vociferously for a fallible Bible, he treated it as if it were propositionally true.

The neoorthodox view of inspiration as articulated by Barth is on the one hand existential: the Bible becomes the word of God when God speaks through it to the individual. On the other hand, it is virtually identical to the Protestant doctrine of illumination.

Radical objectivity. An implicit universalism based on the radical understanding of the nature of the atonement runs through at least the work of Barth. While Barth refused to affirm or deny this universalism, it is hard to avoid this conclusion from a traditional logical analysis. This perception runs counter to historic orthodox understanding and ironically ultimately compromises human freedom.

Heavily contextualized in existentialism. Neoorthodoxy arose out of the Zeitgeist of the early twentieth century. It no longer speaks as powerfully to the culture as it once did. This is not to say that it is wrong; rather, it is a recognition that all theological systems and approaches have a limited life span. While neoorthodoxy's heyday was between the world wars and profoundly influenced the broader theological landscape at that time, during the latter half of the twentieth century, it influenced evangelicalism profoundly.

BIBLIOGRAPHY

Barth, Karl. *Dogmatics in Outline.* New York: Harper & Row, 1959. • ———. *Evangelical Theology.* Grand Rapids: Eerdmans, 1963. • **Bloesch, Donald G.**

Jesus Is Victor. Nashville: Abingdon, 1976. • **Bolich, Gregory G.** *Karl Barth and Evangelicalism.* Downers Grove, IL: InterVarsity Press, 1980. • **Bonhoeffer, Dietrich.** *Creation and Fall.* New York: Macmillan, 1959. • ———. *Ethics.* New York: Macmillan, 1955. • ———. *Letters and Papers from Prison.* New York: Macmillan, 1976. • ———. *Life Together.* New York: Harper, 1954. • **Bromiley, Geoffrey W.** *Introduction to the Study of Karl Barth.* Grand Rapids: Eerdmans, 1979. • **Brunner, Emil.** *Dogmatics.* Translated by Olive Wyon. Philadelphia: Westminster, 1950–62. • ———. *Man in Revolt.* London: Lutterworth, 1939. • **Grenz, Stanley J.**, and **Roger E. Olson**. *Twentieth-Century Theology.* Downers Grove, IL: InterVarsity Press, 1992. • **Humphrey, J. Edward.** *Emil Brunner.* Waco: Word, 1976. • **Jüngel, Eberhard.** *Karl Barth: A Theological Legacy.* Philadelphia: Westminster, 1986. • **Kliever, Lonnie.** *H. Richard Niebuhr.* Waco: Word, 1977. • **Mueller, David L.** *Karl Barth.* Waco: Word, 1972. • **Niebuhr, Reinhold.** *Moral Man in an Immoral Society.* New York: Scribner, 1952. • ———. *The Nature and Destiny of Man.* Louisville: Westminster John Knox, 1996. • **Parker, T. H. L.** *Karl Barth.* Grand Rapids: Eerdmans, 1970. • **Patterson, Bob E.** *Reinhold Niebuhr.* Waco: Word, 1977. • **Ramm, Bernard.** *After Fundamentalism.* San Francisco: HarperSanFrancisco, 1983. • **Roark, Dallas M.** *Dietrich Bonhoeffer.* Waco: Word, 1972.

NOTES

[1]This theory states that the Pentateuch was not written by one person, but consists of multiple strands of tradition woven together by editors/composers centuries after Moses. The four strands are J (using Jahweh as God's name), E (using Elohim as God's name), D (the Deuteronomist), and P (the Priestly source).

[2]See Bernard Ramm, *After Fundamentalism* (San Francisco: HarperSanFrancisco, 1983), 15.

[3]Although Rudolf Bultmann is sometimes cited as a third *B* of neoorthodoxy, with Barth and Brunner, this is in fact a misapprehension of both the neoorthodox agenda and Bultmann's position. In the early years, Bultmann may legitimately have been called a cobelligerent with Barth and Brunner, but he blazed his own path. Bultmann became the dominant force in New Testament studies in the mid-twentieth century and had much more in common with historic liberalism than with neoorthodoxy.

[4]The following section is drawn largely from David L. Mueller, *Karl Barth* (Waco: Word, 1972), 13–48.

[5]Karl Barth, *Credo* (London: Hodder & Stoughton, 1936).

[6]Ibid., 43.

[7]Karl Barth, *The Word of God and the Word of Man* (Boston: Pilgrim, 1928; repr., Grand Rapids: Zondervan, 1935), 100, author's italics.

[8]Barth, *Credo.*

[9]Barth's friend and fellow Swiss theologian Emil Brunner was the first to call attention to its epoch-making character in his review of *Der Römerbrief.*

[10]Karl Barth, *The Epistle to the Romans,* trans. from the 6th ed. by Edwyn C. Hoskyns (London: Oxford University Press, 1933), 10.

[11]Karl Barth, *Word of God,* 195–96.

[12]Heinrich Heppe, *Reformed Dogmatics* (Grand Rapids: Baker, 1978), v.

[13]Karl Barth, *The Doctrine of the Word of God,* vol. 1, pt. 1 (Edinburgh: T. & T. Clark, 1936), ix.

[14]Barth, *Credo,* 184.

[15]Karl Barth, *How I Changed My Mind* (Richmond: John Knox, 1966), 42–43.

[16]David L. Mueller, *Karl Barth* (Waco: Word, 1972), 38.

[17]Karl Barth, *Anselm: Fides Quaerens Intellectum* (Richmond: John Knox, 1960), 13–14.

[18]Karl Barth, *Church Dogmatics,* vol. 4., pt. 4 (Edinburgh: T. & T. Clark, 1936–77), vi.

[19]J. Edward Humphrey, *Emil Brunner* (Waco: Word, 1976), 19.

[20]Ibid., 20.

[21]Years later he commented that if he could do it over again, he would entitle the work *Immoral Man in an Immoral Society.*

[22]One hears echoes of Tillich's analysis of the human condition at this point. *Systematic Theology* (Chicago: University of Chicago Press, 1957): 2:44–58.

[23]Quoted by Eberhard Bethge, *Costly Grace: An Illustrated Biography of Dietrich Bonhoeffer*, trans. Rosaleen Ockenden (San Francisco: Harper & Row, 1979), 98–99.

[24]See above, B.1.c.

[25]Barth, *Church Dogmatics,* vol. 1, pt. 2, 499.

[26]Ibid., vol. 1, pt. 2, 529.

[27]Ibid., vol. 1, pt. 2, 237.

[28]Ibid., vol. 1, pt. 1, 123.

[29]These terms are generally translated as "history" and "meaning/significance" (although some see *Geschichte* as meaning separated from actual occurrence, an "upper-story religious leap" unrelated to space-time occurrence). An example of the distinction is salvation history, which is often referred to by the German *Heilsgeschichte,* since it shows the inner meaning of history. It could not be called *Heilshistorie,* since the mere facts and verifiable data of history do not reveal meaning and significance, only sequence.

[30]John Macquarrie makes this point explicitly in *An Existential Theology,* in his discussion about Bultmann's rejection of the resurrection (New York: Harper & Row, 1965), 185–89.

[31]H.H. Rowley, *The Unity of the Bible* (Philadelphia: Westminster, 1953).

[32]Brevard Childs, *Biblical Theology in Crisis* (Philadelphia: Westminster, 1970), 141–42.

[33]While many challenge his perspective, Stendahl's article in the *Interpreter's Dictionary of the Bible* continues to be the definitive statement on biblical theol-

ogy (*Interpreters Dictionary of the Bible* [Nashville: Abingdon, 1962], s.v. "Biblical Theology").

[34]Gerhard Hasel, *Old Testament Theology* (Grand Rapids: Eerdmans, 1972), 35–55; Gerhard Hasel, "Biblical Theology Movement," in *Evangelical Dictionary of Theology*, ed. Walter Elwell (Grand Rapids: Baker, 1984).

[35]See Roy Harrisville and Walter Sundberg, *The Bible in Modern Culture* (Grand Rapids: Eerdmans, 1995), 2, 5, 10–31.

OUTLINE OF CHAPTER 16

A. The Background of Liberation Theologies
   1. Orthodoxy versus Orthopraxis
   2. Moltmann's Theology of Hope

B. Latin American Liberation Theology
   1. The Context of Latin American Liberation Theology
      a. Historical Background
      b. "Institutional Violence" and Its Consequences
      c. Who Are the Poor?
   2. The Twentieth-Century Response: Liberation Theology
      a. The Emergence of Liberation Theology
      b. The Theological Justification for Liberation Theology
      c. The Method of Liberation Theology
      d. Key Themes in Liberation Theology
      e. The Agenda of Liberation Theology

C. Black Theology
   1. Origins
   2. Radicalization

D. Feminist Theology
   1. Hermeneutical Issues
   2. Christological Issues

E. Critique
   1. Hermeneutics
   2. Latin American Liberation Theology
   3. Black Theology
   4. Feminist Theology

CHAPTER 16

LIBERATION THEOLOGY

A. THE BACKGROUND OF LIBERATION THEOLOGIES

1. Orthodoxy versus Orthopraxis

Traditional theological systems are mostly intellectual in character; they are concerned with organizing and presenting the truth of God in a systematic form. But the second half of the twentieth century saw the rise of an approach to theology that centered not on right *belief* (orthodoxy) but on right *practice* or *praxis* (orthopraxis).

This new approach was characterized by a strong emphasis on divine immanence (in part as a reaction against Karl Barth's radical emphasis on divine transcendence). It was at the same time a response to numerous forms of concrete human oppression. This approach was hailed as "a whole new way of doing theology" and resulted in a cluster of theologies that are referred to collectively as "liberation theologies." These theologies focus on rectifying the concrete realities of oppression rather than on human sin and redemption, and they see the task of theology as the overthrow of oppressive structures—if necessary, according to some, even by means of violent revolution.

Liberation theology is "a collection of contemporary theological movements interpreting salvation and the mission of the church primarily as the changing of oppressive social structures—economic, political, and social—rather than as redemption from personal guilt and sin."[1]

The new theologians took to heart the atheistic critique that Christianity is "pie in the sky" and nothing more than "ivory-tower" intellectual arguments. They determined to create a theology that was vitally involved in the historical process, especially the experience of the downtrodden and oppressed. Theologies of liberation claim to be a biblical and profoundly christological quest for genuine Christian orthopraxis, an orthopraxis that results from a juxtaposition of critical reflection on the church's pastoral activity and its historical interpretation in light of divine revelation.

Liberation theologies presuppose two things. The first presupposition is that all theology is, and always has been, historically and socially conditioned, as the discipline of the sociology of knowledge shows. While a radical application of this insight can lead to a cognitive relativism that locks the knower inexorably into his or her framework (as, for example, radical postmodernism claims), liberation theologians do not fall victim to such reductionism. Instead, they espouse a "critical consciousness" or "dialectical thinking" that subjects even one's own beliefs and interests to criticism.

A second presupposition, equally important, is that sin is more than personal. There is a structural/institutional aspect to sin, evil, and oppression that victimizes the poor to the benefit of those in positions of wealth and power.

2. Moltmann's Theology of Hope

The inspiration for a host of political theologies, including black theology, feminist theology, and most important, Latin American liberation theology, came from Jürgen Moltmann's "theology of hope." The theme of hope came out of Moltmann's personal experience as a German prisoner of war in the British camps during World War II, where he came to see that hope is essential for life itself. "Hope rubbed itself raw on the barbed wire [surrounding the POW camp]! A man cannot live without hope! I saw men in the camp who lost hope. They simply took ill and died. When life's hopes flounder and crack up, a sadness beyond comforting sets in. But on the other hand, hope disturbs and makes one restless. One can no longer be content with his situation, with the way things are."[2]

Jürgen Moltmann

This experience led Moltmann to a position of looking toward the future and to the final establishment of the kingdom of God on earth in fulfillment of the biblical promises.[3]

Besides his own experience, Moltmann's thought has two main contributors. First, as a young theologian, he came under the sway of the neoorthodox theology of Karl Barth. Moltmann absorbed Barth's christocentricity and added a profoundly eschatological-historical focus. "We learned the origin of the Christian faith in the suffering of him who was crucified and in the liberating power of the risen Christ."[4] Christian hope is grounded in both history and experience. The center of the Christian faith is not oriented toward the past but toward the future, toward the establishment of the kingdom of God in glory, the kingdom that will fulfill the promises given in Scripture. Moltmann's theology is thus fully eschatological.

The second influence on Moltmann was the Jewish-Marxist-atheist philosopher Ernst Bloch. Bloch's contribution came in a massive treatise entitled the *Principle of Hope.* Bloch used Jewish and Christian eschatology and Marxist social analysis in his attempt to explain the human drivenness to overcome the inherent sense of alienation and to achieve a utopia. Moltmann adapted Bloch's fundamental thesis while rejecting his atheism: "Christian hope is not an abstract utopia but a passion for the future that has become 'really possible' thanks to the resurrection of Christ."[5]

Moltmann's colleague at Tübingen, Johannes Menz, laid the groundwork for the distinctive method of liberation theology, with political praxis as the starting point of theological reflection.

B. LATIN AMERICAN LIBERATION THEOLOGY

Basic to liberation theology is that unjust structures and oppression in society have a dehumanizing effect and are contrary to God's design. God is immanent in the historical process, and his action in history is aimed at humanization, "to make and to keep human life." From this naturally flows the concept of revolution. Whereas God has for centuries been seen to be allied through the church with the agents of dehumanization, in reality he was aligned with the poor and their humanization. The route to that humanization is through (violent) political revolution.

1. The Context of Latin American Liberation Theology

a. Historical Background

Liberation theology has taken root especially in the Latin American context of Roman Catholicism. The Spanish and Portuguese conquests in Latin America and the subjugation of the indigenous people took place with the tacit approval of the church. Both Spain (through, e.g., Hernan Cortes and Francisco Pizarro) and Portugal (through, e.g., Pedro Alvares Cabral) colonized most of Latin America, beginning in the early sixteenth century. During the subjugation of Latin America, the Roman Catholic Church was in many ways complicit in this domination and subjugation and even the slaughter of the native populations.[6] In this context, the church became an agent of oppression. Since the colonial days, the political system in Latin America has been one of a large, economically and politically oppressed majority held in subjugation by a tiny but incredibly wealthy minority.

b. "Institutional Violence" and Its Consequences

A weak but nevertheless fitting illustration may help us understand the principle of "institutional violence." In nineteenth-century America, the mining companies at times paid their workers in scrip rather than dollars. This scrip was good only at the "company store." The system was designed to keep the company laborers in economic slavery by cynically pricing the necessities of life slightly higher than the wage the laborer could earn. Workers thus had no choice but to rack up an ever-increasing tab at their employer's store and could not quit while they still owed money. As Tennessee Ernie Ford put it in "Sixteen Tons," "I owe my soul to the company store."

In that system the workers were victims of economic slavery at the hand of an individual employer. However, in Latin America the oppression and injustice are systemic and pervasive. *The very structures of society are designed to keep the poor in poverty.*

Statistics cannot convey the desperate realities that have been the impetus for liberation theologies. Anecdotal descriptions come closer. Thus two liberation theologians, Leonardo Boff and Clodovis Boff, relate a number of experiences. In one case, "a woman of forty, who looked as old as seventy," went up to the priest after Mass to explain why she had taken Communion without first going to confession as the church requires. She said, "For three days I have had only water and nothing to eat; I'm dying of hunger. When I saw you handing out the hosts, those little pieces of white bread, I went to Communion just out of hunger for that little bit of bread." Then they add, "The priest's eyes filled with tears. He recalled the words of Jesus: "My flesh [bread] is real food ... whoever feeds on me will draw life from me" (John 6:55, 57)."[7]

Clodovis Boff tells of the night he went to see Manuel, a catechist of a base community.[8] "Father," he said to me, "this community and others in the district are coming to an end. The people are dying of hunger. They are not coming: they haven't the strength to walk this far. They have to stay in their houses to save their energy."[9]

These and other stories told by liberation theology are not intended to be dramatic or to elicit pity. Rather, they reflect the deadly realities in Latin America that call for holy anger and resolve.

c. Who Are the Poor?

Who are the poor? Liberation theologians identify the poor as consisting of two groups, the socioeconomically poor and the evangelically poor. The *socioeconomically poor* consist of several subgroups, all of whom have suffered oppression in one form or another. They include

- Those who lack or are deprived of the basic necessities of life
- Those who are unjustly poor because of exploitation of labor
- Those who are discriminated against because of race
- Those who are discriminated against because of gender
- Those who are discriminated against because of their culture (indigenous peoples)

The *evangelically poor* are those who have seen the oppression of their neighbors who are socioeconomically poor and have identified themselves with their suffering. Ideally this involves a renouncing of worldly possessions and a commitment of themselves to labor on behalf of the socioeconomically poor.

2. The Twentieth-Century Response: Liberation Theology

a. The Emergence of Liberation Theology

Over the decades and centuries, individual priests and bishops at times spoke out against the injustice and suggested that the Spaniards and Portuguese were putting their own salvation in jeopardy by their practices. But by and large these appeals fell on deaf ears. It was not until the middle of the twentieth century that some of these voices of challenge began to be heard.

The birth of liberation theology is generally placed at the 1968 gathering of Roman Catholic bishops in Medellin, Colombia. This conference condemned the church's traditional alliance with the political powers and described the situation as one of "institutionalized violence." It "initiated a revolution in Latin American church life that will finally mean a revolution in Latin American history."[10]

The primary textbook, *A Theology of Liberation* by Gustavo Gutierrez, a Peruvian theology professor, followed in 1971. Gutierrez insists that liberation theology is

> a theology of liberating transformation of the history of (humankind) and also therefore that part of (humankind)—gathered into *ecclesia*—which openly confesses Christ. This is a theology that does not stop with reflecting on the world, but rather tries to be part of the pro-

cess through which the world is transformed. It is a theology which is open—in the protest against trampled human dignity, in the struggle against the plunder of the vast majority of people, in liberating love, and in the building of a new, and just and fraternal society—to the gift of the Kingdom of God.[11]

Gustavo Gutierrez

Liberation theology seeks to bring the harsh realities of life into critical dialogue with the text of Scripture, often questioning the received interpretative tradition. Its hermeneutic is in a sense a hermeneutic of suspicion—not of the text, but of the culture and exegetical methods normally employed. It is a hermeneutic that seeks a new understanding of Scripture as the Word of God that will set free the community in which the theologian ministers and to which he or she is accountable. The theologian thus becomes God's agent in transforming the particular historical-cultural-political situation.[12] This hermeneutical approach allows the community to discover texts and stories in the Bible that provide answers that arise out of the historical praxis of the community.

b. The Theological Justification for Liberation Theology

The proponents of liberation theology realize that theirs is a radical methodological departure from traditional paradigms. For this reason, they have articulated a multipronged *apologia* for this "new way to do theology."

1. Scripture portrays God as giver and sustainer of life. He is impelled to come to the aid of the poor (Exod. 3:7, 9; cf. Isa. 1:10–17; 58:6–7; Mark 7:6–13). "By opting for the poor, the church imitates our Father who is in heaven (Matt. 5:48)."[13]

2. There is also the example of Christ, who made the poor the chief recipients of his message. Not only the example of Christ but also his teaching is invoked. Looking at the teaching of Christ, liberation theologians conclude that at the judgment one's acceptance or rejection of the poor will be a major factor in one's final salvation (Matt. 25:31–46). Only those who participate in this life with the poor and needy will in the end be with Christ.

3. A twofold apostolic motivation is also invoked: the example of the early apostolic church, which held all things in common, and the charge to Paul as he took the gospel to the Gentiles to "remember the poor" in the proclamation of the gospel (Gal. 2:10).

c. The Method of Liberation Theology

Theology. In the past, under the influence of the European university system, theology has been viewed as giving the theoretical and regulative truths for Christianity in the form of orthodoxy. Liberation theology inverts the traditional order and sees action as preceding reflection. Theology thus becomes orthopraxis, as Costas says: "Theology is a critical reflection on praxis in light of the Word of God" (see n. 11). It is understood to be a second act, since theory should *follow* action. Theology is then an effort to articulate the action of faith rather than to abstractly understand God or his actions. This shift away from the traditional construction involves a new paradigm of knowledge that sees knowledge arising from human encounter with reality.

Commitment and Scripture. In keeping with the idea that praxis precedes theology, liberation theologians hold that God is not known through doctrine or propositions but by entering in *obedient commitment* into God's own project in history, that is, the poor. It is only *after* engaging in God's project that Scripture enters into the method: after they are involved in the process of liberation, they go to Scripture to read and understand. Commitment must precede understanding, because "there is no truth outside or beyond the concrete historical events in which men are involved as agents. Therefore there is no knowledge except in action itself, in the process of transforming the world through participation in history."[14]

Bible and revelation. The Bible is understood as a subspecies of Christian theology. It is the normative record of God's liberating activity for his people. However, the normative nature of Scripture does not preclude revelation from other sources. Liberation theologians assert that the final norms of judgment come from revealed truths that are accepted by faith and not from praxis itself. But these final norms, or the "deposit of faith," are not understood as a set of indifferent, catalogued truths; rather, the "deposit of faith" lives in the church and rouses commitments in accordance with God's will as well as providing criteria for judging them in the light of God's Word. Revelation is wider than the Bible, but the Bible is the primary and normative record of God's liberating activity for his people. But in contrast to traditional theological constructions, praxis has precedence and theory arises as a critical description of praxis.

Marxism. Liberation theologians have adopted Marxism (*not* communism), particularly its interpretation of history, as a tool for social analysis and to provide solutions to the problem. Capitalism is seen as inherently evil and socialism as the ideal form of economics. Although this socialism is not identified directly with the kingdom of God in theory, the emphasis of some liberation theologians seems to cross the line and make this identification. The goal is a violent overthrow of the existing economic order and establishment of a just society.

Eschatology. This hope gives an eschatological bent to history. The liberation theologians reject developmentalism, the gradual transformation of society through pulling the poor up by their economic bootstraps. The goal is not merely better living conditions; it is a radical change in the structures of society, a social revolution. More than that, it is envisioned as continuous creation, an endless new way to be human, a permanent cultural revolution.

Levels of Liberation Theology

	PROFESSIONAL	PASTORAL	POPULAR
Discourse	detailed and rigorous	organically related to practice	diffuse and capillary, almost spontaneous
Logic	the logic of erudition: methodical, systematic, dynamic	the logic of action: specific, prophetic, propulsive	the logic of life: in words and deeds, sacramental
Method	socio-analytical, hermeneutical, and theoretico-practical	seeing, judging, acting	confrontation: the gospel and life
Locus	theological institutes, seminaries	pastoral institutes, study centers	Bible study groups, base communities
Promoted through	theological congresses	pastoral congresses	training courses
Practitioners	theologians, professors, teachers	pastoral ministers: priests, religious, laypersons	members of base communities and their coordinators
Spoken works	conference papers, lectures, seminar papers	sermons, talks	commentaries, celebrations, dramatizations
Written works	books, articles	pastoral instructions, guidelines	notes, letters

From Leonardo Boff and Clodovis Boff, *Introducing Liberation Theology* (Maryknoll, NY: Orbis, 1987), 13.

FIGURE 16.1.

d. Key Themes in Liberation Theology

The liberation perspective can be summarized in a number of key points:

- Living and true faith includes the practice of liberation.
- The living God sides with the oppressed against the pharaohs of this world.
- The kingdom is God's project in history and eternity.
- Jesus, the Son of God, took on oppression in order to set us free.
- The Holy Spirit, "Father of the poor," is present in the struggles of the oppressed.
- Mary is the prophetic and liberating woman of the people.
- The church is a sign and instrument of liberation.
- The rights of the poor are God's rights.
- Liberated human potential becomes liberative.[15]

e. The Agenda of Liberation Theology

Liberation theology is not a hit-and-miss approach but has an agenda that encompasses all available options (see figure 16.1).

C. BLACK THEOLOGY

The religious heritage of African Americans is rich. The black spiritual experience born out of slavery and the economic oppression that followed gave birth to a tradition that expressed its faith through the medium of "Negro spirituals." The themes that were woven through this expression of Christianity included the equality of all individuals, the reality of divine justice, and the ultimate triumph of the cause of the black community in spite of the present experience of injustice and frustration. The Jesus of the black churches is the one who stands beside and with his people, who suffered himself and therefore can enter into their concrete suffering and lead them to freedom. In the white churches, on the other hand, Jesus is most often the Christ of the atonement who reconciles us with God, the Christ of theology.[16]

One of the sources of black theology was a resurgence of the thought of Dietrich Bonhoeffer, but whereas Bonhoeffer's followers in the academy looked to his ideas to solve intellectual problems of a secular culture, the concern of the black community was the black American experience. Bonhoeffer's resistance to injustice provided critical motivation and guidance. The endeavor involved the use of biblical imagery to advance the condition of the black community. Key to the struggle here was the question of how the Christian conception of God could be relevant to the black community, which was oppressed at the hands of those calling themselves Christians.

1. Origins

The origins of black theology as a movement can be traced to the nonviolent civil rights movement of the 1960s under the leadership of Dr. Martin Luther King Jr. and the Black Power movement that arose alongside the civil rights movement but advocated violent means to achieve its goals. In 1969 a group of black leaders issued the Black Manifesto at the Interreligious Foundation for Community Organization in Detroit. It set forth the new theological agenda, a theology contextualized for the black community experience.

> Black theology is a theology of black liberation. It seeks to plumb the black condition in light of God's revelation in Jesus Christ, so that the black community can see that the gospel is commensurate with the achievement of black humanity. Black theology is a theology of "blackness." It is the affirmation of black humanity that emancipates black people from white racism, thus providing authentic freedom for both white and black people. It affirms the humanity of white people in that it says No to the encroachment of white oppression.[17]

This articulation makes it clear that black theology is a variation of liberation theology, although the early work of black theology was done without an awareness of the developing liberation theologies in the Third World context. Whereas Latin American liberation theology has been predominantly Roman Catholic, black theology is North American and Protestant. Although trained under neoorthodox and liberal theologians, the leadership of the black theological movement has found European intellectual theology largely too abstract to be of practical use.

2. Radicalization

The late 1960s saw a radicalization of the black theological movement. In 1969 James Cone, who is among the most prominent and militant of the black theologians, explained black theology as

> the religious counterpart of the more secular term Black Power … the religious explication of the need for black people to define the scope and meaning of black existence in a white racist society. While Black Power focuses on the political, social and economic condition of black people, Black Theology puts black identity in a theological

> context, showing Black Power is not only consistent with the Gospel of Jesus Christ, but it is the Gospel of Jesus Christ.[18]

While Cone's tone is the most militant of the major figures, his linking of black identity with the gospel of Jesus Christ is fundamental to the entire movement. This perspective arises out of the history of black oppression in the United States and gives this racial oppression theological significance.

James Cone

The elevation of ethnicity into a theological category is both the most controversial feature of black theology and its defining characteristic. The designation "black" communicates more than skin color; it refers to a whole perspective on life and a particular worldview. It is a black reading of the Scriptures, giving a black hearing of Jesus as the black liberator of black people. It produces a black spirituality experienced by the worshiping community, which in turn validates black theology. This elevation of ethnicity into a theological category has led many, even within the black community, to question whether this theology could be seen as Christian. To this criticism black theologians answer that black people did not reject the gospel brought by the whites but instead had a different perception of it. In fact, the black perception of the truth of the gospel found its authentication in their own experience of suffering and produced in the black mind a religion aimed toward freedom and the welfare of humanity.

While it may be startling to hear of Jesus as "black," what is meant is that black people find in Jesus' gospel a message of liberation, a liberation denied them by the whites who brought them the gospel. In keeping with this theme, there is an insistence that salvation is to be found only by entering into the black experience of oppression and experiencing Jesus as liberator. The affinity with Latin American liberation theology is clearly seen at this point. Black theology is an alternate framework of interpretation that rejects the white gospel that blacks experienced as dehumanizing.

In Cone's *A Black Theology of Liberation*, his most influential work, he clearly sets forth the liberating agenda of black theology. He asserts that theology is not merely an abstract description of the being of God; it is involved with God's liberating activity in the world, enabling the oppressed to "risk all for earthly freedom, a freedom made possible in the resurrection of Christ."[19] Cone is heavily indebted to Barth but takes Barth's teaching of the character of revelation and radically transforms it. Revelation is a black event, that is, what black people are doing about their liberation.[20] Revelation thus becomes more than simple divine self-disclosure. It is *disclosure in the event of liberation.* The task of theology is to keep in tension the biblical community of faith and the modern community, and thus to be able to speak to the contemporary situation in a significant manner.

Cone argued that the core of theology is the assertion of the blackness of God; that is, God is involved with the struggle for justice wherever there is oppression. Cone goes so far as to assert that the very nature of God is to be found in liberation. This concept informed his anthropology. The image of God as found in man is found in the liberation struggle against the structures of oppression. To be human means to be involved in the struggle for liberation from oppression. From this it follows that Jesus was also black in that he was "the Oppressed One whose earthly existence was bound up with the oppressed of the land."[21] Since the early 1970s, Cone has sought to ground his thinking more deeply in black concepts rather than borrowing a white conceptualization of issues. He has also more heavily emphasized the socio-political aspects of the gospel and insisted on the application of the social sciences in the analysis and articulation of white racism.

Whereas black theology has advocated power and at times violence as it found fertile soil in the apartheid political climate of South Africa, in the United States it has been more closely associated with the influence of Martin Luther King Jr. and his commitment to nonviolence. Allan Boesak, a leading South African theologian, has declared, "Following the direction pointed out to us by Martin Luther King Jr., Black Theology takes Christian love very seriously, opting for agape, which stands at the very center of God's liberating actions for his people."[22] Identifying black theology with a particular political agenda is rejected. Rather, "blackness" is identified with humanness, with blacks taking their rightful place as human beings, and is to be identified with wholeness.

D. FEMINIST THEOLOGY

Feminist theology, like Latin American liberation theology and black theology, is a product of the 1960s. Feminism as a movement is identified with the publication of Betty Friedan's *The Feminine Mystique* in 1963. The feminist movement sought to bring to women the rights and freedoms enjoyed by men in every area of life. Theological feminism is the application to religion of the goal of equality in the face of a male-dominated religious establishment. The intent is to actualize the Pauline pronouncement of Galatians 3:26–28 that in Christ there are no class, ethnic, or gender distinctions; all are one in him. The types of feminist theology run the gamut from evangelical, with a high view of Scripture as divinely inspired and authoritative, to the radical, which would dismiss Scripture and substitute the agenda of promoting the equality (or even superiority) of women.

Within the Christian context, feminist theology looks at the perceptions about women as well as at their activities, roles, and practices as found in the Bible, traditions, and theologies of the Christian heritage. This work has served to uncover the historical sources of negative views about women both in Scripture and in more recent Christian thought. A threefold ideology about women has been discerned. In the Bible and the earliest Christian sources, women were viewed as property. Later theologians viewed women as polluting, sexually dangerous, and carnal. Finally, a romantic and idealized view of women developed, and they were seen as morally superior to men but in need of protection and therefore to be relegated to the private realm. Many who embraced this ideology excluded women from full participation in the image of God and thus from church leadership in the areas of preaching, teaching, and ordination. Despite the historic marginalization of women, feminist theologians have shown the noteworthy influence women have exercised throughout the ages, even while they were formally viewed as inferior.

1. Hermeneutical Issues

As with other types of liberation theology, the hermeneutical principle of feminist theology differs from the generally accepted method. The starting point is a critique of the status quo, "the androcentrism and misogyny of patriarchal theology."[23] These patriarchal features are seen even in the Scriptures themselves, particularly in 1 Timothy 2:12: "I do not permit a woman to teach or to have authority over a man; she must be silent." This perspective, considered by many feminist theologians as non-Pauline, has continued throughout the history of the church and has been a major contributing factor to the ongoing oppression of women.

Feminist theologians propose several methods for dealing with the patriarchalism of the Scriptures.

1. Some, following the mode of liberation theology, argue for a "prophetic liberating tradition of biblical faith,"[24] which can be found in certain biblical texts. These in turn function as a norm by which other texts can be judged. This procedure essentially sets up a canon within the canon, with the biblical

prophetic tradition determining which texts are to be viewed authoritatively and which are to be seen as reflecting the cultural bias of the author.

2. Another position seeks to recover passages that have been either overlooked or twisted by patriarchal hermeneutics. This perspective reexamines passages, looking for countercultural implications ignored by patriarchal hermeneutics. It also focuses on passages in which the chief characters are women and explores the function of those women apart from patriarchal presuppositions. One author who has done some particularly fine work in this area is Phyllis Trible in her *God and the Rhetoric of Sexuality.*[25] Her work on Eve in Genesis 2–3 is particularly thought provoking.

3. A third and more radical position in practice comes close to rejecting the canon and essentially asserts that the Bible itself is a result of patriarchal hermeneutics and thus is filled illegitimately with ideas of female inferiority and subordination. Some go so far as to seek new directions outside the Scriptures. One of the most vocal, Rosemary Radford Reuther, states:

> Feminist theology, then is not just engaged in a reformation to some original good movement in the past, some unblemished period of origins, because no such period can be discovered for women, either in the Judeo-Christian tradition or before it. Even for those who claim some continuity with the Jewish or Christian traditions, feminist theology must stand as a new midrash or a third covenant, that ... makes a new beginning, in which the personhood of woman is no longer at the margins but at the center.[26]

Feminist theologians are quick to point out that while most references to God are masculine, there are significant references that picture God as female, particularly in a maternal role. It is an error to conceive of God as male as opposed to female. Such a perception projects a patriarchal bias onto the text rather than taking Scripture as it presents itself. Many feminist theologians call for the use of multiple metaphors with reference to God rather than filtering all understanding through the dominant male metaphor, arguing that no one metaphor can capture the fullness of God's relationship to humanity. While the metaphor *father* is undoubtedly the predominant scriptural metaphor, others include *mother* and *friend.* These other metaphors must be given full weight in theologizing in order to escape the patriarchal trap.

Another area of critique involves the concept of sin. The feminist critique holds that the dominant form of sin that is emphasized is pride. This, it is argued, presupposes a masculine perspective and does not reflect the experience of women. Feminists argue that a woman more often suffers the "sin" of lack of self-esteem and lack of personal focus and ambition. She slips into an existence of triviality rather than achieving her God-given potential. While acknowledging that women can fall victim to the same sins as men, more often they fail to develop a sense of self and personal agency and responsibility. In the feminist perspective, sin is predominately understood as breaking relationship with God, with other people, and even with nature and life itself. When sin is viewed from this perspective, salvation is sometimes reformulated as the healing of broken relationships.

2. Christological Issues

It is in the area of Christology that feminists find doctrine most often used against women. It is particularly the historical maleness of Jesus that is the focus. This aspect of Jesus' human existence has been used historically to justify the maleness of God. In answer to this, feminists argue that maleness is a contingent rather than a necessary feature of Jesus' earthly existence, on the order of his language, his Jewishness, or his profession as a carpenter. Rather than focusing on Jesus' gender, feminist theology focuses on the radical inclusiveness of the marginalized of society in all of Jesus' life and preaching.

> Though the observation is frequently made by those who oppose women in leadership roles that Jesus chose no women to be among his twelve disciples, by any reading of the Gospels, Jesus' attitude toward women was revolutionary. Contrary to Jewish custom, he freely socialized with women.... In the home of Mary and Martha (Luke 10:38–42), Jesus related to Mary as a teacher to a disciple and tacitly defended her right to a role which was commonly denied to Jewish women. Talking to the Samaritan woman at the well (John 4:1–42), Jesus broke conventions again in the freedom with which he related to this woman whom he would have scorned had he followed the conventions of his day.... But it is not only his actions which were positive towards women, his teachings were also revolutionary.... By declaring that a man commits adultery in his heart when he looks at a woman with the purpose of lusting after her (Matt 5:28), he affirmed that women have rights of their own and are not things to be used.[27]

An area of diverse understanding among feminist theologians is the nature of humanity. One position holds that, apart from biological differences, women and men are the same and that differences attributed to the sexes are culturally constructed and have led to the subjugation of women. The other position holds that women and men are essentially different and stress the importance of understanding physical existence as embodiment. This position stresses the capacity of childbearing and motherhood with all this entails. These thinkers stress that women's physical embodiment provides insight that has been overlooked and needs to be taken seriously in theological and ethical thought.

Feminist theology, like other liberation theologies, is a theology of protest. It is not monolithic; it is multifaceted, ranging from the moderate evangelical feminism of the Council for Biblical Equality to the radical feminist agenda that reenvisions God or invokes the Goddess.

E. CRITIQUE

From a positive perspective, the various theologies of liberation have recognized a problem that has often characterized traditional theologies. They have become orthodoxy without having a necessary orthopraxy connected to them. Thus many theologies and theologians might be characterized as hearers of the Word without being doers. In addition, liberation theologians have rightly seen the social and structural elements of sin so often neglected in theological history.

Liberation theologians have also rightly seen that the implications of the gospel are deeper than can be established by proper historical-grammatical exegesis, that is, by grasping what the text meant to its original hearers. We could point to the church's ultimate recognition of the immorality of slavery, especially race-based slavery, as one example of how the church at large has seen the deeper implications of the gospel.[28]

1. Hermeneutics

On the other hand, liberation theologies present a profound hermeneutical question. While bringing issues to the table and engaging in dialogue with Scripture may be legitimate as an entry point into theological study, there is a twofold danger here. First, the burning issue at hand easily becomes a procrustean bed, and all texts that do not address the issue are cut off and left on the floor. Related to the first danger is a second: Scripture becomes a tool to advance a cause rather than the Word of God with a coherent message addressed to humanity. Instead of examining the totality of Scripture to establish a theology, liberation theologies of whatever stripe look for scriptural texts and stories that mesh with their agenda. In so doing, they establish a canon within the canon, which becomes the controlling factor in their theologizing. The theologian at that point hears what she or he wants to hear rather than being confronted by, as Paul puts it, the "whole counsel of God." When such a reductionism takes place, the divine redemptive message is muted and human tradition is substituted.

2. Latin American Liberation Theology

A key concern is the place Marxism plays in the analytical process of liberation theology. In their use of Marxism to analyze the poverty of Latin America, liberation theologians have concluded that capitalism is inherently evil and that socialism is the ideal economic system. While liberation theologians have productively used Marxism as a tool for sociological analysis, the tool is not value free. A key tenet of Marxism is that of economic alienation, but the idea of economic alienation is tied to Marx's view of the person as a self-creation through his work, rather than as a creation of God. The tools used in the theological process have a way of directing the conclusion. Latin American liberation theologians argue that the use of Marxism is not methodologically different than Thomas Aquinas's use of Aristotle or the patristic use of Plato. Yet as the history of theology has shown, one must be critically aware when one embraces a philosophical position in doing theology, lest the philosophy become master rather than servant.

Highly problematic is the contention that praxis precedes reflection. Many critics, even those sympathetic to the goals of liberation theology, have made this point. How can one have right praxis if one does not have a prior view of what is in fact right? Is not Scripture the ultimate norm for the Christian? British evangelical J. Andrew Kirk has argued that Gutiérrez's method must be inverted. If this does not happen, human ideology rather than Scripture becomes the ultimate norm.

For this reason, the task of modern theology should be a consciously critical reflection on God's Word in light of a contemporary praxis of liberation. If this is not the order of our methodology, then the phrase "in light of God's Word" (in Gutiérrez's definition) ultimately becomes emptied of content."[29] As Kirk concludes, "Right praxis ultimately depends on right theory."[30]

While liberation theologians acknowledge the necessity of personal repentance and faith, their emphasis is so weighted toward structural societal issues that one wonders if statements about repentance and faith are mere lip service. This suspicion grows when one encounters statements such as, "Since the incarnation, humanity, every human being, history, is the living temple of God. The 'profane' ... no longer exists."[31] Given the perspective of liberation theologians, one wonders if God exists outside of history, if sin is anything more than oppressive structures, and if salvation is more than participation in liberation. Is liberation anything more than social action on behalf of the poor?[32]

3. Black Theology

A central problem of black theology is its ethnocentricity. The ethnocentricity appears at its root to be opposed to the message of the gospel as summarized by the apostle Paul in Galatians 3:28. A second problem is the elevation of experience to the final norm. In this it has much in common methodologically with old liberalism, but in this case the norm is not universal human experience but the black experience of oppression.[33]

4. Feminist Theology

A key area of critique is that authority is not rooted in anything other than the feminist consciousness. A crucial aspect of any theology is that it be prophetic. To be prophetic it must have the ability to be self-critical.[34] While feminist theology is critical of the culture around it, it has no vehicle that supports self-criticism. Donald Bloesch has noted, "When a theology becomes consciously ideological, as in some forms of feminist and liberation theologies, it is bound to lose sight of the transcendent divine criterion, the living Word of God, by which alone it can determine the validity of its social valuations."[35] Even some feminist theologians have recognized this weakness. Pamela Dickey Young has observed:

> Basically the person employing the term [*Christian*] can use it however he or she wishes. This means, then, that whereas feminist theologians may claim the use of "Christian" for whatever liberates women, if there is nothing that can be derived from the tradition itself that can be used normatively to argue that this is what Christianity is all about, then others can use the tradition in less liberating ways.[36]

She goes on to suggest that the feminist method of determining "Christian" doctrine leads directly to relativism.[37]

The proclivity to assume that hierarchy is patriarchy and thus inherently evil has led in many cases to a denial of God as Father and in some cases even to a denial of God as parent. God or goddess is frequently identified with the natural order, leading feminism ultimately to paganism as opposed to Christianity. Noted biblical scholar and theologian Elizabeth Achtemeier has observed:

No religion in the world is as old as this immanentist identification of God with creation. It forms the basis of every nonbiblical religion except Islam; and if the church uses language that obscures God's holy otherness from creation, it opens the door to corruption of the biblical faith in the transcendent God who works in creation only by his Word and Spirit. Worshipers of a mother goddess ultimately worship the creation and themselves rather than the Creator.[38]

BIBLIOGRAPHY

Boff, Leonardo, and **Clodovis Boff**. *Introducing Liberation Theology*. Maryknoll, NY: Orbis, 1987. • **Brown, Robert McAffee**. *Gustavo Gutierrez: An Introduction to Liberation Theology*. Maryknoll, NY: Orbis, 1990. • **Cone, James H.** *A Black Theology of Liberation.* Philadelphia: Lippincott, 1970. • **Cone, James H.**, and **Gayraud S. Wilmore**. *Black Theology*. Maryknoll, NY: Orbis, 1993. • **Grenz, Stanley J.**, and **Roger E. Olson**. *Twentieth-Century Theology*. Downers Grove, IL: InterVarsity Press, 1992. • **Gutierrez, Gustavo.** *A Theology of Liberation*. Maryknoll, NY: Orbis, 1972. • **Kirk, J. Andrew.** *Liberation Theology: An Evangelical View from the Third World.* Atlanta: John Knox, 1979. • **Miller, Ed. L.**, and **Stanley J. Grenz**, *Fortress Introduction to Contemporary Theologies*. Minneapolis: Fortress, 1998. • **Nash, Ronald**, ed., *Liberation Theology.* Grand Rapids: Baker, 1984. • **Ruether, Rosemary Radford**. *Sexism and God Talk*. Boston: Beacon, 1983. • ———. *Women-Church*. San Francisco: Harper & Row, 1986. • **Trible, Phyllis.** *God and the Rhetoric of Sexuality*. Philadelphia: Fortress, 1978. • **Young, Pamela Dickey.** *Feminist Theology/Christian Theology: In Search of Method.* Minneapolis: Fortress, 1990.

NOTES

[1]John Jefferson Davis, *Theology Primer* (Grand Rapids: Baker, 1981), 28.

[2]Jürgen Moltmann, foreword in Douglas Meeks, *Origins of the Theology of Hope* (Philadelphia: Fortress, 1980), x–xi.

[3]In the process, his own theological journey took on the characteristics of an exploration: "I have never done theology in the form of a defence of ancient doctrines or ecclesiastical dogmas. It has always been a journey of exploration. Consequently my way of thinking is experimental—an adventure of ideas—and my style of communication is to suggest.... So I write without any built-in safeguards, recklessly as some people think. My own propositions are intended to be a challenge to other people to

think for themselves" (Jürgen Moltmann, *The Coming of God* [Minneapolis: Fortress, 1996], xiv).

[4]Moltmann, in Meeks, *Origins of the Theology of Hope*, xi.

[5]Marcel Neuch, *The Sources of Modern Atheism* (New York: Paulist, 1982), 211.

[6]This situation was graphically portrayed in the 1986 film *The Mission.*

[7]Leonard Boff and Clodovis Boff, *Introducing Liberation Theology* (Maryknoll, NY: Orbis, 1987), 1.

[8]A base community is defined as a Roman Catholic term meaning "a lay group, especially in South America, practicing nonliturgical religious devotions and striving for socioeconomic improvement in the community" (*The American Heritage Dictionary of the English Language,* 3rd ed. [Boston: Houghton Mifflin, 1992], 153).

[9]Boff and Boff, *Introducing Liberation Theology*, 1. Clodovis relates another experience: "One day, in the arid region of northeastern Brazil, one of the most famine-stricken parts of the world, I (Clodovis) met a bishop going into his house; he was shaking. 'Bishop, what's the matter?' I asked. He replied that he had just seen a terrible sight: in front of the cathedral was a woman with three small children and a baby clinging to her neck. He saw that they were fainting from hunger. The baby seemed to be dead. He said: 'Give the baby some milk, woman!' 'I can't, my lord,' she answered. The bishop went on insisting that she should, and she that she could not. Finally, because of his insistence, she opened her blouse. Her breast was bleeding; the baby sucked violently at it. And sucked blood. The mother who had given it life was feeding it, like the pelican, with her own blood, her own life. The bishop knelt down in front of the woman, placed his hand on the baby's head, and there and then vowed that as long as such hunger existed, he would feed at least one hungry child each day."

[10]Robert McAffee Brown, *Gustavo Gutiérrez: An Introduction to Liberation Theology* (Maryknoll, NY: Orbis, 1990), 11.

[11]Gustavo Gutiérrez, *A Theology of Liberation* (Maryknoll, NY: Orbis, 1972), 15. According to Orlando Costas, a theology of liberation involves "critical reflection on praxis in light of the Word of God. *Praxis* is the creative and transforming action of God's people in history, accompanied by a critical reflection and prophetic process that seeks to make the obedience of faith ever more efficacious" (Orlando E. Costas, "The Subversiveness of Faith: A Paradigm for Doing Liberation Theology," in *Doing Theology in Today's World*, ed. John D. Woodbridge and Thomas Edward McCoskey [Grand Rapids: Zondervan, 1991], 378).

[12]Costas, "Subversiveness of Faith," 379.

[13]Boff and Boff, *Introducing Liberation Theology*, 44.

[14]Samuel Escobar, "Liberation Theology," in Alister McGrath, ed., *Blackwell Encyclopedia of Modern Christian Thought* (Oxford: Blackwell, 1993), 331.

[15]Boff and Boff, *Introducing Liberation Theology*, 43–65.

[16]This is an oversimplification, but it approximates the two understandings of Christ (cf. Kelly Brown Douglas, *The Black Christ* [Maryknoll, NY: Orbis, 1994], esp. 1–34).

[17]"Statement by the National Committee of Black Churchmen, June 13, 1969," reprinted in James H. Cone and Gayraud Wilmore, *Black Theology* (Maryknoll, NY: Orbis, 1993).

[18]James Cone, quoted in *The New Dictionary of Theology*, ed. Sinclair B. Ferguson and David F. Wright (Downers Grove: InterVarsity Press, 1988), s.v. "Black Theology."

[19]James H. Cone, *A Black Theology of Liberation* (Philadelphia: Lippincott, 1970), 20–21.

[20]Ibid., 65.

[21]Ibid., 183.

[22]Quoted by K. Bedicko, *Black Theology* (Downers Grove, IL: InterVarsity Press, 1988), 104.

[23]Rosemary Radford Reuther, "Feminist Theology in the Academy," *Christianity and Crisis*, March 4, 1985, 58.

[24]Mary Ann Tolbert, "Defining the Problem: The Bible and Feminist Hermeneutics," *The Bible and Hermeneutics, Semeia* 28, ed. Mary Ann Tolbert (Chico, CA: Scholars, 1983), 122.

[25]Phyllis Trible, *God and the Rhetoric of Sexuality* (Philadelphia: Fortress, 1978).

[26]Reuther, "Feminist Theology," 61.

[27]Roger L. Omenson, "The Role of Women in the New Testament Church," *Review and Expositor* 83 (Winter 1986): 15–16.

[28]See William J. Webb, *Slaves, Women and Homosexuals* (Downers Grove: InterVarsity Press, 2001).

[29]J. Andrew Kirk, *Liberation Theology: An Evangelical View from the Third World* (Atlanta: John Knox, 1979), 193.

[30]Ibid., 198.

[31]Gutiérrez, *Theology of Liberation*, 110.

[32]Stanley Grenz and Roger Olson, *Twentieth-Century Theology* (Downers Grove: InterVarsity Press, 1992), 224.

[33]Ibid., 209–10.

[34]Ibid., 234.

[35]Donald G. Bloesch, *The Battle for the Trinity: The Debate over Inclusive God-Language* (Ann Arbor: Servant, 1985), 84.

[36]Pamela Dickey Young, *Feminist Theology/Christian Theology: In Search of Method* (Minneapolis: Fortress), 74.

[37]Ibid., 77.

[38]Elizabeth Achtemeier, "The Impossible Possibility: Evaluating the Feminist Approach to Bible and Theology," *Interpretation* 42 (January 1988): 57.

PART 3

SIGNIFICANT PEOPLE AND TERMS

CHAPTER 17

BIOGRAPHICAL SKETCHES OF MAJOR THEOLOGIANS AND PHILOSOPHERS

PETER ABELARD (ABAILARD) (1079–1142)

Roman Catholic

French scholastic theologian, philosopher, and teacher who emphasized the role of reason in theology. Born near Nantes in northern France, Abelard is considered one of the brightest twelfth-century European scholars. He developed the *moral influence theory* of the atonement (emphasizing the love of God, which motivates individuals, in turn, to respond in love). Because of the place of reason in his theology, he influenced the rationalism of the thirteenth century. His *Sic et Non* (*Yes and No*) (1122), is a compilation of contradictory statements from the Scriptures and church fathers, leaving the reconciliation of the contradictions to his students and readers. In so doing, Abelard contributed to the rise of reason in the medieval period: "Nothing is to be believed unless it is first understood."

Abelard's views on the Trinity brought strong opposition from Bernard of Clairvaux, who accused Abelard of compromising biblical faith for philosophy. After Abelard refused to retract his writings, Bernard charged him with heresy and succeeded in his excommunication by two different councils, the second in 1141. He was later reconciled to Bernard and moved to the monastery at Cluny, where he soon died.

ALBERTUS MAGNUS (c. 1206–80)

Roman Catholic

The "universal doctor" and teacher of Thomas Aquinas. Also known as Albert the Great. He was an outstanding scholastic philosopher who was the first medieval Christian scholar to master the entire writings of Aristotle. A scientific observer whose main interest lay in natural science, Albert tried to square the ideas of Aristotle with the doctrines of Christianity. He taught the superiority of revelation over human reason but also affirmed the right of scholars to use all of human knowledge in the investigation of divine mysteries.

ALEXANDER OF ALEXANDRIA (c. 273–328)

Orthodox/catholic[1]

Bishop of Alexandria (c. 313–328) and leader of the Orthodox party at the Council of Nicea (A.D. 325), called to deal with the teaching of Arius. The controversy concerning the unorthodox Arian views of the eternal divine nature of the Logos eventually led to the condemnation and excommunication of Arius in 321 by the synod of Alexandria, called by Alexander. Alexander held firmly to his Trinitarian views, insisting that the preincarnate Son was *homoousias* (of the same substance) as God the Father and shared with the Father eternal deity. Alexander and his pupil Athanasius represented the position that was declared orthodox at the Council of Nicea.

AMBROSE OF MILAN (c. 339–97)

Orthodox/catholic

One of the four doctors of the ancient period of the Roman Catholic Church (along with Jerome, Augustine, and Gregory the Great) and, as bishop, preacher, and teacher, a champion of orthodox Christianity. Ambrose was born at Trier in Gaul into a Christian family. He aspired to follow his father, the Praetorian prefect of Gaul, into an administrative career. After practicing law, he was appointed governor of Aemilia-Liguria (370), and then, in 374, after the death of Auxentius (the Arian bishop of Milan), Ambrose was appointed bishop of Milan by popular acclaim even though he was unbaptized at the time. As bishop he began to share his wealth with the poor, and he fought paganism and Arianism. Among his works are *De Fide*, *De Spiritu Sancto*, and *De Mysteriis*.

Ambrose influenced Augustine of Hippo, whom he eventually saw converted in 386 and whom he also baptized and taught. A fearless churchman, he refused Communion to Emperor Theodosius until the emperor openly did penance for the slaughter of thousands in Thessalonica while putting down a seditious rebellion. He declared, "The emperor is within the church, not over it."

MOISE AMYRAUT (1596–1664)
Reformed

French Protestant theologian and pastor, whose distinctive teachings are known as Amyraldism. (See chapter 11.B.5.)

ANSELM OF CANTERBURY (c. 1033–1109)
Roman Catholic

Archbishop of Canterbury, theologian, philosopher, and monk, considered a founder of scholasticism. Born in Aosta, Italy, he resisted family pressure to enter politics and instead entered the Benedictine monastery at Bec, in northwestern France, becoming an abbot in 1078. Through his reputation, Bec became a leading school of philosophy and theology. Then, while on an inspection tour of monasteries in England, Anselm became friends with King William I. In 1093 William I's son and successor, William II, appointed Anselm archbishop of Canterbury. He was canonized a saint in 1163 and declared a doctor of the church in 1720.

Anselm's main works were the *Monologion* (*Monologue*), the *Proslogion* (*Addition*), and the *Cur Deus Homo?* (*Why Did God Become Man?*). All were outstanding attempts to use reason to explain belief. He wrote, "I do not seek to understand in order that I may believe, but I believe in order that I may understand. For this I also believe, that unless I believe I will not understand." Anselm proposed the ontological argument for the existence of God, arguing that based on the fact that finite man conceives of a perfect being and that one attribute of perfection is existence, one can deduce that the very idea of a perfect being implies that God exists. Anselm also advanced the "satisfaction" theory of atonement in *Cur Deus Homo?* arguing that man owed God as his Lord the debt of obedience. Man has failed to render to God the obedience he is due and has thus offended God's honor. While man has the obligation to repay this debt, man does not have the ability to repay the honor of which God has been defrauded, because man incurs daily a greater indebtedness of obedience. God has the resources to repay the debt but not the obligation. The answer to this dilemma is the incarnation, which brings together in one person the resources to satisfy God's offended honor (arising from Christ's deity) and the obligation to repay what has been robbed (arising from Christ's humanity). His satisfaction theory represented an advance over the *Christus victor* view popular in the early church.

APOLLINARIUS (APOLLINARIS) (c. 310–c. 390)

Orthodox/catholic

Bishop of Laodicea in Syria whose Christology minimized the humanity of Christ. Growing up in Laodicea, Apollinarius began as a reader under the Arian bishop Theodotus and also read the pagan classics. When Emperor Julian deprived the Christians of the classics,[2] Apollinarius and his father, a grammarian from Beirut, created poetic meters and philosophical dialogues from the Bible. Passion and purpose in the midst of controversy marked his adult life. He was briefly excommunicated about 332 for attending a pagan function, yet he was a staunch defender of Nicene orthodoxy. In 346 he welcomed back Athanasius from exile but was excommunicated again by the Arian bishop George. However, during the conflict between the Nicenes and the Arians, he became bishop of Laodicea in 361. His views came into conflict with the Alexandrine leadership in the Council of Alexandria, who condemned them (but not him) in 362. After initially clearing himself, the conflict concerning his Christology grew until 375, when he seceded from the Orthodox Church. He was condemned by the Western Council of Rome (377), the Eastern councils of Alexandria (378) and Antioch (379), and finally Constantinople (381). Decrees in 383–88 forbade Apollinarian worship and outlawed his adherents. However, he was a man of unusual godly character so that even his opponents paid tribute to his character.

The Christology Apollinarius developed forced the church to clarify its doctrine of the Son. Being a thinker in the Alexandrine tradition, Apollinarius's difficulty lay in his explanation of the relationship of the deity and humanity in the incarnate Christ. Using Platonic psychology that saw humanity as tripartite—body, soul, and spirit (the spirit was understood as the mind/rational faculty of man)—he asserted that in the person of Christ the divine Logos replaced the human mind. This view was attacked because it robbed Jesus of a human mind, making his human nature incomplete and passive. The soteriology this entailed brought a strong reaction from the Alexandrines: If the Son was anything less than human, he could not restore fallen humanity, since it required his complete identification with humanity. The Council of Constantinople affirmed Christ's full humanity and full deity, anathematizing Apollinarius's teaching.

THOMAS AQUINAS (c. 1225–74)

Roman Catholic

Considered by most to be the greatest philosopher and theologian of the medieval church, Aquinas proposed a new synthesis of theology with the philosophy of Aristotle.

The son of Count Landulf of Aquino, Thomas went to the Benedictine school at Monte Cassino, with his parents believing him destined for the Benedictine order. In 1239 he began studies at the University of Naples, where he was attracted to the recently formed Dominican order. His family discovered this, and in their opposition, his four brothers kidnapped him and held him for fifteen months at Roccesecca, his birthplace. Nevertheless, he joined the Dominicans in 1244.

In 1245 Aquinas began studies under Albertus Magnus at the Convent of St. James in Paris. Magnus introduced him to Aristotelian thought. Aquinas accompanied Albert to Cologne to teach there and a few years later returned to Paris to teach at the university. There he became a master of theology, defended the Mendicant order[3] against the secular doctors of the University of Paris, and began writing his *Summa contra Gentiles*, an apologetic work for missionaries that contains a defense of natural theology. From 1259 to 1268, he taught at the papal curia in Italy, where he became friends with a leading translator of Aristotle's works, William Moerbeke. Here he began his *Summa Theologica*, a three-part work focusing on God the Creator, the restoration of humanity to God, and the manner in which the person and work of Christ bring about the salvation of humanity. He was recalled to Paris in 1269, where he combated the philosophical doctrines of Siger of Brabant, John Peckham, and Stephen Tempier, bishop of Paris. Being in ill health, he was on his way to the Second Council of Lyons when he died on March 7, 1274, in the Cistercian monastery of Fossanova. Aquinas was canonized in 1326, made a doctor of the church in 1567, and had his system declared the official teaching of the Catholic Church by Pope Leo XIII in 1880. (See also chapters 2.A.1.a; 7.A.3.b; 18, "Five Ways.")

ARIUS (c. 256–336)

Orthodox/catholic/Heretic

Leader in the dominant christological controversy of the fourth century. Little is known about Arius's early life, and scholars disagree on many details. It appears he was a Libyan by birth and trained under Lucian of Antioch. He was probably ordained by Bishop Peter of Alexandria, who later excommunicated him as a member of the Melitian sect. He was reordained a priest by Peter's successor, Achillas, and given charge over Baucalis, one of the principal churches of Alexandria.

Sometime around the installation of Alexander as bishop of Alexandria (c. 321), Arius championed the subordinationist view of Christ (denying the eternality of Jesus Christ and making him merely a being created by God), which spread rapidly, creating what is now known as the Arian controversy. Very likely, Arius desired to maintain the integrity of the singularity of deity in the Father and—based on passages that speak of the Son as "only begotten"—believed that "there was a time when the Son was not." The factions developed with Arius and Eusebius of Nicomedia on one side and Alexander and his disciple Athanasius on the other. Constantine's attempted settlement through Hosius failed, and he called for an ecumenical council to convene at Nicea in 325, with Eusebius of Nicomedia representing Arius at the council. The debate raged, with Alexander defining the Catholic faith in the coeternality and coequality of the Father and the Son through the use of *homoousion* (lit. "of the same substance"), and bringing about the rejection of the Arian position. The Council of Nicea developed the Nicene Creed, thereby condemning Arius and his views.

After several years of exile in Illyria, Arius was aided by Eusebius of Nicomedia's political connections to come back to Alexandria in about 334, where Athanasius refused the order to take him back into communion. In light of Constantine's wavering and the political connections involved, Arius's view did not die out after his death in 336 but actually grew in strength and was at times the dominant belief. When Constantius succeeded his father, Constantine, as emperor, he favored Arianism and allowed the heresy a period of ascendancy. Thus Arianism remained influential until Julian the Apostate ascended the throne and withdrew all imperial support from the church, hoping the theological warfare would destroy it. During this period, the brilliant expositions of the Nicene faith by the Cappadocians (Basil the Great, Gregory of Nazianzus, and Gregory of Nyssa), the orthodox Nicene party was able to theologically defeat Arianism, which was then condemned again at the Council of Constantinople in 381. After Constantinople, Arianism became a minor sectarian heresy reappearing occasionally throughout history (e.g., Jehovah's Witnesses and extreme Unitarians) but never as the primary position of the church.

JAMES (JACOB) ARMINIUS (1560–1609)

Arminian

Dutch theologian who, in response to rigid Calvinism, put forth a theological perspective centered on the concept of human freedom and responsibility. (See chapter 12.A.2–3.)

ATHANASIUS (c. 297–373)

Orthodox/catholic

Bishop of Alexandria and a staunch defender of Nicene orthodoxy. Athanasius served as a presbyter under Bishop Alexander at the time of the Arian controversy. At the council at Nicea (A.D. 325), Athanasius, although present, did not have the ecclesiastical authority to speak. In 328, when Bishop Alexander died, Athanasius succeeded him. He became the greatest theologian of the fourth century and the chief defender of Nicene Trinitarianism against Arianism. He endured banishment from his see on five occasions for a total of seventeen years, exiled four times by Arian emperors and once by Julian the Apostate because of his strict adherence to the doctrine of the Trinity.

Athanasius's publication *On the Incarnation of the Word of God* upheld the orthodox understanding of Scripture that the Logos is the eternal Son who by union with manhood, death, and resurrection is Savior.

AUGUSTINE OF HIPPO (354–430)

Orthodox/catholic

Augustine is rightly called the most influential theologian in all of Western Christianity. His theological articulation forms the fountainhead of both the Catholic and the Protestant perspectives to this day. His views on anthropology (human depravity) remain dominant in Protestantism.

Born in Tagaste, North Africa, to a pagan father (Patricius) and a devout but overbearing Christian mother, Monica, Augustine developed a passion for truth after reading Cicero's *Hortensius*, and he began a quest that would last for more than a decade. During this time, he rejected Christianity and was involved successively with Manichaeism and Neoplatonism. After becoming a professional teacher of rhetoric in Milan, he attended Christian services to hear Bishop Ambrose, the greatest preacher of the day. Although his interest lay in Ambrose's rhetoric, he came under conviction by the message and was converted to Christianity at age thirty-three. He then returned to Tagaste and joined a monastic community. At age thirty-seven, Augustine visited Hippo, where he was forced into the priesthood. Later he founded a monastery and also became bishop of Hippo. He died as the Vandals ransacked the city.

Augustine was the last of the early Christian writers and the most quoted source in the theology produced in the Middle Ages. He is recognized as one of the four doctors of the ancient Roman Catholic Church (along with Ambrose, Jerome, and Gregory the Great); additionally the Reformation was built squarely on his shoulders, making him a force in the Protestant movements as well. Catholic theologians see Augustine's theology of the church (visible versus invisible) and sacraments (regular and valid) as his greatest contribution; Protestants focus on his thinking in anthropology (depravity of man) and soteriology (salvation by grace alone). Throughout the Middle Ages, the church misinterpreted Augustine's views on anthropology and soteriology, and it was not until the Reformation that his teaching was discovered firsthand.

Augustine formulated his doctrine of original sin and consequent total depravity from the teachings of the apostle Paul, filtered through the lens of his personal struggles with sexual temptation and sin. His doctrine of depravity and inability provoked an intense response by Pelagius, a prominent British monk teaching in Rome. (See "Pelagius" below and "Pelagianism" in chapter 18.) Between 411 and 431, several councils addressed the Pelagian controversy. It was in this setting that Augustine argued vigorously for the doctrine of original sin as the inherited liability, guilt, and corruption of Adam. Furthermore, Augustine argued for predestination, that all humanity was in a mire of sin and that God elected some to receive salvific grace.

Augustine greatly influenced Martin Luther, John Calvin, and the other Reformers, especially with the doctrines of depravity, predestination, and perseverance. His two most celebrated works, *Confessions* and *City of God*, remain classics.

KARL BARTH (1886–1968)

Reformed/Neoorthodox

Swiss theologian and the father of neoorthodoxy, best known for his massive *Church Dogmatics.* (See chapter 15.B.1.)

BASIL THE GREAT (c. 330–79)

Orthodox/catholic

Bishop of Caesarea, who was instrumental in the establishment of the Nicene faith and one of the theological architects who oversaw the final defeat of Arianism. Basil grew up in Caesarea, then went to Athens to study law. There he met Prince Julian (later to become Emperor Julian the Apostate) and became good friends with Gregory of Nazianzus. Basil, his brother Gregory of Nyssa, and his friend Gregory of Nazianzus would come to be known in history as the "Three Cappadocians" who battled for the triumph of the Nicene faith.

After returning to Caesarea, Basil visited various monasteries in Palestine, Syria, and Egypt, then settled in a small communal hermitage. When Bishop Eusebius of Caesarea called on him to help in the fight against the Arians, Basil began to produce writings that championed the Trinitarian theology of the Council of Nicea, for example, *Against Eunomius*. When Eusebius died, Basil was elected to succeed him as bishop of Caesarea. He died in 379, his life shortened due to a lifetime of severe physical asceticism.

Most of Basil's writings are apologetic in nature, directed toward the Arian controversy over the Trinity. His work *On the Holy Spirit* dealt with the deity of the Holy Spirit, a topic not addressed before the fourth century. Basil also developed and established the monastic system in Pontus. He preferred communal monasteries, and some of his writings address the rules and organization of these communities.

FERDINAND CHRISTIAN BAUR (1792–1860)

Liberal

German Protestant theologian and New Testament scholar and critic. Baur spent most of his life as a professor at the University of Tübingen, and his approach to New Testament interpretation came to be known as the Tübingen School of New Testament criticism. He applied Hegel's dialectic to the development of Christianity and the New Testament. Baur's critical conclusions marked a dramatic shift in New Testament studies, and his perspective became the fountainhead of critical thinking for over a century.

The best exposition of Baur's understanding is contained in his extensive work *Paul the Apostle of Jesus Christ* (two volumes, 1845). Baur saw a historical dialectic operative at the inception of Christianity that was represented by three parties. The first was the Jewish party, led by Peter, which was in opposition to the second group, a Gentile party led by Paul. Conflict abounded between these two groups, but it was resolved in the late second and third centuries by a conciliatory group (also called the Catholic group), which formed a synthesis of the two opposing positions.

HERMAN BAVINCK (1854–1921)

Reformed

Dutch Reformed theologian, leading theologian (with Abraham Kuyper) of the neo-Calvinist revival that began in the Dutch Reformed Church during the late nineteenth century. (See chapter 11.F.2.)

THOMAS BECKET (À BECKET) (c. 1118–70)

Roman Catholic

English archbishop and martyr. Born in London, Thomas à Becket (or Thomas Becket) was educated in England and France. In 1155 Henry II made him chancellor of England. After the death of Archbishop Theobald in 1162, Henry appointed Becket, his trusted adviser and confidant, archbishop of Canterbury, with hopes of regaining control over the English church, which had been lost under his predecessor, King Stephen. Becket, however, became a staunchly independent and capable church leader who firmly defended the rights of the church. He served the pope and demonstrated full allegiance while remaining a favorite with the people.

Becket fell into conflict with his former friend, the king, which led to his temporary relocation to France. But in 1170 he reconciled with Henry and returned to Canterbury, only to become involved in another controversy. Later that year he was murdered in the Cathedral of Canterbury by a band of the king's supporters. As a result, the pope ordered Henry to abandon the constitution and do public penance at Becket's graveside. Becket was canonized shortly thereafter, and his tomb became a popular pilgrimage destination immortalized by Geoffrey Chaucer in the *Canterbury Tales.*

BENEDICT OF NURSIA (c. 480–c. 547)

Orthodox/catholic

Italian monk and founder of monasteries. Benedict was born at Nursia in Umbria into a wealthy family and later pursued an education in Rome. But he disapproved of the immoral lifestyle demonstrated by others at school and promptly dropped out. At age fourteen he began to live as a hermit in a cave at Subiaco and later gathered several cells with thirteen monks in each. He became abbot, overseeing all of the monks and monasteries.

In 529 Benedict left Subiaco and founded a monastery at Monte Cassino on a mountain between Rome and Naples. It was here that organized monasticism in general as well as the Benedictine order in particular originated. He oversaw this order for fourteen years and composed the Benedictine rule of poverty, chastity, and obedience. This rule, which became a model for future monastic orders, included requiring monks to copy manuscripts, study, do physical work, and attend to the things of the soul.

LOUIS BERKHOF (1873–1957)

Reformed

Prominent twentieth-century American Reformed theologian. (See chapter 11.F.3.)

G. C. BERKOUWER (1903–96)

Reformed

Dutch Reformed theologian regarded as one of the significant theological minds of the twentieth century. Berkouwer's willingness to dialogue with modern movements in theology while remaining within the boundaries of traditional Reformed theology has made him a key figure in contemporary theology.

Born in Amsterdam, Berkouwer matriculated at the Free University of Amsterdam in 1922. Two theologians who consecutively served as professor of systematic theology had created the milieu of this theological institution: Abraham Kuyper, followed by Herman Bavinck. After receiving his doctorate in 1932, Berkouwer entered the pastorate and in 1945 was appointed to the chair of dogmatics at the Free University.

During Berkouwer's years at the university, his theological insights were recorded in his fourteen-volume *Studies in Dogmatics*. Each volume considers a different topic in theology, and the set covers the entire field of theological inquiry. Significant new contributions in theology are dealt with judiciously (e.g., the neoorthodoxy of Karl Barth), avoiding reductionistic characterizations. Berkouwer is sometimes innovative, as seen in his concept of the central message of Scripture as it interacts with inerrancy, and he is immensely practical. He challenges all a priori assumptions present when Scripture is systematized and urges that a theologian should not go further than the Word of God.

Berkouwer's emphasis on dialogue that turns to the Bible for answers is a paradigm that seems essential in the continuing task of the theologian. G. C. Berkouwer personified this method and applied it to the theology of Karl Barth and the Roman Catholic Church. Perhaps it is this attitude of critical interaction that will be most remembered by future theologians.

BERNARD OF CLAIRVAUX (c. 1090–1153)

Roman Catholic

Medieval mystic, monastic reformer, and founder of the Cistercian monastery in Clairvaux. Bernard has been called the "most powerful churchman of twelfth-century Europe" as well as "father of Western mysticism." In his youth he tended toward asceticism and encouraged others to follow his devoted way of living. At age twenty-three he entered the famous monastery at Citeaux, from which came the Cistercian order of monks. In 1115 he then founded the famous Clairvaux monastery, presiding as abbot until his death in 1153.

Bernard was a counselor to kings and popes, was a preacher to large crowds, and was highly influential in Germany and Italy. As a defender of Catholic orthodoxy, he condemned the scholastic teachings of Peter Abelard and the anti-papal views of Arnold of Brescia. Bernard was a man of holy reputation and a skilled speaker. He demonstrated a passionate love for God and brought about new devotion to Christ in the church. His theology emphasized the infinite love and mercy of God over judgment. He wrote a number of religious treatises and hymns, including "Jesus the Very Thought of Thee" and "O Sacred Head Now Wounded." He was canonized in 1174 and was made a church doctor in 1830.

THEODORE BEZA (1519–1605)

Reformed

French Reformed theologian and successor to Calvin in Geneva. Born into a noble family in Vezelay, Burgundy, Beza's early education was directed by Melchior Wolman, a crypto-Lutheran who taught him both the classics and Luther's views on justification by faith. At age fifteen, Beza began the study of law in Orleans. He was licensed to practice in 1539. However, his passion was the classics, which he pursued with innate ability. In 1548 Beza published a book of Latin poetry, *Poemata Junenilia*, which established him as the finest Latin poet of the day.

The crisis that changed Beza's course in life was a severe illness. After recovering from the illness, he renounced Catholicism and embraced Protestantism. He was appointed professor of Greek at Lausanne, where he labored from 1549 to1558. In 1558 Calvin asked him to come to Geneva as a professor of Greek at the newly founded Academy. When Calvin died in 1564, his mantle fell to Beza, who carried it until his death at the age of eighty-six.

As a student of the classics, Beza contributed to the area of textual criticism of the New Testament, and his works on textual criticism influenced the translators of the Authorized Version. His theological works were *Confession of the Christian Faith* (1560) and *Theological Treatises* (1570–82). While claiming to simply continue the doctrine of Calvin, Beza differed methodologically from Calvin and subtly changed the emphasis of Calvin's theology. He made predestination a topic to be contemplated under the heading of the attributes of God and insisted on limited atonement, a conclusion Calvin suggests only inconsistently. The presbyterian form of church government, only suggested by Calvin, was required by Beza of all Reformed churches. Under Beza's direction, Calvinism moved from its original form into the scholastic mode, a more logical and hard form of Calvin's thought. This transition set the stage for the debates between Arminians and Calvinists that would characterize the seventeenth century.

GEORG BLAUROCK (c. 1492–1529)

Anabaptist

Early Anabaptist preacher credited with initiating the practice of believer's baptism as opposed to infant baptism. Blaurock was a priest in the small town of Chur, Switzerland, when he first heard Zwingli preach. He was converted under Zwingli's ministry sometime prior to 1523 and later became one of the founding Anabaptists. He is known for being the first person to be rebaptized by Conrad Grebel when the Anabaptists broke off from Zwingli in 1525 (which began what has been called the Radical Reformation, or the left wing of the Reformation). Called "the second Paul" because of his eloquence, Blaurock became through his preaching the most influential Anabaptist.

In 1525 Blaurock planted a church in Zollikon, a small town just outside Zurich. The congregation quickly grew to 150 members, but local authorities responded by arresting Blaurock and other leaders of the church. In 1527 Blaurock was banished from Switzerland. During the next few years, he toured Europe as an evangelist, and thousands responded to his message. It was Blaurock who first brought the Anabaptist message to Tyrol, where the Moravians became one of the most devoted groups of Anabaptists. In 1529 he was arrested and tortured and burned at the stake as a heretic at Clausen in Tyrol.

DONALD BLOESCH (1928–)

Reformed

Prominent twentieth-century theologian. Coming from a background that exposed him to philosophy, sociology, liberalism, pietism, and neoorthodoxy,

Bloesch has become a powerful force in the evangelical movement. His work reflects sympathy with Barth and takes issue with aspects of both fundamentalism and liberalism.

Bloesch's father was a pastor in the Evangelical and Reformed Church (which was later merged into the United Church of Christ). The Lutheran pietism of this denomination influenced the young Bloesch. At Elmhurst College, the denominational school, he received his first exposure to liberal theology, and he chose to attend Chicago Theological Seminary, a school dominated by process theology. After earning his Ph.D. in 1956, he joined the faculty at Dubuque Theological Seminary, a Presbyterian institution, where he has remained throughout his career.

Bloesch's journey from liberalism to evangelicalism had many steps. He had considerable exposure to many of the contemporary trends in theology, such as process theology, neoorthodoxy, and existential theology. Although each of these influenced his thinking, it was a wholesale reliance on the Bible that transformed Bloesch into an evangelical. He rejected the ideologies that shaped these other views and strove to understand the framework of the Scriptures. This ideological awareness has allowed him to chart a course within the larger evangelical framework while steering clear of the extremes in this tradition.

A prolific author who has written or edited more than twenty-five books and some three hundred articles, he has made his major contribution to systematic theology in his *Essentials of Evangelical Theology*. This two-volume set deals with issues that have tended to divide the church (e.g., salvation by grace, the priesthood of all believers, the personal return of Christ) and reveals Bloesch's passion for ecumenism among believers. His strong belief in a God-focused gospel with social imperatives has forged a balance in his thinking that is rarely maintained with such potency among evangelicals. This two-volume set has been followed by his seven-volume magnum opus *Christian Foundations* surveying the breadth of Christian doctrine.

DIETRICH BONHOEFFER (1906–45)

Lutheran

German Lutheran pastor, theologian, and martyr, deeply influenced by Karl Barth. With Barth, Bonhoeffer was instrumental in the creation of the Barmen Declaration in 1934 and became a leader of the confessing church that opposed the Nazis. Prior to World War II, he was forbidden to speak or publish, and although he could have found refuge in America, he decided in 1939 that if he were to serve his fellow Germans, he would have to remain in his homeland and suffer. He became involved in the movement that opposed Hitler and in a plot to take Hitler's life. He was imprisoned in a Nazi camp from 1943 to 1945, where he spent much time deep in thought and wrote several books. His works include *Ethics*, *The Cost of Discipleship*, *Letters and Papers from Prison*, and *Creation and Fall*. He was not a systematic thinker, but his works influenced many late-twentieth-century theological movements, especially liberation theology, and those who have suffered persecution under oppressive political regimes. Bonhoeffer was executed for treason on April 9, 1945, just days before the end of World War II. (See chapter also 15.B.4.)

BONIFACE VIII (1235–1303)

Roman Catholic

The pope at the nadir of papal influence over the monarchy. Born Benedetto Gaetani, Boniface VIII was pope from 1294 to 1303, and he inherited the papal power that had been established under Innocent III (1160–1216). The struggle between secular rulers and those within the hierarchy of the church had been going on for centuries, and during Boniface's reign, papal influence over the monarchs reached its lowest point.

Philip IV of France repeatedly challenged Boniface. The first incident was over Philip's right to tax the clergy. Boniface issued a bull, *Clericos Laicos*, forbidding all clergy from paying any tax that was not sanctioned by the pope. In response, Philip stopped sending church revenue from his countries. This retaliation forced Boniface to capitulate to Philip.

The second incident concerned a French bishop accused of treason. Philip claimed jurisdiction, but Boniface maintained that the clergy were exempt from secular authority. In defense of his claim, Boniface issued a bull, *Unum Sanctum*, declaring the absolute authority of the pope over all earthly authorities. *Unum Sanctum* asserted that the spiritual authority of the church could never be judged by any earthly authority, but only by God. Moreover, only those who were in subjection to the pope could be saved, inferring that those who opposed him in France would face eternal condemnation for their actions. In response, a French synod leveled a number of accusations against Boniface, including murder, and an armed band of men was sent to Italy to arrest Boniface. The men never reached Rome, but Boniface died a few months after their attempt.

While Boniface attempted to extend the power established by Innocent III, the changing political conditions proved the practical impotence of the ecclesiastical hierarchy in exercising authority over secular powers.

EMIL BRUNNER (1889–1966)

Neoorthodox

Swiss Reformed theologian who, along with Karl Barth, was a major figure in neoorthodox theology. For much of his career, he was professor of systematic and practical theology in Zurich; later in life he taught at the International Christian University of Tokyo. Among his many works are *Man in Revolt* and his three-volume *Dogmatics.*

Brunner rehabilitated the doctrines of sin, the incarnation, and the resurrection, restating them for the twentieth century. He was instrumental in helping to reestablish Scripture as normative for faith and practice in the church. This personal emphasis reflected the influence of Søren Kierkegaard and Martin Buber. Brunner sided with Barth in his opposition to theological liberalism but disagreed with Barth on the question of general revelation. Brunner's thought, like Barth's, evidenced a high Christology but with this difference: Brunner emphasized a personal relationship with Jesus as the centerpiece of the Christian faith. Flowing from this was an ethical perspective that attempted to retain the tension between individual liberty and life in community. To this was added the concept of the church as a dynamic fellowship based on individual existence in Christ rather than on the external organization. (See also chapter 15.B.2.)

JOHANN HEINRICH BULLINGER (1504–75)

Reformed

Churchman and Reformer who led Swiss Protestantism after Zwingli's death. Bullinger's adoption of Reformation thought was also influenced by the writings of Luther and Melanchthon. For several years, he studied evangelical doctrine, and in 1531 he succeeded Zwingli as pastor of the Grossmünster Church in Zurich. In 1536 he was one of the authors of the First and Second Helvetic Confessions, hoping to find the correct understanding of the Eucharist as well as common ground with other Reformed groups. In 1549 he worked with John Calvin in writing the *Consensus Tigurinus* (Consensus of Zurich) of the Lord's Supper, ending the dogmatic disputes in Protestant Switzerland. In 1566 he drafted the Second Helvetic Confession.

Bullinger maintained wide correspondence with both political and ecclesiastical leaders, including Henry VIII, Edward VI, and Elizabeth of England. He was considered an eloquent preacher, a devoted pastor, a solid thinker, and a consistent witness. He consistently followed the doctrines of the

Reformed Church over against the views from Roman Catholics, Anabaptists, and Lutherans. He was willing to listen to other positions but remained uncompromising in his own convictions.

RUDOLF BULTMANN (1884–1976)

Liberal/Existential

The leading New Testament scholar of the mid-twentieth century. Bultmann taught at the University of Marburg from 1921 to 1951. He applied the form criticism pioneered by German scholar Hermann Gunkel to the New Testament documents to the point of methodological skepticism. He posited a radical disjuncture between history and faith and contended that if the New Testament were to be accepted by modern man, it had to be demythologized and reinterpreted existentially in a modern context. He envisioned this project as one that asserts the primacy of faith in Jesus, who calls humanity to accept his radical demand to recognize himself as one in whom God is savingly present. But Bultmann's radical historical skepticism left nearly nothing of the historicity of the New Testament, except for the reality of the crucifixion.

While often associated with Barth and Brunner as part of the neoorthodox movement, in reality Bultmann's thought is an amalgamation of a dialectic method, a Lutheran insistence on *sola fide*, and a continuation of the basic rationalistic assumptions of nineteenth-century theological liberalism.

JOHN BUNYAN (1628–88)

Puritan

Puritan preacher and writer, best known for the literary classic *Pilgrim's Progress.* Born at Elstow, near Bedford, England, Bunyan was a tinker by trade and a Baptist by theological conviction. During the Restoration in 1660, he was imprisoned for twelve years for preaching without a license or permission from the established church. In jail he wrote a number of books, including *Pilgrim's Progress*, *The Holy War*, and his famous autobiography, *Grace Abounding to the Chief of Sinners.* In the latter part of his imprisonment, he was given a great deal of freedom and was even allowed to preach outside the jail on occasion. The Act of Pardon led to his release in 1672, giving him permission to preach. He worked with independents in Bedford and did evangelistic work. The last years of his life were spent pastoring at the Bedford Baptist Church.

HORACE BUSHNELL (1802–76)

Liberal

American Congregational minister recognized as the father of American theological liberalism. Bushnell had planned for a career in law but after conversion chose the ministry and attended Yale Divinity School. Drawing most of his ideas from practical experience as a pastor at Hartford's North Church (1833–59), Bushnell fashioned a new approach to and synthesis of theology. Noting that all language is metaphoric, he concluded that doctrinal arguments are relative. His *Christian Nurture* (1847) argued that conversion should be a gradual educative process rather than instantaneous. Subjectivism and experience of spiritual matters became more important to Bushnell as he argued in *God in Christ* (1849) that language is inadequate to represent spiritual realities. In *Nature and the Supernatural* (1858) he posited the metaphysical cosmos as an organic whole, with no sharp distinctions between categories such as the natural and the supernatural, individual and society, humanity and divinity. Rather, he held that there is constant penetration and interaction between aspects where one affects the other, where God reunites the world to himself through reconciling love instead of punishment. Bushnell's influence paved the way for the acceptance of European liberalism in America.

JOSEPH BUTLER (1692–1752)

Anglican

English theologian, apologist of the Church of England, and bishop of Durham, best known for his work discrediting deism. Butler served as preacher at the Rolls Chapel in London, later was bishop of Bristol, and then served in Durham until his death. He was offered the position of archbishop of Canterbury in 1747 but declined.

Living in the "golden age of English deism," Butler became famous for his *Analogy of Religion*, which attacked deism and tried to find a rational foundation for Christianity in the world of nature. This book was a required text in apologetics for years in both English and American universities. He is considered to be among the greatest exponents of natural theology since the Reformation.

JOHN CALVIN (1509–64)

Reformed

French Reformer and theologian, father and systematizer of Reformed theology, and one of the most influential theologians in the history of the church. (See chapter 11.A.)

JOHN MCLEOD CAMPBELL (1800–1872)

Reformed

Scottish theologian. Educated at Glasgow and Edinburgh, Campbell in 1825 was appointed curate of Row in Strathclyde. The next year he became convinced of the doctrine of "assurance of faith," which led to his arraignment before the Dunbarton Presbytery. In 1831 the general assembly found him guilty of preaching the doctrine of universal atonement and propounding that assurance is of the essence of faith. He was removed from his position. Subsequently Campbell maintained a ministry to an independent congregation at Glasgow from 1833 to 1859. In *The Nature of the Atonement* (1856), Campbell argued against the penal substitution of Christ's atonement, stating that Christ's spiritual sufferings atoned for all humanity and fulfilled the condition of forgiveness. He saw in his work a purging of Calvinistic gloom. Campbell's theological contribution to Scottish theology was recognized by Glasgow University when it conferred on him an honorary doctor of divinity.

ANDREAS VON CARLSTADT (KARLSTADT) (1480–1541)

Lutheran

German Protestant Reformer. Carlstadt studied at Erfurt and Cologne and later taught at the new University of Wittenberg. He was originally an adherent of the scholastic system of Thomas Aquinas but later repudiated his beliefs and became a supporter of the Protestant movement. In 1518 he wrote against Johann Eck in support of Luther, emphasizing the authority of Scripture above the church and its councils. In 1519 he debated Eck. Since Carlstadt was a better scholar than debater, Luther came to his aid in the debate. In 1520 a papal bull condemned Carlstadt, Luther, and others.

While Luther was in hiding at Wartburg, Carlstadt and Philip Melanchthon became the leaders of the Reformation. On Christmas Day 1521, Carlstadt led the Wittenberg community in Communion in the Castle Church; he omitted the most essential features of Roman liturgy and offered the cup to the laity. He married in 1522, and he taught that all ministers could marry.

He opposed church music, religious images, begging, and religious fraternities, and he also destroyed icons. Luther had originally been in favor of these changes but later felt uneasy about them. The two men parted company over these differences. Carlstadt saw Luther as not going far enough to reform the church, and Luther saw Carlstadt as being an extremist to the point of endangering the Reformation.

Luther went to Wittenberg to address the situation Carlstadt had created, while Carlstadt went to Orlamünde, where he became a popular preacher. In 1524 Luther went to Orlamünde to debate Carlstadt at the request of the Saxon authorities. Later Carlstadt was banished, eventually settling in Switzerland, where his symbolic understanding of Communion was accepted. There he joined forces with Zwingli. Carlstadt was a professor at Basel until his death.

EDWARD JOHN CARNELL (1919–67)

Reformed

Twentieth-century American theologian known for his intellectual contributions to conservative evangelical theology. Carnell was born into the home of a fundamentalist Baptist minister in Wisconsin. He received his undergraduate education at Wheaton College, where Gordon H. Clark had a profound influence on him. Carnell's apologetic work would always utilize the law of noncontradiction on which Clark so often relied. Carnell went on to study apologetics at Westminster Theological Seminary under Cornelius Van Til and later obtained a Th.D. from Harvard and a Ph.D. from Boston University.

Carnell taught at Gordon College and Divinity School, then at Fuller Theological Seminary. From 1954 through 1959, he was the president of Fuller, after which he resumed teaching. His book *An Introduction to Christian Apologetics* made him prominent among evangelicals, but he was attacked by many fundamentalists for his association with Fuller Seminary. Perhaps because of the pain of that time, he later wrote a scathing attack on fundamentalism in his work *The Case for Orthodoxy* (1959). Throughout his life, Carnell struggled with clinical depression, and he died of an overdose of his antidepressant.

As evangelicalism matured in the post–World War II era, Carnell was instrumental in giving orthodoxy an intellectual and apologetically persuasive voice. His development of the verificational method represented a new avenue in apologetics, and he influenced the next generation of theologians (e.g., Colin Brown and Gordon Lewis). Finally, although his critique was harshly worded, Carnell's words to fundamentalists served to distinguish that extreme group from the remainder of the evangelical community.

LEWIS SPERRY CHAFER (1871–1952)

Dispensational

American Presbyterian clergyman, theologian, and educator who advanced premillennial dispensational theology in the early twentieth century. Originally trained as a musician, Chafer began his ministry as a gospel singer and evangelist, then turned to education. He met and was influenced by C. I. Scofield in 1901, joined the faculty of Philadelphia College of the Bible in 1914, and moved to Dallas in 1923 to pastor Scofield Memorial Church. There, in 1924, he established the Evangelical Theological College (renamed Dallas Theological Seminary in 1936), where he became president and professor of systematic theology.

Chafer strengthened premillennial and dispensational theology through his teaching and academic work. Chafer edited the journal *Bibliotheca Sacra* and wrote books on topics such as Satan, evangelism, the kingdom of God, grace, and the Christian life. His *Systematic Theology* (1947) laid a detailed foundation for dispensational theology.

MARTIN CHEMNITZ (1522–86)

Lutheran

German Lutheran Reformer. Chemnitz was recognized early for his intellectual skill and was sent to the Latin school at Wittenberg, only to leave to help in his family's business. He returned to school at Magdeburg, then attended the University of Wittenberg to study under Philip Melanchthon. Moving to Königsberg when the Smalcald War broke out, he developed a deep interest in the study of theology and earned the degree of magister. Subsequently he served as librarian of the ducal library, as a professor at Wittenberg, and finally as a preacher in Brunswick. He also founded the University of Helmstedt.

Chemnitz had an immense impact on the Lutheran movement. His *Examen Concilii Tridentini* analyzes the Tridentine assertions against the teachings of Scripture and the early fathers, as well as the sacraments and the abuses of the Roman Catholic Church. It is considered a masterpiece of Reformational Lutheran exposition. His work on the Formula of Concord helped forge unity among Lutheran pastors. It has been said that if Martin Chemnitz had not come, Martin Luther hardly would have survived.

JOHN CHRYSOSTOM (c. 347–407)

Orthodox/catholic

A doctor of the Greek church and the second leading influence on the Reformers (behind only Augustine). Chrysostom was raised in Antioch, Syria, by his widowed Christian mother. After studying and practicing law, which he found unsatisfying, he pursued Christian asceticism. Baptized by Bishop Melitius and instructed by Diodorus at the Antiochene school, he devoted himself to his mother and lived as a monk. After his mother died, Chrysostom pursued a more rigorous monasticism in the mountains, which ultimately ruined his health and drove him back to Antioch, where he was recognized for his wisdom, preaching skill, scholarship, and piety while serving first as a deacon, then as an elder.

In 398 Chrysostom was unwillingly appointed patriarch of Constantinople, where he set out to reform the leadership of the church. This met with resistance from the emperor's wife, who, along with Patriarch Theophilus of Alexandria, set out to depose him. After several attempts, they were successful as he defied an imperial order in 404. He was exiled to the eastern frontier, where his influence was still felt. He was ordered to march to a more remote location three years later and died on the way due to exhaustion and exposure. He was later vindicated posthumously, and in 438 his remains were honorably interred in Constantinople.

Chrysostom's teaching was based on a literal and grammatical exegesis, yet he is not known as systematic, precise, or original in his theology. His passion was for the people to whom he ministered, with an emphasis on the spiritual and moral applications drawn primarily from the Pauline writings and the gospels of Matthew and John. His reputation grew to the point where the sixth-century churchmen regularly referred to him as "Chrysostomos" (golden-mouthed).

GORDON H. CLARK (1902–86)

Reformed

A deductive rationalist who advanced the intellectual depth of evangelicalism during the rise of modernism in the first half of the twentieth century. Clark earned a Ph.D. in philosophy from the University of Pennsylvania, where he also began his teaching career. In 1936 he moved to Wheaton College in Illinois, where he had a deep influence on many evangelicals, including Carl F. H. Henry, who called him "one of the profoundest evangelical Protestant philosophers of our time." While he was at Wheaton and later at Butler

University in Indianapolis, his work brought a notable respectability to a rather unsophisticated fundamentalism, which helped to give balance to evangelicalism and to Reformed doctrine in particular. Among his most notable works is *A Christian View of Men and Things* (1951). Clark also served as a contributing editor of *Christianity Today.*

CLEMENT OF ALEXANDRIA (c. 150–c. 215)

Orthodox/catholic

Athens-born pagan who was converted to Christianity, known as one of the first systematizers of theology. Clement also defended orthodoxy against the Gnostics, stressing the eternal preexistence, incarnation, and redemptive work of the Logos. He went to Alexandria, succeeding his teacher as head of the catechetical school in 190. He laid the foundation for the concept of philosophy as the servant to theology. Clement's work is found in four complete preserved writings and fragments, *Protreptikos*, *Paedagogos*, *Stromata*, and *Hypotyposes*. He left Alexandria in 202 under persecution and apparently never returned.

Crucial to Clement's understanding was the Logos, Creator of all things, who guides all good men and is the originator of all right thought. Consequently, Greek philosophy was a partial revelation and prepared the Greeks for Christ, the final revelation, as the law had done for the Jews. Against the Gnostics, Clement saw faith as the necessary first principle and foundation for knowledge, itself the perfection of faith. People attain to God's likeness when, by love and contemplation, they rid themselves of passions and arrive at impassability. Thus Clement insisted that orthodoxy is the true *gnosis* and its followers are the true Gnostics. Clement profoundly influenced Greek Christian spirituality and soteriology with this idea.

JOHANNES COCCEIUS (1603–69)

Reformed

Linguist and the German father of covenant theology who argued dogmatically based on biblical thought. As a teacher in Bremen, his birthplace, Cocceius defended the Bible against philosophy and secular thought. He moved to Franeker, Holland, and became a professor of languages, later the chair of Hebrew studies, and then professor of theology.

While Cocceius was a self-professed Calvinist, he found problems with Calvinistic scholastic orthodoxy on the grounds that key presuppositions were logical but not necessarily biblical. He developed a biblical theology through which he concluded that God had developed three different kinds of covenants with man: (1) With Adam, God established a covenant of works; this was replaced by (2) a covenant of grace, which was finalized through Christ as the (3) new covenant. Cocceius's teachings evolved into a system of thought known as *federal theology*. Those who subscribed to his views following his death were accused of unorthodoxy. Yet his understanding eventually became the dominant view of the divine-human relationship within Reformed theology. His best-known work is the *Doctrine of the Covenant and Testaments of God*.

JAMES HAL CONE (1938–)

Liberation

Twentieth-century African-American theologian known for developing the contemporary black liberation theology movement. The racial turbulence of the 1960s shook the United States, and many of the leaders of the nation's black community were pastors, such as Martin Luther King Jr. Although there was a definite black expression of Protestant religion, it was not until Cone published his book *Black Theology and Black Power* (1969) that black theology was born.

Cone began his graduate education at Garrett Theological Seminary and finished with a Ph.D. from Northwestern University. After a number of teaching appointments, he became a faculty member of Union Theological Seminary in New York, where he is currently the Charles A. Briggs Professor of Systematic Theology. Cone acknowledges that he drew inspiration from the work of Karl Barth and Paul Tillich as he formulated his understanding of the liberation message.

The core of Cone's appraisal of the gospel is liberation for oppressed people. As is also true in other liberation theologies, a particularly symbolic biblical event is the exodus, when God delivers his people from the hands of political and economic oppression. The term *Black Power* had been used to express the secular movement of equal rights for the African-American, and Cone believes that the gospel supports and gives ethical underpinnings to the cause of Black Power.

CONSTANTINE THE GREAT (c. 288–337)

Orthodox/catholic

The first Christian emperor of Rome. Constantine initiated tolerance of and favor toward the practice of Christianity among his people, making it a lawful religion in Roman society. As a believer himself, he strove to bring church and state together through various policies and legislation. Socially, he demonstrated a Christian attitude toward individuals and groups who were in need of extended rights and privileges. His laws concerning the treatment of slaves and prisoners show the influence of Christian teachings. He was baptized shortly before his death.

In 313 Constantine issued the Edict of Milan, which gave Christians the right to practice their religion openly. By 323 he had taken over rule of the entire Roman world. At that time Arianism threatened to split the Christian church into two camps. To settle the matter, Constantine called an ecumenical, or worldwide, council of bishops at Nicea in Asia Minor in 325. He presided at the council and suggested the term *homoousios* to express the relationship between the Father and the Son. An overwhelming majority condemned the Arian view as heresy. The council drew up the Nicene Creed, which stands to this day as the foundational doctrinal statement of those who call themselves Christian.

THOMAS CRANMER (1489–1556)

Reformed/Anglican

The first archbishop of Canterbury of the Church of England, who put the English Bible in parish churches, contributed to the formation of the *Thirty-nine Articles*, and drew up the *Book of Common Prayer*. Cranmer helped Henry VIII in making the churches in England independent from Rome.

Educated at Cambridge, Cranmer became an outstanding religion scholar. He favored the "new way of thinking" that resulted from Martin Luther's revolt against the Roman Catholic Church. Cranmer's involvement in the interpretation of church law to Henry's benefit came about by chance, but the king immediately became supportive of him and in 1533 appointed him archbishop of Canterbury. When Edward VI became king after Henry died, Cranmer led the Anglican Church to a thoroughgoing Protestant stance. He led in the renewal of the English liturgy and helped in circulating the Bible in the English language.

Upon Mary Tudor's ascension to the throne, Cranmer was arrested and charged with treason. He was convicted and sentenced to death, but Mary spared his life. Three years later he was tried for heresy and convicted. He recanted under duress, but when taken to the stake to be burned on March 21, 1556, he renounced his recantation and held his right hand in the fire until it dropped off and he died.

CYPRIAN (c. 200–258)

Orthodox/catholic

Bishop of Carthage who was the first African bishop to be martyred. Cyprian demonstrated impressive literary knowledge and knew the Scriptures as well as the writings of Tertullian thoroughly. He became a Christian in midlife and eventually devoted himself to asceticism. As the head of the North African clergy, he sought to maintain the unity of the church when an attempt was made to excommunicate those who had lapsed from the faith during persecution. Cyprian favored tolerance for these people, though only after penance and suitable delay. He emphasized penance and baptism as means of grace and left the church a number of important works. Refusing to renounce his faith after banishment by the Roman emperor Valerian, he was beheaded while crying out, *"Deo Gratias!"* He was later proclaimed a saint and is viewed as a hero and a loyal Christian, encouraging many through his faithfulness.

CYRIL OF ALEXANDRIA (c. 376–444)

Orthodox/catholic

Bishop of Alexandria. Cyril was so zealous for orthodoxy that he closed Novatian churches (see below, "Novatian"), declaring them to be filled with heretics, and expelled Jews from the city after ordering an onslaught of their synagogues. His greatest theological battle was the Nestorian controversy, in which he opposed Nestorius, patriarch of Constantinople, over the ascription of *theotokos* ("God-bearer") to Mary. While politically ruthless, he was a brilliant theologian and defender of Alexandrine theology, employing skill in reasoning and paying close attention to accuracy.

JOHN NELSON DARBY (1800–1882)

Brethren/Dispensational

Born in London and once a lawyer, Darby entered the ministry with the Church of Ireland in 1825. He became disillusioned by the apostasy he perceived there, left the established church, and joined the movement later known as the Plymouth Brethren. He developed a distinctive ecclesiology, believing that the church was not to be identified with any institution but was a spiritual fellowship. This ecclesiology became the catalyst for dispensationalism as a system. He posited a radical discontinuity between the church and Israel, asserting that God had two separate peoples and was working out two separate programs in history. This discontinuity makes it incumbent, in keeping with 2 Timothy 2:15, to "rightly divide the Word of truth," discerning which passages are addressed to Israel and which to the church. This idea of discontinuity, coupled with a futurist view of biblical prophecy and the doctrine of the pretribulational rapture of the church, gave coherence to incipient dispensationalism.

The views and ideas of the Brethren movement spread to North America. Although few left their established denominational affiliations, Darby and Brethren expositors and evangelists gained a wide hearing, particularly among Presbyterians and Baptists, significant numbers of whom adopted the dispensational historiography. The Niagara Bible Conference, founded in 1876, became fertile soil for dispensationalism and a forebear of many Bible conferences extant today.

JOHANN ECK (1486–1543)

Roman Catholic

German Roman Catholic theologian, orator, and principal contemporary opponent of Martin Luther and the early Reformers. Eck wrote *Obelisci* (1518) in response to Luther's Ninety-five Theses. Eck also engaged Luther in public debate in Leipzig in 1519 and was responsible for the papal bull *Exsurge Domine* (1520) that excommunicated Luther. He taught theology at Ingolstadt from 1510 until his death.

JONATHAN EDWARDS (1703–58)

Reformed

Arguably the greatest philosopher/theologian America has ever known. Edwards was also a brilliant and gifted preacher. By age thirteen he knew Greek, Hebrew, and Latin and was enrolled at Yale. He served as a pastor in Northampton, Massachusetts, from 1724 to 1750, and it was under the influence of his preaching that the First Great Awakening occurred in America. In defense of the awakening, he penned *Narrative of Surprising Conversions* and *Religious Affections.* He was elected president of Princeton in 1757 but died of a smallpox injection the next year.

Edwards's Calvinistic theology led him to write *Original Sin* and *Freedom of the Will.* His strong beliefs against allowing the unregenerate at the Lord's Supper ultimately cost him his pastorate in Northampton. He spent the following six years as a missionary among the Indians. These years were his most productive theologically, for the ministry allowed him time to write. He was described as a man with a mind like Augustine, and he sought to devote himself completely to Jesus Christ. He failed to see the separation between "heart" and "head" that has often been found in evangelicalism.

ELIZABETH I (1533–1603)

Anglican

Protestant English monarch popularly known as the "Virgin Queen" and "Good Queen Bess." As daughter of Henry VIII, Elizabeth Tudor became queen at age twenty-five after the death of her Catholic half-sister, Mary, in 1558. Disliking both Catholics and Calvinists, she became architect of the Church of England as the via media that could encompass the religiously divergent groups within England under one broad umbrella. Under her influence, the decidedly Calvinistic forty-two articles of religion of the Church of England were revised to a more theologically ambivalent thirty-nine articles. Likewise, the wording surrounding the Eucharist became less Calvinistic and more theologically ambivalent. England prospered under her leadership, and by her death at age sixty-nine, England was enjoying its greatest literary period and had established itself as a world leader. Her reign is significant in that her policies involved the abolition of papal power in England, which facilitated a Protestant mind-set.

RALPH WALDO EMERSON (1803–82)

Unitarian

American essayist and poet who as a former Unitarian minister advanced transcendentalism (the notion that humans possess an intuitive faculty enabling them to know truth apart from empirical evidence). Emerson believed that all could have knowledge about God's love because God indwells every human heart. Emerson rejected the doctrine of original sin. His most popular essay, *Self-Reliance*, makes a strong defense of rugged individualism. His line, "Trust thyself: every heart vibrates to that iron string," has influenced not only American culture in general, but ultimately the culture of American church ecclesiology, where emotional distancing is more the norm.

EUSEBIUS OF CAESAREA (c. 260–c. 340)

Orthodox/catholic

The father of church history. Eusebius became associated with Pamphilus, the founder of the theological school in Caesarea, and as a youth, assisted him in preparing an apology for the teachings of Origen. He became bishop of Caesarea in 314, and in 325 he led the moderate party at the Council of Nicea. He was responsible for the first draft of the Nicene Creed. After discovering how radical Arius's subordination views were, Eusebius moved toward the Athanasian party. He is best remembered for his *Ecclesiastical History* and *Life of Constantine.*

GUILLAUME FAREL (1489–1565)

Reformed

French Reformer of Germany and Switzerland as well as an eloquent preacher and lifelong associate and friend of John Calvin. Guillaume (William) Farel persuaded Geneva to accept Reformed doctrines and is considered the pioneer of Protestantism in western Switzerland. When Calvin visited the city in 1536, Farel persuaded him to become Geneva's principal preacher and teacher of theology. However, strong opposition forced Farel and Calvin to flee to France in 1538. While Calvin returned to Geneva two years later, Farel stayed in Neuchâtel and continued his evangelistic work in France until his death.

CHARLES GRANDISON FINNEY (1792–1875)

Arminian

American lawyer, theologian, and revivalist, known as a fiery preacher of the Second Great Awakening. Raised in upstate New York, Finney became a lawyer. After he experienced a dramatic conversion, he became a Presbyterian minister. His revivals were immensely successful, with an estimated half million conversions under his ministry. His methods of evangelism included protracted meetings of nightly gatherings with large crowds and the "anxious bench," where souls under conviction could pray for salvation.

Although Finney was from a Calvinistic tradition, he had Arminian leanings, especially toward free will and final apostasy. His optimistic view of human ability to respond to grace, which caused him to encourage people to exert themselves in becoming Christians and to overcome social ills such as slavery, has been criticized by many as teetering on the edge of Pelagianism. The Holiness movement grew in part out of his revivals and the efforts of his followers. From 1835 on, he taught theology at Oberlin College, also serving as president from 1851 to 1866. A perfectionist theology of sanctification became Oberlin's trademark. Finney's books include his *Memoirs*, *Lectures on Revivals of Religion*, and *Systematic Theology.*

GEORGE FOX (1624–91)

Quaker

English mystic and founder of the Society of Friends (Quakers). As a youth, Fox was influenced by his Puritan upbringing and his family's association with the Anabaptists. At age twenty-two, he set out to visit various preachers in search of enlightenment. Besides his native England, he traveled through Scotland, Holland, and America, attracting many as he spoke. He developed a following and in 1648 led a dissolved Anabaptist congregation at Nottingham, England.

Fox came to the conviction that man can have direct communication with God as a result of the indwelling work of the Holy Spirit. Thus he often felt impelled to speak out against various evils as well as the uselessness of external ordinances. In 1649 he was jailed for interrupting a church service in Nottingham with a biblical appeal to follow the Holy Spirit's leading. This, along with a denunciation of churches, clergymen, lawyers, and soldiers, made him a victim of mob hatred and imprisonment many times. A judge in Derby nicknamed Fox's group "Quakers" in 1650 after Fox exhorted the magistrates to "tremble" before the Lord. He built up a strong organization of Friends in England and America.

WASHINGTON GLADDEN (1836–1918)

Liberal

American Congregational minister with liberal social and religious views, known for being a leader of the social gospel movement. Gladden graduated from Williams College and served churches in New England before taking his main pastorate at First Congregational Church in Columbus, Ohio (1882–1914), where he championed his liberal social and political ideas. Theologically, he drifted from traditional conservative orthodoxy, adopting higher critical methods, human potential, and evolutionary views of origins. He once urged his denomination to refuse a substantial donation from Standard Oil Company, calling it "tainted money." He is famous for the words of the hymn "O Master, Let Me Walk with Thee."

GOTTSCHALK (c. 804–c. 869)

Roman Catholic

German Benedictine monk and theologian. Gottschalk's study of Augustine's anti-Pelagian writings led him to an absolute view of predestination (i.e., God has predestined some to eternal life in heaven and others to eternal damnation; also known as double predestination). This teaching was later condemned by the archbishops of Mainz and Reims, who supported the widely accepted semi-Pelagian views. Gottschalk (also known as Godescalus) was condemned by two councils and confined to monastic imprisonment for the last twenty years of his life. Among his writings are a letter to his contemporary, the medieval theologian Ratramnus, as well as an attack on the views of the Trinity held by Hincmar, archbishop of Reims.

GREGORY I (c. 540–604)

Roman Catholic

Benedictine monk considered the father of the medieval papacy. Also known as Gregory the Great, he was pope from 590 until his death. Gregory is the fourth and last of the Latin doctors of the church. He became the official interpreter of Augustine for the medieval church and promoted the teachings and practices of good works and penance, purgatory, Mass, transubstantiation, and liturgy in worship. Gregory altered the monastic and papal systems and sent Augustine of Canterbury to England, making him the first Roman Catholic archbishop in the British Isles. Gregory also consolidated the papal supremacy after being elected pope against his will. Furthermore, he was the first pope to assume secular power after the emperor abandoned Rome. Although he was a trained Roman lawyer and a successful preacher, he was not a man of profound learning, a philosopher, nor even a theologian. Nevertheless, Catholics regard him above all as a "physician of souls and a leader of men."

GREGORY VII (HILDEBRAND) (c. 1021–85)

Roman Catholic

Benedictine monk regarded by many as the greatest of the medieval popes. Originally named Hildebrand, he was educated at a Benedictine monastery in Rome and later became a monk. In 1047 he spent a year in Cluny. He became cardinal in 1049 and then served as the power behind the papacy until 1073 when he became pope. As cardinal he advised and had great influence over five popes. He had a strong desire to see reform in the Roman Catholic Church but also believed in the position and power of the papacy.

Condemning the evils of lay investiture and declaring the supremacy of the church throughout the world, he was defied by Henry IV, the German emperor, who declared Gregory deposed. Gregory excommunicated Henry, who crossed the Alps in the winter and knelt barefoot in the snow at Canossa in 1077 to receive absolution. In the unrest that followed, Rome was invaded, and Gregory died in exile in Salerno, Italy.

GREGORY OF NAZIANZUS (c. 330–c. 390)

Orthodox/catholic

One of the "Three Cappadocians." Gregory loved monasticism but was repeatedly drawn into ecclesiastical and theological endeavors. He served as patriarch of Constantinople in the late fourth century. For his great contribution at defending and explaining the Nicene faith, he earned the reputation and title "The Theologian." His Arian opponents argued that the members of the Trinity are differentiated either by essence or by action. If by essence, then the Son must be subordinate to the Father, since they are not of the same essence. If by action, then the Father is creator and not the Son; therefore the Son was created and is part of creation.

Gregory held that the members of the Trinity are differentiated, not by essence or action, but by relation. Therefore the Son is begotten (in terms of relation, not of time since there was never a time when the Son did not exist), and the Spirit proceeds from the Father (again in terms of relation, not of time). He also argued against the Apollinarian reduction of Christ's full humanity.

GREGORY OF NYSSA (c. 331–c. 395)

Orthodox/catholic

One of the "Three Cappadocians," and brother of Basil the Great. Gregory was not as skilled a writer and orator as Gregory of Nazianzus, and he was not as accomplished a leader and organizer as his brother. But because of his broad classical education, he was perhaps the greatest theologian of the three. He was skilled in philosophy and constantly read the writings of Origen. His defense of the Nicene faith accelerated the defeat of the Arian heresy. Gregory's contribution was the refutation of Arianism's subordination of the Logos, a defense against tritheistic arguments, and a clear distinction between the two natures (divine and human) in Christ.

GERHARD GROOTE (GERRIT DE GROOTE) (1340–84)

Roman Catholic

Dutch religious Reformer. After Groote's conversion in 1374, he strongly desired to live a devoted Christian life and served as a monk and later as a missionary preacher. In his speaking, he denounced church abuses, and when his preaching license was withdrawn, he founded the monastic lay order known as the Brethren of the Common Life. He stressed a communal and simple lifestyle, devotion to Christ, service to the world, and a commitment to education. Groote kept a diary of his life, and some scholars believe it to be the same work attributed to Thomas à Kempis called the *Imitation of Christ.*

HUGO GROTIUS (1583–1645)

Arminian

Dutch Reformer who embraced and advanced the beliefs of his mentor, Jacob Arminius, and the Remonstrants. Grotius was trained in the classics, wrote poetry at eight, attended the University of Leyden at eleven, and earned his doctorate at age fifteen from the University of Orléans. He served in Dutch politics as pensionary of Rotterdam at a time of tension between Calvinists and Arminians. When the Union of Utrecht (a declaration of independence from Catholic Spain) commenced, Dutch provinces were free to determine their religious allegiances. In a political-religious struggle between Arminian-leaning leaders and Calvinist supporter Prince Maurice, Grotius was condemned to life in prison. Grotius was able to escape prison and flee to France, where he lived out most of the rest of his life.

As a lawyer, Grotius proposed the "governmental theory of the atonement" in his work *De Satisfactione Christi.* This view regards God as a ruler who can relax his law concerning death and condemnation for sin and allow Christ to suffer as a penal example. Grotius also published commentaries on the New Testament and sought to bring peace and unity to the Protestant church.

ADOLF VON HARNACK (1851–1930)

Liberal

German Lutheran church historian and greatest of the liberal theologians. In 1890 Harnack joined the faculty of the University of Berlin, remaining there for thirty-eight years. As one of the leaders of the critical school of theology, he was a teacher of Karl Barth. He became an authority on Ante-Nicene church history and saw Christian dogma as reflecting Greek philosophy more than the teaching of Jesus. He believed it was the historian's task to strip off the husks of Hellenism that had encrusted the gospel and to return to the pure teachings of Jesus. These he set forth (in *What Is Christianity?*) as the fatherhood of God, the brotherhood of man, the example of Jesus, and the establishment of the kingdom of God on earth. His important works are many and include *Outlines of the History of Dogma, The Expansion of Christianity in the First Three Centuries, The Apostles' Creed, Marcion,* and *Luke the Physician.*

CARL F. H. HENRY (1913–2003)

Reformed

American Baptist theologian considered one of the leading proponents of evangelicalism in the twentieth century. Henry studied at Wheaton College; at Northern Baptist Theological Seminary (Th.D.), where he also taught; and Boston University (Ph.D.). In 1947 he became a professor at Fuller Theological Seminary.

He was the founding editor of *Christianity Today*, which is still a popular voice among mainline evangelicalism. Henry was chairman of the 1966 World Congress on evangelism, a lecturer-at-large for World Vision, and a visiting professor and international speaker. He published and edited many works, including the book *Jesus of Nazareth*, in which various scholars deal with some of the modern theories concerning biblical criticism and the historicity of Jesus. His major theological work is the six-volume *God, Revelation and Authority* (1973–83), in which he defends theism, the inerrancy of Scripture, and supernaturalism.

ARCHIBALD ALEXANDER HODGE (1823–86)

Reformed

American Presbyterian theologian and eldest son of theologian Charles Hodge. He was named after Archibald Alexander, who had started the Calvinist tradition that was begun at Princeton Theological Seminary. After his studies at Princeton College and Seminary, he and his wife were sent as missionaries to Allahabad, India. Illness brought Hodge and his family back to America, but his experience left him with a lifelong taste for foreign missions. He pastored several churches and in 1846 became professor of didactic theology at Western Seminary in Pittsburgh.

In 1877 Hodge went to Princeton Seminary to assist his ill father. Following in his father's footsteps, he proclaimed his commitment to systematic theology and biblical preaching. He also coauthored with B. B. Warfield the article entitled "Inspiration," in which they defended the doctrine of verbal plenary inspiration. This article led to the definition of the doctrine of inerrancy. Hodge also put forth Reformed theology as a basis for establishing cultural values.

CHARLES HODGE (1797–1878)

Reformed

American Presbyterian theologian who defended Reformed orthodoxy in the nineteenth century as the architect of "Princeton theology." Educated at the

College of New Jersey (now Rutgers) and Princeton Seminary, Hodge began teaching at Princeton in 1822, first as professor of biblical and oriental literature and later of New Testament exegesis, and taught there for the rest of his life. In 1825 he started the journal *Biblical Repository*, later renamed the *Princeton Review*, to which he contributed many articles, mostly in defense of Calvinism and attacking theologies he saw to be incongruent with Calvinistic orthodoxy.

Hodge was a prolific writer. Among his works are commentaries on Romans, Ephesians, and 1 and 2 Corinthians as well as books on contemporary problems. His greatest work is his three-volume *Systematic Theology*. He was committed to the authority of the Bible and to Calvinism, and he believed in the necessity of holy living. Scottish Common Sense categories can be seen in his writings, though not to the same extent as those of his colleagues. He has been called the greatest American Calvinist theologian since Jonathan Edwards.

JAN HUS (JOHN HUSS) (c. 1372–1415)
Roman Catholic

Czech Reformer, well-known preacher, rector of the University of Prague, and a forerunner of Protestantism. Like many of his time, Hus called for the reform of the church. His aim was not to change doctrine but simply to confront corrupt practices. When John Wycliffe's writings became the focus of intense debate at the University of Prague, Hus joined the side favoring Wycliffe. The opposition raised doubts about the orthodoxy of Wycliffe and of those sympathetic to him. The church hierarchy attempted to silence Hus's calls for reform, and Hus decided that he was obligated to disobey. He justified this decision by stating that a pope acting out of self-concern rather than out of concern for his sheep must not be obeyed.

Hus drew still more attention when he opposed the efforts of the pope to finance a war against the Christian nation of Naples by the sale of indulgences. In an attempt to bring about a calmer resolution of these issues, Hus left his preaching post to write on behalf of reform. The emperor invited Hus to present his views at the Council of Constance. He was given a pledge of safe-conduct, but after he arrived he was arrested and ordered to recant his heresies. Hus was not allowed to debate issues, and after he refused to recant, he was publicly burned at the stake.

Outrage over Hus's fate led to the formation of a resistance movement, whose aims are summarized in its *Four Articles*: permission for the Bible to be freely preached; the cup and not just the bread to be given to the laity during the Lord's Supper; the clergy to be stripped of its wealth; and blatant sin in the church to be punished. After prolonged dispute and armed resistance, peace returned with a compromise over the *Four Articles*.

IGNATIUS OF ANTIOCH (c. 35–c. 107)

Orthodox/catholic

Bishop of Antioch, martyred by Emperor Trajan. Ignatius was likely a native of Syria and a pupil of the apostle John. Little is known about him except for what he wrote in the seven letters addressed to different churches and Polycarp, warning them against docetism and urging obedience to bishops. Ignatius opposed the Ebionite heresy, which enforced the keeping of Jewish law as a means of salvation, and suggested Christians meet on the Lord's Day (Sunday) rather than on the Sabbath. He helped develop the episcopacy and very well may have been the first person to use the term "catholic church," implying unity of faith.

IGNATIUS OF LOYOLA (1491–1556)

Roman Catholic

Spanish nobleman and founder of the Society of Jesus (Jesuits). Born into a noble family at the castle of Loyola, Ignatius was influenced through reading about the lives of Christ, St. Dominic, and St. Francis and was converted at age thirty. He joined a Dominican monastery; he was strictly ascetic and despaired over his personal sins and the issue of forgiveness, nearly committing suicide. Eventually he found peace through yielding to the church and the authority of the pope. In 1522 he began to dream of forming a military order committed to the leadership of Christ and defending the teachings of the church. In 1534 he was joined by six companions and founded the Society of Jesus, of which he served as general the rest of his life. The Jesuits became a great power for the papacy and for Catholicism and had a leading role in the Counter-Reformation. Loyola was canonized by Pope Gregory XV in 1622.

INNOCENT III (c. 1160–1216)

Roman Catholic

The pope at the zenith of medieval papal authority. Upon becoming pope in 1198, Innocent III committed himself to restoring the prestige of the papacy. An able leader, he organized a number of crusades and summoned the Fourth Lateran Council in 1215, considered to be the greatest church council of the Middle Ages. He exercised authority over many countries and, had it not been for the rise of nationalism, might have subjugated all Christendom to the political and spiritual supremacy of the church. He wrote, "The Lord left to Peter the governance not only of the Church but also of the whole world."

IRENAEUS (c. 130–c. 200)

Orthodox/catholic

Church father and bishop of Lyons in Gaul, noted for his systematization of Christian theology. He is also known for two works, *Against Heresies* (a defense of the Christian faith against the Gnostics and other heretics) and *The Demonstration of the Apostolic Preaching*, both strongly based on the Bible. Irenaeus was probably a native of Smyrna in Asia Minor and a pupil of Polycarp. He maintained that the Father and the Son cooperated in both revelation and redemption, and he expounded the recapitulation theory of the life of Christ—the view that Jesus' life of perfect obedience recapitulated the career of Adam, reversing the curse Adam had brought on humankind. Little is known about Irenaeus after 190, though he is believed to have been martyred under the persecution of Septimus Severus.

JEROME (EUSEBIUS HIERONYMUS) (c. 342–c. 420)

Orthodox/catholic

Biblical scholar and church father. Born in Dalmatia, Jerome went to Rome at age twelve for eight years of study and became proficient in Latin, Greek, and pagan authors. He had a dream or vision at age nineteen, in which Christ told him, "You are not a Christian." He was baptized by the pope, renounced his classical studies, learned Hebrew, and began to proclaim an ascetic form of Christianity. Intending to imitate the devotion and martyr spirit demonstrated by previous church fathers, he spent the last half of his life in a monastery at Bethlehem meditating, studying, writing, translating, and supervising his monks. He wrote biblical commentaries and made a translation of Scripture that became the basis of the Vulgate, replacing all other Latin translations. He corresponded with Augustine and denounced Arianism, Origenism, and Pelagianism. Christian art often represents Jerome with a red hat or robe and/or with a lion.[4]

JOHN OF DAMASCUS (c. 675–c. 749)

Orthodox

Church father and hymn writer of the Greek church who fought iconoclasm (in the literal sense of opposing icons). In three treatises (726–30), John defended the use of icons, arguing that they stimulated Christian devotion. He was the last great theologian among the Greek fathers, and he wrote extensively. He is famous for his work *Fount of Knowledge*, a systemization of Aristotle's dialectics and theology. That work gave him the title "father of scholasticism" as it became a method adopted by theologians in the Middle Ages.

JUSTIN MARTYR (c. 100–c. 165)

Orthodox/catholic

Leading apologist for Christianity in the second century. As a Samaritan Christian who was also an apologist, Justin Martyr studied the works of stoicism, Aristotelianism, Pythagoreanism, and Platonism. He sought to show that Christianity is the embodiment of the noblest concepts of Greek philosophy. He saw Christianity as the full revelation of truth because Christ himself was the incarnation of the divine Logos. In history he is known as the first great Christian thinker after the apostle Paul. He was beheaded in Rome.

IMMANUEL KANT (1724–1804)

Enlightenment Philosopher

German philosopher often referred to as the "Aristotle" or the "Plato" of the eighteenth century. As the last of the Enlightenment philosophers, he created a link between the idealists and the empiricists, becoming the father of epistemological phenomenalism. He is best known for his *Critique of Pure Reason*, in which he differentiated between material things of the world and things of the mind. He said that things in the world are real, but only the mind can give them order and form in order to see the relationship between them. He also developed the "categorical imperative": one should judge every action by whether it represents a universal law. If it would be acceptable as a universal law, then as an action it is acceptable. (See chapter 14.A.2.)

SØREN KIERKEGAARD (1813–55)

Lutheran

One of the most influential modern thinkers, considered the founder of existentialism. Although he studied for ordination in the Danish Lutheran Church, Kierkegaard never entered the ministry but devoted most of his life to studying and writing. He wrote much about the predicament of life, and through his studies he came to vehemently oppose Hegelian philosophy. After undergoing a profound religious experience in 1848, he began to reflect on the chasm between what he called authentic Christianity and the Christianity he observed in his Danish Lutheran church. Kierkegaard argued for the need for a personal, subjective engagement with the truth. He also emphasized existence over essence. His writings include *Stages on Life's Way*, *Philosophical Fragments*, *Works of Love*, *Sickness unto Death*, and *Attack on Christendom*. (See also chapter 3.B.6.)

JOHN KNOX (c. 1513–72)

Reformed

Principal Protestant Reformer of Scotland. Knox studied under John Calvin at Geneva and made Presbyterianism the religion of Scotland. His preaching attacked the queen, Mary Stuart, who occupied the throne from 1560 to 1567. She forbade him to preach and later had him arrested for treason, but he was acquitted. After Mary's abdication, Knox preached at the coronation of her son James VI as King of Scotland.

A fiery preacher and controversialist, his great contribution to theology was in the relationship of church and state. Seeing the church and state as coterminus communities, he looked to the Old Testament as the model for good government in the civil realm. He argued for the right of people to disobey ungodly rulers when the civil authority violated divine law. Late in his career, he argued that it was the responsibility of the godly to overthrow ungodly (i.e., Roman Catholic) rulers.

HANS KÜNG (1928–)

Roman Catholic

Roman Catholic theologian who questioned the traditional Catholic claims for infallibility. Born in Switzerland, Küng attended a coed Latin high school in Lucerne, then went to Rome for religious studies in a Jesuit environment. His thesis on Sartre formed the basis for one of his later works, *Does God Exist?* in which he describes and evaluates several atheists, calling them "prophets" of Western culture. Küng was ordained to the priesthood in 1955 and the next year became Licentiate in Theology. His studies in Rome familiarized him with Protestant theology, dialectical theology, and secular existentialism, laying the groundwork for his later influence in Vatican II. Küng also became proficient in the thought of Barth and Hegel and in 1957 earned a doctorate from the Catholic Institute at the University of Paris (Sorbonne) for his work on Barth's understanding of justification. Theologians Karl Rahner and Yves Congar sparked Küng's thinking on Catholic Church reform issues.

Küng has stirred much controversy, but never for controversy's sake. Under Pope John XXIII, he pushed for an ecumenical council and discussion on the church's policy toward non–Roman Catholic Christians. As professor of dogmatics at the University of Münster, he wrote *The Council, Reform, and Reunion*, which drew fire from various Catholic leaders for his ideas on reform and reunion with the Reformation.

In 1963 he questioned the absolute authority of the councils and the divine right of the pope to preside over them—this came after Küng's role as a high-profile theological adviser for Vatican II in 1962. With the death of Pope John XXIII and the election of the more conservative Paul VI in 1963, Küng's position and credibility in the Roman Catholic Church changed from prospect to suspect. One problem was Küng's use of the dialectic method, leading him to propose that a functional rather than ontological Christology was essential for contemporary relevance. Another was his questioning of the authority of the church.

A more open conflict developed in 1979 as a result of the publication of his *Infallible?* in 1970. The reaction from the hierarchy led to his dismissal from his post at the University of Tübingen. He then moved to the Institute for Ecumenical Research in Tübingen, from which he has promoted the ecumenical movement.

ABRAHAM KUYPER (1837–1920)

Reformed

Dutch Calvinistic political and theological leader in the Netherlands. Kuyper founded the Reformed (*Gereformeerde*) Church and the Free University of Amsterdam (i.e., free from church and state control). He stood for classical Reformed doctrines and has been influential theologically in the United States and Germany. The son of a Reformed minister, Kuyper was a student in Leyden, where he drifted into modernism. As a young pastor, he was drawn to the deep Calvinistic piety of his village parishioners. At thirty he moved to Amsterdam, where he joined the anti-revolutionary political views of Calvinist theorist Groen van Prinsterer and eventually succeeded him as the Anti-Revolutionary Party leader. Kuyper sought to make orthodox Calvinism a political force. He promoted his view of state support for religious schools and other social causes, and he became prime minister in 1901. Among his coalition were the Catholics, who wanted state funding for their schools as well. Kuyper believed in a broad view of common grace. He recognized that various institutions were autonomous and had God-given rights to pursue their functions; therefore the state was responsible for supporting them. (See also chapter 11.F.1.)

LEO I (THE GREAT) (c. 400–461)

Roman Catholic

Pope (440–461) and doctor of the church who saved Italy from destruction by the Hun invaders and the Vandals. Leo's *Tome of Leo* became the basis for the christological definition adopted by the Council of Chalcedon in 451: Christ as one person with two natures. He opposed the Manichaeans, Monophysites, and Pelagians. He is also known for his strengthening of Rome by combining Roman law with church ecclesiastical procedure and structure.

CLIVE STAPLES (C. S.) LEWIS (1898–1963)

Anglican

English teacher, writer, and Christian apologist, often called "the apostle to the skeptics." One of the most widely read authors on Christian themes in the Western world, Lewis plays a significant role in helping people to understand Christian theology.

Lewis was born in Belfast, Ireland, and educated by a private tutor and then at Malvern College in England for a year before attending University College, Oxford. An outstanding classical scholar, he taught at Magdalen College in Oxford from 1925 to 1954. From 1954 until his death he was professor of medieval and Renaissance English literature at Cambridge University.

Lewis gained his greatest audience as an apologist for Christianity. In his attempt to formulate a core of Christian understanding, Lewis wrote a number of highly readable books—intelligent, imaginative, and often witty. These include *The Problem of Pain*, *Miracles*, *The Screwtape Letters*, and *Mere Christianity* (1952). He also wrote a trilogy of religious science fiction novels: *Out of the Silent Planet*, *Perelandra*, and *That Hideous Strength*. One of his most popular works is the Chronicles of Narnia, a series of seven children's tales beginning with *The Lion, the Witch, and the Wardrobe.* His autobiography, *Surprised by Joy*, was published in 1955.

LUCIAN OF ANTIOCH (c. 250–312)

Orthodox/catholic

Theologian and martyr, presbyter of Antioch, and founder of Antioch's theological school. Lucian was born at Samosata to distinguished parents and later completed his education at the theological school in Antioch, of which he eventually became the head. Both Arius and Eusebius of Nicomedia attended this school.

In response to the allegorical teachings of Origen, Lucian supported a literal interpretation of the Bible. He believed in the preexistent Christ but did not agree that Christ's existence was eternal. Lucian is considered the father of Arianism, but only a few of his writings remain. It is believed that the second of the four creeds offered by the Council of Antioch in 341 was Lucian's work. As a biblical student, he also revised the Greek text of the Bible.

MARTIN LUTHER (1483–1546)

Lutheran

Founder of the German Reformation. (See chapter 10.B.1.)

J. GRESHAM MACHEN (1881–1937)

Reformed

Defender and apologist of conservative scholarship in the Old Princeton theology tradition. Born in Baltimore into a distinguished Southern family, Machen studied at Johns Hopkins University and then Princeton Theological Seminary, where he encountered B. B. Warfield and R. D. Wilson. Machen's article on the virgin birth was published in the *Princeton Theological Review.* Upon graduation, unsure of his call to ministry, he spent a year in Germany at the universities of Marburg and Göttingen. Although attracted to the liberal theology of Wilhelm Hermann, he finally settled on the infallibility of Scripture and the traditional emphases of historic Reformed theology.

Beginning in 1906, when he began teaching New Testament at Princeton, Machen became increasingly prominent in the conservative movement. Following World War I, he became acutely aware of the shift taking place in the Northern Presbyterian Church. Both it and Princeton were changing from traditional Calvinism to modernism. When Warfield died in 1921, the conservative leadership in the seminary fell to Machen. The struggle between the modernists and conservatives escalated and led to a split in the faculty, with an administrative reorganization in 1929 bringing a marked shift toward liberalism. Machen led several, including Cornelius Van Til, Oswald T. Allis, and R. D. Wilson, out of Princeton and began Westminster Seminary in Philadelphia.

Machen saw how the theological forces affected mission work. In response, he founded the Independent Board for Presbyterian Missions in

1933. This created conflict with the church, and the church tried him without giving him the opportunity to defend himself from Scripture or theology and finally suspended him from ministry. In 1936 Machen led in the organization of what is now the Orthodox Presbyterian Church. He also dissolved the Covenant Union, the organization of Bible-believing members of the Presbyterian Church (USA), the last bridge between the two denominations. Machen died on a preaching tour the next year.

Machen's major works include *Christianity and Liberalism*, *What Is Faith?* and *The Christian Faith in the Modern World.*

ALISTER E. MCGRATH (1953–)

Reformed

Evangelical Anglican theologian of the late twentieth century. McGrath has contributed to the resurgence of evangelical theology in both the academic and popular spheres. An authority on Luther, Calvin, the doctrine of justification by faith, theological method, science and theology, and Christology, McGrath brings to the theological task an expertise in the sciences (Ph.D. in molecular biology) as well as expertise in historical theology. His numerous scholarly works include *Justitia Dei*, *Luther's Theology of the Cross*, *The Making of Modern German Christology*, *John Calvin* (biography), *The Intellectual Origins of the European Reformation*, *J. I. Packer* (biography), *A Scientific Theology* (three volumes), and *The Genesis of Doctrine.*

PHILIP MELANCHTHON (1497–1560)

Lutheran

Second most important German Lutheran Reformer, after Martin Luther. Melanchthon entered the University of Heidelberg at the age of thirteen, where he excelled in Greek. He then studied at Tübingen, where his scholarship attracted the attention of Erasmus, and in 1518 he joined the faculty at Wittenberg as a professor of Greek. At Wittenberg he met Luther and became involved in the German Reformation. In 1521 Melanchthon wrote *Loci Communes*, a systematic formulation of Luther's ideas.

Melanchthon composed the Augsburg Confession and the Augsburg Apology, both of which became key statements of Lutheran beliefs. After Luther's death, Melanchthon became the leader of the German Reformation. A humanist by training and in spirit, Melanchthon was at heart a peacemaker. As Lutheranism hardened after Luther's death, his gentle spirit and willingness to compromise made him the object of suspicion in Lutheran circles. In the face of opposition, he sought peace and argued that there were certain Roman Catholic ideas that were *adiaphora*, nonessential to the faith.

Because of his mild demeanor, conscientious character, and introverted personality, Melanchthon has been called "the quiet Reformer." In addition to his contributions to the Reformation, he also helped in the development of schools and universities. (See also chapter 10.B.2.)

MENNO SIMONS (1496–1561)

Anabaptist

Known as the father of the Mennonites, although he did not actually begin the movement. Simons was an evangelical who held to the major doctrines of the faith. He differed from the Reformers in that he taught the baptism only of believers. He also taught peace and nonresistance. He was born in Friesland, where he prepared for the Roman Catholic priesthood and in 1524 was consecrated a priest.

In his first year as a priest, Simons came to doubt the doctrine of transubstantiation. After turning to Scripture, he rejected this doctrine. He then began to read more intensively, not only the Bible, but also the writings of Luther and other Reformers. In 1531 he heard of the martyrdom of Sicke Snijder, who was rebaptized as an Anabaptist. This led Simons to the conclusion that baptism should follow conversion. In 1536 he renounced Roman Catholicism, siding with the Anabaptists, and went into hiding. The next year he was baptized and ordained an elder in the province of Groningen, in an Anabaptist group founded by Obbe Philip. Menno Simons soon became a leader among the Anabaptists, promoting evangelical doctrines and opposing extremist groups within the movement.

JÜRGEN MOLTMANN (1926–)

Protestant

Father of the "theology of hope." He has been professor of systematic theology at the University of Tübingen since 1967. His major works include three complementary volumes: *Theology of Hope*, *The Crucified God*, and *The Church in the Power of the Spirit.* He also is producing a set of studies in dogmatics, each with a particular focus, including *The Trinity and the Kingdom of God* (1980–81), *God in Creation* (1985), *The Way of Jesus Christ* (1989–90), and *The Spirit of Life* (1991–92), with more to follow on eschatology and theological method.

Moltmann's thinking has especially influenced and has been contextualized by liberation theologians, including the proponents of black, Asian, Native American, and feminist theologies, and has found its most powerful expression in Latin America.

MONTANUS (SECOND CENTURY)

Orthodox/catholic/Heretic

Phrygian Christian, ultimately condemned as a heretic. Montanus perceived that the church had fallen into laxity and needed to return to a state of purity, and he believed he was the person through whom the Holy Spirit was calling for renewal. He saw Christ's return as imminent, and thus the church needed to be prepared. Two women, Priscilla and Maximilla, prophesied along with Montanus. Most of their activity occurred in Phrygia in Asia Minor, where they believed Christ would usher in his millennial reign. They gained a large following, mostly among the religiously excitable. Tertullian was attracted to Montanism by the strict morality promoted by the group.

Doctrinally Montanus stressed the imminent return of Christ, miraculous gifts, ecstatic utterances, prophecy, and progressive revelation. After his death, his followers went to such an extreme that they gave more weight to the words of Montanus than to the words of Scripture. Montanism was ultimately condemned by the early church as heretical.

DWIGHT LYMAN (D. L.) MOODY (1837–99)

Protestant

One of the most prominent American evangelists. Moody grew up in Northfield, Massachusetts, and sought a career in Boston, where he was converted and joined a Congregational church. Later he moved to Chicago, where he was a successful shoe salesman and also developed an interest in evangelism. After the Civil War he became the president of the YMCA in Chicago.

From 1873 to 1875, Moody and his singing associate, Ira Sankey, traveled to the British Isles and reportedly preached to more than two and a half million people. They continued their evangelism upon their return to America, preaching to the poor as well as to middle-class audiences who were attracted by Moody's businesslike style.

Moody was sympathetic toward many denominations and cooperated with them in various revival campaigns. He avoided taking a rigid stance on the emerging premillennial movement, but he had a strong influence on later

American fundamentalism and evangelicalism. He also founded the trans-denominational Moody Bible Institute in Chicago.

NESTORIUS (DIED 451)

Orthodox/catholic

Patriarch of Constantinople who attained notoriety for his opposition to the term *theotokos* as applied to Mary and was ultimately convicted of heresy at the council of Ephesus (431). A native Syrian, Nestorius studied under Theodore of Mopsuestia and served as a monk and presbyter in Antioch before being appointed patriarch. His first official act as patriarch was the burning of an Arian chapel.

Nestorius began to challenge the standard title of Mary as *theotokos* ("God-bearer") out of concern that it entailed a mixing of the human and divine natures in Christ, and thus a reduction of both natures. In its place, he proposed the term *Christotokos* ("Christ-bearer") for Mary. He was opposed by Cyril of Alexandria, who accused him of heresy for his failure to see an organic joining of the two natures in Christ. The Council of Ephesus (431) condemned Nestorius's teaching and exiled him to a monastery in Antioch. He was later banished to Upper Egypt, where he died. Because of the scarcity of primary sources, Nestorius's views remain a matter of dispute today; some hold that he was a heretic, while others contend that he was misunderstood and a victim of church politics.

JOHN HENRY NEWMAN (1801–90)

Roman Catholic

Leader of the Oxford Movement, Anglican convert to Catholicism, and later a cardinal. The most influential English convert to Roman Catholicism of the nineteenth century, Newman grew up and was led to faith in a Calvinistic evangelical Anglican home. He studied at Oxford and initially rejected the liberal currents he was exposed to. While other evangelicals returned to the Reformation, he was driven to patristics.

In 1828 Newman was appointed vicar of St. Mary's, the university church at Oxford, where he had a significant teaching and preaching ministry. His patristic studies led to an attempt to reconcile the Anglican Church and the Roman Catholic Church through stressing the power and authority of a bishop and the unity of the church. This met with resistance from the Evangelical Anglicans and Broad Churchmen. Newman resigned St. Mary's in 1843 and was accepted into the Roman Catholic Church in 1845.

A primary doctrine for Newman became the assertion of the ecclesial and corporate nature of Christianity. This concept involved authority, which for Newman was interpreted through the Vincentian Canon that only what has been believed "always, everywhere, by all" is to be considered genuinely Christian. He also sought to distinguish true development from false, suggesting seven tests (later "notes"), as recorded in his *Essay on the Development of Christian Doctrine* (see chap. 9, n. 8). This essay mandated that Christianity is a revealed religion to be maintained by an infallible expounder, Rome. He used this argument for his move to Roman Catholicism and was rewarded by being chosen cardinal in 1879.

REINHOLD NIEBUHR (1892–1971)

Neoorthodox

American neoorthodox theologian and proponent of American "Christian realism." Niebuhr entered the ministry after studying theology at Eden Theological Seminary and Yale Divinity School. As a pastor, he focused on the problems of both the church and the nation and for a while was a member of the socialist party. He ran unsuccessfully for Congress in 1930. While he set aside his political beliefs with the advent of World War II, Niebuhr nonetheless remained active in social and ethical causes. To promote social action, he founded the journal *Christianity and Crisis* in 1941. He was also involved in forming Americans for Democratic Action and the Liberal Party in New York.

Niebuhr was heavily influenced by Barth and Brunner but departed from them by arguing that Christianity is to have a "vital prophetical voice" in society. Through a number of books—including *Moral Man and Immoral Society* and *The Nature and Destiny of Man*—Niebuhr communicated his belief that humanity is not perfectible. Rather, man ought to think of himself in light of the dialectical relationships Scripture offers. He was often criticized for putting more emphasis on humanity and social issues than on the saving work of Jesus Christ. His opponents argued that he used Scripture primarily for the study of humanity rather than for its general message. (See also chapter 15.B.3.)

NOVATIAN (DIED C. 258)

Orthodox/catholic/Schismatic

Antipope, best known for his role in what is called the "Novatian Schism." Little is known about Novatian, a presbyter of Rome. He emerged against the backdrop of the Decian persecutions (249–50). After Pope Fabian was martyred in January 250, no successor was elected until the spring of 251, with the majority vote going to Cornelius, who favored full acceptance of those who had lapsed during the persecution. The bishops believed otherwise and opposed this decision, choosing Novatian, who was known for his outstanding orthodox work, *On the Trinity*, as pope. Thus the young church was divided.

Resolution of the matter began when Cyprian of Carthage clarified the absolute need for a unified church to receive back the lapsed, since salvation was impossible outside the church. Novatian and his followers held that this was true only as long as the church was preserved in purity without the defilement of those who had not proven to be steadfast. A synod of local bishops was called to decide the matter, and the Novatians were excommunicated due to their schismatic nature. The Novatians, wishing to avoid compromise with sin, established a separate church. Novatian died a martyr during the persecutions under Emperor Valerian. The church bearing his name was recognized as orthodox, though schismatic, at the Council of Nicea (325). Conditions were given there for the readmittance of its members back into the Catholic body. Many reassimilated, but the Novatian Church itself continued as an identifiable entity until the fifth century.

ORIGEN (ORIGENES ADAMANTIUS) (c. 185–c. 254)

Orthodox/catholic

Alexandrine theologian, philosopher, exegete, and writer, and most influential theologian in the early Eastern church. Born in Egypt, he succeeded Clement as head of the catechetical school of Alexandria when he was eighteen years old. He became an ascetic and founded a theological school at Caesarea in Palestine. Greek father, scholar, theologian, and apologist, he gained a reputation as a prolific writer, interpreter and critic of Scripture, and Christian thinker. He brought new insights to theology and apologetics, buttressing Christian doctrine with his massive knowledge of Greek and Gnostic thought. Among his most significant works were *De Principiis* (On First Principles), one of the first attempts to systematize theology, and *Hexapla*, a parallel edition of the Old Testament containing Hebrew and various Greek texts and transliterations. His exegesis was often allegorical and typological, yet he viewed Christ as the center of all Scripture. He also viewed Scripture as historically and literally true.

Although he exercised a continuing massive influence over subsequent Alexandrine theology, he was declared a heretic three centuries after his death.

JAMES ORR (1844–1913)

Reformed

Scottish theologian, lecturer, and writer who advanced evangelicalism in the heyday of liberalism. After graduating from Glasgow University, Orr ministered in the United Presbyterian Church, taught church history in its theological college, and then taught apologetics and dogmatics at Trinity College of Glasgow. Among his best-known works are *The Sabbath: Scripturally and Practically Considered* and the apologetic work *The Christian View of God and the World.* His lectures in the United States in 1897 were published as *The Process of Dogma and Neglected Factors in the Study of the Early Progress of Christianity.*

While evangelical in his beliefs, Orr was familiar with modern German and British philosophy and theology, and this bred a desire to see Christianity interwoven with modern trends in these areas. He saw the church and its doctrine as constantly moving forward, evolving as it better grasped the truth of Scripture. He was criticized by some within the Scottish Free Church for advancing a "modified Calvinism" and a moderate view of inspiration.

ALBERT COOK OUTLER (1908–89)

Wesleyan

Methodist ecumenical theologian who interpreted John Wesley as a practical theologian with a catholic breadth. Outler studied at Emory University and obtained a Ph.D. from Yale. He taught theology at Duke, Yale, and Southern Methodist universities. Outler also served on the editorial board of the Wesley Works Project and as president of the American Theological Society and the American Society of Church History. His contribution to Wesleyan theology includes the understanding of how patristic fathers influenced John Wesley, particularly Wesley's doctrine of soteriology.

JAMES I. PACKER (1926–)

Reformed

Anglican theologian and apologist and prolific author on Reformed theology and biblical Christianity. Packer's greatest contribution has been as an exponent of the inspiration and authority of Scripture. His works include *Knowing God, God Has Spoken, "Fundamentalism" and the Word of God,* and *Evangelism and the Sovereignty of God.* Packer is professor emeritus of systematic and historical theology at Regent College in Vancouver, British Columbia.

WOLFHART PANNENBERG (1928–)

Protestant

German Protestant theologian and most influential theologian of the latter twentieth century. Pannenberg's theology has been characterized by the phrase "revelation as history." As professor of theology at Munich since 1968, he has championed the historical nature of the resurrection of Christ. His work is in some ways a response to the existential emphasis in both Karl Barth and Rudolf Bultmann. Pannenberg contends that divine revelation is open to critical investigation by the methodology shared with other scholarly disciplines. His emphasis, while healthy, has drawn criticism for a failure to seriously integrate the noetic effects of sin and the work of the Holy Spirit. Critical realists have sharply criticized his neo-Hegelian epistemology. Pannenberg's works include *Jesus—God and Man*, *Theology and the Kingdom of God*, *Theology and the Philosophy of Science*, and *Systematic Theology.*

BLAISE PASCAL (1623–62)

Roman Catholic

French theologian, philosopher, mathematician, scientist, and Christian apologist. He is credited with many scientific advancements in physics (Pascal's Law) and Euclidean geometry and inventing the first mechanical calculator and the first wristwatch. Influenced by Jansenism, Pascal attacked the Society of Jesus (Jesuit) doctrines and sought to make a defensible case for essential Christianity. He also fought against Descartes' rationalism by advancing an apologetic emphasizing the overwhelming evidence in favor of the historical faith, especially in fulfilled prophecy, the witness of history, and other external evidences.

In November 1654, Pascal had a mystical experience that convinced him of the importance of a personal encounter with the Savior. He described the experience on notes and later sewed them into the lining of his coat, which was found after his death. In his *Pensées*, published posthumously from his notes, he emphasized the importance of faith in Christ as Savior: "The heart has its reasons, which reason does not know."

PELAGIUS (c. 360–c. 420)

Orthodox/catholic/Heretic

British monk and founder of Pelagianism, a school of thought that taught humankind's inherent capacity for good. He utterly rejected Augustine's doctrine of original sin. Little is known about his early life, but Pelagius seems to have begun as a British monk who came to Rome to preach. He was trained in law and taught among the aristocracy in Rome, but he left the city when the Vandals invaded it. Known as a very disciplined and pious man, Pelagius was a prolific writer, his main extant works being *Expositions of the Thirteen Epistles of Paul* and *Book of Faith.* In 405 he read Augustine's *Confessions* and took issue with the emphasis of grace over human choice.

He and Augustine became adversaries. Augustine authored a steady stream of writings against Pelagianism, and Pelagius suffered a number of excommunications, appeals, and reinstatements into the church. In 424 Pelagius was condemned and left for Egypt, where he remained in obscurity the rest of his life. The last action taken concerning his views was their condemnation as heresy at the Council at Ephesus in 431.

One condition that gave rise to Pelagius's views was the moral laxity that pervaded the church. The excuse for this lack of moral purity was that a Christian was only human and had a sinful nature that could not be mastered until the next life. Pelagius considered this wrong thinking, for he could not imagine that God would call his people to holy living without providing a means of obeying those commands. Pelagius emphasized that God gave free will to humans to enable them to choose good over evil. He denied that there was any depraved nature inherited from Adam, only a bad example. He held that Adam's sin was charged only to Adam on the grounds that God would not be just in condemning all humankind because of one man's choice.

The Pelagian position on sin and human nature has appeared repeatedly during the history of the church. This position has been called "the natural religion of the human heart."

WILLIAM PERKINS (1558–1602)

Reformed

English scholar who advanced Puritan theological concepts to the laity through his writings. Perkins was educated at Christ's College, Cambridge, and from 1595 taught at Great St. Andrews, Cambridge.

Perkins was thoroughly Puritan in his thinking. He was known for having the ability to communicate complex theological truths in clear terms without losing any important qualities of a doctrine. *De Praedestinatione* (On Predestination) was so popular that it evoked a written response from Arminius. Perkins was also an able commentator on Scripture and a patristic scholar, and he published polemics against the Roman Catholic Church, witchcraft, and astrology.

As a teacher, Perkins inspired many of the future leaders of the Puritan movement, the most famous of whom was William Ames. Perkins's work *A Golden Chaine* is an example of the type of spiritual guidance he believed should be part of every believer's experience. The Church of England was influenced by his emphasis on practical piety, and his works form a foundation on which the pietism of the seventeenth century was built.

PETER LOMBARD (c. 1100–c. 1160)

Roman Catholic

Italian theologian and bishop, recognized for his contribution to medieval scholasticism. Born in Lombardy in northern Italy, he was educated in Bologna and then Paris, where he became acquainted with many scholastic theologians, including Peter Abelard, Bernard of Clairvaux, and Hugo of St. Victor. In 1141 he became a professor of theology (called a "canon") at Notre Dame. Peter was appointed bishop of Paris a year before he died.

Peter's summary of theological thought entitled *Libri Quatuor Sententiarum* (Four Books of Sentences, often called *The Sentences*) became the standard theological textbook for the next five centuries. Until the sixteenth century, all B.A. degree candidates at Notre Dame were required to pass an examination on his work. Albertus Magnus, Bonaventura, and Thomas Aquinas wrote commentaries on it. Although it was used by some as late as the seventeenth century, it was eventually replaced by Aquinas's *Summa.* Peter Lombard is still known as the "master of the Sentences."

PETER MARTYR (1500–1562)

Reformed

Italian monk and scholar who advanced Reformation ideals, especially among the English. Born Pietro Martire Vermigli in Florence, Italy, he was dedicated by his father to saint Peter Martyr (1205–52). He was educated by the Augustinian order and became a monk. He was a first-rate scholar who was familiar with patristics, rabbinic literature, and much of the work of the scholastics. Through his studies, he encountered the writings of Martin Bucer and Ulrich Zwingli, and soon he was won over to Protestantism. Fleeing Italy, Peter arrived in Germany in 1542 in the midst of the Reformation.

Peter's scholarly skills led Martin Bucer to help him get a teaching position at the university in Strasbourg. While there, he met and married Catherine Dummartin, a former nun in the Roman Catholic Church. Later he began to teach at Oxford and under Edward VI helped to advance the reform movement in the Church of England. However, after Mary took the throne, he left England and returned to Strasbourg. His differences with Lutherans regarding the sacraments eventually led him to resign and move to Zurich. It was there that he truly felt at home with other English refugees who had fled the English persecution.

PLOTINUS (c. 205–270)

Philosopher

Egyptian philosopher and mystic, and founder of Neoplatonism. Plotinus was educated in Alexandria under the teaching of Ammonius Saccas but later moved to Rome and began his own school of philosophy. Plotinus developed a system of philosophy that synthesized various schools of philosophy and became known as "Neoplatonism." One of his students was Porphyry, who compiled Plotinus's essays in *Enneads*, a book published posthumously in A.D. 300. Along with the essays, the work contains a biography that details four mystical experiences of Plotinus and remains a classic in mystical literature.

Neoplatonism had a profound effect on the church, for it deeply influenced the theological school that sprung up in Alexandria and through this the whole Eastern theological mind-set. For example, the Eastern insistence on apophatic theology (defining God only by negation) has its roots in Neoplatonism. The three levels of existence contributed to the affirmation of an allegorical hermeneutic used in Alexandria, where Clement and Origin affirmed three levels of meaning in every text. This influence was also felt in the West, where Augustine was greatly influenced by the Neoplatonism he learned in Rome.

POLYCARP (c. 70–c. 155)

Orthodox/catholic

Greek bishop of Smyrna, church father, and martyr. At his trial, Polycarp declined to swear allegiance to the emperor and curse Christ, which would have gained him his freedom. He said, "For eighty-six years I have served him, and he has done me no evil. How could I curse my King, who saved me?" This early martyr is recognized as a faithful pastor, champion of apostolic tradition, and pillar of catholic orthodoxy.

As a young man, Polycarp had at least talked with John the apostle, according to Irenaeus. He was influenced by Ignatius of Antioch (c. 35–111), who had both visited the bishop and written to him to encourage him. Polycarp maintained a letter-writing ministry, although only one letter—to the Philippians—is extant; in it he warns against docetism, heresy, and avarice. He had an amiable disagreement with Bishop Anicetus on the Quartodeciman issue (the celebration of Easter). He also clashed with the heretic Marcion. Yet he was instrumental in converting Valentinians and Marcionites. *The Martyrdom of Polycarp* (written within a year of his death) is the earliest extant account of a martyr.

KARL RAHNER (1904–84)

Roman Catholic

German Jesuit priest and scholar who influenced twentieth-century Roman Catholic theology. Rahner became a Jesuit, then was ordained a priest, and still later a teacher at Innsbruck University and München University. He upheld supernaturalism, but as Karl Barth did for Protestantism, Rahner integrated contributions from existentialism and modern philosophy into orthodox Catholic doctrines. He was a good communicator, with a pastoral and evangelistic manner, and is recognized as one of Roman Catholicism's outstanding expositors.

WALTER RAUSCHENBUSCH (1861–1918)

Protestant

Baptist clergyman in the United States who is known as the father of the "social gospel." He preached, lectured, and taught at German Baptist Theological Seminary and Rochester Theological Seminary.

As a pastor in Hell's Kitchen in New York's Lower East Side, Rauschenbusch encountered the effects of poverty, crime, and labor exploitation. This experience led him into a fresh study of the Bible and resulted in his first book, *Christianity and the Social Crisis* (1907). He wrote polemics against American capitalism and advanced what he called a "Christian socialism" in works such as *Christianizing the Social Order*, *The Social Principles of Jesus*, and *A Theology for the Social Gospel.* His theology continued to be evangelical (sinners must first repent and believe in the gospel), but he also made this then-provocative statement: "Social religions, too, demand repentance and faith: repentance for our social sins; faith in the possibility of a new social order." So he was an evangelical liberal who maintained that the root problems are not necessarily with the "system" but are buried in sinfully wicked hearts that need redemption.

JOHANNES REUCHLIN (1455–1522)

Roman Catholic

Outstanding German humanist and Hebraist. Reuchlin was an avid scholar who studied under the Brethren of the Common Life in Schlettstad, studied law and Latin and Greek at various universities, compiled a Latin lexicon, and later wrote two Latin comedies. He also served as an interpreter (on a trip to Rome in 1482) and later as an adviser and ambassador for Count Eberhard of Württemberg. In 1502 he became one of three justices in the Swabian League. In the meantime, his study of Hebrew with the help of learned Jews resulted in his writing several works on the subject of cabalistic doctrines. But his most important publication was a Hebrew grammar and lexicon called *Rudimenta Hebraica* (1506), which revived both the academic study of Hebrew and the study of the Old Testament in the original.

In later life, Reuchlin became embroiled in controversy with theologians Johannes Pfefferkorn and Jakob Hoogstraten and the Dominican friars of Cologne, all of whom demanded the destruction of Jewish books. Reuchlin disagreed on the grounds that they should be retained for scholarship. He was charged with heresy by Hoogstraten, and even though the humanists and many Reformers rallied to his defense in Rome, Pope Leo X decided against him in 1520.

Reuchlin, who never left the Roman Catholic Church, was the great-uncle of Philip Melanchthon. He attempted to detach his nephew from Luther, yet he prevented Luther's books from being burned at Ingolstadt.

ALBRECHT BENJAMIN RITSCHL (1822–89)

Liberal

German liberal theologian who advanced a moralistic and ethical understanding of justification. Ritschl studied at various universities and taught first at Bonn and then at Göttingen. He was influenced by F. C. Baur, Hermann Lotze, and Immanuel Kant. Ritschl distinguished between judgments of facts, which could be proven empirically, and judgments of values, which involved subjective interpretation. Thus, to Ritschl, the divinity of Christ was to be understood not as a statement of fact but as an expression of the relational value he gives to the church. Although he spoke of justification as God's acceptance of sinners, he did not view the atonement in orthodox terms. The atonement was not to satisfy penal wrath; rather, Christ's death was martyrdom. Jesus simply died as a result of his ultimate loyalty to his vocation. Consequently, Jesus serves as a supreme moral example for us of the extent to which we are to change our attitudes and accept God's standards for living ethically. (See also chapter 14.B.2.)

SABELLIUS (THIRD CENTURY)

Orthodox/catholic/Heretic

Little is known about Sabellius except through the movement that bears his name, Sabellianism. Some scholars hold that he was from Libya or the Pentapolis (near the Dead Sea). It is known that at one point he was in Rome, where he was instrumental in propagating his heresy.

Sabellianism is also known as modalistic Monarchianism or Patripassianism. It posits an extreme understanding of the unity of God who expresses himself not in three persons but in three modes. As Father, this divine monad presented itself as creator and lawgiver; as Son it was redeemer; and as Holy Spirit it was the grace giver after the ascension. Sabellius's line of thought depersonalizes the Logos as simply the inherent rationality of God, thereby denying the personal subsistence of the preincarnate Word.

Sabellianism was defeated in the Roman Catholic Church primarily by Tertullian, the great legal mind of the early church, who defended the concept of the Trinity in his work *Against Praxeus*. The view is still found, however, in Unitarianism, in the work of Friedrich Schleiermacher, and in Horace Bushnell's writings.

GIROLAMO SAVONAROLA (1452–98)

Roman Catholic

Italian Reformer, preacher, and martyr. In his youth, Savonarola was especially interested in the works of Thomas Aquinas. He became a Dominican monk in Bologna. He aspired to be a great preacher and, despite some early failures, became one. In 1490 his superiors ordered him to go to Florence, where he preached boldly against the abuses of the church and its leaders and of the government of Lorenzo de'Medici.

Savonarola's preaching not only brought about a great religious revival but also made him so powerful as a religious and political reformer that he became the virtual dictator of Florence. He introduced a democratic government and began to reform the bureaucracy. This brought opposition from Savonarola's political enemies and corrupt clergy. Under pressure to silence Savonarola, Pope Alexander VI ordered him to stop preaching. When Savonarola defied the order, the pope excommunicated him. The Florentine people turned against Savonarola after his failure to bring about a promised miracle, and he was soon arrested. Even though his teachings were essentially the same as those of the church, Savonarola was condemned, hanged, and burned as a heretic.

FRANCIS A. SCHAEFFER (1912–84)

Reformed

Twentieth-century evangelical missionary, philosopher, and author who called attention to the decline of the Judeo-Christian worldview in Western culture. Schaeffer was born into a Lutheran family in Philadelphia. As a teen, he became agnostic and studied to become an engineer. He was converted while a student at Drexel Institute in Philadelphia. Afterward he studied at Hampden-Sydney College (Southern Presbyterian) and Faith Theological Seminary.

While serving as a missionary in Switzerland, Schaeffer formed a community in the Alps called L'Abri, meaning "shelter." It became a haven for thousands of youth who stopped in for a time of reflection and discussion regarding secular issues and faith. His ministry gained worldwide recognition through his lecturing and writing, in which he confronted philosophical issues from a biblical perspective. In his books, he blames Hegel's advancement of metaphysical relativism (no absolutes) for the decline of morals in Western society. Schaeffer was perhaps the first evangelical to call late-twentieth-century America a "post-Christian" culture.

Schaeffer's most noted works include two film series, *Whatever Happened to the Human Race?* and *How Should We Then Live?* In these he argues that secular humanism has replaced deontological Christian ethics with relativism. The result will be dehumanization, a decline in culture, and ultimately political tyranny. He also called Christians to advance their worldview: "As Christians we are not only to know the right world view, the world view that tells us the truth of what is, but consciously to act upon that world view so as to influence society in all its parts." Schaeffer especially advanced this ideology as he called the church to speak and act against abortion. In one of his final works, *The Great Evangelical Disaster*, he presented inerrancy as the church's watershed issue of his time.

PHILIP SCHAFF (1819–93)

Reformed

Swiss-American theologian and church historian. Known also as an ecumenical pioneer, Schaff became professor at the German Reformed Church's theological seminary in Mercersburg, Pennsylvania, the breeding ground for the controversial Mercersburg theology. With J. W. Nevin, Schaff promoted this system of thought, a mixture of German idealism and American Protestantism. It included Schaff's belief that Protestantism and Catholicism would someday fuse together into a unified, evangelical system of faith.

A prolific writer, Schaff's works include *A History of the Christian Church* (eight volumes, 1908–12), *Creeds of Christendom* (three volumes), and the *Schaff-Herzog Encyclopedia of Religious Knowledge*. He was involved in the development of Sunday school, the Evangelical Alliance, and the translation of the Revised Version of the Bible. In 1888 he was one of the founders of the American Society of Church History and served as its first president.

FRIEDRICH SCHLEIERMACHER (1768–1834)

Liberal

The father of modern (liberal) theology and possibly the greatest theologian to live between the time of John Calvin and Karl Barth. (See chapter 14.B.1.)

ALBERT SCHWEITZER (1875–1965)

Liberal

German theologian, medical missionary, organist, and music historian whose theological influence remains at work in those trying to recover the "historic Jesus." Schweitzer earned a doctorate in philosophy in 1899 and a doctorate in theology a year later. He served as a pastor in Strasbourg and later became head of the Theological College of St. Thomas. He was also a leading interpreter of the organ music of Johann Sebastian Bach.

Schweitzer's deeply religious nature led him to put these achievements behind him. At age thirty he entered medical school and, as a medical missionary, set up a tiny hospital in Lambarene (in what is now the Republic of Gabon). While in the jungle, he wrote books on theology and philosophy. In *The Philosophy of Civilization* and other books, he explained his belief in reverence for life as the key to understanding the universe and the human mind and spirit. For Schweitzer, reverence for life included all living things.

His book *The Quest of the Historical Jesus* (1906) pictures Jesus as one who believed he was the fulfillment of the messianic promises but never realized it because he did not set up his kingdom on the earth. To Schweitzer this meant that Jesus was driven by a mistaken understanding of himself.

JOHANN SALAMO SEMLER (1725–91)

Lutheran/Rationalist

German Lutheran theologian and biblical critic. The son of a pastor, Semler attended the University of Halle. He served as professor at Coburg and Altdorf and then at Halle. He is best known for his work in biblical and historical criticism, in which he investigated the origins of the New Testament books. He developed a threefold classification of Greek manuscripts that enabled textual criticism to go beyond quantity to quality, based on age and geographical origin. However, in *Treatise on the Free Investigation of the Canon* he maintained that religious doctrine and ethics are primarily culture bound. Thus he resisted the notion that all Scripture is inspired.

LAELIUS SOCINUS (1525–62)

Unitarian/Rationalist

Italian religious teacher who became the founder of Socinianism, a rationalistic, anti-Trinitarian version of Christianity. He taught that Jesus was the revelation of God but was only a man. Socinus's writings were used by his nephew, Faustus Socinus (1539–1604), to establish the new movement, which was a forerunner of modern unitarianism.

PHILIPP JAKOB SPENER (1635–1705)

Lutheran

German Lutheran pietist. Raised in a religious atmosphere, Spener studied theology at Strasbourg and, after becoming acquainted with Reformed theology, became a free preacher in Frankfurt-on-Main. There he became the leader of the pietist movement. His influence lay in his reform of religious instruction: he focused on preaching through entire books of the Bible and setting aside days for fasting and prayer. He appealed for conversion and holy living and created conventicles for pastors and lay leaders to pray and study the Bible together for mutual edification. His conventicle concept spread to other Reformed and Lutheran bodies. His pietistic teachings made him famous but also controversial, and some of his disciples were even expelled from Leipzig in 1690. Though little of his work was original, his emphasis on conversion and holy living undermined the position of scholastic orthodoxy, and it served to revitalize German Lutheranism.

AUGUSTUS H. STRONG (1836–1921)

Reformed

Baptist theologian and educator in the United States, noted for his *Systematic Theology.* Strong was born in Rochester, New York, and studied at Yale and at Rochester Theological Seminary. In 1872 he was named both president and professor of the seminary and served there for thirty years. Strong was a voice for conservative orthodoxy in the midst of rising modernism and theological liberalism, but unlike his Presbyterian counterpart Charles Hodge, he was open to using modern scholarship and critical methods in his work. He served for three years as president of the Northern Baptist Convention, which eventually became the American Baptist Church. Along with his three-volume *Systematic Theology*, Strong published *Philosophy and Religion*, *Christ in Creation*, and *Ethical Monotheism* (in which he allowed for theistic evolution).

JOHANN TAULER (c. 1300–1361)

Roman Catholic

German Dominican mystic who bridged the gap between scholasticism and mysticism by translating the academic into the practical. Born in Strasbourg, he entered the Dominican order of preachers around 1315. His writings and sermons became popular as he emphasized that spiritual health is not only for the spiritual elite, but also for commoners. During the period of the Black Death in Europe, Tauler devoted himself to serving the sick. Martin Luther was influenced by his writings.

TERTULLIAN (c. 160–c. 225)

Orthodox/catholic

North African church father, apologist for Christianity, and first theologian to write in Latin. Known as the father of ecclesiastical Latin, Tertullian was the first to contend that "the blood of the martyrs is the seed of the church." He was well educated and probably practiced law. When he was in his late thirties, he was converted and went on to serve the church in Carthage, where he decried the moral laxity among professing Christians. Consequently he became a Montanist and separatist but remained orthodox in other beliefs. Because he was drawn toward asceticism, his views on Christian living and morality tended toward the extreme. In *Apology*, considered his masterpiece, he argued effectively for the toleration of Christianity. Tertullian's influence has contributed to the legal cast of all Western theology. Moreover, he is responsible for coining hundreds of theological terms, many of which are still widely used.

JOHANN TETZEL (c. 1465–1519)

Roman Catholic

German Dominican whose abuse in selling indulgences prompted Martin Luther's Ninety-five Theses. He studied at Leipzig and entered a Dominican convent. In 1517 Pope Leo X named him the inquisitor and commissioner of indulgences for Germany. Tetzel abused the system, promising his hearers—contrary to the approved teaching of Roman Catholicism—that money for an indulgence would release a soul from the torment of purgatory. He was also accused of questionable financial dealings with Augsburg bankers and earned a rebuke from C. von Miltitze, the papal legate, for sexual improprieties.

THEODORE OF MOPSUESTIA (c. 350–428)

Orthodox/catholic

Syrian exegete, bishop, and theologian best known for advancing the Antiochene Christology of two independent natures of Christ. Theodore preferred the historical rather than the allegorical interpretation of Scripture. Considered the most brilliant exegete of the ancient church, he was considered orthodox in his lifetime but was condemned posthumously at the councils of Ephesus and Constantinople for the teaching associated with his pupil Nestorius.

HELMUT THIELICKE (1908–86)

Lutheran

Voice for evangelical theology in Germany in the twentieth century. Prior to World War II, Thielicke received doctorates in theology and philosophy and taught at several German universities, including Erlangen and Heidelberg. During the war, the Nazis prohibited Thielicke from speaking because he had spoken out against Nazi racial policy. After World War II, Thielicke became a popular preacher and writer. He emphasized personal regeneration and the responsibility of responding to social issues based on the principles of the Bible. His nearly two dozen works include *The Evangelical Faith*, *A Little Exercise for the Young Theologian*, and *Theological Ethics*.

THOMAS À KEMPIS (c. 1380–1471)

Roman Catholic

German monk, mystic, and ascetic writer best known for his efforts to reform church institutions and bring spirituality to the common people of the Low Countries. Thomas was educated in the Netherlands by the Brethren of the Common Life. There he became an Augustinian monk. While he produced many devotional works, the best-known book attributed to him is *The Imitation of Christ.* Thomas's work, along with that of the other Brethren, contributed to the success of the Reformation in the Low Countries.

PAUL TILLICH (1886–1965)

Protestant

German theologian and philosopher. The son of a Lutheran pastor, Tillich was schooled in Berlin, Tübingen, Halle, and Breslav. He served as a chaplain in World War I and then taught at Berlin, Marburg, Dresden, Leipzig, and Frankfurt. After joining the religious socialist movement, he came to oppose Hitler and national Socialism and was dismissed from his position at Frankfurt. He then came to America and taught at Union Theological Seminary, Columbia University, Harvard, and the University of Chicago. His theology, which is based on Platonism, medieval mysticism, German idealism, and existentialism, is best understood through his *Method of Correlation,* which contends for complementary roles of philosophy and theology. Philosophy poses the problems and theology answers them. Tillich taught that existentially man derives his being by participating in the ground of being—which is God—and that Jesus Christ is the "New Being," who became transparent to the ground of being at the cross. The major criticisms of Tillich are his dependence on idealism, which tends toward pantheism and impersonal deity, and his failure to grasp the Protestant principle of *sola scriptura.*

FRANCIS TURRETIN (1623–87)

Reformed

Leading figure of Reformed scholasticism, whose thought influenced "Princeton theology" centuries later. (See chapter 11.B.4.)

WILLIAM TYNDALE (c. 1494–1536)

Roman Catholic/Anglican

English Reformer who translated the Bible into English. Tyndale was educated at Oxford and Cambridge, where he studied Greek and Hebrew. He made it his life goal to translate the entire Bible into English. When he could not find a place to do his work, he moved to Germany to do his translation and publication. There he became acquainted with Luther's writings. In 1525 he completed the New Testament and began smuggling copies into England. Before he could complete the Old Testament, he was arrested and sent to Brussels, where he was imprisoned. After a year in prison he was brought to trial, then strangled and burned at the stake. His associate, Miles Coverdale, completed the Old Testament translation. Tyndale's vigorous translations profoundly influenced subsequent English versions of Scripture. He advocated the doctrines of justification by faith and the authority of Scripture.

CORNELIUS VAN TIL (1895–1987)

Reformed

Dutch-American apologist and theologian who argued for presuppositional truth. Born in the Netherlands, Van Til came to the United States with his family in 1905. He attended Calvin College, Princeton Theological Seminary, and Princeton University. He is best known for his writings and his forty years of teaching apologetics at Westminster Theological Seminary. His approach to apologetics is presuppositional, and he argued that the infallible truth of Scripture and the existence of the triune God are the necessary presuppositions. His books include *The New Modernism*, *Common Grace*, *The Defense of the Faith*, and *A Christian Theory of Knowledge.*

VOLTAIRE (1694–1778)

Rationalist

French rationalist philosopher and writer who opposed orthodox Christianity during the Enlightenment. Born Jean François-Marie Arouet, Voltaire was educated by Parisian Jesuits. Despite his religious upbringing, Voltaire was throughout his life violently opposed to the Roman Catholic Church and criticized it for deceit, superstition, and fanaticism. He was twice imprisoned and then banished for three years to England for his political activism. In his *Lettres Philosophiques* (1734), he viewed England as the land of rationalist philosophy, just social institutions, and religious toleration. While in exile, Voltaire came in contact with Isaac Newton and John Locke, who influenced his deistic beliefs. Although he did not view God as a personal God, Voltaire attacked atheism on the grounds that a belief in God is necessary for the masses because atheism can only lead to anarchy.

PETER WALDO (c. 1140–1217)

Roman Catholic

The founder of the Waldenses, a group that called for reform prior to the Reformation. Waldo was a wealthy merchant in Lyons, France. Upon conversion he decided to give up his wealth in order to preach to the common people. He gathered a group of men about him who became known as the "poor men of Lyons." At the Third Lateran Council, they sought permission to preach to the common people in the vernacular and to work for reformation in the church. It was decided that they were allowed to preach only if they were invited by the local priests. They obeyed for a time but then began to tour the country preaching, saying that they would rather obey the voice of God than man. Their movement spread rapidly, and in 1184 they were excommunicated by Pope Lucius III. In 1229 the Council of Toulouse decreed a forceful suppression of the heresy. The Waldenses endured much suffering under the Inquisition but continued as a movement and ultimately merged into the Reformation.

JOHN F. WALVOORD (1910–2002)

Dispensational

Dispensational theologian, writer, and president of Dallas Theological Seminary. Walvoord earned his Th.D. in 1936 during his initial pastorate. He then joined the faculty of Dallas Theological Seminary, becoming president after Lewis Sperry Chafer's death in 1952. He led the school for twenty-eight years, and under his administration, the seminary emerged as a primary proponent of dispensational theology. Walvoord was the author of numerous works, including *The Millennial Kingdom*, *The Blessed Hope and the Tribulation*, *Israel in Prophecy*, and commentaries on Daniel and Revelation.

BENJAMIN B. WARFIELD (1851–1921)

Reformed

Conservative Northern Presbyterian theologian and educator during the rise of liberalism. Warfield is known as the last of the great conservative Princeton theologians who defended Calvinistic orthodoxy. Born in Kentucky, he studied at Princeton University, Princeton Theological Seminary, and the University of Leipzig. He became assistant minister at First Presbyterian Church of Baltimore. He taught New Testament language and literature at Western Theological Seminary, Pittsburgh, then succeeded A. A. Hodge at Princeton Seminary as professor of didactic and polemical theology.

Warfield remained a staunch Calvinist and had a high regard for the Westminster Confession of Faith. He fought relentlessly for biblical inerrancy and waged an ongoing battle with Charles A. Briggs and Henry Preserved Smith over the issue. In 1881 he published, with A. A. Hodge, the famous essay "Inspiration," which defended the infallibility and truthfulness of Scripture. Subsequently Warfield published numerous other essays on biblical inspiration and authority that have influenced American evangelicals to the present. His collected works, covering bibliology, Christology, apologetics, and numerous topical studies, fill ten volumes.

CHARLES WESLEY (1707–88)

Methodist

English Methodist leader, hymn writer, and brother of John Wesley. Charles was the eighteenth child and youngest son of Susanna and Samuel Wesley. He studied at St. Peter's College in London and later went to Christ Church, Oxford. There he helped form the "Holy Club," whose members practiced spiritual disciplines, visited prisoners, helped the poor, and maintained a school for neglected children. Both George Whitefield and, later, John Wesley were members. In 1735 Charles was ordained and sent to Georgia with John, but dissatisfaction and ill health led Charles to return to England only a year later. Charles came under the influence of Peter Bohler, a Moravian, and on Whitsunday 1738, Charles experienced an evangelical conversion, claiming to finally have peace in God, rejoicing in the hope of loving Christ. Charles's greatest contribution is the multitude of hymns he wrote. It has been said that what John Wesley preached, Charles Wesley sang. His hymns include *Hark! the Herald Angels Sing*, *And Can It Be That I Should Gain?* and *O for a Thousand Tongues to Sing.*

JOHN WESLEY (1703–91)

Methodist

The founder of Methodism and a leading figure of the evangelical revival in England and the First Great Awakening in America during the eighteenth century. (See chapter 12.B.)

GEORGE WHITEFIELD (1715–70)

Reformed

Methodist evangelist of Calvinist persuasion who, with John and Charles Wesley, led the English revival in the eighteenth century. In America he was prominent in the Great Awakening. Whitefield was born in Gloucester, England, and met the Wesleys while a student at Oxford. There he had an evangelical conversion (1735) and, after being ordained by the Church of England, began preaching the necessity of spiritual regeneration for salvation. When churches began closing their doors to him, he started preaching in open fields. Whitefield and the Wesleys worked together for a few years and then parted in 1741, as Whitefield was more convinced by Calvinistic arguments regarding predestination than by the Wesleys' sympathy with Arminian understandings.

Whitefield's voice was powerful, and he had the ability to capture audiences numbering in the thousands. It is reported that during his thirty-four-year ministry, he preached over fifteen thousand times and to millions of people. He preached throughout the British Isles and made seven trips to the American colonies. He died in Newburyport, Massachusetts. Many consider Whitefield the founder of American revivalism, as he inspired Jonathan Edwards and others.

ALFRED NORTH WHITEHEAD (1861–1947)

Philosopher

English mathematician and Harvard professor and philosopher. Whitehead was the father of process philosophy, which views change as being as fundamental to reality as permanence. Whitehead conceived of God as limited and gradually developing. His philosophy emphasized the atomistic nature of reality and God as "dipolar" or "bipolar," having a primordial (eternal) aspect and a subsequent aspect (which is subject to change and development). Whitehead's work became the fountainhead for process theology. Among his works are *Process and Reality*, *Religion in the Making*, and *Essays in Science and Philosophy*.

WILLIAM OF OCCAM (OCKHAM) (c. 1285–c. 1347)

Roman Catholic

Medieval Franciscan scholastic and theologian renowned for his philosophy. A leader in the school of nominalism, Occam denied the common doctrine of universals and abstraction, holding that only specific, individual things exist. He traced the basis of morality and of existence itself to the will of God. This led to the contention that knowledge is reached through intuition and that reason can neither prove nor disprove things of faith. Occam denied the pope's temporal authority and held that Scripture is the only source of infallible authority. He believed that the laity should have a greater voice in church affairs and that knowledge of God is apprehended by faith. Thus he greatly influenced John Wycliffe and Martin Luther. For a time, he was imprisoned for his beliefs. While he had profound influence on late medieval thinking, he is most often remembered today for his "razor," i.e., the principle of economy in thinking. The principle states that one should not make more assumptions than the minimum needed to solve a problem. This principle is used to "shave off" concepts, variables, or constructs that are not actually needed to explain phenomenon under scrutiny.

ROGER WILLIAMS (c. 1604–83)

Protestant

The founder of Rhode Island and advocate of the separation of the church and state. Williams was an English Anglican clergyman who became first a Puritan, then a Baptist leader, and finally a seeker after the "pure church." After voicing his belief in religious liberty, he was banished from the Massachusetts colony and went to Rhode Island, where he founded a new colony. This became a haven from religious oppression for those "distressed in conscience." Williams sought to live in peace with the Indians and succeeded until the beginning of King Philip's War. He argued against the state's involvement in church affairs, contending that while the state has authority to preserve law and order, it has no jurisdiction over church matters of doctrine, practice, and government.

JOHN WYCLIFFE (c. 1329–84)

Roman Catholic

The "Morning Star of the Reformation." Wycliffe (or Wiclif) was an Oxford professor and English rector whose criticism of wrongs he found in the Roman Catholic Church led to his fame as a Reformer and his condemnation as a heretic. He attacked indulgences, penance, and transubstantiation, asserting the authority of the Bible against the decisions of the church. Wycliffe believed that the best way to prevail against the abuses of the church is to make the Scriptures available to all people in their own language. His followers produced the Wycliffe Bible (the first English translation from Latin), and his work foreshadowed the Protestant Reformation. In 1428 his remains were exhumed and burned by order of the Council of Constance.

NIKOLAUS LUDWIG VON ZINZENDORF (1700–1760)

Pietist

Lutheran minister who helped pioneer the Moravian Church, which promoted an ecumenical effort to spread the gospel. Born in Dresden, Zinzendorf came to faith in Christ at an early age and was educated at Halle and Wittenberg universities, where he studied both law and theology. Through his family and education, Zinzendorf was influenced by pietism and Lutheranism, and he devoted much of his life to bringing unity between the two.

In 1721 Zinzendorf was appointed the king's counselor at Dresden and there opened his home to those seeking spiritual renewal. Soon he began ministering to people from other traditions, including a remnant of the Bohemian Brethren (Unitas Fratrum). Although he remained Lutheran in doctrine and became an ordained Lutheran minister, his new methods created discord. Controversy arose as Zinzendorf's nontraditional ministry expanded to the community he founded near Dresden named "Herrnhut" (The Lord's Watch). Zinzendorf was eventually exiled, and he established other settlements patterned after Herrnhut in the Baltic Provinces, Holland, England, the West Indies, and America.

Zinzendorf emphasized nontraditional ecclesiastical methods, particularly the emotionally therapeutic aspects of conversion and mysticism. He was persuaded that the common ground for Christians is saving faith made visible in love to the world.

ULRICH ZWINGLI (1484–1531)

Reformed

Swiss Protestant Reformer. Zwingli became an admirer of the humanist Erasmus and taught himself Greek and studied patristics. After ordination to the priesthood, Zwingli attacked abuses in the church and broke with Catholicism in 1519, as seen in his lectures on the New Testament. He included expository preaching in his church services and attacked teachings on purgatory, invocation of the saints, and monasticism. Through a series of public disputations with the Roman Catholic representatives, the Reformation in Zurich took hold under Zwingli's leadership. He continued to lead the German-speaking Swiss Reformation until his death at the battle of Cappel (Kappel), which was waged during the struggle between Catholics and Protestants.

Zwingli claimed to have developed his reformation convictions independent of Martin Luther, and his break with church traditions was more radical than Luther's. This was especially pronounced in Zwingli's view of the Lord's Supper, or Eucharist, which he interpreted as simply a memorial in contrast with both the transubstantiation of Catholicism and the consubstantiation of Lutheranism.

NOTES

[1]*Orthodox* with a capital "O" refers to the Eastern Orthodox tradition, while *catholic* with a small "c" refers to the unified tradition of the West (and East) that antedates the rise of the Roman Catholic Church. The term *orthodox* with a small "o" is more generic and can be used across lines of Christian traditions—e.g., orthodox Lutheran, orthodox Presbyterian.

[2]Julian "the Apostate" (331/2–63) converted publicly to paganism in 361 and prohibited Christians from teaching the sciences and the arts, so that young people had access to the classics only through pagan teachers.

[3]There are a number of mendicant orders that support themselves through alms. One of these is the Dominican order.

[4]A red hat or robe, befitting a cardinal, because of his services for Pope Damascus; a lion, because from one's paw, so legend goes, he once withdrew a thorn—although that tradition rightly belongs to St. Gerasimus, according to Catholic hagiography.

CHAPTER 18

A BRIEF DICTIONARY OF THEOLOGICAL AND PHILOSOPHICAL TERMS

An asterisk * indicates an entry in chapter 17, "Biographical Sketches of Major Theologians and Philosophers."

adiaphora. Lit. "indifferent things." Issues that are not essential to the faith and are neither commanded nor forbidden in Scripture. This term gained prominence especially during the Reformation as Protestants sought some basis for unity with the Roman Catholic Church. *Adiaphora* encompassed matters that could be tolerated to minimize ecclesiastical and theological conflict.

adoptionism. Theological position that holds that Jesus was born a fully human person who at some later point in his life was adopted by God as his Son. At the point of adoption, he assumed divine power as given by the Holy Spirit. Dynamic monarchianism, a teaching that took root in the second century A.D. and was later condemned as heretical, held that the man Jesus Christ became God when at his baptism the Holy Spirit came upon him, but even then he was not fully God until his resurrection. Thus, at his baptism, Jesus was "adopted" as the Son of God.

agnosticism. Belief that there is no *proof* for the existence of God but without denying the *possibility* that God exists. Coined by T. H. Huxley, the word has now come to describe a belief that God is irrelevant to life. Agnosticism is distinct from theism, which affirms the existence of God, and from atheism, which denies divine existence. Modern agnosticism can be traced to David Hume and Immanuel *Kant.

Alexandrian school/theology. A theology, rooted in Neoplatonism, that originated in third-century Alexandria. Its chief architect was *Origen. It included (1) a self-conscious Neoplatonic philosophical perspective, (2) an emphasis on the Logos doctrine to unite God and the world, (3) an allegorical interpretation of Scripture, and (4) a tendency to emphasize Christ's divinity at the expense of his humanity. This school of thought stood in opposition to the school of Antioch, which held to a literal interpretation.

allegory. In its strictest sense, an oral, literary, or other artistic device that attempts to communicate immaterial truths in concrete forms. It usually occurs as extended metaphor in narrative form, moving point for point between the intangibles under discussion and representations recognizable to the intended audience. To understand the allegory, the audience must be familiar with the thought forms of the author.[1] Allegory is different from the method of interpretation known as *allegorism*, *allegorizing*, or *allegorical interpretation*, which is characterized by the search for deeper meaning in the literal statements of a text than is readily apparent or intended by the author. Allegorism became a dominant hermeneutic during the patristic period and continued to be influential until the Reformation. (See also *typology*.)

amillennialism. See *millennialism*.

Amyraldism. See chapter 11.B.5.

Anabaptist. See *Radical Reformation*.

analogy of being (*analogia entis*). The theory that a correspondence or analogy exists between the created order and God as a result of the divine creatorship. This concept theoretically justifies drawing conclusions about God from the known objects and relationships of the natural order and is especially associated with Thomas *Aquinas. Karl *Barth rejected it on the basis of the wholly "otherness" of God, meaning that we cannot know anything of God unless God reveals it to us.

analogy of faith (*analogia fidei*). A term with a range of meanings, all centered on the hermeneutical principle that an obscure text of Scripture may be illumined by other, clearer texts. As an exegetical principle, it means that an interpretation of Scripture must not contradict what is taught elsewhere in Scripture. Roman Catholicism extended it to include the principle that the Bible must be interpreted so as to agree with tradition.

analytic judgment. See *justification by faith*.

Anglicanism. The Church of England. As formulated by *Elizabeth I, the Anglican Church was designed to be a via media between Protestantism and Catholicism, broad enough theologically to encompass both groups. Its theology and worship are found in the *Thirty-nine Articles of Religion* and the *Book of Common Prayer*. Historically, the authority of the church has rested with the clergy, but in 1970 synodical government was introduced, resulting in laity having equal authority in church councils.

annihilationism. The doctrine that the final state of sinners is the complete destruction of the individual, body and soul. Immortality is only for the righteous, while the wicked are raised, not for eternal torment, but for judgment and then final death. In recent decades, this view has been adopted by a number of prominent evangelicals, including John R. W. Stott and Clark Pinnock.

anthropology (Gk. *anthropos*, "man"). The study of humanity. In theological usage it deals with humanity in relation to God mainly in three areas: (1) The *content* of the image of God (rational faculties, spiritual capacity, dominion over creation, maleness and femaleness, or sonship). (2) The *origin* of the soul (God is the immediate creator of the human soul [creationist], or the substances of soul and body are propagated together in a mediate procreative process [traducianist]). (3) The extent of the freedom of the will. (See *Augustinianism*; *Pelagianism*.)

anthropomorphism (Gk. *anthropos + morphe*, "man + form"). A literary device that attributes human characteristics to nonhuman objects (e.g., "the trees clap their hands"). The use of anthropomorphic language to speak of God, especially in the Old Testament, is ultimately merely an attempt to express the inexpressible by means of a parallel: it communicates things about God in concrete, comprehensible terms (e.g., God is our Father; the "eye of God" refers to his omniscience). Anthropomorphism as a literary device is to be distinguished from the polytheistic pagan religions that saw the gods as idealized projections of humanity.

Antinomianism (from Gk. *anti + nomos*, "against + law"). Generally used to refer to those who reject moral law, especially the Mosaic law, as binding. Paul's stress on the inadequacy of the law to save and on justification by faith apart from "works of the law" (Rom. 3:20–28; Eph. 2:8–9; Titus 3:5) led to antinomian heresies, which began to emerge early on as some interpreted the exemption from Mosaic obligation as permission to disregard *all* moral law in determining their conduct. (For Paul's reaction, see especially Romans 6 and 8.)

antinomy (from Lat. *antinomia*, "conflict of laws"). In theological usage, the contradiction, or logical incompatibility, between two propositions, both of which contain truth. Examples of theological antinomies include God's sovereign election versus a human's freedom to choose; Jesus Christ being fully God yet fully man; and God's justice demanding a consequence for sin in contrast to his grace and willingness to forgive people their wrongdoing.

Antiochene school/theology. A patristic school of theology that practiced literal, historical, and grammatical exegetical methodology as opposed to the allegorism of the school of Alexandria. Theologically, Antioch focused its attention on the incarnate Jesus Christ and had particular interest in his humanity. Antiochene theology was the background for the Nestorian heresy, which denied an organic union between the humanity and deity of Christ. (See also *Alexandrian school/theology*; *Nestorianism*.)

anti-Pelagian writings. The works of *Augustine that elucidated his opposition to *Pelagius and his doctrines, especially in the theological areas of anthropology, soteriology, and hamartiology. (See also chapter 7.C.4.a.)

apocalyptic (Gk. *apokalypsis*, "unveiling"). A literary genre that originated during the intertestamental period. Apocalyptic literature contains, or claims to contain, revelations and imagery of the events that will accompany the end of the world and the inauguration of the new heavens and new earth. Apocalyptic generally shows the elect being oppressed and the triumph of God over the oppressors by supernatural means. Apocalyptic is highly figurative, employing allegory and striking and bizarre imagery to portray future events. The books of Ezekiel and Daniel contain apocalyptic scenes, as does the New Testament (Matt. 24 and Revelation).

Apollinarianism. See chapter 5.C.1.b and chapter 17: *Apollinarius.

apologetics. A defense (Gk. *apologia*) of the faith. Apologetics involves systematic, argumentative discourse in defense of the divine origin and the authority of the Christian faith. It is justifiable from 1 Peter 3:15 and has always been an implicit part of evangelism, as Christianity makes explicit truth claims that demand substantiation. For the two primary types of apologetics, see *presuppositionalism* and *evidentialism*.

apophatic (Gk. *apophasis*, "denial"). The theological position that maintains that God is in himself absolutely transcendent and rationally unknowable. Thus he can be described only by the language of negation, that is, only by what he is *not* like rather than by assertions about what he *is* like. Eastern theology has tended to be more apophatic than Western theology, which has tended toward cataphatic, that is, positive assertions (Gk. *kata-*

phasis, "affirmation") about God on the basis of God's self-revelation. (See also chapter 8.B.1.)

apostasy. A willful repudiation of one's previously confessed faith and practice. The term is understood in different ways, depending on a theological tradition's view of the possibility of a true believer apostatizing from orthodox faith.

Apostles' Creed. An early summary of Christian doctrine that according to legend was authored by the twelve apostles. This statement of Christian faith is harmonious with the teaching of the apostles, but modern scholarship generally denies apostolic authorship. The creed is derived from the Old Roman Symbol or Creed (a second-century doctrinal summary that was an expansion of the apostolic church's baptismal formula). The present form of the creed is to be dated somewhere around A.D. 700.

apostolic era. The earliest period of church history, normally delimited by the death of Christ (c. A.D. 30) and the passing of the last apostle, John (c. A.D. 100).

apostolic fathers. A term used specifically of the early-second-century writers who came immediately after the original apostles. Those commonly included are Clement of Rome, *Ignatius, *Polycarp, Papias, and Hermas, as well as the authors of the anonymous works *The Epistle of Barnabas*, *2 Clement*, the *Epistle to Diognetus*, and the *Didache*. Their writings were primarily pastoral in nature.

apostolic succession. A view developed in the late second century that the apostolic tradition, including its teaching and authority, was handed down from the apostles to the ordained clergy. In the Roman Catholic view, this becomes the foundation for the papacy, since the bishop of Rome traces his authority back to Peter, to whom Christ said, "I will give you the keys of the kingdom of heaven" (Matt. 16:19).

appropriation. Ascribing the action of the Godhead to one member of the Trinity. For example, sanctification is appropriately understood to be the work of the Holy Spirit, though both the Father and the Son are also involved in the sanctification process.

Arianism. An early-fourth-century christological heresy advanced by *Arius, then presbyter of Alexandria. In an effort to maintain absolute monotheism, Arius taught that the preincarnate Christ was a created being, the firstborn of all creation. ("There was a time when the Son was not.") The Arian controversy led to the first Council of Nicea in A.D. 325, which resulted in the condemnation of the Arian view in favor of that espoused by Alexander, bishop of Alexandria, and his disciple, *Athanasius.

Arminianism. See chapter 12.A.

atheism (Gk. *a* + *theos*, "not + god"). A doctrine that denies the existence of deity. Absolute atheism is the dogmatic denial of God's existence. Atheism differs from agnosticism, which holds that there is no *proof* for the existence of God. The term atheism simply means a rejection of deity in any form. Many have been incorrectly called atheists merely because they reject a particular concept of divinity. Thus, to the Romans the early Christians were atheists because they denied the visible Roman gods. Similarly, Muslims are not atheists, even though they deny biblical theism.

atonement. Reparation for a given offense. In Christian thought, atonement refers primarily to the death of Christ on the cross whereby he effected salvation for humanity, reconciling humans and God. Numerous explanations have been given as to the exact *nature* of the meaning of the death of Christ (ransom paid to Satan, *Christus victor* [victory over sin and death], satisfaction, penal substitution, governmental example, and moral influence, et al.). There are also different views regarding the *extent* of the atonement: is it extended only to the elect (see *limited atonement*) or to both the elect and nonelect (*unlimited atonement*)?

attributes of God. The basic inherent characteristics by which God in his trinitarian fullness can be described. They are permanent characteristics that God has always possessed and will always possess. God cannot gain additional attributes, nor can he lose any. God's attributes are correlated with his actions, i.e., his actions will always be congruent with his nature. Theologians often distinguish between the *incommunicable* attributes (those that God alone possesses—e.g., immortality, omniscience, omnipotence, omnipresence) and the *communicable* attributes (those that God shares with humanity—e.g., love). Attributes can be divided into a number of categories. In the *supernatural* realm, God is unique in that he is eternal, self-existent, and unchanging. *Intellectually*, God is omniscient, wise, and faithful. *Ethically*, God is loving, merciful, and completely just. *Emotionally*, God is personal, compassionate, and intimately involved in every area of our life. *Existentially*, God is unique, free to do whatever he chooses, and omnipotent.

Augustinianism. A theological system developed by *Augustine, bishop of Hippo, derived from Scripture and expressed through the underlying categories of Neoplatonic philosophy. Augustine maintained that humans are born with original sin and can be saved only through the sovereign grace of God as expressed through absolute predestination and election. Augustinianism has been the starting point for both the Catholic and Protestant traditions. (See chapter 5.C.1.c.)

Babylonian captivity. (1) The period of time in which the Jews were exiled in Babylon and Mesopotamia, beginning with the fall of Jerusalem in 586 B.C. and continuing until the rebuilding of the temple in 538 B.C. (2) The period of time in which the popes of the Roman Catholic Church were exiled from Rome to Avignon in France (1309–77). (3) The title of a work by Martin *Luther, *The Babylonian Captivity of the Church* (1520), the subject of which is the sacramental system of the Roman Catholic church.

baptismal regeneration. The doctrine that baptism is the means to the new birth.

Barthianism. Neoorthodoxy. The theological thought of Karl *Barth, considered the most significant theologian of the twentieth century. (See chapter 15.B.1.)

bibliology. The branch of systematic theology that studies the Bible, including the categories of inspiration, authority, revelation, inerrancy, and illumination.

black theology. See chapter 16.C.

blasphemy. Irreverence, insult, contempt, or slander against God. Blasphemy can also be a matter of attributing deity to a human being, either by self or by others. In a more general sense, it is appropriating for oneself glory that belongs solely to God, whether in word, deed, or belief.

Calvinism. See chapter 11.A.

canon of Scripture. The books received by the church as having been inspired by God and bearing the divine imprimatur. The church from its infancy accepted the Hebrew Old Testament as canonical and therefore authoritative. The canon of the New Testament evolved slowly. By the end of the second century, the four Gospels, Acts, and the Pauline Epistles were widely recognized as canonical. The other books, including many of the Catholic Epistles, were the last to be generally recognized. By the end of the fourth century, the New Testament canon was fixed for practical purposes, although no universal formal pronouncement on the extent of the canon was made until the time of the Reformation, when the Protestant canon of sixty-six books was affirmed, while the Roman Catholic canon also included the Apocrypha.

Cappadocian fathers. Three theologians—*Basil the Great, *Gregory of Nazianzus, and *Gregory of Nyssa—who worked in Cappadocia (east-central Turkey). They expounded the orthodox doctrine of the Trinity in the second half of the fourth century in response to the views of *Arius. (See chapter 8.B.2.)

cataphatic. See *apophatic.*

catechism (Gk. *katecho*, "to teach," "to instruct"). Instruction manual that provides basic summaries of Christian doctrine for those being instructed in the Christian faith. One of the earliest was the *Didache*, a second-century manual of church discipline. Cathechisms are often structured in a question-and-answer format. Notable catechisms from the Reformation era include Martin Luther's Small Catechism (1529), John Calvin's French catechisms (1537, 1541), and the Shorter and Larger Catechisms of the Westminster Assembly (1647).

Chalcedonian definition. The definitive statement of the ancient church with reference to the relationship of the human and divine natures in the incarnate person of Jesus Christ, declaring that two natures were present in the one person of Christ without any division, change, or confusion. (See chapter 5.C.1.b.)

charismatic movement. A movement that began in the late 1950s. As people were looking for spiritual renewal, churches around America embraced what was then known as the "neo-Pentecostal" movement. The movement emphasized the work of the Holy Spirit in and through people by means of the charismata (Gk., "grace gifts"). While earlier Pentecostalism had tended toward anti-intellectualism and theological separatism, the charismatic movement took root in historic Protestant denominations. The movement has been called the "second wave" of the Spirit, while the so-called third wave (also called the neocharismatic movement) is a worldwide phenomenon that is highly diverse both culturally and doctrinally but shares an emphasis on the Holy Spirit, spiritual gifts, and signs and wonders. In 2000 there were 66 million Pentecostals, 176 million charismatics, and 296 million neocharismatics worldwide.[2]

chiliasm. See *millennialism.*

Christology. The study of the person and work of Jesus Christ. Christology received its classic expression at the Council of Chalcedon in 451 (see *Chalcedonian definition*). Christian orthodoxy holds that Christ is the

Messiah, both Son of God and Savior of humankind. He is a coequal member of the Trinity and a perfect and sinless man. In his incarnate state, he was both fully human and fully divine at the same time (possessing two different and yet complementary natures, organically joined). As purposed by God in eternity, Christ died for the sins of the world and was resurrected from the dead three days later. He redeems his people forever and provides the only source of salvation available to humankind (see chapter 5.C.1.b). While the nature of the person of Christ has been "defined," the exact nature of his atoning death has never been universally established (see *atonement*).

circumincession. See *perichoresis.*

common grace. See *grace.*

confession. (1) The personal acknowledgment of Christ, particularly in the confession of Christ as the Son of God (Matt. 16:16; 1 John 4:15). (2) Confession of one's sins, publicly, privately, or to a priest or minister. (3) A theological statement of faith espoused by a denomination or theological tradition, e.g., the Westminster Confession (Reformed) and the New Hampshire Confession (Baptist). (4) *Confession* was also used to refer to the profession of faith made by a martyr during the Roman persecution. Those who refused to give in to their persecutors were labeled "confessors."

congregationalism. A system of church government that places emphasis on the congregation in the governing of church affairs. Congregationalism holds that the individual Christian has complete and free access to God and that no human authority is necessary for mediatorial purposes. Therefore, collectively Christians (the local congregation) are to be autonomous and not subject to a higher governing body, whether that body be *episcopal* or *presbyterian* in form. Baptist churches today demonstrate the congregational model, as do many independent and Bible churches.

consubstantiation. See *Eucharist.*

contextualization. "The translation of the unchanging gospel of the kingdom into verbal forms meaningful to peoples in their separate cultures and within their particular existential situation" (Bruce J. Nichols).[3] (See chapter 2.C.)

conversion. The change of one's personal relationship to God. In Protestantism it involves repentance and is generally linked to regeneration, the new life in Christ. (See also *baptismal regeneration.*)

correlation, method of. A method, proposed by Paul *Tillich, of structuring a theological system. It begins with the questions that arise from the human condition and situation and correlates them with relevant principles of God's Word.

correspondence theory of truth. The view that truth can be found when a belief is in correspondence with the actual state of affairs in the world, i.e., with objective reality. This view has historically been held in evangelicalism. This approach underlies evidentialist apologetics (see *evidentialism*) as well as the doctrine of the inerrancy of Scripture. From a Christian perspective, the modern scientific insistence that *all* truth must be empirically verifiable is reductionistic because reality is more than merely material.

cosmological argument. One of Thomas *Aquinas's "Five Ways." The cosmological argument holds that the existence of the created order argues for a sufficient first cause, who is to be identified as the creator. While the argument has been popular with both theologians and philosophers, those proceeding from a materialistic perspective have denied that the argument *proves* God's existence. (See *Five Ways*.)

covenant theology. A theological system that views God's dealings with human beings under a series of covenants (covenant of works, covenant of grace), emphasizing the unity of humankind, the unity of the Old and New Testaments, and the unity of the church and Israel. Covenant theology began in the Reformed tradition of *Zwingli and *Bullinger, was developed by *Cocceius, and was adopted in the Westminster Confession. (See chapter 11.C and D.1.)

creed (Lat. *credo*, "I believe"). A concise, formal, summary of Christian doctrine, authorized by the councils of the early church. Three primary creeds are the Apostles' Creed, the Nicene Creed, and the Athanasian Creed. Note that *creeds* belong to the church as a whole, *confessions* to a specific church or denomination. (See chapter 2.A.2.)

critical philosophy. A philosophy that originated with Immanuel *Kant (1724–1804). It asserts that humankind's understanding of reality is a result, not simply of empirical data as observed by the senses, but rather of those data as interpreted through the rational mind. Thus reality cannot be apprehended in and of itself. Kant rejected all proofs for the existence of God. Nonetheless, humans are able to know God as their conscience assures them of the validity of divine truth in a manner that reason could never achieve.

cultural conditioning. The effect of cultural factors on the written form and substance of revelation. (See *contextualization.*)

death of God school. A school of theology that achieved a limited following in the 1960s. Theologians of this school (Thomas J. J. Altizer, William Hamilton, and Paul Van Buren) attempted to respond to a culture that found God to be no longer relevant. The secular realm is where God now operates, and it is in secular terms that we must speak about Christianity (without referring to "God").

decrees of God. The comprehensive plan and purpose of God for the world and his creation. As normally formulated, the decrees include creation, election, fall, and redemption. (See chapter 11.B.1.)

deism. Deism believes that God's relationship to the world is like a clock maker who creates a watch, winds it up, and leaves it to run by itself via inviolable natural laws. The five basic doctrines of deism are: (1) belief in a supreme being, (2) the obligation to worship, (3) the obligation of ethical conduct, (4) the need for repentance from sins, and (5) divine rewards and punishments in this life and the next. Deism denies, however, the Trinity, the incarnation, the uniqueness of Jesus Christ, the atoning death of Christ, and the depravity of man. It was the religion of the leaders of the American Revolution, such as Thomas Jefferson, Thomas Paine, and Benjamin Franklin.

demythologization. An approach to biblical interpretation, advanced by Rudolf *Bultmann, who argued that the New Testament encapsulates the kerygma (the essential Christian message) in a "mythological" worldview that uses language symbols and images that are no longer comprehensible to us. Bultmann did not want to eliminate myth from the Bible, but rather to reinterpret the mythological language of the Bible in such a way as to make the kerygma comprehensible and meaningful to the twentieth-century scientific mind-set.

dialectical theology. The early theological approach of Karl *Barth that emphasized the "dialectic" between God and humanity. (See chapter 15.C.1.)

dichotomism (Gk. *dichotomia*, "division into two"). The theological view that human beings have two components—an immaterial and a material one, or body and soul (Matt. 10:28). Soul, spirit, mind, and heart are merely different terms for the immaterial part. *Trichotomism* (Gk. *trichotomia*, "division into three"), on the other hand, sees three components: body, soul, and spirit (1 Thess. 5:23).

Didache (Gk., "teaching"). A writing from the late first century or early second century, probably from Palestine or Syria, that presents "the teaching of the apostles" (the full title of the work) for new converts.

dispensationalism. A theological movement within evangelicalism that stresses an apocalyptic understanding of history. (See chapter 13.)

docetism (Gk. *dokein,* "to seem"). A late-first-century Christian heresy that regarded the human aspects of Christ, including his sufferings, as apparent rather than real. In the dualistic view of the time, matter and the physical world are evil, but the spiritual world is good. Therefore, if Christ were God, he could not suffer; if he did suffer, he could not have been divine. Hence, since Christ is God, his sufferings could not have been real.

doctrine/dogma. *Doctrine* (from Lat. *docere,* "to teach") is that which is taught by a teacher, a group, or a church. By contrast, *dogma* (Gk., "opinion"), includes only teachings contained in the confessions of the church. Doctrines are therefore much more diverse and may be much more detailed than dogmatic statements.

dogmatic theology. The study of primarily creedal and confessional statements of the church and their development.

Donatism. A fourth-century separatist movement in North Africa. The followers of Donatus, bishop of Carthage (A.D. 313–47), held that the priest's part in sacraments was substantial, not only instrumental. Consequently, following the Diocletian persecution (303–5), those priests who had given up the Bible were adjudged to be traditors (traitors) whose ordination was invalid, as were any sacraments they performed. The Donatist church survived in North Africa until the Muslim conquests in the seventh century. (See also *traditors.*)

Dort, Synod of (also Dordt). An international assembly of the Reformed churches, convened in Dort, Netherlands, by the Dutch Reformed Church to address the Arminian controversy (1618–19). At this synod five main tenets of Calvinism (The "TULIP") were formulated in response to the Remonstrance. (See chapter 11.B.3.)

double predestination. The doctrine that God has predestined some to eternal life and others to eternal damnation. (See *predestination* and chapter 11.A.2.d.)

dualism. Any explanation of reality that invokes two distinct and irreducible principles, e.g., spirit vs. matter, light vs. darkness, form vs. substance. It is opposed to both monism (one principle) and pluralism (many principles). In Plato's philosophy there is an ultimate dualism of ideas and matter. *Kant posits an ontological dualism between the phenomenal and the noumenal. (Cf. *docetism*, *Gnosticism*.)

Ebionitism. An early Jewish-Christian heresy. Ebionitism (also known as Ebionism) is the position that Jesus was made the Anointed One at his baptism and was made so because he had kept the law perfectly. This position thus emphasizes the humanity of Jesus to the exclusion of an essential deity in the nature of the Logos. The fundamental criticism is that if Jesus loses his essential dissimilarity from those he came to redeem, then he is unable to redeem them. (Ebionitism holds to the same presuppositions as the later dynamic monarchianism. See *monarchianism*.)

ecclesiology. The area of theology dealing with the study of the church and issues such as its purpose, nature, character, government, institutions (especially sacraments), and mission. How one develops answers to these determines one's ecclesiology.

ecumenical councils. Assemblies convened for determining church doctrine, sometimes resulting in the condemnation of certain teachings as heretical. The early councils of Nicea (325), Constantinople (381), Ephesus (431), and Chalcedon (481) were particularly important in the trinitarian and christological debates, finally resulting in the establishment of an orthodox Christology. In the early church, ecumenical councils included all churches, both Eastern and Western. The Roman Catholic Church still convenes "ecumenical councils," although they do not include the Eastern and Protestant churches. The most recent such council was Vatican II (1962–65).

election. The biblical and theological concept asserting the sovereignty of God whereby some are chosen for blessing, as ultimately seen in some being elected unto salvation. Election is a crucial doctrine within Reformed theology, which teaches God's unconditional election of certain individuals for blessing. In this understanding, faith is the consequence rather than the cause of election. In contrast, conditional election (the Arminian view) maintains freedom of the human will by positing that God predestines based on foreknowledge of who will believe and who will not. (See chapter 11.A.2.d.)

encyclical. In the Roman Catholic and Anglican churches, a letter from a bishop or bishops to their diocese as an exposition of Christian belief and practice. The best-known encyclicals of modern times are those issued by popes for their worldwide constituency and those issued by the Anglican bishops at the end of the Lambeth Conferences that are held every ten years.

Enlightenment, the. An intellectual movement born during the seventeenth century that elevated human reason to near-divine status and ascribed to it the ability to discern truth of all types without appeal to supernatural divine revelation. Reason, natural law, and human progress were the themes of the seventeenth and eighteenth centuries, also called the Age of Reason. The intellectuals of this time rejected external authority (church, Bible, government) and promoted reason as the standard for all beliefs and actions. The cry was *"Sapere aude!"* ("Dare to use your own judgment"). Prominent Enlightenment thinkers were Descartes, *Voltaire, Jean-Jacques Rousseau, John Locke, and Immanuel *Kant. The end of this era was ushered in by the realities of revolution in France and the Napoleonic conquest in Europe.

episcopalianism (Gk. *episkopos*, "bishop"). A form of church government that places emphasis on bishops, priests, and deacons in the governing of church affairs. Episcopal forms of government exist today in the Roman Catholic Church, the Orthodox churches, the Anglican Church, the Episcopal Church, and the Methodist tradition.

epistemology. The branch of philosophy concerned with the ground and nature of human knowledge. Epistemology investigates the source, conditions, rationale, and limits of knowledge. Religious epistemology focuses on the theory of the knowledge of God, whether God can be known through justifiable grounds of empiricism, cosmology, or rationalism.

eschatology (Gk. *eschatos* + *logos*, "last + word"). The study of the last things. Eschatology deals with the end of the world and includes the second coming of Christ, the resurrection, judgment, the millennium, and the new heavens and new earth. It also deals with the last things for the individual: physical death, the intermediate state of a person between death and the final resurrection, and the final state (heaven or hell).

ethics. The study of principles of right conduct. Systems of ethics are generally classified as deontological or teleological. Deontological systems contain the motif of obedience to laws or norms. These laws come from either reason or divine revelation. Teleological systems contain the motif of the pursuit of human good. Common categories of philosophical ethics include egoism (Which alternative best benefits self?), situational ethics (Which alternative is considered appropriate in this culture at this time?), utilitarianism (Which alternative serves the greatest number for the greatest common good?), Kantian (Which alternative serves my duty to treat others with respect and dignity?), and virtue (Which alternative would a person of virtue and character choose?). Biblical ethics, on the other hand, are founded in humankind's relationship with God and its objective obligations to obedience. Christlike character, or "virtue ethics," is the goal of realized biblical ethics.

Eucharist. The sacrament instituted by Christ at the Last Supper. All Christian churches celebrate the Eucharist, which is variously known as "Mass," "the Lord's Supper," and "Holy Communion." There is significant disagreement over the nature of the Eucharist. The fundamental issue is whether the bread and wine somehow change. (1) *Transubstantiation* means that the bread and wine become the actual body and blood of Christ, even though the outward appearance does not change. (2) *Consubstantiation*, associated with Martin *Luther, holds to the simultaneous presence of both bread and the body of Christ at one and the same time. (3) *Memorialism* holds that the Eucharist is a memorial of the sufferings of Christ; it is associated with Ulrich *Zwingli. (4) *Spiritual presence*, *Calvin's view, seems to be a mediate position between Luther and Zwingli.

Eutychianism (monophysitism). See *monophysitism; hypostatic union.*

evangelical. In the American context, an evangelical is identified by his or her theological stance, not by denominational or institutional affiliation. The term identifies a Protestant who believes in the inspiration and authority of Scripture, the depravity of man, the need for God's gracious gift of salvation through faith in Christ, Jesus' commission to evangelize the lost, and the second coming of Christ. In the early twentieth century, these beliefs identified a person as a fundamentalist, but the term *evangelical* emerged during the 1940s and 1950s to distinguish between those who held these theological beliefs without accepting the separatist and political nuances that became associated with fundamentalism.

evidentialism. A theory of apologetics that seeks to prove the claims of Christianity through historical evidences available to both the believer and unbeliever. This is much different than building credibility through an appeal to a revelational starting point or subjective data. Proponents include John Warwick Montgomery and Josh McDowell.

exegesis. See *hermeneutics.*

exemplarism. This explanation of the meaning of the atonement, first suggested by Peter *Abelard, has also been called the "moral influence theory." This view sees the death of Christ as the ultimate expression of God's love for humanity. By realizing the depth of this love, a person is compelled to respond by turning from sin and following the example of Christ. In this theory, the atonement is directed toward humanity and has no meaning for God outside of being an expression of his love.

existentialism. A philosophical approach that originated with Søren *Kierkegaard and is opposed to the conventional moral values and authoritarian codes of conduct. Individuals have to determine their own existence as they live. Experience precedes existence. Existentialism is by its nature often easier to present in a play (Jean Paul Sartre) or a novel (Albert Camus) than in scholarly papers. Christian existentialism is most prominent in theologians such as Rudolf *Bultmann, John Macquarrie, and Paul *Tillich. (See also chapter 3.B.6.)

expiation. While the term *propitiation* includes not only the forgiveness of sin but also the turning away of God's wrath upon humans, *expiation* is the simple annulment of sin. Some have argued that the New Testament understanding of the death of Christ excludes the idea of turning away wrath inherent in propitiation and insist that expiation better reflects the tenor of the New Testament. Others hold that "expiation," while a biblical concept, is unsatisfactory as a term to describe comprehensively the nature of Christ's death.

exposition. See *hermeneutics.*

Fathers. The term used generically of the church leaders of the ancient church up through about A.D. 600. The Fathers are subdivided into three groups: the apostolic fathers, the generation of Christian writers immediately following the original apostles; the ante-Nicene fathers, who lived prior to the Council of Nicea (A.D. 325); and the Nicene and post-Nicene fathers, who lived up to c. A.D. 600.

feminism. At its core, the view that women deserve the same political, economic, and social rights as men. Although there are many different expressions of feminism, the points of agreement tend to be reproductive rights, including legalized abortion; equal economic rights; and elimination of traditional gender roles. Most also favor the elimination of sexist language by using, e.g., *humanity* instead of *man*, and protest the stereotypical images of women promoted by the media. In the late twentieth century, a theological trend toward egalitarianism emerged among evangelicals. Egalitarianism is the perspective that both women and men share equal status and function within domestic and ecclesiastical roles.

fideism. The view that faith rather than reason is the means to knowledge of God. The term is often used in a somewhat pejorative sense of a theology that focuses on subjective experience to the exclusion of reason.

Five Ways. The five a posteriori ways, postulated by Thomas *Aquinas, to rationally prove the existence of God. They center on ultimate causality as deduced from reason: (1) from motion to an Unmoved Mover, (2) from effects to a First Cause, (3) from contingent being to a Necessary Being, (4) from degrees of perfection to a Most Perfect Being, and (5) from design in nature to a Designer.

foreknowledge. An understanding of God's omniscience whereby all things in human and cosmological history, past, present, and future, are open to God, who knows all things about his creation, including all choices and all motives in the human heart. Calvinism sees foreknowledge as *active prescience*, i.e., as synonymous with the decrees and election. Arminianism, on the other hand, distinguishes foreknowledge from foreordination; that is, God foreordains that all who receive God's gift of salvation will be saved, and by his foreknowledge (*passive prescience*), he knows who will choose salvation and will persevere.

form criticism. A critical methodology that looks at the text of Scripture and attempts to see the "prehistory" of that text by tracing it through its oral and written stages. This is coupled with the *sitz im leben* ("setting in life") to which the text was addressed in order to enhance understanding. The approach originated with Hermann Gunkel, who applied it to the narratives of Genesis and to the Psalms.

fourth gospel. See *Synoptic Gospels.*

fundamentalism. A term coined in 1915, the traditional meaning of which refers to a theological movement that holds to the "fundamentals" of Christian doctrine, especially the virgin birth, bodily resurrection, and biblical inerrancy and authority. As a movement, fundamentalism arose in the United States in the early 1900s in response to theological liberalism, Darwinianism, modernism, and German higher criticism. Fundamentalists have traditionally held to a literal hermeneutic and a historically orthodox understanding of doctrine. In the context of the theological warfare it engaged in, the movement became anti-intellectual and culturally obscurantist. After World War II, fundamentalism began to divide and gave rise to evangelicalism. Fundamentalism and evangelicalism share the same orthodox "fundamentals," but evangelicalism seeks a more rigorous and scholarly approach to theology and has adopted an openness to culture. While fundamentalism had the stigma of being anti-intellectual, intolerant, and unconcerned with social ills, evangelicalism became less militant and anti-intellectual, and more tolerant and concerned with social problems. By the 1980s, fundamentalists became a political force and voting bloc (the "Religious Right") against liberal policies, pacifism, and some education efforts.

genre. A particular type of literary writing, such as poetry, historical narrative, or fiction. An understanding of genres is of critical importance in biblical interpretation.

glorification. Along with justification and sanctification, an aspect of the doctrine of *soteriology*. Glorification is the final and full realization of salvation for the faithful, the result of which is eternal life. Glorification takes place for the human spirit at physical death and for the body at the *parousia*. Those dead in Christ will be given a resurrected body suitable for the final eschatological state (Rom. 8:23; 1 Cor. 15:53).

glossolalia (Gk. *glossa* + *lalia*, "tongue + talk, chatter"). Speaking in tongues. Speaking, in a state of ecstasy, in a pattern of speech different from languages known to the speaker or different from normally intelligible patterns. In modern charismatic circles, the practice of glossolalia is viewed as a prayer or praise language uttered to God.

Gnosticism (Gk. *gnosis*, "knowledge"). A vaguely defined group of religious perspectives in the early Christian era that focused on the acquisition of special "insider" knowledge, available only to the initiated. It reflected various permutations of pagan religions, Greek philosophy, and Christianity. Presupposing a spirit-matter dualism, it adopted a dualistic view of God. It saw the creator God of the Old Testament (the demiurge) as an evil deity who had power over the evil world of matter. The demiurge was viewed as the antithesis of the true God, who offers salvation through *gnosis* (knowledge). Since the true God cannot have anything to do with evil matter, Gnosticism rejected the idea that Jesus was God incarnate. Christ's death provides humans with knowledge, not salvation. In response to this view, early Christian creeds and documents took a firm stand against Gnosticism.

grace. Generally speaking, blessings that cannot be merited or earned. Rather, they are freely bestowed on people by God. God shows his grace to humanity especially in the incarnation and death and exaltation of his

Son. Grace is usually divided into common grace and special grace. *Common grace* is available to all of humankind. It is a general, universal form of grace that God equally bestows on all people, as evidenced in the way he cares and provides for his creation. *Special grace* is the merciful response of God to redeem his people. Under special grace are *prevenient grace* (grace that precedes all human decisions and efforts), *efficacious grace* (grace that brings to completion the purpose for which it is given), *irresistible grace* (grace that cannot be rejected), and *sufficient grace* (grace that is adequate to save a believer for eternity). (See also *prevenient grace.*)

Great Awakenings. A term referring to two great revivals experienced in the United States. The First Great Awakening (c. 1735–43) had as its key figures Jonathan *Edwards, George *Whitefield, and John and Charles *Wesley. Both Edwards and Whitefield were powerful Calvinistic preachers. The Wesleys emphasized not only conversion, but also sanctification in their ministry. The Second Great Awakening (c. 1795–1830) was less Calvinistic and had heightened millennial expectations, as well as revival "camp meetings" characterized by powerful calls to repentance.

Great Schism, the. The definitive split between the Eastern Orthodox Church and the Western church that took place in 1054. (See chapter 8.A.)

hermeneutics. Classically, the theory of the interpretation of literary texts, particularly the rules and principles used in the interpretation of particular texts. More recently the field has been broadened to encompass the entire communication process. With reference to the interpretation of the Bible in the ancient church, two dominant schools of interpretation arose, the *allegorical* and the *literal* (grammatico-historical). The allegorical method gained prominence in the ancient church and maintained its dominance until the Reformation, during which the Reformers gravitated to the grammatico-historical with its emphasis on understanding the author's intent. While classical Protestant hermeneutics has insisted that meaning resides in authorial intent, the advent of postmodernism has displaced authorial intent and insisted that meaning is created by the reader (reader-response criticism). *Exegesis* (Gk. *exegeo*, "to lead out") uses the hermeneutical principles in the critical analysis, interpretation, and explanation of a text, seeking to "lead out" the intended meaning of the author. In biblical studies, the term *exegesis* is applied to the detailed study of the text in its original language (Hebrew, Aramaic, Greek) and original historical situation (historical-cultural context). *Exposition*, finally, is the explanation of the text of Scripture, based on hermeneutics and exegesis, to the contemporary hearer in his or her present situation and application of the text.

higher criticism. The study of Scripture as literature, examining its literary sources, its various genres, and its authors and their contextual perspectives. It is different from lower criticism (also called "textual criticism"), which deals with the origin and transmission of the text of the documents. Higher criticism, while a legitimate discipline in itself, has often proceeded from antisupernaturalistic presuppositions when applied to the Bible, denying the possibility of revelation and approaching the Scriptures as merely human documents. (See *textual criticism.*)

historical Jesus. A reference to Jesus as a human, historical figure who can be studied with the tools of historical research. Numerous quests for the "historical Jesus" were undertaken during the mid to late nineteenth century, particularly by rationalistic German New Testament scholars. The first quest was pronounced a failure by Albert *Schweitzer in the early twentieth century. A second quest was based on the work of Rudolf *Bultmann, and a third quest was inaugurated by Ernst Käsemann.

historicism. A philosophical approach that holds that all matters of truth and knowledge must be interpreted in light of their historical context. Developed in the nineteenth century out of Hegelian thought, it says that sociocultural phenomena are historically determined and can be properly understood only as we set aside our preconceptions and try to enter into the thinking and attitudes of past periods.

homoousios (Gk. *homos* + *ousios*, "same + substance"). A significant theological term in the polemics of the Arian controversy in the fourth century. *Homoousios* ("of the *same* substance") was used to describe the true nature of Christ—that is, he was indeed fully God, being of the same nature and substance of God the Father. The term was included in the Nicene Creed (A.D. 325). Arius expressed his position with the term *homoiousios*, "of *like* substance" (Gk. *homoios* + *ousios*, "like, similar + substance").

humanism. See chapters 10.A.1; 11.A.1.a.

hypostatic union. The inseparable union of the divine and human natures of Christ in one person without compromising either nature. This union was realized at the incarnation. This doctrine is in contradistinction to Nestorianism, which divided Christ into two separate natures, and to Eutychianism, which merged the two natures into one. It also emphasizes the continuity of Christ's nature and thus opposes adoptionism, the doctrine that says the divine and human natures were united at Jesus' baptism.

hypothetical universal predestination. See *Amyraldism* and chapter 11.B.5.

illumination. The ministry of the Holy Spirit that enables a person to understand the truth of Scripture, especially with regard to its salvific message. The unregenerate mind is unable to understand spiritual truth without the Holy Spirit opening the heart and mind to God's grace.

image of God (*imago Dei*). The aspects of human existence that reflect the nature and being of the Creator and set humans apart from the rest of creation. The image has been conceived variously as rational faculty, spiritual capacity, male and female, dominion, and sonship. Scripture attests to the fact of the image and to its continuance after the fall, but it also attests to the image having been damaged by sin and to its progressive renewal in salvation.

immaculate conception. The Roman Catholic doctrine that the soul of the Virgin Mary was free from original sin. It is not to be confused with the virgin birth. A festival of the immaculate conception was celebrated in the Eastern church as early as the fifth century and in the Western from the seventh century. Opposition to the doctrine arose in the twelfth century by *Bernard of Clairvaux and in the thirteenth century by *Aquinas. In 1854 Pope Pius IX issued a decree declaring the immaculate conception to be dogma and essential for the belief of the universal church.

incarnation. The act by which the eternal Logos, the second person of the Trinity, without any compromise of his full deity, took on full humanity in the person of the God-man Jesus Christ. The incarnation is understood to have taken place at the moment of conception by the Virgin Mary and the Holy Spirit.

inerrancy. The belief that the Bible is without error in all that it affirms, including historical and scientific facts. Inerrantists recognize that this is a faith position and that the validity of the doctrine cannot be demonstrated beyond challenge. However, inerrancy is held to be a necessary corollary of God's absolute truthfulness, which must also be expressed in the details of the divine inspiration of the Bible. The doctrine of inerrancy has historically been the chief touchstone of American evangelicalism. (See chapters 5.A.1.a; 6.A.2.)

infralapsarianism (also called "sublapsarianism"). In a Calvinistic understanding of the decrees, a belief that God issued the decrees of election and reprobation *after* the fall of man (Lat. *infra* + *lapsus*, "below/after + fall"). This is contrary to supralapsarianism, which holds that God predestined some to salvation and others to eternal damnation *before* he made the decision to allow the fall of man (Lat. *supra* + *lapsus*, "above/before + fall"). (See chapter 11.B.1.)

inspiration (Lat. *inspirare*, "to breathe in"; Paul uses *theopneustos*, "God-breathed," in 2 Tim. 3:16). The process whereby God guided the authors of Scripture in the recording of his revelation. A number of views have been held. (1) *Concept inspiration.* God inspired the ideas of Scripture but left to the human authors the task of choosing the actual words to employ in expressing the inspired ideas. (2) *Plenary inspiration.* Scripture is fully (extensively) the Word of God. As originally employed, the term implied a verbal aspect, but as debates about the nature of Scripture continued, further refinement was introduced into the discussion. (3) *Verbal inspiration.* God inspired both the ideas of Scripture and the words employed by the human authors to express those ideas. (4) *Verbal-plenary inspiration.* An intensification of the idea of plenary inspiration that makes explicit that both extensively (*all* of Scripture) and intensively (the very words) the Scriptures are divine in origin and therefore totally trustworthy. The corollary doctrine is inerrancy.

justification by faith. The judicial declaration by God that the sinner is "not guilty," or righteous (i.e., in the right relationship with God), based on the righteousness of Christ (Rom. 3:24–26; 4:25; 5:16–21). The result of justification is peace with God (Rom. 5:1) and the indwelling of the Holy Spirit (Rom. 8:9). Protestantism and Catholicism hold to different understandings of the doctrine of justification by faith. (1) *Analytic judgment.* The Roman Catholic perspective sees justification as a divine judgment based on actual divine righteousness imparted to and inherent in a person's life by God's grace. This righteousness comes through the sacraments and good works done in faith through the power of the Holy Spirit. (2) *Synthetic judgment.* The Protestant perspective that sees justification as a divine judgment based on a righteousness synthesized from the alien righteousness of Christ and imputed to the sinner's account at the moment of trust in Christ. Protestants contend that such an understanding is the clear teaching of Paul and is the only basis for assurance of one's acceptance before God.

kenosis, kenotic (Gk. *kenoo*, "to empty"). The self-limitation or self-emptying by Christ of certain divine attributes at the incarnation. The idea of *kenosis* finds its root in Philippians 2:7, Jesus "emptied himself" (NIV "made himself nothing"). Various kenotic theories have been proposed since the nineteenth century. Some of the more radical theories contended that Christ laid aside his deity during his incarnation to take it up again after the resurrection. Other kenotic explanations have been more moderate, suggesting that Christ's "emptying" consisted of the voluntary disuse of his incommunicable attributes during his earthly life.

kerygma (Gk., "proclamation"). As used in modern thought, the essential Christian message, especially as it relates to Christ, faith, and salvation.

Liberal Protestantism. See chapter 14.

Liberation Theology. Liberation theology is "a collection of contemporary theological movements interpreting salvation and the mission of the church primarily as the changing of oppressive social structures—economic, political, and social—rather than as redemption from personal guilt and sin." (See chapter 16.)

limited atonement. Also called "particular redemption." The view that Jesus died for only the elect. Most Reformed theologians have held this view (see chapter 11.B.1). Unlimited atonement, which holds that Christ died for all of humanity, is held by other Christian traditions. (See chapter 12.A.2.)

liturgy (Gk. *leitourgia*, "work of the people"). Its general meaning is worship by the people of God, regardless of worship style. The word has come to refer especially to more formal styles of worship with a relatively fixed order and content. Roman Catholics, Eastern Orthodox, Anglicans (particularly the High Church), and Lutherans are commonly referred to as liturgical churches.

logic. A branch of philosophy dealing with the principles of valid reasoning and argument. Logicians strive to determine the conditions under which one is justified in passing from premises to valid conclusions that are claimed to follow from the premises.

logical positivism. The philosophical movement that emerged in Vienna during the early twentieth century and asserts that all meaningful statements are either analytic, verifiable, or confirmable by empirical observation. Science, central to logical positivism, is regarded as a description of experience. All statements that fail the test of verifiability are considered to be technically meaningless, or "non-sense," with regard to objective content.

lower criticism. See *textual criticism.*

Lutheranism. See chapter 10, especially 10.C.

Marxism. A philosophy proposed by Karl Marx that has been the theoretical foundation of communism. Marxism is built on the concepts of dialectical materialism (Hegel's dialectic applied to the historical development of economic systems), inevitable class conflict, violent revolution on behalf of the working class, the belief that religion is essentially a weapon wielded by the powerful to prevent the lower classes from rising up, and the belief that the masses should collectively own all property and industrial resources. Marxism has been used as a tool for social analysis by Latin American liberation theologians. (See chapter 16.)

metaphysics. The branch of philosophy dealing with the nature of ultimate reality. Metaphysics inquires into matters such as ontology, the nature of existence, causality, true reality versus perceived reality, and determinism. Christianity requires certain metaphysical commitments, such as God being true reality and the origin of the created order.

millennialism; **millenarianism** (Lat. *mille* + *annus*, "thousand years"). Also called "chiliasm" (Gk. *chilios*, "thousand"). The belief that Christ will return and reign on earth for a thousand years. Some who hold a millenarian view of the end of history believe that the "thousand years" should be understood symbolically rather than literally, for example, as a symbol of the church age. There are three prominent millenarian views: (1) *amillennialism*—the kingdom reign of Christ is within the heart of a believer and in the collective church; (2) *postmillennialism*—the return of Christ will come after the millennium, which will be inaugurated by efforts of the church to Christianize culture; (3) *premillennialism*—Christ's return will precede and precipitate the establishment of the millennial kingdom.

modalism (Lat. *modus*, "form, mode"). Originating early in the third century, modalism rejects the doctrine of the Trinity and contends that the one God revealed himself to the world in different and successive modes but that each of these manifestations was the one true God. In the Old Testament, he revealed himself as Father, in the Gospels as Son, and after the resurrection as Spirit. The church fathers responded by contending that if Christ were the Father, it was the Father who suffered on the cross (Lat. *patripassus*, "the Father having suffered"). Modalism is also known as modalistic monarchianism, Sabellianism (after its proponent Sabellius), and patripassianism.

monarchianism (Gk. *monarchia*, "one origin/rule"). A radically monotheistic and antitrinitarian doctrine that denies distinctions within the Godhead. For the monarchian, God is one but not "three in one." There are two varieties of monarchianism, both from the late second century—*modalistic monarchianism* (see *modalism* above) and *dynamic monarchianism*, which states that Christ was a man who was acted on by an impersonal divine force that came from the Father.

monergism. See *synergism*.

monism. The metaphysical understanding that views everything in the universe as being an extension of a single reality. Ultimately all is absorbed into the one source. Differentiation is an illusion. All forms of monism are in conflict with Christianity.

monophysitism (Gk. *mono*, "one," *physis*, "nature"). Monophysitism (also called "Eutychianism") asserts that after the incarnation Christ did not have both a divine and a human nature. Rather, the divine absorbed the human, or the divine and human formed what could be called a semi-divine nature. The debate over this came to a climax at the Council of Chalcedon (see *Chalcedonian definition*). The view of the monk Eutyches that Christ had two natures before the incarnation but one after was rejected. A later, derivative heresy is monothelitism ("one will").

monotheism. Monotheism is the belief that there is only one God. It is opposed to pantheism (everything is god) and polytheism (there are many gods). The Shema (Deut. 6:4, "The LORD our God, the LORD is one") is an early, unambiguous statement of monotheism.

Montanism. A late-second-century ecstatic/prophetic, apocalyptic, and ascetic movement founded by *Montanus, a recently converted pagan priest from Phrygia (northern Asia Minor). While the sect affirmed the orthodox theological tenets, its extreme emphasis on prophecy coupled with asceticism and a courting of martyrdom brought opposition and eventual condemnation by synods in Rome and Asia. *Tertullian, with his natural inclination toward asceticism, was the most prominent convert to the sect.

natural theology. An approach whose goal is to establish truths about God through observation of nature and the natural order (general revelation) apart from special revelation (Scripture). A focus on natural theology is found primarily in the Roman Catholic tradition. Protestants have tended to resist natural theology, objecting that human reason has been damaged by the fall and is therefore not capable of making objective deductions about spiritual realities apart from faith.

neoorthodoxy. See chapter 15.

Nestorianism. A movement that emphasized the dual human-divine nature of Christ at the expense of the unity of his person. *Nestorius was a vigorous defender of Antiochene Christianity (see *Antiochene school/theology*). He was understood to be advancing the notion that the human nature and the divine nature of Christ existed side by side within Christ's body without being organically unified. After Nestorius's views were condemned at the Council of Ephesus in 431, he was banished to an Antiochene monastery and later to Egypt, where he died.

new hermeneutic. According to Rudolf *Bultmann, events in the external world are not the basis of spiritual realities; rather, they are used in a narrative to illustrate spiritual truth. This is the genre of myth used by the biblical writers. Biblical events that seem to contradict the findings of modern science and history are not to be taken literally, since they are the result of elaboration employed to communicate spiritual realities. Therefore the Scriptures, and especially the Gospels, must undergo a demythologization, or reinterpretation, of those mythical elements that have no application or relevance to contemporary concerns.

Nicene Creed. A statement of Christian beliefs formulated by fourth-century ecumenical councils in response to the Arian heresy (see *Arianism*). Emperor *Constantine, seeking to use Christianity as the means to unify the empire, called the first ecumenical council of the church in Nicea in 325 to settle the issue. The council condemned the Arian view and formulated the Nicene Creed. The creed uses various phrases to describe Christ, including "... true God from true God, begotten not made, of one substance with the Father." The focus of the Nicene Creed in its original form was on the relationship of the Son to the Father. During the period immediately following Nicea, the discussion widened to include the Holy Spirit's relationship to the Father and the Son. The contemporary form of the creed comes from the Council of Constantinople (A.D. 381) and includes further definition of the person and role of the Holy Spirit as a coequal member of the Trinity.

Ninety-five Theses. A list of ninety-five propositions prepared and nailed to the door of Castle Church in Wittenberg on October 31, 1517, by Martin *Luther as an open challenge for academic debate at the University of Wittenberg. This document is generally regarded as the catalyst of the Protestant Reformation. The theses, written in Latin, dealt with the abuses of the sale of indulgences in the Roman Catholic Church, a practice whereby forgiveness of sin could be purchased with money, not only for this life, but also for those already in purgatory. Others translated the theses into German and circulated them throughout Germany, where they aroused a storm of protest.

noetic effects of sin (Gk. *noetikos*, "intellectual"). The blinding of the human mind by sin, resulting in the inability to accurately apprehend reality, especially spiritual reality, and to respond to salvific, scriptural truth. Only by the grace of God is one able to be enlightened to biblical truth and to exercise action toward obedience. The noetic effects of sin are not wiped away by regeneration. Christians must ever be wary that their understanding is skewed by the lingering effects of sin on the mind.

nominalism. A philosophical movement that holds that "universals" are creations of the mind as opposed to having objective reality. Nominalism arose in opposition to Platonic *realism* that saw universals as having independent existence. It provided the foundation for *William of Occam's work in theology, *Centilogium*. Occam's reliance on nominalism led him to see the systematization of theology as futile, and he believed that only through faith could God be known. As a philosophy, nominalism challenged the reigning scholastic theological methodology.

ontological argument (Gk. *ôn* + *logos*, "being + study"). Argument "from being" for the existence of God, first formulated by *Anselm of Canterbury and later refined by Descartes. It states that God is, by definition, the highest being above which nothing higher can possibly be thought of. But if God did not exist, then existing beings would be higher, since existing beings are greater than nonexisting beings. Therefore God exists. Both *Aquinas and *Kant criticized this argument on the ground that perfection may not be a true predicate and that a proposition can be logically necessary without being true in fact.

original sin. A view of sin as originating in the sin of Adam and being transmitted to all his posterity. *Augustine first formally articulated the doctrine, arguing that each person is born with a predisposition toward sin, whereby sin is not merely the result of individual transgression but is inherited as part of the corrupted human nature. The term may refer to a corruption of human nature or to guilt (with accompanying liability for punishment). The Reformed tradition generally contends that each person born is guilty of the sin of Adam, who acted as the head of the race (federalism). Others see all humanity as present in Adam and participating in the first sin (realism). Still others see humanity as inheriting a corrupt nature without being personally guilty of Adam's sin.

orthodoxy. (1) Eastern Orthodoxy (see chapter 8). (2) Beliefs that are in conformity with the historic, established doctrine of the church.

panentheism (Gk. *pan* + *en* + *theos*, "all + in + God"). In contrast to pantheism, which identifies God with the created order, panentheism holds that God is radically immanent in the world but not identical with the world. God is thus both immanent and transcendent.

pantheism (Gk. *pan* + *theos*, "all + God"). Affirms that God is everything—that is, God is the world and the world is God. God is the ground for the existence of everything, including evil. For the pantheist, God is not a personal being but an impersonal force. *Absolute pantheism* states that all reality is God. *Modal pantheism* affirms that everything is a mode in the infinite essence. Some forms of pantheism affirm various levels of reality, as in Hindu pantheism.

parousia (Gk. *parousia*, "coming, arrival, presence"). The second coming of Christ. The term is used in 1 Thessalonians 4:15 to designate Christ's coming to raise the righteous dead.

patristics. The branch of theological studies that deals with the writings of the church fathers (see *Fathers*).

Pelagianism. Late-fourth- and early-fifth-century heresy that denied human depravity and the absolute necessity of the work of Christ for salvation. Pelagianism made freedom of the will absolute and taught the plenary ability of humans to please God apart from any divine intervention. Pelagianism was opposed by *Augustine, who argued for original sin, total depravity, total inability, and predestination. *Semi-Pelagianism* is the position that the human condition has been injured by sin and that humans are spiritually sick and need rescuing but that humans retain some measure of freedom to turn to God apart from the prior work of the Holy Spirit.

perichoresis (Gk., "penetration" = Lat. *circumincessio*, "mutual indwelling" or "mutual interpenetration"). Perichoresis is a necessary implication of orthodox Trinitarian thought. Each person of the Trinity has "being in each other without any coalescence" (John of Damascus). In Christology, perichoresis is used to describe the mutual interpenetration of the Lord's two natures.

person(s). The Latin term *persona* (Gk. *hypostasis*) is used to refer to the unique *individual* aspects of the divine trinitarian life that distinguish the centers of divine consciousness as Father, Son, and Holy Spirit. The term *substantia* (Lat.; Gk. *ousia*) is used to refer to that which is eternally *common* to all members of the Trinity.

pietism. Initially (but not exclusively) a German movement in the late-seventeenth-century Lutheran Church that emphasized the need for personal faith and holy living. It was a reaction against Lutheran scholasticism that had fallen into a cold, rationalistic creedalism. The initial impetus for the movement came from Philipp Jakob *Spener, whose tract *Pia desideria* (Pious Longings) advocated six requirements for reform: better knowledge of the Bible by the people, restoration of mutual Christian concern, emphasis on good works, avoidance of controversy, better spiritual training for ministers, and reformation of preaching with fervency. Under Spener's successor, August Francke, the movement spread rapidly and affected Count Nikolaus von *Zinzendorf, whose Moravian followers in turn had an impact on John *Wesley and early Methodism. Spener also had corresponded with the New England Puritan Cotton Mather, who consequently strove to encourage pietistic vitality in the New World. The Great Awakening of the 1730s and 1740s exhibited pietistic features.

point of contact. A term used in the debates between Karl *Barth and Emil *Brunner, referring to the existential engagement of the gospel and fallen man. God and man meet through personal encounter, the point of contact being the preaching of Scripture (Barth), or through a sense of human guilt, the witness of the Holy Spirit, the testimony of the saints, or biblical revelation (Brunner).

postliberalism. A contemporary theological movement challenging the intellectual and cultural credibility of liberalism (rooted in Enlightenment presuppositions of universal rationality) that has arisen in conjunction with postmodernism and has reasserted the distinctinctiveness of Christianity. It reasserts Scripture as the supreme source of Christian ideas and virtues and the centrality of Christ in the life of the church. Leading postliberal thinkers include George Lindbeck, Stanley Hauerwas, and Hans Frei.

postmillennialism. See *millennialism*.

postmodernism. A contemporary movement consisting of a rejection of the "modern" mind as it has developed out of the Enlightenment project and the philosophical/epistemological foundationalism upon which it is built. Postmodernism rejects the idea of "objective truth" open for all, of a universal rationality and a legitimate "metanarrative." It insists that all truth is "local," arising from one's particular group. Claims for universal truth must be "deconstructed" to expose the power and domination being exerted. Reality is understood to be socially constructed, and relativism extends beyond individual perception of truth to the essence of truth itself. Taken to its logical extreme, this leads to an all pervasive pluralism and relativism in which all interpretations are equally valid (or meaningless).

pragmatism. A philosophical position that contends that the truth of an idea or statement is to be measured by its consequences. A statement is valid if it is workable in human experience, that is, over a period of time in the lives of many people. All conclusions are open to modification if further experience so indicates. Philosophical pragmatism is considered an integral part of the American worldview.

predestination. A term referring to the divine foreordination of human events. This doctrine encompasses a wide spectrum of views, ranging from the broad understanding that God ordains all that comes to pass to a narrower concept that God sovereignly elects certain individuals to salvation. The doctrine of predestination carries the derivative doctrine of election. At the heart of the debate over predestination is the sovereignty of God versus the freedom of man. The Reformed tradition uniformly sees divine predestination as unconditional, that is, not based on God's *passive prescience* of future events. Other Christian traditions see predestination as conditional on divine foreknowledge, i.e., *active prescience.* Double predestination sees the elect as having been predestined for salvation and all others as having been predestined for damnation. (See chapters 11.A.2.d; 12.A.2.)

premillennialism. See *millennialism.*

presbyterianism. A system of church government that emerged in the Reformed tradition during the Reformation. It places the responsibility and authority in church affairs with a group of elders, who are in turn accountable to regional and national bodies, such as the session or classis, the synod, and the general assembly.

presuppositionalism. A theory of apologetics that holds that biblical revelation is the necessary presupposition to any coherent system of truth. Presuppositionalism was popularized in North America by Cornelius *Van Til. As an apologetic system, presuppositionalism denies any point of contact or common ground between the biblical revelation and the unregenerate mind. As a philosophy of apologetics, it is opposed to *evidentialism*.

prevenient grace. The preparatory work of the Holy Spirit in the heart of sinners, preparing them for salvation. *Augustine first developed the concept of prevenient grace as grace that necessarily precedes human action and is solely the initiative of God. This term is generally used by those in the Wesleyan tradition. There is an affinity between the Wesleyan doctrine of prevenient grace and the Reformed doctrine of efficacious grace, but where the Reformed see in efficacious grace an inevitable and irresistible moving of the Spirit in working salvation in the elect, Wesleyans view the Spirit's activity as enabling all humanity to respond to this grace without making this response inevitable.

process theology. A philosophical theology that holds that reality is a process of becoming, not a static universe of objects. A personal God enters into relationships in such a way that he is affected by the relationships, and to be affected by relationships is to change. Thus God too is in the process of growth and development. Process theology is largely based on the metaphysical system posited by Alfred North *Whitehead in his work *Process and Reality*.

procession of the Spirit. At the heart of the *filioque* (Lat., "from the Son") controversy is the question whether the Spirit proceeds from the Father and from the Son or only from the Father. Though not part of the original Nicene Creed of 325, the term was added to a version of the creed at the Council of Toledo in 589. The Orthodox Church of the East objected to this addition, and eventually it became a primary issue resulting in the Great Schism of 1054.

proofs for the existence of God. See *Five Ways*.

propitiation. The turning away of God's wrath. Human sin is deserving of divine wrath; the atonement through Christ's sacrificial and substitutionary death averts such divine wrath (Heb. 2:17; 1 John 2:2; 4:10).

Protestantism. A label, originally derived from the term "protestation" used at the Diet of Speyer in 1529, that denotes the whole movement that originated in the sixteenth-century Reformation. It includes the Lutheran, Reformed (Calvinist), Anglican, and Anabaptist traditions.

Radical Reformation. Also known as the Third Reformation, or the left wing of the Reformation. The term refers primarily to the Anabaptist reaction to the reforms instigated by *Luther and *Zwingli. They did not baptize their children as the Lutheran and Zwinglian churches did, but only adults who had made a personal, public profession of faith. Hence the name Anabaptist (lit. "rebaptizer"). Other traits include a general distrust of external authority and an emphasis on pacifism and nonresistance. The radicalizing aspect emerges in the understanding of faith and practice: the true believer will believe and do only what is explicitly taught in Scripture. The Anabaptists, unlike the Lutheran and Reformed churches, saw a fundamental separation between church and government. The most significant leader was *Menno Simons, after whom the Mennonites are named.

realism. See *nominalism.*

redaction criticism. In biblical studies, the critical analysis of the various sources and contexts from which the authors of Scripture developed their writings. Redaction criticism sees the biblical authors as theologians in their own right who shaped (redacted or edited) their material according to their theological and literary purposes. It is particularly interested in seeing the unique purpose and perspective of each gospel writer. Evangelicals affirm the goals of redaction criticism with the caveat that the gospel writers did not subordinate historical fact to theological or literary interests.

Reformed theology. See chapter 11.

Remonstrants. The Dutch Protestant followers of James *Arminius. This group presented the *Remonstrance* in 1610, which reflected their departure from scholastic Calvinism on such points as limited atonement, irresistible grace, and the freedom of the will. (See chapter 12.) At the Synod of Dort (1618), Arminianism was condemned.

revelation. God's self-disclosure to humankind, including God's divine interaction in human history. *General revelation* refers to the disclosure of certain divine attributes, such as his power, through the natural world to all persons in all places at all times. *Special revelation* refers to God's self-disclosure through his written Word and is addressed to humans in their sinful condition with a view to salvation.

Sabellianism. See *modalism.*

sacerdotalism. The view that the rites of the church, including baptism and Communion, are effective only when they are administered by one who has been ordained by the church, and that these rites convey grace to the recipient. The roots of sacerdotalism lie in the concern of the early church for the maintenance of the apostolic tradition and succession, in which the bishop passed down the teaching and authority of the apostles.

sacrament. A religious rite, service, or ceremony instituted or affirmed by Christ. Each sacrament is seen as manifesting an inward, spiritual grace through an outward, visible sign or symbol. Protestants recognize two sacraments, the Lord's Supper and baptism, while the Catholic tradition adds the sacraments of marriage, confirmation, anointing of the sick (formerly called "extreme unction"), penance, and ecclesiastical order.

salvific. Adjective meaning "having the intent or power to save."

sanctification. Along with justification and glorification, an aspect of soteriology. Sanctification is the continuing work of the Holy Spirit in the life of believers by which moral righteousness and godly character are imparted and matured. Sanctification is understood to commence initially at the moment of justification and continue to the moment of glorification. Within traditional Reformed circles, sanctification is viewed primarily as a process. In Keswick and Wesleyan models, sanctification is viewed as involving a deeper work of the Holy Spirit, or as a second work of grace, characterized as a crisis experience.

schism. Division in the church. The Great Schism took place in A.D. 1054, permanently dividing the Eastern church and the Western church. (See chapter 8.A.)

scholasticism. See chapters 9.A.4 (medieval scholasticism) and 7.C.4.d (post-Reformation scholasticism).

Scotism. A theological and philosophical tradition developed by John Duns Scotus, a thirteenth-century Scottish-born scholastic philosopher. In opposition to Thomas Aquinas, Duns Scotus held that faith is a volitional matter and not a result of reasoned logic. He taught that divine revelation supplements and perfects natural knowledge; consequently no contradiction can exist between them. Whereas Aquinas defined theology as primarily a speculative discipline, Duns Scotus saw theology as primarily a practical science, concerned with theoretical issues only insofar as they contribute to the goal of saving souls.

Scripture principle. A theological principle that holds that Scripture is the final arbiter of truth in matters of life practice and faith. As such, principles taught in Scripture are applicable to the Christian's life and to the life of the church.

semi-Pelagianism. See *Pelagianism.*

Septuagint (Lat. *septuaginta*, "seventy"; the usual symbol for the Septuagint is the Roman numeral seventy, LXX). Translation of the Hebrew Old Testament into Greek, dated third to first century B.C. Legend claims that the work was done by seventy-two (or seventy) scholars in seventy days. Today the LXX is the official Old Testament text in the Greek Orthodox Church.

social gospel. See chapter 14.D.1.

Socinianism. Sixteenth-century theologian Laelius *Socinus believed in a rationalistic interpretation of Scripture that led him to deny the Trinity and the deity of Christ. He emphasized the sin nature but saw Christ's death only as an example of love, not as the propitiatory death of Protestant orthodoxy. Therefore salvation was achieved through good works, not through faith. (See chapter 12.A.5 and E.)

soteriology. The study of salvation. The branch of systematic theology that sets forth the saving work of Christ under the rubrics of the atonement, forgiveness of sin, justification, and sanctification. The doctrine presupposes the sinfulness of humanity and the necessity of atonement on humanity's behalf.

special grace. See *grace.*

sublapsarianism. See *infralapsarianism.*

substantia, **substance.** In the Trinity, see *person(s).*

supralapsarianism. See *infralapsarianism.*

syncretism. A blending of different, often contradictory, religious and/or philosophical beliefs or practices to form a new belief or practice in such a way that—at least on the surface—the contradictions between them are resolved. The Old Testament portrays the syncretistic tendencies of the Israelites in their incorporation of various pagan religious practices in the worship of Yahweh.

synergism (Gk. *synergos*, "working together"). *Synergism* is the view that both God and humans participate in salvation; it is mostly associated with semi-Pelagianism and Arminianism. The Reformed tradition holds to *monergism* (Gk. *monergos*, "working alone"): it is the Holy Spirit alone who effects salvation. While those in the Reformed/Augustinian tradition deny synergism with reference to justification, they affirm that sanctification is a synergistic process.

Synoptic Gospels (Gk. *synoptikos*, "a seeing together"). Matthew, Mark, and Luke are called the "Synoptic Gospels," or "Synoptics," because, unlike the book of John, they present many events in a similar order and often with similar wording. The fourth gospel, John, is unique in form and theological emphasis. It contributes a great deal to Christology (Jesus = Logos = Messiah), the personal nature of God ("Father"), and the role of the Holy Spirit (Spirit of truth). It was probably written several decades after the Synoptics.

synthetic judgment. See *justification by faith.*

teleological argument (Gk. *telos*, "end, purpose"). One of the arguments for the existence of God, it posits that since the cosmos seems to demonstrate design and order, there must therefore be a Designer of that order. (See *Five Ways.*)

textual criticism. Also called "lower criticism." In literary study, the examination and analysis of documents with the goal of determining the original form of a given document. Thus textual criticism, as applied to the study of Scripture, seeks to accurately reconstruct the original text of Scripture through critical comparison of extant manuscripts.

theodicy. A defense of God's goodness, love, and omnipotence in the face of the existence of evil and suffering.

theology. The study of God and God's interaction with humankind and the cosmos. Systematic theology is an attempt to organize these doctrines and typically includes theology proper (the doctrine of God), Christology (the person and work of Christ), soteriology (salvation), anthropology (humanity), pneumatology (the Holy Spirit), ecclesiology (the church), and eschatology (the last things).

theology proper. The doctrine of God.

Thirty-nine Articles. The doctrinal standard of both the Episcopal and Anglican churches, published in 1563. Largely a result of the English Reformation of the sixteenth century, this document embodies much of German Reformation thought.

Thomism. See chapters 2.A.1.a and 7.C.4.b.

total depravity. The doctrine, first articulated by Augustine and held by the Reformers, that sin has permeated every aspect of human existence so that people are completely unable to do anything on their own to build a bridge back to God.

traditors. A name given in the African church to early Christians who saved their lives during Diocletian's persecution by surrendering copies of the Scriptures to their persecutors. At the Council of Arles (A.D. 314) the decision was made that persons who had been consecrated by traditors should be duly recognized. See *Donatism.*

transubstantiation. The Roman Catholic belief that in the Eucharist the whole substance of the bread and wine are converted into the whole substance of the body and blood of Jesus, while only the accidents (the *appearance* of the bread and wine) remain. (See also *Eucharist.*)

trichotomism. See *dichotomism.*

Tridentine (Lat. *Tridentum*, "[city of] Trent"). Adjective meaning "of, by, or relating to [the council of] Trent."

Trinity (Lat. *trinitas*, "triad"). The central and foundational doctrine of the Christian faith specifying that the one God exists as three distinct persons (God the Father, Jesus the Son, and the Holy Spirit) yet as one divine essence, one unified substance. The Athanasian Creed states, "We worship one God in trinity, and trinity in unity, neither confounding the persons, nor separating the substance." Although the term *Trinity* is not found in the Bible, the concept is supported throughout Scripture.

two natures, doctrine of. The belief that in the single, undivided person of Jesus Christ complete human nature and complete Deity subsist together in harmony and organic union. The Council of Chalcedon (451) declared that Christ possessed these two natures "without confusion, without change, without division, without separation."

typology (Gk. *typos*, "copy, image, example"). A type of spiritualizing hermeneutic that attempts to interpret many parts of the Old Testament, such as the Tabernacle, as predictive images (prefigurements) of New Testament truth and especially of Christ. Typology has been a popular hermeneutical methodology in dispensational circles, although that popularity has declined in recent years.

unitarianism. Sometimes called antitrinitarianism, it is a system of religious thought that rejects the doctrine of the Trinity and the deity of Christ. Its origin lies in the fourth-century Arian controversy (see *Arianism*). It was revived by Socinus in the seventeenth century and became increasingly rationalistic and less supernaturalistic, until in the nineteenth century all supernatural elements were stripped away. Unitarians believe in the goodness of human nature and believe that a genuine religious community can be created without doctrinal conformity. Consequently, they reject the doctrines of the fall, the atonement, and eternal damnation. Their only requirement is openness to divine inspiration. (See *universalism.*)

universalism. The belief that every soul will eventually be restored to God, regardless of one's belief in Christ. It dates back to the early church and can be found in several traditions, including Gnosticism, Anabaptism, and mysticism. *Clement of Alexandria, *Origen (who believed that eventually the devil himself will be saved), and *Gregory of Nyssa all held this view. After almost a millennium of invisibility, universalism was revived during the Reformation in some of the Anabaptist writings. The first universalist congregation in America was organized in 1779. By 1942 the group welcomed all humane men, Christian or not. In 1961 the universalists merged with the Unitarians, forming the Unitarian-Universalist Association.

unlimited atonement. See *limited atonement.*

Vulgate. The Latin version of the Bible, based on the work of *Jerome, who initially worked with Old Latin manuscripts but became convinced that it was necessary to use the Hebrew text. Thus he made a fresh translation that was completely independent of the Greek. At the Council of Trent in 1546, the Latin Vulgate was declared to be the only authentic Latin text of the Scriptures.

Waldenses. See Peter *Waldo.

Wesleyanism. See chapter 12.

Westminster Confession. A document completed in 1647 by the Westminster Assembly convened in an attempt to harmonize the theological traditions of Scotland and the Church of England. It resulted in the premier affirmation of Calvinistic theology in the English language and has become the most prominent confession of the modern church, embraced by many Reformed traditions today.

will of God. The focus of many theological discussions based on distinctions drawn between God's decretive, perceptive, and permissive will. The *decretive will* is secret and effective, determining what will occur; it is only known after the fact. God's *perceptive will* is also called his moral will, by which he reveals his moral standards for humanity; this will may be either obeyed or disobeyed by humans as morally responsible agents. God's *permissive will* refers to those acts that while not in accord with the divine character are nonetheless permitted by God and used in accomplishing his sovereign purpose (Gen. 50:20; Rom. 8:28).

Zwinglianism. The rationalistic Protestant theology of Swiss Reformer Ulrich *Zwingli. Like Lutheran theology, Zwinglianism is opposed to penance and relics and is strongly predestinarian in its understanding of election.

It looks for scriptural warrant in understanding certain issues. Thus it rejects church practices that are neither commanded nor prohibited in the Bible. This tendency is an important reason Zwingli rejected the view of Christ's sacramental presence during the Lord's Supper (affirmed by Luther) in favor of the memorial view.

NOTES

[1]An example of this need for familiarity with the author's thought forms is C.S. Lewis's *A Pilgrim's Regress*, which is an allegory. It is probably Lewis's least-read work, mostly because we are no longer very familiar with the philosophical debates this work addresses.

[2]Statistics from David B. Barrett, *World Christian Encyclopedia*, 2nd ed. (New York: Oxford University Press, 2001).

[3]Bruce J. Nichols, "Theological Education and Evangelization," in *Let the Earth Hear His Voice*, ed. J. D. Douglas (Minneapolis: World Wide, 1975), 647.

APPENDIX

A SUGGESTED APPROACH TO FINDING ANSWERS

1. *State the problem.* Identify the issue to be examined and state it in the form of a question. State the issue clearly and simply. Note the significance of the issue. Clarify the parameters of the discussion. Do not obscure the matter by introducing other valid questions that are not germane to the specific issue you are examining. For example, if you are going to examine the issue of believer's baptism versus household baptism or paedobaptism, do not complicate the discussion with questions relating to mode.

Be very careful in phrasing the question. As in scientific inquiry and experimentation, the question asked will to some degree determine the answer found. Avoid false dichotomies; that is, "Is the answer *this* or *that*?" Do not limit the options at the outset. It is possible that the answer to the question may not be a simple one or the other. The answer may possibly be a third alternative not anticipated in the simple *this* or *that*, or the answer may incorporate elements of *this* and *that.*

2. *Do a preliminary inductive study.* Using your present knowledge of Scripture and of the question, determine the key teaching passages relating to the question. Study them inductively to determine the basic teachings of each passage.

If you discover very few passages dealing with your issue, reexamine the way you have asked the question to determine whether you are focusing on a significant theological question as opposed to a topic that is rooted in a more fundamental question. For example, if you are asking a question regarding abortion, you will find very few passages dealing with the issue. More fundamental questions have to do with personhood and the taking of life. If this is the case, rework your question, focusing on the more basic theological issues.

3. *Examine proposed hypotheses/solutions.* Consider and examine the different answers to the question that have been proposed. Look at both contemporary and historical treatments, as well as at solutions from a wide variety of traditions. Treat each as a proposed hypothesis to the problem. (Remember, everyone makes mistakes, but not all make the same mistakes.) Include the position you hold or have been taught, and treat it as a proposed hypothesis also. (Do not give your current understanding a privileged position in your study.) At this juncture you are, as it were, donning the white coat of the researcher looking for evidence and hypotheses that adequately explain the evidence. Note for each hypothesis the presuppositions, supporting passages, interpretations, and key arguments to the best of your ability (Prov. 18:17). State each position accurately so that one who holds the position would be satisfied with your statement. Do not be satisfied with an examination of only popular (as opposed to scholarly) statements of the views. Also, you must refer to original sources whenever possible; that is, you must allow the area of disagreement to be stated by the proponents themselves. (In this day of electronic data retrieval via the Internet, your task as a researcher is made much easier than in previous generations even if you do not have easy access to a theological library.) For example, if you are going to discuss the inadequacies of postmillennialism from a premillennial point of view, let a postmillennialist state that position. Further, if you are going to discuss the postmillennialism of a theonomist, read a theonomist rather than a classical postmillennialist.

4. *Do a biblical theological survey.* Survey the issue under consideration by tracing the development of the concept historically throughout Scripture, being sensitive to the progress of revelation. Be sure not to read later revelation back into earlier revelation. For example, do not make the common mistake of reading the New Testament revelation of God as Trinity back into the Old Testament. Remember that biblical theology looks at the Scriptures from the point of view and categories of the original authors. This step is a vital check to make sure that systemic conclusions are not read back into the text as the "plain meaning" of the Bible.

5. *Do Scripture exegesis.* List the primary and secondary passages used to support each of the positions. Examine each major biblical passage advanced in support of all sides of the issue and determine the correct interpretation of each, avoiding as much as possible all prejudgment other than the firmly established doctrines of orthodoxy. Examining the various views will help you see aspects of the passages you might otherwise overlook as well as find pas-

sages whose relevance are not initially recognized. Be sure to note passages or teachings that each view emphasizes or neglects. Also, be alert as to whether the exegetical conclusions are in harmony with the biblical theology of the specific passages or whether the proponents of the various positions on the question have imported presuppositions from their systems into their exegesis.

6. *Examine the arguments.* Likewise, examine each logical premise and presupposition that is offered so as to determine any logical flaws in the argument. Examine each in terms of the three tests for truth:

A. Agreement with the facts
B. Logical consistency
C. Existential viability

For example, if you are considering the perseverance of the saints, all key problem passages for each view must be considered and one view must be found that can harmonize them all without strained exegesis. Also, the logic of such statements as "Eternal life would not be eternal if there is no security for the believer" or "The evidence of many backsliders disproves any doctrine of security," must be evaluated. Additionally, if you are analyzing various views of revelation, note the philosophical as well as the theological and biblical presuppositions of the views. If you are dealing with christological viewpoints, the history of the doctrine is very important.

7. *List crucial questions and issues that must be solved.* Be alert for critical questions and issues raised by each view. Issues should flow out of your examination of the questions asked and differences between the proposed solutions, your exegesis of Scripture, and your examination of arguments. This includes issues of biblical interpretation, culture, history, grammar, word meanings, logical arguments, relationships between passages, and so on. It also includes noting such things as historical, scientific, social-scientific, philosophical, theological, and biblical data to which appeal is made in the hypotheses. This list should not be static but should give rise to a more careful examination of the hypotheses, Scripture, and arguments, which in turn should give rise to more questions.

8. *Evaluate data.* Gather the exegetical and theological insights gained from the previous steps. Following are guidelines for evaluation of the data.

A. Evaluate the proposed solutions in light of Scripture and theological orthodoxy, with the priority always on the Scripture. Theories are always regulated by the biblical data. Do not allow an initially adopted view on an issue to cause you to strain interpretation of passages or to treat the data selectively. For example, do not let one's view of security force an interpretation of the warning passages in Hebrews or lead you to ignore gospel passages that speak to the believer's security.

B. Evaluate the collected data in light of such things as the analogy of the faith; careful exegetical procedure (watching for undue use of word studies apart from contextual and syntactical considerations and for misuse of Greek tense distinctions); consistent use of grammatico-historical-hermeneutical principles (including the differentiation between descriptive and prescriptive biblical statements); proper use of logic; and examination of all pertinent biblical data in both Old and New Testaments.

C. Identify the major biblical doctrine(s) involved in the matter and determine how a decision one way or another on the problem will impinge on that/those doctrine(s). Remember that you are examining one particular problem in light of the whole of theology. For example, what effect may a given conclusion about human depravity have on your doctrine of elective grace? How will your resolution of the problem of human "free will" influence your view of the attributes of God?

9. *Formulate a statement.* Bring all the data together into a cohesive statement as a solution to the original problem. Select the hypothesis that best fits these two criteria:

A. *Quantitative criterion.* The theory that best accounts for *all* the relevant data (scriptural data and other relevant data).

B. *Qualitative criterion.* The theory that best accounts for these data in the manner that is most faithful to the individual teachings of the data. Which hypothesis best incorporates the most data? What modifications need to be made in that hypothesis to incorporate more of the data?

This statement should answer the questions/issues raised in step 7. It should also incorporate the scriptural data discovered in step 5 and be consistent with the logical arguments formed in step 8. It must pass the three tests of truth stated under step 6.

NOTE: This should be just the first stage in a continual circle of revising theological statements in light of a growing understanding of Scripture and of insights gleaned from general revelation, new arguments, new recognition of implications for life and ministry, and so on.

CAUTIONS

1. *Avoid the kind of blind dogmatism and absolute statements that close the door to further inquiry and understanding and that suggest that all of the data on a disputed issue has been identified and correctly interpreted.* Note that this is not rejecting the proper place of dogmatism or the possibility of confident statements of conclusion. The key words are *blind* and *absolute.* For example, reaching conclusions prior to examination of the evidence is a sure way to short-circuit learning and the discovery of truth. On the other hand, some things, once settled, may only need reaffirmation (for example, the saving work of Christ as personally appropriated by faith).

2. *Beware of extreme statements, whether they be claims, assertions, conclusions, or even suggestions, even when clothed in the respectability and authority of biblical statement, unless they are documented with unimpeachable evidence.* For example, beware of the theonomist who calls for a Christian form of government wherein the details of the Mosaic law are the governing principles and include capital punishment for incorrigible children.

3. *No proposed answer to a theological problem is beyond accountability.* While not to be treated lightly, denominational or religious preference, historical creeds, and schools of theological thought must be both internally consistent and biblically sound.

BIBLIOGRAPHIC RESOURCES FOR THE STUDY OF THEOLOGY

The range of theological literature is overwhelming. This bibliography is based on previously published bibliographies and updated with recent material.

TOOLS FOR LOCATING JOURNAL ARTICLES AND BOOK REVIEWS

Adams, Charles J., ed. *A Reader's Guide to the Great Religions*. 2nd ed. New York: Free Press, 1965, 1977.
Bibliographic guide to world religions.

Bollier, John A. *The Literature of Theology: A Guide for Students and Pastors*. Philadelphia: Westminster, 1979.
A concentration on reference and bibliographic tools.

Catholic Periodical and Literature Index. Formerly *The Catholic Periodical Index*. Haverford, PA: Catholic Library Association, 1967/68 to date.
Annual indexing of 133 Catholic periodicals; also includes book reviews.

Christian Periodical Index. Buffalo, NY: Christian Librarian's Fellowship, 1956/60 to date.
An index to subjects, authors, and reviews in some fifty-nine popular and scholarly periodicals, mostly evangelical. Useful for locating articles not listed in *Religion Index One*.

"Elenchus Bibliographicus" in *Ephemerides Theologicae Lovanienses*. University of Louvain. Gembloux: Duculot, 1924 to date.
A comprehensive bibliographic guide to theological literature in English and foreign languages prepared by Catholic scholars at the University of Louvain in Belgium. Includes books, reviews, journal articles, and pamphlets; no abstracts.

Index to Book Reviews in Religion. Chicago: American Theological Library Association, 1986–present.

Montgomery, John W. *The Writing of Research Papers in Theology.* N.p., 1959.
Bibliography: Introduction to theology. Contains a list of "150 basic reference tools for the theological student," pp. 22–36.

The Philosopher's Index. Bowling Green, OH: Philosophy Documentation Center, c. 1978; a retrospective index to U.S. publications from 1940.
Comprehensive indexing of periodical literature in philosophy. Subjects and book reviews; author index with abstracts.

Religion Index One: Periodicals. Formerly *Index to Religious Periodical Literature.* Chicago: American Theological Library Association.
Subject indexing for 210 theological and religious periodicals; includes author index with abstracts. An indispensable bibliographic tool.

Religion Index Two: Multi-Author Works. Chicago: American Theological Library Association.
Indexing by subject, author, and editor for multiauthor books.

Religious and Theological Abstracts. Myerstown, PA: Religious and Theological Abstracts, 1958 to date.
Abstracts from some 150 journals covering biblical, theological, historical, practical, and sociological subjects. Author and subject indexes for each volume.

Wainwright, William J. *Philosophy of Religion: An Annotated Bibliography of Twentieth-Century Writings in English.* New York: Garland, 1978.
A valuable bibliographic tool for philosophical theology and apologetics. Includes abstracts of both books and journal articles.

DICTIONARIES AND ENCYCLOPEDIAS

The Ecole Initiative. www2.evansville.edu/ecoleweb/
A hypertext encyclopedia of early church history on the World Wide Web.

Encyclopaedia Britannica Online. www.eb.com/
The online version of the published encyclopedia. Fourteen-day free trial subscription.

Fieser, James, gen. ed. *The Internet Encyclopedia of Philosophy. www.utm.edu/research/iep/*

World Wide Encyclopedia of Christianity. www.ccel.org/php/wwec.php
A hypertext encyclopedia hosted by Calvin College.

Zalta, Edward N., ed. *Stanford Encyclopedia of Philosophy. http://plato.stanford.edu/*

Catholic

Bouyer, Louis. *Dictionary of Theology*. Translated by Charles Underhill Quinn. Tournai, Belgium: Desclee, 1965.
A work designed "to give precise definitions of theological terms—and a concise synthesis of Catholic doctrine." Brief articles with references to Scripture and ecclesiastical documents; no bibliography. A very helpful reference for traditional Catholic teaching.

The Catholic Encyclopedia. 15 vols. with index. New York: Encyclopedia Press, 1907–12.
Dated but valuable source for Catholic thought and scholarship in its historical development. Available online at *http://www.newadvent.org/cathen/*

Davis, H. Francis; Aidan Williams; Ivo Thomas; and Joseph Crehan, eds. *A Catholic Dictionary of Theology*. London: Thomas Nelson and Sons, 1962ff.
Comprehensive signed articles with bibliography. Citations from Scripture and church fathers.

New Catholic Encyclopedia. 17 vols. New York and Washington, DC: McGraw-Hill, 1967, 1974, 1979.
"An international work of reference on the teachings, history, organization, and activities of the Catholic Church, and on all institutions, religions, philosophies, and scientific and cultural developments affecting the Catholic Church from its beginning to the present." Prepared by an editorial staff at the Catholic University of America; a successor to the *Catholic Encyclopedia* of 1907–12.

Parente, P., A. Piolanti, and S. Garofalo. *Dictionary of Dogmatic Theology*. Translated by E. Doranzo. Milwaukee: Bruce, 1951.
Brief definitions of theological terms, with bibliography.

Rahner, Karl, ed. *Encyclopedia of Theology: The Concise Sacramentum Mundi*. New York: Seabury, 1975.
A valuable and convenient reference tool for recent Catholic thought.

Rahner, Karl, and Herbert Vorgrimler. *Theological Dictionary*. Edited by Cornelius Ernst. New York: Herder and Herder, 1965.
"The book is intended to provide brief explanations, in alphabetical order, of the most important concepts of modern Catholic dogmatic theology for readers who are prepared to make a certain intellectual effort."

Rahner, Karl, et al. *Sacramentum Mundi: An Encyclopedia of Theology*. 6 vols. New York: Herder and Herder, 1968–70.
A valuable source for developments in post–Vatican II Catholicism.

Vacant, A., E. Mangenot, and F. Amann, eds. *Dictionnaire de Theologie Catholique*. 15 vols. Paris: Librairie Letouzey et Aue, 1930–50.

A scholarly work in French on Catholic doctrine and ecclesiastical history.

Protestant

Atkinson, David J., David F. Field, Arthur Holmes, and Oliver O'Donovan, eds. *New Dictionary of Christian Ethics and Pastoral Theology*. Downers Grove, IL: InterVarsity Press, 1995.

Cross, F. L., ed. *The Oxford Dictionary of the Christian Church*. London: Oxford University Press, 1958.
Over 6,000 concise articles, with nearly 4,500 brief bibliographies. "Its aim is to provide factual information on every aspect of Christianity, especially in its historical development." An invaluable reference tool.

Douglas, J. D., ed. *The New International Dictionary of the Christian Church*. Grand Rapids: Zondervan, 1974, 1978.
Over 4,800 signed articles, mostly without bibliography. Convenient for quick reference; conservative Protestant in orientation.

Edwards, Paul, ed. *Encyclopedia of Philosophy*. 8 vols. New York: Macmillan, 1967.
Signed articles with bibliography covering the whole range of philosophy. Reflects the empirical and analytic tradition of Anglo-Saxon philosophy. Useful to both the novice and the specialist.

Elwell, Walter, ed. *The Evangelical Dictionary of Biblical Theology.* Grand Rapids: Baker, 1996.
A one-volume collection of brief signed articles, with bibliography. Comes with searchable CD-ROM electronic edition. Available online at *http://bible.crosswalk.com/Dictionaries/BakersEvangelicalDictionary/*

———, ed. *The Evangelical Dictionary of Theology.* 2nd ed. Grand Rapids: Baker, 2001.
A one-volume collection of brief signed articles, with bibliography.

Evans, A. Craig, and Stanley E. Porter. *Dictionary of New Testament Background.* Downers Grove, IL: InterVarsity Press, 2000.
A one-volume collection of signed articles, with bibliography.

Ferguson, Sinclair B., David F. Wright, and J. I. Packer, eds. *New Dictionary of Theology*. Downers Grove, IL: InterVarsity Press, 1988.
A one-volume collection of brief articles.

Freedman, David Noel, ed. *The Anchor Bible Dictionary*. New York: Doubleday, 1992.

Green, Joel B., and Scot McKnight, eds. *Dictionary of Jesus and the Gospels.* Downers Grove, IL: InterVarsity Press, 1992.
A one-volume collection of signed articles, with bibliography.

Halverson, Marvin, and Arthur A. Cohen, eds. *Handbook of Christian Theology.* Cleveland and New York: World, 1958.

Harrison, Everett F., ed. *Baker's Dictionary of Theology*. Grand Rapids: Baker, 1960.
A one-volume collection of brief signed articles, with bibliography, by conservative American and British scholars. Dated.

Hart, Trevor, ed. *The Dictionary of Historical Theology*. Grand Rapids: Eerdmans, 2000.
A one-volume collection of brief signed articles, with bibliography, by British and American scholars.

Harvey, Van A. *A Handbook of Theological Terms*. New York: Macmillan, 1964.
Quick reference for terms in systematic and philosophical theology. Cross-references; no bibliography.

Hastings, James, ed. *Encyclopedia of Religion and Ethics*. 12 vols. and index. Edinburgh: T. & T. Clark; New York: Scribner, 1908–27. Reprint, New York: Scribner, 1959.
A dated but still valuable work. Lengthy articles with bibliographies, including material on anthropology, mythology, folklore, and sociology.

Hawthorne, Gerald F., and Ralph P. Martin, eds. *Dictionary of Paul and His Letters*. Downers Grove, IL: InterVarsity Press, 1993.
A one-volume collection of brief signed articles, with bibliography.

Jackson, S. M., ed. *The New Schaff-Herzog Encyclopedia of Religious Knowledge*. 12 vols. and index. New York: Funk and Wagnalls, 1908–12. Reprint (13 vols.), Grand Rapids: Baker, 1949–50.
A valuable but dated work treating theology, Bible, church history, denominations, and missions. Includes bibliographies. Available online at *www.ccel.org/s/schaff/encyc/*

Loetscher, Lefferts A., ed. *Twentieth-Century Encyclopedia of Religious Knowledge*. 2 vols. Grand Rapids: Baker, 1955.
Updating of *The New Schaff-Herzog Encyclopedia of Religious Knowledge*.

Martin, Ralph P., and Peter H. Davids, eds. *Dictionary of the Later New Testament and Its Developments*. Downers Grove, IL: InterVarsity Press, 1997.
A one-volume collection of brief signed articles, with bibliography.

McGrath, Alister E., ed. *The Blackwell Encyclopedia of Modern Christian Thought*. Cambridge, MA: Blackwell, 1993.
A one-volume dictionary of the modern theological landscape, heavily continental in orientation. Signed articles, with bibliography.

M'Clintock, John, and James Strong, eds. *Cyclopaedia of Biblical, Theological, and Ecclesiastical Literature*. 12 vols. New York: Harper and Brothers, 1867–87.
A dated work still valuable for scholarly information on historical and doctrinal subjects.

Richardson, Alan, ed. *A Dictionary of Christian Theology*. Philadelphia: Westminster, 1969.

Brief signed articles with bibliography, mostly by British scholars. "Emphasis is laid upon development of thought rather than biographical details or events of church history."

BIBLICAL THEOLOGIES

Old Testament

Barr, James. *The Concept of Biblical Theology: An Old Testament Perspective.* Minneapolis: Fortress, 1999.

Brueggemann, Walter. *Old Testament Theology: Essays on Structure, Theme, and Text*. Minneapolis: Fortress, 1992.

Childs, Brevard S. *Old Testament Theology in a Canonical Context.* Philadelphia: Fortress, 1985.

Dyrness, William. *Themes in Old Testament Theology.* Downers Grove, IL: InterVarsity Press, 1979.

Eichrodt, Walther. *Theology of the Old Testament.* Translated by J. A. Baker. Philadelphia: Westminster, 1961–67.

Hasel, Gerhard F. *Old Testament Theology: Basic Issues in the Current Debate.* Grand Rapids: Eerdmans, 1975.

Jacob, Edmund. *Theology of the Old Testament.* New York: Harper, 1958.

Kaiser, Walter. *Towards an Old Testament Theology*. Grand Rapids: Zondervan, 1978.

Oehler, Gustav Friedrich. *Theology of the Old Testament.* Edinburgh: T. & T. Clark, 1873.

Sailhamer, John. *Introduction to Old Testament Theology: A Canonical Approach*. Grand Rapids: Zondervan, 1995.

von Rad, Gerhard. *Old Testament Theology*. 2 vols. Translated by D. M. G. Stalker. New York: Harper, 1962–65.

Zuck, Roy B., Eugene H. Merrill, and Darrell L. Bock, eds. *A Biblical Theology of the Old Testament*. Chicago: Moody Press, 1991.

New Testament

Caird, G. B. *New Testament Theology*. Completed and edited by L. D. Hurst. New York: Oxford University Press, 1994.

Goppelt, Leonhard. *Theology of the New Testament.* Translated by John E. Alsup; edited by Jürgen Roloff. 2 vols. Grand Rapids: Eerdmans, 1981–c. 1982.

Guthrie, Donald. *New Testament Theology*. Downers Grove, IL: InterVarsity Press, 1981.
Conservative and evangelical in orientation.

Ladd, George Eldon. *A Theology of the New Testament*. Edited by Donald A. Hagner. Eerdmans, 1993.
Conservative and evangelical in orientation following the *Heilsgeschichte* approach.

Morris, Leon. *New Testament Theology*. Grand Rapids: Zondervan, 1986.
Conservative and evangelical in orientation.

Richardson, Alan. *An Introduction to the Theology of the New Testament*. New York: Harper, 1959.

Schlatter, Adolf. *The Theology of the Apostles*. Translated by Andreas J. Köstenberger. Grand Rapids: Baker, 1998.
Dated but still valuable.

Stevens, George Barker. *The Theology of the New Testament*. New York: Scribner, 1910.

Zuck, Roy B., ed. *A Biblical Theology of the New Testament*. Chicago: Moody Press, 1994.

Pauline

Bruce, F. F. *Paul: Apostle of the Heart Set Free*. Grand Rapids: Eerdmans, 1983.

Davies, W. D. *Paul and Rabbinic Judaism*. London: S.P.C.K., 1948.

Dunn, James D. G. *The Theology of Paul the Apostle*. Grand Rapids: Eerdmans, 1998.
British evangelical work heavily influenced by E. P. Sanders's "new perspective on Paul."

Ridderbos, Herman N. *Paul: An Outline of His Theology*. Translated by John Richard De Witt. Grand Rapids: Eerdmans, 1975.

Sanders, E. P. *Paul and Palestinian Judaism*. Philadelphia: Fortress, 1977.
Seminal work for the "new perspective on Paul."

Schreiner, Thomas. *Paul, Apostle of God's Glory*. Downers Grove, IL: InterVarsity Press, 2001.

Stevens, George Barker. *The Pauline Theology: A Study of the Origin and Correlation of the Doctrinal Teachings of the Apostle Paul*. New York: Scribner, 1918.

Whitely, D. E. H. *The Theology of St. Paul*. Oxford: Blackwell, 1964.

HISTORICAL THEOLOGIES

Berkhof, Louis. *The History of Christian Doctrines*. Edinburgh: Banner of Truth Trust, 1937.
Very helpful survey of the development of individual doctrines by the noted systematic theologian.

Fischer, George Park. *History of Christian Doctrine.* New York: Scribner, 1923.

Gonzalez, Justo. *A History of Christian Thought.* 3 vols. Nashville: Abingdon, 1970–75.
Fine introduction to the subject.

Hagenbach, Karl Rudolf. *A History of Christian Doctrines*. Edinburgh: T. & T. Clark, 1880–81.

Harnack, Adolf von. *History of Dogma.* 7 vols. Boston: Little, Brown, 1897–1900.
Standard interpretation of dogma. Classic liberal in orientation.

McGiffert, Arthur Cushman. *History of Christian Thought.* 2 vols. New York and London: Scribner, 1932–33.

McGrath, Alister. *Historical Theology*. Malden, MA: Blackwell, 1998.
College-level survey of the history of Christian theology.

Neander, Johann August Wilhelm. *Lectures on the History of Christian Dogmas.* 2 vols. Edited by J. L. Jacobi. Translated by J. E. Ryland. London: Bell & Daldy, 1866.

Neve, J. L., and Otto W. Heick. *A History of Christian Thought.* 2 vols. Philadelphia: United Lutheran Publication House, 1943–46.

Olson, Roger. *The Story of Christian Theology.* Downers Grove, IL: InterVarsity Press, 1999.
A good introduction to the topic that traces the development of theology in a narrative format.

Pelikan, Jaroslav. *The Christian Tradition: A History of the Development of Doctrine.* 5 vols. Chicago: University of Chicago Press, 1971–89.
Exhaustive, detailed contemporary treatment.

Schaff, Philip. *History of the Christian Church.* 8 vols. Grand Rapids: Eerdmans, 1950.
The classic church history up through the Refomation. Includes much historical theological history. Available online at *www.ccel.org/s/schaff/history/*

Seeberg, Reinhold. *Text-Book of the History of Doctrines.* 2 vols. in 1. Grand Rapids: Baker, 1977.

Shedd, William G. T. *History of Christian Doctrines.* New York: Scribner, 1891.

Solid tracing of the history of doctrine by the noted systematic theologian.

Sheldon, H. C. *History of Christian Doctrine.* New York: Harper, 1895.

SYSTEMATIC THEOLOGIES

Aulen, Gustaf. *The Faith of the Christian Church.* Philadelphia: Fortress, 1960.
Swedish Lutheran. An attempt at a middle course between fundamentalism and modernism.

Barth, Karl. *Church Dogmatics.* Edited by G. W. Bromiley and T. F. Torrance. Translated by G. T. Thomson and Harold Knight. 4 vols. Edinburgh: T. & T. Clark, 1936–77.
The most voluminous work in twentieth-century theology by one of the church's greatest theologians.

Bavinck, Herman. *Our Reasonable Faith.* Grand Rapids: Eerdmans, 1956.
Dutch Reformed.

Berkhof, Hendrikus. *Christian Faith: An Introduction to the Study of the Faith.* Grand Rapids: Eerdmans, 1979.
Dutch Reformed. Fruitful interaction with contemporary thought; neoorthodox approach to Scripture.

Berkhof, Louis. *Systematic Theology.* Grand Rapids: Eerdmans, 1941, 1949.
Dutch Reformed. A standard text.

Berkouwer, G. C. *Studies in Dogmatics.* 14 vols. Grand Rapids: Eerdmans, 1952–76.
The most extensive twentieth-century work in Dutch Reformed theology.

Bloesch, Donald. *Essentials of Evangelical Theology.* 2 vols. San Francisco: Harper & Row, 1978–79.
A recent expression of American evangelical theology. Generally Reformed in orientation, Bloesch makes use of positive insights from Roman Catholicism and Karl Barth.

———. *Christian Foundations.* 7 vols. Downers Grove, IL: InterVarsity Press, 1994–2004.

Brunner, Emil. *Dogmatics.* 3 vols. Philadelphia: Westminster, 1949–60.
Swiss neoorthodox. A work that stresses existential rather than cognitive aspects of Christian faith; generally more readable than Barth.

Buswell, J. O., Jr. *A Systematic Theology of the Christian Religion.* Grand Rapids: Zondervan, 1962.

American Calvinist, attempting to keep theology and biblical exegesis closely tied.

Calvin, John. *Institutes of the Christian Religion.* 2 vols. Edited by J. T. McNeill. Translated by Ford Lewis Battles. Library of Christian Classics. Philadelphia: Westminster, 1960.
An all-time classic in Protestant theology. The McNeill edition has helpful annotations. The nineteenth-century edition translated by Henry Beveridge is available online at *www.ccel.org/c/calvin/institutes/institutes.html*

Chafer, L. S. *Systematic Theology*. 8 vols. Dallas: Dallas Seminary Press, 1947–48.
Classic American dispensational statement. Chafer taught for many years at Dallas Theological Seminary.

Cone, James H. *A Black Theology of Liberation*. Philadelphia and New York: J. B. Lippincott, 1970.
An interpretation of the gospel as essentially a message of liberation from oppression; written from the perspective of black experience in America.

Dabney, Robert L. *Lectures in Systematic Theology*. First published in 1878. Grand Rapids: Zondervan, 1972.
American Calvinist. Dabney was a leading nineteenth-century theologian of the Southern Presbyterian Church.

Demarest, Bruce, and Gordon Lewis. *Integrative Theology*, 3 vols. Grand Rapids: Zondervan, 1987, 1990, 1994.
A contemporary evangelical systematic theology focusing on a six-step theological method from statement of the issue under discussion to its practical significance to faith and life.

DeWolf, L. H. *A Theology of the Living Church*. New York: Harper, 1953.
Liberal Methodist.

Erickson, Millard J. *Christian Theology.* 2nd ed. Grand Rapids: Baker, 1998.
Contemporary evangelical Baptist.

Finney, Charles G. *Lectures on Systematic Theology*. Oberlin, OH: E. J. Goodrich, 1887.
American Arminian. Finney was a notable nineteenth-century evangelist and social reformer. The 1851 edition is available online at *http://gospeltruth.net/1851Sys_Theo/index1851st.htm*

Garrett, James Leo. *Systematic Theology: Biblical, Historical, and Evangelical.* 2 vols. Grand Rapids; Eerdmans, 1990, 1995.
Detailed treatment from a baptistic perspective.

Grenz, Stanley J. *Theology for the Community of God.* Nashville: Broadman & Holman, 1994.

A contemporary evangelical systematic theology self-consciously organized and presented from the categories of the postmodern mind.

Grudem, Wayne. *Systematic Theology.* Grand Rapids: Zondervan, 1994.

Hammond, T. C. *In Understanding Be Men.* Revised by D. F. Wright. Downers Grove, IL: InterVarsity Press, 1968.
Anglican evangelical. An introductory handbook of Christian doctrine suitable for church study classes.

Henry, Carl F. H., comp. *Fundamentals of the Faith.* Grand Rapids: Zondervan, 1969.
American evangelical. Previously published essays on theological themes by evangelical authors.

Hodge, A. A. *Outlines of Theology.* First published in 1860. Grand Rapids: Zondervan, 1972.
American Calvinist. Lectures by the son of Charles Hodge; still valuable.

Hodge, Charles. *Systematic Theology.* 3 vols. First published in 1872. Grand Rapids: Eerdmans, 1975.
American Calvinist. The major work by the major theologian of the "Old Princeton" school.

Hoeksema, Herman. *Reformed Dogmatics.* Grand Rapids: Reformed Free Publishing Association, 1966.
Dutch Reformed. Hoeksema defends a supralapsarian view of election.

Irenaeus. *Demonstration of the Apostolic Preaching. www.ccel.org/i/irenaeus/preaching/htm/i.htm*
One of the earliest systematic presentations of the church's theological understanding.

Kaufman, G. D. *Systematic Theology: A Historicist Perspective.* New York: Scribner, 1968.
Liberal Mennonite. Kaufman teaches at Harvard Divinity School.

Kuyper, Abraham. *Principles of Sacred Theology.* First published in 1898. Grand Rapids: Eerdmans, 1954.
Dutch Calvinist. Discussion of matters of prolegomena; helpful chapter on noetic effects of sin.

Lecerf, Auguste. *Introduction to Reformed Dogmatics.* London: Lutterworth, 1949.
French Reformed. A good discussion of principles of canonicity.

Litton, E. A. *Introduction to Dogmatic Theology.* London: Robert Scott, 1912.
Traditional Anglican. Written in the tradition of the Thirty-Nine Articles of the Church of England.

Macquarrie, John. *Principles of Christian Theology.* New York: Scribner. 1966.
Liberal Anglican. In his philosophical orientation, Macquarrie reflects the existentialist stance of Martin Heidegger.

McGrath, Alister, *Christian Theology: An Introduction.* Cambridge, MA: Blackwell, 1997.
College-level introduction. Heavily historical in orientation.

Miley, John. *Systematic Theology.* 2 vols. New York: Eaton and Mains, 1892.
Wesleyan Arminian. Old but still valuable.

Moltmann, Jürgen. *Theology of Hope.* New York: Harper & Row, 1967.

Mueller, J. T. *Christian Dogmatics.* St. Louis: Concordia, 1934.
Missouri Synod Lutheran. Largely a restatement of Franz Pieper's *Christliche Dogmatik.*

Mullins, E. Y. *The Christian Religion in Its Doctrinal Expression.* Philadelphia: Judson, 1917.
By a longtime professor at the Southern Baptist Theological Seminary in Louisville, Kentucky. An attempt to steer a middle course between Calvinism and Arminianism.

Oden, Thomas C. *Systematic Theology.* 3 vols. San Francisco: HarperCollins, 1987–1992.
A consensual theology tracing the doctrines held in common by the major branches of Christianity—Roman Catholic, Orthodox, and historic Protestant. Invaluable.

Pannenberg, Wolfhart. *Systematic Theology.* 3 vols. Translated by Geoffrey W. Bromiley. Grand Rapids: Eerdmans, 1991–98.
Leading late-twentieth-century German theologian for whom "revelation as history" is a central motif.

Peters, Ted. *God—The World's Future.* Minneapolis: Fortress, 1992.
A contemporary Lutheran introductory survey of systematic theology addressed to the postmodern world.

Pieper, Franz. *Christian Dogmatics.* 4 vols. St. Louis: Concordia, 1950–57.
Missouri Synod Lutheran. Perhaps the best conservative Lutheran text in English.

Pohle, Joseph. *Dogmatic Theology.* 12 vols. St. Louis: Herder, 1911, 1946.
American Roman Catholic. A comprehensive treatment; pre–Vatican II perspective.

Pope, W. B. *A Compendium of Christian Theology.* 2nd ed. 3 vols. New York: Phillips and Hunt, n.d.
Nineteenth-century English Methodist.

Prenter, Regin. *Creation and Redemption.* Philadelphia: Fortress, 1967.
Danish Lutheran. Neoorthodox in his view of revelation; emphasis on integral connection of creation and redemption.

Rahner, Karl. *Foundations of Christian Faith.* New York: Seabury, 1978.
Theology grounded within the horizon of human experience, drawing philosophical resources from existentialism and phenomenology.

Russell, Letty M. *Human Liberation in a Feminist Perspective: A Theology.* Philadelphia: Westminster, 1974.
An approach to the the incarnation, salvation, and ecclesiology from a feminist perspective.

Schleiermacher, Friedrich. *The Christian Faith.* 2 vols. First published in 1821–22. New York: Harper & Row, 1963.
By the "father of liberal theology," who held that theology is primarily an articulation of religious feeling and experience rather than an expression of propositional truth or a system of ethics.

Shedd, W. G. T. *Dogmatic Theology.* 3 vols. New York: Scribner, 1888–94.
American Presbyterian; Reformed. Comprehensive and still valuable. Shedd taught for many years at Union Theological Seminary of New York.

Stevens, W. W. *Doctrines of the Christian Religion.* Grand Rapids: Eerdmans, 1967.
Southern Baptist. Written primarily for college rather than seminary use.

Strong, A. H. *Systematic Theology.* First published in 1907. Valley Forge, PA: Judson, 1962.
American Baptist; Reformed. For many years a leading text in Baptist seminaries.

Thielicke, Helmut. *The Evangelical Faith.* 3 vols. Grand Rapids: Eerdmans, 1974, 1982.
German Lutheran; generally neoorthodox in orientation. An important contribution by a leading European theologian.

Tillich, Paul. *Systematic Theology.* 3 vols. Chicago: University of Chicago Press, 1951–63.
German-American neoliberal. A comprehensive correlation of Christian revelation and human culture by one of the most influential figures in twentieth-century American theology. Philosophically indebted to Martin Heidegger and German idealism.

Warfield, B. B. *Biblical and Theological Studies.* Philadelphia: Presbyterian and Reformed, 1952.
A collection of doctrinal essays by a notable representative of the "Old Princeton" school.

Wiley, H. Orton. *Christian Theology.* 3 vols. Kansas City, MO: Beacon Hill, 1960.
American; Church of the Nazarene. Perhaps the best recent text in the Arminian tradition.

REVELATION

Baillie, John. *The Idea of Revelation in Recent Thought.* New York: Columbia University Press, 1956.
Neoorthodox.

Berkouwer, G. C. *General Revelation.* Grand Rapids: Eerdmans, 1955.
A review of the Barth-Brunner debate on natural theology and other issues related to the topic of general revelation.

Brunner, Emil. *Revelation and Reason.* Philadelphia: Westminster, 1946.
A stress on "personal" rather than "propositional" revelation; neoorthodox.

Downing, F. Gerald. *Has Christianity a Revelation?* London: SCM Press, 1964.
Analysis of the problems arising with the use of the concept of God's self-revelation in recent theology, especially in neoorthodoxy.

Henry, Carl F. H. *God, Revelation, and Authority.* Vols. 1–4. Waco: Word, 1976, 1979.
A major evangelical contribution. Interacts extensively with contemporary thought; stresses cognitive element of revelation.

Latourelle, Rene. *Theology of Revelation.* Staten Island, NY: Alba House, 1966.
Roman Catholic.

Masselink, William. *General Revelation and Common Grace.* Grand Rapids: Eerdmans, 1953.
A work dealing with the controversies on common grace, general revelation, and apologetics involving Cornelius Van Til and others in Dutch and American Reformed circles.

McDonald, H. D. *Ideas of Revelation: 1700–1860.* New York: Macmillan, 1959.

———. *Theories of Revelation: 1860–1960.* New York: Humanities Library, 1963.
Valuable studies in the history of the doctrine.

Morris, Leon. *I Believe in Revelation.* Grand Rapids: Eerdmans, 1976.
Good evangelical overview of the subject.

Niebuhr, H. R. *The Meaning of Revelation.* New York: Macmillan, 1941.
Wrestling with problems of revelation, faith, and historical relativism.

Pannenberg, Wolfhart, ed. *Revelation as History.* New York: Macmillan, 1968.
Essays by Pannenberg and other German scholars intended to counteract the separation of revelation and history by Barth and Bultmann.

Pink, A. W. *The Doctrine of Revelation.* Grand Rapids: Baker, 1975.
Biblical exposition by a popular conservative writer.

Ramm, Bernard. *Special Revelation and the Word of God.* Grand Rapids: Eerdmans, 1961.
A leading American evangelical theologian holding together both the redemptive and the cognitive aspects of special revelation.

Van Til, Cornelius. *Common Grace and the Gospel.* Nutley, NJ: Presbyterian and Reformed, 1973.
Essays on common grace, with reference to apologetics and natural theology.

SCRIPTURE

Conservative

Bannerman, James. *Inspiration: The Infallible Truth and Divine Authority of the Holy Scriptures.* Edinburgh: T. & T. Clark, 1865.

Berkouwer, G. C. *Holy Scripture.* Grand Rapids: Eerdmans, 1975.
The argument that inerrancy should be distinguished from historical and scientific exactness.

Bloesch, Donald G. *Holy Scripture: Revelation, Inspiration and Interpretation.* Downers Grove, IL: InterVarsity Press, 1994.

Boettner, Loraine. *The Inspiration of the Scriptures.* Grand Rapids: Eerdmans, 1937.

Cunningham, William. *Theological Lectures.* London: Nisbet, 1878.
Pages 269–469: discussion of inspiration and canonicity.

Custer, Stewart. *Does Inspiration Demand Inerrancy?* Nutley, NJ: Craig Press, 1968.
Pages 93–114: discussion of various problem texts.

Davis, Stephen T. *The Debate about the Bible.* Philadelphia: Westminster, 1977.
A review of the contemporary debate, concluding that "infallibility in faith and practice" rather than inerrancy should be the evangelical stance.

Engelder, Theodore. *The Scripture Cannot Be Broken.* St. Louis: Concordia, 1944.

France, R. T. *Jesus and the Old Testament.* London: Tyndale, 1971.
A revised version of the author's doctoral dissertation.

Gaussen, Louis. *The Inspiration of the Holy Scriptures.* Chicago: Moody Press, n.d.
A work first published in 1840; still helpful.

Gerstner, John H. *A Bible Inerrancy Primer.* Grand Rapids: Baker, 1965.

Giesler, Norman, ed. *Inerrancy.* Grand Rapids: Zondervan, 1979.
Essays addressing the concept of biblical inspiration and authority by evangelical scholars.

Harris, R. Laird. *The Inspiration and Canonicity of the Bible.* Grand Rapids: Zondervan, 1957.
A staunch defense of verbal inspiration; argues that inspiration is the principle of canonicity.

Harrisville, Roy A., and Walter Sundberg. *The Bible in Modern Culture.* Grand Rapids: Eerdmans, 1995.
An excellent history of the influence of the historical-critical method from its inception to the present.

Henry, Carl F. H. *God, Revelation, and Authority.* Vol. 4. Waco: Word, 1979.
A massive treatment of biblical authority; good discussion of inerrancy.

Henry, Carl F. H., ed. *Revelation and the Bible.* Grand Rapids: Baker, 1958.
Essays by various evangelical scholars, including G. C. Berkouwer, Paul K. Jewett, Gordon H. Clark, J. I. Packer, Roger Nicole, Edward J. Young, Bernard Ramm, and F. F. Bruce. Note essay by Geoffrey Bromiley on history of doctrine of inspiration.

Hodge, A. A., and B. B. Warfield. *Inspiration.* Grand Rapids: Baker, 1979.
Reprint of the famous article that originally appeared in the April 1881 issue of the *Presbyterian Review*; with an introduction and bibliography by Roger R. Nicole.

Kistemaker, Simon, ed. *Interpreting God's Word Today.* Grand Rapids: Baker, 1970.

Kline, Meredith. *The Structure of Biblical Authority.* Grand Rapids: Eerdmans, 1970.
The argument that the concept of canon should be understood on the basis of the treaty documents of the ancient Near East.

Kretzmann, P. E. *The Foundations Must Stand.* St. Louis: Concordia, 1936.

Kuyper, Abraham. *Principles of Sacred Theology.* Grand Rapids: Eerdmans, 1954.
See especially pp. 341–563.

Lecerf, Auguste. *Introduction to Reformed Dogmatics.* London: Lutterworth, 1949.
See pp. 319–74 on canonicity and inspiration.

Lee, William. *The Inspiration of Holy Scriptures.* New York: Carter, 1857.

Pages 51–93: a review of the patristic data.

Lightner, Robert P. *The Saviour and the Scriptures.* Grand Rapids: Baker, 1966.
A defense of inerrancy based on Christ's view of Scripture.

Lindsell, Harold. *The Battle for the Bible.* Grand Rapids: Zondervan, 1976.
Highly polemic. A work that added fresh fuel to the debate with the claim that there is evidence of significant erosion on inerrancy in various evangelical denominations and schools.

M'Intosh, Hugh. *Is Christ Infallible and the Bible True?* Edinburgh: T. & T. Clark, 1901.
Extensive discussion of various criticisms of Christ's infallibility as a teacher. Still valuable.

Montgomery, John W., ed. *God's Inerrant Word.* Minneapolis: Bethany Fellowship, 1974.
Essays by Montgomery, J. I. Packer, John Gerstner, Clark Pinnock, R. T. France, Peter Jones, and R. C. Sproul; very helpful.

Morris, Leon. *I Believe in Revelation.* Grand Rapids: Eerdmans, 1976.
A somewhat brief treatment of various issues, including general revelation and the question of revelation outside Christianity.

Orr, James. *Revelation and Inspiration.* New York: Scribner, 1910.
A noted Scottish evangelical of an earlier generation, who held that minor errors of detail are not incompatible with divine inspiration.

Pache, Rene. *The Inspiration and Authority of Scripture.* Chicago: Moody Press, 1969.
Pages 120–58: Good discussion of inerrancy and biblical difficulties.

Packer, J. I. *"Fundamentalism" and the Word of God.* Grand Rapids: Eerdmans, 1958.
A clear and cogent statement of the evangelical view of Scripture. Packer is in the process of preparing a new edition to respond to James Barr's *Fundamentalism.*

Pesch, Christiano. *De Inspiratione Sacrae Scripturae.* Freiburg, Germany: Herder, 1906.
A scholarly treatment of the history of the doctrine; can be used to locate patristic references even by those with no knowledge of Latin.

Pinnock, Clark H. *Biblical Revelation.* Chicago: Moody Press, 1971.

———. *A Defense of Biblical Infallibility.* Philadelphia: Presbyterian and Reformed, 1967.

———. *The Scripture Principle.* San Francisco: Harper & Row, 1984.
See also *Theology, News and Notes*, special issue, 1976.

Preus, Robert D. *The Theology of Post-Reformation Lutheranism: A Study of Theological Prolegomena.* St. Louis: Concordia, 1970.
See pp. 254–403 for discussion on the doctrine of Scripture.

Ramm, Bernard. *The Pattern of Authority.* Grand Rapids: Eerdmans, 1957.
Brief discussion of Scripture in relation to various understandings of religious authority, including Roman Catholicism, modernism, and neoorthodoxy.

Rogers, Jack B., and Donald K. McKim. *The Authority and Interpretation of the Bible: An Historical Approach.* San Francisco: Harper & Row, 1979.
The most important recent expression of the "limited inerrancy" position in American evangelicalism.

Runia, Klaas. *Karl Barth's Doctrine of Holy Scripture.* Grand Rapids: Eerdmans, 1962.
A careful criticism of Barth's view of Scripture from a Reformed perspective.

Scroggie, W. G. *Is the Bible the Word of God?* Philadelphia: Sunday School Times, 1922.

Stonehouse, N. B., and Paul Woolley, eds. *The Infallible Word.* Grand Rapids: Eerdmans, 1946, 1953.
A symposium by members of the faculty of Westminster Theological Seminary.

Tenney, Merrill C., ed. *The Bible: The Living Word of Revelation.* Grand Rapids: Zondervan, 1968.
Essays by evangelical scholars.

Van Kooten, Tenis. *The Bible: God's Word.* Grand Rapids: Baker, 1972.
Pages 200–220: analysis of various deviant views.

Walvoord, John F., ed. *Inspiration and Interpretation.* Grand Rapids: Eerdmans, 1957.
Essays by various members of the Evangelical Theological Society. Note essay by Kenneth Kantzer on Calvin's view of Scripture.

Warfield, B. B. *The Inspiration and Authority of the Bible.* Philadelphia: Presbyterian and Reformed, 1948.
Reprints of exegetical and theological articles by Warfield that have never, in some respects, been surpassed. Note especially the article " 'It Says:' 'Scripture Says:' 'God Says.' "

———. *Limited Inspiration.* Philadelphia: Presbyterian and Reformed, 1962.
Reprint of an article that originally appeared in volume 5 (1894) of the *Presbyterian and Reformed Review.* In his reply to Professor Henry P. Smith, Warfield criticizes the view that inspiration may be limited to matters of "faith and morals."

Wenham, John W. *Christ and the Bible.* London: Tyndale, 1972.
A valuable work that interacts with recent biblical scholarship.

Young, E. J. *Thy Word Is Truth.* Grand Rapids: Eerdmans, 1957.
A former professor of Old Testament at Westminster Theological Seminary. Chapter 7 discusses several problem texts.

Nonconservative

Barr, James. *The Bible in the Modern World.* New York: Harper, 1973.

———. *Fundamentalism.* London: SCM, 1977.
The latter volume: a full-scale attack on the evangelical view of Scripture and conservative theology in general.

Beegle, Dewey M. *Scripture, Tradition, and Infallibility.* Grand Rapids: Eerdmans, 1973.
A review and enlargement of the earlier 1963 work, *The Inspiration of Scripture.* Beegle contends that infallibility and inerrancy apply only to God and Christ, not the Bible.

Briggs, Charles A. *The Bible, the Church and the Reason.* New York: Scribner, 1892.
Briggs's views on inerrancy and higher criticism that led to his trial for heresy in the Presbyterian Church.

Burtchaell, James T. *Catholic Theories of Biblical Inspiration since 1810.* Cambridge: Cambridge University Press, 1969.
A historical study that criticizes Catholic theories of verbal inspiration and inerrancy.

Dillistone, F. W., ed. *Scripture and Tradition.* London: Lutterworth, 1955.
Essays by various British scholars.

Dodd, C. H. *The Authority of the Bible.* New York: Harper, 1929.
Liberal Protestant. The Bible is authoritative because it "is the instrument of the Spirit in creating an experience of divine things … in inducing in us a religious attitude and outlook."

Dods, Marcus. *The Bible: Its Origin and Nature.* Edinburgh: T. & T. Clark, 1905.
Liberal Protestant. Critical of concepts of verbal inspiration and infallibility.

Fosdick, Harry E. *The Modern Use of the Bible.* New York: Macmillan, 1924.
A former pastor of Riverside Church in New York City, and a modernist leader in the modernist-fundamentalist controversy.

Gore, Charles, and H. R. Mackintosh. *The Doctrine of the Infallible Book.* London: Student Christian Movement, 1924.
The argument that the Bible, while inspired in varying degrees and modes, is not infallible.

Huxtable, J. F. *The Bible Says.* London: SCM, 1962.
Pages 64–71: criticism of J. I. Packer and other conservative writers.

Ladd, George T. *The Doctrine of Sacred Scripture.* 2 vols. New York: Scribner, 1883.
A lengthy discussion by a liberal Protestant scholar who taught at Yale during the nineteenth century.

Levie, Jean. *The Bible: Word of God in Words of Men.* New York: P. J. Kenedy and Sons, 1961.
Liberal Roman Catholic.

Rahner, Karl. *The Inspiration of the Bible.* New York: Herder and Herder, 1961.
Nontraditional Roman Catholic.

Reid, J. K. S. *The Authority of the Scriptures.* New York: Harper, 1957.
Neoorthodox in orientation, arguing that Luther and Calvin did not hold to strict verbal inspiration.

Richardson, Alan, and Wolfgang Schweitzer, eds. *Biblical Authority for Today.* Philadelphia: Westminster, 1951.
A World Council of Churches symposium.

Sanday, William. *Inspiration.* London: Longmans, Green, 1893.

Smart, J. D. *The Interpretation of Scripture.* Philadelphia: Westminster, 1961.
Neoorthodox.

Smith, Henry P., and Llewelyn J. Evans. *Biblical Scholarship and Inspiration.* Cincinnati: Clarke, 1891.
In Smith, a coauthor who held that there are "minor errors" in Scripture and became embroiled in a controversy over inerrancy in the Presbyterian Church in the 1890s.

Vawter, Bruce. *Biblical Inspiration.* Philadelphia: Westminster, 1972.
Roman Catholic; post–Vatican II in attitude toward biblical criticism.

HERMENEUTICS

Achtemeier, Paul J. *An Introduction to the New Hermeneutic.* Philadelphia: Westminster, 1969.
A readable introduction to a somewhat obscure movement.

Berkhof, Louis. *Principles of Biblical Interpretation.* Grand Rapids: Baker, 1950.
Dutch Reformed.

Bray, Gerald. *Biblical Interpretation, Past and Present.* Downers Grove, IL: InterVarsity Press, 1996.
Detailed survey of the history of interpretation.

Briggs, Charles Augustus. *The Study of Holy Scripture.* New York: Scribner, 1899.
A significant expansion of *Biblical Study* (1883). Thorough and helpful.

Briggs, R. C. *Interpreting the New Testament Today.* Nashville: Abingdon, 1969.
A helpful introduction to issues in New Testament interpretation.

Carson, D. A. *Exegetical Fallacies.* Grand Rapids: Baker, 1984.
Basic survey detailing and illustrating the pitfalls to which interpreters regularly fall prey.

Cottrell, Peter, and Max Turner. *Linguistics and Biblical Interpretation.* Downers Grove, IL: InterVarsity Press, 1989.
Valuable survey applying the discipline of linguistics to biblical interpretation.

Fairbairn, Patrick. *The Typology of Scripture.* Edinburgh: T. & T. Clark, 1870.
A classic on the subject by a nineteenth-century Scottish scholar.

Farrar, Frederic W. *History of Interpretation.* London: Macmillan, 1885.
A standard treatment.

Grant, Robert M., with David Tracy. *A Short History of the Interpretation of the Bible.* Philadelphia: Fortress, 1984.
A concise and helpful account.

Hendricks, Howard G., and William D. Hendricks. *Living by the Book.* Chicago: Moody Press, 1991.
A popularization of the inductive method of Bible study developed by Robert Traina in *Methodical Bible Study.*

Kaiser, Walter, and Moisés Silva. *An Introduction to Biblical Hermeneutics.* Grand Rapids: Zondervan, 1994.
A contemporary conservative survey introduction to the field.

Klein, William W., Craig L. Blomberg, and Robert L. Hubbard Jr. *Introduction to Biblical Interpretation.* Dallas: Word, 1993.
Comprehensive survey text from an evangelical perspective.

Kuitert, H. M. *Do You Understand What You Read?* Grand Rapids: Eerdmans, 1970.
An emphasis on the time-bound character of biblical truth that favors a nonliteral view of early Genesis.

Marle, Rene. *Introduction to Hermeneutics.* New York: Herder and Herder, 1967.
A Roman Catholic discussion of issues in modern theological hermeneutics.

Marshall, I. H., ed. *New Testament Interpretation.* Grand Rapids: Eerdmans, 1977.

Valuable essays by various evangelical scholars, mostly British.

Mickelsen, A. Berkeley. *Interpreting the Bible.* Grand Rapids: Eerdmans, 1963.

Good evangelical treatment of biblical hermeneutics.

Osborne, Grant. *The Hermeneutical Spiral.* Downers Grove, IL: InterVarsity Press, 1991.

A comprehensive introduction to hermeneutics from an evangelical perspective. Invaluable.

Palmer, Richard. *Hermeneutics.* Evanston, IL: Northwestern University Press, 1969.

A valuable guide to the hermeneutical discussions of Friedrich Schleiermacher, Wilhelm Dilthey, Martin Heidegger, and Hans-Georg Gadamer.

Ramm, Bernard. *Protestant Biblical Interpretation.* Boston: W. A. Wilde, 1956.

A standard conservative text. Dated.

Robinson, James M., and John B. Cobb Jr., eds. *The New Hermeneutic.* New York: Harper & Row, 1964.

Essays by Robinson, Gerhard Ebeling, Ernst Fuchs, and others.

Ryken, Leland. *How to Read the Bible as Literature.* Grand Rapids: Zondervan, 1984.

Introduction to the literary genres found in Scripture, explaining the way each works and the principles for approaching each.

———. *The Literature of the Bible.* Grand Rapids: Zondervan, 1974.

Ryken, Leland, and Tremper Longman III, eds. *A Contemporary Literary Guide to the Bible.* Grand Rapids: Zondervan, 1993.

A book-by-book survey of the literature of the Bible.

Schultz, Samuel J., and Morris Inch, eds. *Interpreting the Word of God.* Chicago: Moody Press, 1976.

A noteworthy essay by Gordon Fee on pp. 103–27.

Silva, Moisés, *Biblical Words and Their Meaning.* Grand Rapids: Zondervan, 1983.

Introduction to linguistics and semantics to the practice of word studies.

Silva, Moisés, ed. *Foundations of Contemporary Interpretation.* Grand Rapids: Zondervan, 1996.

A compilation in one volume of the earlier series of monographs. Extremely valuable.

Thiselton, Anthony C. *New Horizons in Hermeneutics.* Grand Rapids: Zondervan, 1992.
Exhaustive survey of contemporary hermeneutical theory.

———. *The Two Horizons.* Grand Rapids: Eerdmans, 1980.

Vanhoozer, Kevin J. *Is There a Meaning in This Text?* Grand Rapids: Zondervan, 1998.
Detailed analysis of the question of meaning in light of the postmodern ethos.

GOD

Adeney, W. F. *The Christian Concept of God.* London: National Council of Evangelical Free Churches, 1909.

Aquinas, Thomas. *Summa Theologica Ia.1–49.* New York: McGraw-Hill, 1963.
Discussions on the doctrine of God by one of the greatest theologians of all time. The Benziger Brothers edition of 1947 is available online at *www.ccel.org/a/aquinas/summa/home.html.*

Baillie, John. *Our Knowledge of God.* New York: Scribner, 1939.
Lectures by a Scottish contemporary of Karl Barth and Emil Brunner.

Bavinck, Herman. *The Doctrine of God.* Grand Rapids: Baker, 1951.
A comprehensive treatment taken from volume 2 of the author's systematic theology. Dutch Reformed.

Bloesch, Donald G. *God, the Almighty.* Downers Grove, IL: InterVarsity Press, 1995.

Calvin, John. *Institutes of the Christian Religion.* 2 vols. Edited by J. T. McNeill. Translated by Ford Lewis Battles. Library of Christian Classics. Philadelphia: Westminster, 1960.
Classic discussion of the knowledge of God by the definitive theologian of the Reformed tradition.

Charnock, Stephen. *The Existence and Attributes of God.* Evansville, IN: Sovereign Grace, 1958.
The classic Puritan study on the subject.

Dewan, W. F. *The One God.* Englewood Cliffs, NJ: Prentice Hall, 1963.
Roman Catholic.

Dowey, E. A. *The Knowledge of God in Calvin's Theology.* New York: Columbia University Press, 1952.
A valuable study of Calvin's theological epistemology.

Erickson, Millard. *God in Three Persons.* Grand Rapids: Baker, 1995.

Farley, Edward. *The Transcendence of God.* Philadelphia: Westminster, 1960.

A study of the transcendence of God as viewed by Reinhold Niebuhr, Paul Tillich, Karl Heim, Charles Hartshorne, and Henry Nelson Wieman.

Ferré, Nels. *The Christian Understanding of God.* New York: Harper, 1951.
A philosophically oriented work.

Fortman, E. J., ed. *The Theology of God: Commentary.* Milwaukee: Bruce, 1968.

France, R. T. *The Living God.* Downers Grove, IL: InterVarsity Press, 1970.
A brief, popular helpful survey of biblical teaching.

Garrigou-Lagrange, Reginald. *God: His Existence and His Nature.* 2 vols. St. Louis: Herder, 1936.
An important apologetic work by a modern Catholic theologian in the Thomistic tradition.

Gollwitzer, Helmut. *The Existence of God as Confessed by Faith.* Philadelphia: Westminster, 1965.
Interaction with Rudolf Bultmann, Paul Tillich, and other European theologians; neoorthodox in perspective.

Headlam, Arthur C. *Christian Theology: The Doctrine of God.* Oxford: Clarendon, 1934.
A text prepared for divinity students in the Church of England.

Henry, Carl F. H. *Notes on the Doctrine of God.* Boston: W. A. Wilde, 1948.
Essays by a well-known evangelical apologist.

Hick, John. *Arguments for the Existence of God.* New York: Seabury, 1971.
Pages 136–46: a helpful bibliography on the theistic proofs.

John of Damascus. *The Orthodox Faith.* In *St. John of Damascus: Writings.* Translated by F. H. Chase Jr. New York: Fathers of the Church, 1958.
The statement of Eastern Orthodox theology by its final recognized father/theologian.

Kaufman, Gordon D. *God the Problem.* Cambridge: Harvard University Press, 1972.
Various essays in philosophical theology by a professor at Harvard Divinity School.

Knudson, A. C. *The Doctrine of God.* New York: Abingdon-Cokesbury, 1934.
Moderately liberal.

Lightner, Robert P. *The First Fundamental: God.* Nashville: Thomas Nelson, 1973.

Mackintosh, H. R. *The Christian Apprehension of God.* New York: Harper, 1929.

Lectures given at Union Theological Seminary of Virginia in 1928.

Matczak, Sebastian A., ed. *God in Contemporary Thought: A Philosophical Perspective.* New York: Learned Publications, 1977.
Scholarly essays on concepts of God in both Christian and non-Christian traditions, with bibliographies.

Mozley, J. K. *The Impassibility of God.* Cambridge: Cambridge University Press, 1926.
A valuable historical study of one particular aspect of the divine nature.

Ogden, Schubert. *The Reality of God and Other Essays.* New York: Harper, 1966.
Essays by a contemporary American process theologian.

Otto, Rudolf. *The Idea of the Holy.* London: Oxford University Press, 1923.
Noted study of an essential characteristic of the religious experience.

Owen, H. P. *Concepts of Deity.* New York: Herder and Herder, 1971.
An excellent comparative study of classical theism and various modern views.

Packer, J. I. *Knowing God.* Downers Grove, IL: InterVarsity Press, 1973.
A modern classic on the essential relation of Christian theology and the Christian life.

Pike, Nelson. *God and Timelessness.* New York: Schocken Books, 1970.
The argument that the concept of God's timelessness was imported from Platonism.

Robinson, J. A. T. *Explorations into God.* London: SCM, 1966.
A dubious attempt to move "beyond the God of theism."

Tozer, A. W. *The Knowledge of the Holy.* New York: Harper, 1961.
A popular but valuable discussion of the attributes of God in relation to the Christian life.

Wenham, John. *The Goodness of God.* Downers Grove, IL: InterVarsity Press, 1974.
A fine biblical study of God's goodness in relation to the problems of suffering, evil, and retribution.

Trinity

Augustine. *On the Holy Trinity.* In *The Nicene and Post-Nicene Fathers*, vol. 3. Grand Rapids: Eerdmans, 1956.
A classic source.

Barth, Karl. *Church Dogmatics.* Vol. 1, pt. 1. Edited by G. W. Bromiley and T. F. Torrance. Translated by G. T. Thomson and Harold Knight. Edinburgh: T. & T. Clark, 1936.

Chapter 2 presents Barth's discussion of the Trinity.

Fortman, E. J. *The Triune God.* Philadelphia: Westminster, 1972.
A comprehensive discussion of the history of the doctrine.

Franks, R. S. *The Doctrine of the Trinity.* London: Duckworth, 1953.
The case for a view combining elements of Friedrich Schleiermacher, Aquinas, and Karl Barth.

Hodgson, Leonard. *The Doctrine of the Trinity.* New York: Scribner, 1944.
The case for the "social" rather than the "psychological" analogy.

Knight, G. A. F. *A Biblical Approach to the Doctrine of the Trinity.* Edinburgh: Oliver and Boyd, 1953.
An emphasis on the value of Old Testament theology.

Mikolaski, S. J. "The Triune God," in *Fundamentals of the Faith*, edited by Carl F. H. Henry. Grand Rapids: Zondervan, 1969.
A brief overview.

Rahner, Karl. *The Trinity*. New York: Herder and Herder, 1970.
The relation of Trinity to Christology and pneumatology, arguing for "three distinct manners of subsisting" rather than three persons.

Richardson, C. C. *The Doctrine of the Trinity.* New York: Abingdon, 1958.
Questioning of the traditional formulations of Trinitarian doctrine.

Wainwright, A. W. *The Trinity in the New Testament.* London: SPCK, 1962.
A helpful biblical study.

Warfield, B. B. "Trinity," in *Biblical and Theological Studies.* Philadelphia: Presbyterian and Reformed, 1952.
A good discussion of the biblical data.

Welch, Claude. *In This Name: The Doctrine of the Trinity in Contemporary Theology*. New York: Scribner, 1952.
A significant contribution by an American scholar; favors the "psychological" rather than the "social" model of the Trinity.

Election and Predestination

Aquinas, Thomas. *Summa Theologica*, 1.23; 3.24. New York: McGraw-Hill, 1963.

Augustine. *Anti-Pelagian Works.* In *The Nicene and Post-Nicene Fathers*, vol. 5. New York: Christian Literature Company, 1887.

———. "On the Predestination of the Saints." In *Four Anti-Pelagian Writings.* Washington, DC: Catholic University of America Press, 1992.

Barth, Karl. *Church Dogmatics.* Vol. 2, pt. 2. Edited by G. W. Bromiley and T. F. Torrance. Translated by G. T. Thomson and Harold Knight. Edinburgh: T. & T. Clark, 1957.
See chapter 7 for Barth's discussion of election.

Berkouwer, G. C. *Divine Election.* Grand Rapids: Eerdmans, 1960.
The view that election can be understood only within the context of faith and the gospel; rejects logical symmetry of election and reprobation.

Boettner, Loraine. *The Reformed Doctrine of Predestination.* Philadelphia: Presbyterian and Reformed, 1932.
A clear statement of the Calvinistic position.

Calvin, John. *Institutes of the Christian Religion.* 2 vols. Edited by J. T. McNeill. Translated by Ford Lewis Battles. Library of Christian Classics. Philadelphia: Westminster, 1960. Bk. 3.21–24.
A classic treatment.

Edwards, Jonathan. *Freedom of the Will.* London: James Duncan, 1831.
Penetrating discussions by one of America's greatest theologians.

Forster, Roger T., and Paul V. Marston. *God's Strategy in Human History.* Bromley, England: Send the Light Trust, 1973.
Exegetical discussion from an Arminian perspective.

Pinnock, Clark, ed. *The Grace of God, the Will of Man: A Case for Arminianism.* Grand Rapids: Zondervan, 1989.

Pinnock, Clark, ed. *Grace Unlimited.* Minneapolis: Bethany Fellowship, 1975.
Various essays from an Arminian perspective.

Creation and Providence

Barbour, Ian G. *Issues in Science and Religion.* Englewood Cliffs, NJ: Prentice Hall, 1966.
An important work in the area of science and religion; written from a perspective sympathetic to process theology. See also Barbour's *Myths, Models and Paradigms.* San Francisco: Harper & Row, 1976.

———. *Religion and Science: Historical and Contemporary Issues.* San Francisco: HarperCollins, 1997.

Barnette, H. *The Church and the Ecological Crisis.* Grand Rapids: Eerdmans, 1972.
Brief discussion of biblical basis for environmental concern.

Behe, Michael. *Darwin's Black Box.* New York: Free Press, 1996.
The case argues against the possibility of Darwinism from the concept of irreducible complexity on the biochemical level.

Berkouwer, G. C. *The Providence of God.* Grand Rapids: Eerdmans, 1952.
A good treatment of the subject, including discussion of issues raised by the scientific worldview. Reformed in perspective.

Clark, Robert Edward David. *The Universe: Plan or Accident?* Philadelphia: Muhlenberg, 1962.

Discussions of issues in science and Scripture, including a defense of the argument from design.

Dillenberger, John. *Protestant Thought and Natural Science.* London: Collins, 1961.
A useful work tracing developments from the Reformation to the present; written from a neoorthodox perspective.

Farmer, H. H. *The World and God.* London: Nisbet, 1936.
A study of prayer, providence, and miracle; stresses religious experience rather than Scripture as starting point for theology.

Gilkey, Langdon. *Maker of Heaven and Earth.* Garden City, NY: Doubleday, 1965.
An important recent discussion relating creation to issues in philosophy, the sciences, and studies in myth and symbol. Neoorthodox.

Hick, John. *Evil and the God of Love.* London: Macmillan, 1966.
Excellent discussion of the problem of evil in historical and theological perspective.

Hooykaas, R. *Religion and the Rise of Modern Science.* Edinburgh: Scottish Academic Press, 1972.
The view that biblical thought was as important as, if not more important than, Greek thought in the rise of modern science.

Johnson, Phillip. *Darwin on Trial.* Downers Grove, IL: InterVarsity Press, 1993.
An examination of the Darwinist construct from the perspective of logical argumentation, which finds it wanting.

Kerkut, G. A. *The Implications of Evolution.* London: Pergamon, 1960.
A highly technical but quite valuable discussion of the assumptions behind modern evolutionary theories.

Klotz, John W. *Genes, Genesis, and Evolution.* St. Louis: Concordia, 1955, 1970.
A Missouri Synod Lutheran and trained biologist who favors special creation and an old earth. Good survey of scientific data.

Kuyper, Abraham. *Lectures on Calvinism.* Grand Rapids: Eerdmans, 1931.
The Stone lectures given at Princeton in 1898; valuable discussions of Christianity and culture from a Reformed perspective.

Lewis, C. S. *Miracles.* New York: Macmillan, 1947.
A fine defense of miracles by a noted evangelical apologist.

Macbeth, Norman. *Darwin Retried.* Boston: Gambit, 1971.
An incisive and readable critique of Darwinian and neo-Darwinian theories.

McGrath, Alister. *Science and Religion: An Introduction.* Cambridge, MA: Blackwell, 1999.

Lucid introduction by a noted evangelical theologian with scientific training.

Mascall, E. L. *Christian Theology and Natural Science.* London: Longmans, 1956.
Various issues at the interface of science and theology discussed by an Anglican scholar indebted to the Thomistic tradition.

Meynell, Hugo. *God and the World.* London: SPCK, 1971.
A fine defense of classical theism against contemporary attacks by a Roman Catholic scholar. Includes chapters on evil, miracles, and prayer.

Orr, James. *The Christian View of God and the World.* New York: Scribner, 1893.
A classic by a Scottish evangelical of an earlier generation.

Pokinghorne, John. *Science and Theology: An Introduction.* Minneapolis: Fortress, 1998.
Fine introduction to the topic by a noted scientist.

Pollard, W. G. *Chance and Providence.* New York: Scribner, 1958.
A somewhat dualistic approach to relating science and religion, by a physicist who is also an Episcopal priest.

Ramm, Bernard. *A Christian View of Science and Scripture.* Grand Rapids: Eerdmans, 1954.
Evangelical discussion of questions relating to astronomy, geology, biology, and anthropology. Old-earth, "progressive"creationist perspective.

Ridderbos, N. *Is There a Conflict between Genesis 1 and Natural Science?* Grand Rapids: Eerdmans, 1957.
The argument for a nonliteral framework hypothesis for Genesis 1. Brief but helpful.

Rushdoony, R. J. *The Mythology of Science.* Nutley, NJ: Craig, 1967.
Critique of scientism by a conservative Calvinist. Several chapters devoted to creation and evolution.

White, Andrew Dickson. *A History of the Warfare of Science with Theology.* A work first published in 1896. New York: Dover, n.d.

Wilder-Smith, A. E. *Man's Origin, Man's Destiny.* Wheaton: Harold Shaw, 1968.
A criticism of evolutionary theories of human origins by a competent scientist. Second half of the volume is more speculative.

MAN

Anderson, Ray S. *On Being Human.* Grand Rapids: Eerdmans, 1982.

Insightful and challenging discussion that relates the doctrine of man to its pastoral implications.

Berkouwer, G. C. *Man: The Image of God.* Grand Rapids: Eerdmans, 1962.

Brunner, Emil. *Man in Revolt.* Philadelphia: Westminster, 1947.
Important discussions by a leading neoorthodox theologian.

Cairns, David. *The Image of God in Man.* London: Collins, 1973.
Good survey of the history of the doctrine.

Hoekema, Anthony. *Created in His Image.* Grand Rapids: Eerdmans, 1986.
Competent Reformed evangelical treatment.

Hughes, Philip E. *The True Image.* Grand Rapids: Eerdmans, 1989.
Fine study arguing that a true understanding of humanity as the image of God is found in the incarnation.

Johnson. A. R. *The Vitality of the Individual in the Thought of Ancient Israel.* Cardiff: University of Wales, 1949.
Detailed exegetical study of Hebrew anthropology. Valuable.

Kummel, Werner G. *Man in the New Testament.* Philadelphia: Westminster, 1963.
A study in New Testament theology. Kummel sees both unity and diversity in the New Testament view of man.

Machen, J. Gresham. *The Christian View of Man.* Grand Rapids: Eerdmans, 1947.
Popular discussions originally presented as radio lectures by a well-known Reformed scholar.

Moltmann, Jürgen. *Man: Christian Anthropology in the Conflicts of the Present.* Philadelphia: Fortress, 1974.
Moltmann relating his theological understanding to issues in social ethics.

Niebuhr, Reinhold. *The Nature and Destiny of Man.* 2 vols. New York: Scribner, 1949.
A classic of modern American theology; especially discussion of sin. Neoorthodox.

Orr, James. *God's Image in Man.* London: Hodder and Stoughton, 1905.
Apologetic discussions by a Scottish theologian; somewhat dated.

Pannenberg, Wolfhart. *What Is Man?* Philadelphia: Fortress, 1970.
Interaction with various trends in modern thought; philosophical rather than exegetical in approach.

Robinson, H. W. *The Christian Doctrine of Man.* 3rd ed. Edinburgh: T. & T. Clark, 1934.

An important work combining exegetical, historical, and theological data and emphasizing Hebrew psychology as basis of New Testament and patristic thought.

Rust, Eric C. *Nature and Man in Biblical Thought.* London: Lutterworth, 1953.
A biblical theology of man related to the philosophy of nature.

Schnelle, Udo. *The Human Condition.* Minneapolis: Fortress, 1996.
Biblical theological study of the New Testament teachings of Jesus, Paul, and John.

Smith, C. Ryder. *The Bible Doctrine of Man.* London: Epworth, 1951.
A comprehensive biblical study.

Torrance, T. F. *Calvin's Doctrine of Man.* London: Lutterworth, 1949.
A valuable historical study. Note especially discussion of noetic effects of sin and natural theology.

Sin

Berkouwer, G. C. *Sin.* Grand Rapids: Eerdmans, 1971.
One of the best modern treatments of the subject; Reformed perspective.

Buswell, J. Oliver. *Sin and Atonement.* Grand Rapids: Zondervan, 1937.
A brief biblical study.

Fairlie, Henry. *The Seven Deadly Sins Today.* Notre Dame, IN: University of Notre Dame, 1978.
Insightful reflections by an author who does not consider himself a believer.

Kierkegaard, Søren. *Sickness unto Death.* Princeton: Princeton University Press, 1946.
Classic discussion of despair by the father of existentialism.

Menninger, Karl. *Whatever Became of Sin?* New York: Hawthorn Books, 1973.
Stimulating insights by a leading American psychiatrist.

Muller, Julius. *The Christian Doctrine of Sin.* 2 vols. Edinburgh: T. & T. Clark, 1885.
A significant work from a leading nineteenth-century German mediating theologian.

Murray, John. *The Imputation of Adam's Sin.* Grand Rapids: Eerdmans, 1959.
Detailed exegetical discussion of theories of imputation of original sin; defends representative view.

Orr, James. *Sin as a Problem Today.* London: Hodder and Stoughton, 1910.

A somewhat dated work.

Peck, Scott. *People of the Lie.* New York: Simon & Schuster, 1983.
An examination of evil by a prominent psychiatrist.

Peters, Ted. *Sin, Radical Evil in Soul and Society.* Grand Rapids: Eerdmans, 1994.
A challenging contemporary study.

Plantinga, Cornelius, Jr. *Not the Way It's Supposed to Be: A Breviary of Sin.* Grand Rapids: Eerdmans, 1995.

Smith, C. Ryder. *The Bible Doctrine of Sin.* London: Epworth, 1953.
A helpful biblical study; a bit weak on original sin.

Tennant, F. C. *The Sources of the Doctrine of the Fall and Original Sin.* Cambridge: Cambridge University Press, 1903.
An important scholarly work; critical and nonliteral view of Genesis account of the fall. Note also by the same author *The Concept of Sin* (Cambridge: Cambridge University Press, 1912) and *The Origin and Propagation of Sin* (Cambridge: Cambridge University Press, 1908).

Warfield, B. B. *Studies in Tertullian and Augustine.* New York: Oxford University Press, 1930.
A work that contains a valuable essay on Augustine and the Pelagian controversy.

Williams, N. P. *The Ideas of the Fall and Original Sin.* London: Longmans, 1927.
A comprehensive scholarly work; critical view of biblical accounts. Proposes theory of precosmic fall.

CHRISTOLOGY

Person of Christ

Athanasius. *On the Incarnation.* Crestwood, NY: St. Vladimir's Press, 1975.

www.spurgeon.org/~phil/history/ath-inc.htm

www.philthompson.net/pages/library/ontheincarnation.html
Classic work by one of the most prominent defenders of the deity of Christ.

Baillie, Donald M. *God Was in Christ.* New York: Scribner, 1948.
An attempt to relate traditional christological understanding to questions arising in modern biblical scholarship. Generally conservative conclusions.

Berkouwer, G. C. *The Person of Christ.* Grand Rapids: Eerdmans, 1954.

Bloesch, Donald G. *Jesus Christ: Savior and Lord.* Downers Grove, IL: InterVarsity Press, 1997.

Cullmann, Oscar. *The Christology of the New Testament.* Philadelphia: Westminster, 1959.
A study of New Testament christological titles from the perspective of *Heilsgeschichte* (salvation history).

Dawe, Donald G. *The Form of a Servant.* Philadelphia: Westminster, 1963.
A review of the development of kenotic Christologies advocating a functional rather than metaphysical approach.

Dorner, I. A. *History of the Development of the Doctrine of the Person of Christ.* 5 vols. Edinburgh: T. & T. Clark, 1876–82.
Comprehensive survey of history of doctrine from early church to nineteenth century. Generally conservative.

Forsyth, P. T. *The Person and Place of Jesus Christ.* Grand Rapids: Eerdmans, 1964.
Originally published in 1909. Forsyth, sometimes called a "Barthian before Barth," stresses the moral power of the cross. Stimulating.

Grillmeier, H. *Christ in Christian Tradition.* New York: Sheed and Ward, 1964.
A masterful treatment of the development of Christology from the apostolic age to Chalcedon by a Jesuit scholar.

Liddon, H. P. *The Divinity of Our Lord and Savior Jesus Christ.* New York: Longmans, Green, 1890.
Classic defense of the deity of Christ by a conservative Anglican.

Longenecker, R. N. *Christology of Early Jewish Christianity.* Naperville, IL: Alec R. Allenson, 1970.
A competent study by an American evangelical biblical scholar.

Machen, J. G. *The Virgin Birth of Christ.* New York: Harper, 1930.
A scholarly defense of the virgin birth.

Marshall, I. H. *I Believe in the Historical Jesus.* Grand Rapids: Eerdmans, 1977.
Careful review of research into the life of Jesus from an evangelical perspective.

Pannenberg, Wolfhart. *Jesus—God and Man.* Philadelphia: Westminster, 1968, 1977.
An important work by a leading German theologian. Advocates a "from below" method in Christology; stresses resurrection as key to Jesus' divinity.

Torrance, Thomas F. *Space, Time, and Incarnation.* London: Oxford University Press, 1969.
Penetrating discussions of the incarnation in relation to issues in science by a conservative Scottish neoorthodox theologian.

Turner, H. E. W. *Jesus, Master and Lord.* London: Mowbray, 1964.

A helpful survey and synthesis of modern New Testament studies by a conservative Anglican.

Vos, Geerhardus. *The Self-Disclosure of Jesus.* New York: Doran, 1926.
A study of Jesus' messianic self-consciousness; conservative Calvinist perspective.

Warfield, B. B. *The Lord of Glory.* New York: American Tract Society, 1907.
See also Warfield's *Christology and Criticism.* New York: Oxford, 1929.

Work of Christ

Anselm. *Cur Deus Homo?* La Salle, IL: Open Court, 1962.
A classic exposition of the satisfaction theory of the atonement from the eleventh century. Available online at *www.ccel.org/a/anselm/basic_works/AnselmsCurDe.htm*

Aulen, Gustaf. *Christus Victor.* London: SPCK, 1950.
The case for the importance of the "classic" theory of the atonement in the early church and Luther.

Berkouwer, G. C. *The Work of Christ.* Grand Rapids: Eerdmans, 1965.
Able treatment by a Dutch Reformed scholar.

Brunner, Emil. *The Mediator.* Philadelphia: Westminster, 1947.
A work considered by many to be a twentieth-century classic in Christology. Neoorthodox.

Cave, Alfred. *The Scriptural Doctrine of Sacrifice and Atonement.* Edinburgh: T. & T. Clark, 1890.
An older conservative work.

Dale, R. W. *The Atonement.* London: Congregational Union, 1905.
British evangelical.

Denney, James. *The Death of Christ.* New York: Hodder and Stoughton, 1911.
A careful study of the death of Christ in the New Testament; evangelical.

Forsyth, P. T. *The Work of Christ.* London: Independent Press, 1938.

Franks, R. S. *The Work of Christ: A Historical Study of Christian Doctrine.* New York: Nelson, 1962.
A comprehensive survey of the history of doctrine.

Hodge, A. A. *The Atonement.* First published in 1867. Grand Rapids: Guardian Press, n.d.

Hughes, Thomas H. *The Atonement: Modern Theories of the Doctrine.* London: Allen and Unwin, 1949.

A study of modern British theories of the atonement concluding with the author's own speculative view.

Mackintosh, Robert. *Historic Theories of the Atonement.* London: Hodder and Stoughton, 1920.
A review of the history of the doctrine. The author's position has affinities with satisfaction theories.

Morris, Leon. *The Cross in the New Testament.* Grand Rapids: Eerdmans, 1965.
Fine biblical study by a well-known evangelical scholar. See also Morris's *Apostolic Preaching of the Cross.* Grand Rapids: Eerdmans, 1965.

Murray, John. *Redemption Accomplished and Applied.* Grand Rapids: Eerdmans, 1955.
A fine study by a well-known Reformed scholar.

Nicole, Roger. "The Nature of Redemption," in Carl F. H. Henry, ed., *Christian Faith and Modern Theology.* New York: Channel Press, 1964.
A good treatment of the New Testament language of redemption by a conservative Reformed scholar.

Rashdall, Hastings. *The Idea of the Atonement in Christian Theology.* London: Macmillan, 1925.
A major modern statement of the moral-influence theory. Denies elements of penal substitution.

Smeaton, George. *The Doctrine of the Atonement.* Edinburgh: T. & T. Clark, 1870.
An older but still valuable conservative work.

Taylor, Vincent. *The Atonement in New Testament Teaching.* London: Epworth, 1940.
Part of an important scholarly trilogy including *Jesus and His Sacrifice* (New York: St. Martin's Press, 1959) and *Forgiveness and Reconciliation* (London: Macmillan, 1946). Opposes concepts of propitiation and penal substitution.

Warfield, B. B. *The Person and Work of Christ.* Philadelphia: Presbyterian and Reformed, 1950.
Posthumously published essays by a notable Princeton theologian.

SALVATION AND THE HOLY SPIRIT

Berkouwer, G. C. *Faith and Justification.* Grand Rapids: Eerdmans, 1954.
A careful treatment by a Dutch Reformed theologian. See also *Faith and Perseverance* (Grand Rapids: Eerdmans, 1954), and *Faith and Sanctification* (Grand Rapids: Eerdmans 1966), by the same author.

Bruner, F. D. *A Theology of the Holy Spirit.* Grand Rapids: Eerdmans, 1970.

An important scholarly study of the Pentecostal experience.

Buchanan, James. *The Doctrine of Justification.* First published in 1867. Grand Rapids: Baker, 1977.
Still one of the finest treatments of the subject.

Burkhardt, Helmut. *The Biblical Doctrine of Regeneration.* Downers Grove, IL: InterVarsity Press, 1978.
A helpful but brief study of the doctrine of regeneration.

Citron, B. *The New Birth.* Edinburgh: Edinburgh University Press, 1951.
A scholarly survey of Calvinistic, Lutheran, Roman Catholic, and Methodist understandings of conversion.

Dunn, J. D. G. *Baptism in the Holy Spirit.* Naperville, IL: Alec R. Allenson, 1970.
One of the most significant recent contributions to the subject.

Fee, Gordon. *God's Empowering Presence.* Peabody, MA: Hendrickson, 1994.
Exhaustive study of the Pauline teaching on the Spirit.

Green, Michael. *I Believe in the Holy Spirit.* Grand Rapids: Eerdmans, 1975.
Helpful bibliography.

Heron, Alasdair I. C. *The Holy Spirit.* Philadelphia: Westminster, 1983.

Kuyper, Abraham. *The Work of the Holy Spirit.* First published in 1900. Grand Rapids: Eerdmans, 1941.
A classic treatment by a Dutch Calvinist. Available online at *www.ccel.org/k/kuyper/holy_spirit/htm/i.htm*

Marshall, I. H. *Kept by the Power of God: A Study of Perseverance and Falling Away.* London: Epworth, 1969.
A work concluding that the possibility of falling away is a real one.

McGrath, Alister. *Iustitia De: A History of the Christian Doctrine of Justification.* 2nd ed. New York: Cambridge University Press, 1998.
Scholarly study by a prolific Reformed evangelical Anglican theologian.

Packer, J. I. *Evangelism and the Sovereignty of God.* Grand Rapids: Eerdmans, 1961.
The argument that the sovereignty of God provides a firm foundation for evangelism.

Ryle, J. C. *Holiness.* London: James Clarke, 1952.
Reprint of the classic work of a Reformed evangelical bishop of the Church of England.

Shank, Robert L. *Life in the Son: A Study of the Doctrine of Perseverance.* Springfield, MO: Westcott, 1960.
Arminian perspective. See also *Elect in the Son* (Springfield, MO: Westcott, 1970).

Smeaton, George. *The Doctrine of the Holy Spirit.* First published in 1882. Edinburgh: Banner of Truth, 1958.
An older conservative work by a minister of the Church of Scotland.

Stott, John R. W. *The Baptism and Fullness of the Holy Spirit.* Downers Grove, IL: InterVarsity Press, 1964.
A clear, concise treatment.

Swete, Henry Barclay. *Spirit in the New Testament.* London: Macmillan, 1910.
Older but valuable biblical study. See also the author's *The Holy Spirit in the Ancient Church.* New York: Macmillan, 1912.

Thomas, W. H. Griffith. *The Holy Spirit of God.* First published in 1913. Grand Rapids: Eerdmans, 1963.
A fine study of the biblical, historical, and theological data. Conservative Anglican.

Wallace, R. S. *Calvin's Doctrine of the Christian Life.* Grand Rapids: Eerdmans, 1959.
A careful and sympathetic study of Calvin's views, drawing from sermons and commentaries as well as his *Institutes.*

Warfield, B. B. *The Plan of Salvation.* Grand Rapids: Eerdmans, 1942.
Lectures originally delivered in 1914; Reformed perspective.

Webb, R. A. *The Theology of Infant Salvation.* Richmond: Presbyterian Committee of Publication, 1907.
The case that that all who die in infancy are elect. Southern Presbyterian.

Wells, David F. *The Search for Salvation.* Downers Grove, IL: InterVarsity Press, 1978.
A helpful comparison of evangelical and nonevangelical views of salvation.

Wesley, John. *A Plain Account of Christian Perfection.* London: Epworth, 1952.
A classic work in the Wesleyan tradition. Available online at *www.ccel.org/w/wesley/perfection/*

CHURCH

Bannerman, Douglas. *The Scripture Doctrine of the Church.* First published in 1887. Grand Rapids: Baker, 1976.
Reprint of a Scottish Presbyterian work.

Bannerman, James. *The Church of Christ.* First published in 1860. Carlisle, PA: Banner of Truth Trust, 1960.
Scottish Presbyterian. Still valuable; note discussion of infant baptism.

Berkouwer, G. C. *The Church.* Grand Rapids: Eerdmans, 1976.

A noteworthy study of the unity, catholicity, apostolicity, and holiness of the church. Dutch Reformed.

Best, Ernest. *One Body in Christ.* London: SPCK, 1955.
A study of Pauline ecclesiology, concluding that the church as the "body of Christ" is neither a collection of individuals nor an extension of the incarnation.

Bloesch, Donald. *The Reform of the Church.* Grand Rapids: Eerdmans, 1970.
A call for renewal in Protestant worship, sacramental theology, and discipline. Evangelical and Reformed.

Brunner, Emil. *The Misunderstanding of the Church.* Philadelphia: Westminster, 1953.
An emphasis on the nature of the church as fellowship rather than organization.

Cerfaux, L. *The Church in the Theology of St. Paul.* New York: Herder and Herder, 1959.
An important study arguing for considerable development in the apostle's thought on the subject.

Cole, R. A. *The Body of Christ.* Philadelphia: Westminster, 1964.
A study of the biblical metaphor of the church as the body of Christ; Anglican.

Küng, Hans. *The Church.* New York: Sheed and Ward, 1967.
A significant work by a controversial Roman Catholic theologian.

Minear, Paul. *Images of the Church in the New Testament.* Philadelphia: Westminster, 1960.
Very helpful biblical study.

Schnackenburg, Rudolf. *The Church in the New Testament.* New York: Herder and Herder, 1965.
Significant work.

Snyder, Howard. *The Problem of Wineskins.* Downers Grove, IL: InterVarsity Press, 1975.
Challenging and insightful discussions concerning church structure and renewal. See also by the same author *The Community of the King* (Downers Grove, IL: InterVarsity Press, 1977).

Stibbs, A. M. *God's Church: A Study in the Biblical Doctrine of the People of God.* London: Inter-Varsity Press, 1959.
A brief biblical study by a British evangelical.

Sacraments

Aland, Kurt. *Did the Early Church Baptize Infants?* Philadelphia: Westminster, 1963.

The answer no by a German New Testament scholar to the question posed in the title.

Baillie, D. *The Theology of the Sacraments.* New York: Scribner, 1957.
Posthumously published lectures of a well-known Scottish Presbyterian theologian.

Beasley-Murray, G. R. *Baptism in the New Testament.* Grand Rapids: Eerdmans, 1973.
An extensive exegetical study; holds believer's baptism.

Berkouwer, G. C. *The Sacraments.* Grand Rapids: Eerdmans, 1969.
Dutch Reformed perspective.

Calvin, John. *Institutes of the Christian Religion.* 2 vols. Edited by J. T. McNeill. Translated by Ford Lewis Battles. Library of Christian Classics. Philadelphia: Westminster, 1960. Bk. 4.14–17.
Classic presentation of the Reformed view. Argues for "spiritual" presence in Eucharist.

Clements, R. E., et al. *Eucharistic Theology Then and Now.* London: SPCK, 1968.

Cochrane, A. C. *Eating and Drinking with Jesus.* Philadelphia: Westminster, 1974.
Discussions of the Eucharist by a student of Karl Barth.

Cullmann, Oscar. *Essays on the Lord's Supper.* Richmond: John Knox, 1958.

Fey, H. E. *The Lord's Supper: Seven Meanings.* New York: Harper, 1948.
A brief overview of various understandings of the sacrament.

Jeremias, Joachim. *Infant Baptism in the First Four Centuries.* 1960. Reprint, London: Wipf & Stock, 2004.
A defense of infant baptism. See also the author's *Origins of Infant Baptism* (1963; repr., London: Wipf & Stock, 2004).

Jewett, Paul. *Infant Baptism and the Covenant of Grace.* Grand Rapids: Eerdmans, 1978.
A critique of infant baptism.

Kingdon, David. *Children of Abraham.* Cambridge: Carey, 1973.
"A Reformed Baptist view of Baptism, the Covenant, and Children."

Kline, M. G. *By Oath Consigned.* Grand Rapids: Eerdmans, 1968.
The rite of baptism related to covenant ceremonies of ancient Near East; advocating paedobaptism.

MacDonald, A. J., ed. *The Evangelical Doctrine of Holy Communion.* Cambridge: W. Heffer and Son, 1936.
A valuable historical study by evangelical Anglican scholars. Contains bibliographies.

Marcel, Pierre. *The Biblical Doctrine of Infant Baptism.* London: James Clarke, 1953.
A detailed argument for infant baptism by a French Reformed theologian.

Stone, Darwell. *A History of the Doctrine of the Holy Eucharist.* London: Longmans, Green, 1909.
A comprehensive survey of the history of the doctrine.

ESCHATOLOGY

Allis, Oswald T. *Prophecy and the Church.* Philadelphia: Presbyterian and Reformed, 1945.
Criticism of dispensationalism; amillennial.

Archer, Gleason L., Jr. *Three Views on the Rapture: Pre-, Mid-, or Post-Tribulation?* Grand Rapids: Zondervan, 1996.
A symposium on issues concerning the timing of the rapture, dispensational.

Bass, Clarence. *Backgrounds to Dispensationalism.* Grand Rapids: Eerdmans, 1960.
A survey and critical analysis of dispensationalism.

Berkhof, Louis. *Systematic Theology.* Grand Rapids: Eerdmans, 1941.
See the section on eschatology for a presentation of the amillennial view.

Berkouwer, G. C. *The Return of Christ.* Grand Rapids: Eerdmans, 1972.
Discussion of a broad range of eschatological issues; amillennial.

Blaising, Craig, and Darrell Bock. *Progressive Dispensationalism.* Wheaton: BridgePoint, 1993.
Best exposition of the contemporary state of dispensational understanding.

Boettner, Loraine. *The Millennium.* Philadelphia: Presbyterian and Reformed, 1957.
Postmillennial.

Brown, David. *Christ's Second Coming.* 6th ed. Edinburgh: T. & T. Clark, 1867.
Postmillennial. Old but still valuable.

Campbell, Roderick. *Israel and the New Covenant.* Philadelphia: Presbyterian and Reformed, 1954.
A view of Israel and Old Testament prophecy; postmillennial in perspective.

Chafer, Lewis Sperry. *Systematic Theology.* 8 vols. Dallas: Dallas Seminary Press, 1947–48.
In volume 7: eschatology; classic dispensational.

Clouse, Robert G., ed., *The Meaning of the Millennium.* Downers Grove, IL: InterVarsity Press, 1977.
A very helpful symposium of four millennial views.

Cohn, Norman. *The Pursuit of the Millennium.* New York: Oxford University Press, 1970.
A study of millenarian thought during the Middle Ages, suggesting analogies with modern revolutionary social movements.

Davis, John Jefferson. *Christ's Victorious Kingdom: Postmillennialism Reconsidered.* Grand Rapids: Baker, 1986.
A postmillennial perspective.

Erickson, Millard J. *Contemporary Options in Eschatology.* Grand Rapids: Baker, 1977.
A helpful survey of the major views. Premillennial, posttribulational.

Froom, Leroy. *The Prophetic Faith of Our Fathers.* 4 vols. Washington, DC: Review and Herald, 1946–54.
A Seventh-day Adventist history of prophetic interpretation containing much otherwise obscure information.

Frost, Henry W. *The Second Coming of Christ.* Grand Rapids: Eerdmans, 1934.
A survey of the biblical data from a premillennial perspective.

Gundry, Robert H. *The Church and the Tribulation.* Grand Rapids: Zondervan, 1973.
A posttribulational, dispensational presentation.

Hodge, Charles. *Systematic Theology.* New York: Scribner, 1871.
American Reformed postmillennial outlook.

Kik, J. Marcellus. *An Eschatology of Victory.* Nutley, NJ: Presbyterian and Reformed, 1974.
Valuable treatment of Matthew 24. Postmillennial.

Klausner, Joseph. *The Messianic Idea in Israel.* New York: Macmillan, 1958.
A definitive study by a noted Jewish scholar. Note appendix, "The Jewish and Christian Messiah."

Kyle, Richard. *The Last Days Are Here Again.* Grand Rapids: Baker, 1999.
A historical survey of eschatological interpretations. Very helpful.

Ladd, George E. *The Blessed Hope.* Grand Rapids: Eerdmans, 1956.
Evangelical criticism of pretribulational rapture doctrine. Also see Ladd's *Crucial Questions about the Kingdom of God* (Grand Rapids: Eerdmans, 1974); *The Gospel of the Kingdom* (Grand Rapids: Eerdmans, 1974); and *The Presence of the Future* (Grand Rapids: Eerdmans, 1974).

Morris, Leon. *Apocalyptic.* Grand Rapids: Eerdmans, 1972.

A brief but helpful study of apocalyptic in the New Testament.

Murray, Iain. *The Puritan Hope.* London: Banner of Truth, 1971.
An important study of the impact of the postmillenarian hope in Puritanism on the cause of Protestant missions.

Pache, Rene. *The Return of Jesus Christ.* Chicago: Moody Press, 1955.
A study of the second coming; dispensational.

Payne, J. Barton. *Encyclopedia of Biblical Prophecy.* New York: Harper & Row, 1973.
A comprehensive reference work; premillennial in perspective.

Pentecost, J. Dwight. *Prophecy for Today.* Grand Rapids: Zondervan, 1961.
Dispensational.

———. *Things to Come.* 1958. Reprint, Grand Rapids: Zondervan, 1964.
Exhaustive treatment of eschatological understanding from a classic dispensational perspective.

Reese, Alexander. *The Approaching Advent of Christ.* London: Marshall, Morgan, and Scott, 1937.
A scholarly criticism of the views of J. N. Darby from the perspective of classical premillennialism.

Ryrie, Charles C. *Dispensationalism Today.* Chicago: Moody Press, 1965.
The best exposition of the "revised" dispensational point of view.

Scofield, C. I. *Rightly Dividing the Word of Truth.* New York: Fleming H. Revell, 1907.
A classic work by a key figure in spreading the dispensational perspective. See also the notes in *The Scofield Reference Bible* (1909) and *The New Scofield Reference Bible* (1967).

Strong, A. H. *Systematic Theology.* 3 vols. Valley Forge, PA: Judson, 1907.
Volume 3: the case for postmillennialism.

Toon, Peter, ed. *Puritans, the Millennium and the Future of Israel.* Cambridge: James Clarke, 1970.
A series of essays on Puritan eschatology from 1600 to 1660.

Vos, Geerhardus. *The Pauline Eschatology.* Grand Rapids: Eerdmans, 1930.
Valuable exegetical discussions; amillennial.

Walvoord, John F. *The Millennial Kingdom.* Findlay, OH: Dunham, 1959.
Dispensational. See also *The Rapture Question* (Grand Rapids: Zondervan, 1977) by the same author.

Warfield, B. B. *Biblical Doctrines.* New York: Oxford University Press, 1929.
See especially the chapter "The Prophecies of St. Paul" for a postmillennial interpretation of 1 Corinthians 15:20–28.

INDEXES

NAMES INDEX

SUBJECT INDEX

A

B

C

D

Q

R

S